T0311862

Banking the World

Banking the World

Empirical Foundations of Financial Inclusion

Edited by Robert Cull, Aslı Demirgüç-Kunt, and
Jonathan Morduch

The MIT Press
Cambridge, Massachusetts
London, England

© 2013 Massachusetts Institute of Technology

All rights reserved. No part of this book may be reproduced in any form by any electronic or mechanical means (including photocopying, recording, or information storage and retrieval) without permission in writing from the publisher.

This book was set in Palatino by Toppan Best-set Premedia Limited, Hong Kong.

Library of Congress Cataloging-in-Publication Data

Banking the world : empirical foundations of financial inclusion / edited by Robert Cull, Asli Demirgüç-Kunt, and Jonathan Morduch.
 p. cm.
Includes bibliographical references and index.
ISBN 978-0-262-01842-5 (hardcover : alk. paper), 978-0-262-54401-6 (pb)
1. Finance—Developing countries. 2. Banks and banking—Developing countries. 3. Financial institutions—Developing countries. I. Cull, Robert J. II. Demirgüç-Kunt, Asli, 1961– III. Morduch, Jonathan.
HG195.B356 2013
332.109172′4—dc23
2012016234

Contents

1 Introduction: Banking the World

Robert Cull, Aslı Demirgüç-Kunt, and
Jonathan Morduch

The story most often told when explaining the global microfinance revolution focuses on new financial products. Those innovations—especially the "group lending" loan contract pioneered by Bangladesh's Grameen Bank and, more recently, the spread of mobile banking in Africa—provide financial institutions with better ways to serve low-income markets. The microfinance revolution has now given way to a broader push to extend financial markets, and this push introduces new products, new providers, and new target markets. The original narratives of product innovation have been so powerful that it's been easy to lose sight of the simultaneous developments in regulation, investment, and business organization that enabled the initial steps. If we are to realize the hope of extending banking services to the planet's unbanked half—the hope of truly "banking the world"—we will continue to need progress on all fronts. That progress, in turn, requires different varieties of evidence and ideas.

The global financial crisis touched off in 2007–2008 provides a sharp reminder that expanding financial access can create opportunities and risks simultaneously (Demirgüç-Kunt and Servén 2010). The crisis also reminds us that narrowly micro views of financial dysfunction (e.g., those that focus only on how loan defaults follow from particular features of credit contracts) show only one part of the story. Large risks in the financial crisis turned out to be systemic: political, regulatory, and tied to macro imbalances and the broader illiquidity of the financial system.

That's a helpful context for understanding the contribution of randomized controlled trials (RCTs) to financial product innovation. The randomized trials have put an important focus on impact evaluations (Banerjee and Duflo 2011; Karlan and Appel 2011), and many of the important applications have been to finance. The new results are contributing to a broader restitching of understandings of household

demand. Randomized trials have proved well suited for critical micro questions, such as how borrowers respond to interest rates and the impacts of access to microcredit or saving accounts. But the likely legacy of the push for randomized trials will be less in the specific method than in the renewed stress on rigorous research.

As chapters 12 and 13 demonstrate, randomized trials deserve attention because they provide a new way to tackle long-recognized biases that undermine the reliability of empirical work, biases created because it is far from random who does and doesn't seek finance and where banks do and do not operate (Bauchet and Morduch 2010). In the end, however, banking the world will require much evidence that randomized trials cannot deliver: for example, the effects of economy-wide regulation, understandings of corporate governance, analyses of bank-level subsidy and profit, and meaningful descriptions of the financial lives of the poor.

We have learned a great deal in recent years, even as the context of financial access steadily changes.[1] The changes are driven in part by humility in the wake of the 2007–2008 financial crisis, which put a spotlight on mismatches between the financial products being supplied and those demanded. The crisis has also driven a push for greater consumer protection and regulation. Alongside those changes has come the innovation—in technology, product, and service—that is altering the definition of financial access and who has it. In Kenya today, 1 million citizens use their mobile phones to make financial transactions (Jack and Suri 2010). In India, private-sector microfinance institutions and government-sponsored self-help groups have grown at such remarkable pace that the new agenda hinges on fears of over-indebted customers and overly intrusive politicians (Sinha 2009). In Brazil, smart cards and point-of-service devices contribute to slashing the costs that limit bank access.

The changing context makes it all the more important to bring evidence to bear on fundamental questions—who has financial access? Who lacks it? Why? Which ideas show the most promise for extending access to the poor? Where are the big unknowns? *Banking the World* collects studies by leading scholars that frame these global shifts and their implications for practice and policy.

Lifting the Veil on the Financial Lives of the Poor

The growing inclusiveness of financial systems is often associated with *microcredit*: the idea of extending small, uncollateralized loans designed

to unleash the productivity of cash-starved entrepreneurs. The rapid growth and the attention given to microcredit—and its associated marketing narrative—have driven interest in other elements of financial access. That process has not only allowed us to create a more complete picture but has also led us to rethink assumptions about microcredit itself.

Fine-grained evidence from "financial diaries" in Bangladesh, India, and South Africa reveals the surprising complexity of the financial lives of poor families, with rapidly changing portfolios composed of a mix of services from formal and informal providers (Collins et al. 2009). Historically, the assumption has been that poor households are unsophisticated and sparing users of financial services simply because their incomes are so small—and because their main interest is in loans for running businesses. The evidence from the financial diaries suggests the opposite. In fact, it suggests that financial dealings are complex precisely *because* households are poor, operating on tight margins with few convenient, cost-effective options for meeting financial emergencies.

The financial diaries reveal patterns that change how we think about financial access: (1) even very poor families can save and do save, though they often do so outside of the formal sector and most often for expenses within a year; (2) families seek small loans, but most often for purposes beyond business finance; and (3) dealing with risk is difficult because lump sums are needed quickly and the resources of family and friends are quickly exhausted. Perhaps most fundamentally, an ongoing need for families is to find ways to translate small, irregular cash flows into "usefully large sums" (Rutherford 2010).

The financial diaries are best seen as delivering a set of patterns and hypotheses. They are helping us extend theoretical frameworks rather than formally testing existing frames. For the latter, larger samples are needed, and the focus must be on establishing causal pathways.

The financial diaries reorient expectations for the net impacts of extending financial access. The diary evidence emphasizes priorities placed on financial management rather than business investment. That sense comes through in new evidence from randomized trials (Morduch 2011), such as evidence from the Philippines that fails to find strong positive impacts of microcredit on business but finds suggestive evidence of risk mitigation (Karlan and Zinman 2011). It similarly emerges in a U.S. study by Morgan and Strain (2008), which finds that in U.S. locales where payday loans were made illegal, bankruptcies, bounced checks, and complaints about debt collectors spiked.

But credit is just a beginning. Financial inclusion means more than access to small loans—it also means access to better ways to save, to transfer funds, and to insure against loss. Trials of savings products, including traditional savings and commitment savings products as well as microinsurance are shedding light onto the demand (and barriers to demand) and positive impact of these equally important financial tools. In a small experiment in Kenya, Dupas and Robinson (2011) found large positive effects of low-cost savings accounts for female shopkeepers who managed to use them (while male account owners benefited far less). Ashraf, Karlan, and Yin (2008) tested a structured contractual savings product in the Philippines and found the level of uptake surprisingly high for such a constrained savings product. A recent study of the impact of access to a similarly structured savings device offered to tobacco farmers in Malawi nicely shows the links between improved saving across seasons, greater investment, higher profit, and increased household consumption—though the pathways from the savings device to household impact remain unclear (Brune et al. 2011).

The Emerging Research Agenda

In a very general sense, the benefits of financial inclusion are widely accepted. Country-level analysis suggests that financial development leads to economic growth and can contribute to poverty reduction. For example, Beck, Demirgüç-Kunt, and Levine (2007) use cross-country data to show that financial development disproportionately raises the incomes of the poorest quintile, both by directly reducing income inequality and, more strongly, through impacts on aggregate economic growth. Even after controlling for the impact of economic growth, there remains an association between financial development and the fraction of a country's population living on less than $1 a day per person. Not surprisingly, the findings so far suggest pent-up demand for better financial products.

Banking the World aims to provide both answers and questions for providers, policymakers, and academics concerned with financial access. The body of the book provides evidence from leading researchers on different pieces of the financial access puzzle. We begin by describing data and methods needed to form baselines on access to formal bank accounts. From there, we look at research on the impact of financial access, cautionary tales on the downsides of financial access,

and finally research on the role of technology, financial literacy, and social capital in improving access to financial services. The independent chapters come together to form a vision that is dynamic, highly empirical, and creative, marked by a return to tests of basic principles.

Part I: Where Are We Now?

We set the stage by detailing more reliable estimates of the state of financial access in each region of the world than have previously been available. Chapter 2 presents a joint McKinsey-NYU effort to make the measure of the unbanked more precise, showing that in the early 2000s about 2.5 billion adults—just over half of the world's adult population—lacked what we have historically considered the metric of financial access: a bank account. (A similar global estimate was subsequently found in data for 2011 analyzed by the World Bank Development Research Group 2012.) Of these unserved adults, 2.2 billion live in Africa, Asia, Latin America, and the Middle East. The dataset is built from the best available data from multiple sources, especially Patrick Honohan's earlier World Bank research (Honohan 2008).

These estimates provide grounding for the belief that the poor are bankable—a belief that continues to be debated despite the continuing expansion of microfinance. This chapter shows that there are more than 800 million living on under $5 per day in purchasing power parity (PPP) terms who use formal financial services. In several regions, this group of lower-income adults makes up a significant majority of the users of formal financial services.

The estimates lay the groundwork for future research. The underlying data on financial access needs to be improved, certainly. But even the limited data currently available show that rates of financial access depend on factors beyond income or urbanization. There is a wide variability in financial penetration between countries with similar demographic and sociographic profiles. That suggests that policies, providers, and products make a difference in extending financial access. Exploring exactly how is a rich vein for research that the following chapters begin to mine.

Part II: Better Data

Although the estimates of global access are a step forward from prior work, understanding financial access requires reliable data on the users

and potential users of financial services. Until recently, little was known about how to collect such demand-side information in a systematic, sustainable manner. The pioneering FinScope surveys have used a product-based approach in more than ten countries, predominantly in Africa.

The FinScope surveys, carried out from 2003 to 2008 in eleven African countries and Pakistan, represent one of the most significant recent steps forward in the collection of information from a representative sample of individual users of financial services in developing countries. The surveys collect data for a range of financial products, the types—and in some cases the identities—of the providers of those services, reasons for nonuse, and awareness of different types of products and providers. In addition to standard demographic information (age, gender, education, income, etc.), the FinScope surveys also collect information that can be used to assess financial literacy, attitudes regarding money, saving, and investment and to construct simple psychological profiles.

Honohan and King's examination of the FinScope data in chapter 3 reveals detailed information about the causes and consequences of use of financial services. On the use side of the equation, income and proximity play their expected positive roles, but attitudes have a surprisingly large impact.

Although the FinScope surveys are richly detailed and revealing, they have a downside: they are so well tailored to the economic and social context that the surveys display considerable variation in detail across countries. This is in some ways a strength, but it also limits the extent to which these data can be used for cross-country comparisons. Other survey vehicles are more likely to produce comparable cross-country data in a cost-effective manner, albeit in a less detailed fashion.

But it's not just an issue of asking questions. Many efforts to measure use of financial services rely on information that is generated with funders, investors, regulators, and supervisors in mind. Such supply-side data gathering approaches, although valuable, cannot replace direct surveys of users and potential users of financial services, especially if one wants to understand the nature of financial exclusion and design policies to combat it.

Surveying people about their use of financial services is considerably more complex than was first understood. What questions are asked, how the questions are asked, and who is asked have a significant

influence on how people respond to financial surveys. In chapter 4, Cull and Scott, drawing on research from Ghana and Timor Leste, find that the identity of the survey respondent (head of household, non–head of household, or a full enumeration of all household members) and the inclusion of detailed product-based cues in the questions affects the reported levels of usage of financial services. In Ghana, rates of household usage are almost identical when the head reports on behalf of the household or when the rate is tabulated from a full enumeration of household use. But others in the household don't provide as complete a summary of household use of financial services as the other two methods. Asking about product types also produces better data than asking about providers, especially for formal sources of credit, insurance, and informal savings. By contrast, in Timor-Leste, the identity of the respondent and the inclusion of product-specific cues in survey questions have little effect on reported usage rates. Cull and Scott's work shows that data gathering must be afforded the same care as data analysis.

Collins continues the conversation in chapter 5, describing the financial diaries method for collecting data based on cash flows. In South Africa (as part of a multinational data gathering exercise), 152 households were interviewed every fortnight for a year to create financial diaries that accurately captured the uneven nature of income and expenses in poor households. The interview protocol included reconciling statements about income and expenses during the interviews. Using this technique, Collins finds that the diaries are able to reduce the "margin of error"—the difference between reported income and expenses (including savings deposits)—in each period to an average of 6 percent. She then uses this dataset to examine what data is most likely to be omitted in other data collection methodologies, giving us not just greater precision but also evidence on a wider range of activities than is usually captured.

Collins's approach joins that of Samphantharak and Townsend (2009) in using the tools of empirical corporate finance combined with a "financial portfolio" view. In this way, families can be seen to patch income sources and put together resources from a variety of instruments simultaneously. The study shows that when researchers investigate one instrument at a time, we can lose sight of how families actually view the instruments (i.e., as a contribution to a collection of devices, and thus with an eye to their incremental contributions to the total).

Part III: Creating Impact

The quality of data on financial access is improving, and with the insights of Honohon, King, Scott, Cull, and Collins, there's reason to believe that major improvements in data are on the way. Data is just a tool, however. Ultimately, the goal of better data is better understanding of the impact of financial access and how to maximize the positive impact on such issues as hunger, business growth, and household welfare.

Bruhn and Love begin this section by exploring the impact of increasing financial access by taking advantage of a unique, rapid increase in availability of formal financial services in Mexico. In 2002, Banco Azteca opened branches inside more than 1000 Grupo Elektra retail stores, overnight creating the second largest network of bank branches in the country. By comparing municipalities with Grupo Elektra stores to those without, a measure can be made of the impact of financial access—and the authors do find substantial impact, particularly in the informal sector. Informal businesses owned by men increased 7.6 percent in municipalities with Banco Azteca branches and the percentage of women earning wages also increased. Overall income levels increased 7 percent for men and women. The study is a unique episode establishing the links between household behavior, income, and increased availability of financial services.

Bruhn and Love's work indicates the potential impact of financial access on incomes. There are other channels of development through which financial access could improve household welfare. In chapter 7, Claessens and Feijen explore the impact of financial development on hunger. Their work uses cross-country data to give evidence of a link between increased financial access and a decrease in undernourishment. The mechanisms for this increase in welfare seem to be increased use of fertilizer and tractors, which translates into increases in agricultural productivity and cereal yields. There are spillover effects from the increase in agricultural inputs: not only do the incomes of agricultural households rise but there are also reductions in the price of food that benefit all as quantity expands.

One of the clear theoretical benefits of formal financial access is ready availability of financing for entrepreneurial ventures. However, the practical evidence of increasing financial access affecting the success of small and medium enterprises is limited. Demirgüç-Kunt, Klapper, and Panos explore the link in the Western Balkans in chapter 8. They

find that having an existing relationship with a formal bank doesn't have an impact on the decision to start a new business but does have a major impact on the survival and job creation rates of a startup. Although the formal and informal financial sectors are typically considered as distinct buckets by researchers and policymakers, Demirgüç-Kunt, Klapper, and Panos's work suggests the importance of linking the two finding that individuals with some experience in the informal sector—particularly those with access to informal loans and informal sources of finance—are more likely to start a formal business and survive the difficult first year. In their research, informal and formal finance are not substitutes but complements in creating viable formal businesses.

Part IV: Cautionary Tales

The choices of policymakers and providers would be far easier if financial access only had upsides for the poor, but like all else, there are dangers to beware and pitfalls to avoid. Not all forms of financial inclusion have a positive impact, and there are substantial possibilities for actual harm, both for the poor and for providers (and therefore ultimately for the poor also by limiting access to other financial services) if policies and products are not carefully designed.

This part begins with a look at the disappointing impact of remittances in Vietnam. Given the large sums that flow globally through international remittances—several multiples of official aid to developing countries—many have hoped that remittances could prove a valuable channel for financial inclusion and development. Some work has buttressed this hope. Demirgüç-Kunt et al. (2007) find that the percentage of households that receive remittances in Mexico has a positive impact on use of deposit services and the penetration of bank branches. Ashraf et al. (2011) find that formal savings accounts with control by the remitter increases remittances and savings. But the evidence on the broader development impacts of remittances is still limited. In chapter 9, Viet Cuong, van den Berg, and Lensink, using data from the two most recent Vietnam Household Living Standard Surveys, estimate the effects of international remittances on per-capita income, per-capita expenditure, work effort, poverty, and inequality. Though they find that increases in remittances unsurprisingly increase household incomes and expenditures, they also find downsides. First, they see evidence that remittances increase disincentives to work, limiting the

long-term impact of remittances. Second, they find that remittances, at least in the short term, increase inequality. The bottom line is that although there are a number of clear benefits to recipient households, the picture is more complicated with regard to the hope that international remittances can play a major role in alleviating poverty in developing countries.

Chapter 10 turns to the rapid growth of the mortgage finance market in Central and Eastern Europe. Beck, Kibuuka, and Tiongson seek to highlight problems of over-indebtedness using household survey data from 2005 to 2007. They focus on who gets access to mortgage finance, the most rapidly expanding form of finance in many EU countries prior to the global financial crisis. The context is fast-rising levels of household debt in new EU member countries. Still, the study provides no evidence that mortgage holders were financially more vulnerable than renters or outright owners. Nor were mortgage holders more likely to suffer financial distress than non–mortgage holders. The study shows how overall economic conditions matter: the overall incidence of financial vulnerability fell from 2005 to 2007, owing in part to the strong income growth experienced by many of the new EU countries. The crisis changed much, however, and it will be valuable to continue the investigations as the post-crisis rounds of the household surveys become available.

Part V: More than Products

Extending financial access isn't just about finding the right policies and right products; it also requires getting the risks and costs right. The progress in financial access made in the last few decades can largely be attributed to innovative approaches that have lowered costs and credit risks for providers, with microcredit contracts as a leading example.

Still, even with the innovations, the costs of serving the poorest customers are still high—putting a floor beneath the interest rates that must be charged—and the risk mitigation strategies such as group lending, weekly meetings, and social pressure clearly have downsides in terms of cost, both for providers and clients (Cull, Demirgüç-Kunt, and Morduch 2009). These additional costs of the typical microcredit product can limit demand (Dehejia, Montgomery, and Morduch 2012), despite evidence from field experiments indicating that the returns to capital investments in microenterprises are substantially higher than market interest rates (de Mel, McKenzie, and Woodruff 2008). The

sector thus continues to seek a wider range of risk mitigation strategies. One promising approach is being led by Asim Khwaja and the Entrepreneurial Finance Lab (Winter 2010). Their work has found that psychometric testing for latent traits (of the sort used to screen job applicants in developed countries) can be a useful tool for predicting repayment and default among microcredit clients more effectively and more cheaply than loan officers.

In chapter 11, Karlan, Mullainathan, and Robles examine other sources of information that might improve credit risk assessment, including borrower personality traits, qualitative social capital measurement surveys, and general personality indexes. They show that in a sample from the Philippines, although personality traits such as high psychosomatic moral costs predict lower default rates, neither social capital measures nor general personality indexes proved useful. Although it is not an emphasis of the chapter, an alternative interpretation of the study is that the primary locus of default is either external to the borrower—adverse events presumably beyond their control—or tied to incentives created by the credit contract and borrowing process. Beyond the specific findings, the chapter illustrates how an openness to nontraditional tools opens new possibilities for microcredit. The search for additional cost-effective methods for lowering risk should continue.

The next three chapters of the section broaden the scope of inquiry to factors not directly related to financial services that influence their spread and positive impact. The three chapters also provide good examples of how interventions can be disentangled and assessed in order to spur learning and innovation.

In chapter 12, Cole, Sampson, and Zia examine financial literacy training—an intervention that many assume must be a key part of any pro-poor efforts to extend financial access. Indeed, survey evidence indicates that financial illiteracy is associated with higher costs of borrowing, failure to build assets, and lower rates of usage of formal financial services. But the causal link, and which direction it flows, is unclear. Employing a randomized control trial, Cole, Sampson, and Zia attempt to untangle the relationship.

Using a sample of households in Indonesia that reported not having a bank account, participants were randomly assigned to a control group or to a treatment group that was offered free training in basic financial literacy. In addition, financial incentives were randomly assigned to participants to open bank accounts, independent of whether they were

offered financial literacy training. This approach allows for financial literacy training and direct financial incentives to be compared in terms of their effects on the acceptance of bank accounts. (As Karlan, Morduch, and Mullaithan 2010 report, rates of adoption of financial innovations are often surprisingly low.)

Cole, Sampson, and Zia find that financial incentives had a stronger effect on opening a bank account than financial literacy training. But financial literacy training did have a significant positive effect on the least educated participants. This finding suggests that financial literacy could be a useful tool for expanding take-up of accounts if it is properly targeted, but raises questions about the cost-effectiveness of training versus simply providing conditional grants as a mechanism to increase use of formal bank accounts. Drexler, Fischer, and Schoar (2011) similarly find a mixed result, showing that teaching simple "rule of thumb" financial accounting training had significant effects on profits and cash flow for shopkeepers in the Dominican Republic in months with poor sales (while more formal accounting training didn't have measurable effects).

The use of technology, especially in the form of mobile phones, is expanding rapidly in the regions with the lowest rates of formal financial services adoption. One use of technology even in poor communities in these regions is to deploy more reliable and secure forms of identification (which can make transactions more secure for clients as well as limit default risks for providers of credit), for example, by employing biometric scanning. In chapter 13, Giné, Goldberg, Sankaranarayanan, Sheerin, and Yang detail an experiment in Malawi that sheds light on the impact of reliable individual identification on credit provision and usage.

Paprika farmers who applied for agricultural input loans were randomly assigned to a control group or to a treatment group in which each member had a fingerprint collected as part of their loan application. Knowledge that they could be reliably identified (and knowledge that the information would be combined in a credit reporting mechanism) led to 40 percent higher rates of repayment among the highest risk group of borrowers. The mechanism induced the group to take smaller loans and increase their use of other agricultural inputs—essentially, this group became more risk averse. Meanwhile, fingerprinting had no effect on repayment rates or behavior of lower risk groups of borrowers. The findings of Giné and colleagues indicate there

is promise in unique identification systems as a way of limiting risks and therefore lowering costs of serving these populations, which in turn could lead to faster expansion of access.

In chapter 14, we return to the FinScope surveys, this time specifically in Uganda, to examine the role that social capital plays in access to formal and informal finance. Heikkilä, Kalmi, and Ruuskanen examine the FinScope surveys and find that different types of trust play roles in financial access. Individual social capital has a clear positive association with access to credit from informal financial groups, unsurprisingly. However, general interpersonal trust matters more for formal financial institutions than less formal lenders. These are important findings for policymakers, as they illustrate the importance of trust, a factor enhanced by reliable and rule-bound engagements between providers and customers. The finding is striking when viewed alongside the finding from chapter 11 that social capital measures do not predict default in microcredit in the Philippines sample.

Conclusion

Together, the work compiled in this volume significantly advances the state of knowledge about the extent of financial access, pathways to improve data in the field, the impact—positive, negative, and neutral— of expanding financial access, and the interplay of nonfinancial factors in determining the impact and success of efforts to bank more of the world. Every chapter provides new answers and also raises new questions. Overall, the studies illustrate exciting possibilities, but also prompt humility about the scope of the remaining research agenda. In the closing chapter of the book, Morduch offers ten research questions about financial access and its impact to be answered by research.

Note

1. For a policy-focused overview, see World Bank 2007. For a broad, analytical overview, see Armendáriz and Morduch 2010. For a market-based overview, see Cull, Demirgüç-Kunt, and Morduch 2009. For a research-focused overview, see Karlan and Morduch 2010.

References

Armendáriz, Beatriz, and Jonathan Morduch. 2010. *The Economics of Microfinance*. 2nd ed. Cambridge, MA: MIT Press.

Ashraf, Nava, Dean Karlan, and Wesley Yin. 2008. Tying Odysseus to the Mast: Evidence from a Commitment Savings Product in the Philippines. *Quarterly Journal of Economics* 121 (2): 635–672.

Ashraf, Nava, Diego Aycinena, Martinez A. Claudia, and Dean Yang. 2011. Remittances and the Problem of Control: A Field Experiment among Migrants from El Salvador. Working Paper, University of Michigan.

Bauchet, Jonathan, and Jonathan Morduch. 2010. An Introduction to Impact Evaluations with Randomized Designs. Financial Access Initiative working paper.

Banerjee, Abhijit, and Esther Duflo. 2011. *Poor Economics*. New York: PublicAffairs.

Beck, Thorsten, Aslı Demirgüç-Kunt, and Ross Levine. 2007. Finance, Inequality and the Poor. *Journal of Economic Growth* 12 (1): 27–49.

Brune, Lasse, Xavier Giné, Jessica Goldberg, and Dean Yang. 2011. Commitments to Save: A Field Experiment in Rural Malawi. World Bank Policy Research Working Paper 5748.

Collins, Daryl, Jonathan Morduch, Stuart Rutherford, and Orlanda Ruthven. 2009. *Portfolios of the Poor: How the World's Poor Live on $2 a Day*. Princeton, NJ: Princeton University Press.

Cull, Robert, Aslı Demirgüç-Kunt, and Jonathan Morduch. 2009. Microfinance Meets the Market. *Journal of Economic Perspectives* 23 (1): 167–192.

de Mel, Suresh, David McKenzie, and Christopher Woodruff. 2008. Returns to Capital in Microenterprises: Evidence from a Field Experiment. *Quarterly Journal of Economics* 123 (4): 1329–1372.

Dehejia, Rajeev, Heather Montgomery, and Jonathan Morduch. 2012. Do Interest Rates Matter? Credit Demand in the Dhaka Slums. *Journal of Development Economics* 47 (2): 437–499.

Demirgüç-Kunt, Aslı, Ernesto López Córdova, Maria Soledad Martinez Pería, and Christopher Woodruff. 2007. Remittances and Bank Services: Evidence from Mexico. World Bank, Development Research Group, Washington, DC.

Demirgüç-Kunt, Aslı, and Luis Servén. 2010. Are All the Sacred Cows Dead? Implications of the Financial Crisis for Macro- and Financial Policies. *World Bank Research Observer* 25:91–124.

Dupas, Pascaline, and Jonathan Robinson. 2011. Savings Constraints and Microenterprise Development: Evidence from a Field Experiment in Kenya. National Bureau of Economic Research, Working Paper No. 14693.

Drexler, Alejandro, Greg Fischer, and Antoinette Schoar. 2011. Keeping It Simple: Financial Literacy and Rules of Thumb. London School of Economics, working paper.

Honohan, Patrick. 2008. Cross-Country Variation in Household Access to Financial Services. *Journal of Banking & Finance* 32 (May): 2493–2500.

Jack, William and Tavneet Suri. 2010. The Economics of M-Pesa: An Update. Sloan School, MIT, working paper.

Karlan, Dean, and Jacob Appel. 2011. *More than Good Intentions*. New York: Dutton.

Karlan, Dean, and Jonathan Morduch. 2010. Access to Finance. In *Handbook of Development Economics*, vol. 5, ed. Dani Rodrik and Mark Rosenzweig, 4704–4784. Amsterdam: Elsevier.

Karlan, Dean, Jonathan Morduch, and Sendhil Mullainathan. 2010. Take-Up: Why Micro-finance Take-Up Rates Are Low and Why It Matters. Financial Access Initiative working paper.

Karlan, Dean, and Jonathan Zinman. 2011. Microcredit in Theory and Practice: Using Randomized Credit Scoring for Impact Evaluation. *Science* 332 (6035): 1278–1284.

Morduch, Jonathan. 2011. Why Finance Matters. *Science* 332 (6035): 1271–1272.

Morgan, Donald P., and Michael R. Strain. 2008. Payday Holiday: How Households Fare after Payday Credit Bans. Federal Reserve Bank of New York Staff Reports, no. 309.

Rutherford, Stuart. 2010. *The Poor and their Money*. 2nd ed. Rugby, UK: Practical Action.

Samphantharak, Krislert, and Robert Townsend. 2009. *Households as Corporate Firms: An Analysis of Household Finance Using Integrated Household Surveys and Corporate Financial Accounting*. Cambridge: Cambridge University Press.

Sinha, Frances. 2009. *Microfinance Self-Help Groups in India: Living Up to Their Promise?* Rugby, UK: Practical Action.

Winter, Caroline. 2010. A Test to Identify Entrepreneurs. *Bloomberg Business Week*, July 15, 2010. http://www.businessweek.com/magazine/content/10_30/b4188020389751.htm (accessed October 12, 2011).

World Bank. 2007. *Finance for All? Policies and Pitfalls in Expanding Access*. Washington, DC: The World Bank.

World Bank Development Research Group. 2012. The "Global Findex" Global Financial Inclusion Database. April.

I Where Are We Now?

2 Half the World Is Unbanked

Alberto Chaia, Aparna Dalal, Tony Goland, Maria
Jose Gonzalez, Jonathan Morduch, and Robert Schiff

Over the past quarter-century, the microfinance movement has pro-
pelled a global expansion of formal and semiformal financial services[1]
for the world's poor. The Microcredit Summit Campaign, a leading
advocacy group, counted 205 million clients worldwide at the end of
2010. That is impressive, but it is just a start relative to the unmet
demand. Experts agree that unmet demand for formal finance is large,
but the exact number (or even a rough but credible number) has been
hard to pin down, with estimates ranging from half a billion people to
3 billion.

Limited information on the size and nature of the global population
using financial services limits policymakers' abilities to identify what's
working and what's not in terms of increasing financial access. Just as
important, it limits financial service providers' ability to identify new
markets and opportunities for new products. Both regulators and pro-
viders have little opportunity to learn from others' experiences.

In an effort to begin closing the information gap, we've built on a
dataset compiled from existing cross-country data sources on financial
access and socioeconomic and demographic characteristics to generate
an improved estimate of global financial access. Insight into the size
and nature of the global population that does and does not use formal
financial services is an important first step in driving more detailed
research that will allow real progress in extending financial access.

By analyzing this data, making conservative assumptions about the
use of financial services among the poor, we believe we can reliably
estimate that 2.5 billion adults—just over half of the world's adult
population—do not use formal financial services to save or borrow. The
financial access gap between populations in OECD (Organization for
Economic Cooperation and Development) countries and others is sig-
nificant. Of the 2.5 billion unserved adults, 2.2 billion live in Africa,

South or East Asia, Latin America, and the Middle East. In the best-performing of these regions, South Asia and Latin America, still nearly 60 percent of adults do not use formal financial services. Meanwhile, only 8 percent of the adult population in high-income OECD countries is unbanked.

Because hard data on financial inclusion was hard to come by, there has been a great deal of debate on the factors that determine levels of formal financial access and those factors' levels of importance. The "minimalist" view has been that financial access follows in the footsteps of socioeconomic and demographic factors such as income and urbanization. We found that levels of financial inclusion are not determined by socioeconomic or demographic factors alone. In fact, our estimates uncover that the majority of users of formal financial services—at least two-thirds of the financial services market—in Africa, Asia, and the Middle East live on less than $5 per day.[2] In other words, there are now more than 800 million people worldwide who recently would have been thought of as "unbankable" who are actively using formal financial services.

Additionally, there is considerable variance among countries of similar national levels of per capita income and urbanization in financial services usage. For instance, countries including India and Thailand have far wider usage of formal financial services than would be predicted by their level of gross domestic product (GDP) or urbanization. Our research indicates that regulatory and policy environments, as well as the actions of individual financial services providers, shape the financial inclusion landscape in a country or region and are, to a large extent, independent of countries' socioeconomic and demographic characteristics. That finding suggests, of course, that well-considered policy and practice may be able to increase financial inclusion even in the absence of broader socioeconomic or demographic changes.

Our findings provide empirical grounding for what many in the field already believe to be true. It is possible to serve low-income communities at scale with financial services, but there are still billions left to reach.

Approach

We began our analysis of the state of financial access by building a dataset with four components of country-level data. The country-level data for these components is included in table 2.1:

1. Percentage of adults with a credit or savings account measured from Honohan (2008). Honohan presents estimates, for more than 160 countries, of the fraction of the adult population using formal and semiformal (i.e., from unregulated microfinance institutions) financial services by combining data from banks and microfinance institutions with household surveys. Honohan's financial measures are based on population data from 2003.

2. 2005 population data from the United Nations Human Development Index online database. We define adult population as individuals ages 15 years or older.[3]

3. Percentage of population living on more than and less than $5 per day, PPP-adjusted, using most recently available data from the World Bank's PovcalNet.[4]

4. 2005 per capita income and level of urbanization from the Human Development Index online database.

Using this dataset we were then able to analyze several areas of interest to policymakers, providers, and researchers alike. First we considered the number of adults who do and do not use formal financial services. We then examined levels of usage for people living above and below $5 per day PPP-adjusted. We then compared levels of usage across various countries and regions to find if there were any correlations between levels of financial services use and income and urbanization.

In our research we use some key terminological distinctions that are worth emphasizing: use of financial services, rather than access; and using households and adults interchangeably.

Use of Financial Services
In the world of financial inclusion, experts often go back and forth between "use" of financial services and "access." There are important conceptual debates about which of these makes for more appropriate policy goals—do we aim for people to have the opportunity to use formal financial services, or are there some services that we want all people to use (e.g., savings, health insurance)? This chapter uses data that is explicitly focused on usage, in large part because that is what was available. Access is more difficult to measure (though it can be approximated by, for example, measuring proximity to formal financial services outlets). Access, by definition, is always larger than usage so the numbers here put a lower bound on access. Being underserved

Table 2.1
Country-level data on adult population from United Nations Human Development Index, financial service usage from Honohan 2008, and income data from World Bank's PovcalNet

Source	HDI 2007/8 "Build your own tables"	HDI 2007/8 "Build your own tables" Calculated	Honohan (2008)	Calculated	HDI 2007/8 "Build your own tables"	HDI 2007/8 "Build your own tables"	PovcalNet (World Bank)	PovcalNet (World Bank)
Country	Population (m, 2005)	Population >15 (m, 2005)	Use of financial services (%, adults)	Adults using financial services (m)	GDP per capita (PPP, $ Intl, 2005)	Urban (%, 2005)	<$5 per day (%)	<$5 per day (year of data)
Afghanistan	25.1	13.303	No data	No data	No data	No data	No data	No data
Albania	3.2	2.3584	34	0.801856	No data	No data	0.5924	2005
Algeria	32.9	23.1616	31	7.180096	7062	0.633	0.7644	1995
Angola	16.1	8.6296	25	2.1574	2335	0.533	0.9134	2000
Argentina	38.7	28.4832	28	7.975296	14280	0.901	0.2846	2006
Armenia	3	2.376	9	0.21384	No data	No data	0.9296	2003
Australia	20.3	16.3415	No data	No data	No data	No data	No data	No data
Austria	8.3	6.9886	96	6.709056	No data	No data	No data	No data
Azerbaijan	8.4	6.2748	17	1.066716	No data	No data	0.7584	2005
Bahamas	0.3	0.2172	53	0.115116	18380	0.904	No data	No data
Bahrain	0.7	0.5159	No data	No data	No data	No data	No data	No data
Bangladesh	153.3	99.3384	32	31.788288	2053	0.251	0.9777	2005
Barbados	0.3	0.2433	56	0.136248	0	0.527	No data	No data
Belarus	9.8	8.2614	16	1.321824	No data	No data	0.1229	2005
Belgium	10.4	8.632	97	8.37304	No data	No data	No data	No data
Belize	0.3	0.1872	46	0.086112	7109	0.483	No data	No data

Table 2.1
(continued)

Benin	8.5	4.743	32	1.51776	1141	0.401	0.9667	2003
Bhutan	0.6	0.402	16	0.06432	0	0.111	0.862	2003
Bolivia	9.2	5.6948	30	1.70844	2819	0.642	0.6088	2005
Bosnia and Herzegovina	3.9	3.2136	17	0.546312	No data	No data	0.1718	2004
Botswana	1.8	1.1592	47	0.544824	12387	0.574	0.819	1993.9
Brazil	186.8	134.8696	43	57.993928	8402	0.842	0.3931	2007
Brunei Darussalam	0.4	0.2816	No data	No data	No data	No data	No data	No data
Bulgaria	7.7	6.6374	56	3.716944	No data	No data	0.3673	2003
Burkina Faso	13.9	7.4782	26	1.944332	1213	0.183	0.9748	2003
Burma (Myanmar)	48	34.896	19	6.63024	0	0.306	No data	No data
Burundi	7.9	4.3371	17	0.737307	699	0.1	0.9941	2006
Cambodia	14	8.736	20	1.7472	2727	0.197	0.9461	2004
Cameroon	17.8	10.3596	24	2.486304	2299	0.546	0.9095	2001
Canada	32.3	26.6152	96	25.550592	No data	No data	No data	No data
Cape Verde	0.5	0.3025	40	0.121	5803	0.573	0.7951	2001
Central African Republic	4.2	2.4066	19	0.457254	1224	0.38	0.9731	2003
Chad	10.1	5.4338	No data	No data	No data	No data	0.9786	2002.5
Chile	16.3	12.2413	60	7.34478	12027	0.876	0.2509	2006
China	1313	1029.392	42	432.34464	6757	0.404	0.8006752	2005
Colombia	44.9	31.2953	41	12.831073	7304	0.727	0.5987	2006
Comoros	0.8	0.464	20	0.0928	1993	0.37	0.8984	2004
Congo, Dem. Rep.	58.7	30.9936	No data	No data	No data	No data	0.9652	2005.5
Congo, Rep.	3.6	2.0916	27	0.564732	1262	0.602	0.9472	2005

Table 2.1
(continued)

Costa Rica	4.3	3.0788	29	0.892852	10180	0.617	0.3573	2005
Côte d'Ivoire	18.6	10.8438	25	2.71095	1648	0.45	0.8644	2002
Croatia	4.6	3.887	42	1.63254	No data	No data	0.0059	2005
Cuba	11.3	9.1304	45	4.10868	0	0.755	No data	No data
Czech Republic	10.2	8.6904	85	7.38684	No data	No data	0.0104	1996
Democratic People's Republic of Korea	23.6	17.8888	No data	No data	No data	No data	No data	No data
Denmark	5.4	4.3848	99	4.340952	No data	No data	No data	No data
Djibouti	0.8	0.492	No data	No data	No data	No data	0.8668	2002
Dominican Republic	9.5	6.3175	29	1.832075	8217	0.668	0.4722	2006
Ecuador	13.1	8.8294	35	3.09029	4341	0.628	0.4391	2007
Egypt	72.8	48.5576	41	19.908616	4337	0.428	0.8478	2004.5
El Salvador	6.7	4.4153	26	1.147978	5255	0.598	0.5398	2005
Equatorial Guinea	0.5	0.288	No data	No data	7874	0.389	No data	No data
Eritrea	4.5	2.565	12	0.3078	1109	0.194	No data	No data
Estonia	1.3	1.1024	86	0.948064	No data	No data	0.2205	2004
Ethiopia	79	43.845	14	6.1383	1055	0.16	0.9817	2005
Fiji	0.8	0.5368	39	0.209352	6049	0.508	No data	No data
Finland	5.2	4.2952	99	4.252248	No data	No data	No data	No data
France	61	49.776	96	47.78496	No data	No data	No data	No data
Gabon	1.3	0.8333	39	0.324987	6954	0.836	0.6885	2005
Gambia	1.6	0.9408	21	0.197568	1921	0.539	0.8927	2003

Table 2.1
(continued)

Georgia	4.5	3.6495	15	0.547425	No data	No data	0.7828	2005
Germany	82.7	70.7912	97	68.667464	No data	No data	No data	No data
Ghana	22.5	13.725	16	2.196	2480	0.478	0.9063	2005.5
Greece	11.1	9.5127	83	7.895541	No data	No data	No data	No data
Grenada	0.1	0.0658	37	0.024346	7843	0.306	0.6267	2006
Guatemala	12.7	7.2263	32	2.312416	4568	0.472	0.9812	2003
Guinea	9	5.094	15	0.7641	2316	0.33	0.9758	2002
Guinea-Bissau	1.6	0.8416	No data	No data	No data	No data	0.5785	1998
Guyana	0.7	0.4823	20	0.09646	4508	0.282	0.9294	2001
Haiti	9.3	5.766	15	0.8649	1663	0.388	0.6312	2006
Honduras	6.8	4.08	25	1.02	3430	0.465	No data	No data
Hong Kong	7.1	6.0279	38	2.290602	No data	No data	0.0622	2004
Hungary	10.1	8.5042	66	5.612772	No data	No data	No data	No data
Iceland	0.3	0.2337	No data	No data	No data	No data	0.9730299	2004.5
India	1134.4	760.048	48	364.82304	3452	0.287	0.9306022	2005
Indonesia	226.1	161.8876	40	64.75504	3843	0.481	0.4952	2005
Iran	69.4	49.4128	31	15.317968	7968	0.669	No data	No data
Iraq	28	16.38	17	2.7846	0	0.669	No data	No data
Ireland	4.1	3.2513	88	2.861144	No data	No data	No data	No data
Israel	No data	No data	No data	No data	No data	No data	0.4032	2004
Italy	58.6	50.396	75	37.797	No data	No data	No data	No data
Jamaica	2.7	1.8441	59	1.088019	4291	0.531	0.4706	2006
Japan	127.9	110.1219	No data	No data	No data	No data	No data	No data
Jordan	5.5	3.454	37	1.27798	5530	0.823	0.7079	2003
Kazakhstan	15.2	11.5216	48	5.530368	No data	No data		

Table 2.1
(continued)

Kenya	35.6	20.4344	10	2.04344	1240	0.207	0.8197	2005.4
Kuwait	2.7	2.0574	No data	No data	No data	No data	No data	No data
Kyrgyz Republic	5.2	3.588	1	0.03588	No data	No data	0.9304	2004
Laos	5.7	3.4314	No data	No data	No data	No data	0.9761	2002.2
Latvia	2.3	1.9688	64	1.260032	No data	No data	0.1654	2004
Lebanon	4	2.856	79	2.25624	No data	No data	No data	No data
Lesotho	2	1.192	17	0.20264	3335	0.187	0.8982	2002.5
Liberia	3.4	1.8054	11	0.198594	0	0.581	0.994	2007
Libyan Arab Jamahiriya	5.9	4.1123	27	1.110321	0	0.848	No data	No data
Lithuania	3.4	2.8288	70	1.98016	No data	No data	0.2228	2004
Luxembourg	0.5	0.4075	99	0.403425	No data	No data	No data	No data
Macedonia (the former Yugoslav Republic of)	2	1.606	20	0.3212	No data	No data	0.3115	2003
Madagascar	18.6	10.4532	21	2.195172	923	0.268	1	2005
Malawi	13.2	6.9828	21	1.466388	667	0.172	0.9876	2004.3
Malaysia	25.7	17.6302	60	10.57812	10882	0.673	0.476	2004
Maldives	0.3	0.198	No data	No data	1033	No data	No data	No data
Mali	11.6	6.0668	22	1.334696	1033	0.305	0.9693	2006
Mauritania	3	1.791	16	0.28656	No data	No data	0.873	2000
Mauritius	1.2	0.9072	54	0.489888	12715	0.424	No data	No data
Mexico	104.3	72.1756	25	18.0439	10751	0.76	0.3364	2006
Micronesia	0.1	0.0614	No data	No data	No data	No data	No data	No data
Moldova	3.9	3.12	13	0.4056	No data	No data	0.8368	2004

Table 2.1
(continued)

Mongolia	2.6	1.8486	25	0.46215	2107	0.567	0.9342	2005
Montenegro	0.6	0.4824	No data	No data	No data	No data	No data	No data
Morocco	30.5	21.2585	39	8.290815	4555	0.587	0.6582	2007
Mozambique	20.5	11.439	12	1.37268	1242	0.345	0.9896	2002.5
Namibia	2	1.218	28	0.34104	7586	0.351	0.8172	1993
Nepal	27.1	16.531	20	3.3062	1550	0.158	0.9616	2003.5
Netherlands	16.3	13.3008	100	13.3008	No data	No data	No data	No data
New Zealand	4.1	3.2185	No data	No data	No data	No data	No data	No data
Nicaragua	5.5	3.4155	5	0.170775	3674	0.59	0.7222	2005
Niger	13.3	6.916	31	2.14396	781	0.168	0.98	2005
Nigeria	141.4	78.7598	15	11.81397	1128	0.482	0.9782	2003.7
Norway	4.6	3.6984	84	3.106656	No data	No data	No data	No data
Oman	2.5	1.655	33	0.54615	15602	0.715	No data	No data
Pakistan	158.1	99.2868	12	11.914416	2370	0.349	0.9603	2004.5
Palestine	3.8	2.0558	14	0.287812	0	0.716	No data	No data
Panama	3.2	2.2272	46	1.024512	7605	0.708	0.4528	2006
Papua New Guinea	6.1	3.6234	8	0.289872	2563	0.134	0.8815	1996
Paraguay	5.9	3.7878	30	1.13634	4642	0.585	0.4641	2007
Peru	27.3	18.6186	26	4.840836	6039	0.726	0.5378	2006
Philippines	84.6	53.9748	26	14.033448	5137	0.627	0.8347	2006
Poland	38.2	31.9734	66	21.102444	No data	No data	0.2146	2005
Portugal	10.5	8.8515	84	7.43526	No data	No data	No data	No data
Qatar	0.8	0.6264	No data	No data	No data	No data	No data	No data
Republic of Korea	47.9	38.9906	63	24.564078	No data	No data	No data	No data
Romania	21.6	18.2088	23	4.188024	No data	No data	0.4649	2005

Table 2.1
(continued)

Russian Federation	144	122.256	69	84.35664	No data	No data	0.2602	2005
Rwanda	9.2	5.198	23	1.19554	1206	0.193	0.9861	2000
Saint Lucia	0.2	0.1442	40	0.05768	6707	0.276	0.8453	1995
Saint Vincent and the Grenadines	0.1	0.0707	45	0.031815	6568	0.459	No data	No data
Samoa	0.2	0.1184	19	0.022496	6170	0.224	No data	No data
São Tomé and Príncipe	0.2	0.1168	15	0.01752	2178	0.58	No data	No data
Saudi Arabia	23.6	15.458	62	9.58396	15711	0.81	No data	No data
Senegal	11.8	6.8204	27	1.841508	1792	0.416	0.9354	2005
Serbia	9.9	8.0685	No data	No data	No data	No data	No data	No data
Sierra Leone	5.6	3.2032	13	0.416416	806	0.407	0.9592	2003
Singapore	4.3	3.4615	98	3.39227	No data	No data	No data	No data
Slovakia	5.4	4.4928	83	3.729024	No data	No data	0.0874	1996
Slovenia	2	1.718	97	1.66646	No data	No data	0.0076	2004
Solomon Islands	0.5	0.2975	15	0.044625	2031	0.17	No data	No data
Somalia	8.2	4.5838	No data	No data	No data	No data	No data	No data
South Africa	47.9	32.5241	46	14.961086	11110	0.593	0.724	2000
Spain	43.4	37.1504	95	35.29288	No data	No data	No data	No data
Sri Lanka	19.1	14.4778	59	8.541902	4595	0.151	0.8618	2002
Sudan	36.9	21.8817	15	3.282255	2083	0.408	No data	No data
Suriname	0.5	0.351	32	0.11232	7722	0.739	0.6211	1999
Swaziland	1.1	0.6622	35	0.23177	4824	0.241	0.9648	2000.5
Sweden	9	7.434	99	7.35966	No data	No data	No data	No data

Table 2.1
(continued)

Switzerland	7.4	6.1642	88	5.424496	No data	No data	No data	No data
Syria	18.9	11.9826	17	2.037042	3808	0.506	No data	No data
Tajikistan	6.6	3.9996	16	0.639936	No data	No data	0.9337	2004
Tanzania	38.5	21.406	5	1.0703	744	0.242	0.9999	2000.4
Thailand	63	49.329	59	29.10411	8677	0.323	0.5742	2004
Timor-Leste	1.1	0.605	13	0.07865	No data	No data	0.9673	2001
Togo	6.2	3.5154	28	0.984312	1506	0.401	0.9647	2006
Tonga	0.1	0.0625	No data	No data	No data	No data	No data	No data
Trinidad and Tobago	1.3	1.0114	53	0.536042	14603	0.122	0.5333	1992
Tunisia	10.1	7.474	42	3.13908	8371	0.653	0.5674	2000
Turkey	73	52.341	49	25.64709	No data	No data	0.4349	2005
Turkmenistan	4.8	3.2736	No data	No data	No data	No data	0.8912	1998
Uganda	28.9	14.6234	20	2.92468	1454	0.126	0.9604	2005
Ukraine	46.9	40.0057	24	9.601368	No data	No data	0.2369	2005
United Arab Emirates	4.1	3.2882	No data	No data	No data	No data	No data	No data
United Kingdom	60.2	49.364	91	44.92124	No data	No data	No data	No data
United States	299.8	237.4416	91	216.071856	No data	No data	No data	No data
Uruguay	3.3	2.5146	42	1.056132	9962	0.92	0.2808	2006
Uzbekistan	26.6	17.7688	16	2.843008	No data	No data	0.9734	2003
Venezuela	26.7	18.3429	28	5.136012	6632	0.934	0.4308	2006
Vietnam	85	59.84	29	17.3536	3071	0.264	0.8975	2006
Yemen	21.1	11.4151	14	1.598114	930	0.273	0.9162	2005
Zambia	11.5	6.2445	15	0.936675	1023	0.35	0.9655	2004.3
Zimbabwe	13.1	7.9255	34	2.69467	2038	0.359	No data	No data

does not necessarily mean that these populations lack access. This is especially true for low income populations who lead active financial lives, and choose to use informal financial instruments even though they have access to formal services. Informal tools offer flexibility and convenience that might be missing from more structured financial services. However, informal financial services lack the reliability (e.g., consistent quality and availability), security (e.g., insured savings accounts, sound insurance), affordability and value (e.g., lower interest rates, positive real interest on savings), and potential for scale that formal financial services offer. The challenge in expanding use for policymakers and financial providers is how to provide financial services that match the flexibility afforded by informal tools, and are also reliable, secure, affordable, and value-creating on a large scale.

Adults and Households

Honohan's data uses the concepts of adults and households interchangeably. We realize that policymakers and financial providers might value the estimates differently. For many policymakers, especially those concerned about financial inclusion as a tool for poverty alleviation, household-level data may be more appropriate due to the focus on how many families can benefit from formal financial services. Financial services providers may care about households for some products (e.g., credit), while others, such as savings accounts, payments products, or health insurance, may be relevant at the individual level. Honohan's data sources provide a mix of household-level and adult-level information. "Some of the surveys are based on household units (such as those from the LSMS program); others, such as Finscope, use individual adults as the unit" (Honohan 2008, 2496). In the future, it will be helpful to get usage data at both the household and adult levels in a comparative way to correct for a potential bias where data at the household level suggests more widespread usage than is taking place. For instance, if there are two adults in each household, and in half of all households one adult is using financial services, household data could tell us that 50 percent of households are using financial services, while only 25 percent of adults are using services. This level of analysis would be particularly helpful to providers in understanding how to target products.

Key Findings

Counting the Unbanked

To obtain the total number of adults who do and do not use financial services, we multiplied the percentage of adults who use financial services in each country from Honohan's study with the number of adults in each country based on 2005 population data.

In 2005, out of a total world population of 6.4 billion people, 4.7 billion were adults. As illustrated in figure 2.1, only 2.2 billion of these adults used some form of formal financial services to borrow and/or save. Just over half of the world's adult population, 2.5 billion adults, did not use any formal financial services.

We had complete adult population and usage data for 95 percent of the population. To conduct the analysis for the remaining countries for which we had adult data but no data on usage, we used a "scaling-up" approach, as shown in tables 2.2 and 2.3. We first conducted the analyses for all countries with complete data. We created a multiplier for each region (e.g., East Asia, Latin America, Sub-Saharan Africa) by dividing adult population for all countries by adult population for countries with complete data. We then multiplied the usage data drawn

Adults who use and do not use formal or semiformal financial services globally

Billions of adults

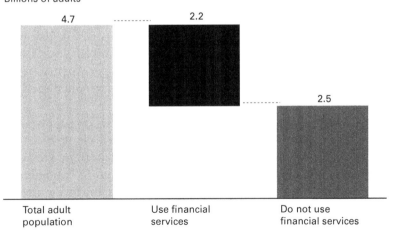

| Total adult population | Use financial services | Do not use financial services |

Figure 2.1
2.5 billion adults globally do not use formal or semiformal financial services. *Sources:* Honohan 2008; United Nations 2010

Table 2.2
Total usage of financial services for 149 countries with data on adult population and financial services usage

Region	Adult population (m)	Using financial services (m)	Not using financial services (m)	% using
Arab states	191.7022	63.283081	128.419119	33
Central Asia and Eastern Europe	381.8651	194.997908	186.867192	51
East Asia	1471.1953	607.900493	863.294807	41
High-income OECD	588.9427	539.652729	49.289971	92
Latin America and the Caribbean	387.1273	136.815373	250.311927	35
South Asia	1039.4968	435.756134	603.740666	42
Sub-Saharan Africa	370.0234	74.426923	295.596477	20
Total	**4430.3528**	**2052.832641**	**2377.520159**	**46**

from countries with complete data with this multiplier to compute usage data for all countries.

Our confidence in the data is increased through confirmation of the bottom- line figure of 2.5 billion unbanked adults—half of the world population—in an independent household-level survey collected in 2011 in 148 economies as part of the Gallup World Survey (with funding from the Bill & Melinda Gates Foundation and oversight from the World Bank Development Research Group). The Gallup survey also counts about 2.5 billion unbanked adults in 2011, which is, like our estimate, half of the global sample (Demirgüç-Kunt and Klapper 2012). The Gallup survey includes about 1,000 households per country (with more from India, China, and Russia), interviewed by telephone and in face-to-face meetings.

Another way to measure financial access is to focus on supply side data. The *Financial Access 2010* report by the Consultative Group to Assist the Poor (CGAP 2010) does just that. CGAP used data from a survey of financial regulators from 142 countries to estimate the number of unbanked adults in the world. They begin by counting the total number of deposit accounts in countries and then dividing by 3 (a rough estimate of the number of deposit accounts per banked adult worldwide). The result from this approximation is that 2.7 billion adults are unbanked, a number that is again very similar to ours. Wherever possible, data on households or individuals seems most appropriate for

Table 2.3
Total usage of financial services scaled-up to 177 countries that had data on adult population but no data on usage

Region	Multiplier to scale-up	Adult population (m)	Using financial services (m)	Not using financial services (m)	% using
Arab states	1.060321165	203.2659	67.10039016	136.1655098	33
Central Asia and Eastern Europe	1.030965124	393.6896	201.0360423	192.6535577	51
East Asia	1.01476738	1492.921	616.8775906	876.0434094	41
High-income OECD	1.220591239	718.8583	658.6953932	60.16290678	92
Latin America and the Caribbean	1	387.1273	136.815373	250.311927	35
South Asia	1.012988015	1052.9978	441.4157412	611.5820588	42
Sub-Saharan Africa	1.101498986	407.5804	81.98118024	325.5992198	20
Total		**4656.4403**	**2203.921711**	**2452.518589**	**47**

Note: We created a multiplier for each region based on total adult population for all countries (adult population column in table 2.3) divided by adult population for each region from table 2.2. We used this multiplier to scale-up the figures for financial services usage.

Adults who do not use formal financial services
Millions of adults

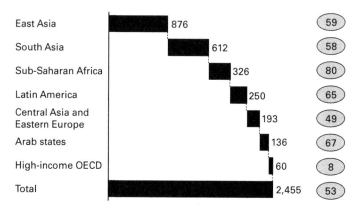

Figure 2.2
Nearly all of the world's financially unserved adults live in Africa, Asia, and Latin America. Regional groupings based on UN Human Development Index. *Sources:* Honohan 2008; United Nations 2010; World Bank 2010

measuring financial usage, but it is helpful to know that a supply-side approach yields similar results.

Where Are the Unbanked?

Figure 2.2 depicts the geographical distribution of the adults who do not use formal financial services. The exhibit plots the number and percentage of unserved adults against the following regions: East Asia, South Asia, Sub-Saharan Africa, Latin America, Central Asia and Eastern Europe, Arab states, and high-income OECD countries.

Nearly all of the 2.5 billion unserved adults live in Africa, Asia, and Latin America. For these regions, the total percentage of unserved adults climbs to 62 percent of the adult population. The greatest number of unserved adults, almost 1.5 billion, reside in East and South Asia. In Sub-Saharan Africa, 80 percent of the adult population—325 million people—remains unserved, as compared to only 8 percent in high-income OECD countries.

Who Are the Unbanked?

Given that financial inclusion is a stated goal for many governments, estimating the depth of financial services is a useful first step for policy

making. We examined usage by income distribution using a conservative assumption about the penetration of formal financial services among those living on less than $5 per day.

We divided countries' population into two segments: the percentage of population living on more than $5 per day and the percent living on less than $5 per day. We assumed a positive one-to-one correlation between use of financial services and income level, meaning that formal financial usage becomes universal above $5 per day.

This is an inherently conservative approach to estimating how far down-market financial services provision goes, as it is unlikely that every adult living on more than $5 per day uses formal financial services. In other words, our figures almost certainly underestimate the use of formal financial services below the $5 per day threshold. We use India as an example in figure 2.3 to illustrate our approach:

• In 2005, India had 760 million adults.

• Using Honohan estimates, we knew that 48 percent of these adults, 365 million, used formal financial services.

Methodology used to estimate the profiles of the banked and unbanked

Indian adult population by income segment
Percent, 100% = 760 million adults
(15+ years old), 2005

1 Segment India's population by income segment, using PPP-adjusted PovcalNet

<$5/day

97% 3%

>$5/day

2 Place line at point equivalent to total access to financial services, and assume all adults use financial services up to this line and no adults use them below it.

48% of Indians use formal financial services, according to Honohan 2008

3 Estimate usage by income segment

Estimated number of adults using formal financial services in India
Millions of adults

365

345 20

| Using financial services and earning <$5/day | Using financial services and earning >$5/day | Use financial services |

Figure 2.3
We have taken a conservative approach to estimating the "depth" of financial services penetration. *Sources:* Honohan 2008; United Nations 2010; World Bank 2010

• We assumed that financial services usage begins top-down, meaning that the first set of adults to use formal services were the richest adults.

• Approximately 20 million adults live on more than $5 per day, PPP-adjusted.

• We assume that all of the adults who live on more than $5 per day are included in the approximately 365 million adults who use formal financial services.

• We then assume that the remainder of adults using financial services live on less than $5 per day.

• This means that approximately 345 million adults live on less than $5 per day and use formal financial services.

Tables 2.4 and 2.5 apply the same approach to countries in Africa, Asia, and the Middle East. We omitted high-income OECD countries, Central Asia and Eastern Europe, and Latin America because of the relatively small percentage of the population living on less than $5 per day, PPP-adjusted, in comparison to the amount of financial services usage.

Given these conservative assumptions, the number of people below the $5 per day threshold will surprise many. Figure 2.4 depicts the number of adults who live on less than $5 per day and more than $5 per day in East Asia, South Asia, Sub-Saharan Africa, and the Middle East who use formal financial services.

Although there are many people unserved by formal financial services, the news is not all bad. In these regions, 1.2 billion adults use

Table 2.4
Usage by income for countries with usage and income data

Region	Adult population (m)	Usage <$5 per day (m)	Usage >$5 per day (m)	Total served (m)	# of countries with data
Arab states	115.3208	15.90756064	25.48714036	41.394701	6
East Asia	1386.8666	308.128521	262.618309	570.74683	10
South Asia	1039.4968	391.0915648	44.6645692	435.756134	7
Sub-Saharan Africa	358.5089	48.9139094	22.0031356	70.917045	36
Total	**2900.1931**	**764.0415558**	**354.7731542**	**1118.81471**	59

Note: Figures based on 57 countries with population, usage, and income data across the Arab states, East Asia, South Asia, and Sub-Saharan Africa.

Table 2.5
Scaled-up usage by income data for all countries

Region	Multiplier to scale-up	Adult population (m)	Usage <$5 per day (m)	Usage >$5 per day (m)	Total served (m)
Arab states	1.762612642	203.2659	28.03886749	44.92395581	72.96282
East Asia	1.076470513	1492.921	331.691267	282.7008658	614.3921
South Asia	1.012988015	1052.9978	396.1710679	45.2446733	441.4157
Sub-Saharan Africa	1.136876658	407.5804	55.60908184	25.01485126	80.62393
Total		3156.7651	811.5102842	397.8843461	1209.395

Note: Figures scaled-up to cover all of Arab states, East Asia, South Asia, and Sub-Saharan Africa. A similar approach is described in table 2.2.

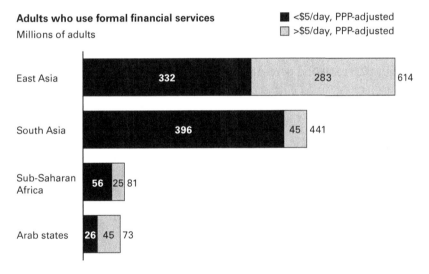

Adults who use formal financial services
Millions of adults

■ <$5/day, PPP-adjusted
☐ >$5/day, PPP-adjusted

East Asia: 332 | 283 | 614

South Asia: 396 | 45 | 441

Sub-Saharan Africa: 56 | 25 | 81

Arab states: 26 | 45 | 73

Figure 2.4
Hundreds of millions of adults who use financial services live on less than $5 per day, PPP-adjusted. *Sources:* Honohan 2008; United Nations 2010; World Bank 2010

formal financial services. About 800 million adults, two-thirds of the served population, actually live on less than $5 per day. In South Asia alone, financial providers serve 396 million low-income adults (mostly in India).

The key message from these analyses is that hundreds of millions of adults living on less than $5 per day are already being reached with formal financial services. Serving these segments at scale is not only possible but is also to a large extent already happening.

Drivers of Inclusion

We compared the data on financial services usage separately with national levels of per capita income and urbanization to identify possible drivers of financial inclusion through a standard correlation. Our dataset included complete data for 102 countries in Africa, the Middle East, Asia, and Latin America. We did not include the high-income OECD countries or Central Asia and Eastern Europe because we wanted to focus on the poorest countries.

Figure 2.5 plots the percentage of population that uses formal financial services against GDP per capita (we had GDP per capita data for 94 of the 102 countries). We found a moderate to strong positive correla-

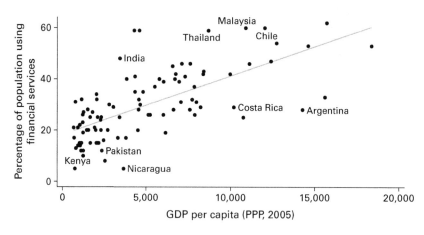

Figure 2.5
There is a moderate to strong relationship between GDP per capita and usage of financial services. The gray line indicates the linear prediction. *Sources:* Honohan 2008; United Nations 2010; World Bank 2010

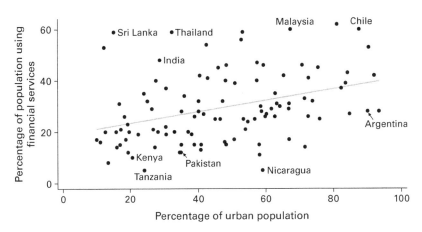

Relationship between urban population and financial services
All countries

Figure 2.6
There is a weak positive correlation between usage of financial services and urbanization. The gray line indicates the linear prediction. *Sources:* Honohan 2008; United Nations 2010; World Bank 2010

tion between usage levels and per capita income across countries. Figure 2.6 plots the percentage of population that uses formal financial services against level of urbanization. We found a weak positive relationship between use of services and urbanization.[5]

Many countries do not fit the overall pattern. For example, India and Thailand have relatively low per capita income and a large rural population but have greater use of financial services than many richer and more urban countries. These differences also occur within regions—for instance, Chile has far more citizens using formal financial services than Costa Rica, a nation with generally well-regarded governance and policy.

These findings support the idea that countries can improve levels of financial inclusion by creating effective regulatory and policy environments and enabling the actions of individual financial services providers.

Improving Data

The quality of these analyses hinges largely on the quality of Honohan's cross-country data on financial services usage. This data is widely

cited and is used in *Finance for All*, the World Bank's 2008 publication on access to financial services (World Bank 2008).

We constructed an alternative measure for twelve countries using more recent select financial services country-specific data from domestic news sources and others' analyses. The countries account for 2 billion people, almost one-third of the world's total population.[6] In general, Honohan's data held up well against this testing. Using these alternative financial access measures, we estimate that 2.4 billion adults do not use formal financial services, compared to our original estimate of 2.5 billion. The number of unserved adults in Asia, Africa, the Middle East, and Latin America drops from 2.2 billion to 2.1 billion. These differences are relatively small and do not change the fundamental findings.

Another consideration is that our estimates are based on population data from around 2005. The global financial crisis that started in 2008, twinned with a growing policy focus on financial inclusion, have created forces to both increase and decrease global financial access after the surveys reflected here. In that light, it's notable how closely our benchmark estimate that 2.5 billion adults are unbanked lines up with the 2011 Gallup World Survey estimate (Demirgüç-Kunt and Klapper 2012).

We undertook this analysis to create a reasonable estimate of financial services usage. This effort, even with its limitations, provides a quantitative starting point for future studies on the nature and amount of usage of financial services.

Conclusion

This study brings together available data to frame important debates on financial inclusion. The findings are striking: (1) approximately 2.5 billion adults do not currently use financial services, about half of the world's adults; (2) existing practice shows that it is possible to serve low-income populations on a large scale; (3) socioeconomic status and demographics are not deterministic factors in financial access. Yet billions of people—and especially those who live on under $5 per day—are not using formal financial services, which can inhibit their ability to build wealth, increase their income, and manage uncertainty.

This research is just a start. Updating and refining these analyses (and perhaps even refuting them) requires more detailed household and/or adult-level data. The Gallup World Survey is now helping

in efforts to identify gaps and pin down numbers more firmly (Demirgüç-Kunt and Klapper 2012). Those efforts are crucial to our understanding of the factors, policies, regulatory frameworks, and products that will have a materially positive effect on financial access. It is absolutely necessary to have a better understanding of the scope of formal financial access today. But even as these estimates of access improve, they will not be sufficient to realize the hope indicated in our estimates: increasing financial access is possible and within the grasp of policymakers and financial services providers. Banking the world is not only possible but already happening, yet much work remains to be done.

Notes

1. A version of this chapter was published as "Counting the World's Unbanked" by Chaia, Goland, and Schiff in *The McKinsey Quarterly* (March 2010). The research here considers the use of formal and semiformal financial services. We exclude informal financial sources such as moneylenders or informal rotating savings and credit schemes. Semiformal sources include microfinance institutions, which might not be subjected to the same regulation as traditional banks. To keep things simple through this chapter, when we refer to "formal financial services," we include semiformal services such as those provided by microfinance institutions.

2. This chapter uses regional definitions from the United Nations (UN) Human Development Index. High-income OECD countries, as well as Central Asia and Eastern Europe and Latin America and the Caribbean are excluded from this analysis because the methodology employed is ineffective for these regions, because of their relatively high incomes in comparison to the levels of usage. Please see the methodology section for further discussion.

3. A new version of the UN Human Development Index that uses 2007 population data is available at http://hdr.undp.org/en/statistics/data/.

4. The World Bank's PovcalNet is an online computational tool that provides regional and country-level poverty measures.

5. The coefficient of correlation between percentage of population using financial services and GDP per capita is 0.64, and the coefficient between percentage of population using financial services and urbanization is 0.36. Both are significant at 1 percent.

6. The countries are Botswana, Brazil, India, Indonesia, Kenya, Mexico, Namibia, Nigeria, South Africa, Tanzania, Uganda, and Zambia. The alternative data sources included Finscope Africa surveys, Reserve Bank of India reports, World Bank surveys on Brazil, Business Latin America, and Bank Rakyat of Indonesia studies.

References

Consultative Group to Assist the Poor (CGAP). 2010. Financial Access 2010: The State of Financial Inclusion through the Crisis. September.

Demirgüç-Kunt, Aslı, and Leora Klapper. 2012. Measuring Financial Inclusion: The Global Findex Database. Policy Research Working Paper 6025, World Bank, Washington, DC.

Honohan, Patrick. 2008. Cross-country variation in household access to financial services. *Journal of Banking & Finance* 32 (May): 2493–2500.

United Nations. 2010. Human Development Index dataset.

World Bank. 2008. Finance for All? Policies and Pitfalls in Expanding Access. World Bank Policy Research Report. World Bank, Washington, DC.

World Bank. 2010. PovcalNet.

II Better Data

3 Cause and Effect of Financial Access: Cross-Country Evidence from the FinScope Surveys

Patrick Honohan and Michael King

Access to financial services is widely considered essential for the economic well-being of households in low-income countries. Savings, payment, and credit services facilitate household-level consumption smoothing, help insure against risk, and allow investment in education and other forms of capital. Yet levels of access to financial services vary widely, with up to 2.5 billion people globally outside the formal banking system (Morduch et al. 2009). In Africa, estimates from the FinScope surveys suggest that the proportion of the population with access to formal financial services ranges from 8 percent in Mozambique to 54 percent in neighboring South Africa.

Although innovations in microfinance have taken center stage in efforts to expand financial access over the last two decades, attention is now shifting to opportunities to reform formal banking systems to open savings, loan, and insurance products up to the financially excluded (Karlan and Morduch 2009). Despite growing interest in formal banking systems, there was until recently only limited availability of detailed surveys of household usage of financial services in sub-Saharan Africa, especially at the cross-country level (Beck and Demirgüç-Kunt 2008). Addressing this weakness, a wave of financial access surveys known as the FinScope surveys have been conducted across sub-Saharan Africa since their launch in 2004, and this chapter provides the latest estimates of formal banking penetration in eleven sub-Saharan African countries.[1]

By pooling eleven nationally representative FinScope surveys, we exploit commonalities in survey design to comprehensively examine the role of individual, geographic, and national characteristics in influencing the use of financial services in sub-Saharan Africa. Our efforts complement recent research conducted on Mexico and transition economies

in Eastern Europe that has shed light on the characteristics of households with formal financial access (Djankov et al. 2008; Beck and Brown 2010).

In our pooled dataset of eleven countries, we confirm that income and education are key demand-side determinants of access to formal banking. We find that the more sophisticated an individual's financial sector knowledge, the higher their likelihood of being formally banked, and that trust in banks is associated with a significant increase in the chances of being formally banked. Geographical location also plays a role. We confirm the supply-side constraint of location, as measured by the urban-rural divide or mobile phone usage, in determining the financial status of households in sub-Saharan Africa. However, though we maintain the view that distance to financial services is a central determinant of financial access in Africa, notwithstanding recent advances in mobile banking, our "time to grocery store" variable is not significantly related to financial access. Although the role of gender is confirmed as an important correlate of financial access in summary statistics and univariate tests, it is revealing that when psychometric variables and education are controlled for, gender is not statistically significantly related to financial access.

This chapter also contributes to the literature on the impact of access to financial services on individual level income at the micro level. We argue for the validity of trust in banks as an instrumental variable for the use of banking services and believe this approach contributes to the related literature. In our pooled dataset, we specifically find, using this instrumental variable approach, that access to formal banking services increases an individual's monthly income by 1.67 percent, which in economic terms represents an increase of $1.41 in monthly income when evaluated at the mean.

Literature Review

Accumulated evidence at the national level on penetration rates of formal finance has identified some of the main country characteristics that influence these penetration rates and offered preliminary estimates of the magnitude of the effects (Honohan 2008a, 2008b). Mean income, the quality of national institutions, and indicators of geographic isolation such as population density or mobile phone penetration are strongly related to household financial penetration rates, with additional factors such as age distribution also playing a role.

At the household level, recent research documenting access to formal banking services in Mexico and transition economies has shed light on the characteristics of households with formal financial access. In their study of Mexican households using data collected by BANSEFI and the Mexican Ministry of Agriculture, Djankov, Miranda, Seira, and Sharma (2008) find that households with bank accounts enjoy higher levels of consumption and possess greater assets and that members of such households are more likely to be college educated. Beck and Brown (2010) use the European Bank for Reconstruction and Development's (EBRD) Life in Transition Survey (LITS) database to assess the correlates of access for formal banking services. At the household level, they find that the likelihood of holding a bank account or bank card increases with income, wealth, and education in most transition countries. They also find evidence of a statistically significant role played by religion and minority status as well as the urban-rural divide.

Economic theory suggests that financial development can have ambiguous outcomes for poverty and inequality reduction at the national level. The empirical evidence is however suggestive of the positive role played by financial development in reducing poverty and easing inequality. Beck, Demirgüç-Kunt, and Levine (2007) find that financial development reduces income inequality, and Honohan (2004) shows that financial depth helps explain the level of poverty, measured as the proportion of people with incomes of less than $1 or $2 a day.

At the household and individual level, economic theory suggests that access to financial services can contribute to poverty reduction. Access to finance should allow poor households to save, invest in the future in the form of physical and human capital, and insure against income and health shocks. The most striking fact about the current state of knowledge is the disconnect between evidence on the effects of national financial depth (seen as an imperfect proxy for overall financial development) and the effects of household financial penetration (Beck, Demirgüç-Kunt, and Honohan 2009; Honohan 2004; World Bank 2008). Thus, although considerable evidence at both the cross-country and sectoral levels confirms a causal role for financial sector development in contributing to economic growth and economic welfare—a confirmation not overturned by the recent severe collapses, following overextension, in the financial systems of most advanced economies— surprisingly little evidence has so far been obtained to confirm a robust link at the micro level between financial penetration and the welfare of

individuals and households. Many recent empirical studies have suggested a direct link between access to microfinance and welfare outcomes but failed to adequately take into consideration selection bias in their econometric strategies. However, some recent research has pointed to a possible link. Addressing the issue of selection bias, Burgess and Pande (2005) find that rural branch expansion significantly reduces poverty at the household level by examining the state-led rural bank expansion in India between 1977 and 1990. In the area of microfinance, there is reason to believe that well-managed, innovative, community-based financial products can lead to poverty reduction (Morduch and Hayley 2002), although controversies remain.

Data and Methodology

Data

Our data come from the FinScope surveys conducted between 2004 and 2009 across sub-Saharan Africa. The eleven surveys were carried out using broadly similar stratified multistage random sampling, and the sample size varies from 1,200 in Botswana and Namibia to 21,110 in Nigeria, giving us a total of 55,762 individual observations.[2] Although eight of the surveys are nationally representative, three of the more recent surveys—Malawi, Mozambique, and Nigeria—capitalized on greater resources available to oversample rural areas and interview a broadly equal number of people in different districts, provinces, and states, respectively. These surveys as well as the remaining eight surveys use adult weights, and for the purpose of summary statistics we use these adult weights to transform the eleven datasets into nationally representative datasets. In addition, all regression analyses conducted in this chapter, including our pooled regressions, take these weights into consideration.

The surveyed countries include some of the poorest in the world, and it is not surprising that they display very low penetration of financial services. Previous survey estimates have put usage of formal financial services as low as 5 percent in Tanzania, for example, although FinScope's more probing interviews estimate this number as somewhat higher (Honohan 2008a). On the other hand, three of the countries in Southern Africa—Botswana, Namibia, and South Africa—are middle-income countries with some of the highest mean incomes in sub-Saharan Africa, although they also have exceptionally high levels of inequality.

The FinScope surveys contain significant detail on individuals' awareness and usage of different financial products and service providers, and although the surveys collect details on some individual characteristics, unlike the Living Standards Measurement Survey (LSMS) surveys they do not attempt to build a rounded profile of each household's economic activities. The questions asked are not exactly the same for each country, as is to some extent inevitable given the different product and provider ranges and cultural settings, but there is enough commonality between the surveys to allow quite a degree of cross-country comparison.

The FinScope surveys take a country-specific approach to assessing whether an individual is formally, informally banked, or financially excluded. In each country, respondents are asked whether they currently use a financial product, for up to thirty different such products. Although it is obvious for the vast majority of the financial products which are formal or informal, there may be a difference of opinion for some of the marginal cases.[3] Two significant differences between our approach and the official FinScope methodology are worthy of note. First, we have included a small number of additional products for Malawi, Namibia, Rwanda, and Zambia to improve consistency in approach between the countries. Second, the absence of a published methodology for Mozambique, Tanzania, and Uganda means that we are unable to compare our list of formal financial products with the list used by FinScope.

Although variables such as *age, urban, mobile,* and *female* are instantly comparable across datasets, considerable work is required to ensure that *education, personal monthly income, financial sector knowledge, bank trust, risk aversion,* and *time to grocery store* are comparable.[4]

Education is first standardized on a scale of 1–8 from "no formal education" up to "completed university education," but for the purposes of our multivariable regressions we derive four binary measures of education: less than primary education, completed primary education, completed secondary education, and above secondary education.

The financial sector knowledge score is a normalized score (on a scale of 1 to10) achieved in a financial sector knowledge quiz given during the interview. For nine countries, a series of financial products/terms are mentioned and the individual receives two points for "I understand," one point for "I have heard of," and zero points for "never heard of/don't understand." For example, in Namibia respondents are

asked whether they understand or have heard of sixteen financial terms/products: ATM, interest rates, bad debts, application process, bond/mortgage loan, credit bureau, credit record, the Bank of Namibia, and eight others. The one exception is Uganda, where we are forced to rely on the response to the question, "What do we call an increase in prices?" Different scores are given for each of seventeen possible answers.

To support our analysis, we derive two important psychometric variables for each individual: risk aversion and trust in banks. For seven of the countries, our measure of risk aversion is calculated using an individual's response to the statement, "To get ahead in life, one needs to take some risks," but for three of the countries we had to use more innovative approaches to ascertain the level of risk aversion at the individual level, with varying degrees of success. For Tanzania, an individual is classified as risk averse if they responded positively to having insurance or agreeing with the statement, "I would like to have insurance but I cannot afford it." For Malawi and Rwanda, risk aversion is ascertained by the respondent mentioning a number of risks to their household that was above a certain threshold. For nine of the countries, the *banktrust* variable is determined by the question "I trust banks" or similar, but in the case of Tanzania, trust in banks is defined as a positive response to the statements "Banks are my ideal financial service provider" or "I don't use banks at the moment but would really like to," excepting those who say that their lack of trust in banks is the reason they don't have a bank account or the reason they don't save with banks.

Although the mobile banking revolution in Africa is reducing the need for large-scale rural bank branch expansion to improve financial inclusion, distance or time to banking infrastructure is likely to continue to remain a significant barrier to multilayered financial services for the rural poor. To capture this barrier accurately, data on distance or time to nearest bank branch would be ideal. Unfortunately, for the FinScope surveys data of this kind is available only for Rwanda. Instead, for the remainder of the counties we rely on a time to grocery store as a proxy for distance to banking infrastructure. Tanzania is an exception for which we use distance to where people usually conduct business transactions. Of course, in remote rural areas in Africa, grocery stores are significantly more abundant than banking infrastructure, and as a result it is important to consider our results with this distinction in mind.

Monthly personal income is mostly recorded in the FinScope surveys as a categorical variable with up to twenty possible bands, with the exception of Nigeria, which records the exact income. For the purposes of our pooled dataset, we have taken the midpoint of these categories and converted the amount into U.S. dollars according to the average exchange rate for the year of the survey.[5]

For most of the analyses in this chapter, Kenya drops out because FinScope Kenya does not include many of our variables of interest such as income, trust in banks, financial sector knowledge, or risk aversion. The remainder of the pooled dataset has good coverage of our variables of interest, with the exception of no observations for time to grocery store for Mozambique and Uganda and an unorthodox approach to calculating personal income in Uganda that leads to 80 percent missing values.[6]

In table 3.1, we present the summary statistics of the percentage of adults with access to formal financial services in general and with various attributes for our eleven countries of interest. In addition, we graph the underlying distribution of four nonbinary variables of interest: financial sector knowledge, education, monthly natural log income, and time to store, for both the banked and unbanked populations (see figures 3.2–3.9).

At the country level, formal financial service penetration rates are higher in the relatively more affluent countries of South Africa (53.9 percent), Namibia (47.4percent), and Botswana (43.4 percent) and lower in the poorer countries of Kenya (17.0 percent), Malawi (16.0 percent), Rwanda (15.3 percent), Tanzania (14.3 percent), Zambia (14.5 percent), and Mozambique (7.9 percent). The exception is Nigeria, which records a low financial sector penetration rate (21.1 percent) despite its relative affluence among sub-Saharan African peers. Figure 3.1 shows a graphical representation of the relationship between gross national income (GNI) per capita and financial penetration at the national level and highlights Nigeria's underperformance.[7]

Previous estimates of access to formal financial services, such as Honohan (2008a), use country-level correlates to predict the level of financial penetration (based on equation 3.4 in Honohan 2008a). In table 3.2, we compare the FinScope estimates of formally banked with Honohan's (2008a) estimates of warranted penetration rates and the Mark IIIe estimates.[8] The FinScope surveys have raised the estimates of formally banked in Kenya, Namibia, Nigeria, South Africa, and Uganda. As one might expect, the predicted (warranted) penetration

Table 3.1
Formal financial service penetration for individuals with various characteristics (percentage of surveyed adults in each category)

	Botswana (2004)	Kenya[a] (2006)	Malawi[b] (2008)	Mozambique[b] (2009)	Namibia (2004)	Nigeria[b] (2008)	Rwanda (2008)	South Africa (2006)	Tanzania (2006)	Uganda[a] (2006)	Zambia (2005)
Total	43.4	17.0	16.0	7.9	47.4	21.1	15.3	53.9	14.3	26.1	14.5
Region											
Urban	56.8	29.2	40.9	19.3	64.9	39.1	26.5	69.7	22.0	31.9	24.5
Rural	37.0	13.0	11.2	2.0	35.7	14.1	13.3	44.2	11.3	24.2	9.2
Gender											
Female	41.3	12.9	14.5	6.0	47.9	15.0	13.5	53.2	11.5	21.9	11.4
Male	45.9	21.3	17.7	10.1	46.9	26.7	17.7	54.5	17.4	30.7	17.5
Education											
Did not complete primary	22.9	5.6	4.2	5.7	19.6	2.2	4.5	27.5	6.3	20.0	1.8
More than completed secondary school	66.9	40.9	51.9	14.7	77.2	43.7	50.0	79.9	36.0	31.2	42.1
Income[c]											
Under $1 per day	16.7	N/A	4.2	3.2	14.5	13.2	9.8	20.2	6.3	N/A	8.7
Above $1 per day	64.5	N/A	31.4	11.3	60.3	31.8	35.8	65.2	19.4	N/A	20.3
Age											
60 +	37.9	15.0	10.2	6.6	44.0	20.9	10.9	41.5	12.3	16.8	15.8
50–59	45.1	22.5	16.2	8.1	49.8	22.3	15.1	61.2	11.9	27.9	26.2
40–49	46.1	21.1	17.5	8.6	53.6	25.7	18.4	58.4	20.1	27.4	27.3
30–49	54.2	21.0	19.4	8.9	57.9	23.3	20.0	66.0	14.9	32.1	22.5
16–29	38.0	12.1	14.9	7.3	40.6	17.9	10.2	46.0	13.1	24.6	8.0

[a] Income figures for Kenya not available and not sufficient coverage for Uganda.
[b] Malawi, Mozambique, and Nigeria are figures calculated using adult weights to ensure summary statistics are nationally representative.
[c] 30.4 days per month.

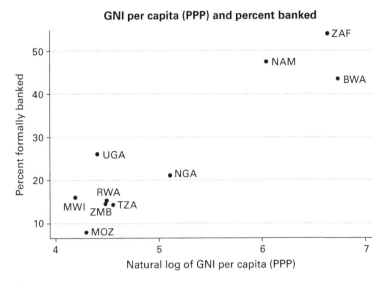

Figure 3.1
Mean income and percentage with bank account in FinScope surveys. *Sources:* FinScope surveys and World Bank 2012

rate using the fitted values for a country with the same GDP per capita, age dependency, ownership of mobile phones, and quality of institutions index enjoys mixed success when compared with either the original Mark IIIe estimates or the FinScope estimates.

There are lower financial sector penetration rates among the poorest individuals in sub-Saharan Africa, defined as those who earn less than $1 a day. The differences are particularly striking in countries with higher inequality, such as South Africa, Botswana, and Namibia. In Namibia, for example, 60.3 percent of those earning above $1 per day have personal access to formal financial services, while only 14.5 percent of those earning less than $1 per day have access. Graphical inspection of the income distribution histograms for the pooled banked and unbanked populations (figures 3.2 and 3.3) confirm the country-level results of table 3.1.

The relationship between education and access to formal banking services is confirmed in table 3.1, which provides the financial penetration rates for those with education beyond the secondary level and those who did not complete primary education. Individuals with less than full primary education display very low levels of financial access, with the poorly educated in Kenya, Malawi, Mozambique, Nigeria,

Table 3.2
Formal penetration rates: Estimated and warranted

	Mark IIIe estimate[a]	Warranted[b]	Over-performance[c]	FinScope formally banked
Botswana	47.0	46.8	0.1	43.4
Ghana	16.2	26.0	−9.8	–
Kenya	10.0	14.8	−4.8	17.0
Lesotho	17.0	29.7	−12.7	–
Malawi	21.1	15.0	6.2	16.0
Mozambique	11.8	17.6	−5.8	7.9
Namibia	28.4	38.5	−10.2	47.8
Nigeria	14.8	11.0	3.8	21.1
Pakistan	12.2	21.3	−9.1	11.0
Rwanda	22.9	11.7	11.1	15.3
South Africa	46.0	51.1	−5.1	53.9
Swaziland	35.3	27.9	7.4	–
Tanzania	5.0	16.3	−11.3	14.3
Uganda	20.2	17.7	2.6	26.1
Zambia	15.4	17.2	−1.8	14.5

[a]Honohan 2008a.
[b]Fitted value from equation 3.4 in Honohan 2008a showing expected penetration percentage for a country with the same GDP per capita, age dependency, ownership of mobile phones and quality of institutions index.
[c]Mark IIIe estimates minus warranted.

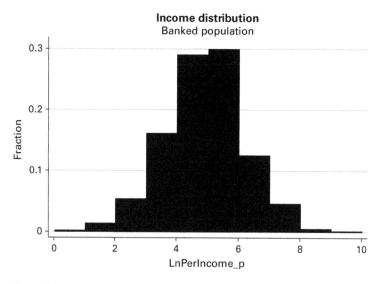

Figure 3.2
Distribution of natural log of income, formally banked population.

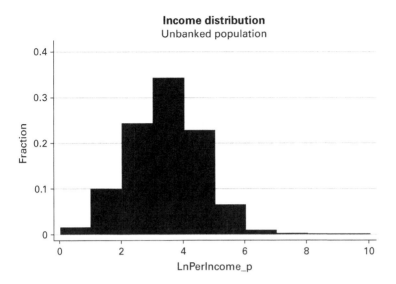

Figure 3.3
Distribution of natural log of income, unbanked population.

Rwanda, Tanzania, and Zambia recording penetration rates between 2 and 6 percent. In contrast, individuals with low levels of education in relatively more affluent countries—South Africa, Botswana, and Namibia—display penetration rates of 28, 23, and 20 percent, respectively, reflecting the greater depth in local financial infrastructure. The level of financial inclusion of less well educated individuals in Uganda especially stands out at 20 percent. More generally, figures 3.4 and 3.5 graphically illustrate the underlying distributions of education level for the banked and unbanked populations for our pooled dataset and confirm our conclusion based on the country-level summary statistics.

In line with previous studies, we find that urban penetration rates are considerably higher than those in rural areas. There is greater formal financial penetration among men than women for ten sub-Saharan African countries, with the exception of Namibia, and more middle-aged individuals tend to participate in financial services than the youngest and oldest age categories, but the differences here are slight.

Figures 3.6 and 3.7 illustrate the clear differences in the distribution of financial sector knowledge between the banked and unbanked populations. The differences are less clear for time to grocery store, but the banked population is still more likely to experience a shorter time to store (see figures 3.8 and 3.9).

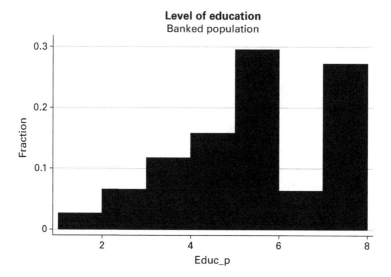

Figure 3.4
Distribution of education levels, formally banked population.

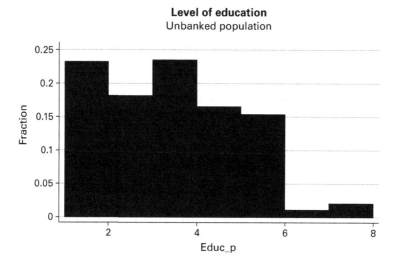

Figure 3.5
Distribution of education levels, unbanked population.

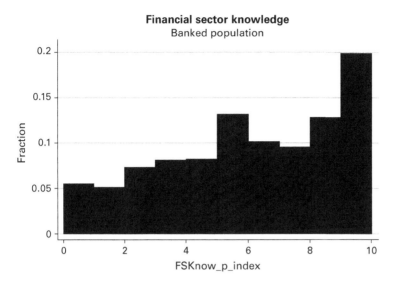

Figure 3.6
Distribution of financial sector knowledge, formally banked population.

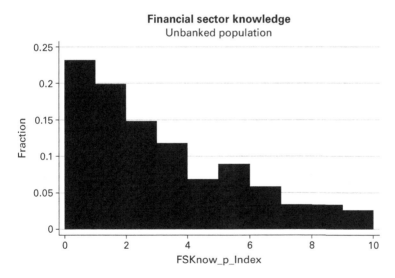

Figure 3.7
Distribution of financial sector knowledge, unbanked population.

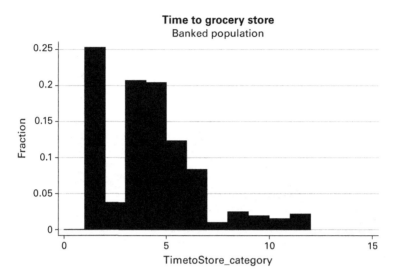

Figure 3.8
Distribution of time to grocery store, formally banked population.

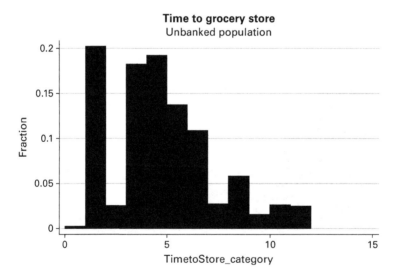

Figure 3.9
Distribution of time to grocery store, unbanked population.

Methodology

The first part of our analysis ascertains the determinants of access to formal financial services at the individual level. Following a series of univariate tests, we employ a multivariable probit model (equation 3.1). The simplest model to assess the probability of a household or individual i in country n having an account ($Use = YES$) is

$$\Pr\{Use_{i,n} = YES_{i,n}\} = f(IND_{i,n}, GEO_{i,n}, NAT_n^f, NAT_n^{nf}), \qquad (3.1)$$

where $IND_{i,n}$ are characteristics of the individual respondent, $GEO_{i,n}$ are characteristics of that individual's local environment, NAT_n^f are country characteristics that are thought of as being subject to the influence of financial access policy, and NAT_n^{nf} are other country characteristics or nonfinancial characteristics. Individual characteristics can be broken down into socioeconomic and psychometric variables such as monthly income, education, financial sector knowledge, age, gender, and risk aversion and trust in banks, respectively. Individual-level geographical variables include an urban dummy, time to grocery store (agnostic to the mode of transport), and whether an individual has a mobile phone. With ten countries in our pooled dataset, it was deemed prudent to use country controls or dummy variables rather than to include a myriad of country-level financial characteristics and other country-level variables, an approach taken by Beck and Brown (2010).

In addition, to help control for unobserved regional heterogeneity and the related problem of omitted variables, a series of subnational district controls are included. Specifically, we control for 5 Ugandan provinces, 5 Rwandan provinces, 9 South African provinces, 9 Zambian provinces, 11 Mozambique provinces, 13 regions in Namibia, 25 districts in Botswana, 26 regions in Tanzania, 30 districts in Malawi, and 37 states in Nigeria.[9]

Reflecting the literature, we expect the demand-side determinants such as income and education to have strong positive coefficients. Our measure of financial sector knowledge, which is related to education level, is also likely to be significant and positively related to the likelihood of being formally banked. We expect that trust in banks will have a positive influence on being banked but are less certain on the relationship our measure of risk aversion will display.

In line with the findings of Beck and Brown (2010), we anticipate that the location of the respondent in relation to banking services (proxied by distance to the nearest grocery store) will be significantly and negatively related to the likelihood of being banked. The interpretation of

the mobile coefficient is more complex. At least in the early stage of the rollout of mobile telecommunications, possession of a mobile phone is likely to indicate proximity to services as well as individual wealth. As mobile phones increasingly reach rural areas, the ability to interpret the mobile dummy as a measure of proximity to services becomes less clear. However one interprets the mobile phone variable, we consider it an important control variable.

In the second step of our analysis, we attempt to find a causal link between access to formal banking services and income. We model the determinants of monthly personal income using equation 3.2 as follows:

$$\text{Income} = f(Banked_{i,n}, IND_{i,n}, GEO_{i,n}, NAT_{i,n}) . \tag{3.2}$$

Instrumental Variables

There is reason to suspect that access to financial services may not be exogenous, which could lead to misleading estimates. The channel whereby access to financial services influences income is at least as plausible as the likely mechanism whereby passing a threshold level of income opens up the opportunity for an individual to access formal banking services. If this is the case reverse causality is likely to lead to inconsistent estimation of the role played by access to financial services in determining income in our ordinary least squares (OLS) estimates.

An additional form of bias in OLS estimates can occur when unobserved heterogeneity at the individual level—such as ambition, ability, or conscientiousness—may make the individual more likely to simultaneously have a higher income and a formal bank account. Such endogeneity may lead to an overestimation of the role played by formal banking in determining income in our OLS estimates.

As the potential endogeneity of access to formal financial services brings into question the validity of our OLS estimates, we propose the use of trust in banks as an instrumental variable for bank use. Trust in banks has been suggested in the literature as a reason for exclusion from the formal banking system (Bertrand, Mullainathan, and Shafir 2004). We expect the first-stage regression to show that bank trust is significantly related to access to formal banking and that when we control for an individual's innate level of risk aversion, trust in banks is not related to income level.

We must go further than proving the relevance of trust in banks as an instrumental variable and argue that *banktrust* is not correlated with omitted variables (the source of the endogeneity); in essence, that there

is no covariance between *banktrust* and the error term in the second-stage regression (Cov{ε, Z} = 0), and that there is sufficient exogenous variation in *banktrust*. We argue that the relationship between psychometric variables such as trust and attitudes to risk and monthly income are complex and unlikely to exhibit any predictable relationship. When it comes to determining future monthly income, we argue that although trust in others—whether colleagues, customers, or fellow villagers—is likely to have a positive influence on income at least outside of dysfunctional institutions, trust in banks is not likely to influence future income. If the decision to trust banks were related to a general preference to be risk averse, and risk aversion had a systematic relationship with income, then *banktrust* might not be a good instrument. However, as we include a measure for risk aversion in our model, we can rule out this channel—at least as far as our measure of risk aversion captures the psychometric phenomenon of risk aversion.

Intuition would suggest that *banktrust* should be correlated with education level and level of financial sector knowledge, and this is confirmed in basic cross tabulations. In particular, there is reason to believe that banktrust may be related to the level of annual banking transactions an individual engages in, although we do not have a measure of this. However, we argue that there is some exogenous element to bank trust that is independent of all potential correlates, emerging from an inner trustfulness to part with one's money that is sufficient, in the African context, to allow the use of trust in banks as an instrument. As a result, the instrumental variables strategy is supported by an attempt to control for as many potential correlates of *banktrust* as possible, including the use of a series of interaction terms.

Our instrumental variable estimates allow us to test for the endogeneity of those formally banked by comparing the coefficients between the OLS and instrumental variables (IV) estimators, otherwise known as the Hausman test. If we find a considerable difference in the coefficients, then it was necessary to instrument in the first place to derive accurate estimates. We use a bootstrapped approach to calculating the Hausman test statistic because of our adherence to robust standard errors.

We remain open to the idea that an individual's education is in fact endogenous in our specification, and we did attempt to use instrumental variables to overcome this problem. We investigated the use of time to grocery store as a potential instrument, but in truth, the nature of the datasets and the precise nature of the time to grocery store variable

precludes an obvious instrument for education. Likewise, financial sector knowledge may be considered endogenous to banking status, and while an argument could be made that financial sector knowledge is endogenous to income, the endogeneity of this relationship is less obvious. In any case, we present the results with and without financial sector knowledge as a control variable.

Results

Determinants of the Formally Banked

We report the results of univariate tests that compare the differences in means for the subsamples of formally banked and non–formally banked respondents in table 3.3. This first step of the analysis confirms the predictions from the literature. First, in terms of measures of household location, we find that banked respondents are more likely to be urban dwellers, experience a shorter time to the local grocery store, and have a mobile phone as the difference in the means of the two subsamples for each of these variables are statistically significant at the 1 percent level. Gender differences are relevant in the two subsamples: we find that men are more likely to have access to formal banking services.

In accordance with our expectations, our univariate tests find that level of education, financial sector knowledge, and monthly income are all higher for the formally banked subsample of the population. As for

Table 3.3
Univariate tests: Determinants of formally banked

	All households	Banked		T-statistic	Sample test
		Yes	No		
Female	0.509	0.412	0.537	24.58	***
Mobile	0.350	0.753	0.238	−120.00	***
Urban	0.318	0.506	0.266	−51.61	***
BankTrust	0.396	0.724	0.303	−86.84	***
RiskAversion	0.322	0.259	0.334	16.15	***
FSKnow	3.719	6.058	3.047	−110.00	***
Time to store	4.134	3.734	4.262	18.27	***
Educ	3.412	5.083	2.942	−130.00	***
LnIncome	3.652	4.722	3.304	−74.29	***

*, **, and *** denote the significance level of the results of the linear independent sample tests. The sample tests are conducted on an unweighted pooled dataset.

psychometric variables, our central prediction of lower trust in banks among the unbanked population is confirmed by the univariate tests. We also find that the unbanked population displays higher levels of risk aversion compared with those integrated into the formal banking system.

In the next step of our analysis, we investigate the determinants of the use of formal bank services more systematically using multivariable probit regressions and find some interesting results. The results are presented in table 3.4. The table reports the marginal effects, defined as the change in the probability of an individual making formal use of banking services for an infinitesimal change in each independent, continuous variable, and by default, the discrete change in the probability for dummy variables or other discrete variables. We provide results of the model without country controls (columns 1, 4, and 7), but we place greater emphasis on the results with country controls (columns 2, 5, and 8) and district controls (columns 3, 6, and 9). The more comprehensive the geographical controls are, the more unobserved regional heterogeneity is controlled for. Not only are the eleven countries in the dataset likely to be characterized by heterogeneous economic, financial, and social circumstances, but different districts within each country are likely to exhibit different geographical and economic characteristics.

Reading from column 9, the importance of education and financial literacy is confirmed. We find that those who have completed primary education increase their chances of being banked by 4 percent compared with the omitted category of less than primary education or illiteracy, and when we consider those with completed secondary education (13 percent increase in the likelihood of being banked) and those with higher than secondary education (43 percent increase in the likelihood of being banked), the relationship strengthens. In similar fashion, increasing financial sector knowledge by one unit increases the likelihood of being formally banked by 3 percent.

We find that a 1 percent increase in monthly personal income increases the chances of being banked by 3 percent and having a mobile phone increases the probability of being banked by 12 percent. This result adds weight to the reasonable suspicion of potential two-way causality between formally banked and income. Having trust in banks is associated with a 11 percent increase in the chances of being banked, a result that is statistically significant with or without country controls and under different specifications of the model. We find that risk aversion is inversely related to formally banked in our full specification

Table 3.4
Determinants of formally banked: Marginal effects

Variables	(1)	(2)	(3)	(4)	(5)	(6)	(7)	(8)	(9)
LnPerIncome	0.04***	0.03***	0.03***	0.04***	0.03***	0.03***	0.04***	0.03***	0.03***
	(0.004)	(0.009)	(0.002)	(0.005)	(0.008)	(0.002)	(0.005)	(0.007)	(0.002)
Primary_completed	0.09***	0.07***	0.06***	0.09***	0.06***	0.05***	0.08***	0.05**	0.04***
	(0.017)	(0.018)	(0.011)	(0.019)	(0.014)	(0.011)	(0.017)	(0.015)	(0.011)
Secondary_completed	0.22***	0.23***	0.21***	0.19***	0.17***	0.15***	0.17***	0.15***	0.13***
	(0.022)	(0.035)	(0.018)	(0.026)	(0.015)	(0.016)	(0.022)	(0.017)	(0.015)
Some_third_level	0.58***	0.63***	0.63***	0.51***	0.48***	0.47***	0.47***	0.44***	0.43***
	(0.028)	(0.064)	(0.030)	(0.031)	(0.029)	(0.027)	(0.029)	(0.030)	(0.026)
Age/100	0.93***	0.98***	0.90***	0.90***	0.99***	0.93***	0.90***	0.97***	0.91***
	(0.129)	(0.157)	(0.101)	(0.138)	(0.175)	(0.107)	(0.127)	(0.138)	(0.100)
Age/100_sq	-0.77***	-0.85***	-0.80***	-0.68***	-0.83***	-0.80***	-0.70***	-0.83***	-0.79***
	(0.142)	(0.210)	(0.120)	(0.148)	(0.233)	(0.126)	(0.138)	(0.177)	(0.116)
Female	-0.01	-0.03**	-0.03***	0.00	-0.01	-0.01*	0.00	-0.01	-0.01
	(0.007)	(0.008)	(0.005)	(0.007)	(0.007)	(0.005)	(0.007)	(0.007)	(0.005)
Mobile	0.20***	0.20***	0.18***	0.18***	0.15***	0.14***	0.16***	0.13***	0.12***
	(0.013)	(0.026)	(0.009)	(0.015)	(0.019)	(0.008)	(0.013)	(0.019)	(0.009)

Table 3.4
(continued)

Variables	(1)	(2)	(3)	(4)	(5)	(6)	(7)	(8)	(9)
Urban	0.07***	0.07***	0.07***	0.05*	0.03**	0.03***	0.05*	0.03**	0.03***
	(0.017)	(0.013)	(0.008)	(0.023)	(0.011)	(0.008)	(0.021)	(0.009)	(0.008)
TimetoStore				0.01**	0.00	0.00	0.01**	0.00	0.00
				(0.003)	(0.002)	(0.002)	(0.003)	(0.001)	(0.002)
FSKnow				0.02***	0.04***	0.04***	0.02***	0.03***	0.03***
				(0.003)	(0.002)	(0.002)	(0.003)	(0.001)	(0.002)
BankTrust							0.14***	0.11***	0.11***
							(0.016)	(0.008)	(0.007)
RiskAversion							−0.02*	−0.02**	−0.02***
							(0.009)	(0.006)	(0.006)
Country Controls					Yes	Yes		Yes	Yes
District Controls		Yes	Yes						
Observations	43,788	43,788	43,774	36,759	36,759	36,747	36,062	36,062	36,050

Notes: Mozambique and Uganda are excluded when time to grocery store is included. Country controls involve a series of country dummies and clustered standard errors at the country level. District controls involve a series of district dummies and clustered standard errors at the district level. Robust standard errors in parentheses.

*$p < 0.05$, **$p < 0.01$, ***$p < 0.001$.

with country controls, but additional country-level analysis indicates that this result in the pooled dataset is largely driven by the Nigerian data.

Although the role of gender is confirmed as an important correlate of financial access in summary statistics and univariate tests, it is revealing that when psychometric variables and education are controlled for, gender is not statistically significantly related to financial status. As indicated earlier, our time to grocery store cannot be considered time to nearest bank branch, and we find that the time to grocery store variable is not significantly related to financial status when country or district level controls are included. However, living in an urban environment does increase the likelihood that an individual is formally banked.

Our country-level analysis confirms these pooled results—but with some striking differences between countries (see table 3.5). The extent of the roles played by income level, education, and financial sector knowledge varies by country. In Namibia, South Africa, Tanzania, and Botswana, we find that a 1 percent increase in monthly personal income increases the chances of being banked by 14 percent, 11 percent, 11 percent, and 10 percent, respectively, compared with a less economically significant relationship in some of the poorer countries in the sample such as Mozambique and Zambia, as well as Nigeria (which weighs down the result for the pooled estimates due to its significant sample size).

Our results from the pooled regression in relation to education are broadly confirmed in our country-level regressions, particularly for the most educated groups. At lower levels of education, the relationship with financial access loses statistical significance in countries such as Mozambique, Nigeria, South Africa, Tanzania, Uganda, and Zambia. Our location variables reveal some interesting results. Although the effect of having a mobile phone is uniformly positive for the majority of countries, the coefficients on time to store and living in an urban area reveal some points worthy of note. Mozambique, Nigeria, and Uganda are the only countries in the sample that record a positive and significant relationship between urban dwelling and formally banked. In Botswana, the opposite result is achieved, indicating that living in an urban environment means an individual is less likely to use formal banking services when all other variables are controlled for. In contrast, the coefficient for time to grocery store remains insignificant for all countries when district controls are included.

The absence of a role of gender in determining financial access when all other variables are included can be seen in the majority of the country-level regressions. However, in Nigeria and Uganda being female reduces the likelihood that an individual is formally banked, whereas in Rwanda the opposite is the case. In relation to trust in the financial system, we find that trust in banks increases the likelihood of being formally banked in all countries, with the exception of Uganda and Zambia.

Financial Access and Income

Although financial access is likely to have a slow-burning effect on an individual's welfare, it may nevertheless be possible to detect such an effect in cross-sectional data, if access changes only gradually. Table 3.6 displays the results of our multivariable investigation into the causal relationship between personal income and financial access within our pooled dataset.

Our OLS estimates (columns 1–4) in table 3.6 confirm our prior finding that having access to formal financial services is associated with higher income, estimated at approximately 1 percent higher income per month when either country or district controls are included. Having a mobile phone is both a proxy for location and income/wealth level, and it is unsurprising that it is positively and significantly related to monthly personal income. We find that women make 39 percent lower monthly income than men.

A number of unexpected results are also present in the data. In line with recent concerns over returns to education in Africa, we find no statistically significant relationship between education level and income is found when country controls are concluded (Pritchett 2001). However, when greater regional heterogeneity is controlled for the relationship between education and income is reestablished. Our results show that differences between countries in average education levels and average attitudes to risk are more important than levels of education and risk aversion at the individual level. The R^2 for the OLS models with country controls is 0.19, higher than the model without country controls.

We find that although time to grocery store does not play a role in determining the likelihood that an individual is banked, it does play a statistically significant role in the determination of income. Specifically, we find that at the 0.05 level of significance, time to grocery store is negatively related to income when district controls are included.

Table 3.5
Determinants of formally banked by country: Marginal effects

Variables	Botswana	Malawi	Mozambique	Namibia	Nigeria	Rwanda	S. Africa	Tanzania	Uganda	Zambia
LnPerIncome	0.10***	0.03***	0.01***	0.14***	0.01***	0.07***	0.11***	0.11***	0.08***	0.01***
	(0.011)	(0.004)	(0.002)	(0.035)	(0.001)	(0.007)	(0.011)	(0.011)	(0.022)	(0.002)
Primary_completed	0.22**	0.04***	0.00	0.21*	0.01	0.09***	0.05	0.05	-0.03	0.02
	(0.079)	(0.009)	(0.004)	(0.102)	(0.011)	(0.028)	(0.062)	(0.062)	(0.093)	(0.017)
Secondary_completed	0.23***	0.07***	-0.00	0.34***	0.08***	0.20**	0.18***	0.18***	0.32***	0.12**
	(0.071)	(0.021)	(0.005)	(0.098)	(0.015)	(0.073)	(0.035)	(0.035)	(0.059)	(0.038)
Some_third_level	0.51***	0.37***	0.00	0.37***	0.31***	0.13	0.34***	0.34***	0.34***	0.38***
	(0.079)	(0.102)	(0.006)	(0.101)	(0.026)	(0.149)	(0.055)	(0.055)	(0.040)	(0.076)
Age/100	2.66***	0.37	0.15***	1.70*	0.58***	0.81*	2.56***	2.56***	-0.04	0.88***
	(0.640)	(0.191)	(0.043)	(0.735)	(0.092)	(0.389)	(0.306)	(0.306)	(0.764)	(0.150)
Age/100_sq	-1.82*	-0.34	-0.12*	-1.38	-0.45***	-0.60	-2.88***	-2.88***	-0.10	-0.87***
	(0.788)	(0.223)	(0.052)	(0.884)	(0.095)	(0.465)	(0.430)	(0.430)	(0.798)	(0.178)
Female	0.07	-0.00	-0.00	0.04	-0.01*	0.03***	0.03	0.03	-0.08*	0.00
	(0.045)	(0.009)	(0.002)	(0.035)	(0.006)	(0.005)	(0.033)	(0.033)	(0.042)	(0.007)

Table 3.5
(continued)

Variables	Botswana	Malawi	Mozambique	Namibia	Nigeria	Rwanda	S. Africa	Tanzania	Uganda	Zambia
Mobile	0.17***	0.08***	0.03***	0.06	0.11***	0.04	0.19***	0.19***	0.18***	0.02
	(0.049)	(0.012)	(0.009)	(0.053)	(0.009)	(0.035)	(0.057)	(0.057)	(0.039)	(0.016)
Urban	-0.27***	0.01	0.02***	0.08	0.03***	0.01	0.05	0.05	0.12***	0.01
	(0.050)	(0.027)	(0.005)	(0.046)	(0.007)	(0.030)	(0.062)	(0.062)	(0.015)	(0.010)
TimetoStore	0.00	-0.00		-0.02	0.00	-0.00	0.00	0.00		0.00
	(0.011)	(0.003)		(0.012)	(0.002)	(0.003)	(0.014)	(0.014)		(0.003)
FSKnow	0.10***	0.02***	0.01***	0.05***	0.02***	0.03**	0.06***	0.06***	0.00	0.01***
	(0.020)	(0.002)	(0.001)	(0.011)	(0.002)	(0.009)	(0.010)	(0.010)	(0.005)	(0.002)
BankTrust	0.27***	0.07***	0.06***	0.32***	0.08***	0.07***	0.27***	0.27***	0.02	0.04
	(0.065)	(0.015)	(0.008)	(0.043)	(0.008)	(0.012)	(0.041)	(0.041)	(0.038)	(0.020)
RiskAversion	-0.07	-0.01	0.00	0.10**	-0.02***	-0.02	-0.07	-0.07	-0.02	-0.02*
	(0.076)	(0.008)	(0.002)	(0.038)	(0.005)	(0.017)	(0.042)	(0.042)	(0.103)	(0.007)
District controls	Yes	Yes	Yes	Yes	Yes	Yes	Yes	Yes	Yes	Yes
Observations	1,007	3,964	3,728	993	21,109	1,809	2,773	2,773	580	2,511

Notes: District controls involve a series of district dummies and clustered standard errors at the district level. Robust standard errors in parentheses.

*$p < 0.05$, **$p < 0.01$, ***$p < 0.001$.

Table 3.6
Natural log of personal income and use of banked services

Variables	(1)	(2)	(3)	(4)	(5)	(6)	(7)	(8)
	OLS estimates				IV: Trust in banks			
Banked	1.27***	1.32***	1.04***	0.92***	1.65***	2.01***	1.92***	1.67***
	(0.027)	(0.031)	(0.160)	(0.066)	(0.114)	(0.164)	(0.298)	(0.357)
Primary_completed	0.11***	0.13***	0.10	0.22***	0.08***	0.09***	0.06	0.21***
	(0.020)	(0.025)	(0.147)	(0.054)	(0.023)	(0.028)	(0.123)	(0.054)
Secondary_completed	0.07*	0.16***	0.21	0.38***	-0.00	0.06	0.06	0.30***
	(0.028)	(0.034)	(0.150)	(0.075)	(0.034)	(0.041)	(0.103)	(0.083)
Some_third_level	0.19***	0.28***	0.46*	0.52***	-0.02	-0.04	-0.01	0.22
	(0.043)	(0.052)	(0.171)	(0.099)	(0.071)	(0.089)	(0.193)	(0.177)
Age/100	8.21***	9.08***	8.75***	9.52***	7.82***	8.39***	7.84***	8.79***
	(0.292)	(0.340)	(1.310)	(0.587)	(0.312)	(0.376)	(1.292)	(0.706)
Age/100_sq	-8.58***	-9.51***	-9.14***	-9.17***	-8.25***	-8.95***	-8.32***	-8.54***
	(0.335)	(0.390)	(1.508)	(0.606)	(0.344)	(0.407)	(1.501)	(0.691)
Female	-0.42***	-0.45***	-0.44***	-0.39***	-0.41***	-0.44***	-0.41***	-0.38***
	(0.018)	(0.021)	(0.091)	(0.047)	(0.018)	(0.021)	(0.082)	(0.047)
Mobile	0.30***	0.28***	0.32***	0.42***	0.22***	0.16***	0.14*	0.32***
	(0.022)	(0.026)	(0.058)	(0.037)	(0.033)	(0.039)	(0.064)	(0.061)

Table 3.6
(continued)

Variables	(1)	(2)	(3)	(4)	(5)	(6)	(7)	(8)
	OLS estimates				IV: Trust in banks			
Urban	0.05*	-0.04	-0.06	-0.07	0.02	-0.08**	-0.12	-0.09
	(0.020)	(0.026)	(0.163)	(0.051)	(0.022)	(0.026)	(0.149)	(0.052)
TimetoStore		0.04***		-0.03*		0.03***		-0.02*
		(0.005)		(0.010)		(0.006)		(0.010)
FSKnow		-0.00		0.05***		-0.02***		0.02
		(0.005)		(0.010)		(0.006)		(0.017)
RiskAversion		0.21***		0.02		0.22***		0.03
		(0.023)		(0.041)		(0.024)		(0.041)
Constant	0.93***	0.57***	1.54***	0.69***	1.01***	0.78***		
	(0.060)	(0.072)	(0.317)	(0.136)	(0.066)	(0.087)		
Country controls			Yes				Yes	
District controls				Yes				Yes
Observations	43,788	36,062	43,788	36,062	43,788	36,062	43,788	36,061
R-squared	0.15	0.15	0.19	0.27	0.14	0.14	0.12	0.16
Adj. R-squared	0.15	0.15	0.19	0.27	0.14	0.14	0.12	0.15

Notes: Mozambique and Uganda are excluded when time to grocery store is included. District controls involve a series of district dummies and clustered standard errors at the district level. Country controls involve a series of country dummies and clustered standard errors. Robust standard errors in parentheses.
$*p < 0.05$, $**p < 0.01$, $***p < 0.001$.

The central challenge in assigning causation to access to financial services is the issue of endogeneity. In the methodology section, we proposed the use of trust in banks as an instrumental variable in an exactly identified equation to overcome this issue.

Examining the relevance of trust in banks as an instrumental variable, the first stage regression shows that bank trust is statistically significantly related to personal access to financial services, across a range of specifications and with country and district fixed effects (see table 3.7). We find that the Angrist-Pischke multivariate F-test of excluded instruments is 69.47 (prob. > F = 0.00), significantly higher than the general rule of thumb suggested by Staiger and Stock (1997) and the Stock and Yogo (2005) critical values for the specification that includes country controls and 159.76 for the model with district controls. As a result, we feel comfortable rejecting the null hypothesis of weak instruments.

The central results from the respective country-level first-stage regressions are presented at the bottom of tables 3.8a and 3.8b. We find that bank trust is statistically significantly related to personal access to financial services for eight of the ten countries and that the Angrist-Pischke multivariate F-test of excluded instruments is greater than ten for all but three of the countries.

Making the case that *banktrust* affects personal income only through the use of banking services is more challenging. We argued in the previous section why we believe this to be the case, and in the absence of any formal test of the validity of an instrument, we point to the absence of a relationship with *banktrust* in the multivariable OLS regression examining the determinants of income under any of our specifications and irrespective of whether risk aversion is included in the model.[10]

Our instrumental variable results for this specification are found in columns 5–8 in table 3.6. We present a number of specifications with and without country fixed effects, and our results are consistent throughout. We find that access to formal banking services increases an individual's monthly income by 1.67 percent on average, an economically more significant result than our OLS estimates suggested. Evaluated at the mean, 1.67 percent of monthly income represents $1.41.

Although we remain open to the critique that education is in fact endogenous to income and that our model may require respecification, we have reason to believe that this is not a significant issue for the purposes of our empirical approach. First, the coefficient(s) on education, regardless of whether we use the one variable or the three dummy

Table 3.7
First-stage probit regression

Variables	(1)	(2)	(3)	(4)
BankTrust	0.17***	0.14***	0.16***	0.12***
	(0.003)	(0.004)	(0.020)	(0.009)
Primary_completed	0.04***	0.03***	0.03	0.01
	(0.004)	(0.004)	(0.017)	(0.007)
Secondary_completed	0.14***	0.13***	0.14**	0.09***
	(0.005)	(0.006)	(0.030)	(0.011)
Some_third_level	0.47***	0.44***	0.47***	0.38***
	(0.006)	(0.008)	(0.051)	(0.015)
Age/100	1.02***	1.01***	1.01***	0.97***
	(0.051)	(0.057)	(0.145)	(0.093)
Age/100_sq	−0.87***	−0.84***	−0.91***	−0.85***
	(0.058)	(0.065)	(0.138)	(0.097)
Female	−0.02***	−0.01**	−0.02*	−0.01*
	(0.003)	(0.004)	(0.010)	(0.005)
Mobile	0.20***	0.17***	0.18***	0.13***
	(0.004)	(0.004)	(0.019)	(0.008)
Urban	0.05***	0.04***	0.05**	0.02**
	(0.004)	(0.004)	(0.010)	(0.009)
TimetoStore		0.00*		−0.00
		(0.001)		(0.002)
FSKnow		0.02***		0.04***
		(0.001)		(0.002)
RiskAversion		−0.01**		−0.01**
		(0.004)		(0.005)
Constant	−0.25***	−0.29***		
	(0.011)	(0.012)		
Country controls			Yes	
District controls				Yes
Observations	43,788	36,062	43,788	36,061
Adj. R-squared
Angrist-Pischke F-Stat	2490.66	1304.46	69.47	159.76

Notes: Country controls involve a series of country dummies and clustered standard errors at the country level. District controls involve a series of district dummies and clustered standard errors at the district level. Robust standard errors in parentheses.
*$p < 0.05$, **$p < 0.01$, ***$p < 0.001$.

Table 3.8a
Natural log of personal income and use of banked services by country

Variables	Botswana OLS	Botswana IV	Malawi OLS	Malawi IV	Mozambique OLS	Mozambique IV	Namibia OLS	Namibia IV	Nigeria OLS	Nigeria IV
Banked	1.72***	3.24**	0.66***	2.40***	0.47**	0.83***	1.28***	2.19***	0.75***	1.68**
	(0.228)	(0.998)	(0.081)	(0.576)	(0.128)	(0.240)	(0.206)	(0.506)	(0.074)	(0.580)
Primary_completed	0.26	0.01	0.35***	0.30***	-0.05	-0.05	0.00	-0.13	0.22*	0.24**
	(0.208)	(0.254)	(0.047)	(0.050)	(0.058)	(0.058)	(0.107)	(0.131)	(0.084)	(0.080)
Secondary_completed	0.48	0.18	0.43***	0.18	-0.01	-0.01	0.56**	0.30	0.32**	0.25*
	(0.274)	(0.347)	(0.106)	(0.134)	(0.112)	(0.105)	(0.131)	(0.165)	(0.112)	(0.117)
Some_third_level	1.63***	0.89	1.08***	0.32	-0.11	-0.10	1.35***	1.11***	0.42**	0.04
	(0.285)	(0.506)	(0.156)	(0.302)	(0.133)	(0.123)	(0.238)	(0.216)	(0.133)	(0.266)
Age/100	13.88***	10.14*	4.53***	3.28***	3.24***	3.04***	12.30***	9.88***	10.08***	9.37***
	(3.511)	(5.093)	(0.807)	(0.941)	(0.696)	(0.715)	(1.611)	(1.922)	(0.766)	(0.928)
Age/100_sq	-11.77**	-8.85	-5.55***	-4.34***	-3.39**	-3.20***	-10.27***	-8.09***	-9.78***	-9.19***
	(3.880)	(5.158)	(0.929)	(1.053)	(0.856)	(0.861)	(1.721)	(2.116)	(0.781)	(0.896)
Female	-0.26*	-0.25*	-0.13**	-0.15***	-0.15*	-0.15**	-0.16	-0.17	-0.51***	-0.48***
	(0.111)	(0.100)	(0.039)	(0.040)	(0.054)	(0.052)	(0.107)	(0.100)	(0.076)	(0.077)
Mobile	0.45*	0.19	0.55***	0.31**	0.24***	0.19***	0.18	0.09	0.48***	0.36***
	(0.160)	(0.254)	(0.058)	(0.094)	(0.036)	(0.039)	(0.127)	(0.136)	(0.055)	(0.081)

Table 3.8a
(continued)

Variables	Botswana OLS	Botswana IV	Malawi OLS	Malawi IV	Mozambique OLS	Mozambique IV	Namibia OLS	Namibia IV	Nigeria OLS	Nigeria IV
Urban	-0.07	0.23	0.26	0.19	-0.12	-0.13	0.21	0.12	-0.07	-0.11
	(0.256)	(0.223)	(0.201)	(0.207)	(0.070)	(0.069)	(0.148)	(0.135)	(0.061)	(0.066)
TimetoStore	0.02	0.01	-0.06***	-0.05***	N/A	N/A	0.04	0.06	-0.01	-0.01
	(0.036)	(0.036)	(0.014)	(0.014)	N/A	N/A	(0.025)	(0.032)	(0.021)	(0.020)
FSKnow	0.23***	0.10	0.10***	0.03	0.12***	0.10***	0.07**	0.03	0.04*	-0.01
	(0.053)	(0.100)	(0.015)	(0.024)	(0.018)	(0.022)	(0.018)	(0.030)	(0.015)	(0.028)
RiskAversion	0.19	0.23	0.00	0.02	-0.08	-0.08	0.02	-0.03	0.05	0.07
	(0.135)	(0.171)	(0.057)	(0.053)	(0.105)	(0.101)	(0.110)	(0.125)	(0.073)	(0.074)
Constant	-0.72		1.40***		2.09***		-0.09		0.64**	
	(0.720)		(0.282)		(0.144)		(0.411)		(0.200)	
District controls	Yes	Yes	Yes	Yes	Yes	Yes	Yes	Yes	Yes	Yes
Observations	1,019	1,018	3,964	3,964	3,728	3,728	993	993	21,109	21,109
R-squared	0.53	0.39	0.32	0.14	0.25	0.17	0.47	0.38	0.20	0.13
Adj. R-squared	0.51	0.36	0.32	0.13	0.25	0.16	0.46	0.36	0.20	0.13
First stage		***		***		***		***		***
Banktrust is significant		***								
Angrist-Pischke F-Stat		35.78		19.83		171.78		35.22		85.14

Notes: Robust standard errors in parentheses. District controls involve a series of district dummies and clustered standard errors at the district level.

$*p < 0.05$, $**p < 0.01$, $***p < 0.001$.

Table 3.8b
Natural log of personal income and use of banked services by country

Variables	Rwanda OLS	Rwanda IV	S. Africa OLS	S. Africa IV	Tanzania OLS	Tanzania IV	Uganda OLS	Uganda IV	Zambia OLS	Zambia IV
Banked	0.79***	0.52	1.64***	1.46**	0.39***	2.51	0.31*	2.35	0.41*	1.95
	(0.040)	(0.583)	(0.181)	(0.543)	(0.069)	(1.911)	(0.078)	(4.020)	(0.149)	(1.562)
Primary_completed	0.17*	0.20*	-0.38*	-0.36*	0.22*	0.35*	0.20*	0.18	0.39*	0.38*
	(0.044)	(0.086)	(0.165)	(0.165)	(0.081)	(0.154)	(0.070)	(0.190)	(0.167)	(0.158)
Secondary_completed	0.62*	0.70***	0.07	0.12	0.29**	0.09	0.20	-0.45	0.50	0.35
	(0.143)	(0.117)	(0.163)	(0.198)	(0.100)	(0.209)	(0.151)	(1.374)	(0.219)	(0.190)
Some_third_level	0.71***	0.81***	0.90**	0.97**	0.74***	0.23	0.93**	0.23	0.17	-0.65
	(0.050)	(0.225)	(0.264)	(0.311)	(0.084)	(0.491)	(0.196)	(1.301)	(0.388)	(0.751)
Age/100	3.45*	3.83**	9.65***	9.98***	1.33	0.59	1.28	0.78	20.43**	18.77***
	(0.865)	(1.386)	(1.212)	(1.120)	(0.749)	(1.032)	(1.024)	(2.040)	(4.117)	(5.076)
Age/100_sq	-4.05**	-4.38***	-6.79***	-7.06***	-1.45	-1.01	-1.40	-0.53	-21.99**	-20.39***
	(0.821)	(1.188)	(1.312)	(1.134)	(0.793)	(1.001)	(1.037)	(2.228)	(4.889)	(5.689)
Female	-0.25**	-0.25***	-0.51***	-0.51***	-0.29***	-0.22	-0.09	0.02	-0.29**	-0.28***
	(0.048)	(0.044)	(0.077)	(0.074)	(0.065)	(0.112)	(0.063)	(0.224)	(0.069)	(0.053)
Mobile	0.44**	0.48**	0.65***	0.69***	0.36***	-0.03	0.40**	0.02	0.01	-0.10
	(0.086)	(0.158)	(0.106)	(0.203)	(0.071)	(0.352)	(0.079)	(0.686)	(0.124)	(0.169)

Table 3.8b
(continued)

Variables	Rwanda		S. Africa		Tanzania		Uganda		Zambia	
	OLS	IV	OLS	IV	OLS	IV	OLS	IV	OLS	IV
Urban	0.19*	0.21***	0.28	0.29	0.18**	0.21*	-0.05	-0.21	-0.46	-0.43*
	(0.053)	(0.056)	(0.193)	(0.167)	(0.059)	(0.098)	(0.070)	(0.321)	(0.207)	(0.214)
TimetoStore	-0.04	-0.05*	-0.03	-0.03	0.02	0.01	N/A	N/A	-0.01	-0.02
	(0.022)	(0.022)	(0.033)	(0.033)	(0.010)	(0.015)	N/A	N/A	(0.030)	(0.022)
FSKnow	0.11**	0.12**	0.06*	0.07*	0.06***	-0.03	0.01	-0.01	0.11*	0.08
	(0.022)	(0.043)	(0.026)	(0.030)	(0.011)	(0.082)	(0.015)	(0.019)	(0.033)	(0.054)
RiskAversion	0.07	0.06	0.07	0.06	-0.11	-0.13	0.01	-0.02	-0.28*	-0.23*
	(0.074)	(0.066)	(0.078)	(0.083)	(0.077)	(0.080)	(0.113)	(0.309)	(0.098)	(0.106)
Constant	0.94*		0.25		1.95***		3.25***		-1.69*	
	(0.207)		(0.414)		(0.174)		(0.209)		(0.718)	
District controls	Yes	Yes	Yes	Yes	Yes	Yes	Yes	Yes	Yes	Yes
Observations	1,809	1,809	2,773	2,773	1,884	1,884	582	582	2,511	2,511
R-squared	0.39	0.31	0.38	0.37	0.31	-0.36	0.23	-0.58	0.19	0.14
Adj. R-squared	0.38	0.31	0.37	0.36	0.30	-0.39	0.21	-0.62	0.18	0.13
First stage										
Banktrust is significant		*		***		No		No		*
Angrist-Pischke F-Stat		11.85		51.19		2.49		1.11		6.53

Notes: Robust standard errors in parentheses. District controls involve a series of district dummies and clustered standard errors at the district level.

*p < 0.05, **p < 0.01, ***p < 0.001.

categories, is not significant in our country fixed effect OLS estimation. Second, when we omit education from this model, very modest changes in the coefficient on formally banked are observed.

To enrich the analysis, the model for each individual country is estimated (see table 3.8). In South Africa, Namibia, Botswana, Malawi, Mozambique, and Nigeria, we confirm the positive role played by access to financial services in determining income, noting that in the countries besides South Africa, the relationship becomes economically more significant when we use instrumental variables. Although in all countries we are able to find a correlation between the use of formal services and monthly income through the OLS specification, we are unable to find a relationship in the instrumental variable models for Rwanda, Tanzania, Uganda, and Zambia. Analysis of the respective first stage regressions helps explain these results. In countries where banktrust is statistically significantly related to personal access to financial services at the 1 percent level and the F-test for excluded instruments is greater than 30, the instrumental variables estimator produces statistically significant results. There is also reason to believe that for Uganda this result can in part be attributed to the unorthodox approach to measuring income, whereas the nature of the *banktrust* variable for Tanzania may undermine the IV approach.

The higher IV estimates provide an insight into the nature of the endogeneity between use of formal banking services income level in this dataset. Endogeneity driven by unobservable factors such as ambition, ability, or conscientiousness would have led to an upward bias in the OLS estimates. The IV estimates suggest that this form is not the most significant source of endogeneity. Alternatively, reverse causality can be responsible for either an upward or downward bias in the OLS estimates, and may account for the higher coefficients achieved once formally banked is instrumented for using *banktrust*.

Alternatively, attenuation bias or regression dilution caused by measurement error in the formally banked variable could be responsible for the higher instrumental variables estimate of the relationship between banked in income. It could be plausibly argued that it is household level access to financial services that plays a role in determining income. For example, parental access to financial services can help maintain consistent investments in education that facilitate higher incomes for young adults. An even more reasonable explanation might come from the nature of inter-household transfers and borrowings which can help maintain the income levels of a particular

individual in the household, through helping to overcome health or other income shocks, and prevent against costly divestment of productive assets.

Our country-specific regressions also highlight the different mechanisms at play in determining income across diverse countries in Africa, particularly around the urban-rural divide. Urban dwellers are likely to have higher incomes in Rwanda, and Tanzania, when all other variables are controlled for and district level controls are included. However, the opposite is the case in Zambia. Our binary variable for *female* behaves as expected across all countries but it is not significant in Namibia and Uganda.

Robustness

To lend weight to our instrumental variables approach, we formally test for endogeneity of financial access by comparing the coefficients between the OLS and IV estimators. We use a bootstrapped approach to calculating the Hausman test statistic because of our adherence to robust standard errors. Where we find a considerable difference in the coefficients, then it was necessary to instrument in the first place to derive more consistent estimates. Our test results indicate that there is reason to believe that our formally banked variable is endogenous to income. We strongly reject the null hypothesis of exogeneity when we instrument with *banktrust*, and as a result we confirm the necessity of using instrumental variables.

The comprehensiveness of the control variables helps provide the case for the independence of *banktrust* to the error term. To add further robustness to the analysis, a number of interaction terms were separately added to the model. For all combinations interaction terms for urban, female, education level, financial sector knowledge quartile and risk aversion, the coefficients on the instrumental variable regression are almost identical to the specification without interaction terms as reported in table 3.6.

We have conducted our analyses of the causal role played by access to formal banking services in determining personal income with an important change to the income data. As noted previously, the reported results avoided the technical problems of taking the natural log of an income of zero by assuming that those households (10,632 in total and about 20 percent of our total pooled dataset) reporting zero income truly had very low but nonzero incomes, assumed to be $1 per month. Although we stand by this approach, it may be open to challenge, as

it specifically changes relative income levels, particularly at low incomes. To help assuage such concerns, we performed our investigation into personal income under two alternative approaches: taking the natural log without adding the $1 to monthly personal income and therefore losing 10,632 of the poorest individuals, and using the transformation $x/(1 + x)$ for an alternative scaling—an approach that produces more challenging coefficients for interpretation. The first approach produces a coefficient that is lower but statistically significant at the 0.05 percent level for the same specification represented in column 8 of table 3.6, confirming our central result. However, this result must be considered within the context of the loss of information associated with excluding 10,632 of the poorest individuals from the dataset and hence the likely underestimating of the magnitude of the relationship. The second approach produces coefficients for all equations implied in table 3.6 that are strongly statistically significant and larger than the corresponding OLS estimates.

Conclusion

The FinScope surveys greatly expand the information available on the use of financial services in sub-Saharan Africa and provide a platform for expanded research on financial access in some of the poorest countries in the world, a contribution that will be strengthened only when repeat surveys are completed.

In this chapter, we confirm the importance of wider development efforts to the financial inclusion agenda in our findings that income and education are key demand-side determinants of access to formal banking. In the shorter term, we find some evidence that financial literacy programs may be effective interventions for greater financial inclusion. Specifically, our results show that improving one's financial sector knowledge increases the likelihood of being formally banked and that developing trust in banks leads to a significant increase in the chances of being formally banked. As the expansion of mobile banking in sub-Saharan Africa reaches increasingly more consumers, opportunities exist to overcome the dearth of bank branch infrastructure across the continent, but this growth will take time. In the meantime, we confirm the supply-side constraint of location, as measured by the urban-rural divide, in determining the financial status of households in sub-Saharan Africa.

Using a novel instrument, we have sought to identify a causal role for the use of financial services by individuals in influencing income. In our pooled dataset of ten countries, using instrumental variables, we find that access to formal banking services increases an individual's monthly income by 1.67 percent, which is significant in economic terms. However, our pooled regression results mask significant heterogeneity at the country level.

To assist with the financial inclusion agenda, future research should continue attempts not only to identify the magnitude of the effect of financial access on important socioeconomic outcomes but also to decipher the relative importance of the different channels of causation at the individual and household level. In this chapter, we have capitalized on an unprecedentedly large pooled dataset for eleven sub-Saharan African countries, and we hope that our efforts will be complemented with more experimental approaches.

Nevertheless, there is more to be learned from the cross-country pooled datasets of this kind, notably on the use of different financial products and on attitudes. But it needs to be held in mind that to do justice to the complexity of the financial, economic, and social systems in the different countries, and to account for varying needs of stakeholders funding or implementing the surveys, the FinScope surveys display considerable variation in detail from country to country.

Notes

We are indebted to Darrell Beghin, Andrea van der Westhuizen, Dayo Forster, and Irma Grundling for their generous assistance with the FinScope data, and to Thorsten Beck, Carol Newman, and David Porteous for valuable suggestions.

1. The data for the chapter come from the FinScope surveys; we include Botswana (2004), Kenya (2006), Malawi (2008), Mozambique (2009), Namibia (2004), Nigeria (2008), Rwanda (2008), South Africa (2006), Tanzania (2006), Uganda (2006), and Zambia (2005) in our analysis.

2. Other details of survey methodologies and related techniques are well documented on the FinScope website, http://www.finscope.co.za.

3. The list of products considered formal financial products for each country is available in a table found only in the online version of this chapter: Institute for International Integration Studies (IIIS) Working Paper No. 399, http://www.tcd.ie/iiis/documents/discussion/pdfs/iiisdp399.pdf (accessed June 1, 2012).

4. The online version of this chapter details how country-level variables are made comparable across countries in our pooled dataset and provides an extensive record of the summary statistics.

5. The exact approach taken and the exchange rates used are available for reference in a table found only in the online version of this chapter. A significant number of observations are recorded as zero, which indicates that when we used the natural log of income, we lost a number of observations. Assuming that these individuals truly had very low but nonzero income, to obtain the regression results reported, we have added $1 to every respondent's monthly income (see the conclusion to this chapter).

6. Ugandan respondents were asked for their exact household income from farming enterprises and other nonfarming economic activities. This variable is for the entire household rather than the individual, and there is a significant bias in responses toward agricultural households.

7. Our average income figure for Uganda is likely to be biased downward due to a bias toward agricultural income among respondents.

8. The Mark IIIe dataset for financial access is reported in Honohan 2008a and is based on the author's calculations as well as Beck, Demirgüç-Kunt, and Levine 2007, Christen, Jayadeva, and Rosenberg 2004, Claessens 2006, European Commission 2005, Peachey and Roe 2005 and subsequent revisions. For definitions and method, see Honohan 2008a.

9. Attempts were also made to conduct the analyses in this chapter using controls at the electoral area (EA) or sublocation area. While there was evidence to suggest that the core results of this chapter did not change, the approach was undermined by the fact that there were in fact 5,000 electoral areas for 50,000 observations with some electoral areas only having one or two observations.

10. A series of reduced reform equations was estimated for increasing number of control variables, country, and district fixed effects. We find that trust in banks does not have a statistically significant independent relationship with personal income once formally banked is included as an explanatory variable.

References

Beck, Thorsten, and Martin Brown. 2010. Which Households use Banks? Evidence from the Transition Economies. European Banking Center Discussion Paper No. 2010–25. Tilburg, The Netherlands.

Beck, Thorsten, and Aslı Demirgüç-Kunt. 2008. Access to Finance: An Unfinished Agenda. *World Bank Economic Review* 22 (3): 383–396.

Beck, Thorsten, Aslı Demirgüç-Kunt, and Patrick Honohan. 2009. Access to Financial Services: Measurement, Impact, and Policies. *World Bank Research Observer* 24 (1): 119–145.

Beck, Thorsten, Aslı Demirgüç-Kunt, and Ross Levine. 2007. Finance, Inequality and the Poor. *Journal of Economic Growth* 12 (1): 27–49.

Bertrand, Marianne, Sendhil Mullainathan, and Eldar Shafir. 2004. A Behavioral Economics View of Poverty. *American Economic Review* 94 (2): 419–423.

Burgess, Robin, and Rohini Pande. 2005. Do Rural Banks Matter? Evidence from the Indian Social Banking Experiment. *American Economic Review* 95 (3): 780–795.

Christen, Robert Peck, Veena Jayadeva, and Richard Rosenberg. 2004. Financial Institutions with a Double Bottom Line: Implications for the Future of Microfinance. Occasional

Paper No. 8. CGAP, Washington, DC. http://www.microfinancegateway.org/content/article/detail/21629 (accessed November 15, 2011).

Djankov, Simeon, Pedro Miranda, Enrique Seira, and Siddharth Sharma. 2008. Who Are the Unbanked? World Bank Policy Research Working Paper 4647. Washington, DC.

European Commission. 2005. Public Opinion in Europe on Financial Services. Special Eurobarometer 230. Luxembourg. http://europa.eu.int/comm/consumers/cons_int/fina_serv/cons_experiences/background_en.htm (November 15, 2011).

Honohan, Patrick. 2004. Financial Development, Growth and Poverty: How Close Are the Links? In *Financial Development and Economic Growth: Explaining the Links*, ed. Charles Goodhart, 1–37. London: Palgrave.

Honohan, Patrick. 2008a. Cross-Country Variation in Household Access to Financial Services. *Journal of Banking & Finance* 32 (11): 2493–2500.

Honohan, Patrick. 2008b. Household Financial Assets in the Process of Development. In *Personal Wealth from a Global Perspective*, ed. James B. Davies, 271–292. New York: Oxford University Press.

Karlan, Dean, and Jonathan Morduch. 2009. Access to Finance. In *Handbook of Development Economics*, vol. 5, ed. Dani Rodrik and Mark Rosenzweig, 4704–4784. Amsterdam: Elsevier.

Morduch, Jonathan, Alberto Chaia, Aparna Dalal, Tony Goland, and Maria Jose Gonzalez. 2009. Half the World Is Unbanked. Financial Access Initiative Framing Note, October.

Morduch, Jonathan, and Barbara Haley. 2002. Analysis of the Effects of Microfinance on Poverty Reduction. Working Paper No. 1014. New York University Wagner Working Paper Series.

Peachey, Stephen, and Allan Roe. 2005. Access to Finance: Measuring the Contributions of Savings Banks. Working Paper, World Savings Banks Institute, September.

Pritchett, Lant. 2001. Where Has All the Education Gone? *World Bank Economic Review* 15 (3): 367–391.

Staiger, Douglas, and James H. Stock. 1997. Instrumental Variables Regression with Weak Instuments. *Econometrica* 65 (3): 557–586.

Stock, James H., and Motohiro Yogo. 2005. Testing for Weak Instruments in Linear IV Regression. In *Identification and Inference for Econometric Models: Essays in Honor of Thomas Rothenberg*, ed. Donald W. K. Andrews and James H. Stock, 80–108. Cambridge: Cambridge University Press.

World Bank. 2008. *Finance for All: Policies and Pitfalls in Expanding Access*. Washington, DC: The World Bank.

World Bank. 2012. World Development Indicators. http://data.worldbank.org/data-catalog/world-development-indicators (accessed February 20, 2012).

4 How to Ask Households about Financial Services: Experimental Evidence from Ghana and Timor-Leste

Robert Cull and Kinnon Scott

In recent years, data collection to measure financial inclusion has moved beyond supply-side measures of the depth of financial sectors to include more detailed surveys of the users of financial services and measure the breadth of financial sectors.[1] Because supply-side measures of depth, such as the ratio of credit extended to the private sector to GDP, provide no information about the average size of a loan (or deposit), they provide only an imperfect sense of the outreach of the financial sector. A highly concentrated banking sector in which a small number of relatively wealthy depositors and borrowers were responsible for a large share of banking activity could score comparatively well in terms of financial depth with limited breadth of outreach.

Perhaps the major reason why financial sector breadth has been understudied is the difficulty in collecting data. Whereas measures of financial depth can be derived from the balance sheets that financial institutions already furnish to supervisory agencies such as central banks, the same information is not readily available—certainly not in a consistent form across countries—for financial sector breadth. Recent attempts to collect data on financial sector breadth have pushed beyond balance sheet information, using both demand- and supply-side approaches. On the supply side, measures of the outreach of the financial sector often focus on the number of accounts of providers of financial services. For example, Beck, Demirgüç-Kunt, and Martinez Peria (2007, 2008) collect information on the aggregate number of deposit and loan accounts from bank regulators in ninety-nine countries. They also collect information on the number of bank branches and ATMs in each country as a proxy for physical access to financial services. A limitation of those data is that they are primarily derived from information about banks, which—though important or even dominant providers of financial services in many countries—are not the full story.

Honohan (2008) therefore combines the commercial bank accounts from Beck and colleagues with accounts at microfinance institutions (Christen, Jayadeva, and Rosenberg 2004) and at savings banks that are members of World Savings Bank Institute (Peachey and Roe 2006) to produce the most comprehensive, though admittedly still rough, accounts-based estimates of access to date.[2] Although this information represents a step forward, the accounts-based approach provides little information about the account holders themselves and thus about the nature of financial exclusion in a given country.

As described shortly, the number of demand-side surveys of access to and use of financial services has multiplied, but little is known about whether the data generated are comparable across countries or within the same country over time because different data collection methods are employed. To help fill some of these knowledge gaps, this chapter reports results from a field experiment designed to test whether the identity of the survey respondent and the format of the questions affects the reported rate of financial usage. The experiment was first undertaken in Ghana; a part of it was then repeated in Timor-Leste to gauge the consistency of results across different environments.

To foreshadow our findings, both the identity of the respondent and the question format do affect reported financial usage in Ghana. In Timor-Leste, we confirm the importance of the identity of the respondent, specifically that heads of households are reliable (and cost effective) providers of financial usage information on behalf of the entire household. We were unable to conduct the part of the experiment on question format in Timor-Leste, but given the low usage rates of services from formal providers there that we report in this chapter, it seems unlikely that including product-specific cues in questions would have increased usage rates much (as it did in Ghana for some services). We speculate that because income levels are somewhat lower and financial institutions more rudimentary in Timor-Leste than in Ghana, concerns about question wording are likely to be of second-order importance.

In the part of the experiment focused on how the identity of the survey respondent affects reported household usage of financial services, there were three treatments used in Ghana. The first treatment used the most comprehensive approach to measuring household financial usage, a full enumeration in which each member of the household reports on personal use of financial services and individual responses are then aggregated to the household level. Other treatments used an

informant—either the head of household or a randomly selected adult—to provide information on the usage of financial services by all members of the household. In Timor-Leste, we were able to include treatments for only the head of household and the full enumeration. In both countries, the experiment was therefore designed to test whether the household financial usage information provided by an informant is as complete as that provided by a full enumeration. Full enumeration is more time consuming and costly than reliance on an informant; these results provide an indication of the services for which a sole informant can provide reliable, cost-effective information.

A second key dimension on which surveys vary is the way in which questions are asked. For ease of implementation, lower costs, and low respondent burden, a short set of questions that aggregate individual items into more global questions is preferred. However, research in other areas has shown that such questions may lead to accidental omissions or memory lapses, thus lowering reported incidence or use. For example, experiments in measuring household consumption have shown that including a greater number of items in the questionnaire leads to higher reported consumption (Jolliffe 2001; Pradhan 2001; Steele 1998; Statistical Institute of Jamaica 1994). As important, in consumption measurement at least, is that aggregation affects certain types of consumption more than others and can lead to reranking of households on overall consumption (Jolliffe 2001).

To test whether reported usage of financial services varies with question format, we rely on two popular survey methodologies. The first, which is the approach taken by the FinMark Trust, relies on the stand-alone FinScope survey of financial usage and asks detailed questions about specific financial products. Though potentially costly and time consuming to administer, this approach should reduce the accidental omission of service use. Questions on product use are supplemented by others regarding the respondent's attitudes toward financial institutions, risk, and coping strategies in times of economic hardship, among other issues. To date, the FinScope survey (http://www.finscope.co.za) has been deployed in fifteen African countries and Pakistan.

A second widely used approach is the embedding of a small module of questions on financial usage within a larger survey designed to cover another topic (e.g., household expenditures or labor market participation) or multiple topics, as in the Living Standards Measurement Surveys (LSMS), which originated at the World Bank. This approach (referred to hereafter as the LSMS approach) generally asks about

financial services use at an aggregate rather than a product level and focuses more on relationships with types of financial services providers. Although such an approach is simpler and less costly to implement, the concern is that certain types of product usage are likely to be omitted when responding to general questions about dealings with types of financial services providers. This issue may be of particular concern in terms of financial services, given the heterogeneity of knowledge of financial instruments in the population. If there is more room for misunderstanding among respondents, it may lead to greater underreporting.

A third approach to data collection, involving so-called financial diaries, has also emerged in recent years (Collins et al. 2009; Collins, chapter 5, this volume). This is the most costly and time-consuming of the methods, but it appears to yield more reliable data on financial usage than the other methods. By meeting with households on a regular basis, establishing trust between respondents and interviewers, and tracking all flows of funds into and out of the household, the diary approach yields a more complete picture of financial usage. Experience has shown that the quality and completeness of the information provided by respondents improves over the first handful of interviews and then remains consistent.

Although that information casts some doubt on whether one-shot approaches are sufficiently reliable methods for collecting data on financial usage, we note that diaries are prohibitively costly in most contexts and that measurement of financial inclusion in a reasonably consistent manner over time and across countries will not likely be possible using that approach. Moreover, the problems associated with incomplete provision of financial usage information differ across services. Informal services such as savings clubs and some forms of credit (from moneylenders, local stores, friends, and family) were reported completely in the earliest visits from diary interviewers. Information became more complete over time (i.e., usage rates went up) for cognitively more complex products from formal providers. The biggest increases were for services from banks (accounts and loans) and especially insurance, pension/provident funds, and retirement annuities (Collins, chapter 5, this volume). Interestingly, we found large increases in reported usage for the product-specific FinScope question format over the institution-based LSMS format for many of the same services (namely, credit from banks and other formal financial institutions and insurance products).[3] The overlap in the services for which the diaries

and product-specific cues in question format produce higher usage rates suggests that both methods offer improvements over other approaches. Given the cost advantages of the product-based format, improving that approach would seem to offer the best chance to expand coverage in a consistent, reliable way over time and across countries.

Country Context

Ghana and Timor-Leste were chosen as the settings for our experiment not because of the characteristics of their financial sectors but rather because there was an opportunity to append our experiment onto a survey that had recently been in the field. In order to develop and implement the experiment in Ghana, we worked with the national statistical office, the Ghana Statistical Service (GSS). The GSS carries out a series of national household surveys and other statistical activities. The most comprehensive of the household surveys, the Ghana Living Standards Survey (GLSS), is an LSMS survey designed to provide information on multiple aspects of living conditions: human capital, productive activities, consumption, and access to and use of public services, inter alia. The survey uses a national probability sample of households stratified by region and urban versus rural areas developed to present results at the level of the three ecological zones of the country (GSS 2006). The survey has been implemented five times since the 1980s, with the most recent one—GLSS5—carried out in 2005–2006.

The GLSS5 presented us with a significant opportunity. Research experiments are usually constrained by how much information can be collected in one questionnaire. However, by revisiting a subsample of the GLSS5 households, we were able to take advantage of the information already collected. This information eliminated many constraints on the experiment survey, meaning that more data could be collected on financial issues in the Financial Service Survey (FSS) as questionnaire space was not needed for gathering data on other characteristics of the household or individuals. Additionally, a more complex design was possible because interviewers needed to be trained only on financial questions and data collection. And more risks could be taken, as the government's national survey was in no way at risk from the work: the GLSS5 is not a panel survey, so any effect of the FSS on households' willingness to respond to future surveys or to specific questions would not be affected by the experimental work.[4]

In Timor-Leste, the experimental opportunity arose for similar reasons. In 2007–2008, the Timor-Leste Survey of Living Standards (TLSLS) was conducted for the second time by the Direcção Nacional de Estatística (DNE). The TLSLS2 followed the lines of the LSMS survey and thus resembles fairly closely the GLSS5. Both surveys collected detailed information on household welfare, along with a host of demographic and economic variables.[5] In collaboration with the DNE and a private firm, an extension of the Timor-Leste TLSLS2 survey was carried out from June to August in 2008. As in Ghana, this extension survey (TLSLS-X) aimed to take advantage of the work already done by revisiting a subset of TLSLS2 households and collecting additional information on the households that could then be linked to the original data. The extension survey was administered to approximately one-third of the households from the TLSLS2 (see World Bank 2009 for more information).

Although the experimental environments were chosen because of the research opportunities afforded by existing surveys, there are differences between the two countries that could help explain the relative rates of financial usage in the two countries and that should be borne in mind when interpreting the results from the experiment. Overall, the two countries are quite different, and not just in population and land size. Ghana has been an independent country for more than fifty years; Timor-Leste has existed for less than a decade. The economy of Ghana grew substantially over the fifteen years before the GLSS5; that of Timor-Leste suffered from serious disruptions due to the independence struggle and ongoing conflict. The formal sector in Timor-Leste is extremely small (less than 12 percent of those working in 2007 were engaged in formal activities), and it is estimated that the economy generates only 400 formal sector jobs a year (World Bank and Asian Development Bank 2007). Ghana's formal sector accounts for 21 percent of the working population. Although it is small, it is almost twice that of Timor-Leste. And unlike that of Timor-Leste, the Ghanaian economy added substantial numbers of new formal sector jobs (in both government and industry) in the period 2001–2006 (Coulombe and Wodon 2007). As in most developing countries, agriculture plays an important role in both countries. In Ghana, half the working population is in agriculture. The level is much higher in Timor-Leste. According to the 2004 census, 76 percent of the labor force worked in subsistence agriculture; the TLSLS2 survey data show that over 80 percent of the working population are farmers, sharecroppers, or farm laborers.

Table 4.1
Means of payment types received and main source of income, Timor-Leste (standard errors in parentheses)

	Means
Income in check	0.63
	(0.27)
Income in direct deposit	0.72
	(0.25)
Income in cash	25.97
	(3.49)
Income received in kind	73.00
	(3.12)
Farm income	66.88
	(2.97)
Wage income	9.57
	(1.41)
Self-employment income	20.00
	(2.08)
Public transfer income	0.27
	(0.17)
Remittance income	0.21
	(0.12)
Other income	3.07
	(0.64)
Number of observations	1,559

Sources: Timor-Leste Survey of Living Standards-Extension 2008; authors' calculations.

The usefulness of full experiments in countries like Timor-Leste may be limited in that the economy as a whole is not completely monetized and the bulk of the population works outside of both the formal labor sector and the formal monetary sector as well. In addition to very low levels of bank access, less than 2 percent of Timorese households receive income payments by check or direct deposit. A quarter of all households receive their income in cash; slightly less than three-quarters receive income in-kind (table 4.1). Although similar questions on payment mechanisms were not asked in Ghana, the greater number of banks in the country, the larger formal sector, and smaller subsistence agriculture sectors suggest that the Ghanaian economy has a greater degree of monetization.

Design of Experiment and Indicators of Financial Usage

Identity of Respondent

As part of the extension surveys in Ghana and Timor-Leste, a financial experiment was developed to assess the quality of information on household usage of financial services obtained from respondents (either head of household or another randomly selected adult) versus from all adults via a full enumeration of individual usage of financial services—in other words, to determine whether there is a downward bias if we ask only the head of household or another adult about the overall use of financial services by the household.

The implementation of the survey differed in two ways between the two countries. First, and as noted previously, in Ghana all three treatments regarding respondent identity (head of household, other randomly selected adult, and full enumeration) were used, whereas in Timor-Leste only the head of household and full enumeration treatments were compared. Second, although the design in Timor-Leste called for full enumeration in the second treatment, the firm involved in the survey work was not able to ensure that this step was actually carried out. Instead, in this second group, although data were collected for each person separately, in many cases the head of household provided this information. Thus instead of full enumeration, we have cases in which the head of household is essentially prompted to recall the details of each person's financial service use. In other areas of data collection, such as consumption, there is evidence that greater prompting (more disaggregation) leads to higher reported levels. Thus, although the reported use of financial services in the second treatment group is not as high as it might have been if true full enumeration were done in all households, it does seem reasonable to think that prompting the head of household could lead to greater observed financial service use.[6]

We constructed seven different indicators of the use of financial services from this part of the experiment. For the institution-based questions that we asked of a household informant (either the head of household or a randomly selected adult who is not the head in the Ghana case), the seven indicators and the survey questions from which they derive were as follows:

1. *Banked* Some people like to keep their money in an account with a bank. Do you or any member of your household have a bank account?

2. *Indirect access to an account* Do you or other members of your household perform banking transactions using someone else's account?

3. *Formal nonbank savings* Now think of all the ways that you and members of your household save money. We are not talking about investing in a business or buying land, but only about where you or other household members put their money to use later. Have you or anyone in your household used a nonbank institution such as a credit union or savings association to save money in the past twelve months?

4. *Formal credit* Many people borrow money to buy things on credit. Have you or any other member of your household used an institution such as a credit union, savings association, or bank to borrow money or to buy on credit in the past twelve months?

5. *Informal savings* Have you or any other member of your household used a welfare scheme or savings club to save money in the past twelve months?

6. *Informal credit* Have you or any member of your household used a welfare scheme or savings club to borrow money in the past twelve months?

7. *Insurance* Many people insure themselves and their possessions against unexpected circumstances. Have you or any member of your household used an institution to insure yourselves (life, health) or property (household goods, house, vehicle, and the like) in the past twelve months? That is, do you or anyone in the household have any long- or short-term insurance policies with any institution?

Questions 1, 2, and 3 were asked identically in both Ghana and Timor-Leste. Other questions needed to be adapted slightly to the specific country context. For example, regarding usage of informal savings, the most prevalent rotating credit and savings arrangement in Timor-Leste, the "arisan," was explicitly mentioned in question 5. In Ghana, those schemes were referred to under the more generic "savings clubs and welfare schemes" as listed. However, "susu" collectors were mentioned explicitly in the Ghana experiment in questions 4 and 5. For a small fee, susu collectors provide an informal means for Ghanaians (and other West Africans) to securely save and access their own money and gain some limited access to microcredit. Money placed with a susu collector is held in a susu account.

The main differences in the way questions were asked across the two countries were with respect to insurance and credit. To our surprise, in

Timor-Leste there are no formal providers of insurance, and thus that question was not asked, leaving only six financial usage indicators for that experiment. For credit, the questions were more detailed because translating from English to the native Tetum (a visual language) proved difficult. Phrases such as "formal institutions" and "savings association" did not resonate with respondents. The basic credit question therefore became: "In the last twelve months, how many times did you, or others members of your household, borrow or obtain funds that you had to (or have to) repay from the following sources?" For the formal credit question, the options were (1) credit union, cooperative, or NGO, and (2) bank. For the informal credit question the options were (1) family member, friend, or other individual, (2) employer or landlord, and (3) moneylender or pawnshop. In short, aside from a more specific listing of formal and informal sources of credit in Timor-Leste, the questions regarding household usage of financial services were very similar in the two countries.

For the full enumeration treatments, we asked the same questions but with respect to individual use. For example, for the *banked* indicator, we asked simply, "Do you have a bank account?"[7] Reponses were aggregated across all members of the household to derive our measure of household usage. In other words, if one member of the household reported having a bank account, then the whole household was considered banked for the full enumeration treatments.

Question Format

This experiment was designed to compare reported usage of financial services under the institution-based questions described in the previous subsection (the LSMS format) with that derived from a series of product-specific questions (the FinScope format). We expected that reported usage would be higher for the product-specific question format under the hypothesis that such cues help to spur more complete recall by respondents. It was not feasible to conduct this part of the experiment in Timor-Leste, so the results pertain only to Ghana. Again, however, we speculate that product-specific cues might not spur greater recall in nonmonetized financial systems such as the one in Timor-Leste, especially cues related to services from formal providers.

To calculate product-based indicators of financial usage, we relied on a series of questions used in FinScope surveys. For example, a respondent was considered banked if he or she responded yes to any of the following questions:

1. Do you currently have an ATM card?

2. Do you currently have a debit card?

3. Do you currently have a Savings Plus account?

4. Do you currently have a current account (checking)?

5. Do you currently have a savings account at a bank?

6. Do you currently have a PostBank account or a post office savings account?

7. Do you currently have a bank loan?

8. Do you currently have a bank overdraft facility?

The questions underlying each of the indicators appear in the appendix. Note that there is no product-based indicator for indirect access because there was only one question on that topic and it was asked in the same way in both the product-based and institution-based questionnaires. That indicator is therefore dropped from subsequent tables. Although we selected questions from those that had been used in past FinScope surveys, we also invested considerable effort in adapting the product-based questions to the Ghanaian context. The questionnaires were developed in close collaboration with the GSS. In addition to their own experiences in other surveys, the GSS called upon various experts and sources in the country to determine the comprehensive list of financial services that existed and the range of service providers. The GSS staff also worked to determine the best terminology and how to minimize translation problems.

Finally, we focused on individual use of financial services in this part of the Ghanaian experiment so as not to conflate the effects of the method of eliciting household usage information (informant versus full enumeration) with the effects of asking product- versus institution-based questions.

Results

Identity of Respondent
For informants and the full enumeration, table 4.2 reports the percentage of Ghanaian households that use a financial service for each of our seven indicators. For five of the seven indicators—banked, indirect access, formal nonbank savings, informal savings, and informal credit—household usage rates are almost identical when the head of household is the informant or when a full enumeration is undertaken. For formal

Table 4.2
Percentage of households that use financial services, Ghana (standard errors in parentheses)

	Banked	Indirect access	Formal nonbank saving	Formal credit	Informal savings	Informal credit	Insurance
Respondents							
Head of household	26.5%	6.4%	3.0%	3.3%	19.7%	4.2%	11.3%
	(1.7%)	(1.0%)	(0.7%)	(0.7%)	(1.6%)	(0.8%)	(1.3%)
$n = 638$							
Random household member	10.0%	3.3%	1.7%	1.5%	17.7%	4.2%	10.6%
	(1.4%)	(0.8%)	(0.6%)	(0.5%)	(1.7%)	(0.9%)	(1.4%)
$n = 480$							
Full enumeration	25.5%	5.1%	2.5%	1.9%	17.3%	4.2%	7.9%
	(1.7%)	(0.9%)	(0.6%)	(0.5%)	(1.5%)	(0.8%)	(1.1%)
$n = 643$							
T-tests of equivalence of means							
Head vs. random	7.05	2.33	1.41	1.94	0.86	0.05	0.35
p-value	0.00	0.02	0.16	0.05	0.39	0.96	0.73
Head vs. full enumeration	0.40	0.99	0.54	1.61	1.15	0.03	2.04
p-value	0.69	0.32	0.59	0.11	0.25	0.98	0.04
Full enumeration vs. random	6.69	1.46	0.94	0.52	0.19	0.03	1.55
p-value	0.00	0.14	0.35	0.60	0.85	0.98	0.12

Sources: Ghana Financial Service Survey 2006; authors' calculations.

credit, usage rates reported by the head of household are slightly higher than those from the full enumeration treatments, though we cannot reject the hypothesis that the two rates are equal to one another. In all, however, the head of household reports information that is very similar to that generated by full enumeration.[8]

Similarly, in Timor-Leste there is little difference across the board between usage rates reported by the head of household when asked about the household as a whole and those reported by full enumeration (or the head prompted to recall usage for each individual in the household). Heads answering for the household tend to report slightly less banking, informal savings, and informal credit than the other respondents, but the differences are insignificant for all six indicators (table 4.3). It is also interesting that the head is able to report household usage rates similar to those from a full enumeration of individual usage in strikingly different environments. In Ghana, although there is substantial usage of informal savings, banks appear to dominate in the provision of financial services. In Timor-Leste, informal credit arrangements dominate and there is very little usage of formal banking services. Yet the experiments indicate that the head of household has a good knowledge of financial services use by other members of the household in either context.

This evidence is good news because interviewing only the head is much cheaper than interviewing all adult members of a household.

Table 4.3
Household financial services use by respondent type, head vs. full enumeration/ prompted, Timor-Leste (standard errors in parentheses)

	Banked	Indirect banked	Formal nonbank savings	Informal savings	Formal credit	Informal credit
Respondents						
Full enumeration/ prompted	3.71	0.03	4.77	5.33	6.12	40.46
$n = 807$	(1.26)	(0.03)	(1.56)	(1.06)	(1.55)	(3.15)
Head (unprompted)	3.28	0.11	6.33	4.57	7.69	38.07
$n = 752$	(1.15)	(0.05)	(2.16)	(1.06)	(2.31)	(2.72)
T-test equivalence of means						
Head vs. full/ prompted	−0.24	1.34	1.30	−0.54	1.00	−0.70
p-value	(0.81)	(0.18)	(0.20)	(0.59)	(0.32)	(0.48)

Sources: Timor-Leste Survey of Living Standards-Extension 2008; authors' calculations.

However, some surveys with a financial services module, such as labor force participation surveys, are designed to interview all members of a household. Our results provide good news in those cases, too, because the information generated via the full enumeration appears to be a good substitute for that generated by the head of household. Because the household usage rates calculated from responses to institution-based questions are comparable using either method, there appears to be potential to expand comparisons across a much broader set of countries.

On the other hand, the results from Ghana also indicate that a randomly selected adult from the household (who is not the head) does not provide information comparable to that generated by the head or via full enumeration (table 4.2). Randomly selected informants produce usage rates that are lower than those for the other two methods and significantly lower for banked, indirect access, and formal credit. This pattern suggests that the random informant has substantially less knowledge about household use of financial services than does the head of household. We also note that the disparities are greatest for services provided by formal institutions. For both informal savings and informal credit, the usage rates produced by random informants are almost identical to those produced by the head of household or via full enumeration. This similarity could be because many of the informal savings and credit arrangements revolve around social activities (meetings) that all household members know about.[9]

Results are also similar for regressions that control for both the treatment type and household characteristics (table 4.4). The only significant regression coefficient when the head reports on behalf of the household is for informal savings in Timor-Leste, but that is significant at only the 10 percent level and the marginal effect is only 2 percent. The differences seen in average reported usage rates between a head of household and a randomly selected informant (nonhead) answering on behalf of the household are mirrored in the regression results. The random adult respondent coefficient in the banked regression is negative, significant, and large in absolute value (−17%). That coefficient is also negative in the indirect access, formal credit, and informal credit regressions, though it approaches significance only in the indirect access specification. The effects are all measured relative to the omitted category in our regressions: full enumeration. Provided that treatments were randomly assigned across the population of households, it should come as little surprise that the regression results are similar to those

Table 4.4
Marginal effects of treatments on reported use of financial services, Ghana, Timor-Leste (standard errors in parentheses)

Respondent	Banked	Indirect access	Formal nonbank saving	Formal credit	Informal savings	Informal credit	Insurance
Ghana							
(Omitted category = full enumeration)							
Head of household	0.02	0.01	0.00	0.01	0.02	-0.00	0.03
	(0.02)	(0.01)	(0.01)	(0.01)	(0.02)	(0.01)	(0.02)
Random household member	-0.17***	-0.01	0.01	-0.00	0.00	-0.00	0.03
(Nonhead)	(0.02)	(0.01)	(0.01)	(0.01)	(0.03)	(0.01)	(0.02)
Timor-Leste							
(Omitted category = full enumeration)							
Head of household	0.00	0.01	0.00	0.01	-0.02*	-0.01	n.a.
	(0.00)	(0.01)	(0.01)	(0.01)	(0.01)	(0.03)	

Sources: Ghana Financial Services Survey 2006; Timor-Leste Survey of Living Standards-Extension 2008; authors' calculations.
*, **, and *** represent significance at the 10, 5, and 1 percent levels.

obtained by calculating average usage rates across treatments. In both countries, we regressed treatment dummies on the household characteristics and found no significant coefficients indicating that assignment was indeed random. For brevity, we do not present those regressions in this chapter.

Question Format

Table 4.5 shows that the product- and institution-based questions produce very similar usage percentages for basic services, such as banked and formal nonbank saving. The same is also true for informal credit, suggesting that respondents understand well the meaning of informal credit without needing to be cued about specific types of arrangements. By contrast, the product-based questions yield much higher usage percentages than do the institution-based questions for formal credit (2.8% vs. 0.8%), informal savings (18.8% vs. 8.9%), and insurance (18.4% vs. 5.7%), and all of those differences are statistically significant. For these—arguably more complex—financial services, product-related cues appear to produce a much more complete picture of usage.

We would expect that, by definition, the level of individual use of financial services could not exceed the level of household use. Comparing tables 4.2 and 4.5, we can see that this is true in Ghana for all services except for insurance. For that indicator, the individual usage rate based on product-related questions far exceeds the household usage rate calculated from the institution-based question. We take this as a sign that our institutional insurance question is not a good substitute for a series of product-related questions. In fact, insurance appears to be a particularly difficult service to measure. Subsequent cognitive testing of finance questions showed that people use different cognitive and emotional concepts for insurance relative to other financial services (Cosby 2009).[10]

Nor does the problem appear to stem from the financial knowledge of the respondent. We would presume that the head of household is likely to be the most financially knowledgeable member of the family, but even when the head is asked about his or her own personal use of insurance products, the product-based usage rate is much higher than the institution-based measure (table 4.6). A similar pattern holds for formal credit and informal savings and for both household heads and for nonheads, and the differences between the product- and institution-based usage rates are statistically significant. The evidence in table 4.6

Table 4.5
Percentage of individuals that use financial services: Product vs. institutional questions, Ghana (standard errors in parentheses)

Survey type	Banked	Formal saving banks + Nonbanks	Formal credit	Informal savings	Informal Credit	Insurance
Questions on use of products	14.3%	14.2%	2.8%	18.8%	2.0%	18.4%
$n = 2201$	(0.7%)	(0.7%)	(0.4%)	(0.8%)	(0.3%)	(0.8%)
Questions on use of institutions	13.3%	13.8%	0.8%	8.9%	2.2%	5.7%
$n = 1568$	(0.9%)	(0.9%)	(0.2%)	(0.7%)	(0.4%)	(0.6%)
T-tests of equivalence of means						
Products vs. institutions	0.88	0.39	4.32	8.49	0.46	11.57
p-value	0.38	0.70	0.00	0.00	0.65	0.00

Sources: Ghana Financial Services Survey 2006; authors' calculations.

Table 4.6
Percentage of individuals that use financial services: Product vs. institutional questions, Ghana (standard errors in parentheses)

Survey type	Banked	Formal saving banks + Nonbanks	Formal credit	Informal savings	Informal Credit	Insurance
Household heads						
Questions on use of products	22.8%	22.7%	4.6%	21.9%	2.4%	20.8%
n = 2201	(1.3%)	(1.3%)	(0.7%)	(1.3%)	(0.5%)	(1.3%)
Questions on use of institutions	23.8%	24.5%	1.4%	12.7%	2.7%	7.5%
n = 1568	(1.7%)	(1.7%)	(0.5%)	(1.3%)	(0.6%)	(1.0%)
T-tests of equivalence of means						
Products vs. institutions	0.48	0.81	3.50	4.70	0.40	7.29
p-value	0.63	0.42	0.00	0.00	0.69	0.00
Non-household heads						
Questions on use of products	7.4%	7.4%	1.4%	16.3%	1.6%	16.4%
n = 2201	(0.8%)	(0.8%)	(0.3%)	(1.1%)	(0.4%)	(1.1%)
Questions on use of institutions	6.0%	6.5%	0.4%	6.3%	1.8%	4.4%
n = 1568	(0.8%)	(0.8%)	(0.2%)	(0.8%)	(0.4%)	(0.7%)
T-tests of equivalence of means						
Products vs. institutions	1.29	0.89	2.25	7.10	0.34	8.91
p-value	0.20	0.37	0.02	0.00	0.73	0.00

Sources: Ghana Financial Services Survey 2006; authors' calculations.

points to across-the-board difficulties for all respondents with using institution-based questions to gather information on formal credit, informal savings, and insurance.

Similar to the experiment regarding respondent identity, regressions that control for individual and household characteristics also produce results that are very similar to the average usage rates calculated across treatments: usage is significantly higher for formal credit, informal savings, and insurance when the product-based question format is used. Because those regressions are reported and discussed in detail in Cull and Scott 2010, we do not report them here.

In summary, the comparisons across treatment groups indicate that the identity of the respondent and the way questions are asked does affect reported usage of some financial services. Full enumerations of all household members produce usage rates similar to those reported by the head of household, and interviewing a randomly selected nonhead produces lower levels of household usage for some indicators. Product-related cues appear to be important to gain a full understanding of usage of insurance, formal credit, and informal savings but do not appear necessary for more basic services such as bank accounts, formal savings, and informal credit.

Discussion and Conclusions

Surveys of individuals and households about their use of financial services hold promise for measuring the depth of outreach of financial sectors, but their cost and other logistical hurdles have made it difficult to develop a standard method of questioning that would generate comparable financial usage data across countries and within countries over time. The experimental analyses described in this chapter were designed to contribute to our understanding about the comparability of financial usage data generated under different approaches.

Our main finding is that rates of household usage are similar when the head reports on behalf of the household or when the rate is tabulated from a full enumeration of individual use. By contrast, randomly selected informants provide a less complete picture of household use of financial services than do the other two methods. The comparability of data provided by the head of household and the full enumeration is potentially important because interviewing only the head is much less costly than interviewing all household members. This

pattern holds in both Ghana, a country where banks provide a large share of financial services, and Timor-Leste, a weakly monetized economy in which there is little use of financial services from formal providers such as banks and in which informal financial arrangements dominate.

As an aside, although our survey indicated that there was no insurance from formal providers in Timor-Leste, the prevalence of informal credit and savings arrangements suggests that those could be a form of insurance, especially in terms of access to informal sources of credit during times of hardship. Our surveys were not designed to tease out the uses of informal credit, but it would not be difficult to design surveys that asked respondents about the uses of different sources of credit. Indeed, the LSMS and FinScope surveys already do this to some extent. The use of financial diaries has also shed light on the uses of various sources of funds, both formal and informal (Collins et al. 2009).

We also find that question format can have an effect on reported usage. More usage was reported when questions were asked about specific financial products rather than about the respondents' dealings with types of financial institutions with respect to formal credit, informal savings, and insurance. Product-related cues appear to be important for all respondents regarding these services, not just those whom we would expect to be less financially knowledgeable. To obtain a more complete picture of financial services use, the institution-based questions used in the financial modules of larger, sometimes multipurpose surveys should therefore be adapted to include product-based cues that are appropriate to the country context.

In short, the combination of a reliable informant (i.e., the head of household) and a question format that incorporates product-specific cues for some types of services would appear to be an efficient way to gain a reasonably accurate understanding of household usage of financial services. Moreover, the cost advantages of such an approach are likely to increase as countries develop and financial usage becomes more prevalent. In Ghana, for example, the full enumeration product-based format took 20 to 30 percent more time to administer when members of the household used banking or insurance services than when they did not.

Appendix

Construction of Indicators from Product-Level Questions

Banked:	Q2	ATM card
	Q4	Debit Card
	Q6	Savings Plus Account
	Q8	Current Account
	Q10	Savings Account at Bank
	Q12	PostBank Account, Post office savings account
	Q36	Bank Loan
	Q54	Bank Overdraft Facility
Indirect:	Q16	Use of someone else's account
Formal Savings:	Q6	Savings plus account
	Q10	Savings Account at bank
	Q12	PostBank Account, Post office savings account
	Q14	CDs, treasury bills, notes, money market funds
	Q22	Savings w/regulated MFI
	Q24	Savings w/credit union
	Q30	Shares, Investment funds
	Q32	Provident fund
	Q34	Pensions fund
Informal Savings:	Q26	susu scheme
	Q28	Welfare scheme, other savings club (e.g., with religious organization)
Formal Credit:	Q36	Bank loan
	Q38	Loan from government
	Q40	Loan from credit union
	Q42	Loan from MFI
	Q44	Loan from employer
Informal Credit:	Q46	Loan from moneylender
	Q48	Welfare scheme, susu, savings club
	Q50	Loan from friend, family member
Insurance:	Q60	Vehicle
	Q62	Property
	Q64	Homeowners
	Q66	Debts
	Q68	Travel
	Q70	Life
	Q72	Debts if you die
	Q74	Disability from employer
	Q76	Other disability
	Q78	Professional
	Q80	Funeral policy w/institution
	Q84	Health/Medical
	Q86	Children's education

Notes

1. See Beck, Demirgüç-Kunt, and Levine 2000 for a description of supply-side measures of financial sector depth.

2. Chaia et al. (chapter 2, this volume) build upon the Honohan (2008) data to provide estimates of the number of adults worldwide who lack access to financial services from formal and semiformal providers, and they also estimate the number of the unserved who fall under various poverty lines. Finally, they use alternative data on financial inclusion from country-specific sources to validate the Honohan (2008) estimates for twelve large countries comprising 2 billion people.

3. Note that specific questions were asked in Ghana in the treatments that used the FinScope format about pension and provident funds. The increase in reported usage of formal savings was small and insignificant when those product-specific cues were included (FinScope format) compared with the LSMS institution-based question format. This finding suggests that financial diaries are a more effective way of understanding use of financial services for retirement than the types of surveys tested in this chapter.

4. As noted, in the Ghanaian case there were two separate experiments with three treatments in one of them. Rather than field five separate surveys, we combined treatments in ways that made sense in order to maintain our sample size and thus the power of our statistical tests. For example, under one survey, household usage questions were asked of the household head using the institution-based LSMS approach, and then a randomly selected adult (other than the head) was asked questions about his or her own financial usage under the FinScope product-based approach. The way treatments were fitted together in the Ghana experiment (and why) is explained in depth in Cull and Scott 2010, and thus we do not cover it in detail in this chapter.

5. There are some minor differences between the two surveys that affect the variables available on the household that we use as controls in our regressions, but overall, the two surveys are very comparable.

6. Note that it is not possible among the second group of households to determine which did full enumeration and which had the head responding but prompted for each individual in the household.

7. Again, however, the survey team in Timor-Leste did not always ask questions about financial usage to each member of the household individually. In those cases, the interviewers asked the head of household questions of the form "Does household member X have a bank account?"

8. Although the head of household and the full enumeration tend to yield very similar usage rates, there is one exception in the Ghana case: insurance. One would expect that the full enumeration would provide the most complete information and thus produce the highest usage levels. Yet the percentage of households that have insurance is 11.3 percent when information is provided by the head of household and only 7.9 percent when a full enumeration of individual usage is collected. It is conceivable that the head of household purchased insurance for other household members without the knowledge of those members. However, it seems more likely that the institution-based question could simply be a poor method of collecting information on insurance use and that thus none of the estimates for that indicator are reliable. Certainly, the results from Collins et al. 2009 and Collins (chapter 5, this volume) indicate that insurance is one of the

products for which reported usage increases after repeated visits using the financial diaries approach.

9. Similarly, and as noted previously, informal credit and savings arrangements were reported completely in the earliest visits to households under the diaries approach to collecting financial usage information (Collins, chapter 5, this volume).

10. This work took place in Jamaica but was explicitly designed as a follow-up to the findings in Ghana.

References

Beck, Thorsten, Aslı Demirgüç-Kunt, and Ross Levine. 2000. A New Database on the Structure and Development of the Financial Sector. *World Bank Economic Review* 14 (3): 597–605.

Beck, Thorsten, Aslı Demirgüç-Kunt, and Maria Soledad Martinez Peria. 2007. Reaching Out: Access to and Use of Banking Services across Countries. *Journal of Financial Economics* 85 (1): 234–266.

Beck, Thorsten, Aslı Demirgüç-Kunt, and Maria Soledad Martinez Peria. 2008. Banking Services for Everyone? Barriers to Bank Access and Use around the World. *World Bank Economic Review* 22 (3): 397–430.

Christen, Robert P., Veena Jayadeva, and Richard Rosenberg. 2004. *Financial Institutions with a Double Bottom Line: Implications for the Future of Microfinance.* Consultative Group to Assist the Poor, Occasional Paper No. 8.

Collins, Daryl, Jonathan Morduch, Stuart Rutherford, and Orlanda Ruthven. 2009. *Portfolios of the Poor: How the World's Poor Survive on $2 a Day.* Princeton, NJ: Princeton University Press.

Cosby, Jarold. 2009. Financial Services and Products: Cognitive Interviews. Report to the World Bank.

Coulombe, H., and Q. Wodon. 2007. Poverty, Livelihoods and Access to Basic Services in Ghana. In World Bank, *Ghana: Meeting the Challenge of Accelerated and Shared Growth* (Country Economic Memorandum), Volume 3. Washington, DC: The World Bank.

Cull, Robert, and Kinnon Scott. 2010. Measuring Household Usage of Financial Services: Does It Matter How or Whom You Ask? *World Bank Economic Review* 24 (2): 199–223.

Ghana Statistical Service. 2006. Sample Design for Round Five of the Ghana Living Standards Survey (GLSS 5). Mimeo.

Honohan, Patrick. 2008. Cross-Country Variation in Household Access to Financial Services. *Journal of Banking & Finance* 32 (11): 2493–2500.

Jolliffe, Dean. 2001. Measuring Absolute and Relative Poverty: The Sensitivity of Estimated Household Consumption to Survey Design. *Journal of Economic and Social Measurement* 27 (1): 1–23.

Peachey, Stephen, and Allan Roe. 2006. Access to Finance: Measuring the Contributions of Savings Banks. World Savings Banks Institute, working paper.

Pradhan, Menno, 2001. Welfare Analysis with a Proxy Consumption Measure: Evidence from a Repeated Experiment in Indonesia. Cornell Food and Nutrition Policy Program Working Paper No. 126, University of Cornell.

Statistical Institute of Jamaica. 1994. *Survey of Living Conditions, 1994.* Kingston: Statitstical Institute of Jamaica.

Steele, Diane, 1998. Ecuador Consumption Items. World Bank. Mimeo.

World Bank. 2009. Basic Information Document: Timor Leste Survey of Living Standards 2-Extension (TLSLS2-X) 2008. Washington, DC: The World Bank

World Bank and Asian Development Bank. 2007. Timor Leste: Economic and Social Development Brief. Working Paper 41072, Washington, DC.

5 Going with the Flow: Measuring Financial Usage in Poor Households

Daryl Collins

Poverty is not measured in money alone but also in terms of what money can buy: access to health, education, and at the most fundamental level, freedom (Sen 1999). However, we increasingly see evidence that financial management, as much as income levels themselves, matter to poor households. In a striking example, Duflo, Kremer, and Robinson (2011) study fertilizer use in western Kenya. They found that the largest barrier to the adoption of new fertilizer was not understanding the benefits, or even knowing its price, but in timing savings in order to have the right amount of money available to buy the fertilizer at the right time. We increasingly see that having the right financial tools, in coordination with income stream and consumption needs, is central to overcoming the vulnerabilities of poverty.

Increased interest in understanding financial access in developing countries has increased cross-country data collection efforts, such as FinScope (a financial-services survey conducted in fifteen different countries across Africa) and the World Bank Access to Finance surveys. However, there is little evidence about the validity of these survey instruments. Sudman, Bradburn, and Schwarz (1996) and Samphantharak and Townsend (2009) both point out that although the literature focuses on the theoretical basis of sampling and survey design, far less attention is focused on interviewing and measurement techniques, leaving questionnaire design largely in the domain of the in-house tradition of survey firms and researchers' personal experience.

Contributions to the micro data survey measurement literature are few, but they have generated key insights into the most appropriate methods of gathering household-level data. Broadly speaking, these investigations support moving beyond asking respondents about a long list of items. Deaton and Grosh (2000) pay particularly close attention to household consumption data and investigate the usefulness of

using such tools as respondent-kept diaries and questioning expenditures over both the long and short terms.

Thus far, existing financial access surveys have not been extensively probed to assess how similarly innovative methods might improve data robustness. One exception is the work of Cull and Scott (2010), who performed experiments in Ghana designed to show who the best household member is to interview as well as how best to capture information on the household's financial products or institutions. This unique work aside, most current surveys ask only whether households have different financial instruments, stopping short of capturing actual balances and flows of data. Yet, as the fertilizer example shows, questions about the timing and size of financial flows across a range of financial products can be crucial to understanding how households manage their money. The problem is that information on financial flows is difficult to collect. These flows can be tiny and very transitory; the structure of informal financial services is not well understood, so the door is opened to misunderstandings between researcher and respondent, and respondents are naturally sensitive about revealing too much. These factors make it particularly difficult to collect survey data on household-level financial management, but having this information could help researchers develop new and innovative methodologies, thereby helping policymakers and private-sector institutions create new products and services that support these financial flows.

This chapter contributes to the literature on household-level data measurement by examining the conceptual and empirical literature and by using a unique, high-frequency panel dataset to interrogate a number of commonly held assumptions about financial data collection.

Theoretical Frameworks

The existing measurement literature, both theoretical and empirical, is focused on two areas of household surveys: consumption and small businesses. Although each is seen as distinct, both point to similar ideas about how household finances should be conceptualized.

Consumption

Both conceptual thinking and empirical evidence are covered comprehensively in Deaton and Grosh's 2000 chapter on measuring consumption. Their comments focus primarily on the context of the Living Standard Measurement Surveys (LSMS) collected by the World Bank.

The LSMS objective is to measure poverty and, to a lesser extent, equity. As Deaton and Grosh relate, these surveys measure poverty via consumption data, rather than income data, for two reasons. First, although income and assets help people obtain goods and services, it is the goods and services themselves that directly generate well-being. Consumption measures what people actually acquire and therefore directly measures their standard of living. Moreover, Deaton and Grosh suggest that the practical outcome of consumption data is a tool to construct indirect utility curves. For this reason, they say, it is necessary to collect a comprehensive set of consumption items. If only a subset of items is collected, the relationship between that subset and the entire basket of consumptions is not stable over time or across households, which weakens a valid representation of the utility curve.

Small Businesses

Within the relationship between small businesses and household finances, Samphantharak and Townsend (2009) have made an important contribution by conceptualizing households as corporate firms. Their framework is based on the view that to date, definitions of critical terms such as household income, consumption, savings, and financing have been unclear. Borrowing the tools of corporate finance, they equate such things as household assets to equity, consumption to dividends, and the household budget constraint to cash flow. This approach allows them to view household concepts through a new lens. For example, in the cash flow statement, savings is seen as a budget surplus rather than asset accumulation. This view provides an important connection between liquidity and performance rather than simply between income and performance. As pointed out at the beginning of this chapter, this issue ties well into evidence suggesting that poor households struggle not simply with low incomes but, more important, in terms of having the right amount of money at the right time—that is, liquidity.

Empirical Literature

The empirical literature focuses on *how* to collect household-level data in the most valid way. This focus includes *which* questions to ask (that is, which measures most aptly operationalize a particular concept), *how* to ask these questions (that is, how to avoid recall errors and other errors), and even *whom* to ask.

Consumption

Deaton and Grosh (2000) provide a good, comprehensive summary of the empirical literature. With respect to the question of *what* to ask, they point to the extensive literature suggesting that even in poor communities, people smooth their incomes over the course of a year (Bhalla 1979, 1980; Musgrove 1978, 1979; Paxson 1992, 1993; Wolpin 1982; Deaton 1997, chap. 6). The implication is that any survey that is administered only once will better reflect living standards throughout the year by measuring consumption rather than income. A second implication arises: if it is feasible to visit households on many occasions throughout the year, thus capturing seasonality in household income, then there is little difference between measuring income and consumption if one measure can be captured as cheaply and accurately as the other.

To back up this suggestion, Deaton and Grosh (2000) checked the accuracy of the consumption modules of the LSMS surveys against each country's National Income and Product Accounts (NIPA) by looking at ratios of annual estimates of expenditure of household surveys over annual estimates of NIPA expenditure.[1] They found general consistency between the two measures, although there were large discrepancies for certain countries and years. However, they were primarily concerned about underreporting of expenditures in household surveys, as respondents tend to want to play down their standards of living. However, they found no evidence of understated expenditures from these household surveys.

In terms of *how* to ask about household consumption data, Neter (1970) provides a typology of collection errors in expenditure surveys:

1. Recall errors associated with fading memories

2. Telescoping of reported events by incorrect dating

3. Reporting errors associated with respondents being overwhelmed by the length of the survey or the number of items covered

4. Prestige errors—that is, reporting errors due to various social pressures

5. Conditioning effects from participating in the survey

6. Respondent effects—that is, respondents' identities affect their answers

7. Interviewer effects

8. Effects associated with instrument design

Deaton and Grosh (2000) point out that most of the empirical literature focuses on items 1 and 2, that is, recall errors and telescoping errors.

Recall errors are essentially progressive forgetting—that is, increased underestimation of expenditures as the recall period increases. Scott and Amenuvegbe (1990) ran a series of experiments with households from the Ghanaian Living Standards Survey; they found that reported expenditures fell an average of 2.9 percent for every day, up to a week, that was added to the recall period. Thus, for a seven-day recall period, expenditures were just 87 percent of what was reported for a single day. A two-week recall period yielded a total expenditure that was another five percentage points lower than that yielded by the one-week period. They also found a difference according to whether questions were phrased in a normative or factual way. Annual recall based on explicitly normative questions (e.g., "How much do you *usually* spend on x?") resulted in an expenditure figure that was 91 percent of the one-day recall, and annual recall based on ostensibly factual questions (e.g., "How much did you spend on x?") gave 113 percent of the one-day recall figure.

Telescoping is slightly different than progressive forgetting and has been formally modeled by Rubin and Baddeley (1989) and by Bradburn, Huttenlocher, and Hedges (1994). These models suggest that respondents remember the *event* of making a large purchase such as a TV, bike, or radio more than the actual date, so they are apt to bring that expenditure forward into the referenced time period. This behavior naturally causes a net upward bias in resulting data—that is, the further in the past the event is, the greater the uncertainty about the date. Thus, the probability that the expenditure will be placed closer to the present is higher than the probability of its being placed farther into the past. In other words, past events are more likely to intrude into the reference period than relevant events are to be lost.

Neter and Waksberg (1964) suggest a fix for telescoping, which they label "bounded recall." In this technique, the interviewer asks about expenditures in the past month but then does a second interview in which respondents are asked about purchases since the first interview. This technique prevents respondents from double-counting purchases close to the boundary between the two interviews.

Silberstein (1990) uses data from the U.S. Consumer Expenditure Survey (CEX) to provide evidence on telescoping. Respondents are interviewed about household purchases on five separate occasions. The first interview (recall over the past month) is discarded, then four more

quarterly interviews are conducted, all asking for expenditures during the past three months, that is, since the last interview. Results from the first interview show much higher expenditures than results from the others. For example, respondents report 40 percent higher expenditures for clothing in the first interview than for the average of the subsequent four interviews.

Sudman, Bradburn, and Schwarz (1996) used themes in cognitive psychology to develop lessons in questionnaire design. This study contends that when recounting expenditures in the short term or recalling important events, respondents estimate their expenditures by counting the events. But when recalling long periods of time that do *not* include important events, respondents instead estimate the frequency of expenditure over a shorter time frame, then multiply the results from this time frame by the length of the reference period. Sudman and colleagues show that the estimation of expenditure itself may be unbiased but the counting methods may be biased either upward for short time periods or downward for longer periods. Respondents are "cognitive misers"—that is, they try to minimize the effort of responding to the interviewer's questions.

One instrument that is frequently used to help minimize data collection errors is a respondent-completed diary.[2] Blaizeau (1998) provides evidence of the experience of using diaries throughout seven African countries. He suggests that such diaries are time consuming because interviewers have to spend a great deal of time visiting households, almost daily, to help respondents complete them. Moreover, he found that they were pertinent only for short-recall items and not for a large proportion of nonfood expenditures because respondents were not motivated to complete them and needed frequent help. Martini and Ivanova (1996) provide additional evidence that respondent fatigue and decreased interest prevent households from completing diaries. They found that expenditures recorded in the second week were about 15 percent lower than those in the first week.

Deaton and Grosh (2000) explain how these lessons have influenced the LSMS attempts to address both recall and telescoping. First, different types of expenditures are separated into different frequency periods. For example, frequently purchased items will have a recall period of a week or two, and more occasional items will be recalled within the past month, quarter, or year. For food expenditures, LSMS uses a bounded-recall technique involving a two-interview process. During the first interview, respondents are asked whether certain foods were consumed

in the last year; during the second interview, respondents are asked about purchases made since the last visit. Respondents are also asked during how many months of the year the household purchased items, how often in each month, and how much they usually spend each time. This approach allows for the computation of both a "last visit" measure and a "usual month" measure. Because there is no demonstrable evidence that this technique is superior to interviews, LSMS surveys have made little use of diaries.

Financial Instruments

Evidence of the validity of financial services measurement is decidedly thinner, largely because financial services have only recently become a substantive part of household questionnaires. Nonetheless, some empirical evidence is offered on which questions are asked and who answers them.

Karlan and Zinman (2008) offer evidence about what may be left out of surveys on financial usage, specifically credit. They use bank records to check survey data in South Africa, finding that borrowers do not report their higher-interest consumer loans in surveys. Moreover, they find differences in data measurement error across population segments that would lead to biased inferences in indebtedness statistics if based purely on self-reported data.

Kochar (2000) uses results from the LSMS surveys to focus on measuring savings. She concentrates on two different estimates of savings: income less consumption and changes in household assets. Using Ghana and Pakistan, she shows substantive differences between savings estimates derived from asset-value changes compared to those computed using income less expenses. She also enumerates several reasons why both measures should be considered suspect.

Cull and Scott (2010) use experiments in Ghana to see how a variety of different financial devices are used. They provide evidence about who should be asked about financial instrument usage as well as which questions to ask. They motivate their paper by drawing on the different methodologies used by LSMS versus FinScope. They find that reported rates of household usage are similar regardless of whether the head of the household reports on behalf of the rest of the household or the household is fully enumerated. They also note that randomly selected informants provide a less complete picture than either of these methods.

With respect to which questions are asked, Cull and Scott (2010) test whether it is better to ask about institutions ("Do you have an account

with a bank?") or specific products ("Do you have an ATM card/debit card/current account/savings account?"). They find that institutional questions are appropriate when asking about basic services like savings. This finding holds true regardless of whether respondents hold savings at banks or formal nonbank institutions (such as credit unions and savings associations) or they hold savings at informal credit institutions (such as deposit collectors). In contrast, Cull and Scott found that some concepts—including formal credit (whether issued by credit unions or banks), informal savings (such as savings clubs), and insurance (such as life insurance)—are more complex and showed that responses were improved by asking more detailed product questions.[3]

Using a New Dataset to Comment on the Literature

The literature has focused on using small experiments focused on specific validity questions. I will take a complementary approach by using the Financial Diaries, a unique dataset on household financial flows in South Africa.[4] This dataset is not a set of self-report "diaries" but a year-long series of fortnightly household interviews to track daily income, expenditure, and financial transactions. The sample is focused on 152 black households in three rural and urban areas of South Africa.[5] With the intent of examining diversity in households within those areas, the sample population includes those with different dwelling types and wealth levels (Collins et al. 2009; Collins 2005).

The Financial Diaries data is aided by a margin-of-error tool that provides both a helpful device for designing innovative questionnaire strategies and a means of testing the robustness of those strategies. A relational database was specially built to aid data collection; it allowed household-specific questionnaires to be generated based on data from the previous interview. Field workers were trained to calculate an on-the-spot reconciliation of household cash flow statements, which allowed them to easily target cash flows that households might have forgotten or avoided discussing. Both these elements offer highly precise recall and reporting, even for small financial transactions.

An example shows how this margin of error is calculated. The following accounts are those of a fifty-year-old woman, Pumza, who lives with her three children and one grandchild in Langa, Cape Town. Table 5.1 shows her complete set of cash flows for April 2004, based on the combined results of two interviews. Pumza supports her family with

Table 5.1
Pumza's sources and uses of funds, April 2004

Sources of funds		Uses of funds	
Operational		*Operational*	
Casual wage	$52	Food	$85
Business revenues	$218	Business inventory	$119
Child grant	$26	Business expenses	$2
Remittances received	$27	Paraffin	$6
Financial		Electricity	$22
Received mashonisa loan	$92	Household products	$46
Savings club payout	$23	Transport to work	$12
		Newspapers, magazines	$1
		Vodacom container	$3
		Penalties and fines	$1
		Personal (haircut)	$2
		Clothing	$17
		Financial	
		Savings club payment	$121
Total	**$438**	**Total**	**$437**

Notes: Data in this table come from the 2004 South African Financial Diaries dataset, described in the chapter. The example shown is one of 152 poor households selected from two urban and one rural site in South Africa. Data on income, expenditures, and financial transactions were collected every fortnight for over a year. Figures in dollars are converted from South African rand at prevailing market rates of $1 = ZAR6.5.

profits from cooking and selling sheep intestines on the street, with a bit of extra income from a monthly government child grant. In addition, in April, her oldest daughter worked a few days at a casual job, and Pumza received some money from her aunt. She and her children also belonged to eight different savings clubs over the year; most were Christmas clubs and one helped fund her cash flow requirements for business inventories. However, she found that the other members in the club she used for business cash flow did not pay on time, so she also took a loan from a moneylender. The club's payout came late in the month, and she used it to pay back the moneylender in May.

As Pumza's cash flows show, the sources of funds coming into the household from income and from financial receipts in April totaled $438, and the uses of those funds for expenditures and financial outflows totaled $437. The difference between the two is the survey margin of error, which was $1 in this example. The survey margin of error is

a measure of how well the Financial Diaries captured all the household cash flow.

What explains the improved margin of error in the Financial Diaries data? First, households came to trust the researchers more over time and thus revealed more over time. (This effect is not necessarily helpful in the context of this chapter, as we are motivating a methodology that could be successfully used in a one-time questionnaire rather than a panel.) However, the second element that helped improve data collection was the introduction of an in-field calculation of the margin of error, which we introduced several months after beginning the field work in February 2004. To perform this calculation, field researchers simply added up the sources of funds less the uses of funds. If there was a high margin of error, the field researchers had an opportunity to probe the household further about what cash flows might be missing. Soon after implementing this field device (which we launched after about three or four months of interviews), we saw a decline in the margin of error.

Empirical Strategy

The empirical strategy used to measure financial usage in poor households is focused on better understanding the major pitfalls in one-off household surveys of financial management. Several types of questions were asked, both about income and expenditure data and about financial-management data.

Income and Expenditure

As discussed previously, most household questionnaires favor capturing expenditures for several reasons, including the irregularity of income and the lack of robust self-reporting. I draw upon the Financial Diaries data to investigate several questions, including:

• What types of income data typically fail to be captured in one-off questionnaires?

• Are income or expenditure data captured more accurately by one-off questionnaires?

• Does this result differ depending on income levels?

Financial Instruments

One of the key challenges of collecting financial information is that households either are not motivated to be honest about their financial

use or do not understand what they are being asked. This section seeks to better determine which types of financial instruments are most likely left out of initial interactions. We can make this determination by comparing which types of financial instruments are not mentioned in the initial interview against information learned from subsequent interviews.[6] We can also estimate how long it takes households to report financial instruments. The collection of each financial device within the Financial Diaries database has two associated time records. The first is the date of interview at which it was detected. The second is the date when the household opened the device. I use these two pieces of information to calculate a variable that I call "LATEFI":

$$LATEFI_f = DATE\ OF\ RECORD_f - DATE\ STARTED_f \qquad (5.1)$$

This variable will be calculated for each type of financial device f.

With this variable in hand, I then explore which other elements were associated with late discovery of a financial device. In particular, I seek to explore whether the type of financial instrument matters—that is, loan, savings, or insurance—and whether informal or formal financial instruments are reported "late" more frequently. I do this by running a cross-section OLS regression:

$$LATEFI_f = \alpha + \beta_1 Savings_f + \beta_2 Loan_f + \beta_3 Formal_f + \beta_4 X_f + \varepsilon_f. \qquad (5.2)$$

Savings and *Loan* are dummy variables (insurance is left out) and *Formal* is a dummy variable indicating whether the instrument is formal or informal. X is a vector of household and individual characteristics. Each variable is measured for each financial instrument used (f).

It would also make sense for LATEFI to be modeled as a survival model because it is, in essence, a time to expiration. I have no a priori expectations about what shape curve this relationship should take, so I fit these data using a Cox Proportional Hazard model.

I also explore the extent to which the flows through financial instruments are accurately reported in a one-off questionnaire as compared to the information revealed by ongoing interviews.

Who Is Best to Ask?
Using the margin of error, I can test the robustness of data measurement, whether interviewing the head of household, taking a full enumeration, or interviewing an alternative family member about not only financial information but about full household information. The Financial Diaries are sometimes done with a household head, sometimes with a spouse, and sometimes with another family member. I can

separate the sample households into those where head of household responded, versus where a non–head of household responded:

$$M_i = \alpha + \beta_1 I_i + \beta_2 X_i + \varepsilon_i,$$ (5.3)

where M is the margin of error for each household i. I is a household interview dummy that would take on four different values depending on whether the main interviewee is the household head, spouse of the household head, child of the household head, or other. X is a vector of covariates such as log per capita household income; share of those receiving regular income; gender of the most often interviewed; age, education, literacy, fatalism, math skills, regularity of income, and marital status of the most often interviewed; and even which researcher interviewed the household. The coefficient of interest is β_1.

Results

Several descriptive tables give us an initial overview of the Financial Diaries data. For all these tables, two data points are compared. First, the data labeled "data from initial questionnaires" is taken from the first three questionnaires, which are administered soon after meeting the respondent for the first time. We argue that these questionnaires are a proxy for a one-off survey. Initial contact with the respondent would have occurred during the survey's recruitment phase, when the team performed participatory wealth rankings to determine the wealthiest and poorest within the neighborhood or village. Soon after, the team would have approached the respondent to gain permission for the interviews. The respondent would then have been interviewed four consecutive times, in what we call the "initial interviews." The first interview covers the household register, dietary habits, living conditions, and a tally of physical assets. The second interview covers income and expenditure. The third interview, which was later split into two sittings because the field workers found it so long, is a full register of financial instruments.

Most of these initial questionnaires, with the exception of the third questionnaire about financial instruments, borrowed heavily from existing national household surveys in South Africa. We would therefore argue that these initial questionnaires yield the type of robust data that would have been gathered from a one-off questionnaire. We then compare the data gathered from these preliminary interviews to the data yielded by the Financial Diaries data—as mentioned previously,

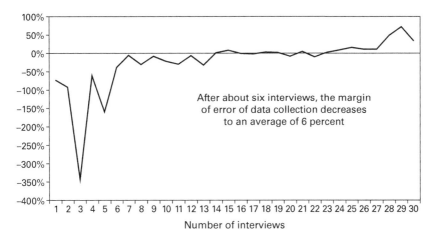

After about six interviews, the margin
of error of data collection decreases
to an average of 6 percent

Number of interviews

Figure 5.1
Financial Diaries: margin of error (percent of sources of funds). *Notes:* Data in this chart come from the 2004 South African Financial Diaries dataset, described in the chapter. Data on income, expenditures, and financial transactions were collected every fortnight for over a year. Margin of error is calculated by subtracting uses of funds from sources of funds, then dividing by sources of funds.

Financial Diaries data collection began two weeks after the completion of the third questionnaire. The Financial Diaries questionnaires ran from November 2003 to December 2004, and respondents were interviewed every other week. As figure 5.1 suggests, only the data after about six interviews, or three months, has a low margin of error. The tables in this chapter therefore include only Financial Diaries data gathered from February to November 2004.

Table 5.2 analyzes income data, comparing the preliminary questionnaire data to the Financial Diaries data. Not surprisingly, the preliminary questionnaires yield a lower income per capita than expected. On average, households report income per month that is R37.40 lower than the level recorded by the Financial Diaries, which is significant at $0.50 per day on a PPP basis.[7] What accounts for the difference? According to table 5.2, respondents report the share of their income coming from government grants and from small businesses at levels that tend to be confirmed by Financial Diaries data. This result for government grants is not surprising, as respondents know exactly how much they receive in grants (so there is little respondent error) and tend not to hide this income. That they accurately report small-business income is more surprising, and we look more closely at small-business details

Table 5.2
Monthly income from initial questionnaire versus diaries

	Data from initial questionnaires	Data from diaries	Average % difference across households
Household income			
Average monthly per capita	$146	$152	−8.8%
Difference by income quartiles			
Lowest quartile			44.9%*
Second lowest quartile			13.1%*
Second highest quartile			5.5%
Highest quartile			−18.2%***
Share of income			
From regular jobs	48.2%	41.8%	10.6%***
From casual work	9.0%	5.8%	9.3%**
From government grants	23.8%	24.0%	−0.5%
From remittances	5.8%	16.7%	−11.2%***
From small business	7.2%	7.1%	0.3%

Notes: Data in this table come from the 2004 South African Financial Diaries dataset, described in the chapter. The sample is 152 poor households selected from two urban and one rural site in South Africa. Data on income, expenditures, and financial transactions were collected every fortnight for over a year. Income quartiles were determined by the diaries per capita income. Figures in dollars are converted from South African rand at a rate of $1 = ZAR6.5. Significance in the difference between the two series is tested using a two-sided paired *t*-test.
*significant at 10 percent; **significant at 5 percent; ***significant at 1 percent.

shortly. Respondents overestimate income from regular jobs, largely (we found) because they reported gross income rather than net. Only once we knew respondents better and they felt comfortable enough to show us their pay slips were we able to see that not only were taxes and other mandatory subtractions taken from gross pay but a number of loan payments were also taken out directly. Casual work was overestimated for a different reason. Respondents simply worked a great deal less than they reported when asked to state the number of days they planned to work in an average month. The biggest difference was in the money respondents received from other family members. Because these remittances were often irregular—both in timing and amounts—and because respondents did not think of them as "income," they would rarely report this important source of income in the preliminary interviews.

These discrepancies differ by income quartile, with more wealthy households reporting a very different, and lower, income in the pre-

liminary questionnaires than in the Financial Diaries. Within the lowest quartiles, the differences are distinctly less significant, with households *overreporting* their income. Sensitivities about reporting income therefore seem to be confined to the highest-income categories.

Table 5.3 reports expenditure items, again comparing data gathering during the (second) preliminary questionnaire compared to the Financial Diaries data. Generally speaking, respondents are far worse at reporting expenditures than income. On average, households in this sample underreported their monthly expenditures per capita by R2862, which works out to underreporting by $35 per day, far more than the $0.50 overreport on income shown in table 5.2 The underreporting seems to be spread across all regular items, but food expenditures are particularly underreported in terms of percentage of income. Moreover, this type of underreporting occurs across all income quartiles.

This is contrary to Deaton (1997)'s suggestion that households should find it easier to report expenditures. I suggest that this discrepancy exists because cash flows for expenditures are much tinier and more frequent and they therefore go missing easily. For example, in the preliminary questionnaire, households estimated that they spent R419 on food per month, while actually spending, on average, R5150 per month. Respondents also overreport the share of income they spend on energy and telephone. Generally speaking, households have little knowledge of exactly how much money slips through their fingers on a monthly basis. This notion is similar to that put forward by Gibson (2002), who suggests that as household size rises, so do the number of food purchases in a time period, and therefore so does measurement error. With these data, I see no such relationship between measurement error and household size, but I suggest that the frequency of food purchases is what drives up measurement error.

I also use several methods to investigate how well households report usage of financial instruments. First, I look at how quickly households report owning the financial instrument. Then I look at how well households report the transactions they make on these instruments. Finally, I look at what makes these financial instruments "appear"—that is, what causes respondents to finally report them—and whether certain types of households underreport financial instruments.

Table 5.4 shows each type of financial instrument we designated for the sample, the total number that we ultimately tracked across the entire sample, and the percentage that were missed in the one-off questionnaire. One might expect loans to be underreported because, as

Table 5.3
Monthly expenditure from initial questionnaire versus diaries

	Data from initial questionnaires	Data from diaries	Average % difference across households
Household expenditure			
Average monthly per capita	$45	$486	−90***
Difference by expenditure quartiles			
Lowest quartile			−88.5%***
Second lowest quartile			−89.8%***
Second highest quartile			−89.5%***
Highest quartile			−92.0%***
Share of expenditure			
For food	54.6%	62.1%	−7.5%***
For energy (including electricity, paraffin)	13.7%	10.6%	3.1%**
For transport (including transport to work, school, shopping)	13.9%	15.6%	−1.7%
For cigarettes	3.3%	1.6%	1.7%***
For beer and alcohol	1.1%	1.3%	−0.2%
For telephone (including landline, cell phone, pay phone)	7.1%	3.7%	3.3%**
Regular monthly items (including rent, water, sanitation, rates and taxes, church fees, union fees)	6.2%	5.0%	1.2%*

Notes: Data in this table come from the 2004 South African Financial Diaries dataset, described in the chapter. The sample is 152 poor households selected from two urban and one rural site in South Africa. Data on income, expenditures, and financial transactions were collected every fortnight for over a year. Household expenditure is defined as the sum of the most common items, which are listed in the table. Expenditure quartiles were determined by the diaries per capita expenditure. Figures in dollars are converted from South African rand at a rate of $1 = ZAR6.5. Significance in the difference between the two series is tested using a two-sided paired *t*-test.
*significant at 10 percent; **significant at 5 percent; ***significant at 1 percent.

Table 5.4
Financial instruments: Instruments not reported in initial interview

Financial instrument type	Number of instruments had by the sample	Percent missed in the initial interview
Bank account	246	24.6%
Pension/provident fund	55	34.5%
Savings clubs	224	4.9%
Funeral insurance	269	25.7%
Retirement annuities	25	56.0%
Insurance (excluding funeral insurance)	53	47.2%
Loans from banks/savings clubs	140	15.0%
Moneylender loan	109	1.8%
Credit/hire purchase	239	7.5%
Credit from a local shop	101	0.1%
Giving loans to an individual	367	1.6%
Taking loans from an individual	232	3.0%
Money guarding—looking after someone's money	17	11.8%
Money guarding—having someone else look after your money	23	4.3%
Saving in the house	163	10.4%
Rent arrears	23	13.0%
Wage advance	30	3.3%
Income arrears	46	0.0%
Giving credit to customers	351	0.3%
Receiving trade credit	1	0.0%
Credit cards	86	0.0%
Salary timing	11	0.0%
Debts under administration	11	18.2%

Notes: Data in this table come from the 2004 South African Financial Diaries dataset, described in the chapter. The sample is 152 poor households selected from two urban and one rural site in South Africa. "Financial instruments" are predefined and asked about in the third of a set of preliminary questionnaires. As householders are probed in subsequent diaries interviews, some revealed that they had held these instruments since the first interview.

Karlan and Zinman (2008) suggested, respondents often lie about borrowing. However, we found that the least-mentioned financial instruments were formal services. Informal instruments such as savings clubs, money guarding, and giving credit to customers were all reported from the beginning of the interviews. Similarly, credit instruments such as moneylender loans, credit from the local store, and borrowing from an individual (such as family, friends or neighbors) were reported faithfully. The least-reported financial instruments were insurance, pension or provident funds, and retirement annuities. None of these instruments can be associated with the "shame" that is supposedly associated with using lending instruments, so there seems to be no clear reason for underreporting these instruments.

We would instead argue that respondents who owned these instruments were largely confused about what they were. Many respondents who held these types of instruments were employed, and the payments came directly out of their paycheck. Financial Diaries data show that these respondents frequently did not understand what these deductions were and that they were reluctant to ask their employers. It was not until we looked at the respondents' pay slips and probed further that we were able to discern whether the instrument was insurance or long-term savings; as mentioned, respondents frequently did not themselves know what the instrument was. Therefore, we argue that this lack of reporting had more to do with a lack of financial understanding rather than deliberately failing to report financial dealings.

Contrary to findings by Karlan and Zinman (2008), table 5.5 suggests that loans are reported far more quickly than savings or insurance instruments. The OLS regression results show that the number of days it took to report a loan or credit instrument was significantly fewer than for savings or insurance instruments. Also interesting was that the fact that the higher the respondent's education, the fewer days it took to report the instrument. Also, the higher the respondent's age, the longer it took to report the instrument. Both results are consistent with a picture of misreporting instruments based on misunderstanding either the question or the types of instruments being asked about. Formal instruments also take longer to be reported, as do instruments owned by men rather than women.

This regression was also specified as a Cox Proportional Hazard model. The sign of the coefficients in this specification is interpreted as the influence of the covariate on the baseline hazard function. Therefore, a variable with a positive coefficient increases the "hazard" of discovering the instrument, and a negative coefficient decreases the

Table 5.5
Regression results: Predictors of the number of days it took for financial instruments to be reported after they had started to be used

Estimator	OLS	Cox Proportional Hazard Model
Dependent variable: log (LATEFI)	coefficient (standard errors)	coefficient (standard errors)
Savings	−0.05 (0.09)	0.06 (0.20)
Loan or credit	−0.35*** (0.08)	1.14*** (0.24)
Formal	−0.14* (0.08)	−0.33* (0.17)
Age of person with instrument	0.01** (0.00)	−0.02*** (0.01)
Education of person with instrument	−0.00*** (0.00)	0.00 (0.00)
Gender of person with instrument	−0.14* (0.07)	0.35* (0.18)
Log (household income per capita)	0.09 (0.09)	−0.11 (0.20)
R-squared	0.19	
Pseudo R-squared		0.03
Number of financial instruments	169	169

Notes: Each regression controls for area dummies. I left out the financial variable type Insurance. Formal instruments are coded 1. Female is coded 1. OLS standard errors are heteroskedasticity-corrected.
*significant at 10 percent; **significant at 5 percent; ***significant at 1 percent.

hazard of discovery. So a loan or credit instrument is at increased hazard of being discovered, compared to an insurance instrument. Likewise, a respondent who is older and female decreases the hazard of finding the instrument, as mentioned previously, and formal instruments have decreased hazards of being found. Interestingly, education is not significant in this specification.

Perhaps the biggest challenge in obtaining financial data from household surveys is getting good estimates of the financial flows going through the reported instruments. Table 5.6 provides the monthly flows, in South African rand terms, going through several financial instruments. On average, households tended to accurately report most financial flows, except for withdrawals from savings in the house and contributions to savings clubs. However, both of these items are significant. First, households may willingly report that they have savings

Table 5.6
Monthly flows into financial instruments: Initial versus actual by instrument

	Rand		
	Data from initial questionnaires	Data from diaries	Average difference across households
Bank account deposits	$316	$323	−$7
Bank account withdrawals	$226	$247	−$21
Savings in house deposits	$41	$47	−$5
Savings in house withdrawals	$25	$37	−$12**
Savings club contributions	$49	$29	$21***
Funeral insurance contributions	$24	$22	$2

Notes: Data in this table come from the 2004 South African Financial Diaries dataset, described in the chapter. The sample is 152 poor households selected from two urban and one rural site in South Africa. Data on income, expenditures, and financial transactions were collected every fortnight for over a year. Figures in dollars are converted from South African rand at a rate of $1 = ZAR6.5. Significance in the difference between the two series is tested using a two-sided paired t-test.
*significant at 10 percent; **significant at 5 percent; ***significant at 1 percent.

in the house, as seen in table 5.4, but they do not accurately report how much they might use this financial instrument. In fact, they considerably underreport withdrawals from savings in the house. Based on a single questionnaire, a researcher could conclude that a respondent is saving significantly more than he or she claims. Savings club contributions are surprisingly also significantly lower than reported in a one-off questionnaire, which frequently occurs because contributions are often made late or not at all and are deducted from the final payout, so respondents may report that they are saving more than they really are.

Finally, I looked at the question of who within the household provided the fullest answer about all household cash flows. To answer this question, I used the absolute value of the margin of error described earlier in an OLS regression against the household role of the month's respondent, as well as household- and individual-level covariates. The results in table 5.7 confirm Cull and Scott's (2010) finding that the head of the household provides the fullest picture of cash flows, that is, the lowest average absolute margin of error. Child of household head is also significant, but there are only five cases in our sample in which the child of the household head is the most-interviewed member, and all are adult children in their thirties and are the de facto household heads.

Table 5.7
OLS regression results—Predictors of absolute value of margin of error

Dependent variable: Absolute value of margin of error	Coefficient (standard error)
Household characteristics	
Log per capita income	−46.50 (30.29)
Share of those receiving regular income (either government grant or salary)	43.92 (43.56)
Household position of person interviewed most	
Head of household	−48.37** (19.43)
Spouse of head	81.98 (66.52)
Child of head	−155.44** (76.81)
Personal characteristics of person interviewed most	
Gender (female = 1)	−44.87 (31.54)
Age	0.78 (0.97)
Education	1.90 (2.30)
Married or partnered	−86.44** (39.86)
Math score	−30.75 (52.09)
Fatalism score	−39.19 (26.85)
Financial literacy score	195.54 (144.25)
Regularity of income	−57.60 (38.46)
R-squared	0.22
Number of households	152

Notes: Each regression controls for area dummies and dummies representing individual enumerators. Math scores are based on a series of eight math questions. Fatalism scores are based on a series of three questions about how much control one has over the future. Financial literacy scores are based on two questions about credit payments. I left out the *Other household member* variable. Married or partnered is coded 1, while divorced, single, or widowed is coded 0. Regularity of income is coded 1 if head of household receives either a salaried wage or a monthly government grant; 0 if other. Standard errors are heteroskedasticity-corrected.
*significant at 10 percent; **significant at 5 percent; ***significant at 1 percent.

I also estimated this regression using first only the positive margin of error (41 percent of the sample) and then the negative margin of error (59 percent of the sample).[8] The regression using the positive margin of error showed a strong negative relationship between the spouse of the household head and the margin of error. The regression using the negative margin of error did not show that any household-place variables were significant but did show a strong negative relationship with the "married" variable. The nonsymmetric results for the positive margin of errors suggests that among household members underestimating uses versus sources, spouses (usually women) provide the most complete information. In other words, the spouse, usually a woman, provides the best information on expenditures.

Conclusions and Suggestions for Collecting Financial Flow Data

The empirical results in the previous section echo the conceptual platforms presented earlier, suggesting an important notion about collecting household-level financial access data. Understanding the economics of poor households means understanding the cash flows they see on a day-to-day basis. As Deaton and Grosh suggest, "Questionnaires should be designed around items that are familiar to the respondent—typically cash flows or flows of goods—provided that enough information is gathered to allow total consumption to be calculated" (2000, 8). The empirical literature, as well as the evidence presented thus far, suggests that the most successfully collected data are those that are the most familiar—that is, informal flows and loans, including those that are lumpy. This conclusion suggests that the respondents' cognitive biases—the tendency to keep thinking about lumpy expenditures and obligations such as loans—keeps these cash flows at the top of the mind. In South Africa, income flows, which tend to be lumpy and regular,[9] are better collected through a one-off questionnaire than through expenditure flows, which are irregular, small, and frequent. In other environments, where income flows are much more irregular and small, such as for casual workers, this may not be the case.

The results also suggest the importance of looking at financial portfolios within context. Using the basic tools of corporate finance, as per Samphantharak and Townsend (2009), household-level financial management can be seen as a daily balancing act rather than being clinically viewed as a series of isolated "types" of behavior or instrument.

Although households may not perfectly report borrowing, for example, they may report borrowing far more frequently than they report insurance.

Both results suggest possible improvements to household surveys about financial use. Though current financial access surveys consist of long lists asking about usage of various financial products,[10] a more fruitful approach includes two additional elements. The first element is a household reconciliation of a full set of cash flows for a recent period (for a month or two weeks, depending on income frequency). These cash flows would include not only financial flows but also expenditure and income data, as well as cash on hand. This element leverages the concepts specified by Deaton and Grosh (2000), by Samphantharak and Townsend (2009), and by the evidence shown here—namely, that financial management is best understood through the cash flow statement; that questions should be familiar to the respondents; and that understanding financial management can be achieved only within the context of the whole of household economic activities.

Finally, the empirical literature on consumption strongly suggests that households clearly recall spending on certain events and large assets, and the Financial Diaries evidence certainly supports the contention that households have difficulty remembering small, high-frequency expenditures. The additional element required to improve financial surveys is therefore finding key events and asset purchases in the respondent's near past, then asking how the respondent financed the purchase and whether the financial instrument that enabled that funding is still in use.[11]

Notes

1. Deaton and Grosh (2000) say that this point should not be taken too seriously because there is no rigorous information about their accuracy and the surveys are from various reports rather than original microdata, so there may be some incomparabilities in their calculations.

2. Earlier work using diaries to test data collection errors can be found in the experiments described in Sudman and Ferber 1971.

3. Although elements of Cull and Scott's (2009) work are tested in this chapter, this is one conclusion on which I cannot comment. The data used in this chapter were specified by product rather than by institution.

4. The Financial Diaries is a research project based at the University of Cape Town and funded by the Ford Foundation, FinMark Trust, and the Micro Finance Regulatory Council of South Africa. Please see http://www.financialdiaries.com for more information.

5. The sample started out with 181 households and had an attrition rate of 19 percent through the survey year. The analysis shown in this chapter is based on the 152 households for which we have a complete set of data.

6. Financial instruments were captured in the third and fourth of a series of four "initial questionnaires" described in the section on results. The financial instruments questions were product based, but they should not be taken as a test of the FinScope survey instruments mentioned earlier. The initial financial instrument questionnaires were not constructed based on the FinScope survey instrument.

7. Using PPP conversation rate of R2.7 per U.S. dollar.

8. Results available upon request.

9. Thanks to a high number of monthly grant recipients and salary earnings.

10. I can include details of these, along with average times they take for respondents to complete.

11. One could also ask questions about how future events, such as weddings or retirement, will be financed, which would pick up financial instruments that may have already been funded, such as fixed deposit accounts, and that have large balances but no associated cash flows.

References

Bhalla, Surjit S. 1979. Measurement Errors and the Permanent Income Hypothesis: Evidence from Rural India. *American Economic Review* 69 (3): 295–307.

Bhalla, Surjit S. 1980. The Measurement of Permanent Income and its Application to Saving Behavior. *Journal of Political Economy* 88 (3): 722–744.

Blaizeau, Didier. 1998. *Household Expenditure and Surveys in Seven UEMOA Countries.* Paris: INSEE.

Bradburn, Norman, Janellen Huttenlocher, and Larry Hedges. 1994. Telescoping and Temporal Memory. In *Autobiographical Memory and the Validity of Retrospective Reports*, ed. Norbert Schwartz and Seymour Sudman, 203–215. New York: Springer-Verlag.

Collins, Daryl. 2005. Financial Instruments of the Poor: Initial Findings from the Financial Diaries Study. *Development Southern Africa* 22 (5): 717–728.

Collins, Daryl, Jonathan Morduch, Stuart Rutherford, and Orlanda Ruthven. 2009. Portfolios of the Poor. Princeton, NJ: Princeton University Press.

Cull, Robert, and Kinnon Scott. 2010. Measuring Household Usage of Financial Services: Does It Matter How or Whom You Ask? *World Bank Economic Review* 24 (2): 199–223.

Deaton, Angus. 1997. *The Analysis of Household Surveys: A Microeconometric Approach to Development Policy.* Baltimore: Johns Hopkins University Press.

Deaton, Angus, and Margaret Grosh. 2000. Consumption. In *Designing Household Survey Questionnaires for Developing Countries: Lessons from 15 years of the Living Standards Measurement Survey*, ed. Margaret Grosh and Paul Glewwe, 91–133. Washington, DC: The World Bank.

Duflo, Esther, Michael Kremer, and Jonathan Robinson. 2011. Nudging Farmers to Use Fertilizer Evidence from Kenya. *American Economic Review* 101 (6): 2350–2390.

Gibson, John. 2002. Why Does the Engel Method Work? Food Demand, Economies of Size and Household Survey Methods. University of Waikato, Department of Economics Working Paper 2/02.

Karlan, Dean, and Jonathan Zinman. 2008. Lying about Borrowing. *Journal of the European Economic Association* 6 (2–3): 510–521.

Kochar, Anjini. 2000. Savings. In *Designing Household Survey Questionnaires for Developing Countries: Lessons from 15 Years of the Living Standards Measurement Survey*, vol. 2, ed. Margaret Grosh and Paul Glewwe, 183–209. Washington, DC: The World Bank.

Martini, Alberto, and Anna Ivanova. 1996. *The Design and Implementation of Income and Expenditure Survey of Belarus*. Washington, DC: Urban Institute.

Musgrove, Philip. 1978. *Consumer Behavior in Latin America*. Washington, DC: Brookings Institution.

Musgrove, Philip. 1979. Permanent Household Income and Consumption in Urban South America. *American Economic Review* 69 (3): 355–368.

Neter, John. 1970. Measurement Errors in Reports of Consumer Expenditures. *Journal of Marketing Research* 7: 11–25.

Neter, John, and Joseph Waksberg. 1964. A Study of Response Errors in Expenditure Data from Household Interviews. *Journal of the American Statistical Association* 59: 18–55.

Paxson, Christina. 1992. Using Weather Variability to Estimate the Response of Savings to Transitory Income in Thailand. *American Economic Review* 82 (1): 15–33.

Paxson, Christina. 1993. Consumption and Income Seasonality in Thailand. *Journal of Political Economy* 101 (1): 39–72.

Rubin, David, and Alan Baddeley. 1989. Telescoping Is Not Time Compression: A Model of the Dating of Autobiographical Events. *Memory & Cognition* 17: 18–55.

Samphantharak, Krislert, and Robert Townsend. 2009. *Households as Corporate Firms: An Analysis of Household Finance Using Integrated Household Surveys and Corporate Financial Accounting*. Cambridge: Cambridge University Press.

Scott, Christopher. and Ben Amenuvegbe. 1990. Effect of Recall Duration on Reporting of Household Expenditures: An Experimental Study in Ghana. Social Dimensions of Adjustment in Sub-Saharan Africa Working Paper 6. Washington, DC: The World Bank.

Sen, Amartya K. 1999. *Development as Freedom*. New York: Knopf.

Silberstein, Adriana R. 1990. First-Wave Effects in the U.S. Consumer Expenditure Interview Survey. *Survey Methodology* 16 (2): 293–304.

Sudman, Seymour, Norman H. Bradburn, and Norbert Schwarz. 1996. *Thinking About Answers*. San Francisco: Jossey-Bass.

Sudman, Seymour, and Robert Ferber. 1971. Experiments in Obtaining Consumer Expenditures by Diary Methods. *Journal of the American Statistical Association* 66: 725–735.

Wolpin, Kenneth. 1982. A New Test of the Permanent Income Hypothesis: The Impact of Weather on the Income and Consumption of Farm Households in India. *International Economic Review* 23 (3): 583–594.

III Creating Impact

6 The Economic Impact of Expanding Access to Finance in Mexico

Miriam Bruhn and Inessa Love

It is well recognized that financial development is important for economic growth (Levine 2005). In addition, several recent studies have found a positive correlation between access to finance and poverty alleviation at the country level (Beck, Demirgüç-Kunt, and Levine 2007; World Bank 2008; Honohan 2004). However, these studies tend to face identification issues, implying that they do not necessarily establish a causal impact of increasing access to finance on economic outcomes. Similarly, although the microfinance industry has grown exponentially in the past few decades and a number of researchers have written on the topic (e.g., Coleman 1999; Kaboski and Townsend 2005; McKernan 2002; Pitt and Khandker 1998; Pitt et al. 2003), there is still little systematic evidence on the casual impact of microfinance on economic activity (Harford 2008; Karlan and Morduch 2009). There is also little evidence on the channels through which finance may help to reduce poverty.

In this chapter, we use a unique event to evaluate the effect of increased access to financial services for low-income individuals on entrepreneurial activity, employment, and income. Specifically, we evaluate the effect of the opening of Banco Azteca in Mexico in October 2002. This event was unique in that Banco Azteca opened branches in all of the existing stores of its parent company—a large retailer of consumer goods, Grupo Elektra. Almost overnight, Banco Azteca established the second largest network of branches in the country, setting a world record of a bank opening more than 800 branches at once.

An important feature of Banco Azteca was that from the start it catered to low- and middle-income groups, which had mostly been excluded from the commercial banking sector.[1] Capitalizing on Grupo Elektra's decades of experience in making small installment loans for purchasers of its merchandise, its rich data, and its established

information and collection technology, the bank was uniquely positioned to target this segment of the population, which it estimated to comprise over 70 percent of total households. Many of these households were part of the informal economy—operating small informal businesses that lacked the documentation necessary for obtaining bank loans. The nature of Azteca's operations, including low documentation requirements and motorcycle-riding loan officers who come to the borrower's house, as well as the size of the loans offered, make it comparable to microfinance institutions that operated in Mexico at the time of Azteca opening.

We use the predetermined nature of the branch locations—which were opened in all stores of its parent company, Grupo Elektra—to identify the casual impact of Azteca opening on economic activity through a difference-in-difference strategy. Specifically, we compare the changes in outcome variables from before to after Azteca opening across municipalities with preexisting Grupo Elektra branches and those without branches at the time of the bank opening. Using the Mexican Labor Market Survey (ENE), we study the impact of this event on individuals' employment choices and income levels.

Our results show that the new bank opening led to an increase in the proportion of informal businesses by 7.6 percent but did not lead to change in formal businesses. This finding is consistent with anecdotal evidence suggesting that Azteca targeted lower-income individuals and also with Azteca's low documentation requirements. In contrast, formal business owners have easier access to commercial bank credit and likely prefer it because of higher interest rates charged by Azteca.[2]

Second, the increase in informal businesses is significant only for men. However, we find a higher proportion of women working as wage earners in municipalities with Azteca branches after its opening, which possibly signifies an expansion of labor market opportunities for women from homemakers to paid staff. Overall, total employment, including informal business owners and wage earners, rose by 1.5 percent for the complete sample.

Third, the new bank opening led to higher income levels for both men and women by about 7 percent.[3] Burgess and Pande (2005) similarly find that the expansion of bank branches in rural India had a significant impact on alleviating poverty, although Kochar (2011) and Panagariya (2006) cast doubt on their findings.

It is important to point out that our chapter does not establish whether the new bank opening had a direct impact, which it might

have had given its large scale of the operations, or an indirect one—that is, via improvement in the competition in the local financial sector. Azteca was probably competing for clients with existing microfinance organizations and credit unions. Thus, the impact on the economic outcomes we observe could have stemmed from the access to credit and savings provided by Azteca or by a number of other financial institutions.[4] Nevertheless, our evidence suggests that improving access to low-income households has a significant impact on the labor market and income levels.

Our chapter is related to work on U.S. banking deregulation that exploits the natural experiment of the gradual relaxation of restrictions on state-wide branching and on entrance by out-of-state banks. This relaxation of restrictions resulted in increased presence of banks in different states, which is somewhat akin to the entry of Banco Azteca. Some of the results of this literature parallel ours: Jayaratne and Strahan (1996) find an increase in the economic growth rate of 0.51–1.19 percent, and Black and Strahan (2002) find an increase in new firm incorporations of up to 8 percent.

Also closely related to our work, Beck, Levine, and Levkov (2007) find that banking deregulation resulted in a reduction in income inequality through its impact on labor market conditions. In particular, they find a reduction in the income gap between men and women, which parallels our results regarding increased employment opportunities for women. Although we don't test for this question directly, the entrance of Banco Azteca has likely led to increased bank competition, similar to what Cetorelli and Strahan (2006) find in the United States: they argue that deregulation has led to increased competition and a larger presence of small firms. Despite some similarities with previous research, the unique feature of Banco Azteca—namely, the targeting of low-income, previously unbanked individuals—make it an important case for studying the real effects of bank expansion.

Background on Banco Azteca

In March 2002, one of Mexico's largest retailers for electronics and household goods, Grupo Elektra, received a banking license. In October 2002, Grupo Elektra launched Banco Azteca, opening a total of 815 branches in all preexisting Grupo Elektra stores.

As of the opening date, "The bank was the first and only all-Mexican-owned franchise to be licensed by the Finance Ministry since 1994. It

is also the first bank to aim at Mexico's middle and working classes: the 73 million people who live in households with combined family incomes of $250 to $4,000 a month, a mass market largely neglected by Mexico's banking system" (Conger 2002).

Before Azteca, access to credit was largely unavailable to millions of informal businesses, such as taxi drivers, plumbers, or street merchants. Banco Azteca officials claimed that Azteca would make credit more available to Mexico's large informal sector, the small business owners and self-employed who operate outside the regulatory framework (Conger 2002).

Commenting on the opening of Banco Azteca, Ricardo B. Salinas, chairman of the board of Grupo Elektra, stressed that "Banco Azteca will improve access to goods and services for our people. A major impediment to the growth of the Mexican middle class has been the lack of access to credit, one of the main vehicles for personal financial improvement. Banco Azteca will demonstrate the importance of offering financial services to this under-served segment of the Mexican population" (PR Newswire 2002).

Thus, from the outset, Banco Azteca targeted low- and middle-income customers, who were historically underserved by the traditional banking industry. Banco Azteca had a comparative advantage in serving these types of customers because of several unique features. The first feature is the synergies with its retail operations, which provided a rich source of data on their customers. Through Elektra's forty-eight years of know-how in providing installment loans for electronics and household goods to low-income consumers, Banco Azteca obtained information on about 4 million borrowers. Many of those customers buy Elektra's products or receive money transfers from the United States through Western Union service points located in Elektra stores. "We know this segment of Mexican society better than anyone else," says Banco Azteca President Carlos Septien. "The sophisticated technology and collection systems already in place at Grupo Elektra will provide us with invaluable data about our customers' buying habits and financial needs, allowing us to succeed" (Smith 2003).

The second feature is Grupo Elektra's unique information technology. The group has spent $20 million a year over three years on information technology, including high-tech fingerprint readers that eliminate the need for customers to present identification or passbooks. Banco Azteca also requires less documentation than traditional commercial banks, often taking a cosigner instead of valid documents. Many of its

customers are informal business owners who do not have the proof of income required by other banks.

The third feature is Azteca's specialized distribution and collection network. The bank commands a 3,000-strong army of motorcycle-riding loan agents. They carry handheld computers loaded with Elektra's rich database, which includes customers' credit histories and even names of neighbors who might help track down delinquent debtors (Smith 2003). "The difference between Elektra and more established banks is that Elektra has a much better collection system," said Joaquin Lopez-Doriga, an analyst with Deutsche-Ixe. "If you want to address the market that Elektra is addressing, you have to know it very well. That's very labor intensive" (Orlandi 2003).

Because of these unique features, Banco Azteca was able to extend credit to segments of the low-income population that were previously unbankable. Box 6.1 highlights two anecdotal accounts that demonstrate Banco Azteca's unique way of operating and the type of clients it serves.

Box 6.1
Media Accounts of Banco Azteca

Banco Azteca Bikers Reach Out to Mexico's Poor

By Lorraine Orlandi, September 21, 2003, Reuters News, © 2003 Reuters Limited

Loan officers make house calls to investigate potential customers and to ensure that they make payments once a loan is approved. Sometimes they repossess items that are resold at Elektra's Bodega de Remates discount stores, typically at prices higher than the amount due on the loan.

On a recent afternoon Azteca loan officer Manuel Monroy hopped on a Honda 125 to visit Blanca Guevara at home in a working-class neighborhood of Mexico City. The 48-year-old widow had applied to buy a sewing machine for 2,174 pesos (about $210) on credit at Elektra the day before.

Guevara said she could pay 41 pesos a week over 53 weeks, after a 141-peso down payment. But as an off-the-books house cleaner, she had no proof of income.

Once her mother-in-law, who owns their house, agreed to back the loan, Monroy looked over property and identification papers and recorded the information on a handheld computer. The software analyzed the information and within minutes a verdict flashed on the computer's tiny

Box 6.1
(continued)

screen: "Approved." He pressed another button to produce a ticket from a printer on his belt for Guevara to present at the store.

Buy a Toaster, Open a Bank Account: Banco Azteca Caters to the Little Guy—in Appliance Stores

By Geri Smith in Mexico City, January 13, 2003, *BusinessWeek* 54, no. 3815
(© 2003 McGraw-Hill, Inc.)

Pedro Rubio was in a bind. The fifty-six-year-old carpenter needed to come up with thousands of pesos in notary fees to get legal title to his modest cinderblock house. Otherwise, he feared that squatters would stake claim to it when he was away working at construction sites. But Rubio, who earns the equivalent of $600 a month, had no proof of income and no bank account.

So, on a recent morning, he walked through his gritty Mexico City neighborhood to an Elektra appliance store. At the back, behind an aisle of microwave ovens, he sat down with a loan officer from a new bank, Banco Azteca. Unfazed by Rubio's worn jeans and unshaven face, the officer drew up an inventory of his possessions: TV, refrigerator, washing machine—all bought on credit at Elektra in the past three years. Accepting these as collateral, the bank approved Rubio's application within twenty-four hours.

The nine-month, $200 loan carries a 48 percent annual interest rate, usurious by U.S. standards but not in Mexico, where the banking sector is still recovering from the effects of the 1994 peso crash. "It's a little expensive," says Rubio. Still, he says he can swing the weekly $8 payments. In any event, he adds, "I don't really have any other option."

Azteca began its operations by offering savings accounts targeted to low-income customers that could be opened with as little as $5. Within the first month, 157,000 accounts were opened, increasing to 250,000 accounts by the end of December 2002. At its opening in October 2002, Banco Azteca also took over the issuance of installment loans, which were previously issued by Elektrafin, the financing unit of Grupo Elektra's retail stores. Elektra's old consumer financing operation closed down as its borrowers paid off their loans, which had an average maturity of 53 weeks and an average amount of $250. Although these loans were tied to merchandize, they could be used for business purposes. For example, purchasing a new sewing machine or a fridge might allow

a person to start or to sustain their micro business. In 2003, Azteca started offering $500 consumer loans not tied to the merchandize. These amounts were comparable in size to loans offered by several microfinance organizations, which in 2002 amounted to about $360.[5] Toward the end of 2003, Azteca also expanded into the mortgage and insurance business. After less than a year of operations, Banco Azteca had "seen rapid success as it [tapped] Mexico's vast informal economy, thanks to Elektra's long record of serving the working class" (Orlandi 2003).

Although Grupo Elektra was disbursing installment loans before opening Banco Azteca, Banco Azteca's new savings accounts allowed its loan portfolio to expand significantly. Figure 6.1 plots Grupo Elektra's loan portfolio within Mexico over time, showing a steep increase from the fourth quarter of 2002 on. The loan portfolio increased from around 2 billion Mexican pesos at the time of opening Banco Azteca to 10 billion Mexican pesos in the last quarter of 2004. Although this portfolio size is small compared to the total commercial bank credit to the private sector, which was about 550 billion Mexican pesos in the fourth quarter of 2002, it is large compared to the credit disbursed by smaller institutions, which cater to low-income households. The combined portfolio of the largest microfinance institutions in Mexico stood at only 0.5 billion Mexican pesos in the fourth quarter of 2004. In this same quarter, the total amount of outstanding loans from credit unions was 8.7 billion Mexican pesos.

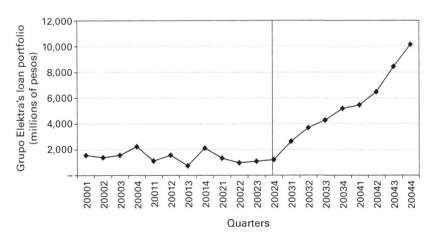

Figure 6.1
Grupo Elektra's loan portfolio within Mexico over time.

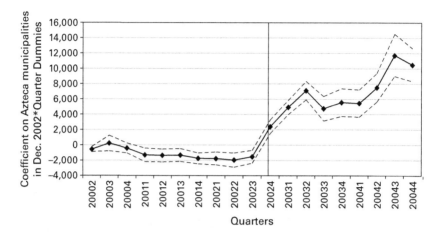

Figure 6.2
Effect of Banco Azteca opening on savings accounts over time.

The number of savings accounts in the banking sector also increased significantly due to Banco Azteca opening. Figure 6.2 shows the relative difference in the number of savings accounts in municipalities with Azteca versus municipalities without Azteca. Data on savings accounts comes from the Mexican bank supervisory body, the Comisión Nacional Bancaria y de Valores (CNBV). There is a clear rapid growth in savings accounts in municipalities with Azteca after December 2002.[6] Thus the opening of Banco Azteca had a nontrivial impact on availability of financial services in municipalities where the branches were present.

Empirical Strategy to Measure the Effect of the Banco Azteca Opening on Economic Activity

In order to identify the effect of Banco Azteca opening on economic activity, we exploit the cross-municipality and cross-time variation in Azteca branches. As discussed previously, Banco Azteca opened in October 2002, only in the municipalities that had preexisting Grupo Elektra stores. Thus we compare pre- to post-Azteca changes in outcome variables in municipalities that had an Azteca branch with those that did not. This is a difference in difference methodology, which allows us to identify the causal effect of the Azteca opening on economic activity.

In our analysis, we use outcome variables from the Mexican National Employment Survey (ENE). The ENE is the survey that the Mexican government relies on for calculating unemployment statistics and for measuring the size of the informal sector. It has been conducted quarterly since the second quarter of 2000 (2000-II) and covers a random sample of approximately 150,000 households each quarter. Households remain in the survey for five consecutive quarters. We use data for 2000-II to 2004-IV (nineteen quarters in total). After 2004-IV, the ENE was changed to a new survey.[7]

We chose to use the ENE data in our analysis for the following reasons. First, it includes detailed questions about a person's economic activity (including self-employment) and reports a person's income from their main occupation. Second, it captures and distinguishes between formal and informal self-employment and firms, making it possible to investigate the effect of Banco Azteca on informal firms. This point is important because the anecdotal reports mentioned in the previous sections suggest that many Banco Azteca clients are informal business owners. Third, the ENE covers a wide range of municipalities for ten quarters before Banco Azteca opened and nine quarters after, allowing us to implement the identification strategy described previously. Fourth, the panel structure of the ENE allows us to describe the effect of Banco Azteca more precisely by looking at the impact on different prereform occupation groups.

The ENE covers a total of 1,222 municipalities, but we drop the ones that do not have any bank because we feel that they would be less comparable to the municipalities with Azteca. We determine which municipalities had a bank branch in the fourth quarter of 2002 and which had an Azteca branch by referring to data from the Mexican bank supervisory body, the CNBV. Our final sample includes 576 municipalities, of which 249 had an Azteca branch in the fourth quarter of 2002 and 327 did not have an Azteca branch but had a branch of a different bank. Almost all the municipalities where Azteca opened also had a branch of a different bank. Only 6 out of the 249 Azteca municipalities in our data did not also have a different bank branch.[8]

Figure 6.3 shows a map of Mexico in which municipalities that had an Azteca branch in the fourth quarter of 2002 are marked in black and municipalities that had a different bank branch but no Azteca branch are marked in gray. Both types of municipalities are distributed throughout Mexico. The white municipalities are not in our sample

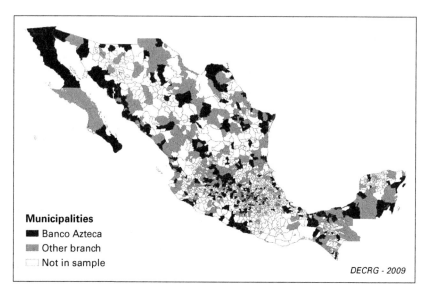

Figure 6.3
Map of municipalities with Banco Azteca branches and other bank branches.

because they either are not included in the ENE data or do not contain a Banco Azteca branch or another bank.

Because our analysis applies to potential Banco Azteca clients who could be economically active, we keep only individuals of working age (between the ages of 20 and 65) in our sample. We then construct three of our main outcome variables by creating dummy variables for each person in the sample, indicating whether the person (1) owns an informal business, (2) owns a formal business, and (3) is a wage earner.[9] These are the three possible occupations for someone who is employed. People who do not fall into either of these categories are not employed (they are either unemployed or not in the labor force).

All dummies are defined for the whole sample, meaning that they denote the percentage of all individuals in the sample who fall into each category. For example, a value of 0.08 of the formal business owner dummy means that 8 percent of all people between the ages of 20 and 65 own a formal business.

Finally, we also use monthly income as an outcome variable. Although the dummy variables are defined for all interviewees in our sample, income is available only for the gainfully employed and is missing for the unemployed, for individuals who are out of the labor

force, and for unpaid workers. Unfortunately, the income data from the ENE is probably not as reliable as the occupation data because it is not the focus of the survey. The survey includes only one question on income, asking for the earnings from the individual's main occupation, and 4.2 percent of employed individuals do not answer this question.

The upper section of table 6.1 includes summary statistics for the outcome variables split up by municipalities that had at least one Azteca branch in the fourth quarter of 2002 and by municipalities that didn't have any Azteca branch at that time but had at least one branch

Table 6.1
Pre-Azteca averages of individual-level variables

	Municipalities with any Azteca branch in Dec. 2002	Municipalities without Azteca, but with other branch in Dec. 2002	Coefficient of Azteca dummy
	(1)	(2)	(3)
Outcome variables levels			
Informal business owner dummy	0.0821	0.1380	−0.0560***
	(0.2745)	(0.3449)	(0.0087)
Formal business owner dummy	0.0790	0.0656	0.0134***
	(0.2697)	(0.2475)	(0.0033)
Wage earner dummy	0.4969	0.4403	0.0566***
	(0.5000)	(0.4964)	(0.0111)
Log monthly income + 1	4.9999	4.4705	0.5294***
	(3.9346)	(3.8103)	0.0918
Outcome variables changes			
Informal business owner change	−0.0023	−0.0010	−0.0013
	(0.0388)	(0.0551)	0.0021
Formal business owner change	0.0049	0.0055	−0.0005
	(0.0264)	(0.0360)	(0.0014)
Wage earner change	−0.0038	0.0031	−0.0068***
	(0.0486)	(0.0690)	(0.0026)
Log monthly income change	0.0311	0.0982	−0.0671***
	(0.3612)	(0.4593)	(0.0182)

Note: Standard errors in parentheses (clustered at municipality level). The employed include wage earners and self-employed/business owners. Changes are changes in ENE municipality averages from one quarter to the same quarter of the next year, using data from 2000-II to 2002-III.
*significant at 10 percent; **significant at 5 percent; ***significant at 1 percent.

from a different bank. The data in table 6.1 are for the pre–Banco Azteca period, including only observations between 2000-II and 2002-III. The averages in columns 1 and 2 of table 6.1 show that in municipalities with Azteca, 8.2 percent of people in the sample owned an informal business in the pre-Azteca period. This number was higher for municipalities without Azteca (13.8 percent). On the other hand, municipalities without Azteca had a somewhat smaller percentage of formal business owners, 6.6 percent, compared to 7.9 percent in municipalities with Azteca. Another 50 percent of our sample worked as wage earners in municipalities with Azteca, while 44 percent were wage earners in municipalities without Azteca. The remaining 34 percent and 36 percent, respectively, of the sample were not employed.

The third column of table 6.1 reports the differences in prereform averages for municipalities with and without Azteca and their statistical significance. Individuals who live in municipalities with Azteca are more likely to work as wage earners and are more likely to own a registered business. However, they are less likely to own an informal business. Moreover, individuals in municipalities with Azteca have a higher average monthly income than individuals in municipalities without Azteca.

These pre-Azteca differences in outcome variables do not necessarily bias our empirical results, as we compare differences in pre and post *changes* in outcome variables across municipalities with and without Azteca, instead of comparing *levels* of outcome variables. Our estimates measure the causal effect of Azteca opening on economic activity under the assumption that the pre and post changes in outcome variables would have been the same in municipalities with and without Azteca in the absence of Azteca opening.

The lower part of table 6.1 indicates that the changes in outcome variables in the pre-Azteca period (from 2000 to 2002) were the same in municipalities with and without Azteca for our measure of formal and informal businesses. However, the number of wage earners and income tended to increase faster in municipalities without Azteca than in municipalities with Azteca from 2000 to 2002. We account for these different trends in our empirical analysis by controlling for municipality-specific time trends. This approach ensures that our results are not simply driven by differences in linear time trends. A more detailed explanation of the empirical analysis and regression results can be found in Bruhn and Love 2009.

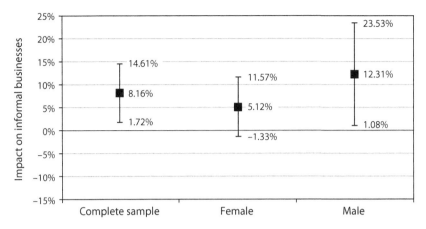

Figure 6.4
Effect of Banco Azteca opening on the number of informal businesses.

The Impact of Banco Azteca Opening on Entrepreneurial Activity, Employment, and Income

We first investigate the impact of Banco Azteca opening on entrepreneurial activity. Figures 6.4 and 6.6 present the impact estimates on the number of informal and formal business owners based on the difference-in-difference regression analysis in Bruhn and Love 2009. The boxes in the figure represent the size of the estimated impact and the lines correspond to the 95 percent confidence intervals around the impact estimates.[10]

Figure 6.4 shows that the number of informal businesses increased by 8.16 percent in the complete sample due to Banco Azteca opening. This effect is statistically significant at the 5 percent level. Figure 6.4 also displays the effect of Banco Azteca on female-owned and male-owned informal businesses separately. There was no statistically significant increase in the number of female-owned business; the number of male-owned businesses increased by more than 12 percent.

Figure 6.5 is a different graphical illustration of the effect of Banco Azteca opening on the fraction of informal business owners. It displays the fraction of informal business owners in municipalities with and without an Azteca branch in 2002-IV over time. We observe a steep increase in the fraction of informal business owners only in Azteca municipalities after Banco Azteca opened; there was no such increase observed in the municipalities without Azteca.

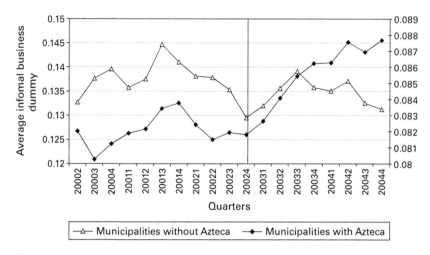

Figure 6.5
Average of informal businesses owner dummy for municipalities with and without
Banco Azteca over time.

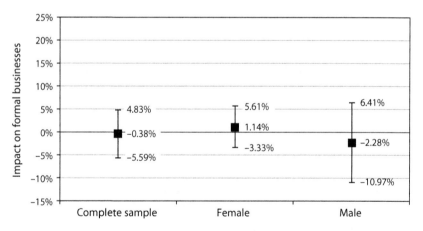

Figure 6.6
Effect of Banco Azteca opening on the number of formal businesses.

The impact estimates for formal business owners are in figure 6.6. We find that Banco Azteca opening had no effect on the number of formal business. This result is perhaps unsurprising, given that Banco Azteca targeted low-income individuals and had low documentation requirements. These features are attractive for informal business owners who would not be able to obtain a loan from a traditional bank. However, formal business owners are likely to prefer credit from traditional banks that charge lower interest rates than Banco Azteca.

Thus, our first set of results suggests that the opening of a new bank geared toward low-income individuals has benefited informal entrepreneurs. We now examine whether Banco Azteca opening led to an increase in the number of wage earners, which could be the case if the increased number of informal businesses hires employees. This outcome is, however, unlikely as informal businesses in Mexico tend to have few employees and are often exclusively staffed by an owner who is self-employed.

Figure 6.7 presents the effect of Banco Azteca opening on wage earners. In the complete sample and for men, there was no statistically significant effect of Azteca opening on wage earners. There was, however, a 2.17 percent increase in the number of female wage earners. This finding suggests that the increased number of informal businesses created additional jobs for women.

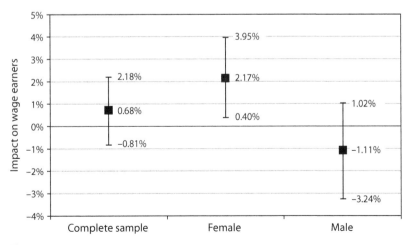

Figure 6.7
Effect of Banco Azteca opening on wage earners.

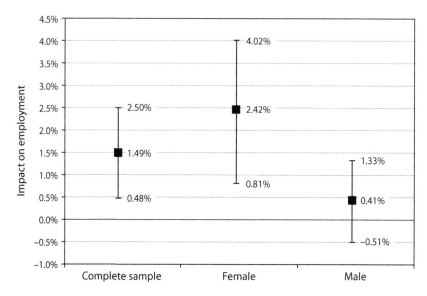

Figure 6.8
Effect of Banco Azteca opening on employment.

The opening of Banco Azteca also led to an increase in overall employment, which is the sum of business owners and wage earners, by 1.5 percent in the complete sample (figure 6.8). Note, however, that this effect is statistically significant only for women. For women, the increase in employment was 2.4 percent; the increase in employment for men was much smaller (0.4 percent), suggesting that the effect of Azteca opening on men was mainly reflected in a switch of occupations toward being informal business owners. Women, on the other hand, joined the labor force and took new jobs in informal businesses or took the jobs that men switched out of.

Finally, we investigate the impact of Banco Azteca opening on income. Figure 6.9 shows that average income in the complete sample increased by 7.6 percent. Income increased for both women and men; however, the impact on female income is larger than the impact on men. Specifically, the average income increase for women is about 9 percent, and the average increase for men is 4.8 percent; the impact on women's income is significant at 5 percent, and the impact on men is significant only at 10 percent (note that the bottom line is below the zero level for men). This increase in income is likely due to the increase in employment, as the increase in employment implies that some indi-

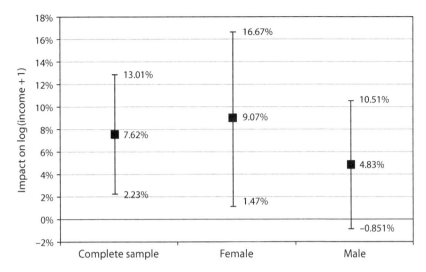

Figure 6.9
Effect of Azteca opening on income.

viduals who previously earned zero income earn positive income after Azteca opened.

Conclusion

This chapter shows that expanding access to finance to low-income individuals can have a positive effect on economic activity. We examine the case of Banco Azteca in Mexico, which opened over 800 branches overnight in 2002, targeting their savings account and loan services mainly to low-income individuals and informal business owners.

Our results suggest that the Banco Azteca opening led to an increased number of informal business owners for men and an increased number of wage earners for women. Total employment increased by about 1.5 percent as a result of the Azteca opening. The increase in informal businesses and wage earners also led to a rise in income of about 7 percent, on average.

Overall, these findings support the existing literature that has pointed toward a connection between access to finance and growth and poverty alleviation. They also shed new light on the channels through which access to finance for low-income individuals promotes economic development, namely by fostering the survival and creation of informal businesses and by increasing labor market participation of women.

Moreover, our results add to the evidence on the effects of microfinance, because operationally Banco Azteca resembles a microfinance institution. It is sometimes argued that micro loans represent a transfer to the poor that is not put to a productive use. However, our results suggest that this not the case and that providing financial services to the poor can indeed generate additional economic activity.

Although our results might be limited to the Mexican context, they suggest that policies aimed at improving access to finance to low-income people will support increased economic activity and poverty alleviation. Such policies might particularly benefit women, who are more likely to become gainfully employed and to earn higher income.

The experience of Banco Azteca demonstrates the importance of flexible lending practices that have low documentation requirements and instead rely on credit information and alternative collection mechanisms. This experience indirectly points to the importance of credit bureaus that contain data on prior repayment history, including payments of appliance installment loans. It also suggests that alternative collateral requirements could be used in low-income lending, such as appliances and cosigners, which allow more access to wider segments of the population.

Notes

1. In fact, Banco Azteca's motto is "We changed banking, now it's your time to change" ("*Cambiamos la banca, cambia tú también*").

2. Azteca charged interest rates of about 50 percent per annum; commercial banks at the time charged rates of 20–40 percent. However, commercial banks rejected all but the most creditworthy customers.

3. Our results on income are not as strong as our results on employment choices because of the nature of the data. The dataset we use is designed to measure labor market participation rather than household income or consumption. This design implies that the quality of the labor market participation data is likely to be higher than the quality of income data available in the survey.

4. We have not been able to examine the market response to Azteca opening by microfinance institutions and credit unions because we do not have data on these institutions at the municipality level.

5. Microfinance loan size is average for all microfinance institutions. Author's calculations using data available on http://www.mixmarket.org.

6. Unfortunately, we cannot perform the same regression analysis for loans because we do not have data on loans before and after the Azteca opening at the municipality level. These effects are also significant in a regression framework that controls for municipality-specific time trends.

7. There are two reasons why we do not use data from the new survey. First, the question that distinguishes informal from formal business owners is different in the new survey, implying that one of our main outcome variables is not consistent across the two surveys. Second, Banco Azteca started opening new branches after initially establishing branches in all existing Elektra stores. Thus our identification strategy is less valid for later years.

8. There are a total of 2,451 municipalities in Mexico, but the ENE does not cover all of them. The ENE is representative for cities but includes only a random sample of rural municipalities. A total of 696 municipalities had a bank branch in Mexico in the fourth quarter of 2002, 120 of which are not covered in our data. However, only 8 municipalities that had an Azteca branch are not in our data.

9. A detailed description of how these variables were constructed is available in Bruhn 2008.

10. To interpret the graphs, if the bottom line is above zero level, the impact is significant at 5 percent.

References

Beck, Thorsten, Aslı Demirguc-Kunt, and Ross Levine. 2007. Finance, Inequality and the Poor. *Journal of Economic Growth* 12 (1): 27–49.

Beck, Thorsten, Ross Levine, and Alexey Levkov. 2007. Big Bad Banks? The Impact of US Branch Deregulation on Income Distribution. National Bureau of Economic Research, Working Paper No. 13299.

Black, Sandra, and Philip Strahan. 2002. Entrepreneurship and Bank Credit Availability. *Journal of Finance* 57 (6): 2807–2833.

Bruhn, Miriam. 2008. License to Sell: The Effect of Business Registration Reform on Entrepreneurial Activity in Mexico. World Bank Policy Research Working Paper WP4538.

Bruhn, Miriam, and Inessa Love. 2009. The Economic Impact of Banking the Unbanked: Evidence from Mexico. World Bank Policy Research Working Paper WP4981.

Burgess, Robin, and Rohini Pande. 2005. Can Rural Banks Reduce Poverty? Evidence from the Indian Social Banking Experiment. *American Economic Review* 95 (3): 780–795.

Cetorelli, Nicola, and Philip Strahan. 2006. Finance as a Barrier to Entry: Bank Competition and Industry Structure in Local U.S. Markets. *Journal of Finance* 61 (1): 437–461.

Coleman, Brett. 1999. The Impact of Group Lending in Northeast Thailand. *Journal of Development Economics* 45:105–141.

Conger, Lucy. 2002. A Bank for Mexico's Working Families. *The New York Times*. December 31.

Jayaratne, Jith, and Philip Strahan. 1996. The Finance-Growth Nexus: Evidence from Bank Branch Deregulation. *Quarterly Journal of Economics* 111 (3): 639–670.

Harford, Tim. 2008. The Battle for the Soul of Microfinance. *The Financial Times*. December 6.

Honohan, Patrick. 2004. Financial Development, Growth and Poverty: How Close Are the Links? World Bank Policy Research Working Paper WP3203.

Kaboski, Joseph, and Robert Townsend. 2005. Policies and Impact: An Analysis of Village-Level Microfinance Institutions. *Journal of the European Economic Association* 3 (1): 1–50.

Karlan, Dean, and Jonathan Morduch. 2009. Access to Finance. In *Handbook of Development Economics, Vol. 5*, ed. Dani Rodrik and Mark Rosenzweig, 4703–4784. Amsterdam: Elsevier.

Kochar, Anjini. 2011. The Distributive Consequences of Social Banking: A Microempirical Analysis of the Indian Experience. *Economic Development and Cultural Change* 59 (2): 251–280.

Levine, Ross. 2005. Finance and Growth: Theory and Evidence. In *Handbook of Economic Growth: Vol. 1*, ed. Philippe Aghion and Steven N. Durlauf, 865–934. Amsterdam: Elsevier Science.

McKernan, Signe-Mary. 2002. The Impact of Microcredit Programs on Self-Employment Profits: Do Noncredit Program Aspects Matter? *Review of Economics and Statistics* 84 (1): 93–115.

Orlandi, Lorraine. 2003. Banco Azteca Bikers Reach Out to Mexico's Poor. Reuters News, September 21.

Panagariya, Arvind. 2006. Bank Branch Expansion and Poverty Reduction: A Comment. Unpublished mimeo., Columbia University.

Pitt, Mark, and Shahidur Khandker. 1998. The Impact of Group-Based Credit Programs on Poor Households in Bangladesh: Does the Gender of Participants Matter? *Journal of Political Economy* 106 (5): 958–996.

Pitt, Mark, Shahidur R. Khandker, Omar Haider Chowdhury, and Daniel L. Millimet. 2003. Credit Programs for the Poor and the Health Status of Children in Rural Bangladesh. *International Economic Review* 44 (1): 87–118.

Panagariya, Arvind. 2006. Bank Branch Expansion and Poverty Reduction: A Comment. Columbia University. http://www.columbia.edu/~ap2231/technical%20papers/Bank%20Branch%20Expansion%20and%20Poverty.pdf (accessed May 14, 2012).

PR Newswire. 2002. Banco Azteca Starts Operations in 749 Branches throughout Mexico. October 29.

Smith, Geri. 2003. Buy a Toaster, Open a Bank Account: Banco Azteca Caters to the Little Guy—in Appliance Stores. *Business Week*. January 13.

World Bank. 2008. Finance for All? Policies and Pitfalls in Expanding Access. World Bank Policy Research Report. http://go.worldbank.org/HNKL9ZHO50 (accessed May 14, 2012).

7 Finance and Hunger: Empirical Evidence of the Agricultural Productivity Channel

Stijn Claessens and Erik Feijen

Although most countries have experienced per capita growth in the twentieth century, extreme income poverty is still widespread. In 2005, GDP per capita in the world, corrected for purchasing power, was on average $23.70 a day. However, more than half of the world population lived on less than $2 a day and more than 1 billion people lived on less than $1 a day, whereas per capita income in a typical developed country at the same time exceeded $90 a day. Income poverty is but one measure of (the lack of) development; another measure is the presence of hunger or undernourishment. Indeed, under the Millennium Development Goals (MDG),[1] income poverty and undernourishment are the two key indicators of incidence of poverty. Unfortunately, undernourishment remains widespread as well, with about 20 percent of the world population undernourished as of the late 1990s. Although many countries have eradicated undernourishment,[2] it remains very high in some countries, such as 70.5 percent in Eritrea.

A large body of literature is devoted to analyzing the links between economic growth, inequality, poverty, and hunger. General findings are that higher growth and lower inequality are associated with lower levels of poverty and hunger. Another large body of literature has found robust evidence that financial sector development spurs economic growth, primarily because it puts capital to its most productive use. Moreover, this line of research has shown that financial development reduces inequality because it levels the playing field and enables (poorer) individuals and (smaller) firms to participate in the formal economy and grow. Recent research has brought these two fields together and found beneficial effects of financial sector development on poverty reduction and inequality. These findings raise the question of whether beneficial relationships also exist between financial development and undernourishment, not just income poverty. And

if so, are there specific channels through which financial development improves undernourishment? In this chapter, we investigate these two questions.

We focus on undernourishment defined as "the condition of people whose dietary energy consumption is continuously below a minimum dietary energy requirement for maintaining a healthy life and carrying out a light physical activity" (FAOSTAT 2006). An individual is considered undernourished when either his or her food intake falls below the minimum requirement or if his or her food intake is insufficient to meet dietary energy requirements continuously. Reducing undernourishment can be regarded as the first and foremost development objective, as being well nourished determines a person's chances of living. Measuring the prevalence of undernourishment involves the comparison of actual household food consumption (expressed in terms of calories per person per day) with a minimum dietary energy requirement (also expressed in terms of calories per person per day) and the classification of those individuals with per capita calorie consumption levels below the minimum requirement as being undernourished.

Obviously, undernourishment is related to the prevalence of (extreme) poverty, but there are distinctive differences. Whereas the measure of the prevalence of undernourishment is based on the distribution of actual household food consumption and availability, the World Bank measure of the prevalence of extreme poverty is based on the distribution of household income (or consumption), adjusted for purchasing power. Undernourishment and poverty can differ, not only because of relative prices, which can mean that a certain income level does not translate in an ability to attain oneself of sufficient food, but also because of insufficient availability of food, as when faced with permanent or temporary insufficient local production. Furthermore, data on undernourishment are available for a different set of countries and different time periods than the poverty data, thus providing another test on the importance of finance for countries' performance and well-being.

Using these data on undernourishment, we study the impact of financial development. Our findings can be summarized as follows. Using cross-country OLS, instrumental variables, and panel regressions for the period 1980–2003, we find a relationship from greater financial sector development to lower undernourishment. Our results imply that a 1 percent increase in private credit to GDP (our main proxy for financial development) reduces the prevalence of undernourish-

ment by 0.19–1.57 percent. This is further evidence of the importance of financial development for countries' growth and well-being. Our findings remain valid with the inclusion of country controls that are known for their relationship with poverty, financial development, and hunger: initial levels of poverty and GDP per capita, average inflation, average trade openness, the fraction of the working population in the agricultural sector, and the fraction of the population in rural areas. The results prevail when including the level of GDP per capita in the panel estimations, showing that the beneficial effects of finance on undernourishment operate beyond the beneficial effects of finance on general economic development.

In addition to the overall effect of finance on lowering undernourishment, we find evidence that financial development decreases undernourishment, especially through its effect on countries' agricultural sectors. There are several channels by which financial development affects the agricultural sector and, in that way, undernourishment. Regarding some channels we can only speculate, but for others we have empirical evidence. Specifically, we find robust evidence that financial development is associated with increases in overall agricultural productivity, livestock production, cereal and crop yields—increases that in turn lead to less undernourishment. It is important that these results remain when controlling for, among other factors, countries' general economic development. One other study also focusing on the links between access to finance and agricultural productivity is Butler and Cornaggia (2011). They show for the United States that following an increase in demand for corn resulting from a 2005 legislative act on increasing renewable fuel additives, corn yields increased more in comparison with soybean yields in counties with greater financial development, as measured by bank deposits.

Furthermore, we find evidence that the productivity-increasing channel operates through greater use of productivity-enhancing equipment such as tractors and fertilizers. As farmers become more productive by being able to obtain more machinery or use more fertilizers, our analysis suggests that a 1 percent increase in private credit to GDP increases value added per worker by 0.22–1.36 percent. In turn, higher productivity leads to lower undernourishment. We find that a 1 percent increase in value added per worker reduces the prevalence of undernourishment by 0.24 to 0.8 percent. We furthermore find some evidence that it is not just financial sector development that matters but also that the outreach of the banking system (its distribution network) matters

specifically for reducing undernourishment, suggesting that access to financial services is important.

Besides these specific, direct channels, it is likely that financial development reduces undernourishment through indirect channels as well. Finance, for example, facilitates the optimal reallocation of resources, which for countries with a large agricultural sector may mean moving away from agriculture toward other, higher valued-added sectors (note that in general higher-income countries have lower agricultural shares of GDP) while at the same time increasing agricultural production. In turn, higher income may lead to lower undernourishment. Finance may also improve the general prospects of people in rural areas previously relying on agriculture and reduce undernourishment by providing jobs and income. Although we do not study these broader and more indirect channels, we show that the direct, productivity-enhancing channel accounts for about a quarter of the overall impact of financial sector development on undernourishment.

Our results, though robust to many different specifications, do come with some provisos. Like many other studies, we have only rough measures of financial sector development—we use private credit to GDP as a proxy and thus do not capture access to financial services for the poor and undernourished households directly. We have data neither on the composition of loans across purposes and sectors, including agricultural, or on the rates of return on these different purposes. We therefore cannot establish *how* people exactly use financial services to decrease undernourishment or which financial services used for agricultural investments drive the increase in productivity. This research has been done on a (country-specific) basis, however, using firm and household surveys and other micro-evidence, which tends to corroborate the large differences in rates of return across purposes and the importance of access to financial services to reducing undernourishment. Although our cross-country application complements this work, more research is needed to pinpoint whether the specific channels apply similarly across countries or whether certain country characteristics and policies affect the impact of financial development on undernourishment.

Related Literature and Hypotheses

There are many papers that describe the links between growth, equality, poverty, and financial development. We classify these papers in

three separate groups: (1) economic growth, equality, and poverty, (2) financial development, growth, and inequality, and (3) financial development and poverty. Using this literature, we develop the hypotheses and empirical tests about the channels through which we expect financial development to affect the prevalence of undernourishment.

Economic Growth, Equality, and Poverty

Research has shown close links between economic growth and income poverty and between inequality and income poverty. One piece of evidence on the importance of growth is that the poorest share in the benefits of overall economic growth. Dollar and Kraay (2002) show that both overall income per capita and the growth rate of income per capita are highly associated with the level of income of the poorest quintile and the growth rate of their income. They show that growth in overall income per capita explains more than 80 percent of the variation in the growth of the income of the lowest quintile. The poor thus do share in overall growth. And the effect is substantial. Besley and Burgess (2003) find that a 2.1 percent increase in per capita world growth rate from 1990 on would cut world poverty in half by 2015 (with poverty defined as living on less than $1 per day, in 1983 U.S. dollars, corrected for purchasing power).

This importance of general economic growth does not negate the roles of the composition and distribution of growth in reducing poverty. Loayza and Raddatz (2007) show that not only the size of economic growth but also its composition matters for poverty alleviation, with the largest contributions from labor-intensive sectors (such as agriculture, construction, and manufacturing). And there is obviously an important role of inequality in reducing poverty. Besley and Burgess (2003) confirm that less inequality leads to a significant reduction in poverty. If one could diminish world inequality with one standard deviation without sacrificing growth, poverty would be reduced by 67 percent.[3] In all, these findings imply that overall economic growth, its composition, and its (reduced) inequality have large effects on poverty.

Financial Development, Economic Growth, and Inequality

Another large empirical body of literature has established that financial development spurs economic growth (much of this literature started with King and Levine 1993; for an overview of the literature, see Levine 2005). A more recent body of work has established that financial sector development also decreases inequality. The latter finding may not be

obvious. Some theoretical studies argue that the rich benefit more from financial development because only they have access to financial services. Others (Aghion and Bolton 1997; Banerjee and Newman 1993; Greenwood and Jovanovic 1990) argue that only in a later stage of development do the poor get access to financial services. And others argue that the beneficial effects of financial development for the poor come about in an indirect way, even when they do not have direct access to financial services.

Empirically, research finds that financial development not only increases growth but also reduces inequality. The effect of financial development on inequality, as measured by the Gini inequality coefficient, is large and is stronger for countries with greater financial development, as measured by more private credit (Clarke, Xu, and Zou 2006). New research has found that financial development also accelerates the decline in inequality. Cross-country evidence shows that higher private credit to GDP leads to a faster decline in the Gini coefficient (Beck, Demirgüç-Kunt, and Levine 2007), even more so in countries with initially high inequality. Moreover, the effect of financial development is strong even after the general level of development (as proxied by GDP per capita growth) is taken into account. This finding suggests that financial development has a disproportionate effect on inequality reduction, although it does not show the direct channels or whether it matters if the poor themselves have access to financial services.

Financial Development and Poverty

The theoretical reasons why financial sector development may matter specifically for poverty are well known: greater access to financial services enables poor people to plan better for the future and invest in productivity-enhancing assets. In accumulating financial assets and availing themselves of financial services to smooth their income, households can reduce the impact of unfortunate events such as drought, disease, or death that are part of daily life in developing countries. In addition, greater income stability prevents households from being forced to sell off productive assets following adverse shocks, inducing an otherwise vicious spiral.

Empirically, financial development has been found to play an important role in reducing poverty via the first two channels in terms of its effects on growth and inequality. Research along the lines of King and Levine (1993) implies that if in 1990 all countries had financial sectors equal to the current (2005) average, there would have been additional

yearly per capita GDP growth of 0.7–0.9 percent. So in principle, financial development alone could provide growth close to about half of the gap identified by Besley and Burgess (2003) needed to cut world poverty in half by 2015. Its effect on inequality would further aid the reduction in poverty.

There is also other evidence, directly measured, that financial development is associated with a lower poverty ratio. Honohan (2003) analyzes relationships between levels of financial development and poverty and finds that a 10 percent increase in private credit to GDP reduces poverty ratios by 2.5–3 percent. This effect persists even when GDP per capita is taken into account, suggesting that beyond its effects on income growth, financial development broadens the opportunities of the poor to participate in productive economic activities. Besides its effects on Gini inequality, Beck, Demirgüç-Kunt, and Levine (2007) find that financial development has a beneficial effect on the incomes of the poorest quintile of the income distribution, with financial development to accelerate improvements in the poverty ratio.[4] Morduch and Haley (2002) provide detailed analyses of the effects of microfinance on poverty reduction using more micro-based evidence, showing some of the channels in action. See Honohan (2004) for a review of recent empirical work on the links between finance and poverty and Claessens and Feijen (2007) for a more general review of the links between financial development and various Millennium Development Goals.

Hypotheses: The Links between Financial Development and Undernourishment

Because there exists a strong relationship between income poverty and undernourishment and because financial development reduces income poverty, financial development can be expected to reduce the prevalence of undernourishment largely via income poverty reduction, that is, to the extent that financial sector development increases the income of the poor, undernourishment will decline. There is ample country-specific and other evidence that income poverty is the main cause of undernourishment. For example, in Indonesia, during 1984–1987 rising income standards reduced malnutrition in the country and the fraction of people living at less than 1,400 calories declined by 26 percent (World Bank 1993). Given these relationships, one would expect an impact of financial development on the prevalence of undernourishment similar to that on prevalence of poverty.

As such, any result that financial sector development reduces under-nourishment might not surprise. Important from a policy and research perspective, though, are the specific channels through which financial sector development affects undernourishment. We focus on the agri-cultural sector, in part because recent empirical work (Loayza and Raddatz 2007) has shown that growth in this sector can particularly help with poverty reduction. From theory, some specific channels working through the agricultural sector can be identified by which financial development may be especially important for reducing undernourish-ment. First, access to financial services such as savings and credit products may reduce undernourishment because it allows for con-sumption smoothing by poor households in the face of income and other shocks, which can be very prevalent in agriculture. Access to financial services can, for example, make agricultural workers less vulnerable to the impact of (economic) shocks, decreasing the need to inefficiently sell off their productive assets (e.g., cows, equipment), which would otherwise force them into a vicious spiral. Second, access to financial services (directly or indirectly) eases the financing of productivity-improving agricultural equipment, thereby increasing agricultural yields and improving the income of those active in agri-culture and living in rural areas, where poverty tends to be higher, thereby reducing undernourishment. Third, there can be a link between financial development and undernourishment even when undernour-ished households do not gain (directly or indirectly) access to finance. Higher agricultural productivity facilitated by financial sector develop-ment, for example, translates into higher food output and lower food prices, which will be beneficial for all the poor, regardless of whether they are active in agriculture.

Data and Methodology

All our data are taken from either the World Bank's *World Development Indicators* (2006) or from the FAOSTAT online database of the Food and Agriculture Organization (FAO) of the United Nations. We start with using data averaged over all observations in the period 1980–2003 to diminish the effects of business cycles and other changes over time. We do, however, also use instrumental variables and panel data regres-sions as robustness tests. As we are interested not only in the effects of financial sector development on undernourishment but also in the channels through which it happens, we conduct several types of analy-

ses using these data and various econometric approaches. First, we study the overall link between financial development and the prevalence of undernourishment. Second, we explore the link between financial development and undernourishment by studying the relationship between agricultural productivity and undernourishment and the link between financial development and overall agricultural productivity per worker as well as other, more specific agricultural productivity indicators. Third, we decompose these links further by investigating the effects of financial development on the use of productivity-enhancing inputs requiring up-front layouts. And fourth, to investigate the importance of (direct) access to financial services, we study the effects of outreach of financial services on undernourishment, agricultural productivity, productivity-enhancing inputs, and prices. To limit problems of endogeneity and simultaneity, we use instrumental variables and panel approaches when necessary and possible.

Sample, Variables, and Descriptive Statistics

In principle, we attempt to cover all countries in the world, but data availability limits the sample of countries, especially in those regressions for which we use more explanatory variables. Table 7.1 provides the description of all the variables we use (panel A) and the list of countries covered in the various regressions (panel B). Table 7.2 presents basic statistics of the variables that are central to our analysis: undernourishment, agricultural productivity, and private credit to GDP.

Main Variables

Our main LHS variable, undernourishment, is defined as the prevalence of undernourished people as a percentage of the total population. Undernourishment comes from the FAOSTAT database of the Food and Agriculture Organization of the United Nations. It is documented only for the period 1980–2003, with most countries having only three observations in the 1990s: 1992, 1995, and 1998. In the basic sample, undernourishment, when present, is on average 19 percent but varies widely across the world. Although most developed countries have very low values of undernourishment—it is zero in almost all developed countries—25 percent of our sample has an undernourishment rate higher than 30 percent. For countries with some undernourishment, undernourishment ranges from 2.5 percent in Poland to 57 percent in Burundi, with a standard deviation of almost 15 percent.

Table 7.1
Description of variables and countries in sample
Panel A

Variable	Description	Source
Main variables		
Undernourishment	Log prevalence of undernourishment as a percentage of the total population, averaged over the period 1980–2003 for which we have observations. For most countries, three observations are available for three periods: 1991–1993, 1994–1996, 1997–1999.	WDI
Private credit to GDP	Log value of credit by financial intermediaries to the private sector as a percentage of GDP averaged over the period 1980–2003 for which we have observations.	WDI
Agricultural productivity	Log yearly productivity per agricultural worker, expressed in constant 2000 US$ corrected for purchasing power averaged over the period 1980–2003 for which we have observations.	WDI
Branches per 1,000 km^2	Number of banking branches per 1,000 km^2	Beck
Productivity measures		
Cereal yield	Log cereal yields per hectare of arable yield in kilograms averaged over the period 1980–2003 for which we have observations.	WDI
Crop production index	Log crop production index (1999–2001=100) averaged over the period 1980–2003 for which we have observations.	WDI
Livestock production index	Log livestock production index (1999–2001=100) averaged over the period 1980–2003 for which we have observations.	WDI
Productivity-enhancing equipment		
Fertilizer use	Fertilizer use in 100 grams per hectare	WDI
Tractors per worker	Number of tractors per agricultural worker	WDI
Country controls		
Poverty	Log of average percentage of the population living on less than $1 per day (in 1983 US$, corrected for purchasing power) in the period 1980–2003 for which we have observations.	WDI
Initial poverty	Log of the first available observation in the period 1980–2003 of the percentage of the population living on less than 1$ per day (in 1983 US$, corrected for purchasing power).	WDI
Initial GDP per capita	Log of the first available observation in the period 1980–2003 of GDP per capita in 2000 US$, corrected for purchasing power.	WDI

Table 7.1
(continued)

Variable	Description	Source
Initial size government	Log of the first available observation in the period 1980–2003 of government expenditures as a percentage of GDP.	WDI
Inflation	The average of the GDP deflator in the period 1980–2003 for which we have observations.	WDI
Trade	Log of average trade as a percentage of GDP in the period 1980–2003 for which we have observations.	WDI
Export – Import	Total food export minus total food import in kg per person per year. The variable pertains to the following food groups: alcohol (incl. beer and wine), animal fats and products, aquatic products, other beverage crops, cereals and products (excl. beer), eggs and products, fish, seafood and products, fruits and products (excl. wine), meat (slaughtered) and products, milk and products, offals (edible), oil crops (excl. prod.), pulses and products, spices, starchy roots and products, sugar and sweeteners, treenuts and products, vegetable oils and products, vegetables and products.	FAO
Rural population	Log of average percentage of population in rural areas in the period 1980–2003 for which we have observations.	WDI
Agricultural employment	Log of average percentage of agricultural workers in the workforce in the period 1980–2003 for which we have observations.	WDI

Notes: This table presents the variables used in our regression analysis and their description. The sources are WDI (World Bank 2006), FAO (Food and Agriculture Organization 2006), and Beck (Beck, Demirgüç-Kunt, and Martinez Peria 2007).

Table 7.1
(continued)
Panel B: Countries in sample

Country name	In smallest sample?
Albania	
Algeria	
Angola	
Argentina	X
Armenia	
Azerbaijan	
Bangladesh	X
Belarus	
Benin	
Bolivia	X
Bosnia and Herzegovina	
Botswana	X
Brazil	X
Bulgaria	
Burkina Faso	X
Burundi	
Cambodia	
Cameroon	X
Central African Republic	
Chad	
Chile	X
China	
Colombia	X
Congo, Dem. Rep.	
Costa Rica	X
Cote d'Ivoire	X
Croatia	
Czech Republic	
Dominican Republic	X
Ecuador	X
Egypt, Arab Rep.	X
El Salvador	X
Eritrea	
Estonia	
Ethiopia	
Gabon	
Gambia, The	X

Table 7.1
(continued)

Country name	In smallest sample?
Georgia	
Ghana	X
Guatemala	X
Guinea	
Guyana	X
Haiti	
Honduras	X
Hungary	
India	X
Indonesia	X
Iran, Islamic Rep.	X
Jamaica	X
Jordan	
Kazakhstan	
Kenya	X
Korea, Rep.	X
Kuwait	
Kyrgyz Republic	
Lao PDR	
Latvia	
Lebanon	
Lesotho	X
Lithuania	
Macedonia, FYR	
Madagascar	X
Malawi	
Malaysia	X
Mali	
Mauritania	
Mauritius	
Mexico	X
Moldova	
Mongolia	
Morocco	X
Mozambique	
Namibia	
Nepal	X
Nicaragua	

Table 7.1
(continued)

Country name	In smallest sample?
Niger	
Nigeria	X
Pakistan	X
Panama	X
Paraguay	X
Peru	X
Philippines	X
Poland	
Romania	
Russian Federation	
Rwanda	X
Saudia Arabia	
Senegal	X
Sierra Leone	X
Slovak Republic	
Slovenia	
Sri Lanka	X
Sudan	
Swaziland	
Syrian Arab Republic	
Tajikistan	
Tanzania	X
Thailand	X
Togo	
Trinidad and Tobago	X
Tunisia	X
Turkey	X
Turkmenistan	
Uganda	
Ukraine	
United Arab Emirates	
Uruguay	X
Venezuela, RB	X
Vietnam	
Yemen, Rep.	
Zambia	X
Zimbabwe	

Notes: List of countries included in the regression with the largest sample size (regression 1, table 7.3). X denotes the countries that are included in the regression with the smallest sample size (regression 3, table 7.3).

Table 7.2
Descriptive statistics
Panel A: Summary statistics

Average value in period 1980–2003 of:	Countries	Mean	Std. Dev.	Min	Max	Average number of observations used
Undernourishment	86	18.72	14.46	2.5	57	2.73
Private credit	86	26.51	20.47	2.8755	112.17	19.62
Agricultural productivity	85	1802.47	2658.80	111.66	21114.54	20.39
Cereal yield	85	2129.82	1170.24	231.20	5877.61	22.17
Fertilizer use	85	5.74	1.61	1.16	8.64	19.83
Tractors per worker	84	0.05	0.09	0.00	0.55	20.07
Branches per 1,000 km^2 (2003–2004)	91	31.03	82.11	0.11	636.07	1

Table 7.2
(continued)
Panel B: Correlations of main variables

	GDP/cap.	Poverty	Undernourishment	Productivity	Cereal yield
Poverty	-0.77				
	(0.00)				
Undernourishment	-0.75	0.77			
	(0.00)	(0.00)			
Agricultural productivity	0.91	-0.76	-0.75		
	(0.00)	(0.00)	(0.00)		
Cereal Yield	0.65	-0.53	-0.52	0.66	
	(0.00)	(0.00)	(0.00)	(0.00)	
Private Credit	0.71	-0.33	-0.30	0.55	0.40
	(0.00)	(0.00)	(0.00)	(0.00)	(0.00)

Table 7.2
(continued)
Panel C: Correlations of productivity measures

	Agric. productivity	Cereal yield	Livestock
Cereal yield	0.66		
	(0.00)		
Livestock	0.27	0.15	
	(0.00)	(0.05)	
Crop	0.32	0.20	0.63
	(0.00)	(0.01)	(0.00)

Panel D: Correlations of productivity-enhancing equipment

	Fertilizer use	Tractors per worker
Tractors per Worker	0.58	
	(0.00)	
Agricultural productivity	0.66	0.83
	(0.00)	(0.00)

Notes: Panel A presents standard descriptive statistics for undernourishment, private credit, and agricultural productivity for the observations in the basic regression of the main result, regression 2 of table 7.3 (except for banking branches per 1,000 km², which pertains to either 2003 or 2004). Average number is the average number of observations with which the average in the period 1980–2003 has been calculated. Panels B, C, and D display correlations and *p*-values pertaining to the main variables, productivity measures, and productivity-enhancing equipment, respectively. Correlations are based on the whole sample.

Our main RHS variable is financial development and, following the literature, we proxy it by private credit to GDP, the value of credit extended by financial intermediaries to the private sector as a percentage of GDP. This measure excludes credits issued by the central bank and development banks, credit to the public sector, credit to state-owned enterprises, and cross-claims of one group of intermediaries on another. This comprehensive proxy for financial development is widely used and has been shown to be a driver of GDP per capita growth. Data on private credit is for most countries available for each year in the period 1980–2003: for ninety-nine countries, we have observations for each year. In the basic sample, private credit has an average value of 26 percent, with a wide variation: the minimum value is 2.9 percent and the maximum is 112 percent.[5]

Agricultural Productivity

To analyze the channels through which financial development operates, we first study the effect of financial development on overall agricultural productivity, defined as the yearly value added per agricultural worker, expressed in constant 2000 U.S. dollars. We have an average of twenty observations per country for the period 1980–2003. The average level of agricultural productivity is about $1,800. However, there is a wide dispersion, with a standard deviation of about $2,650. Rich countries have an average productivity of more than $20,000, whereas poor countries have productivity as low as $100. Agricultural productivity comes from FAOSTAT of the Food and Agriculture Organization of the United Nations.

Besides overall agricultural productivity, we use three specific productivity measures: cereal yields per hectare of arable land, a crop production index, and a livestock production index. The latter two indices have 1999–2001 as the benchmark year (=100) for all countries, and the tests are conducted on how far the initial values are from 100, that is, how high the growth rates have been over the whole period. We have wide coverage for these variables. For example, the calculation of the average cereal yield is based on about 22 observations per country. The average cereal yield over the period 1980–2003 is 2,129 kg per hectare. However, the variation is again high. In some countries, the average yield is as little as 231 kg, whereas in the most productive countries the average yield is as high as 5,877 kg.

Specific Financial Access Measures

In addition to private credit to GDP—and as a first step in assessing the importance of access to finance, especially for those people living in rural areas—we use the number of banking branches per 1,000 square kilometers from Beck, Demirgüç-Kunt, and Martinez Peria 2007. These data are available only for 2003–2004. The average density of banking branches is 30 per 1,000 square kilometers but differs vastly among the approximately 100 countries. Not surprisingly, large and developing countries tend to have lower densities. The number of banking branches per 1,000 square kilometers in Ethiopia, for example, is less than 1. In contrast, rich but small Singapore has more than 600 branches per 1,000 square kilometers.

Productivity-Enhancing Equipment

To analyze the channels through which financial sector development affects undernourishment, we assess the association of private credit

with two productivity-enhancing measures that require upfront outlays: fertilizer use (100 grams per hectare) and the number of tractors per agricultural worker. Average fertilizer use is 80 kg per hectare but varies widely across countries from 319 grams per hectare to 565.3 kg per hectare. The number of tractors per worker is on average 0.046 and also shows much dispersion, with the highest number per worker 0.55 and the lowest virtually 0.

Country Controls
Following Beck, Demirgüç-Kunt, and Levine's (2007) study of the relationship between financial sector development and poverty, we use several country-level variables to control for initial conditions that otherwise would likely affect the relationship between financial development and undernourishment. In almost all regressions using average values of dependent variables, we control for the initial values of the logs of poverty and/or initial level of GDP per capita (in 2000 U.S. dollars and corrected for purchasing power) as indicators of general economic development.[6] And, following the existing literature, we use as additional controls a range of variables including the log of average inflation, the log of initial government expenditures as a percentage of GDP (government size), the log of the average value of trade (exports and imports) as a fraction of GDP, the log of the average fraction of the population in rural areas, and the log of the average fraction of the population employed in the agricultural sector.

We also take into account trade in food that could affect undernourishment. Specifically, in some of our panel regressions we control for the effects of international food trade, using the net food flow that leaves the country yearly, that is, food exports minus food imports, expressed in kilograms per person. For the trade data, we use FAOSTAT data averaged for 1979–1981, 1990–1992, 1993–1995, 1995–1997 and 2001–2003.

Finally, to investigate more general effects of financial development on agriculture, we calculate a local producer price index based on yearly data from 1991 to 2001. The price index is the weighted average price of the following main food categories: wheat, rice, maize, oats, barley, sheep meat, chicken meat, and pig meat. The price of each category is weighted by its share in total production of all categories in the particular country. The prices are in U.S. dollars and are corrected for "green" purchasing power parity (PPP). This PPP is calculated by the FAO using a basket of agricultural products and related producer prices. To retain consistency, we make the periods for the price index

as close as possible to the periods defined by the FAO. Specifically, we average the data over the following periods: 1991–1992, 1993–1995, 1995–1997, and 2001.

Correlations
Panel B in table 7.2 shows the correlations among the most important variables. All these variables are significantly correlated with each other, with the expected sign. Higher levels of GDP per capita and private credit to GDP are associated with lower poverty and undernourishment and higher agricultural productivity. Panel C shows the correlations between our several agricultural productivity measures. All are positively correlated, but to different degrees, with the correlation between overall agricultural productivity and cereal yields as the highest. The two productivity indices, crop and livestock production, are also highly correlated with each other but less with overall productivity and cereal yields. Panel D shows the high correlations among our productivity-enhancing measures as well as with overall agricultural productivity, with the number of tractors per worker the highest in correlation with overall agricultural productivity.

Basic Econometric Model, Instrumental Variables, and Fixed Effects Panel Estimation
In our basic approach, we run cross-country OLS regressions for the period 1980–2003. To reduce endogeneity concerns, however, we also use an instrumental variables approach for this period. To further ameliorate endogeneity and omitted variable problems, we use a fixed effects panel estimation approach with five time periods: 1979–1981, 1990–1992, 1993–1995, 1995–1997, and 2001–2003.[7] We use these techniques for testing the various relationships of interest, using our four basic models to document the general relationship between financial sector development and undernourishment, the role of the agricultural sector, and the specific channels by which financial sector development reduces undernourishment (these relationships are also depicted in panel A of figure 7.1).

The first basic model investigates the general relationship between financial development and undernourishment:

$$undernourish_i = \alpha + \beta_1 FD_i + BX_i + \varepsilon \tag{7.1}$$

where *undernourish_i* is the average prevalence of undernourishment for country i of available data in the period 1980–2000, FD_i is private credit

Panel A: Basic channels

Panel B: Expanded channels

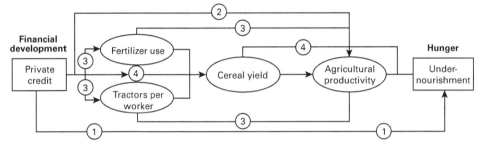

Figure 7.1
Channels from financial development to undernourishment. The channels we test in this chapter from financial development (private credit as a percentage of GDP), via productivity-enhancing equipment (fertilizer use and number of tractors per agricultural worker), via productivity (agricultural productivity), to undernourishment (hunger). The numbers in panel B refer to specific channels that are discussed in table 7.10.

to GDP, and X_i is the vector of our control variables. If higher private credit to GDP indeed reduces undernourishment, we should find β_1 to be negative and economically and statistically significant.

Having investigated the importance of finance for reducing undernourishment, we want to investigate the channels behind these relationships. Before doing so, the second basic model analyzes the relationship between agricultural productivity and undernourishment:

$$undernourish_i = \alpha + \beta_1 productivity_i + BX_i + \varepsilon_i \qquad (7.2)$$

where $productivity_i$ is the average agricultural productivity per agricultural worker or a specific measure of agricultural productivity. If indeed higher productivity reduces undernourishment, we should find that β_1 is negative and economically and statistically significant.

This relationship points us toward investigating the factors driving agricultural productivity. The third basic model therefore

scrutinizes the link between financial development and agricultural productivity:

$$productivity_i = \alpha + \beta_1 FD_i + BX_i + \varepsilon_i \tag{7.3}$$

Our hypothesis predicts that β_1 is positive and economically and statistically significant, which would confirm that financial development increases agricultural productivity.

We next identify in the fourth basic model some specific channels by scrutinizing the links between financial development and productivity-enhancing inputs:

$$productivity_enhancing_i = \alpha + \beta_1 FD_i + BX_i + \varepsilon_1 \tag{7.4}$$

We specifically test whether financial sector development relates positively to the use of productivity-enhancing inputs, fertilizer, and tractor use to investigate the channels through which financial sector development may increase productivity. Our hypothesis predicts that β_1 is positive and economically and statistically significant, confirming that financial development increases the use of productivity-enhancing inputs.

We amplify these four models in more detailed analyses of the channels and robustness tests. Specifically, we expand model 2 by also relating cereal yield, a specific productivity measure, to undernourishment. And we expand model 3 by relating financial sector development to other productivity measures, livestock production, and crop and cereal yield.

The results in the basic four models could all be affected by endogeneity problems. At least in theory, in the first model, a reduction in undernourishment either directly or as a proxy for, say, a reduction in poverty, might stimulate demand for financial services, leading to reverse causality. Similarly, in the second model, less undernourishment could translate into healthier, more productive workers, raising agricultural productivity. In the third model, higher agricultural productivity of workers could raise demand for financial services. And in the fourth model, use of productivity-enhancing inputs can again lead to demand for financial services.

To alleviate these problems, we use an instrumental variables approach. We need two sets of instruments: one for private credit to GDP and one for agricultural productivity. To instrument for private credit to GDP, we rely on the law and finance literature. This literature widely uses the legal origin of countries as an exogenous source of variation that is

highly correlated with financial development measures but not necessarily with undernourishment. This literature finds that property rights are better established in British common law countries and less so in civil law countries (French, German, and Scandinavian origin) (see, e.g., La Porta et al. 1997 and La Porta, Lopez-de-Silanes, and Shleifer 1998). These superior property rights facilitate financial contracting and translate into improved financial development. To instrument for agricultural productivity, we rely on fertilizer use in 100 grams per hectare of arable land and the number of tractors per agricultural worker. Arguably, these two variables are highly correlated with productivity but only indirectly with undernourishment.

We use two tests to validate our instruments: first, we use the Hansen over-identifying restrictions test, which tests whether the instruments are associated with undernourishment or agricultural productivity beyond their ability to explain cross-country variation in private credit to GDP. Under the null, the instruments are valid. We report the p-value of the test as "OIR test" for over-identifying restrictions. The second test assesses whether the instruments are able to explain cross-country differences in financial development or agricultural productivity. This test is provided as an F test in the first stage of the IV regressions. Under the null, the excluded instruments do not explain variation in the dependent variable. We report the p-values of the test as "F Test."

Notably, to further ameliorate concerns about endogeneity problems and omitted variable bias, we use fixed-effects panel estimations whenever sufficient data are available. Data are, however not always available annually. Specifically, as noted, most FAO data are provided only as averages for five different periods. Consequently, we can do panel regressions using these five period averages. We cannot do panel regressions for the specific agricultural productivity indexes—cereal and crop yields—as we have only end-of-period data for these.

Empirical Results

To test the hypotheses that financial development reduces undernourishment via the agricultural sector and through an increase in agricultural productivity specifically, we estimate the following four relationships: (1) between financial development and undernourishment directly, (2) between agricultural productivity and undernourishment, (3) between financial development and agricultural productivity, and (4) between financial development and agricultural productivity-enhancing inputs.

Private Credit and Undernourishment

Table 7.3 shows our main result, which strongly supports the basic hypothesis that financial development reduces undernourishment. Regression 1 presents the basic specification in which undernourishment is the dependent variable and the main independent variable is private credit to GDP and in which we do not use any control variables. Private credit enters negatively and significantly at the 5 percent level. The effect of financial sector development is economically very substantial. Because we use logs, the coefficient implies that a 1 percent increase in private credit to GDP reduces (the degree of) undernourishment by 0.285 percent. To take a specific example, regression 1 implies that in the case of India, an increase in private credit to GDP from India's average level in the period 2001–2003 of 31.2 percent to the sample average of 45.6 percent would mean a reduction of 4.1 percentage points in India's degree of undernourishment from 21 percent to 16.9 percent.

The regression 2 result provides a specification in which we control for the initial levels of poverty and GDP per capita. Although initial poverty and GDP per capita are also very significant, using these very general controls does not change the statistical significance of the financial development variable and keeps the coefficient of similar magnitude, 0.188. Even when using initial GDP per capita and poverty as controls, a concern could remain that private credit correlates with other country factors and that this correlation drives our results. Hence, in regression 3, we use additional country control variables: similar to Beck, Demirgüç-Kunt, and Levine (2007), we include inflation, initial size of government, trade as a percentage of GDP, rural population as a percentage of total population, and agricultural employment as a percentage of the workforce. Our result is robust to this inclusion in sign but not in significance (a *p*-value of 0.303), and the effect of financial sector development decreases in absolute magnitude. However, private credit is significant at the 5 percent level and the coefficient increases slightly in magnitude, –0.202, if we *exclude* inflation (not reported). This result suggests that the expected and well-documented negative relationship between financial development and inflation obscures the relationship between financial development and undernourishment.

To ensure that our results are not driven by richer countries—where financial development is high and undernourishment low—in regression 4 we next drop countries with above-median GDP per capita for

the whole sample from the analysis (a GDP per capita greater than $4671). Not surprisingly, as undernourishment is minimal in developed countries, the result increases further in absolute magnitude (and is again significant), suggesting that the effect of financial development on undernourishment is primarily driven by poorer countries. Using the same specification as regression 2, in regression 5 we also use interactive dummies to explore whether there are statistically significant different relationships between financial development and undernourishment at different levels of general development. Regression 5 confirms that the effects of financial development on undernourishment are stronger (to a statistically significant degree) in low- and middle-income countries than in high-income countries. And the positive sign for the low-income countries dummy shows that undernourishment is higher in poorer countries, as expected.

Next, we want to alleviate endogeneity concerns. In theory, it is possible that lower levels of undernourishment increase demand for financial services. Therefore, following the law and finance literature, we use in regression 6 the same specification as in regression 2 but now employ an instrumental variable (IV) estimation approach in which we instrument private credit to GDP with legal origin dummies. Our tests indicate that the instruments are valid. The regression shows that private credit remains significant and the coefficient even increases in absolute magnitude to −1.567.

To further control for possible endogeneity, we next conduct in regression 7 a panel estimation using country-fixed effects in which we use up to five observations on undernourishment in an unbalanced panel. In the regression, we do not include poverty and GDP per capita because the fixed effects already absorb the average level of poverty and income for each country. Similarly, we drop rural population and agricultural employment, which exhibit much lower time variation and the inclusion of which only reduces the sample size. However, we add food import minus exports because this factor exhibits much time variation. We confirm our main hypothesis of the importance of financial sector development, with private credit having a statistically significant negative effect on undernourishment with a coefficient somewhat smaller than the basic OLS regression in regression 3, −0.103. It is however expected that the panel coefficients are smaller than those of the cross-sectional regressions, as the time covered by each period in the panel is much smaller than the period covered in the cross section. Regression 8 next shows that when we include GDP per capita

Table 7.3
Impact of private credit on undernourishment

| | Average prevalence of undernourishment | | | | | | | |
	(1)	(2)	(3)	(4)	(5)	(6)	(7)	(8)
	Basic	Control for initial levels	All controls	All controls; Poorest 50%	Interact low income dummy	IV	Panel: fixed effects	Panel: fixed effects; control GDP/cap.
Private credit	−0.285	−0.188	−0.118	−0.245	0.124	−1.567	−0.103	−0.080
	(0.128)**	(0.088)**	(0.114)	(0.133)*	(0.190)	(0.434)***	(0.059)*	(0.044)*
Initial poverty		0.384	0.395	0.246	0.396	0.152		
		(0.066)***	(0.078)***	(0.087)***	(0.063)***	(0.207)		
(Initial) GDP/cap.		−0.279	−0.327	−0.253	−0.078	0.252		−0.422
		(0.105)***	(0.161)**	(0.198)	(0.115)	(0.284)		(0.100)***
Low-income dummy					1.763			
					(0.733)**			
Credit * LI dummy					−0.356			
					(0.215)*			
Inflation			0.082	0.015			0.057	
			(0.066)	(0.073)			(0.027)**	
(Initial) size government			−0.246	−0.157			0.196	
			(0.163)	(0.206)			(0.159)	
Trade			0.284	0.003			−0.206	
			(0.189)	(0.210)			(0.136)	
Rural population			0.085	−0.549				
			(0.253)	(0.735)				

Table 7.3
(continued)

| | Average prevalence of undernourishment | | | | | | | |
| | (1) | (2) | (3) | (4) | (5) | (6) | (7) | (8) |
	Basic	Control for initial levels	All controls	All controls; Poorest 50%	Interact low income dummy	IV	Panel: fixed effects	Panel: fixed effects; control GDP/cap.
Agricultural employment			0.018 (0.144)	0.224 (0.148)				
Food import - export							-0.030 (0.033)	-0.023 (0.026)
Observations	116	95	84	49	95	56	233	257
R-squared	0.09	0.61	0.62	0.48	0.66	NA	0.17	0.16
OIR test						0.59		
F test						0.000		
Countries	116	95	84	49	95	56	99	104

Notes: This table reports OLS estimations in regressions 1–5 and a 2SLS estimation in regression 6 for the period 1980–2003. Regressions 7 and 8 report panel fixed effects estimations for the 1990s. All variables are in logs. The dependent variable is the log average prevalence of undernourishment (percent). The main independent variable is average private credit to GDP (percent). Other independent variables are the initial levels of GDP per capita, poverty, and government expenditure as a percentage of GDP in the period 1980–2003. Other controls are average inflation, average poverty, dummy indicating country is a low (middle) income country, percentage trade of GDP, the percentage of the population living in rural areas, and the percentage of the workforce in agriculture. The 2SLS estimations in regression 6 use legal-origin dummies indicating English, French, German, and Scandinavian law as instruments for private credit per GDP. OIR test indicates the *p*-value of the Hansen overidentifying restrictions test, which has the null that the instruments are uncorrelated with the residuals of the second regression. F test indicates the *p*-value of the F test with the null that the excluded exogenous variables do not explain cross-country variation in private credit to GDP in the first-stage estimation. Regressions 7 and 8 are a panel of fixed effects regression with on average 2.5 observations per country. An additional control variable is food import - food export per person (kg). Standard errors are corrected for clustering at the country level. Heteroskedasticity-consistent standard errors are reported in parentheses.

*significant at 10 percent; **significant at 5 percent; ***significant at 1 percent.

in each of the five periods, the coefficient of private credit remains significantly negative, albeit only at the 10 percent level. This result shows that financial sector development has an effect on undernourishment independent of a country's general development, which is a very strong result. Even when we include government size in regression 8, private credit remains significant, although marginally, in the panel regression (*p*-value: 0.118; not reported).

Agricultural Productivity and Undernourishment

We have found strong and robust effects of financial sector development on undernourishment. We next want to investigate the channels from financial development to undernourishment by focusing on how financial sector development affects an intermediate outcome: agricultural productivity. But before investigating the effects of financial sector development on agricultural productivity, we need to show that greater agricultural productivity leads to lower undernourishment. We do this by using aggregate measures of productivity, such as agricultural output per worker, and more detailed measures of productivity, such as cereal yields. In the next section, we show that financial development leads to higher agricultural productivity.

Table 7.4 shows the results for the relation between aggregate productivity and undernourishment. Regression 1 confirms that agricultural productivity decreases undernourishment. The effect is economically large: a 1 percent increase in agricultural productivity decreases undernourishment by 0.592 percent. Regression 2 shows that even when controlling for the initial levels of poverty and GDP per capita, the effect of agricultural productivity on undernourishment remains large: a 1 percent increase in agricultural productivity decreases undernourishment by 0.244 percent. To further ameliorate possible omitted variables bias, we next include our standard country controls (regression 3). This inclusion weakens the effects of agricultural productivity on undernourishment, with a coefficient that is no longer significant (at the 10% level) and magnitude dropping to –0.190. To ensure that the result is not driven by richer countries, we focus again in regression 4 on the poorest countries (with GDP per capita of less than $4671, the median of the total sample). We find that although not significant at the 10 percent level, the effect of productivity on undernourishment increases in absolute magnitude. Although for the last two regressions agricultural productivity is not statistically significant, this lack of significance occurs mainly because we use the same control variables as

in table 7.3. Arguably, this approach is not correct and indeed productivity becomes statistically significant in both regressions if agricultural employment is no longer included.

We would like to know whether private credit to GDP affects undernourishment through agricultural productivity or whether there is a (stronger) other channel. Hence, in regression 5 we include private credit to GDP itself in the regression. We find that financial sector development is not significant, nor is agricultural productivity (both p-values around 0.12). This result might be due to the positive relationship between productivity and private credit reducing the effect of either variable on undernourishment. We next address possible endogeneity problems in our regressions by instrumenting agricultural productivity by fertilizer use and number of tractors per agricultural worker. Regression 6, using the same control variables as Regression 2, shows significant effects (at the 1 percent level) of productivity on undernourishment, with a coefficient of about −0.8, which is a substantial increase in absolute magnitude. Tests indicate again that the instruments are valid. Our last and most comprehensive test for simultaneity and missing variables that otherwise might be affecting the result is a panel estimation using fixed effects (and correcting for clustering at the country level). Regression 7 shows that the main result is maintained, with a strong negative impact of productivity on undernourishment—actually, productivity is the only significant variable. Because the time period in the panel regressions is much smaller, the relatively large coefficient can be interpreted as cereal yields having direct large contemporaneous effects on undernourishment, unlike, for example, private credit to GDP in other panel regressions.

We next study whether a more detailed measure of agricultural productivity, cereal yield, confirms the general results of higher agricultural productivity leading to lower undernourishment. Table 7.5, following the same structure as table 7.4, presents the results. Regression 1 shows that higher levels of cereal yields indeed seem to significantly (at the 5% level) reduce undernourishment, with a coefficient of −0.8. Regression 2 confirms this result even after controlling for the initial levels of poverty and GDP per capita. The coefficient in this case implies that a 1 percent increase in cereal yields decreases undernourishment by 0.27 percent. In regression 3, we add country controls to ameliorate any omitted variable bias. The coefficient becomes marginally larger in magnitude and stays significant at the 5 percent level. Regression 4 excludes countries with above-median GDP per capita and

Table 7.4
Impact of agricultural productivity on undernourishment

	Average prevalence of undernourishment						
	(1)	(2)	(3)	(4)	(5)	(6)	(7)
	Basic	Control for initial levels	All controls	All controls; Poorest 50%	Private credit	IV	Panel: fixed effects
Agricultural productivity	-0.592	-0.244	-0.190	-0.232	-0.206	-0.790	-0.317
	(0.041)***	(0.126)*	(0.147)	(0.213)	(0.131)	(0.254)***	(0.125)**
Initial poverty		0.311	0.369	0.201	0.348	0.213	
		(0.069)***	(0.082)***	(0.087)**	(0.069)***	(0.086)**	
(Initial) GDP/cap.		-0.134	-0.234	-0.136	-0.225	0.380	
		(0.172)	(0.205)	(0.286)	(0.207)	(0.259)	
Private credit					-0.091		
					(0.172)		
Inflation			0.106	0.082			0.030
			(0.063)*	(0.071)			(0.025)
(Initial) size government			-0.324	-0.317			-0.012
			(0.178)*	(0.219)			(0.096)
Trade			0.353	0.136			-0.175
			(0.184)*	(0.210)			(0.142)
Rural population			0.013	-0.497			
			(0.258)	(0.754)			

Table 7.4
(continued)

	Average prevalence of undernourishment						
	(1)	(2)	(3)	(4)	(5)	(6)	(7)
	Basic	Control for initial levels	All controls	All controls; Poorest 50%	Private credit	IV	Panel: fixed effects
Agricultural employment			0.008 (0.138)	0.237 (0.137)*			
Food import – export							-0.035 (0.030)
Observations	111	95	83	49	94	94	230
R-squared	0.55	0.60	0.62	0.46	0.62	NA	0.21
OIR test						0.97	
F test						0.000	
Countries	111	95	83	49	94	94	97

Notes: This table reports OLS estimations in regressions 1–5 and a 2SLS estimation in regression 6 for the period 1980–2003. Regression 7 reports panel fixed effects estimations for the 1990s. All variables are in logs. The dependent variable is the log average prevalence of undernourishment (percent). The main independent variable is average productivity per agricultural worker in constant 2000 US$. Other independent variables are the initial levels of GDP per capita, poverty, and government expenditure as a percentage of GDP in the period 1980–2003. Other controls are average inflation, percentage trade of GDP, the percentage of the population living in rural areas, and the percentage of the workforce in agriculture. The 2SLS estimations use number of tractors per agricultural worker and fertilizer use (100 grams per arable hectare) as instruments for productivity per agricultural worker. OIR test indicates the *p*-value of the Hansen overidentifying restrictions test, which has the null that the instruments are uncorrelated with the residuals of the second regression. F test indicates the *p*-value of the F test with the null that the excluded exogenous variables do not explain cross-country variation in agricultural productivity in the first-stage estimation. Regression 7 is a panel fixed effects regression with on average 2.5 observations per country. An additional control variable is food import - food export per person (kg). Standard errors are corrected for clustering at the country level. White (1981) heteroskedasticity-consistent standard errors are reported in parentheses.

*significant at 10 percent; **significant at 5 percent; ***significant at 1 percent.

Table 7.5
Impact of cereal yields on undernourishment

	Average prevalence of undernourishment						
	(1)	(2)	(3)	(4)	(5)	(6)	(7)
	Basic	Control for initial levels	All controls	All controls; poorest 50%	Private credit	IV	Panel: fixed effects
Cereal yield	-0.790	-0.269	-0.278	-0.410	-0.259	-0.452	-0.516
	(0.115)***	(0.112)**	(0.120)**	(0.209)*	(0.125)**	(0.150)***	(0.153)***
Initial Poverty		0.312	0.344	0.168	0.349	0.283	
		(0.065)***	(0.081)***	(0.080)**	(0.081)***	(0.065)***	
Initial GDP/cap.		-0.345	-0.351	-0.207	-0.337	-0.322	
		(0.084)***	(0.133)***	(0.201)	(0.142)**	(0.081)***	
Private Credit					-0.054		
					(0.117)		
Inflation			0.108	0.071	0.093		0.031
			(0.062)*	(0.072)	(0.067)		(0.027)
(Initial) size government			-0.392	-0.372	-0.368		0.046
			(0.177)**	(0.213)*	(0.185)*		(0.117)
Trade			0.303	0.068	0.295		-0.112
			(0.188)	(0.199)	(0.192)		(0.143)
Food import - export							-0.042
							(0.032)
Rural Population			0.062	-0.222	0.043		
			(0.252)	(0.768)	(0.253)		

Table 7.5
(continued)

		Average prevalence of undernourishment					
	(1)	(2)	(3)	(4)	(5)	(6)	(7)
	Basic	Control for initial levels	All controls	All controls; poorest 50%	Private credit	IV	Panel: fixed effects
Agricultural employment			0.046 (0.145)	0.281 (0.138)**	0.039 (0.147)		
Observations	119	95	83	49	83	94	234
R-squared	0.25	0.60	0.63	0.51	0.63	NA	0.28
OIR test						0.97	
F test						0.000	
Countries	119	95	83	49	83	94	99

Notes: This table reports OLS estimations in regressions 1–5 and a 2SLS estimation in regression 6 for the period 1980–2003. Regression 7 reports panel fixed effects estimations for the 1990s. All variables are in logs. The dependent variable is the log average prevalence of undernourishment (percent). The main independent variable is cereal yields (kg per hectare). Other independent variables are the initial levels of GDP per capita, poverty, and government expenditure as a percentage of GDP in the period 1980–2003. Other controls are average inflation, private credit to GDP, percentage trade of GDP, percentage of the population living in rural areas, and percentage of the workforce in agriculture. The 2SLS estimations use number of tractors per agricultural worker and fertilizer use (100 grams per arable hectare) as instruments for cereal yields. OIR test indicates the *p*-value of the Hansen overidentifying restrictions test, which has the null that the instruments are uncorrelated with the residuals of the second regression. F test indicates the *p*-value of the F test with the null that the excluded exogenous variables do not explain cross-country variation in cereal yields in the first-stage estimation. Regression 7 is a panel fixed effects regression with on average 2.5 observations per country. An additional control variable is food import – food export per person (kg). Standard errors are corrected for clustering at the country level. Heteroskedasticity-consistent standard errors are reported in parentheses.

*significant at 10 percent; **significant at 5 percent; ***significant at 1 percent.

shows that the result is not driven primarily by rich countries: the coefficient increases in magnitude, although it becomes less significant.

In regression 5, private credit is not significant but cereal yields still is. This finding suggests that productivity is an important channel by which private credit reduces undernourishment. Regression 6 shows that our results likely do not suffer from endogeneity problems because, when we instrument cereal yields with fertilizer use and tractors per worker, the coefficient for cereal yields remains statistically significant. The magnitude of the coefficient again further increases to over 0.45 and is significant at the 1 percent level. Tests show that our instruments are again valid. Last, in regression 7 we run an unbalanced panel regression for 99 countries and five periods with an average of 2.5 observations per country, using fixed effects (and controlling for clustering at the country level). Again, cereal yield remains statistically significant and is actually (again) the only significant variable. Overall, the results of table 7.5 confirm the more general results of table 7.4 that agricultural productivity reduces undernourishment. The question we turn to next is whether it is financial development that drives agricultural productivity.

Private Credit and Agricultural Productivity, Overall and Specific

After establishing an effect of agricultural productivity on undernourishment, we next study the link between private credit and agricultural productivity. Table 7.6 provides the results when we use our aggregate measure of agricultural productivity. Regression 1 displays the basic analysis. We find a highly significant effect of private credit on agricultural productivity. The coefficient implies that a 1 percent increase in private credit increases productivity by 0.8 percent. We next control for initial GDP per capita and poverty and find that the effect of financial development on agricultural productivity remains statistically significant but, unsurprisingly, drops in magnitude to 0.223, because initial conditions absorb much of the effects of financial development. Regression 3 confirms the results after including other country variables, as the coefficient remains significant at the 5 percent level and the magnitude decreases slightly to 0.191. To check whether our results are not driven by richer countries, in regression 3 we again drop countries with above-median GDP per capita (greater than $4,671) and find that for this regression, private credit is no longer statistically significant. This result occurs mainly because we use, for comparability, the same control variables as in table 7.3. Arguably, this approach is not correct,

and indeed results for private credit become statistically significant in the regression if agricultural employment and rural population are not included with the magnitude only slightly changed.

Next, we address endogeneity concerns by using an instrumental variables (IV) approach. As in the previous analyses, we instrument private credit with legal origin. In regression 5, private credit has the same positive sign, and the size of the effect increases to 1.358, but it has a p-value of 0.139. As another test for endogeneity, in regression 6 we conduct a panel regression with fixed effects and various other control variables. Here we find that there remains a strong and statistically significant effect of private credit on agricultural productivity, with a coefficient of 0.069. Again, note that this coefficient is expected to be smaller than in the cross-sectional regressions because the length of the period is smaller than in the cross-section.

As a last robustness check, we analyze the impact of private credit on agricultural productivity growth. Growth is calculated by subtracting the logs of the last and the first available observation in the period 1980–2003 and dividing by the time span between these two observations. In regression 7, we rerun the basic specification of regression 2, but we include the initial level of productivity instead of the initial level of poverty. The importance of financial sector development for the growth in agricultural productivity is confirmed, as the coefficient on private credit is statistically significant and positive. The result is again economically significant. Finally, in regression 8 we include, besides initial productivity, the same control variables as in specifications 3 and 4. We find that a 1 standard deviation increase in the log of private credit (1.04) leads to a 0.4–0.8 percentage points increase in productivity growth, statistically significant at the 5 percent level. This finding is substantial because the average growth of rate of productivity was 1.8 percent.

Having established a relationship between private credit and general agricultural productivity, we next ask whether specific agricultural outputs are also affected by private credit. Therefore, we analyze the effect of private credit on cereal yield per hectare of arable land and on growth in livestock and crop production. Table 7.7 presents the results, which indicate that financial development drives agricultural productivity to a substantial extent via these specific measures. Regressions 1 and 2 show that private credit is associated (at the 5 percent and 10 percent levels, respectively) with higher cereal yield. The economic effect is sizeable. The result indicates that a 1 percent increase in private

Table 7.6
Impact of private credit on agricultural productivity

	Average agricultural productivity						Productivity growth	
	(1)	(2)	(3)	(4)	(5)	(6)	(7)	(8)
	Basic	Control for initial levels	All controls	All controls; poorest 50%	IV	Panel: fixed effects	Basic	All controls
Private credit	0.804	0.223	0.191	0.133	1.358	0.069	0.004	0.008
	(0.257)***	(0.071)***	(0.080)**	(0.105)	(0.918)	(0.039)*	(0.002)*	(0.004)**
Initial poverty		−0.178	−0.121	−0.075	−0.003			−0.005
		(0.060)***	(0.056)**	(0.073)	(0.240)			(0.002)**
Initial GDP/cap.		0.891	0.601	0.772	0.521		0.002	0.001
		(0.102)***	(0.148)***	(0.227)***	(0.367)		(0.004)	(0.004)
Inflation			0.001	0.035		−0.091		0.003
			(0.045)	(0.059)		(0.013)***		(0.002)
(Initial) size government			−0.292	−0.336		−0.096		−0.003
			(0.154)*	(0.192)*		(0.078)		(0.005)
Trade			0.381	0.362		0.181		−0.002
			(0.129)***	(0.207)*		(0.085)**		(0.005)
Rural population			−0.561	−0.314				0.003
			(0.246)**	(0.618)				(0.011)
Agricultural employment			−0.118	−0.175				0.004
			(0.068)*	(0.089)*				(0.003)

Table 7.6
(continued)

	Average agricultural productivity						Productivity growth	
	(1)	(2)	(3)	(4)	(5)	(6)	(7)	(8)
	Basic	Control for initial levels	All controls	All controls; poorest 50%	IV	Panel: fixed effects	Basic	All controls
Initial productivity							0.004 (0.003)	0.002 (0.007)
Food import - export						-0.036 (0.033)		
Observations		97	86	50	58	414	149	86
R-squared		0.79	0.83	0.78	NA	0.26	0.22	0.24
OIR test					0.59			
F test					0.000			
Countries		97	86	50	58	126	149	86

Notes: This table reports OLS estimations in regressions 1–4, and a 2SLS estimation in regression 5 for the period 1980–2003. Regression 6 reports panel fixed effects estimations for the 1990s. All variables are in logs. In regressions 1–6, the dependent variable is the log average agricultural productivity per worker in constant 2000 US$. In regressions 7 and 8 the dependent variable is the growth in agricultural productivity per worker in the period 1980–2003. The main independent variable is private credit to GDP (percent). Other independent variables are the initial levels of GDP per capita, poverty, and government expenditure as a percentage of GDP in the period 1980–2003. Other controls are average inflation, percentage trade of GDP, percentage of the population living in rural areas, and percentage of the workforce in agriculture. The 2SLS estimations use legal origin dummies indicating English, French, German, and Scandinavian law as instruments for private credit per GDP. OIR test indicates the p-value of the Hansen overidentifying restrictions test, which has the null that the instruments are uncorrelated with the residuals of the second regression. F test indicates the p-value of the F test with the null that the excluded exogenous variables do not explain cross-country variation in private credit to GDP in the first-stage estimation. Regression 6 is a panel fixed effects regression with on average 2.5 observations per country. An additional control variable is food export - food import per person (kg). Standard errors are corrected for clustering at the country level. Heteroskedasticity-consistent standard errors are reported in parentheses.
*significant at 10 percent; **significant at 5 percent; ***significant at 1 percent.

Table 7.7
Specific channels of private credit: Impact of private credit on several agricultural productivity indicators

	Cereal yield							Initial livestock index	Initial crop yield index
	(1)	(2)	(3)	(4)	(5)	(6)	(7)	(8)	(9)
	Basic	Control for initial levels	All controls	All controls; poorest 50%	IV	Panel: fixed effects	Panel: fixed effects		
Private credit	0.250	0.137	0.235	0.292	1.682	0.081	0.036	−0.202	−0.109
	(0.097)**	(0.071)*	(0.092)**	(0.128)**	(0.890)*	(0.026)***	(0.041)	(0.094)**	(0.050)**
(Initial) GDP/cap.		0.039	−0.051	0.182	−0.440			0.279	0.178
		(0.118)	(0.150)	(0.190)	(0.359)			(0.084)***	(0.059)***
Initial Poverty		−0.169	−0.178	−0.163	0.176			0.032	−0.041
		(0.074)**	(0.074)**	(0.073)**	(0.262)			(0.047)	(0.033)
Inflation			0.042	0.059			−0.063	0.087	0.031
			(0.046)	(0.074)			(0.011)***	(0.049)*	(0.031)
(Initial) size government			−0.467	−0.404			−0.131		
			(0.133)***	(0.153)**			(0.076)*		
Trade			0.063	0.045			0.144		
			(0.119)	(0.170)			(0.057)**		
Food imp. − exp.							−0.048		
							(0.038)		

Table 7.7
(continued)

	Cereal yield							Initial livestock index	Initial crop yield index
	(1)	(2)	(3)	(4)	(5)	(6)	(7)	(8)	(9)
	Basic	Control for initial levels	All controls	All controls; poorest 50%	IV	Panel: fixed effects	Panel: fixed effects		
Rural population			−0.177	0.577					
			(0.206)	(0.530)					
Agricultural employment			0.067	0.072					
			(0.069)	(0.077)					
Obs.	161	96	85	49	58	715	436	94	94
R-squared	0.15	0.25	0.36	0.35	NA	0.03	0.20	0.34	0.31
OIR test					0.74				
F test					0.003				
Countries	161	96	85	49	58	160	135	94	94

Notes: This table reports OLS estimations in regressions 1–4, 8, and 9, and a 2SLS estimation in regression 5 for the period 1980–2003. Regressions 6 and 7 report panel fixed effects estimations for the 1990s. All variables are in logs, except inflation. Regressions 1–7 have cereal yields (kg per hectare) as a dependent variable. In regression 8, the dependent variable is the initial (on average 1981) crop production index (1999–2001 = 100). In regression 9, the dependent variable is the initial (on average 1981) livestock production index (1999–2001 = 100). The main independent variable is private credit to GDP (percent). Other independent variables are the initial levels of GDP per capita, poverty, and government expenditure as a percentage of GDP in the period 1980–2003. Other controls are average inflation, percentage trade of GDP, the percentage of the population living in rural areas, and the percentage of the workforce in agriculture. The 2SLS estimations use legal origin dummies indicating English, French, German, and Scandinavian law as instruments for private credit per GDP. OIR test indicates the *p*-value of the Hansen overidentifying restrictions test, which has the null that the instruments are uncorrelated with the residuals of the second regression. F Test indicates the *p*-value of the F test with the null that the excluded exogenous variables do not explain cross-country variation in private credit to GDP in the first-stage estimation. Heteroskedasticity-consistent standard errors are reported in parentheses.

*significant at 10 percent; **significant at 5 percent; ***significant at 1 percent.

credit increases cereal yields by 0.14–0.25 percent. Regression 3 adds further country controls; the impact of private credit increases actually marginally in magnitude and stays significant at the 5 percent level. The result is also robust to dropping countries that have above-median GDP per capita from the sample (regression 4). The impact increases further to 0.292 and stays significant. To address endogeneity concerns, we again instrument private credit with legal origin (regression 5). Now the magnitude increases to 1.682 and private credit is only marginally significant. Tests also confirm the validity of the instruments.

As another robustness check, we analyze the impact of private credit on cereal yields by using a panel approach with country-fixed effects. Regression 6 shows that at the 5 percent significance level, a 1 percent increase in private credit is associated with a 0.08 percent increase in cereal yields. Again, this coefficient is expected to be relatively small, as the time period in the panel is much shorter than for the cross-sectional regressions. Similar to the other regressions, we also use a panel specification with a number of control variables, inflation, size of government, trade, and food imports minus exports (regression 7). We do not confirm the significant influence of private credit on cereal yields, possibly due to the too many control variables (not including inflation, for example, makes private credit statistically significant). Note that the coefficients for private credit in the cereal yields regressions are generally lower than in table 7.6, in which we analyzed the impact of financial development on overall agricultural productivity. This result suggests that the effect of financial development on cereal yields is perhaps important but is not the only means by which financial sector development drives the increase in agricultural productivity.

We next investigate the association with the two other productivity measures: growth in livestock production and crop production. Because both indices, by construction, have a value of 100 in 1999–2001, we use the initial values for the indexes as the dependent variables, which means that if the initial value was low, growth over the next years was high for that country. Consequently, we would expect a negative sign for private credit if that spurs production. We indeed find this beneficial effect of private credit for both the livestock and crop production indexes, regressions 8 and 9, and significant as well (at the 5% level), even when controlling for initial poverty and inflation. This result shows that financial sector development is also associated with higher productivity growth in crops and livestock.

Private Credit and Productivity-Enhancing Inputs

We have shown that financial development spurs agricultural productivity, but we want to investigate in more depth the channels by which this may happen. We expect financial development to be associated with an increase in the use of productivity-enhancing inputs that require some up-front financing or outlays. Such a result would provide evidence of the specific channels by which financial sector development reduces undernourishment. However, we are constrained by the data to test this hypothesis for a large set of countries using general measures of capital employed in the agricultural sector. Therefore, we use data on fertilizer use and the number of tractors per agricultural worker, inputs that require up-front outlays for which external financing may be important.

Regression 1 in table 7.8 shows that private credit is significantly (at the 1% level) associated with fertilizer use, even after controlling for the initial level of GDP per capita and poverty. The result implies that a 1 percent increase in private credit increases fertilizer use by 0.884 percent. To address a potential endogeneity problem, we instrument in regression 2 private credit with legal origin. The result remains significant and the magnitude of the effect increases (to 1.9). Moreover, the tests confirm the econometric validity of the instruments. In regression 3, we run a panel regression and find a positive correlation, but this time a not significant impact of private credit on fertilizer use.

Next, we assess the impact of financial sector development on the use of tractors per worker. Regression 4, controlling for the initial levels GDP per capita and poverty, shows a positive but not significant impact of financial development on tractor use. When we instrument in regression 5 private credit with legal origin, however, the effect becomes significant at the 1 percent level and increases in size. Here the coefficient implies that a 1 percent increase in private credit leads to a 0.054 percent increase in the number of tractors per worker, which is smaller in magnitude because it covers a shorter time period than the cross-sectional regression. However, the OIR test casts some shadow on the validity of the instruments. We next run regression 6 for tractors per worker and find a significant impact of private credit, with a coefficient of 0.170. This result implies that a 1 percent increase in private credit increases tractor use by 0.17 percent. Together, these findings further confirm an important role of private credit in increasing the use of productivity-enhancing inputs.

Table 7.8
Specific channels of private credit: Impact of private credit on the use of productivity enhancing equipment

	Fertilizer use			Tractors per agricultural worker		
	(1)	(2)	(3)	(4)	(5)	(6)
	OLS	IV	Panel	OLS	IV	Panel
Private credit	0.884	1.910	0.054	0.039	2.008	0.170
	(0.175)***	(0.717)***	(0.089)	(0.147)	(0.918)**	(0.069)**
Initial GDP/cap.	−0.015	−0.217		1.501	1.095	
	(0.298)	(0.467)		(0.171)***	(0.600)*	
Initial Poverty	−0.486			−0.706		
	(0.189)**			(0.121)***		
Trade			0.368			0.217
			(0.183)**			(0.164)
(Initial) size Government			−0.014			0.046
			(0.188)			(0.141)
Inflation			−0.034			−0.047
			(0.030)			(0.022)**

Table 7.8
(continued)

	Fertilizer use			Tractors per agricultural worker		
	(1)	(2)	(3)	(4)	(5)	(6)
	OLS	IV	Panel	OLS	IV	Panel
Food export -import			-0.076 (0.071)			-0.015 (0.051)
Observations	97	97	429	96	97	439
R-squared	0.40	na	0.05	0.73	na	0.08
OIR test		0.19			0.03	
F test		0.000			0.000	
Countries	97	97	131	96	97	133

Notes: This table reports OLS estimations in regressions 1 and 4 and 2SLS estimations in regressions 2 and 5 for the period 1980–2003. Regressions 3 and 6 report panel fixed effects estimations for the 1990s. All variables are in logs. In regressions 1–3, the dependent variable is the log average fertilizer use in 100 grams per hectare. In regressions 4–6, the dependent variable is the log average number of tractors per agricultural worker. The main independent variable is private credit to GDP (percent). Other independent variables are GDP per capita, poverty, trade, government size, and inflation. The 2SLS estimations use legal origin dummies indicating English, French, German, and Scandinavian law as instruments for private credit per GDP. OIR test indicates the *p*-value of the Hansen overidentifying restrictions test, which has the null that the instruments are uncorrelated with the residuals of the second regression. F test indicates the *p*-value of the F test with the null that the excluded exogenous variables do not explain cross-country variation in private credit to GDP in the first-stage estimation. Regressions 3 and 6 are panel fixed effects regressions with on average 3.3 observations per country. An additional control variable is food import - food export per person (kg). Standard errors are corrected for clustering at the country level. Heteroskedasticity-consistent standard errors are reported in parentheses.
*significant at 10 percent; **significant at 5 percent; ***significant at 1 percent.

The Role of Access to Financial Services for the Impact of Finance on Undernourishment

So far, we have used a very aggregate measure of financial sector development, private sector to GDP, and associated increases in that measure with greater access to financial services. But access to financial services may be unequal across households and firms, and it may not be the poor or undernourished that directly benefit from greater financial sector development. Unfortunately, there are no data on access to financial services by individual households or small firms across a large set of countries and covering any consistent time span (see Honohan 2005, 2006 on availability and deficiencies of access data). What we do have are measures of the number of access points to the formal financial system, specifically the number of branches and ATMs for the year 2003–2004. These distribution data can be useful proxies for access and can matter for poverty and undernourishment.[8] Burgess and Pande (2005), for example, show the importance of the banking system distribution in case of India for poverty. And Beck, Demirgüç-Kunt, and Martinez Peria (2007) show that these outreach indicators predict household and firm use of banking services and relate to measures of firm financing constraints.

We use these data, scaled by the size of the country in square kilometers, to get a measure of access to financial services in rural areas. We then use this variable in addition to private credit in our cross-section regressions to distill the joint impact of financial sector development and access to financial services on undernourishment, productivity, and productivity-enhancing inputs. We control in these regressions for the degree of country openness, the size of government, and the degree of inflation. The results are reported in table 7.9.

We find a beneficial effect of the outreach of the financial system on undernourishment (regression 1). The effect of financial outreach is actually so strong as to make private credit no longer statistically significant. This result suggests that our findings shown in table 7.3, that private credit has a significantly negative impact on undernourishment, may be due to the fact that better financial systems offer greater access to financial services, which in turn improves the distribution of food across people. The effects of outreach are also strong for our overall agricultural productivity measure (regression 2). In this regression, there remains a direct and highly statistically significant effect of private credit on productivity, consistent with the earlier regression results. Differentiating productivity somewhat further, we find that

Table 7.9
Impact of outreach of financial services on undernourishment, productivity, and use of productivity-enhancing equipment

	Undernourishment	Productivity	Cereal yield	Tractors per worker	Fertilizer
	(1)	(2)	(3)	(4)	(5)
Branches/1000 km²	-0.175	0.183	0.136	0.285	0.331
	(0.053)***	(0.059)***	(0.037)***	(0.118)**	(0.090)***
Private credit	-0.002	0.338	0.160	0.222	0.640
	(0.185)	(0.120)***	(0.068)**	(0.269)	(0.191)***
Rural Population	0.610	-1.254	-0.187	-1.459	-0.188
	(0.193)***	(0.248)***	(0.082)**	(0.557)**	(0.197)
Trade	-0.404	0.412	0.013	0.642	-0.087
	(0.225)*	(0.243)*	(0.126)	(0.449)	(0.283)
Initial size	-0.343	0.494	-0.445	1.547	-0.638
	(0.302)	(0.302)	(0.198)**	(0.591)**	(0.381)*
Government					
Inflation	-0.050	-0.042	-0.095	-0.093	0.093
	(0.122)	(0.094)	(0.046)**	(0.205)	(0.132)
Observations	59	77	82	80	81
R-squared	0.33	0.66	0.52	0.50	0.50

Notes: This table reports OLS estimations for the period 2001–2003. Dependent variables (all in logs) are prevalence of undernourishment (percent), agricultural productivity per worker (in constant 2000 US$), cereal yield (kg per hectare), number of tractors per agricultural worker, and fertilizer use (100g per hectare). The main independent variable is the log number of bank branches per 1,000 km² in 2003–2004. Other controls are private credit to GDP (percent), percentage government expenditures of GDP, inflation, food export - food import per person (kg). Heteroskedasticity-consistent standard errors are reported in parentheses.
*significant at 10 percent; **significant at 5 percent; ***significant at 1 percent.

both outreach and private credit are statistically significant in explaining cereal yields (regression 3). In terms of productivity-enhancing inputs, we find that outreach matters for tractors and fertilizers usage and that private credit is statistically significant for fertilizer usage (regressions 4 and 5). All in all, although mostly suggestive because we lack good (panel) data on access, these regression results point to the importance of outreach of a financial system for reducing undernourishment.

Comparing the Impact of Finance and GDP per Capita on Undernourishment

We have shown that greater financial sector development significantly reduces undernourishment, but is the impact relatively large? We can gauge the relevance of private credit by comparing the effect of private credit on undernourishment and GDP per capita on undernourishment. Similar to Besley and Burgess (2003), we ask what the reduction would be in undernourishment in seven years (by 2015, the timetable set for meeting the MDGs) caused by increases in private credit and GDP per capita, respectively, if both variables follow their historical average growth rates.

In our sample, the average country GDP per capita growth was 1.198 percent; the average country private credit growth was 1.059 percent. We also need the elasticities of undernourishment to GDP per capita and private credit. The elasticity of undernourishment to GDP per capita is –0.849 (based on a simple regression with only GDP per capita as an explanatory variable; not reported). The elasticity of undernourishment to private credit from a similar basic OLS regression is –0.188 after controlling for the initial levels of GDP per capita and poverty (see regression 2, table 7.3). Based on these elasticities, we can calculate that in seven years, using historical growth rates, increases in GDP per capita would reduce undernourishment for our sample of countries by about 6.83 percent. Historical growth rates for private credit to GDP growth would reduce undernourishment by about 1.38 percent.[9] Hence at almost one-quarter that of GDP per capita, the effect of private credit on undernourishment is substantial.

We can compare these numbers to the study of Burgess and Pande (2005). In 1977, a rule was imposed by the Indian Central Bank under which a commercial bank was to open four branches in areas without banking presence if it opened a branch in an area with bank presence. This so-called 1:4 license rule was subsequently abandoned in 1990.

This rule led between 1977 and 1990 to the opening of almost 30,000 bank branches in rural areas, moving from no formal commercial bank presence to about 100 branches per area, and the share of credit and savings in rural areas rising from 1.5 and 3 percent, respectively, to 15 percent each. The impact of increased access to finance on poverty and output in rural areas was large: Burgess and Pande (2005) estimate that a 1 percent increase in the number of rural banked locations reduced rural poverty by 0.36 percentage points and increased total output by 0.55 percent, due to growth in nonagricultural output. These numbers are thus of comparable magnitude to those we find on the effects of financial development on undernourishment of 0.285 percent (regression 1, table 7.3).

Effects of Private Credit Increases on Undernourishment via Several Channels

The previous section showed that the impact of private credit on undernourishment is relatively large. But via which channels does private credit deliver its largest impact on undernourishment? To explore this question, we calculate the impact of a 1 percent increase in private credit on undernourishment via the several channels we have identified, which allows us to assess to what extent each of these direct channels account for the effect on undernourishment, in relation to the overall effect (direct and indirect) we have found from private credit to undernourishment. We study three direct channels from private credit to undernourishment: (1) via productivity, (2) via productivity-enhancing inputs (fertilizer use and number of tractors per worker), and (3) via cereal yield. These more specific channels are depicted in panel B of figure 7.1.

Table 7.10 presents the findings. In calculating these magnitudes, we use two types of coefficient estimates from our analyses. The first (column 2) are the coefficients taken from OLS regressions, which contain as controls initial GDP per capita and poverty. The second (column 4) are the coefficients taken from IV regressions, which also contain all control variables. By construction, we set the total effect of the private credit to GDP on undernourishment at 100 percent (coefficient OLS: –0.188; coefficient IV: –1.567). And as our comparison, we use the effects of GDP per capita on undernourishment from an OLS regression, the coefficient of which is –0.849 (not reported).

First, we analyze the impact of a 1 percent increase in private credit via the productivity channel on undernourishment. The OLS impact is

Table 7.10
The impact of an increase in private credit on undernourishment via several channels

Effect of a 1 percent increase of private credit on undernourishment:	OLS impact (%)	% of direct impact	% of productivity impact	IV impact (%)	% of direct IV impact	% of IV productivity impact
1. Directly (benchmark case)	-0.188	100.00	NA	-1.567	100.00	NA
2. Via productivity	-0.054	28.94	100.00	-1.073	68.46	100.00
3. Via fertilizer and tractors via productivity	-0.052	27.77	95.96	NA	NA	NA
4. Via cereal yields	-0.037	19.60	70.58	-0.760	48.52	70.87

Notes: This table presents the predicted impact of a 1 percent increase in private credit to GDP on undernourishment via several channels (depicted in panel B of figure 7.1): (1) directly, (2) via productivity, (3) via fertilizer use and number of tractors per worker via productivity, and (4) via cereal yield. To calculate the effect of private credit to GDP on undernourishment via these channels, we use the coefficient estimates from our earlier analysis. The first column in the table reports the effect in percent on the prevalence of undernourishment. In doing so, we use the OLS coefficients that control for the initial levels of GDP per capita and poverty. The fourth column uses the coefficients of IV regressions that control for the initial levels of GDP per capita and poverty. The second (fifth) and third (sixth) columns show the percentages of the direct credit (IV) impact and of the (IV) productivity impact, respectively. The IV calculations for fertilizer and tractor use could not be calculated due to a lack of proper instruments.

–0.054 or 29 percent of the magnitude of the aggregate effect of private credit on undernourishment (the IV effect is –1.07 or 68 percent of the magnitude of the aggregate effect). This finding suggests that although the productivity aspect of financial development plays a large role, there are also other aspects, including the consumption smoothing and transaction facilitating roles of finance.

As a next step, we analyze the effect of a 1 percent increase in private credit via productivity on undernourishment. For this, we regress fertilizer use and the number of tractors per worker on agricultural productivity while controlling for private credit, initial GDP per capita, and poverty. Both fertilizer use and number of tractors per worker are significant at least at the 10 percent level with coefficients of 0.147 and 0.067, respectively (not reported). From this, we calculate the joint impact to be –0.052 or 28 percent of the aggregate impact of private credit on undernourishment and 96 percent of the impact of private credit on undernourishment via productivity. (Because we do not have instruments for the fertilizer and tractor variables, the IV impact estimates are unavailable.) This finding implies that the impact of private credit to GDP on productivity mainly flows through an increase in fertilizer use and number of tractors per worker.

Last, we investigated how much cereal yields contribute to lower undernourishment. We calculate the effect of a 1 percent increase in private credit via cereal yields on undernourishment to be –0.037 or 20 percent of the direct effect of private credit (the IV impact is –0.76 or 49 percent of the direct effect of private credit). This result suggests that increases in cereal yields play an important role in reducing undernourishment, as they represent 71 percent of the impact of productivity.

Conclusions

This chapter shows that financial sector development can play a significant role in reducing undernourishment. First, we find that private credit leads to lower undernourishment. Second, we find that greater agricultural productivity and cereal yields lead to a reduction in undernourishment. Third, in terms of channels, we show that private credit leads to higher agricultural productivity in general and higher livestock, crop, and cereal yields in particular. Fourth, to a large extent, the resultant increased productivity as a result of greater financial sector development can be largely explained by increases in fertilizer use per hectare and tractors per worker. Last, our results suggest that to reduce

undernourishment through these channels, it is not only important to have a well-developed financial system but also to ensure a good distribution of outlets. These results are robust to the inclusion of country controls, different samples, and instrumental variables, as well as to the use of panel estimations when possible.

Our findings are consistent with the hypothesis that access to credit allows agricultural workers to finance productivity-enhancing equipment such as fertilizers and tractors. Even when direct access to financial services is limited for undernourished households, they can still benefit from financial development because they interact with suppliers and others that have access to financial services. More generally, the undernourished can benefit from financial sector development because an increase in agricultural productivity leads to increases in food output. And in addition, there are general beneficial effects of financial development on income and inequality.

These effects are also quantitatively important. Assuming, for example, that private credit and GDP per capita continue to follow their historical country average growth rates, our results imply that by the year 2015 the impact of private credit on undernourishment is about almost one-quarter of the impact of GDP per capita on undernourishment. Using our results, we can also show through which channels an increase in private credit delivers its largest impact on undernourishment and compare the effect of private credit on undernourishment with that of GDP per capita. We report three relative magnitudes: first, productivity is an important channel and accounts for 29 percent to 68 percent of the impact of private credit on undernourishment. The remainder could be due to, for example, the consumption smoothing functions of finance. Second, we find that private credit provides important benefits through increases in productivity-enhancing equipment such as fertilizer and tractors. We find that 96 percent of the impact of private credit via productivity is accounted for by an increase in fertilizer use and the number of tractors per worker. Factors such as education could play a large role to explain the remainder of the impact of productivity. Third, 71 percent of the productivity impact can be accounted for by an increase in cereal yields. This finding suggests that an increase in cereals production is an important source of decreasing undernourishment.

Taken together, our findings imply that financial sector development can contribute substantially to attaining the most important MDG: alleviation of extreme poverty. Policies that could foster financial sector

development with wide access are multiple; they include ensuring a stable macroeconomic environment, enhancing financial sector regulation and enforcement, creating a proper credit information institutional infrastructure, and enforcing property rights. The importance of these policies for financial sector development has been well documented in other research, but our findings give more impetus to furthering financial sector development, especially when it gives access to financial services for a broad class of people. It also gives impetus to more research on finding ways in which financial sector development can specifically help with increased agricultural productivity, as that appears to be an important channel for reducing undernourishment.

Notes

We would like to thank participants in a World Bank seminar, Thorsten Beck (Tilburg University), Jasper Menken (FMO), and Konstantinos Tzioumis (LSE) for helpful comments, and Jonathan Morduch (NYU) for suggestions. The findings, interpretations, and conclusions expressed in this chapter are entirely those of the authors. They do not necessarily represent the views of the IMF or the World Bank, their executive directors, or the countries they represent.

1. During the Millennium Summit in September 2000, 189 nations unanimously adopted the Millennium Declaration. The declaration contains eight specific Millennium Development Goals (MDGs). The main aim of the declaration is to eradicate extreme poverty around the world by 2015. As such, the MDGs are the most ambitious and most broadly supported development goals the world has ever established. One of the most important is the Poverty-MDG, which consists of two parts: (1) reduce income poverty by cutting in half the fraction of the population who live on less than $1 a day and (2) reduce hunger by cutting in half the fraction of the population who suffer from undernourishment.

2. Of the 171 countries for which we have GDP per capita data, all but one of the 29 countries with GDP per capita higher than $16,000 have no undernourishment (the exception is United Arab Emirates, which has a 3 percent prevalence of undernourishment).

3. See further Barro 2000, Banerjee and Duflo 2003, and Forbes 2000 for the relationships between inequality and growth.

4. Analyzing the growth of the poverty gap and financial development in that period produces similar results, in which the poverty gap is the mean distance below the poverty line, expressed as a percentage of the poverty line and the mean is taken over the entire population, counting the nonpoor as having zero poverty gap. The measure reflects the depth of poverty as well as its incidence.

5. In the finance and development literature, stock market capitalization and turnover to GDP are also used as measures of financial development. We expect, however, a more distant relationship between these measures of financial development, and our variables of interest as agricultural activities are less likely to be financed directly by stock markets. Nevertheless, when we use stock markets indicators instead of private credit to GDP, we find qualitatively similar regression results. Another complementary set of financial

development measures would be access to financial services from microfinance institutions. Data on access to microfinance institutions, however, are available only for a more limited set of countries and are generally not available on a time-series basis.

6. Not including these initial values makes all regression results stronger in terms of the effects of financial development on undernourishment and poverty but raises more concerns about potential omitted variables that can drive both initial undernourishment and financial development as well as the subsequent reduction in undernourishment. We therefore generally include initial values.

7. We consider a fixed effects model to be more demanding, and Hausman tests confirm that a fixed effects model is the most suited, but we also used a random effects model, which provided similar (and often stronger) results.

8. We use branches per square kilometer, as that appears to be a better proxy for the (lack of) access to financial services than branches per population because the undernourished tend to live in rural and remote areas. Results are robust though to using the branches per population indicator.

9. $EXP(-0.849 \times 7 \times LN(1.01198)) - 1$ and $EXP(-0.188 \times 7 \times LN(1.010589)) - 1$, respectively.

References

Aghion, Philippe, and Patrick Bolton. 1997. A Theory of Trickle-Down Growth and Development. *Review of Economic Studies* 64 (2): 151–172.

Banerjee, Abhijit V., and Esther Duflo. 2003. Inequality and Growth: What Can the Data Say? *Journal of Economic Growth* 8 (3): 267–299.

Banerjee, Abhijit V., and Andrew F. Newman. 1993. Occupational Choice and the Process of Development. *Journal of Political Economy* 101 (2): 274–298.

Barro, Robert J. 2000. Inequality and Growth in a Panel of Countries. *Journal of Economic Growth* 5 (1): 5–32.

Beck, Thorsten, Aslı Demirgüç-Kunt, and Ross Levine. 2007. Finance, Inequality, and Poverty: Cross-Country Evidence. *Journal of Economic Growth* 12:27–49.

Beck, Thorsten, Aslı Demirgüç-Kunt, and Maria Soledad Martinez Peria. 2007. Reaching Out: Access to and Use of Banking Services across Countries. *Journal of Financial Economics* 85 (1): 234–266.

Besley, Timothy, and Robin Burgess. 2003. Halving Global Poverty. *Journal of Economic Perspectives* 17 (3): 3–22.

Burgess, Robin, and Rohini Pande. 2005. Do Rural Banks Matter? Evidence from the Indian Social Banking Experiment. *American Economic Review* 95 (3): 780–795.

Butler, Alexander, and Jess Cornaggia. 2011. Does Access to External Finance Improve Productivity? Evidence from a Natural Experiment. *Journal of Financial Economics* 99 (1): 184–203.

Claessens, Stijn, and Erik Feijen. 2007, Financial Sector Development and the Millennium Development Goals. World Bank Working Paper 89, Washington, DC.

Clarke, George, Lixin Colin Xu, and Heng-Fu Zou. 2006. Finance and Income Inequality: What Do the Data Tell Us? *Southern Economic Journal* 72 (3): 578–596.

Dollar, David, and Aart Kraay. 2002. Growth Is Good for the Poor. *Journal of Economic Growth* 7 (3): 195–225.

Food and Agriculture Organization. 2006. FAOSTAT. United Nations. http://www .fao.org/corp/statistics/en/.

Forbes, Kristin. 2000. A Reassessment of the Relationship between Inequality and Growth. *American Economic Review* 90 (4): 869–887.

Greenwood, Jeremy, and Boyan Jovanovic. 1990. Financial Development, Growth, and the Distribution of Income. *Journal of Political Economy* 98 (5): 1076–1107.

Honohan, Patrick. 2003. Financial Development, Growth and Poverty: How Close are the Links? World Bank Policy Research Working Paper 3203.

Honohan, Patrick. 2004. Financial Sector Policy and the Poor: Selected Findings and Issues. World Bank Working Paper 43.

Honohan, Patrick. 2005. Measuring Microfinance Access: Building on Existing Cross-Country Data. World Bank Policy Research Working Paper 3606.

Honohan, Patrick. 2006. Household Financial Assets in the Process of Development. World Bank Policy Research Working Paper 3965.

King, Robert G., and Ross Levine. 1993. Finance and Growth: Schumpeter Might Be Right. *Quarterly Journal of Economics* 108 (3): 717–737.

La Porta, R., F. Lopez-de-Silanes, and A. Shleifer. 1998. Law and Finance. *Journal of Political Economy* 106:1113–1155.

La Porta, R., F. Lopez-de-Silanes, A. Shleifer, and R. W. Vishny. 1997. Legal Determinants of External Finance. *Journal of Finance* 52:1131–1150.

Levine, Ross. 2005. Finance and Growth: Theory and Evidence. In *Handbook of Economic Growth*, ed. Philippe Aghion and Steven Durlauf, 865–933. Amsterdam: Elsevier.

Loayza, Norman, and Claudio Raddatz. 2007. The Composition of Growth Matters for Poverty Alleviation. World Bank Research Working Paper Series No. 4077. World Bank, Washington, DC.

Morduch, Jonathan, and Barbara Haley. 2002. Analysis of the Effects of Microfinance on Poverty Reduction. NYU Wagner Working Paper 1014 (paper prepared by RESULTS Canada for the Canadian International Development Agency).

World Bank. 1993. *World Development Report 1993: Investing in Health.* New York: Oxford University Press.

World Bank. 2006. *World Development Indicators.* Washington, DC: World Bank.

8 Entrepreneurial Finance in the Western Balkans: Characteristics of the Newly Self-Employed in Albania, Bosnia and Herzegovina, and Serbia

Aslı Demirgüç-Kunt, Leora F. Klapper, and Georgios A. Panos

After an extensive period of transition and social change, most households in the Western Balkans rely on the labor market for their livelihoods. However, even in countries where a number of important labor market reforms have been implemented in recent years, formal labor participation rates are low and unemployment rates are high. Furthermore, the instance of informal sector activity in the "gray markets" is quite common, particularly among women and youth. Given these facts, job creation and a viable entrepreneurial environment are among the primary policy objectives within this region.

One source of growth in the region is the operation of small and medium-sized firms that dominate the enterprise sector and have contributed to net job creation in several countries (World Bank 2005a). In the transition countries of Eastern Europe and Central Asia, the small and medium enterprise (SME) sector has been the largest creator of new jobs, and the vast majority of these new enterprises are small businesses (Ayyagari, Beck, and Demirgüç-Kunt 2007; Klapper, Sarria-Allende, and Sulla 2002; McMillan and Woodruff 2002). Although these new micro businesses represent a dynamic section of the enterprise sector—with some experiencing very rapid sales growth—there has also been concern about the ability of these firms to survive in the longer term and to secure necessary financing for growth and thus promote constant and continuous job creation (World Bank 2007). The dynamics of this group—including the decision to transition into entrepreneurship, the viability of entrepreneurial activity, and the conditions that promote the initiation and survival of such activity—are an important research and policy issue. However, little is known about these dynamics, particularly in the Western Balkans.

Using panel data from the Bosnia and Herzegovina LSMS (2001–2004), a recent paper examined the correlates of self-employment

transition and viability (Demirgüç-Kunt, Klapper, and Panos 2011): in particular, the role of access to formal and informal means of finance, remittances from abroad, and work experience in "gray markets." For instance, the study found that wealthier households are more likely to engage in viable self-employment and create employment, suggesting an important role for financing constraints. Specifically, although having an existing bank relationship is not significantly related to the entry decision, it is positively related to survival for new entrepreneurs and their employment creation. This chapter also found a nonlinear relationship between remittances and entry, in that individuals not receiving remittances are more likely to enter self-employment; however, conditional on receiving them, the likelihood of starting a business increases in the fraction of wealth received from domestic remittances. Finally, people working in the informal sector are more likely to become viable entrepreneurs, particularly those provided with loans from microcredit organizations. Our chapter extends this analysis for Bosnia and Herzegovina (BiH) to two neighboring countries: Albania and Serbia. The three neighboring countries share several common features in their recent history and transition to market economies.

The results highlight the role of financing constraints. Specifically, wealthier households are more likely to become entrepreneurs and survive the early period of adjustment. However, access to formal means of finance does not have a significant impact on the entry decision in the three countries, a finding highlighting that progress in other fronts is needed for finance to work in the Western Balkans (Johnson, McMillan, and Woodruff 2000, 2002). After the turbulent recent history, the business environment in the three countries is still considered risky, and all three countries rank particularly low in most indicators related to the ease of doing business, contract enforcement, and property rights. For example, property rights need to be established and well defined in order to provide an essential level of security in a stable macroeconomic environment and to allow lenders to take property as collateral (Doing Business 2009). Yet even after reforms are introduced, establishing appropriate norms and sets of incentives to nascent entrepreneurs usually takes a long time (La Porta et al. 2000).

Finally, individuals working in the informal sector—particularly those with access to microloans or informal finance—are more likely to transition to becoming entrepreneurs and more likely to survive in all three countries. The evidence favors a more competitive view of the

informal sector in the Western Balkans (see, e.g., Maloney 1999; Straub 2005), as opposed to a segmentation/necessity view, with important policy implications. A potential link between informal experience and later formal entry has important policy implications (Johnson et al. 1997; Kaufmann and Kaliberda 1996) and can be linked to a number of other arguments, such as: (a) Lazear's (2004) view of entrepreneurs as "jacks of all trades"; (b) the human capital acquisition and skills transferability literature (e.g., Guariglia and Kim 2006;), and (c) Baumol's (1990) idea of a fixed pool of entrepreneurial talent.

The Labor Market and Business Environment in Albania, Bosnia and Herzegovina, and Serbia

In a snapshot, Albania is a country covering 28,700 square kilometers in area, with a population of 3.6 million and a labor force of 1.1 million; BiH covers 51,200 square kilometers, with a population of 4.6 million and a labor force of 1.02 million; and Serbia is a country of 77,500 square kilometers, with a population of 10.15 million and a labor force of approximately 3 million. The three neighboring Western Balkan regions in this chapter share the main common feature of a difficult path of transition since the 1990s. These countries have experienced multiple political and economic shocks, along with the introduction of reforms to their labor markets and business environments.

Albania

Albania has undergone a major economic reform process in the last decade, following a turbulent period starting with the collapse of the communist regime in 1991 and followed by the financial crisis caused by the collapse of the large pyramid schemes in 1997 and the large influx of Kosovo refugees in 1999. However, by the end of the 1990s, Albania had roughly regained its 1990 GDP level, and a satisfactory macroeconomic performance continued after 2000 (World Bank 2004). Several structural reforms have also been carried out since the late 1990s and have involved banking, land reforms, and privatization. Several small and medium enterprises have been privatized, and significant progress has been made in the privatization of strategic sectors. Despite the persistent efforts, however, poverty in Albania has remained high and per capita income, at around US$1,230 in 2002, has remained one of the lowest among transition economies (World Bank 2003). Mostly due to the multiple shocks in Albania during the 1990s, per

capita income did not exhibit a significant increase, even though the economy recorded persistently high growth rates.

Thus Albania is lagging behind its Balkan neighbors in making the transition to a modern open-market economy. Among the negative structural characteristics of the economy are (World Bank 2006a) the following:

1. The country still largely depends on agriculture, which accounts for more than one-fifth of GDP and is held back because of lack of modern equipment, unclear property rights, and the prevalence of small, inefficient plots of land.

2. The energy shortages and antiquated and inadequate infrastructure contribute to Albania's poor business environment and make it difficult to attract and sustain foreign investment.

3. The labor market is hampered by a large informal sector due to the large agricultural sector and the impediments in the labor market. Albanians are known to engage in business activities, but most of these seem to take place under the veil of the gray economy.

4. There are huge worker outflows to neighboring countries (Zezza, Carletto, and Davis 2005; Carletto et al. 2006; Castaldo, Litchfield, and Reilly 2007; Azzari et al. 2008).

Bosnia and Herzegovina
Bosnia and Herzegovina was established after a tragic four-year war in the early 1990s in which 6 percent of a 4.4 million population were killed or missing and another 60 percent were forced to relocate. An estimated 1 million people have left the country (World Bank 2005a). The conflict also generated new categories of unemployed, and in 1996 the official self-reported unemployment rate was 80 percent, which decreased to 35 percent by 2001 (World Bank 2002). The macroeconomic instability caused by the war was characterized by a 75 percent drop in per capita GDP between 1990 and 1995, from its initial US$2,400 level to an estimated US$600. In the following years, high nominal rates of economic growth increased the figure to US$1,200 by the end of 2000 and to its prewar levels as of 2005 (World Development Indicators 2006).

In 1995, the Dayton Peace Accords decentralized BiH and recognized a second tier of government comprised of two entities: the Bosniak/Croat Federation of Bosnia and Herzegovina (FBiH) and the Bosnian Serb–led Republika Srpska (RS). Facing massive

unemployment and a deficient social welfare system, both entities have since taken major steps to transition to market economies, with the continuous support of the international community and the donors. Among them, several initiatives were taken to encourage small and medium enterprises by establishing microenterprise credit institutions,[1] and important reforms to the regulatory framework for the financial environment and the labor market were introduced in 2000–2001.

However, the labor market still faces major challenges such as high and rigid wages in the formal sector, a large and growing share of workers in the informal sector who are not covered by social insurance, and persistent unemployment. BiH has a large informal sector that could account for as much as 50 percent of the official GDP and half of the registered unemployed. Furthermore, the formal sector remains dominated by the public sector and implementation of privatization has been slow. Further regulatory impediments include high taxation of wages and profits and high employer contributions, difficult access and high cost of credit, and lack of systemic trust in the regulatory and financial environment (World Bank 2005b). Among the major challenges are that labor force participation rates are the lowest in the region and the incidence of poverty is also among the highest in the area, once again striking primarily the young and the unemployed.

Given these challenging circumstances, the promotion of microenterprises became a political priority as a gateway out of poverty and/or informality and as a path to sustainable growth. This priority is also based on the fact that BiH had a large entrepreneurial middle class in crafts and services before the war, which received favorable treatment by the centrally planned regime. However, the environment for SMEs is still challenging (World Bank 2002). In World Bank's Doing Business indicators (2005), BiH's "Ease of Doing Business" ranking is higher only than the ranking of Belarus and the Ukraine among Europe and Central Asia (ECA) transition countries. In a total of 154 countries, the country ranks particularly low with respect to ease of starting a business, dealing with licenses, registering property, and trading across borders.

Serbia

Like most former centrally planned economies, Serbia is also experiencing a difficult transition path to a market-based model. After a remarkably turbulent recent history of conflict and political change, Serbia is

trying to catch up with the more successful reformers in ECA. The three most important challenges the country faces are (a) the lack of employment growth; (b) labor market exclusion; and (c) the ineffective social protection for workers (World Bank 2006b). The country introduced major reforms in the labor and tax law, aiming toward a market-oriented system. The 2001 labor law provided greater flexibility in hiring and firing, labor deployment, and collective bargaining, changes necessary during transition. The 2001 tax law was a regressive system that entailed costs for low-wage labor and raised concerns with respect to the distribution of wealth. Since the restructuring and privatization reforms, job losses have been large and job creation in the private sector has been slow despite fairly strong economic growth in recent years.

Thus, despite the economic growth observed after 2000, employment remains low and long-term unemployment is high. Participation rates in the formal labor market are low and a substantial proportion are working in the informal sector. Similar to that of its neighbors, the sizeable informal sector accounts for an important share of employment. The low-educated and the young are overrepresented in the "gray market," the incidence of low pay and poverty among them is high, and the mobility prospects into formal-sector jobs appear low. The result is a weak labor market performance, especially when judged by the standards of the more successful transition countries in East Central Europe (ECE) (e.g., the Czech Republic, Slovenia, and Romania). This weakness appears to disproportionately affect young people who have unemployment rates that are among the highest in Europe. Employment outcomes are also considerably worse for women than for men. Furthermore, almost half of the jobs are still outside the private sector. The remainder is largely in the state sector and in socially owned enterprises (Ersado 2006).

The Business Environments in Albania, Bosnia and Herzegovina, and Serbia Compared

The World Bank's Entrepreneurship and Doing Business databases provide some clear indicators of the particular difficulties of the business environment in the three Western Balkan neighbors. Figure 8.1 presents the rankings of sixteen ECE countries in terms of overall business density and new entry density from the 2008 World Bank Group Entrepreneurship Survey[2]. The figures are averages for the years 2002–2004 (for consistency with the LSMS databases used in the next section).

New entry density
(per 1,000 working age population)

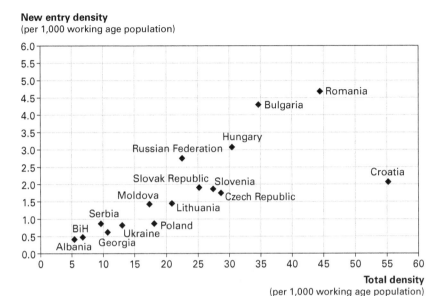

Figure 8.1
Overall business and new entry density in ECE. *Source:* World Bank Group 2008 Entrepreneurship Database (2002–2004 averages); http://go.worldbank.org/C8Q8EGTTH0.

New business entry density is shown on the vertical axis and overall business density is shown on the horizontal. Both figures are numbers per 1,000 of working age population.

Albania, BiH, and Serbia obtain the three lowest rankings when it comes to total business density among the sixteen countries examined. Albania has figures of 5.439 businesses and 0.421 new businesses per 1,000 working-age individuals. The respective figures in BiH are 6.772 total businesses and 0.486 new businesses per 1,000 working-age individuals. Serbia does only slightly better when it comes to new entry, with 9.652 total businesses and 0.874 new businesses per 1,000 working-age individuals. Its ranking is the third lowest for total business density, after Albania and BiH, and the sixth lowest when it comes to new entry density. BiH and Albania also obtain the lowest ranking in the new entry density figures. Thus, the three counties have the lowest ranking in terms of total business density in ECE and also rank particularly low with respect to new entry density. Albania and BiH have the two lowest rankings for the years 2002–2004, and Serbia has the sixth lowest ranking in terms of new entry density, ranking higher than Georgia

and only marginally higher than Ukraine and Poland. The rankings are indicative of a regional effect that has not changed in later years in the data.

This low performance can be complemented by a somehow predictable picture in the World Bank's Doing Business indicators.[3] The ranking for the three neighbors in the year 2009 is shown in figure 8.2. In a total of 183 countries, all three countries rank below the median with respect to ease of doing business, dealing with licenses, employing workers, paying taxes, and enforcing contracts. Bosnia and Herzegovina appears to have a lower ranking in most fronts. However, the three countries perform remarkably better with respect to the ease of getting credit and somewhat better when it comes to protecting investors. These features are both extremely important to the health of the

Figure 8.2
Ease of doing business ranking in Albania, Bosnia and Herzegovina, and Serbia. *Source:* World Bank Group Doing Business Indicators (2009; total of 183 countries); http:// www.doingbusiness.org/.

business environment. However, similar pictures can be obtained for the rankings in previous years.

Given the poor performance of the three neighboring countries in the business environment indicators, it is of great further interest to examine the correlates of new business entry at a microeconomic level. The next sections utilize the World Bank LSMS in an effort to shed some more light on the origins and characteristics of new self-employment entries in the three countries.

The Data: World Bank Living Standards Measurement Surveys

We employ household panel data for Albania, BiH, and Serbia. The three data sources are all part of the World Bank Living Standards Measurement Survey (LSMS) Programme, a multiyear collaborative project among the World Bank, other international institutions and several national statistical agencies aiming to strengthen the government capacity to collect, analyze, and disseminate statistical data for poverty monitoring and policy evaluation.[4] The sample period examined is similar for the three countries, and the coverage in terms of the years is subject to data availability. Thus, the periods covered are Albania (2002–2004), BiH (2001–2004), and Serbia (2002–2003). The data for BiH is also representative at the entity level. The data for Serbia does not include Montenegro, which was still part of the union at the time, and also excludes Kosovo. The samples are representative at the country level and for urban, rural, and mixed municipalities. This unique collection of household panel surveys provides rich demographic and socioeconomic information and an important insight into labor market dynamics in the three countries.

We determine the labor force population aged 16–65 at the time of the interview and classify them into mutually exclusive groups according to their employment status every year. We further select the balanced panels for the three countries to obtain an insight into the dynamics in the labor market by individuals who were continuously present in the surveys. This exercise covers 3,550 individuals observed over three years in Albania (10,650 observations), 4,772 individuals observed for four years in BiH (19,088 observations), and 3,708 individuals observed for two years in Serbia (7,146 observations).

Following the design of the questionnaire, we define self-employed individuals as individuals describing their status as owner/co-owner of: an enterprise/small business that employs workers ("employer") or

an enterprise/small business that does not employ workers ("own account"). We identify "formal" self-employment as including individuals who fall into the first two categories and also declare work-related characteristics such as earnings and hours in self-employment and whose tax, pension, and/or health contributions are paid. If these criteria are not satisfied, the individual is classified as informally self-employed.

Standard International Labour Organization (ILO) definitions classify a person as employed if he or she is presently working or on leave from a job. According to the ILO classification, the informal economy consists of units engaged in the production of goods or services to generate income and employment for themselves. These units typically operate at a low level of organization with little or no division between labor and capital as factors of production and on a small scale. Labor relations—where they exist—are based mostly on casual employment, kinship, or personal and social relations rather than contractual arrangements with formal guarantees. According to the ILO, the informal sector can be regarded as a group of operational units that form part of the household sector as household enterprises or unincorporated enterprises owned by households. In addition, the economic literature commonly uses other operational definitions of the informal sector. One of the widely used definitions is based on the status of a household enterprise, which—being informal—is often not registered with local authorities and as such remains outside the official institutional framework.

For the purposes of this chapter, we distinguish between the formal and the informal sector workers among the group of employed people. We define employees in formal sector paid employment as individuals working in public enterprises and international organizations as well as those in the private sector whose pension and health insurance contributions were paid. Informal sector employment includes three groups: (a) unpaid supporting family members and workers engaged in other activities, such as the sale of agricultural products; (b) workers not employed by public enterprises (or state sector) for which pension and/or health contributions are not paid; (c) workers declaring any other out-of-employment activity but reporting earnings or hours of work. This definition meets previous official classification criteria and informal sector estimates (e.g., World Bank 2002). By default, the unemployed are those who do not have a job at present, are actively searching for employment, and are able to take a job if one were offered to

them. Finally, farmers with their own farm and workers in agriculture are classified as a distinct group. All others of working age are classified as inactive.

We use the classification exercise described previously to calculate the composition of the labor force for the population of the three balanced LSMS panels in Albania, BiH, and Serbia (figure 8.3). Unemployment/inactivity describes a quarter of the working-age population with replies in all waves of the LSMS data in Albania and Serbia; the figure is close to 40 percent in BiH. The former two countries also have a larger agricultural sector. The figure is 33.2 percent in Albania and 17.3 percent in Serbia. The figure for individuals declaring occupations in agricultural activities is much smaller for BiH at 5.6 percent.

Agriculture dominates the labor market in Albania; formal employment is the second-largest activity, with a third of the employed population (17% of the workforce in the balanced panel) working as employees in the public and private sector. One-fifth of the employed population (13% of the workforce) engages in informal employment activity, with one-third of that group (4.9%) conducting informal self-employment activity and two-thirds (8.1%) being informal employees or supporting a household business. Formal self-employment describes 6.8 percent of the working-age population.

Moreover, 10.5 percent of individuals in the sample declare their status as unemployed and 14.3 percent declare their status as be inactive. These figures are close to the official statistics. Finally, an additional 5.2 percent of the population classify themselves as employed abroad. Adding that figure to the numbers of individuals in the informal sector, the total figure for individuals with undetermined informal activity comes close to 20 percent of the population, a size that is similar to the informal sector in BiH.

However, the situation differs somewhat in BiH, due mostly to the structural characteristics of the country. The postwar syndromes are quite evident in the country, as a large number of people were forced to relocate within the region. Furthermore, the instance of disability and the number of people dependent on social assistance increased substantially. Thus, both figures for unemployment and inactivity are large—close to 20 percent each—with a total of 41.2 percent of the sample being out of employment. This figure is among the highest in Europe and is well behind the EU Lisbon Treaty employment standards of 70 percent to be achieved by the year 2010. Agricultural activity

Albania
World Bank LSMS (2002–2004)

Sample averages for 2002–2004
(10,650 observations;
3,550 individuals)

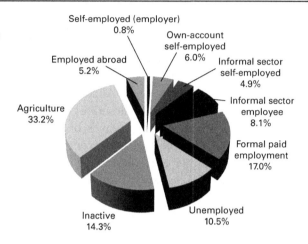

Bosnia and Herzegovina
World Bank LSMS (2001–2004)

Sample averages for 2001–2004
(19,088 observations;
4,772 individuals)

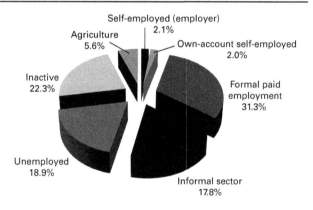

Serbia
World Bank LSMS (2002–2003)

Sample averages for 2002–2003
(7,146 observations;
3,708 individuals)

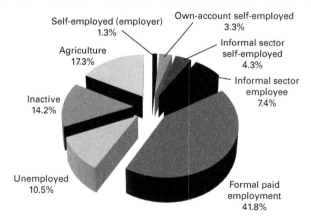

Figure 8.3
Labor force composition in Albania, Bosnia and Herzegovina, and Serbia. *Notes:* The distinction between formally and informally self-employed in Albania can be made based on the tax records of businesses in Wave 1. This distinction cannot be made in Bosnia, but the informal sector category apparently contains both self-employed and employees.

appears quite limited (5.6%), also due to geographical reasons. These two facts might help explain the large role of informality, which appears to include close to a third of the employed population (17.8% of the workforce). This figure contains both informally self-employed and employees; in contrast to the other two countries, the data for BiH does not allow a distinction between the two types of activity. One-half of the employed population (31.3% of the workforce) engages in formal paid employment activity.

Finally, the figure for formal self-employment is quite small (4.1% in total in the balanced panel). An interesting statistic is that half of the formally self-employed classify themselves as employers. This number can be attributed to either the incentives provided by funding projects for the creation of employment or the history of the region. Before the war, BiH had a large entrepreneurial middle class. Compared to most centrally planned economies in Eastern Europe, the regime in the former Yugoslavia tended toward a somewhat different treatment of small businesses, mostly those related to crafts and services. These were encouraged and provided with financing, mostly from local government-owned banks. Their interests were further supported through the formation of local and politically influential crafts unions. Furthermore, BiH was a location where the former regime placed heavy manufacturing industries, on which socialist regimes placed a huge emphasis.

A similar situation with respect to self-employment arises in Serbia, where nearly 5 percent of the balanced sample declares their status as self-employed and paying taxes and contributions. Less than a third of these are employing others in their business; 71 percent—3.3% of the sample—are by their own account self-employed. An additional 4.3 percent appear to be informally self-employed. Previous self-employment estimates give a figure of 7.5 percent self-employed in Serbia (World Bank 2006b) but without distinguishing between formality and informality. The figure is clearly quite low, given the self-employment rates of about 14 percent in the OECD and EU-15, and over 10 percent in other Eastern European economies, such as Slovenia, Hungary, Poland, and the Czech Republic. The figure for the size of

the informal sector in Serbia is close to 12 percent using the definition adopted for this report, that is, a bit less than one-fifth of the employed population. The largest fraction of individuals declare their status in formal paid employment, that is, 41.8 percent of the individuals in the balanced sample. Finally, an additional 17.3 percent of the sample are performing agricultural activities.

The labor force classification used in this report allows us to directly observe transitions to self-employment from year to year. We are able to identify 156 new entries in the three years of the panel for Albania, 222 entries into self-employment status during the course of the four years in the BiH panel, and 88 new entries in the two years of the Serbian panel (table 8.1). The figures for the subsamples of household heads in the three countries are 74, 110, and 38, respectively.[5] Of further interest are the outcomes of the new entries, as business startups bear the higher risk of failure during their first years of operation. Indeed, nearly 40 percent (40 out of 98 new entries of the year 2003) of the newly self-employed in Albania and close to 50 percent in BiH (87 out of 178 new entries in the years 2002–2003) do not make it through their first year in business. This pattern is observed in samples of both individuals and household heads.

These high failure rates could indicate that self-employment entry in BiH is likely to be the outcome of necessity, rather than of opportunity and motivation. Although this interpretation cannot be rejected a priori, it is questionable why an individual would undergo the pains of starting a formal business for a short period in countries where this is not a particularly easy process and informal operation of businesses is very common. Moreover, our data suggests that there are large welfare gains for individuals operating in formal self-employment that do not indicate necessity. Table 8.2 presents some welfare indicators by labor market status for individuals in the sample. The statistics are averages for the years in each sample. It is evident that self-employed individuals rank higher with respect to most welfare indicators. This is the case for both the self-employed who create employment for others and the own-account self-employed, with the former group clearly ranking the highest in all indicators. The self-employed enjoy higher wages and household income/consumption. Moreover, they rank highly in the income, housing, and life satisfaction responses. What is evident from this simple inspection of the data is that unemployed and individuals in the informal sector are the two poorest groups that are also the least satisfied with more aspects of life. Thus, the transition to self-employment is related to higher standards of

Table 8.1
New self-employment entry

	Albania		Bosnia and Herzegovina		Serbia	
	Individuals	HH heads	Individuals	HH heads	Individuals	HH heads
New entry						
2001	–	–	–	–	–	–
2002	–	–	107	49	–	–
2003	98	49	71	37	88	38
2004	58	25	44	24	–	–
Total	156	74	222	110	88	38
Employment generation						
Employers	7	4	83	34	23	15
Own account	149	70	139	76	65	23
Survival in:	2003	2002–2003	–		–	–
Survivors	58	29	91	41	–	–
Failed	40	20	87	45	–	–

Source: World Bank Living Standards Measurement Surveys (LSMS) 2001–2004.
Notes: Figures are for individuals who were not self-employed in the beginning of the panels.

Table 8.2
Labor market status and individual welfare

	Equiv. household consumption decile			Life satisfaction (1–7)		Economic status assessment (1–10)	HH income satisfaction (1–7)	Financial status (1–4)	
	Albania	BiH	Serbia	Albania	BiH	Albania	BiH	Albania	Serbia
Self-employed									
Employer	8.71	7.43	8.27	5.41	5.17	6.71	4.60	2.93	2.97
Own account	7.10	6.96	6.28	4.51	4.64	5.35	3.92	2.25	2.55
Formal paid employment	6.41	6.33	5.80	4.28	4.81	4.16	3.76	1.95	2.42
Informal sector									
Self-employed	6.09	5.49	5.47	3.58	4.28	4.00	3.17	1.77	2.37
Employee	5.23	4.60	5.28	3.49	4.14	3.81	2.62	1.73	2.30
Unemployed	4.27	5.50	4.46	3.38	4.55	3.02	3.25	1.50	1.96
Inactive	5.11	5.84	4.53	3.47	4.47	3.55	3.40	1.70	2.24
Agriculture	4.31	–	4.74	3.53	–	3.31	–	1.77	2.36
Employed abroad	4.55	–	–	3.81	–	3.28	–	1.80	–

Source: World Bank Living Standards Measurement Surveys (LSMS).

living, and formal entry does not appear to be of the necessity type, at least in terms of welfare.

In the following sections of this chapter, we examine the correlates of new self-employment entry in the three countries in more detail. Emphasis is placed on the role of labor market experience and issues of access to finance and financing constraints.

Background and Empirical Strategy

The importance of legitimate business operation for employment creation and growth has been emphasized in the recent literature, particularly for economies in transition. Conceptually, the self-employed can be considered as the smallest but initially the most vital unit of entrepreneurial activity. Furthermore, in the previous section it was shown that the self-employed are less likely to experience poverty and relative deprivation. It was further shown that all three countries experience low rates of formal self-employment, compared to other ECA and OECD countries. It is thus of interest to examine the characteristics of individuals who decide to make the transition to formal self-employment in this challenging environment. Moreover, the interaction of this decision with financial constraints, access to finance, and labor market experience will be explored.

In the first stage of our analysis, we compare differences in human, social, and financial capital between groups of new entrepreneurs and individuals who did not become self-employed. Entrepreneurship has been linked to both economic and social attributes. The literature has distinguished between the role of institutions, socioeconomic factors, individual characteristics, and psychological factors in identifying the correlates of the decision to start an entrepreneurial activity (Djankov et al. 2005; Djankov et al. 2006a, 2006b). Other studies emphasize the importance of labor market characteristics (Earle and Sakova 2000; Dutz et al. 2001), as well as financial wealth and constraints (Paulson and Townsend 2004, 2005; Paulson, Townsend, and Karaivanov 2006). Moreover, we examine the differences between those new entrants who also create employment for others and those who operate as own-account self-employed. Finally, we investigate the correlates of survival in self-employment for more than one year, comparing individuals who made it through their first year as small business operators and individuals who exited before their second year in business.

Our empirical strategy in the regressions examines the relationship between new entry into self-employment in later years of each panel, by individuals not self-employed in the first year, and a set of characteristics of interest. The dependent variable (*Newly Self-Employed*) takes the value 1 if the individual started his or her own business and 0 if not. Our preferred model to examine the relationship between entry and individual and household characteristics is the probit model. The explanatory variables include a vector of the socioeconomic characteristics such as gender; urban or rural region of residence; a second-order polynomial in age; marital status; the logarithm of the number of children, education, and health. Moreover, we distinguish between entities in BiH (Federation of BiH vs. Republica Srpska). Finally, in order to control for within-family effects in self-employment transitions, we examine the impact of the presence of another self-employed member in the family.

In separate specifications, we examine the impact of household financial wealth, the relationship with financial institutions, as well as the role of labor market experience and origins. The wealth proxy we use is the logarithm of equivalized per capita household consumption, which is calculated by adjusting household consumption to the number of equivalent adults and deflated using the regional poverty line.[6] In transition countries, income underreporting and nonreporting biases the calculations based on income. We therefore utilize household consumption in the beginning of the panel as an indicator of overall financial wealth. The use of other wealth proxies, such as property ownership or the ability to "make ends meet," does not change our main results.

In order to examine the labor origins of the new business entries, we create a set of variables capturing labor market status in the first year of each panel. *Formal Sector Employment* takes the value 1 if the individual was employed in the formal sector and 0 if not. *Informal Sector* captures individuals operating in the informal sector, and *Unemployed/ Inactive* captures the individuals who were either unemployed or inactive. *Agriculture* and *Employed Abroad* (for Albania only) are the last two categories of labor market origins. These variables and their interactions with other individual and household characteristics are likely to shed some light on the "push" and "pull" aspects of new business entry in the three countries. Moreover, as the incidence of wage arrears is common in transition economies in ECE, we also distinguish between employees on the formal sector who received delayed payments or lower pay than usual and those who did not. In many transition econo-

mies, people are often paid very irregularly, with several months of wage arrears being common (Earle and Sabirianova 2002; Kim 2005; Boyarchuk, Maliar, and Maliar 2005) and average accrued and paid wages diverging significantly. Our data suggests that 9.2 percent of the population in Albania, 12.3 percent in BiH, and 8.9 percent in Serbia receives delayed or unusual payments. These figures correspond to almost half the individuals in formal paid employment in Albania, a third in BiH, and less than a quarter in Serbia (see table 8.3). Indeed, problematic payment might alter the set of incentives for paid employees in the formal sector, and their transition to self-employment might be motivated more by necessity rather than by any other reason.

Our last set of characteristics of interest is related to access to finance, either formal or informal. Departing from Paulson and Townsend (2004) and Demirgüç-Kunt, Klapper, and Panos (2011), we utilize household affiliation with particular financial institutions and sources of finance in the past and examine their impact on the likelihood of starting a new business. We include a dummy *Micro Loan* variable equal to 1 if the household received a loan from a microcredit institution (such as a credit union, cooperative, or nongovernmental organization [NGO]) in the first year of each panel. We also identify households that received a loan from a bank or government agency, *Bank Loan*, and households that received a loan from a family member, friend, or other individual early in each panel, *Informal Loan*. The figures for bank loans are 0.9 percent in Albania, 11.8 percent in BiH, and 5.6 percent in Serbia. In addition, 0.3 percent of the population received a loan from a microcredit institution in Albania and 2.6 percent in BiH. Finally, the figures for informal loans are 13 percent in Albania, 17.2 percent in BiH, and 4.5 percent in Serbia.

We further examine the relationship between remittances and the switch to self-employment with two variables that make an important distinction between international and domestic remittances: *Domestic Remittances*, which equals 1 if the individual belongs to a household that received any money, gifts, or services from friends or family working in the same country; and *Remittances from Abroad*, which equals 1 if the household receives money, gifts, or services from friends or family working abroad. Most of the literature considers remittances from abroad as the variable of primary interest, though we are also interested in remittances from within each country because following in the turbulent recent years in the Balkans, the numbers of both individuals who immigrated abroad and those who were either displaced or chose to migrate within the country were very large. Albania and BiH in particular are

Table 8.3
Sample averages and mean differences

	Albania			Bosnia and Herzegovina			Serbia		
	Pooled (3,293)	Entry (156)	No entry (3,137)	Pooled (4,538)	Entry (222)	No entry (4,316)	Pooled (3,708)	Entry (88)	No entry (3,620)
Individual and household characteristics									
Male	47.6%	69.2%***	46.5%	51.5%	68.0%***	50.7%	51.5%	64.8%**	51.1%
Age	36.4	38.6**	36.3	35.9	37.3*	35.8	40.67	37.4	40.7***
Married/cohabiting	76.6%	84.6%**	76.2%	62.1%	74.8%***	61.5%	74.9%	67.1%	75.1%*
Number of children	1.12	1.24	1.11	1.39	1.47	1.38	1.34	1.24	1.34
Federation of BiH	–	–	–	54.7%	49.6%	54.9%	–	–	–
Urban region	43.0%	65.4%***	41.9%	42.8%	50.0%**	42.5%	56.6%	68.2%**	56.3%
Low education	63.7%	38.5%	65.0%***	34.1%	22.1%	34.7%***	32.7%	21.6%	33.0%**
Disabled/chronic ill.	6.4%	1.9%	6.6%**	5.2%	2.7%	5.3%*	7.0%	9.1%	7.0%
Another S.E. family member	3.0%	12.2%***	2.5%	6.5%	16.7%***	6.0%	4.6%	8.0%	4.5%
Optimism	29.2%	38.5%***	28.7%	26.6%	32.4%**	26.3%	–	–	–
No social capital	5.4%	3.2%	5.6%	11.0%	4.5%	11.3%***	–	–	–
Wealth and financial characteristics									
Equivalized household Consumption	9,152	11,101***	9,055	2,713	3,318***	2,681	79,294	91,912**	78,986
Property owner	93.2%	91.0%	93.3%	69.6%	70.7%	69.6%	89.4%	94.3%	89.3%
Informal loan	13.0%	7.7%	13.2%**	17.2%	15.3%	17.3%	4.5%	1.1%	4.5%
Microloan	0.3%	1.3%**	0.2%	2.6%	2.7%	2.6%	–	–	–
Bank loan	0.9%	1.3%	0.9%	11.8%	12.6%	11.7%	5.6%	4.6%	5.6%

Table 8.3
(continued)

	Albania			Bosnia and Herzegovina			Serbia		
Domestic remittances	11.8%	5.1%	12.1%***	8.2%	5.4%	8.3%	6.9%	4.6%	6.9%
Remittances from abroad	32.4%	32.7%	32.4%	11.9%	7.2%	12.1%**	6.5%	5.7%	6.5%
Amount of foreign remittances‡	272,348	81,725	281,925**	978	491	992*	28,939	22,000	29,086*
Foreign remit./HH consumption‡	32.55	8.14	33.78**	0.443	0.156	0.452*	0.369	0.315	0.370
NGO/Charity/Grant money	6.1%	4.5%	6.2%	1.8%	2.7%	1.8%	3.0%	2.3%	3.0%
Humanitarian help/Social institutions	23.6%	16.0%	23.9%**	26.2%	20.7%	26.5%*	22.0%	21.6%	22.0%
Labor market characteristics									
Formal sector employee	20.3%	26.3%*	20.0%	35.9%	40.1%	35.7%	42.9%	35.2%	43.1%
... not in wage arrears	11.1%	16.7%**	10.8%	23.6%	30.3%**	23.3%	34.0%	30.7%	34.1%
Informal sector	13.6%	38.5%***	12.4%	14.7%	32.0%***	13.8%	11.7%	40.9%***	11.0%
Unemployed/inactive	24.7%	16.7%	25.1%**	43.6%	21.6%	44.7%***	23.8%	15.9%	24.0%*
Agriculture	36.4%	16.0%	37.5%***	5.8%	6.3%	5.8%	16.8%	8.0%	17.0%**
Employed abroad	5.0%	2.6%	5.1%	–	–	–	–	–	–

Notes: The national currencies at the time of the survey were as follows:

Albania: *Albanian Lek.* The exchange rate in November 2001 was 140.16 Leke per US$1.

Bosnia and Herzegovina: *Konvertibilna Marka* (convertible mark or BAM), introduced in 1998, initially pegged to the German Deutschmark and later to the euro. In 2002, the currency was put on a fixed exchange rate of 1 BAM to €0.511292 (€1 = 1.95583 BAM). The relationship to the dollar in 2001 was 2.1857 BAM per US$1; in 2002–2003, 1.7329 BAM per US$1.

Serbia: *New Yugoslav Dinar.* The exchange rate in January 2002 was 65 new Yugoslav dinars per US$1.

*p< 0.10; **p < 0.05; ***p < 0.01.

‡These two figures for the amount of remittances are among remittance receivers only.

characterized by very large waves of international migration that became a major source of remittances from abroad entering those countries. The impact of remittances from abroad on economic activity and consumption is large (Castaldo and Reilly 2007), but when it comes to the labor market and the motivation to participate and be productive, the effect of remittance receivership does not go without debate.

Our estimates indicate that 11.8 percent of the individuals in the sample for Albania, 8.2 percent in BiH, and 6.9 percent in Serbia receive some form of remittance domestically. Furthermore, the volume of remittances received in Albania amounts to thirty-two times the consumption per capita. In separate specifications, we incorporate variables for the amount of remittances received as a fraction of household consumption, to allow for potential nonlinearity in the relationship between remittance receivership and business entry.

We next identify individuals who receive money from humanitarian and religious institutions that do not need repayment (*Institutional Remittances*). These transactions are of specific interest because they include grants from foreign NGOs and citizen associations provided specifically to promote self-employment and entrepreneurship (Lyman 2005). Finally, we include a dummy variable, set equal to 1 if a member of the individual's household received financial assistance, such as payments from an old age or war veteran's pension program or the like (*Social Remittances*).

The second stage of our analysis examines the employment creation by the newly self-employed and then the correlates of their short-term survival in the first year of business. It is well known that new entrepreneurs bear the highest risk of failure during their first few years of activity. Table 8.1 has already indicated that some 40 percent of individuals becoming self-employed in Albania, and 50 percent of those in BiH quit their new entrepreneurial venture during their first year of activity.[7] We define two variables: *Employment Generation*, which takes the value 1 if the individual is newly self-employed and employs other individuals in his or her business, the value 2 if the individual is own-account self-employed, and the value 3 if the individual did not enter self-employment in 2002–2004. In similar spirit, we define *Business Survival* as a variable that takes the value 1 if the individual remained in business one year upon entry, the value 2 if the individual failed in business during the first year, and the value 3 if the individual did not enter self-employment. We model employment creation and business survival in the multinomial probit framework with individuals not

self-employed as the comparison group. The set of explanatory variables is the same as in the previous section. Although firm- and sector-specific determinants are also of importance, the nature of the database enables only individual-specific analysis. Primary interest in the survival equation is given to the relationship with human capital, labor market origins and access to finance (Holtz-Eakin, Joulfaian, and Rosen 1994; Cooper, Gimeno-Gascon, and Woo 1994; Cressy 1996; Astebro and Bernhardt 2003).

The Transition to Self-Employment

Table 8.3 introduces the variables that will be used in the analysis along with summary statistics and mean differences between the newly self-employed and those who did not become self-employed. With respect to the socioeconomic profile of the newly self-employed, in all three countries the newly self-employed is more likely to be a male, urban region resident with at least some level of secondary education and another self-employed individual in the family. In all three countries, 65–70 percent of the transitions are made by males. Although attitude toward risk is an important factor in determining such decisions, this large difference between the sexes also shows that women have fewer chances in the labor market. The demographic profile of the newly self-employed is more similar between Albania and BiH. In contrast, the newly self-employed in Serbia tend to be younger and less likely to be married compared to their non-self-employed counterparts. Theory on the behavioral patterns of entrepreneurs stresses that the psychological profile and sociological background of individuals are important factors in the decision to initiate one's own business—the impact of social capital and optimism/overconfidence in particular (Puri and Robinson 2007). The data allows the construction of two proxies for optimism and social capital considerations.[8] We find that the newly self-employed in Albania and BiH are more likely to be optimistic about the future and less likely to lack in terms of support from social capital.

An important branch of the literature has examined the links between wealth and entrepreneurship. The existence of borrowing constraints implies that own wealth and personal assets will be positively related to the propensity of individuals to engage in entrepreneurial activities (Evans and Jovanovic 1989; Paulson and Townsend 2004). The summary statistics in table 8.3 suggest that new entrants into self-employment are less likely to be financially constrained in all three countries in

terms of wealth prior to entry. Although there is significant evidence on the positive impact of wealth on entrepreneurial activity, empirical evidence on the role of financial institutions is relatively scarce. We utilize household affiliation with particular financial institutions and sources of finance in the past and examine their relationship with the likelihood of starting a new business. The role of financial institutions is of particular interest in transition economies where the financial sector has undergone major reforms.

The statistics in table 8.3 suggest that the newly self-employed in Albania are less likely to have received informal finance, either in the form of a loan or as domestic remittances that they do not have to repay. They are also more likely to have obtained a loan from a microcredit institution, although the fractions of the population that have obtained such a loan are small: 1.3 percent of the newly self-employed in Albania and 0.2 percent of their comparison group. In BiH, the newly self-employed are less likely to have received remittances from abroad and some type of social assistance; in Serbia, there are no significant differences in the means of the financial institution variables. Moreover, the amount of remittances received in the past, both in currency units and as a fraction of household consumption, is smaller for the newly self-employed compared to nonentrants.

Past employment experience has been shown to exert significant effects on current employment status. An important issue is related to informal sector experience and its relationship to entry into formal self-employment. The relationship between the two is debatable, and the arguments are discussed in detail in Demirgüç-Kunt, Klapper, and Panos 2011. In brief, this relationship could be expected to be either negative or positive, depending on whether informal markets should be viewed as the disadvantaged segment of a dual labor market that provides a subsistence shelter for unmatched employees (Harris and Todaro 1970) or a competitive "gray economy" in which heterogeneous entrepreneurs and workers weigh formal versus informal operation based on the cost of formal entry and the relative efficiency of formal and informal credit mechanisms and their related institutional arrangements (Maloney 1999; Straub 2005; inter alia). In economies under transition, the regulatory environment might not foster formal entrepreneurship and entrepreneurial individuals might choose to operate in the informal sector or shadow economy. Indeed, Djankov and Murrell (2002) document the existence of significant entry costs into formality in the form of registration and license fees. The summary statistics in table 8.3 indicate that individuals with experience in the

informal sector are more likely to enter formal self-employment in all three countries and a third of the new entries are individuals with prior experience in "gray markets." In all three countries, the newly self-employed are less likely to come from unemployment inactivity.

The Correlates of Self-Employment Entry

We model the decision to become self-employed in the probit framework, excluding individuals already self-employed in the beginning of each panel. The list of explanatory variables involves the standard correlates of self-employment activity in the literature. Moreover, in separate specifications we examine the impact of household financial wealth and the relationship with financial institutions, as well as the role of labor market experience and origins. Interaction effects between these variables are also examined.

Table 8.4 presents our two baseline specifications for self-employment entry in Albania, BiH, and Serbia separately. *Specification 1* incorporates the standard socioeconomic variables; *specification 2* includes the wealth proxy. Marginal effects and robust z-statistics of the coefficients are reported in absolute values. Standard errors were clustered at the household level to correct for intrahousehold correlations.

The results for Albania in table 8.4 are consistent with the earlier differences in the means. The newly self-employed are most likely to be male, age thirty-eight, residing in an urban area, married, with some formal education, in good health, and with another self-employed member in the household. The inclusion of the household consumption variable in *Column 2* indicates a significant positive effect of past wealth on current self-employment. This finding suggests that the self-employed are more likely to rely on their own financial means in making their decision. The results from the same sets of estimates for BiH are consistent with Demirgüç-Kunt, Klapper, and Panos 2011. The newly self-employed are more likely to be male, in their early forties, married, with some formal education, and in good health. The inclusion of the household consumption variable in *Column 2* indicates a significant positive effect of past wealth on current self-employment. The magnitude of the coefficient is greater than that for Albania. Finally, the last two columns of table 8.4 present the estimation results for the 2003 self-employment entries in the Serbian LSMS panel, suggesting that these are more likely to be by male and urban area residents. The wealth proxy is of a smaller magnitude and marginally insignificant for Serbia.

Table 8.5 examines the impact of past employment experience in the three countries in our sample. The results indicate that ceteris paribus,

Table 8.4
Self-employment entry

	Albania		Bosnia and Herzegovina		Serbia	
	(1)	(2)	(1)	(2)	(1)	(2)
Male	0.038***	0.039***	0.034***	0.035***	0.013***	0.013***
	[5.93]	[6.04]	[5.70]	[5.98]	[2.67]	[2.68]
Age	0.006***	0.006***	0.006***	0.005***	0.0005	0.0003
	[3.04]	[3.02]	[3.36]	[3.25]	[0.28]	[0.18]
Age squared/1,000	−0.080***	−0.081***	−0.074***	−0.073***	−0.014	−0.012
	[3.17]	[3.23]	[3.31]	[3.41]	[0.64]	[0.55]
Married/cohabiting	0.007	0.009	0.022**	0.021**	0.002	0.002
	[0.76]	[0.98]	[2.30]	[2.38]	[0.28]	[0.22]
Log(number of children)	0.006**	0.005**	−0.005	0.002	−0.004	−0.003
	[2.43]	[2.23]	[0.61]	[0.19]	[0.92]	[0.71]
Federation of Bosnia and Herzegovina	—	—	−0.008	−0.009	—	—
			[1.22]	[1.45]		
Urban region	0.022***	0.019***	0.009	0.006	0.010**	0.010*
	[2.95]	[2.58]	[1.36]	[0.96]	[1.96]	[1.85]
Low education	−0.026***	−0.021***	−0.016**	−0.011*	−0.005	−0.003
	[3.21]	[2.63]	[2.53]	[1.81]	[0.84]	[0.56]

Table 8.4
(continued)

	Albania		Bosnia and Herzegovina		Serbia	
	(1)	(2)	(1)	(2)	(1)	(2)
Disabled	-0.021**	-0.020**	-0.025***	-0.023***	0.011	0.008
	[2.36]	[2.25]	[3.23]	[2.96]	[0.79]	[0.63]
Another self-employed member in the family	0.146***	0.131***	0.089***	0.073***	0.012	0.010
	[3.66]	[3.43]	[3.83]	[3.54]	[0.87]	[0.78]
Log(equivalized household consumption)	—	0.015**	—	0.030***	—	0.007
		[2.18]		[4.95]		[1.47]
Observed probability	0.0474	0.0474	0.0489	0.0490	0.0249	0.0249
Predicted probability	0.0322	0.0314	0.0394	0.0371	0.0219	0.0217
Number of entries	156	156	222	222	88	88
Number of observations	3,293	3,293	4,538	4,531	3,531	3,531
Pseudo R^2	0.109	0.113	0.065	0.080	0.031	0.034
Log-likelihood	-559.8	-556.9	-828.7	-814.8	-399.2	-398.0
Wald χ^2	110.4***	116.7***	111.0***	124.5***	30.2***	30.9***

Notes: Dependent variable: *Newly Self–Employed* (1/0). Probit regressions, marginal effects, and robust z-statistics (absolute values) are presented in brackets. Standard errors are clustered at the household level. The difference in the predicted value for discrete changes (0–1) is reported for the dummy variables. For continuous variables, the derivatives of the predicted dependent variable for small changes in the exogenous variables are reported.

Table 8.5
Self-employment entry and labor market experience

	Albania			Bosnia and Herzegovina			Serbia		
	(1)	(2)	(3)	(1)	(2)	(3)	(1)	(2)	(3)
Male	0.030***	0.031***	0.031***	0.025***	0.027***	0.027***	0.008*	0.008*	0.008*
	[4.57]	[4.68]	[4.74]	[4.46]	[4.83]	[4.93]	[1.85]	[1.87]	[1.89]
Age	0.005**	0.005**	0.004**	0.004**	0.004**	0.004**	0.0001	-0.00001	-0.00002
	[2.47]	[2.47]	[2.39]	[2.40]	[2.41]	[2.51]	[0.03]	[0.01]	[0.01]
Age squared/1,000	-0.063***	-0.063***	-0.061***	-0.054***	-0.056***	-0.058***	-0.008	-0.007	-0.007
	[2.60]	[2.67]	[2.59]	[2.43]	[2.61]	[2.72]	[0.38]	[0.34]	[0.36]
Married/cohabiting	0.006	0.008	0.009	0.020**	0.020**	0.020**	0.002	0.001	0.001
	[0.76]	[0.97]	[1.07]	[2.27]	[2.39]	[2.44]	[0.28]	[0.23]	[0.22]
Log (number of children)	0.006***	0.005**	0.005**	-0.004	0.002	0.002	-0.005	-0.004	-0.004
	[2.58]	[2.37]	[2.34]	[0.52]	[0.23]	[0.25]	[1.12]	[0.94]	[0.94]
Federation of Bosnia and Herzegovina	—			-0.003	-0.005	-0.006	—		
				[0.55]	[0.81]	[1.10]			
Urban region	0.011	0.010	0.009	0.011*	0.008	0.008	0.008	0.007	0.007
	[1.45]	[1.26]	[1.21]	[1.78]	[1.41]	[1.31]	[1.55]	[1.48]	[1.48]
Low education	-0.027***	-0.023***	-0.023***	-0.019***	-0.015**	-0.015**	-0.003	-0.002	-0.002
	[3.40]	[2.88]	[2.96]	[3.07]	[2.49]	[2.53]	[0.48]	[0.31]	[0.28]
Disabled	-0.018**	-0.017*	-0.018**	-0.024***	-0.022***	-0.022***	0.012	0.01	0.01
	[1.99]	[1.91]	[2.08]	[3.52]	[3.23]	[3.26]	[0.90]	[0.78]	[0.78]
Another self-employed family member	0.115***	0.102***	0.099***	0.084***	0.069***	0.067***	0.011	0.011	0.01
	[3.07]	[2.88]	[2.86]	[3.80]	[3.50]	[3.47]	[0.88]	[0.83]	[0.82]

Table 8.5
(continued)

	Albania			Bosnia and Herzegovina			Serbia		
	(1)	(2)	(3)	(1)	(2)	(3)	(1)	(2)	(3)
Log(equiv. household consumption)	—	0.014** [2.18]	0.015** [2.24]	—	0.027*** [4.59]	0.027*** [4.63]	—	0.005 [1.07]	0.005 [1.02]
Formal sector*no wage arrears	—	—	0.022* [1.68]	—	—	0.023** [2.01]	—	—	0.009 [0.84]
Informal sector	0.039** [2.55]	0.041*** [2.64]	0.062*** [2.62]	0.047*** [3.92]	0.047*** [3.98]	0.074*** [3.70]	0.052*** [3.75]	0.052*** [3.76]	0.073** [2.43]
Unemployed/inactive	-0.005 [0.59]	-0.003 [0.34]	0.008 [0.64]	-0.013* [1.77]	-0.009 [1.26]	0.006 [0.57]	-0.003 [0.41]	-0.002 [0.29]	0.006 [0.48]
Agriculture	-0.009 [0.95]	-0.007 [0.72]	0.003 [0.25]	0.029 [1.51]	0.028 [1.48]	0.053* [1.89]	-0.004 [0.57]	-0.004 [0.55]	0.003 [0.26]
Employed abroad	-0.019** [2.36]	-0.018** [2.07]	-0.012 [0.96]	—	—	—	—	—	—
Observed probability	0.0474	0.0474	0.0474	0.0489	0.0490	0.0490	0.0249	0.0249	0.0249
Predicted probability	0.0301	0.0293	0.0290	0.0360	0.0341	0.0337	0.0185	0.0184	0.0183
Number of entries	156	156	156	222	222	222	88	88	88
Number of observations	3,293	3,293	3,293	4,538	4,531	4,531	3,531	3,531	3,531
Pseudo R²	0.133	0.138	0.14	0.09	0.104	0.107	0.081	0.083	0.084
Log-likelihood	-544.5	-541.6	-540.2	-806.4	-794.0	-791.3	-378.2	-377.6	-377.2
Wald χ²	133.5***	139.8***	142.1***	160.2***	176.0***	181.8***	82.8***	82.4***	86.8***

Notes: Comments in table 8.4 apply.

informal sector employees are almost twice as likely to enter self-employment compared to employees in paid employment. The magnitude of the effect is very similar in the three countries and is robust to the inclusion of the wealth variable in the specification. Furthermore, individuals employed abroad are less likely to start their own business in Albania during the sample time. Individuals coming from unemployment inactivity are the ones least likely to start their own business in BiH. Column 3 further distinguishes between the incidences of wage arrears among formal sector employees to allow for the potential of necessity entrepreneurship among formal sector employees. The results contradict this view in Albania and BiH, as employees receiving wage arrears are significantly less likely to make the transition to self-employment, ceteris paribus, compared to employees receiving unusual or delayed payments. The difference between the two groups is insignificant in the Serbian sample.

The positive coefficient for informal sector experience can be interpreted both in favor of the necessity-based "push" to self-employment and/or the latent entrepreneur "pulling." Although the persistence of the pattern both with and without the inclusion of the household income proxy favors the latter view, some further clarifications are needed on this interpretation. In order to shed some more light onto the necessity versus opportunity/motivation discussion, we plot the predicted probabilities of entry by labor market status, versus (a) age and (b) household wealth decile, in figure 8.4. It is evident in both plots that, ceteris paribus, informal sector employees are the group that is most likely to enter formal self-employment at most ages and wealth levels. The latter probability is increasing in wealth level for all groups and countries. If informal sector employees enter formal self-employment due to necessity, then one would expect their entry profile to be nonlinear in wealth. Thus, the evidence is more suggestive of a different explanation than necessity.

Self-Employment Entry and Access to Finance
Table 8.6 examines the relationship between self-employment entry and affiliation with financial institutions, along with informal sources of finance. Departing from the baseline specification, three specifications are implemented. In column 1, the financial variables are added to the baseline specification. Column 2 incorporates household consumption along with the financial indicators, and column 3 controls for labor market experience.

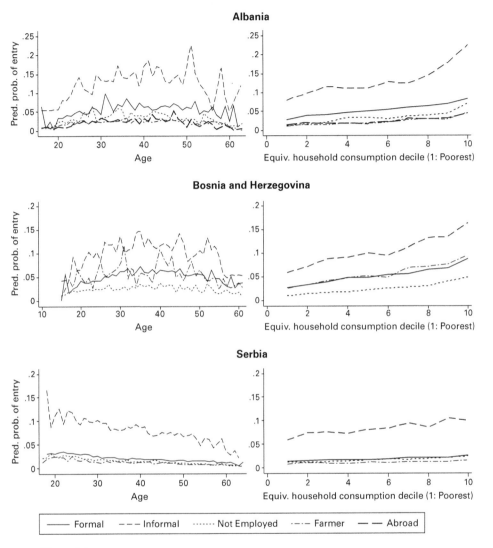

Figure 8.4
Entry probability by labor market status. *Notes:* Predicted probabilities are from specification 2 of table 8.5. The category *Employed Abroad* exists only in Albania.

Table 8.6
Self-employment entry and access to finance

	Albania			Bosnia and Herzegovina			Serbia		
	(1)	(2)	(3)	(1)	(2)	(3)	(1)	(2)	(3)
Male	0.038***	0.038***	0.030***	0.034***	0.035***	0.025***	0.013***	0.013***	0.008*
	[5.93]	[6.03]	[4.60]	[5.74]	[6.02]	[4.53]	[2.74]	[2.76]	[1.87]
Age	0.006***	0.006***	0.004**	0.006***	0.005***	0.004**	0.0004	0.0002	-0.0001
	[3.02]	[2.99]	[2.43]	[3.31]	[3.23]	[2.38]	[0.24]	[0.12]	[0.04]
Age squared/1,000	-0.077***	-0.078***	-0.060**	-0.071***	-0.071***	-0.052**	-0.013	-0.01	-0.006
	[3.16]	[3.20]	[2.56]	[3.27]	[3.42]	[2.42]	[0.61]	[0.51]	[0.33]
Married/cohabiting	0.006	0.008	0.006	0.022**	0.021**	0.020**	0.002	0.002	0.002
	[0.66]	[0.85]	[0.66]	[2.38]	[2.49]	[2.39]	[0.32]	[0.27]	[0.31]
Log (number of children)	0.005**	0.005**	0.005**	-0.005	0.002	-0.004	-0.005	-0.004	-0.005
	[2.09]	[2.00]	[2.32]	[0.57]	[0.30]	[0.49]	[1.06]	[0.91]	[1.21]
Federation of Bosnia and Herzegovina	—	—	—	-0.009	-0.011*	-0.005	—	—	—
				[1.48]	[1.71]	[0.85]			
Urban region	0.023***	0.020***	0.012	0.008	0.005	0.011*	0.011**	0.010**	0.008*
	[3.03]	[2.67]	[1.58]	[1.33]	[0.87]	[1.77]	[2.17]	[2.05]	[1.73]
Low education	-0.022***	-0.019**	-0.024***	-0.016**	-0.011*	-0.019***	-0.005	-0.003	-0.003
	[2.90]	[2.43]	[3.17]	[2.53]	[1.79]	[3.13]	[0.84]	[0.56]	[0.46]
Disabled	-0.019**	-0.018**	-0.016*	-0.024***	-0.021***	-0.023***	0.012	0.009	0.013
	[2.10]	[2.02]	[1.72]	[2.95]	[2.67]	[3.29]	[0.87]	[0.69]	[0.96]

Table 8.6
(continued)

	Albania			Bosnia and Herzegovina			Serbia		
	(1)	(2)	(3)	(1)	(2)	(3)	(1)	(2)	(3)
Another self-employed family member	0.141*** [3.61]	0.129*** [3.40]	0.111*** [3.07]	0.089*** [3.79]	0.072*** [3.48]	0.084*** [3.75]	0.013 [0.96]	0.011 [0.85]	0.012 [0.94]
Log(equivalized household consumption)	—	0.013* [1.77]	—	—	0.031*** [5.20]	—	—	0.008* [1.65]	—
Informal sector	—	—	0.040*** [2.61]	—	—	0.050*** [4.06]	—	—	0.050*** [3.69]
Unemployed/inactive	—		-0.004 [0.47]	—		-0.011 [1.58]	—	—	-0.003 [0.52]
Agriculture	—		-0.008 [0.80]	—		0.031 [1.61]	—	—	-0.004 [0.53]
Employed abroad	—		-0.019** [2.28]	—		—	—	—	—
Informal loan	-0.023 [1.27]	-0.027* [1.74]	-0.025* [1.93]	-0.006 [0.83]	-0.007 [1.05]	-0.007 [1.10]	-0.018*** [3.29]	-0.018*** [3.37]	-0.015*** [2.79]
Microloan	0.241 [0.81]	0.278 [0.88]	0.266 [0.93]	-0.003 [0.19]	-0.007 [0.46]	-0.009 [0.71]	—	—	—
Bank loan	0.040 [0.62]	0.049 [0.69]	0.062 [0.88]	0.004 [0.42]	0.001 [0.14]	0.005 [0.52]	-0.006 [0.68]	-0.007 [0.77]	-0.005 [0.64]

Table 8.6
(continued)

	Albania			Bosnia and Herzegovina			Serbia		
	(1)	(2)	(3)	(1)	(2)	(3)	(1)	(2)	(3)
Domestic remittances	0.02	0.035	0.027	-0.008	-0.007	-0.006	-0.007	-0.008	-0.007
	[0.43]	[0.61]	[0.62]	[0.84]	[0.70]	[0.66]	[0.88]	[1.02]	[1.19]
Remittances from abroad	0.003	0.002	0.002	-0.017**	-0.018***	-0.017**	-0.002	-0.002	-0.001
	[0.45]	[0.30]	[0.31]	[2.29]	[2.60]	[2.42]	[0.16]	[0.22]	[0.05]
Institutional remittances	-0.011	-0.01	-0.01	0.080*	0.098**	0.095**	-0.005	-0.004	-0.007
	[1.10]	[1.05]	[1.07]	[1.90]	[2.10]	[2.03]	[0.37]	[0.34]	[0.72]
Social remittances	-0.012*	-0.009	-0.01	-0.005	-0.004	-0.005	0.004	0.006	0.003
	[1.74]	[1.30]	[1.46]	[0.76]	[0.64]	[0.80]	[0.61]	[0.80]	[0.54]
Observed probability	0.0474	0.0474	0.0474	0.0489	0.0490	0.0489	0.0249	0.0249	0.0249
Predicted probability	0.0312	0.0307	0.0292	0.0384	0.0360	0.0349	0.0210	0.0207	0.0177
Number of entries	156	156	156	222	222	222	88	88	88
Number of observations	3,293	3,293	3,293	4,538	4,531	4,538	3,531	3,531	3,531
Pseudo R^2	0.116	0.119	0.140	0.072	0.089	0.099	0.038	0.041	0.088
Log-likelihood	-555.3	-553.2	-540.4	-822.6	-807.5	-799	-396.3	-394.8	-375.6
Wald χ^2	116.2***	123.6***	140.1***	123.9***	136.3***	173.3***	40.3***	41.9***	102.3***

Notes: Comments in table 8.4 apply.

The estimation results for the three countries indicate that the decision to become an entrepreneur is unrelated to an existing relationship with formal financial institutions, confirming that these institutions rarely finance entry into self-employment. We also fail to see a positive effect of formal microfinance institutions. Furthermore, there is also a significant negative effect by informal loans on the decision to start a new business in Albania and Serbia. However, remittances from abroad exhibit a significantly negative effect on the probability of an individual becoming self-employed in BiH, in accordance with the "disincentive effects" of remittances noted in the literature. This effect is economically significant; that is, an individual switching from not receiving money to getting remittances has a 1.7 percent lower probability to become self-employed (almost 40 percent less likely). To the contrary, the impact of remittance receivership is statistically insignificant in Albania, where the incidence of remittance receivership is much higher. Transfers from institutional sources, such as charities and potentially international NGO initiatives, have a positive impact on the probability to become self-employed in BiH. This result is economically large, although the use of these products is small in the overall sample (about 2 percent of individuals in our sample), which reduces the importance of this effect. These results hold with the inclusion of the wealth proxy and the labor origin variables.

An important aspect of the situation in the Western Balkans, worthy of further attention, is related to remittance receivership. In table 8.6, remittances from abroad are negatively associated with the probability of an individual becoming self-employed in BiH and exert an insignificant impact in the other two countries. However, it is likely that the relationship between entry and remittance receivership is nonlinear. In order to shed some more light onto this issue, we examine the relationship between entry and the amount of remittances received as a fraction of household income. In column 1 of table 8.7, a new variable is introduced in the baseline specification, capturing the amount of remittances from abroad as a fraction of the household income proxy. A dummy for individuals not receiving foreign remittances is also introduced. The estimation results verify that individuals not receiving remittances are more likely to enter self-employment in BiH. However, controlling for foreign remittance receivership, the amount of remittances received as a fraction of household consumption is not significantly associated with entry in the three countries.

Table 8.7
Self-employment entry and remittances from abroad

	Albania		Bosnia and Herzegovina		Serbia	
	(1)	(2)	(1)	(2)	(1)	(2)
Male	0.037***	0.037***	0.034***	0.035***	0.013***	0.013***
	[5.52]	[5.62]	[5.68]	[5.97]	[2.66]	[2.68]
Age	0.006***	0.005***	0.006***	0.005***	0.0005	0.0003
	[3.00]	[2.98]	[3.32]	[3.22]	[0.29]	[0.18]
Age squared/1,000	-0.073***	-0.074***	-0.073***	-0.072***	-0.014	-0.012
	[3.12]	[3.18]	[3.28]	[3.39]	[0.65]	[0.56]
Married/cohabiting	0.006	0.008	0.022**	0.021**	0.002	0.002
	[0.75]	[0.96]	[2.29]	[2.36]	[0.28]	[0.22]
Log(number of children)	0.007***	0.006***	-0.005	0.002	-0.004	-0.003
	[2.86]	[2.74]	[0.54]	[0.27]	[0.92]	[0.71]
Federation of Bosnia and Herzegovina	—	—	-0.009	-0.010	—	—
			[1.38]	[1.61]		
Urban region	0.020***	0.017**	0.008	0.005	0.010**	0.010*
	[2.69]	[2.34]	[1.32]	[0.87]	[1.96]	[1.85]
Low education	-0.024***	-0.020**	-0.016**	-0.011*	-0.005	-0.003
	[3.10]	[2.54]	[2.51]	[1.79]	[0.83]	[0.55]

Table 8.7
(continued)

	Albania		Bosnia and Herzegovina		Serbia	
	(1)	(2)	(1)	(2)	(1)	(2)
Disabled	-0.020**	-0.020**	-0.025***	-0.023***	0.011	0.008
	[2.43]	[2.32]	[3.23]	[2.95]	[0.80]	[0.65]
Another self-employed family member	0.143***	0.129***	0.087***	0.071***	0.012	0.01
	[3.65]	[3.43]	[3.77]	[3.45]	[0.87]	[0.78]
Log(equivalized household consumption)	—	0.014**	—	0.030***	—	0.008
		[2.11]		[4.97]		[1.49]
Does not receive remittances from abroad	0.003	0.005	0.017*	0.018**	0.003	0.004
	[0.19]	[0.36]	[1.96]	[2.37]	[0.25]	[0.41]
Remittances from abroad as a fraction of income	-0.0003	-0.0003	-0.002	0.003	-0.001	0.001
	[1.03]	[0.95]	[0.27]	[0.46]	[0.06]	[0.08]
Observed probability	0.0474	0.0474	0.049	0.049	0.0249	0.0249
Predicted probability	0.0306	0.03	0.0391	0.0367	0.0219	0.0216
Number of entries	156	156	222	222	88	88
Number of observations	3,293	3,293	4,531	4,531	3,531	3,531
Pseudo R²	0.113	0.118	0.068	0.083	0.031	0.034
Log-likelihood	-556.9	-554.1	-826.2	-812.2	-399.1	-397.9
Wald χ²	111.7***	117.3***	111.0***	126.4***	30.4***	31.2***

Notes: Comments in table 8.4 apply.

Figure 8.5
Entry and remittance receivership. *Note:* Predicted probabilities are from specification 2 of table 8.7.

Figure 8.5 plots the predicted probability of entry in each country versus the ratio of foreign remittances to equivalized household consumption. The figures indicate a negative association between the volume of remittances received as a fraction of per capita consumption and the probability of entry in Albania and a more U-shaped profile of this relationship for BiH and Serbia.

Finally, table 8.8 presents estimates of the interaction effects between labor market origins and access to finance, allowing for some additional heterogeneity in the relationship between access to finance and entry. The intuition of this exercise is to explore the relationship of labor market status and the provision of access to (in)formal sources of finance. The

probit models with the interactions between financial and labor market variables are estimated in the framework proposed by Ai and Norton (2003) and Norton, Wang, and Ai (2004) for interaction effects in nonlinear models. The specifications are all similar to column 1 of table 8.4, plus the two variables to be interacted and the interaction term. An interesting difference comes up with respect to the utilization of remittances from abroad in Albania. The interaction effect between remittances and informal sector employment is positive. In contrast, the interaction between remittances and formal sector employment exhibits a negative effect, which may suggest that remittances from abroad cover for the absence of formal financing mechanisms for individuals less likely to gain access to formal finance, such as those in the informal sector. A summary of the interaction terms for BiH suggests a positive interaction between microcredit schemes and informal sector employment. Informal sector employees provided with a microloan are significantly more likely to start their own business. This is not the case with formal sector employees and those not previously employed, none of whom is observed to become self-employed when provided with a loan from a microcredit scheme. Furthermore, interactions between formal means of finance and labor origins suggest a positive effect of the interaction term between bank loans and unemployment inactivity. The interaction effects for Serbia suggest a positive interaction between informality and wealth in the decision to start a new business.

Self-Employment Performance

The results so far suggest two main patterns that appear robust across the three countries and specifications. First, experience in informal markets is positively related to later self-employment, and second, affiliation with institutions providing formal finance is not significantly associated with entry. In this section, we extend the analysis to the correlates of employment creation and business survival.

In table 8.9, we show results from a multinomial probit model in which the dependent variable takes the value 1 if the individual switches to self-employment with employees (*Employer*); the value 2 if the individual switches to self-employment without employees (*Own-Account*); and the value 3 if the individual does not switch to self-employment. An advantage of this model is that it is free of the restrictive Independence of Irrelevant Alternatives Assumption (IIA) without requiring identification restrictions. Djankov et al. (2006a) have

Table 8.8
Self-employment entry and interaction effects

Interaction with	Log(equiv. HH. consumption)		Poverty		Formal sector	Informal sector	Unemployed/ inactive	Agriculture	Employed abroad
Formal sector									
Albania	-0.009	[0.62]	0.032	[1.49]	–	–	–	–	–
BiH	**-0.031****	**[2.12]**	0.010	[0.82]	–	–	–	–	–
Serbia	**-0.035****	**[2.22]**	**0.026***	**[1.95]**	–	–	–	–	–
Informal sector									
Albania	-0.010	[0.23]	0.014	[0.40]	–	–	–	–	–
BiH	**0.033***	**[1.71]**	-0.003	[0.15]	–	–	–	–	–
Serbia	**0.046***	**[1.78]**	-0.036	[1.40]	–	–	–	–	–
Unemployed/inactive									
Albania	0.001	[0.05]	-0.001	[0.02]	–	–	–	–	–
BiH	0.012	[0.22]	**-0.025***	**[1.70]**	–	–	–	–	–
Serbia	-0.005	[0.57]	-0.001	[0.01]	–	–	–	–	–
Agriculture									
Albania	0.014	[0.60]	-0.031	[1.51]	–	–	–	–	–
BiH	-0.015	[0.33]	0.075	[1.56]	–	–	–	–	–
Serbia	0.009	[0.55]	-0.008	[0.70]	–	–	–	–	–

Table 8.8
(continued)

Interaction with	Log(equiv. HH. consumption)	Poverty	Formal sector	Informal sector	Unemployed/ inactive	Agriculture	Employed abroad
Employed abroad							
Albania	-0.034* [1.88]	0.045* [1.84]	–	–	–	–	–
BiH	–	–	–	–	–	–	–
Serbia	–	–	–	–	–	–	–
Informal loan							
Albania	-0.007 [0.356]	-0.024 [0.97]	0.001 [0.02]	0.031 [0.70]	0.018 [0.72]	-0.027 [1.07]	No entry (17)
BiH	-0.026 [1.51]	-0.005 [0.27]	-0.001 [0.07]	-0.006 [0.25]	0.014 [0.88]	-0.068** [1.98]	–
Serbia	-0.005 [0.76]	No entry (55)	0.029* [1.86]	No entry (13)	No entry (44)	No entry (38)	–
Microloan							
Albania	-0.006 [0.01]	-0.026 [0.78]	No entry (4)	No entry (1)	0.064 [0.33]	No entry (1)	-0.055 [0.77]
BiH	-0.019 [0.51]	0.031 [0.77]	No entry (38)	0.178** [1.96]	No entry (51)	No entry (8)	–
Serbia	–	–	–	–	–	–	–
Bank loan							
Albania	-0.021 [0.70]	No entry (7)	0.071 [0.97]	0.154 [0.69]	No entry (11)	No entry (6)	No entry (2)
BiH	-0.016 [0.63]	0.016 [0.61]	-0.052** [2.17]	0.043 [0.86]	0.041* [1.77]	0.030 [0.39]	–
Serbia	0.010 [0.41]	No entry (50)	-0.013 [0.66]	0.008 [0.13]	0.014 [0.83]	No entry (14)	–

Table 8.8
(continued)

Interaction with	Log(equiv. HH. consumption)		Poverty		Formal sector		Informal sector		Unemployed/ inactive		Agriculture		Employed abroad	
Domestic remittances														
Albania	−0.012	[0.62]	−0.015	[0.62]	−0.001	[0.01]	0.005	[0.06]	0.023	[0.84]	−0.015	[0.61]	*No entry (16)*	
BiH	−0.037	[1.48]	0.029	[1.23]	0.012	[0.59]	−0.032	[0.91]	0.002	[0.14]	0.054	[0.63]	–	
Serbia	0.024	[0.72]	*No entry (95)*		−0.006	[0.31]	0.032	[0.57]	*No entry (49)*		*No entry (41)*		–	
Remittances from abroad														
Albania	−0.007	[0.45]	−0.002	[0.12]	**−0.038***	[1.93]	**0.062***	[1.76]	−0.030	[1.60]	0.015	[0.73]	0.032	[1.10]
BiH	−0.013	[0.92]	0.010	[0.59]	−0.013	[0.68]	−0.023	[0.88]	0.016	[0.96]	0.060	[0.84]	–	
Serbia	0.005	[0.25]	0.023	[0.72]	0.021	[0.76]	*No entry (33)*		0.004	[0.19]	0.035	[1.12]	–	
Institutional remittances														
Albania	0.004	[0.01]	0.001	[0.10]	0.020	[0.75]	−0.042	[1.03]	0.001	[0.06]	0.009	[0.36]	–	
BiH	−0.007	[0.04]	0.007	[0.09]	0.180	[1.55]	*No entry (7)*		−0.062	[0.75]	*No entry (3)*		*No entry (6)*	
Serbia	0.051	[0.95]	0.003	[0.10]	0.034	[0.90]	*No entry (26)*		*No entry (30)*		0.056	[1.06]	–	
Social remittances														
Albania	0.042	[1.41]	−0.027	[1.37]	**0.050***	[1.91]	**−0.056****	[2.05]	−0.006	[0.33]	0.015	[0.76]	*No entry (44)*	
BiH	−0.002	[0.18]	0.004	[0.29]	−0.005	[0.35]	0.008	[0.27]	0.008	[0.55]	−0.025	[0.68]	–	
Serbia	0.025	[1.19]	−0.006	[0.43]	−0.003	[0.24]	−0.008	[0.26]	0.007	[0.50]	−0.007	[0.49]	–	

Notes: Marginal effects [z-statistics]. The specifications are as in column 1 of table 8.4, plus *Variable, Interaction Variable,* and *Interaction Term.* The calculation of the interaction effects are based on Ai and Norton 2003 and Norton, Wang, and Ai 2004. No entry (#0bs) indicates that the interaction term predicts no entry perfectly and is dropped from the model. The number of observations dropped is given in the parenthesis.
*$p < 0.10$; **$p < 0.05$; ***$p < 0.01$.

Table 8.9
Employment generation

	Bosnia and Herzegovina			Serbia		
	Employer	Own account	No entry	Employer	Own account	No entry
Male	0.004	0.022***	-0.026***	0.003**	0.003	-0.006
	[1.45]	[5.01]	[5.07]	[1.99]	[0.91]	[1.62]
Age	0.001*	0.002*	-0.004**	0.0005	-0.001	0.0002
	[1.78]	[1.72]	[2.42]	[1.21]	[0.58]	[0.15]
Age squared/1,000	-0.021**	-0.029*	0.050***	-0.006	0.002	0.004
	[1.99]	[1.88]	[2.66]	[1.18]	[0.14]	[0.24]
Married/cohabiting	0.009**	0.009	-0.018**	0.0004	0.006	-0.006
	[2.45]	[1.42]	[2.46]	[0.40]	[1.52]	[1.57]
Log(number of children)	-0.004	0.006	-0.003	-0.0001	0.001	-0.001
	[0.95]	[1.02]	[0.35]	[0.01]	[0.23]	[0.22]
Federation of Bosnia and Herzegovina	-0.006*	-0.0003	0.006	—	—	—
	[1.81]	[0.07]	[1.12]			
Urban region	-0.001	0.008*	-0.007	-0.0002	-0.004	0.004
	[0.22]	[1.74]	[1.36]	[0.18]	[1.08]	[1.06]
Low education	-0.005	-0.009**	0.014**	-0.001	-0.001	0.001
	[1.57]	[2.00]	[2.53]	[0.44]	[0.11]	[0.23]
Disabled	-0.009***	-0.011**	0.019***	-0.0002	0.019	-0.019
	[2.67]	[1.99]	[3.05]	[1.47]	[1.52]	[1.52]
Another self-employed family member	0.011	0.056***	-0.067***	0.005	-0.003	-0.002
	[1.58]	[3.06]	[3.44]	[1.22]	[0.42]	[0.27]
Log(equivalized household consumption)	0.014***	0.011***	-0.026***	0.002***	-0.001	-0.002
	[4.40]	[2.86]	[4.96]	[2.65]	[0.15]	[0.47]
Informal sector	0.002	0.049***	-0.051***	0.021***	0.024**	-0.045***
	[0.57]	[4.23]	[4.16]	[2.68]	[2.47]	[3.69]

Table 8.9
(continued)

	Bosnia and Herzegovina			Serbia		
	Employer	Own account	No entry	Employer	Own account	No entry
Unemployed/inactive	-0.004	-0.002	0.006	0.0001	-0.002	0.002
	[1.11]	[0.33]	[0.90]	[0.40]	[0.41]	[0.41]
Agriculture	0.001	0.032*	-0.033*	0.007*	-0.012***	0.005
	[0.21]	[1.66]	[1.66]	[1.65]	[2.72]	[0.87]
Informal loan	-0.009***	0.002	0.007	0.0002	-0.009**	0.009**
	[3.51]	[0.41]	[1.13]	[1.41]	[1.99]	[1.99]
Microloan	-0.004	-0.006	0.01			
	[0.73]	[0.72]	[0.99]			
Bank loan	0.009*	-0.003	-0.002	-0.0001	-0.004	0.004
	[1.67]	[0.55]	[0.24]	[0.03]	[0.74]	[0.62]
Domestic remittances	-0.003	-0.002	0.005	0.0003	-0.008*	0.007
	[0.57]	[0.37]	[0.64]	[0.17]	[1.67]	[1.54]
Remittances from abroad	-0.011***	-0.005	0.016***	-0.002*	0.003	-0.001
	[4.51]	[0.97]	[2.72]	[1.76]	[0.27]	[0.12]
Institutional remittances	0.049	0.064	-0.113**	0.001	-0.008	0.007
	[1.26]	[1.61]	[2.21]	[0.26]	[1.38]	[1.10]
Social remittances	-0.003	-0.002	0.004	-0.001	0.005	-0.004
	[0.98]	[0.35]	[0.81]	[0.45]	[0.94]	[0.79]
No. of observations	4,531			3,531		
Log-likelihood	-909.5			-405.5		
Wald χ^2	230.9***			160.4***		

Notes: Multinomial probit: marginal effects and z-statistics. In the estimation, robust standard errors were implemented, clustered at the household level.

$*p < 0.10$; $**p < 0.05$; $***p < 0.01$.

used this model in the past to examine self-employment survival. The results are consistent with the previous tables. However, there are some interesting differences. Bank loan affiliation is associated with employment creation upon entering self-employment in BiH. Reasonably, larger firms require greater up-front capital. Moreover, informal sources of finance, such as informal loans and remittances from abroad are less likely to be related to large-scale startups. Finally, employees from the informal sector are more likely to start as own-account self-employed in BiH and appear in both the employer and own-account categories in Serbia.

In table 8.10, we examine the postentry performance of the newly self-employed individuals. The dependent variable takes the value 1 if the individual was still in business in the year following entry (*Survivor*). It takes the value 2 if the individual failed during his or her first year in business (*Failed*) and 3 if the individual did not enter self-employment during the sample lifetime. The year coverage of the panels for Albania and BiH allows this operation. It has already been mentioned that some 40 percent to 50 percent of the newly self-employed in Albania and almost half in BiH fail during their first year in business. It is thus of interest to examine the relationship between individual characteristics such as those prior to entry and the viability of the new business attempts. Marginal effects and robust z-statistics are presented.

The results in table 8.10 suggest that male, older, urban area residents, and those with another self-employed member in the household and greater own wealth have higher chances of survival in business for at least one year. Interestingly, individuals coming from the informal sector also exhibit higher chances of survival. The results suggest that older people, those with another self-employed in the household, and individuals with greater social capital have slightly better chances of success. Informal means of finance, such as domestic remittances, remittances from abroad, and social assistance money bring lower chances of success. Bank financing is associated with greater survival chances in BiH.

Conclusion

In this chapter, we examined and discussed the correlates of new entry into self-employment in three neighboring Balkan countries: Albania, Bosnia and Herzegovina, and Serbia. We made use of the World Bank

Table 8.10
Business survival

	Albania			Bosnia and Herzegovina		
	Survivor	Failed	No entry	Survivor	Failed	No entry
Male	0.012***	0.005*	-0.017***	0.007***	0.009***	-0.016***
	[3.35]	[1.96]	[3.69]	[2.59]	[3.16]	[4.04]
Age	0.002*	0.001	-0.002*	0.003***	0.0004	-0.004***
	[1.87]	[0.72]	[1.88]	[3.67]	[0.55]	[3.03]
Age squared/1,000	-0.023*	-0.008	0.031*	-0.044***	-0.006	0.050***
	[1.90]	[0.78]	[1.95]	[3.79]	[0.54]	[3.17]
Married/cohabiting	-0.001	0.006**	-0.005	0.006	0.004	-0.010*
	[0.19]	[2.31]	[0.91]	[1.63]	[1.04]	[1.81]
Log(number of children)	0.001	0.001	-0.001	0.001	-0.0004	-0.001
	[0.51]	[0.49]	[0.67]	[0.34]	[0.09]	[0.15]
Federation of Bosnia and Herzegovina	—	—	—	0.0001	-0.003	0.003
				[0.04]	[1.09]	[0.72]
Urban region	0.001	-0.001	-0.0001	0.005*	-0.0004	-0.005
	[0.24]	[0.30]	[0.03]	[1.72]	[0.16]	[1.10]
Low education	-0.002	-0.013***	0.015***	-0.008***	-0.003	0.011***
	[0.53]	[2.91]	[2.66]	[2.67]	[1.07]	[2.62]

Table 8.10
(continued)

	Albania			Bosnia and Herzegovina		
	Survivor	Failed	No entry	Survivor	Failed	No entry
Disabled	-0.002	-0.0003	0.002	-0.008***	-0.008***	0.017***
	[0.38]	[0.11]	[0.36]	[2.91]	[2.65]	[3.87]
Another self-employed family member	0.029	0.02	-0.049**	0.028***	0.019*	-0.047***
	[1.57]	[1.31]	[2.03]	[2.73]	[1.65]	[3.07]
Log(equivalized household consumption)	0.008**	-0.001	-0.008	0.012***	0.010***	-0.022***
	[2.16]	[0.21]	[1.61]	[4.06]	[3.43]	[5.19]
Informal sector	0.033**	0.006	-0.040**	0.020***	0.008	-0.027**
	[2.28]	[1.12]	[2.51]	[2.74]	[1.12]	[2.31]
Unemployed/inactive	0.003	-0.001	-0.002	0.004	-0.010***	0.006
	[0.58]	[0.42]	[0.33]	[1.17]	[2.63]	[1.13]
Agriculture	0.002	-0.003	0.001	0.002	0.015	-0.016
	[0.40]	[0.82]	[0.07]	[0.19]	[1.39]	[1.25]
Employed abroad	-0.006	-0.005*	0.011*	–	–	–
	[1.01]	[1.89]	[1.66]			
Informal loan	-0.010**	-0.007***	0.017***	-0.002	-0.004	0.005
	[2.05]	[2.68]	[2.71]	[0.52]	[1.25]	[1.22]
Microloan	0.180	0.127	-0.307	-0.002	-0.001	0.002
	[1.18]	[1.10]	[1.16]	[0.31]	[0.09]	[0.28]

Table 8.10
(continued)

	Albania			Bosnia and Herzegovina		
	Survivor	Failed	No entry	Survivor	Failed	No entry
Bank loan	0.023	0.015	-0.038	0.006*	0.001	-0.007
	[0.87]	[0.87]	[0.88]	[1.77]	[0.31]	[1.24]
Domestic remittances	0.002	0.03	-0.032	-0.008**	0.004	0.003
	[0.15]	[1.05]	[0.90]	[2.53]	[0.60]	[0.45]
Remittances from abroad	-0.001	-0.0001	0.001	-0.006**	-0.010***	0.016***
	[0.13]	[0.02]	[0.11]	[2.12]	[3.63]	[3.98]
Institutional remittances	-0.005	-0.004	0.009*	0.077*	0.015	-0.092*
	[1.10]	[1.42]	[1.68]	[1.69]	[0.58]	[1.81]
Social remittances	0.002	0.004	-0.005	-0.005*	-0.0001	0.005
	[0.41]	[1.40]	[1.04]	[1.92]	[0.02]	[1.25]
No. of observations	58	3,235 40	3,137	91	4,487 87	4,309
Observed frequency	1.79%	1.24%	96.97%	2.03%	1.94%	96.03%
Predicted probability	1.00%	0.60%	98.40%	0.96%	1.05%	97.98%
Log-likelihood		-436.4			-753.1	
Wald χ^2		192.8***			221.3***	

Notes: Comments in table 8.9 hold.

Living Standard Measurement Survey Data available for the region and extended the analysis in Demirgüç-Kunt, Klapper, and Panos 2011 to the role of labor market experience and access to finance. All three countries are on the long difficult path of transition after multiple shocks in the 1990s and have gone through major reform processes with the aim of improving the labor and business environment. The promotion of microenterprise activity has been a key political priority in the region in recent years, as the rates of self-employment and new business entry are still among the lowest in the three countries among transition economies.

Among the primary findings, informal sector employees are the ones most likely to make the transition to formal self-employment—a result that is quite robust for both men and women in the workforce. Furthermore, we find a significantly positive interaction effect between informality and access to finance through microloans and informal sources of finance, such as remittances from abroad. Informal sector employees are also the ones more likely to survive the first year in business. This finding is in accordance with the financed-based, competitive view of informality, suggesting that credit constraints are the driving force behind it. Moreover, it can be linked to a number of arguments, such as: (a) Lazear's (2004) view of entrepreneurs as "jacks of all trades"; (b) the human capital acquisition and skills transferability literature (Guariglia and Kim 2006); and (c) Baumol's (1990) idea of a fixed pool of entrepreneurial talent. In the third case, the increase in the number of self-employed could conform with the reallocation of that talent in more efficient markets.

The informal sector in the Western Balkans can be viewed as an incubator of new entries into formal self-employment by otherwise potentially skilled and entrepreneurial workers who might prefer to stay informal until the institutional environment allows better conditions. This feature indicates that it is not so much the lack of entrepreneurial spirit that contributes to the poor labor market environment as the lack of regulation and motivation to operate formally. A potential link between informal experience and later formal entry has important policy implications (Johnson et al. 1997; Kaufmann and Kaliberda 1996). The most prominent implication shifts the focus from the banning of informality to the operation of the financial market and the provision of incentives for employment growth and viability.

Moreover, wealthier households are more likely to become entrepreneurs and survive the early period in business, emphasizing the

importance of internal finance. Variables indicating financial institution customer affiliation in terms of loans from formal financial institutions, or even informal sources that one needs to repay, have insignificant impact on self-employment transitions. However, an existing prior relationship with a bank significantly increases the chances of survival for new entrepreneurs, suggesting that although banks rarely finance entry decisions, they are still instrumental in survival. Informal finance, on the other hand, is negatively associated with employment creation.

The importance of external finance by formal institutions can have the desirable impact on private sector development only after property rights are established and well-defined in order to provide an essential level of security in a stable macroeconomic environment. Even after reforms are introduced, establishing appropriate norms and sets of incentives to nascent entrepreneurs requires a longer horizon. The creation of an environment that promotes formal self-employment is essential for employment creation and the reduction of informal operations and should ultimately be a target that could promote sustainable growth in the region.

Notes

1. The "Microcredit Organization" law passed the FBiH parliament in 2000 and the RS parliament in 2001, establishing a legal and operational framework for microfinance. Furthermore, several microcredit schemes are active and supervised by the international community, notably the Local Initiatives Project funded by the World Bank, the Micro-Enterprise Bank funded by the EBRD and the International Finance Corporation, and Quick Impact Program funded by the United Nations Development Program/Srebrenica Regional Recovery Programme.

2. The 2008 World Bank Group Entrepreneurship Survey measures entrepreneurial activity in more than a hundred developing and industrial countries over the period 2000–2007. It is a joint effort by the World Bank Development Research Group, the IFC, and the Kauffman Foundation in its third year. The database includes cross-country time series data on the number of total and newly registered businesses collected directly from registrar of companies. For more details, see Klapper et al. 2007 and http://go.worldbank.org/C8Q8EGTTH0.

The sixteen countries presented in figure 8.1 are: Albania, Bosnia and Herzegovina, Bulgaria, Croatia, Czech Republic, Georgia, Hungary, Lithuania, Moldova, Poland, Romania, Russian Federation, Serbia, Slovak Republic, Slovenia, and Ukraine. 2002–2004 averages are presented for reasons of comparability with the LSMS data that will be introduced in the next section.

3. The World Bank's Doing Business project looks at small and medium-size companies and measures the regulations applying to them through their life cycle. The 2008 report covers ten indicator sets in 181 economies with the goal of providing an objective basis for understanding and improving the regulatory environment for business. Doing Business provides a quantitative measure of regulations for starting a business, dealing with

construction permits, employing workers, registering property, getting credit, protecting investors, paying taxes, trading across borders, enforcing contracts, and closing a business as these actions apply to domestic small and medium-size enterprises.

4. For more information on the LSMS data and for the design, the methodology and the samples in the three countries under examination, see Grosh and Glewwe 1998 and the documents at http://www.worldbank.org/LSMS/.

5. This latter subsample is of interest, despite reducing the number of observations, because it is likely to capture new business openings and exclude participation in family enterprises. All results presented in this section are robust to the examination of the household head sample and are available upon request.

6. Income is often considered to be the preferred measure. But income suffers from several defects both in theory and in practice. First, income can be highly volatile, whereas consumption is more readily smoothed by individuals and thus shows more closely the welfare level of an individual at any given time. Second, in transition economies, such as BiH, people are often paid irregularly and wage arrears are common. In this context, consumption is smoothed and income is erratic.

Our main welfare aggregate is total per capita consumption in current 2001 prices. It includes the following expenditure groups: food, alcohol and tobacco, clothing, housing/utilities, furnishings/household equipment, transport, communications, recreation, education, hotels/restaurants, and other miscellaneous expenses. It excludes health expenditure to avoid the presence of outliers. The equivalized measure is calculated by adjusting household consumption to the number of equivalent adults: $EA=(A+aK)^{\theta}$, where A = number of adults; K = number of children; a = economies of scale parameter; and θ = share of public goods consumed parameter. Finally, the measure is deflated at the regional level using the regional poverty line. For full information concerning welfare in Bosnia and Herzegovina and the construction of the 2001 consumption aggregates, see "Welfare in Bosnia and Herzegovina, 2001: Measurement and Findings" (http://siteresources.worldbank.org/INTLSMS/Resources/3358986-1181743055198/3877319-1190298527311/BiH_ANNX_poverty10a_updated.pdf).

7. Observations of an individual in self-employment for two consecutive years do not necessarily establish survival in the same entrepreneurial activity. In order to ensure that survival in self-employment is captured we consider as "survivors," individuals declaring their status as self-employed in at least two consecutive years and with activity tenure more than a year in the second year of observation.

8. We construct a proxy for social capital considerations, *No Social Capital*, using the average of two available questions: (1) "Is there anyone you can count on to listen to you when you need to talk?" and (2) "Is there anyone whom you can really count on to help you out in a crisis?" These variables proxy for social capital in terms of the help people can get from friends, neighbors, and relatives. A second dummy variable approximates *Optimism* in terms of financial expectations in terms of the future. These variables are not used in the regressions of the next section to avoid collinearity with other terms such as wealth and education.

References

Ai, C., and E. C. Norton. 2003. Interaction Terms in Logit and Probit Models. *Economics Letters* 80 (1): 123–129.

Astebro, T., and I. Bernhardt. 2003. Start-Up Financing, Owner Characteristics and Survival. *Journal of Economics and Business* 55:303–319.

Ayyagari, M., T. Beck, and A. Demirgüç-Kunt. 2007. Small and Medium Enterprises across the Globe. *Small Business Economics* 29 (4): 415–434.

Azzari, C., C. Carletto, G. Stecklov, and B. Davis. 2008. Agency, Education and Networks: Gender and International Migration from Albania. World Bank Policy Research Working Paper No. 4507.

Baumol, W. J. 1990. Entrepreneurship: Productive, Unproductive, and Destructive. *Journal of Political Economy* 98 (5): 893–921.

Boyarchuk, D., L. Maliar, and S. Maliar. 2005. The Consumption and Welfare Implications of Wage Arrears in Transition Economies. *Journal of Comparative Economics* 33:540–564.

Carletto, C., B. Davis, M. Stampini, and A. Zezza. 2006. A Country on the Move: International Migration in Post-Communist Albania. *International Migration Review* 40 (4): 767–785.

Castaldo, A., and B. Reilly. 2007. Do Migrant Remittances Affect the Consumption Patterns of Albanian Households? *South Eastern Europe Journal of Economics* 1:25–52.

Castaldo, A., J. Litchfield, and B. Reilly. 2007. Who Is Most Likely to Migrate from Albania? Evidence from the Albania Living Standards Measurement Survey. *Eastern European Economics* 45 (5): 69–94.

Cooper, A. C., F. J. Gimeno-Gascon, and C. Y. Woo. 1994. Initial Human and Financial Capital as Predictors of New Venture Performance. *Journal of Business Venturing* 9 (5): 371–395.

Cressy, R. 1996. Are Business Start-Ups Debt-Rationed? *Economic Journal* 106 (438): 1253–1270.

Demirgüç-Kunt, A., L. F. Klapper, and G. A. Panos. 2011. Entrepreneurship in Post-Conflict Transition: The Role of Informality and Access to Finance. *Economics of Transition* 19 (1): 27–78.

Djankov, S., E. Miguel, Y. Qian, G. Roland, and E. V. Zhuravskaya. 2005. Who Are Russia's Entrepreneurs? *Journal of the European Economic Association* 3 (2–3): 587–597.

Djankov, S., and P. Murrell. 2002. Enterprise Restructuring in Transition: A Quantitative Survey. *Journal of Economic Literature* 40 (3): 739–792.

Djankov, S., Y. Qian, G. Roland, and E. V. Zhuravskaya. 2006a. Entrepreneurship in China and Russia Compared. *Journal of the European Economic Association* 4 (2–3): 352–365.

Djankov, S., Y. Qian, G. Roland, and E. V. Zhuravskaya. 2006b. Who Are China's Entrepreneurs? *American Economic Review* 96 (2): 348–352.

Doing Business. 2005. http://www.doingbusiness.org/ (accessed April 7, 2008).

Doing Business. 2009. http://www.doingbusiness.org/ (accessed September 28, 2009).

Dutz, M., C. Kauffmann, S. Najarian, P. Sanfey, and R. Yemtsov. 2001. Labor Market States, Mobility and Entrepreneurship in Transition Economies. European Bank for Reconstruction and Development Working Paper.

Earle, J. S., and K. Z. Sabirianova. 2002. How Late to Pay? Understanding Wage Arrears in Russia. *Journal of Labor Economics* 20 (3): 661–707.

Earle, J. S., and Z. Sakova. 2000. Business Start-Ups or Disguised Unemployment? Evidence on the Character of Self-Employment from Transition Economies. *Labour Economics* 7:575–601.

Ersado, L. 2006. Rural Vulnerability in Serbia. World Bank Policy Research Working Paper 4010.

Evans, D. S., and B. Jovanovic. 1989. An Estimated Model of Entrepreneurial Choice under Liquidity Constraints. *Journal of Political Economy* 97 (4): 808–827.

Grosh, M. E., and P. Glewwe. 1998. Data Watch: The World Bank's Living Standards Measurement Study Household Surveys. *The Journal of Economic Perspectives* 12 (1): 187–196.

Guariglia, A., and B.-Y. Kim. 2006. The Dynamics of Moonlighting: What Is Happening in the Russian Informal Economy. *Economics of Transition* 14 (1): 1–45.

Harris, J. R., and M. P. Todaro. 1970. Migration, Unemployment and Development: A Two-Sector Analysis. *American Economic Review* 60 (1): 126–142.

Holtz-Eakin, D., D. Joulfaian, and H. S. Rosen. 1994. Sticking It Out: Entrepreneurial Survival and Liquidity Constraints. *Journal of Political Economy* 102 (1): 53–75.

Johnson, S., D. Kaufmann, A. Shleifer, M. I. Goldman, and M. L. Weitzman. 1997. *The Unofficial Economy in Transition. Brookings Papers of Economic Activity* 1997 (2): 159–239.

Johnson, S., J. McMillan, and C. Woodruff. 2000. Entrepreneurs and the Ordering of Institutional Reform: Poland, Slovakia, Romania, Russia, and Ukraine Compared. *Economics of Transition* 8 (1): 1–36.

Johnson, S., J. McMillan, and C. Woodruff. 2002. Property Rights and Finance. *American Economic Review* 92 (5): 1335–1356.

Kaufmann, D., and A. Kaliberda. (1996). Integrating the Unofficial Economy into the Dynamics of Post-Socialist Economies. A Framework of Analysis and Evidence. World Bank Policy Research Working Paper 1691.

Kim, B. Y. 2005. Poverty and Informal Economy Participation: Evidence from Romania. *Economics of Transition* 13 (1): 163–185.

Klapper, L. F., R. Amit, M. F. Guillén, and J. M. Quesada. 2007. Entrepreneurship and Firm Formation Across Countries. World Bank Policy Research Working Paper No. 4313.

Klapper, L. F., V. Sarria-Allende, and V. Sulla. 2002. SME Financing in Eastern Europe. World Bank Working Paper No. 2933.

La Porta, R., F. Lopez-de-Silanes, A. Shleifer, and R. W. Vishny. 2000. Investor Protection and Corporate Governance. *Journal of Financial Economics* 58:3–27.

Lazear, E. P. 2004. Balanced Skills and Entrepreneurship. *American Economic Review* 94 (2): 208–211.

Lyman, T. R. 2005. Legal and Regulatory Environment for Microfinance in Bosnia and Herzegovina: A Decade of Evolution and Prognosis for the Future. Essays on Regulation and Supervision. http://www.microfinancegateway.org/gm/document-1.9.25959/25462_file_Bosnia.pdf (accessed April 7, 2008).

Maloney, W. F. 1999. Does Informality Imply Segmentation in Urban Labor Markets? Evidence from Sectoral Transitions in Mexico. *World Bank Economic Review* 13 (2): 275–302.

McMillan, J., and C. Woodruff. 2002. The Central Role of Entrepreneurs in Transition Economies. *Journal of Economic Perspectives* 16 (3): 153–170.

Norton, E. C., H. Wang, and C. Ai. 2004. Computing Interaction Effects in Logit and Probit Models. *Stata Journal* 4 (2): 103–116.

Paulson, A. L., and R. Townsend. 2004. Entrepreneurship and Financial Constraints in Thailand. *Journal of Corporate Finance* 10:229–262.

Paulson, A. L., and R. Townsend. 2005. Financial Constraints and Entrepreneurship: Evidence from the Thai Financial Crisis. *Economic Perspectives* 29 (3): 34–48.

Paulson, A. L., R. Townsend, and A. Karaivanov. 2006. Distinguishing Limited Liability from Moral Hazard in a Model of Entrepreneurship. *Journal of Political Economy* 114 (1): 100–144.

Puri, M., and D. Robinson. 2007. Optimism and Economic Choice. *Journal of Financial Economics* 86 (1): 71–99.

Straub, S. 2005. Informal Sector: The Credit Market Channel. *Journal of Development Economics* 78:299–321.

World Bank. 2002. Labor Market in Postwar Bosnia and Herzegovina - How to Encourage Businesses to Create Jobs and Increase Worker Mobility. Report No. 24889-BIH, Human Development Unit, South-East Europe Country Unit, Europe and Central Asia Region.

World Bank. 2003. Albania Poverty Assessment. Report No. 26213-AL. Human Development Sector Unit, Europe and Central Asia Region.

World Bank. 2004. Albania: Sustaining Growth Beyond Transition. Report No. 29257-AL. Poverty Reduction and Economic Management Unit, Europe and Central Asia Region.

World Bank. 2005a. Bosnia and Herzegovina Country Economic Memorandum. Poverty Reduction and Report No. 29500-BA, Economic Management Unit, Europe and Central Asia Region.

World Bank. 2005b. Bosnia and Herzegovina, Labor Market Update: The Role of Industrial Relations. Report No. 32650-BA, Human Development Sector Unit, Europe and Central Asia Region.

World Bank. 2006a. Albania: Labor Market Assessment. Report No. 34597-AL. Human Development Sector Unit, Europe and Central Asia Region.

World Bank. 2006b. Serbia: Labor Market Assessment. Report No. 36576-YU. Human Development Sector Unit, Europe and Central Asia Region.

World Bank. 2007. Enterprise Activity, Labor Market Outcomes, and Welfare: Bosnia and Herzegovina 2005–2006.

World Development Indicators. 2006. http://go.worldbank.org/I358WVLTT0 (accessed April 7, 2008).

Zezza, A., Carletto, G., and B. Davis, 2005. Moving Away from Poverty: A Spatial Analysis of Poverty and Migration in Albania. *Journal of Southern Europe and the Balkans* 7 (2): 175–193.

IV Cautionary Tales

9 The Impact of International Remittances on Income, Work Efforts, Poverty, and Inequality: Evidence from Vietnam Household Living Standard Surveys

Nguyen Viet Cuong, Marrit van den Berg, and Robert Lensink

During the last decade, the development impact of international remittance flows has increasingly become the subject of policy discussions because these flows represent a substantial part of financial resources, especially from developed to developing countries (Chami, Fullenkamp, and Jahjah 2003). Foreign direct investment is still the largest flow of external funding for the entire group of developing countries, but international remittances represent the second most important external capital flow (Adams 2006). The average inflow of remittances surpasses even official development flows in middle-income countries and foreign direct investment in low-income countries. In 2005, the total flow of international remittances amounted to US$250 billion and constituted 5–10 percent of total GDP in developing countries (World Bank 2005a). The amount of international remittances to developing countries in 2005 was even 50 percent larger than the level of development aid (World Bank 2008). The rising trend of international remittances is unlikely to reverse in the medium to long term. It is even to be expected that remittance flows keep growing at a 7–8 percent annual rate (World Bank 2005b, 92–93).

The significance of remittances for developing countries also becomes clear by examining the high proportion of households for which remittances are an important source of income. For instance, Rodriguez (1996) shows that 17 percent of Philippines poor households receive international remittances; Cox, Eser, and Jimenez (1998) estimate that about 25 percent of Peruvian households receive remittances; and Edwards and Ureta (2003) find that about 14 percent of the households in El Salvador receive considerable amounts of international remittances.

International remittances are also attracting increasing attention because they are supposed to play a crucial role in improving economic

growth and reducing poverty in developing counties. It is even argued that facilitating international remittances may be very important in achieving the MDGs. Yet the existing empirical evidence shows that many key questions regarding the impact of international remittances on developing countries remain unanswered. The literature points at beneficial but also detrimental effects of international remittances on the economy of the migrant-sending countries. Several studies conclude that on average, remittances positively affect economic growth in developing countries (see, e.g., the survey paper by Rapoport and Docquier [2005, 75]). The channel via which this occurs is still unclear, though. Some authors argue that remittance inflows directly augment income and increase capital availability for consumption in receiving countries. Remittance inflows can also create multiplier effects in local economies on GDP, job creation, consumption, income, and investment (Stahl and Arnold 1986, De Vasconcelos 2005, and Ratha and Shaw 2007). Remittances may provide finance for investment, notably for small-scale projects, and hence may stimulate production (Solimano 2003). Some studies, however, argue that remittances are used unproductively and mostly spent on consumption (see Rapoport and Docquier 2005, 74). Other studies suggest that remittances are used productively. Estimates show that around 10 percent of remittance receipts are being saved, invested, and used for entrepreneurial activity (Orozco and Fedewa 2005, 4). Similarly, Adams's (2006) literature survey concludes that international remittances have a more substantial effect on households investments such as education and housing than on consumption. A large inflow of international remittances can also lower the chance of a financial crisis because it helps to reduce current account reversals (Bugamelli and Paternò 2005). However, a large inflow of remittances may also have negative effects on growth as it may reduce export competitiveness in the remittance-receiving country on account of a sharp currency appreciation (Cordova and Olmedo 2006). Moreover, remittances may promote idleness on the part of the recipients and consequently may have a negative effect on work efforts of recipients (Chami, Fullenkamp, and Jahjah 2003).

One of the most contentious issues regarding the impact of remittances concerns the effect of remittances on poverty reduction and income inequality. Indeed, the impact on poverty reduction and inequality is central in any attempt to examine the overall effect

of international remittances in developing countries. It is argued that international remittances may help reduce poverty in the developing world without increasing debt or administrative burden because remittances are a person-to-person flow of money without government intervention. Yet it is still far from clear whether and how international remittances reduce poverty and income inequality. Several authors find evidence that the inflow of international remittances reduces poverty. For instance, Adams and Page (2005) found a strongly positive correlation between international remittances and poverty reduction in developing countries. Anyanwu and Erhijakpor (2010) in a cross-country study of thirty-three African countries show that international remittances have a significant poverty-reducing effect. In addition, Adams (2006) finds that international remittances reduce poverty in Guatemala and Mexico, for example, because in these countries international migrants come from the poorest group of households and remittances are sent to relatively poor households. Moreover, Adams, Cuecuecha, and Page (2008) show that international remittances have a poverty reducing effect in Ghana. In contrast, Cattaneo's (2009) cross-country study does not find any effect of international remittances on poverty. Stahl (1982) even argues that international remittances may eventually lead to an increase in poverty because poor households would not benefit from the inflow of international remittances. The empirical evidence on the impact of international remittances on income inequality even seems to be more pessimistic. Acosta (2007) suggests that the effect of remittances on inequality is mixed. He finds that in some countries remittances increase inequality, whereas in other countries inequality is reduced. However, Adams, Cuecuecha, and Page (2008) find that international remittances in Ghana increase income inequality. A similar outcome is found by Azam and Gubert (2006). Based on surveys performed in Mali and Senegal, they argue that migrants mainly come from rich families and that the rich families receive most remittances. Hence the existing studies show a wide diversity of empirical results, which calls for more empirical studies to better understand the economic effects of international remittances.

The aim of this study is to provide new empirical evidence on the impact of international remittances. This study has several special features. First, we concentrate on one country: Vietnam. For several reasons, Vietnam is an interesting case. International remittances to

Vietnam are increasing in size and importance. However, few recent empirical analyses on the impact of international remittances on welfare in Vietnam are available. Niimi, Pham, and Reilly (2008) investigate the determinants of remittances in Vietnam, but they concentrate on internal remittances. As argued by Adams, Cuecuecha, and Page (2008), among others, because it is highly likely that international and internal remittances will have differing effects on poverty and inequality, the study by Niimi, Pham, and Reilly (2008) cannot provide any evidence on the impact of international remittances. Phuong and coauthors (2008) study the effects of migration. They also deal with remittances, but only indirectly. Nguyen (2008) uses Vietnam Household and Living Standard Surveys (VHLSSes) in 2002 and 2004 to measure the impact of international remittances on poverty and inequality. However, his discussions on remittances as well as the impact of remittances are rather short and simple. Vietnam is also interesting to look at because over the past decade it has achieved remarkable results in the fight against poverty. The incidence of poverty, according to the international poverty line, declined from 58 percent to 20 percent between 1993 and 2004 (Vietnamese Academy of Social Sciences 2007). The impact of international remittances on household welfare in Vietnam remains an open question, though. Our study aims to provide new evidence on this important issue. Second, this study is the first study that uses data from the two most recent VHLSSes of 2004 and 2006 to estimate the impact of remittances. The use of two years of data allows us to use panel techniques, which enormously improves the estimation strategy, because by using panel data biases that arise due to omitted variables, endogeneity and selection can be addressed. Third, we estimate the impact of international remittances on a series of indicators, so our study provides new evidence for the most important direct effects of remittances. More specifically, we focus on the effect of remittances on per capita income, per capita expenditure (consumption), work efforts, poverty, and inequality. We show that a rise in international remittances increases household income and expenditure. However, we also show that international remittances decrease work efforts, have no impact on poverty reduction, and lead to a minor increase in inequality. Although the empirical analysis deals with Vietnam, we expect our results to be important for a wider group of emerging and developing economies. At the least, our study shows that international remittances are not a panacea for poverty reduction, which may have important policy implications.

Data Set

Since the year 2002, VHLSSes have been conducted by the General Statistical Office of Vietnam (GSO) every two years. At the time of writing, the most recent VHLSSes are the 2004 and 2006 ones. With technical support from the World Bank, these surveys are designed similar to the LSMSes of the World Bank. The sample sizes of the 2004 VHLSS and the 2006 VHLSS are 9,188 and 9,189 households, respectively. The numbers of individuals covered in the 2004 VHLSS and the 2006 VHLSS are 40,437 and 39,071, respectively. These samples are representative for the national, rural and urban, and regional levels.

It is interesting that the 2004 and 2006 VHLSSes result in a panel of 4,216 households for which data is available for both years. The number of urban and rural households is 1,012 and 3,204, respectively.[1]

The sample selection of VHLSSes in 2004 and 2006 follows a method of stratified random cluster sampling. The GSO selected households in all rural and urban provinces of Vietnam—that is, rural and urban areas of all provinces are strata. Among each stratum, communes were selected randomly as a primary sampling unit. The number of communes per stratum is proportionate to the population proportion of the strata over the total population. The number of selected communes in each VHLSS is 3,063. In each commune, about three households were selected randomly.

The surveys collected data by means of household- and community-level questionnaires. Data on households includes basic demography, employment and labor force participation, education, health, income, expenditure, housing, fixed assets and durable goods, and participation of households in poverty alleviation programs. It also contains information on the amount of international remittances that households had received during the twelve months before the interview.

Expenditure and income per capita are collected using detailed questions. Expenditure includes food and nonfood expenditures. Food expenditure includes purchased food and foodstuff and self-produced products of households. Nonfood expenditure comprises expenditure on education; expenditure on health care; expenditure on houses and commodities; and expenditure on power, water supply, and garbage. Household income can come from any source. Income includes income from agricultural and nonagricultural production, salary, wage, pensions, scholarship, loan interest and house rental, remittances, and social transfers. Income from agricultural production comprises crop

income, livestock income, aquaculture income, and income from other agriculture-related activities.

A household is classified as poor if their per capita expenditure is under the poverty line developed by the World Bank and GSO. The poverty line is equivalent to the expenditure level that allows for nutritional needs and some essential nonfood consumption such as clothing, housing, and durables. The poverty lines for 2004 and 2006 are 1,160,000 and 2,560,000 thousands Vietnamese Dong (VND), respectively.[2]

Poverty and Remittances in Vietnam

Poverty rates declined continuously over the period 1993–2006 (figure 9.1). The proportion of poor dropped dramatically from 58 percent in 1993 to 37 percent in 1998 and continued to decrease to 20 and 16 percent in 2004 and 2006, respectively. In rural areas, however, poverty was more prevalent than the country average, with a poverty rate of 20 percent in 2006. The reduction of poverty was associated with a moderate increase in inequality. The Gini index based on expenditure per capita increased from 0.33 in 1993 to 0.36 in 2006.

Recently, international remittances have become an increasing source of external funding for Vietnam. Figure 9.2 shows that international

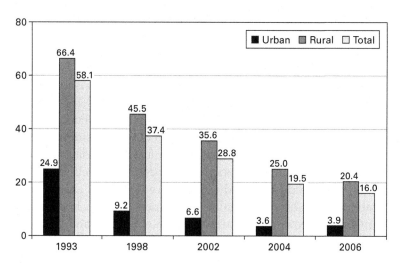

Figure 9.1
Poverty rate over the period 1993–2006 (percent). *Source:* Authors' calculations using VHLSSes in 1993, 1998, 2002, 2004, and 2006

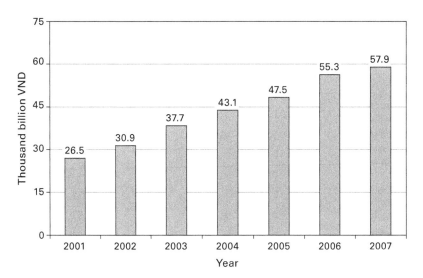

Figure 9.2
International remittances in Vietnam over time (in 2001 prices). *Note:* US$1 = 15084 VND in 2001. *Source:* Vietnam Economy Newspapers (http://www.vneconomy.com.vn)

remittances increased from 26.5 to 57.9 thousand billion VND, in prices of 2001, during the period 2001–2007. Table 9.1 presents the distribution of international remittances over the poor and nonpoor in 2004 and 2006. It shows that international remittances are not pro-poor. In 2004 and 2006, the percentages of the poor receiving remittances were only 1.3 and 1.8 percent, respectively. Moreover, the bulk of international remittances went to the nonpoor. Some 97 percent of the remittances receiving households are nonpoor. In terms of amount, even more than 99 percent of the international remittances inflow is distributed to nonpoor households. The average value of remittances of the nonpoor is more than five times as high as the average value of remittances to the poor. Also, in terms of percentages of household income and expenditure, remittances to the nonpoor are much higher than remittances to the poor.

Table 9.2 shows that urban households are more likely to receive remittances than rural households. In 2006, the proportion of households receiving remittances was 11.6 percent and 5.1 percent in the urban and rural areas, respectively. The average size of international remittances inflows was also larger in urban areas.

Table 9.3 presents changes in welfare and poverty for different household groups over the 2004–2006 period. It appears that households

Table 9.1
International remittances by the poor and nonpoor

	2004			2006		
Indicators	Poor	Nonpoor	All	Poor	Nonpoor	All
% of households receiving remittances	1.3 [0.3]	8.3 [0.4]	7.1 [0.3]	1.8 [0.4]	7.7 [0.4]	6.9 [0.3]
Remittances per capita (thousand VND)*	851.8 [299.1]	4744.1 [390.1]	4626.6 [379.9]	912.0 [228.5]	4919.2 [482.8]	4781.3 [467.7]
Distribution of receiving households	3.0 [0.7]	97.0 [0.7]	100	3.4 [0.8]	96.6 [0.8]	100
Distribution of remittance amount	0.9 [0.4]	99.1 [0.4]	100	0.9 [0.3]	99.1 [0.3]	100
% of remittances in household expenditure	50.5 [17.5]	52.9 [4.0]	52.8 [4.0]	54.7 [13.8]	60.6 [5.9]	60.6 [5.9]
% of remittances in household income	27.6 [7.8]	38.2 [2.1]	38.1 [2.1]	24.8 [5.9]	39.8 [2.7]	39.6 [2.7]
Number of observations	1769	7419	9188	1427	7762	9189

Source: Calculated from VHLSSes 2004 and 2006.
Note: Standard errors in parentheses (corrected for sampling weights and cluster correlation).
*2004 prices.

receiving international remittances in both years have higher income and expenditure per capita and lower poverty than households never receiving remittances. The impact of changes in remittance status is, however, unclear. On the one hand, the strongest decline in the poverty rate is experienced by households receiving remittances neither in 2004 nor in 2006. On the other hand, it appears that households that did receive remittances in 2004 but not in 2006 experienced an increase in poverty, whereas the opposite holds for households who received remittances in 2006 but not in 2004.

If anything, these findings suggest that an increase in international remittances will increase income. However, they also suggest that the effects on poverty reduction are probably minor because international remittances primarily go to the nonpoor. It may even be the case that an increase in international remittances increases inequality. The remainder of this paper analysis these issues in detail.

Table 9.2
International remittances received by urban and rural households

	2004			2006		
Indicators	Urban	Rural	All	Urban	Rural	All
% of households receiving remittances	13.8 [0.9]	4.7 [0.3]	7.1 [0.3]	11.6 [0.9]	5.1 [0.3]	6.9 [0.3]
Remittances per capita (thousand VND)*	5352.5 [633.1]	3861.9 [392.5]	4626.6 [379.9]	5320.4 [828.9]	4319.0 [497.5]	4781.3 [467.7]
Distribution of receiving households	51.3 [2.7]	48.7 [2.7]	100	46.2 [2.7]	53.8 [2.7]	100
Distribution of remittance amount	56.7 [4.6]	43.3 [4.6]	100	50.0 [5.8]	50.0 [5.8]	100
% of remittances in household expenditure	44.9 [4.8]	71.2 [6.9]	52.8 [4.0]	51.3 [7.8]	74.8 [8.5]	60.6 [5.9]
% of remittances in household income	35.2 [2.9]	43.5 [2.8]	38.1 [2.1]	37.9 [4.2]	41.7 [3.0]	39.6 [2.7]
Number of observations	2250	6938	9188	2307	6882	9189

Source: Estimation from VHLSSes 2004 and 2006.
Note: Standard errors in parentheses (corrected for sampling weight and cluster correlation).
*2004 prices.

Methodology

Calculating Impact on Per Capita Income, Per Capita Expenditure, and Work Efforts

We assume a similar specification for estimating the effect of international remittances on per capita income, per capita expenditure, and work efforts (equation 9.1).[3]

$$Y_{ijt} = \beta_0 + G_t\beta_1 + X_{ijt}\beta_2 + D_{ijt}\beta_3 + C_{jt}\beta_4 + u_{ij} + v_j + \varepsilon_{ijt} \, , \, t = 1,2, \qquad (9.1)$$

where Y is a vector including income per capita, expenditure per capita, and different proxies for work efforts. The subscripts i, j, and t refer to household i in commune j at time t. Note that "per capita" refers to the average per household member at period t. For instance, per capita income is calculated as total household income at period t over the amount of household members at period t. G_t is a year dummy, with a

Table 9.3

Per capita expenditure and income (thousand VND), and the poverty indexes of households over the period 2004–2006

	Not receiving remittances in both 2004 and 2006			Receiving remittances in 2004, but not in 2006			Receiving remittances in 2006, but not in 2004			Receiving remittances in both 2004 and 2006		
	2004	2006	Change	2004	2006	Change	2004	2006	Change	2004	2006	Change
Per capita expenditure*	4221.8 [70.5]	4913.4 [94.9]	691.6 [68.5]	8189.7 [673.9]	8427.4 [753.4]	237.7 [487.8]	5488.1 [352.0]	6724.7 [382.5]	1236.6 [272.1]	9437.8 [843.5]	9468.2 [830.9]	30.3 [688.5]
Per capita income*	5542.0 [111.3]	6740.7 [121.3]	1198.7 [90.4]	11015.3 [874.3]	10340.5 [827.1]	−674.7 [675.9]	6869.0 [513.0]	11767.4 [1182.9]	4898.4 [1230.3]	13665.1 [1668.0]	14633.4 [1422.1]	968.4 [1106.3]
Poverty rate (%)	19.01 [0.81]	14.35 [0.73]	−4.67 [0.63]	5.10 [2.07]	5.17 [2.04]	0.07 [2.22]	8.31 [2.07]	5.80 [1.93]	−2.51 [2.57]	1.80 [1.26]	1.70 [1.21]	−0.10 [1.00]
Poverty gap index	0.0460 [0.0026]	0.0338 [0.0022]	−0.0122 [0.0016]	0.0118 [0.0055]	0.0116 [0.0048]	−0.0002 [0.0051]	0.0169 [0.0049]	0.0100 [0.0039]	−0.0069 [0.0051]	0.0014 [0.0011]	0.0045 [0.0036]	0.0030 [0.0026]
Poverty severity index	0.0167 [0.0012]	0.0119 [0.0010]	−0.0048 [0.0008]	0.0040 [0.0021]	0.0031 [0.0014]	−0.0009 [0.0016]	0.0046 [0.0017]	0.0027 [0.0013]	−0.0019 [0.0017]	0.0001 [0.0001]	0.0013 [0.0012]	0.0012 [0.0011]
Number of observations		3800			127			170			119	

Source: Estimation from panel data of VHLSSes 2004 and 2006.

Note: Standard errors in parentheses (corrected for sampling weight and cluster correlation). The poverty indexes are calculated using per capita expenditure and the expenditure poverty line of WB-GSO. The formulas of the poverty indexes are presented in equation (9.5).

*2004 prices.

1 for 2006; this dummy is included to allow the intercept to differ between the two periods. This variable enables to control for common macroeconomic effects. X is a vector of household-level control variables. D is per capita remittances (i.e., average remittances per household member at period t). C is a vector of control variables with community characteristics; u_{ij} and v_j are unobserved time-invariant household and commune characteristics, respectively. ε_{ijt} is an error term. β_0 is a constant. As will be explained later in this chapter, we use a fixed effects and a random effects estimator to estimate equation 9.1. If the random effects estimator is used, β_0 is assumed to be the same for all households. In the fixed effects estimator, however, the constant is allowed to differ per household, that is, $\beta_0 = \beta_{0ij}$. If the fixed effects estimator is used, the time-invariant household and commune characteristics are perfectly correlated with the fixed effects. In that case, $u_{ij} + v_j$ will drop out of the model.

The marginal impact of remittances is measured by β_3. We will also measure the impact of remittances by calculating the Average Treatment Effect on the Treated (ATT) (Heckman, Lalonde, and Smith 1999). ATT is the expected impact of remittances on remittances recipients (with D > 0):

$$ATT_t = E(Y_{ijt}|D_{ijt} > 0) - E(Y_{ijt(D=0)}|D_{ijt} > 0), \qquad (9.2)$$

where $E(Y_{ijt(D=0)}|D_{ijt} > 0)$ is the expected value of the outcome variable of the remittance recipients—that is, income per capita, expenditure per capita, or work efforts—had they not received remittances. This value is not observed and has to be estimated.

Using equation 9.1, we get

$$\begin{aligned} ATT_t &= E\left(Y_{ijt}|D_{ijt} > 0\right) - E\left(Y_{ijt(D=0)}|D_{ijt} > 0\right) \\ &= \left(\beta_0 + G_t\beta_1 + X_{ijt}\beta_2 + D_{ijt}\beta_3 + C_{jt}\beta_4\right) - . \\ &\quad \left(\beta_0 + G_t\beta_1 + X_{ijt}\beta_2 + C_{jt}\beta_4\right) = D_{ijt}\beta_3 \end{aligned} \qquad (9.3)$$

The ATT at time t is thus estimated by equation 9.4:

$$A\hat{T}T_t = \frac{1}{n_t}\sum_{i-1}^{n_t} D_{ijt}\hat{\beta}_3, \qquad (9.4)$$

where n_t is the number of the remittance recipients at the time t.

We estimate the standard error of the ATT estimates by using a nonparametric bootstrap technique. This bootstrap is implemented by repeatedly drawing samples from the original sample of the VHLSS panel data. Because the VHLSSes sample selection follows stratified random

cluster sampling, communes instead of households are bootstrapped in each stratum (Deaton 1997). In other words, the bootstrap is made of communes (i.e., clusters) within strata. The number of replications is 500.[4]

Calculating Impact on Poverty and Inequality

We calculate poverty by three Foster-Greer-Thorbecke poverty indexes, which can all be calculated using the formula in equation 9.5 (Foster, Greer, and Thorbecke 1984):

$$P_\alpha = \frac{1}{n} \sum_{i=1}^{q} \left[\frac{z - Y_i}{z} \right]^\alpha , \qquad (9.5)$$

where Y_i is a welfare indicator for person i. We use consumption expenditure per capita as the welfare indicator because, as is well known, consumption is a better proxy for well-being than income. z is the expenditure poverty line, n is the number of people in the sample population, q is the number of poor people, and α can be interpreted as a measure of inequality aversion.

When $\alpha = 0$, we have the headcount index H, which measures the proportion of people below the poverty line. When $\alpha = 1$ and $\alpha = 2$, we obtain the poverty gap PG, which measures the depth of poverty, and the squared poverty gap P_2, which measures the severity of poverty, respectively.

To measure inequality, we use three common measures of inequality: the Gini coefficient, the Theil-L index of inequality, and the Theil-T index of inequality. The Gini index can be calculated from the individual expenditure in the population, as shown in equation 9.6:

$$G = \frac{1}{n(n-1)\overline{Y}} \sum_{i=1}^{n} \sum_{j=1}^{n} |Y_i - Y_j|, \qquad (9.6)$$

where \overline{Y} is the average per capita expenditure.

The value of the Gini coefficient varies from 0 to 1. The closer the Gini coefficient is to 1, the more unequal the expenditure distribution.

The Theil-L index of inequality is calculated as shown in equation 9.7:

$$Theil_L = \frac{1}{n} \sum_{i=1}^{n} \ln\left(\frac{\overline{Y}}{Y_i} \right). \qquad (9.7)$$

The Theil-L index ranges from 0 to infinity. A higher value of Theil-L indicates more inequality.

The Theil-T index of inequality is calculated as shown in equation 9.8:

$$Theil_T = \frac{1}{n}\sum_{i=1}^{n}\frac{Y_i}{\overline{Y}}\ln\left(\frac{Y_i}{\overline{Y}}\right).$$ (9.8)

The Theil-T index ranges from 0 (lowest inequality) to $\ln(N)$ (highest inequality).

The impact of remittances on the poverty indices of remittances receivers in period t is calculated as shown in equation 9.9:

$$\Delta P = P(D_t > 0, Y_t) - P(D_t > 0, Y_{t(D=0)}),$$ (9.9)

where the first term on the right-hand side is the poverty measure of the remittances receiving households given their remittances. This term is observed and can be computed directly from the sample data. However, the second term on the right-hand side of equation 9.9 is the counterfactual measure of poverty, that is, poverty indexes of the receiving households had they not received remittances. This term is not observed directly and is estimated by using equation 9.1 and substituting these estimates of expenditure into equation 9.5.

We also measure the impact of remittances on total poverty (equation 9.10):

$$\Delta P = P(Y_t) - P(Y_{t(D=0)}),$$ (9.10)

where $P(Y_t)$ is the observed poverty index of the entire population and $P(Y_{t(D=0)})$ is the poverty index of the entire population if the recipients had not received the remittances. The difference between equations 9.10 and 9.9 is that the latter only looks at the effect on remittances receivers, and the former considers the effect on the entire population. Regarding inequality, we measure the impact of remittances only on inequality of the entire population. The impact on the inequality index is given by equation 9.11:

$$\Delta I = I(Y_t) - I(Y_{t(D=0)}),$$ (9.11)

where $I(Y_t)$ is observed inequality, which is calculated using the observed expenditure data. $I(Y_{t(D=0)})$ is an inequality index in the absence of the remittances, which is estimated using the predicted counterfactual expenditure without remittances, using equation 9.1. The standard errors of the estimates of impacts on poverty and inequality are estimated using the same bootstrap technique as for ATT.

Impact Estimation Results

This section presents the estimation results regarding the effects of international remittances on per capita income, per capita expenditure, work efforts, and aggregate poverty and inequality. We use panel data from VHLSS 2004–2006 to regress income per capita, expenditure per capita, and different proxies for work effort, on remittances per capita, and for other control variables. We use fixed and random effects regression. The advantage of these techniques is that they control for time-invariant unobserved variables that are correlated with both income (expenditure) and remittances.

Control variables include household composition, education of household members, land and housing, villages, urbanity, and regional variables. It should be noted that we use two village-level variables: distance to the nearest market and a dummy variable indicating whether the village has a road. The VHLSS data sets provide information on these variables only for the rural area. Because our sample includes urban and rural areas, we had to come up with estimates for the urban areas. We assumed that for urban areas, the variables "distance to market" and "have a road" are equal to 0 and 1, respectively. This is a reasonable assumption given that in all cities there is a market and at least one road.[5]

The complete list of the variables and summary statistics is presented in table A9.1. In order to control for inflation, we have deflated all variables in terms of 2004 prices.

Impact on Per Capita Expenditure and Income

Tables A9.2 and A9.3 present the regression results with respect to the impact of remittances on per capita income and per capita expenditure, respectively. We present both random effects and fixed effects estimates, without and with sampling weight and cluster correlation. Because the Hausman tests strongly favor the fixed effects estimates, we focus on these.

International remittances had a significant positive effect on per capita income and per capita expenditure. For all regressions presented, the coefficient for international remittances is highly significant. An increase in remittances had however a much smaller impact on consumption than on income. An increase of 1 VND in per capita remittances resulted in an increase of 0.85 VND in per capita income and of only 0.08 VND in per capita expenditure. This result suggests that

Table 9.4
Impact of international remittances measured by ATT

	2004			2006		
	Y_1	Y_0	ATT $(Y_1 - Y_0)$	Y_1	Y_0	ATT $(Y_1 - Y_0)$
Income per	11052.6***	7905.0***	3147.5***	11281.8***	7679.9***	3601.9***
capita	[500.1]	[432.5]	[317.8]	[507.9]	[364.8]	[432.1]
Expenditure	7984.8***	7700.2***	284.7**	7445.4***	7119.7***	325.8**
per capita	[331.2]	[349.7]	[132.3]	[289.4]	[314.3]	[158.9]
Difference			2862.9***			3276.1***
in ATT			[309.7]			[413.9]
between						
income and						
expenditure						

Source: Estimation from VHLSSes 2004 and 2006.
Note: Figures in parentheses are standard errors. Standard errors are corrected for sampling weights and estimated using bootstrap (nonparametric) with 500 replications. *significant at 10 percent; **significant at 5 percent; ***significant at 1 percent.

households made only limited use of remittances for daily consumption. Improvement and construction of houses appear to be an important alternative use: these expenses, which are not included in the total expenditure measure used in the remainder in the paper, increased by 0.3 for each VND of remittances. This finding accounts for about 40 percent of the difference between income and expenditures. We did not find a significant direct effect of remittances on the purchase of physical assets (tools, implements, etc.), but these may require more long-term saving.[6]

Table 9.4 presents the ATT for the effect of remittances on per capita income and per capita expenditure. The advantage of ATT over the regression coefficient is that it gives a better estimate of the total increase in per capita income and expenditure caused by remittances. Because ATT depends on the size of remittances, it differs for 2004 and 2006. The table shows that remittances on average increase per capita income of recipients by 3,148,000 and 3,602,000 VND in 2004 and 2006, respectively. In other words, remittances help increase per capita income of the recipient by around 40 and 47 percent in 2004 and 2006, respectively. The effect of international remittances on per capita expenditure, however, is much smaller: only 285,000 and 326,000 VND in 2004 and 2006, respectively.

Impact on Per Work Efforts

Table A9.2 indicates that some crowding out of remittances takes place because there is not a one-to-one increase in income if remittances increase, which might be caused, for example, by a decrease in work efforts. We try to present some evidence for this hypothesis by presenting regression results on the impact of remittances on different proxies for working time. More specifically, we estimate the effect of remittances on the percentage of household members that work (for persons older than age fourteen), the number of working household members, the total annual working hours per capita, and total working hours per working household member.[7] These regression results are reported in tables A9.4 and A9.5. The tables show that remittances lead to a significant reduction in the percentage of household members that work and in per capita annual working hours.

In order to better understand the effect of remittances on working time, we also calculate the ATT for these variables.[8] The results are presented in table 9.5. The table shows that remittances reduce the ratio of working people above fourteen years old by approximately 3 percentage points. As a result, working hours per capita of the receiving households were reduced by 45 and 59 hours in 2004 and 2006, respectively. However, the effect of remittances on the number of annual working hours per working person is small and statistically insignificant.

Impact on Poverty and Inequality

Table 9.6 presents the impact of international remittances on poverty and inequality. The data suggest that an increase in international remittances does not reduce poverty: not one of the three poverty indices is significantly reduced. Our results also show that international remittances have a significant but very small effect on inequality: inequality increased slightly due to an increase in remittances. Both effects do not come as a surprise, given that most remittances go to the nonpoor and that although remittances substantially increase income, they have a limited effect on expenditures (see "Poverty and Remittances in Vietnam" earlier in this chapter).

Conclusions

This chapter estimates the impact of international remittances on per capita income, per capita expenditure (consumption), work efforts, and

Table 9.5
Impact of remittances on annual working hours (ATT)

	2004			2006		
	Y_1	Y_0	ATT $(Y_1 - Y_0)$	Y_1	Y_0	ATT $(Y_1 - Y_0)$
Ratio of members engaged in productive activities to the total household members older than 14	65.2*** [1.3]	68.0*** [1.4]	−2.7*** [0.8]	65.4*** [1.2]	68.8*** [1.5]	−3.4*** [0.9]
Annual working hours per working household member	1985.7*** [47.6]	1998.2*** [52.7]	−12.5 [25.4]	1978.1*** [43.6]	1994.6*** [55.4]	−16.5 [33.6]
Annual working hours per capita	993.0*** [30.1]	1038.2*** [34.9]	−45.2** [19.5]	1014.6*** [31.2]	1074.0*** [40.7]	−59.4** [25.0]

Source: Estimation from VHLSSes 2004 and 2006.
Note: Working people are those who are above fourteen years of age and are working, and working hours are calculated for working people. Figures in parentheses are standard errors. Standard errors are corrected for sampling weights and estimated using bootstrap (nonparametric) with 500 replications.
*significant at 10 percent; **significant at 5 percent; ***significant at 1 percent.

poverty and inequality in Vietnam using the two most recent VHLSSes for 2004 and 2006. We show that an increase in international remittances leads to a significant increase in income. Yet we did not find evidence that international remittances reduce poverty. Our analysis even suggests that in the short run, international remittances might increase inequality. These effects on poverty and inequality seem unfortunate. However, they are not unexpected, given the fact that in Vietnam mainly the nonpoor receive remittances. Moreover, it appears that the direct impact of international remittances on per capita consumption is small because a substantial part of international remittances is being saved and invested.

It should be noted that our estimates show only direct effects. The estimates do not allow for spillover effects. Especially if international remittances are used productively, indirect effects on the poor may be substantial. On the other hand, we do not control for home earnings

Table 9.6
Impact of international remittances on poverty and inequality

	2004			2006		
	With remittances	Without remittances	Impact	With remittances	Without remittances	Impact
Poverty of remittance recipients						
P0	0.0412***	0.0591***	-0.0179	0.0406***	0.0593***	-0.0188
	[0.0098]	[0.0162]	[0.0129]	[0.0098]	[0.0153]	[0.0122]
P1	0.0081***	0.0111***	-0.0029	0.0105***	0.0193***	-0.0088
	[0.0026]	[0.0054]	[0.0048]	[0.0033]	[0.0137]	[0.0135]
P2	0.0027***	0.0035***	-0.0008	0.0038***	0.0097***	-0.0059
	[0.0010]	[0.0068]	[0.0068]	[0.0015]	[0.0473]	[0.0474]
All poverty						
P0	0.1949***	0.1962***	-0.0013	0.1597***	0.1610***	-0.0013
	[0.0058]	[0.0058]	[0.0009]	[0.0059]	[0.0060]	[0.0009]
P1	0.0472***	0.0474***	-0.0002	0.0383***	0.0389***	-0.0006
	[0.0019]	[0.0019]	[0.0003]	[0.0019]	[0.0021]	[0.0009]
P2	0.0170***	0.0170***	-0.0001	0.0137***	0.0141***	-0.0004
	[0.0009]	[0.0011]	[0.0005]	[0.0009]	[0.0035]	[0.0034]
All inequality						
Gini	0.3698***	0.3687***	0.0012***	0.3580***	0.3577***	0.0003
	[0.0050]	[0.0050]	[0.0004]	[0.0046]	[0.0046]	[0.0005]
Theil-L	0.2235***	0.2221***	0.0014**	0.2117***	0.2110***	0.0008
	[0.0062]	[0.0062]	[0.0006]	[0.0056]	[0.0055]	[0.0006]
Theil-T	0.2407***	0.2389***	0.0018**	0.2268***	0.2265***	0.0003
	[0.0077]	[0.0077]	[0.0007]	[0.0074]	[0.0074]	[0.0007]

Source: Estimation from VHLSSes 2004 and 2006.
Note: Figures in parentheses are standard errors. Standard errors are corrected for sampling weights and estimated using bootstrap (nonparametric) with 500 replications.
*significant at 10 percent; **significant at 5 percent; ***significant at 1 percent.

had the migrant stayed at home, which might imply that our estimates are too positive. Estimating the indirect effects of international remittances, allowing for spillover effects, and controlling for home earnings had the migrant stayed at home is beyond the scope of this chapter yet certainly important for future research.

Overall, our analysis suggests that international remittances do not play an important role in reducing poverty or in improving equality. International remittances may play an important role in enhancing production and investment and hence in reducing poverty in the long run. However, to reduce poverty and inequality in the short run, the government of Vietnam could probably better rely on income distribution and poverty reduction programs that are more directly targeted at the poor. Also, for other developing countries, the role that international remittances may play in terms of poverty reduction should not be exaggerated. Especially for some Asian developing countries with a similar economic structure as Vietnam such as the Philippines, Indonesia, Lao, and Cambodia, there is no reason to expect international remittances to have a profound poverty-reducing effect. Our study clearly casts doubts on the hypothesis of many academics and politicians who argue that international remittances may play a crucial role in reducing poverty in developing countries. International remittances may have positive economic effects, especially in the longer run, but are certainly not a panacea for poverty reduction in the short run.

Appendix: Regressions and Impact Estimation Results

Table A9.1
Descriptive statistics for households with and without international remittances

Variables	Type	2004		2006	
		Households with remittances	Households without remittances	Households with remittances	Households without remittances
Outcome and program variables					
Income per capita (thousand VND)	Continuous	11052.6 [500.1]	5325.7 [107.6]	11281.8 [507.9]	6509.8 [125.4]
Expenditure per capita (thousand VND)	Continuous	7984.8 [331.2]	4057.2 [71.4]	7445.4 [289.4]	4666.7 [81.1]
Expenditure per capita on fixed-assets (thousand VND)	Continuous	240.1 [89.4]	312.5 [37.2]	465.7 [158.7]	269.7 [24.8]
Expenditure per capita on housing and land (thousand VND)	Continuous	1477.6 [265.2]	774.1 [71.2]	1581.9 [315.4]	878.5 [87.7]
International remittances per capita (thousand VND)	Continuous	4042.1 [594.6]		4691.7 [818.6]	
Labor variables					
Members engaged in productive activities/total household members older than 14	Continuous	0.652 [0.013]	0.804 [0.006]	0.654 [0.012]	0.784 [0.004]
Number of household members engaged in productive activities	Discrete	2.457 [0.096]	2.692 [0.030]	2.611 [0.098]	2.774 [0.032]

Table A9.1
(continued)

Variables	Type	2004		2006	
		Households with remittances	Households without remittances	Households with remittances	Households without remittances
Annual working hours per capita	Continuous	993.0 [30.1]	1013.0 [9.7]	1014.6 [31.2]	1049.8 [10.4]
Annual working hours per household member engaged in productive activities	Continuous	1985.7 [47.6]	1830.7 [17.8]	1978.1 [43.6]	1829.1 [14.3]
Control variables					
Household variables					
Ratio of members younger than 16 to total household members	Continuous	0.2390 [0.0136]	0.2683 [0.0041]	0.1969 [0.0121]	0.2409 [0.0039]
Ratio of members older than 60 to total household members	Continuous	0.1107 [0.0109]	0.0937 [0.0030]	0.1223 [0.0110]	0.0973 [0.0028]
Household size	Discrete	5.0762 [0.1659]	4.8768 [0.0406]	4.8805 [0.1142]	4.9183 [0.0466]
Household size squared	Discrete	29.7 [2.2]	26.9 [0.6]	26.5 [1.3]	27.6 [0.7]
Ratio of members with technical degree to total household members	Continuous	0.0885 [0.0112]	0.0573 [0.0029]	0.0838 [0.0118]	0.0651 [0.0028]
Ratio of members with postsecondary degree to total household members	Continuous	0.0624 [0.0103]	0.0258 [0.0022]	0.0546 [0.0101]	0.0310 [0.0024]

Table A9.1
(continued)

Variables	Type	2004 Households with remittances	2004 Households without remittances	2006 Households with remittances	2006 Households without remittances
Area of annual crop land per capita (m²)	Continuous	510.8 [72.2]	709.6 [28.1]	437.4 [58.6]	763.6 [33.2]
Area of perennial crop land per capita (m²)	Continuous	290.1 [141.5]	208.2 [17.9]	169.7 [35.8]	243.4 [19.7]
Forestry land per capita (m²)	Continuous	37.6 [26.2]	224.0 [39.9]	108.9 [45.1]	279.3 [51.0]
Aquaculture water surface per capita (m²)	Continuous	32.7 [15.9]	56.8 [9.3]	75.4 [39.5]	65.4 [12.2]
Commune variables					
Road to village (yes = 1)	Continuous	0.9456 [0.0145]	0.8509 [0.0099]	0.9131 [0.0211]	0.9049 [0.0079]
Distance to nearest daily market (km)	Continuous	0.9565 [0.1818]	2.2521 [0.1380]	1.0502 [0.1773]	2.4313 [0.1723]
Regional variables					
Household in Red River Delta	Binary	0.1786 [0.0281]	0.2116 [0.0114]	0.1405 [0.0244]	0.2149 [0.0115]

Table A9.1
(continued)

Variables	Type	2004		2006	
		Households with remittances	Households without remittances	Households with remittances	Households without remittances
Household in North East	Binary	0.0323 [0.0102]	0.1239 [0.0085]	0.0862 [0.0177]	0.1201 [0.0084]
Household in North West	Binary	0.0063 [0.0045]	0.0345 [0.0046]	0.0091 [0.0057]	0.0345 [0.0046]
Household in North Central Coast	Binary	0.1479 [0.0280]	0.1383 [0.0108]	0.1310 [0.0257]	0.1397 [0.0110]
Household in South Central Coast	Binary	0.0701 [0.0164]	0.0880 [0.0075]	0.1034 [0.0226]	0.0854 [0.0074]
Household in Central Highlands	Binary	0.0408 [0.0162]	0.0645 [0.0072]	0.0293 [0.0120]	0.0656 [0.0074]
Household in North East South	Binary	0.3192 [0.0415]	0.1374 [0.0108]	0.2658 [0.0395]	0.1406 [0.0111]
Household in Mekong River Delta	Binary	0.2048 [0.0302]	0.2017 [0.0110]	0.2347 [0.0289]	0.1993 [0.0109]
Household in Living in urban areas	Binary	0.4646 [0.0403]	0.2370 [0.0121]	0.4171 [0.0378]	0.2395 [0.0124]
Observations		563	8625	584	8605

Source: Estimation from VHLSSes 2004 and 2006.
Note: Standard errors in parentheses.

Table A9.2
Impact of remittances on per capita income

Explanatory variables	Random effect (no sampling weights)	Fixed-effect (no sampling weights)	Fixed-effect (sampling weights and cluster correlation)	Random effect (no sampling weights)	Fixed-effect (no sampling weights)	Fixed-effect (sampling weights and cluster correlation)
International remittances (thousand VND)	0.917*** [0.021]	0.853*** [0.024]	0.849*** [0.041]	0.896*** [0.019]	0.848*** [0.023]	0.848*** [0.043]
Members younger than 16/total household members				−1849.669*** [317.177]	−744.764 [592.755]	−448.3 [712.882]
Members older than 60/total household members				−2020.407*** [275.009]	−1446.877** [644.009]	−1604.552* [927.439]
Household size				−687.284*** [115.694]	−1140.166*** [197.594]	−1312.333*** [220.586]
Household size squared				30.233*** [10.292]	64.304*** [17.162]	79.102*** [18.724]
Members with technical degree/total members				5398.712*** [351.413]	2377.630*** [510.939]	2749.986*** [740.022]
Members with postsecondary degree/total members				11452.856*** [518.597]	2970.618*** [942.386]	3091.188* [1655.836]
Area of annual crop land per capita (m^2)				0.579*** [0.035]	0.589*** [0.059]	0.622*** [0.144]

Table A9.2
(continued)

Explanatory variables	Random effect (no sampling weights)	Fixed-effect (no sampling weights)	Fixed-effect (sampling weights and cluster correlation)	Random effect (no sampling weights)	Fixed-effect (no sampling weights)	Fixed-effect (sampling weights and cluster correlation)
Area of perennial crop land per capita (m²)				0.420*** [0.043]	−0.069 [0.063]	−0.131 [0.192]
Forestry land per capita (m²)				0.036 [0.024]	0.033 [0.034]	0.033 [0.062]
Area of aquaculture water surface per capita (m²)				0.639*** [0.088]	0.320*** [0.118]	0.310** [0.126]
Road to village (yes = 1)				357.211** [157.162]	393.357** [200.113]	552.909** [234.068]
Distance to nearest daily market (km)				−29.269*** [8.982]	−7.937 [11.123]	−8.394 [5.629]
Red River Delta	Base-omitted					
North East	−554.983** [225.195]					
North West	−1817.819*** [349.823]					
North Central Coast	−987.195*** [238.329]					
South Central Coast	−284.653 [255.609]					

Table A9.2
(continued)

Explanatory variables	Random effect (no sampling weights)	Fixed-effect (no sampling weights)	Fixed-effect (sampling weights and cluster correlation)	Random effect (no sampling weights)	Fixed-effect (no sampling weights)	Fixed-effect (sampling weights and cluster correlation)
Central Highlands				−821.533***		
				[311.587]		
North East South				1373.413***		
				[240.520]		
Mekong River Delta				294.476		
				[210.262]		
Urban				2401.531***		
				[210.365]		
Time effect (2006 variable)	1272.601***	1276.351***	1240.674***	1041.546***	1127.202***	1086.619***
	[74.338]	[74.227]	[84.223]	[74.567]	[75.390]	[81.476]
Constant	5469.512***	5485.500***	5756.272***	6670.533***	8511.186***	9023.166***
	[86.716]	[52.821]	[44.378]	[373.428]	[576.197]	[651.007]
Observations	8432	8432	8432	8432	8432	8432
Number of i	4216	4216	4216	4216	4216	4216
R-squared	0.17	0.17	0.17	0.39	0.25	0.24
Hausman test χ^2 (prob)	30.0 (0.000)			194.5(0.00)		

Source: Estimation from panel data VHLSSes 2004 and 2006.
Note: Standard errors in parentheses.
*significant at 10 percent; **significant at 5 percent; ***significant at 1 percent.

Table A9.3
Impact of remittances on per capita expenditure

Explanatory variables	Random effect (no sampling weight)	Fixed-effect (no sampling weight)	Fixed-effect with sampling weight and cluster correlation	Random effect (no sampling weight)	Fixed-effect (no sampling weight)	Fixed-effect with sampling weight and cluster correlation
International remittances (thousand VND)	0.161*** [0.012]	0.084*** [0.013]	0.077** [0.031]	0.166*** [0.011]	0.080*** [0.013]	0.077*** [0.029]
Members younger than 16/total household members				-1751.376*** [176.039]	-653.115** [323.282]	-587.531* [346.572]
Members older than 60/total household members				-917.851*** [152.759]	-892.519** [351.235]	-832.818 [651.192]
Household size				-596.769*** [64.184]	-973.662*** [107.765]	-1139.451*** [167.845]
Household size squared				27.810*** [5.709]	51.371*** [9.360]	65.656*** [15.224]
Members with technical degree/total members				3234.433*** [194.720]	903.029*** [278.660]	923.699** [420.860]
Members with postsecondary degree/total members				8450.103*** [287.800]	1480.861*** [513.966]	1,447.67 [1054.883]
Area of annual crop land per capita (m^2)				0.107*** [0.020]	0.102*** [0.032]	0.094*** [0.025]

Table A9.3
(continued)

Explanatory variables	Random effect (no sampling weight)	Fixed-effect (no sampling weight)	Fixed-effect with sampling weight and cluster correlation	Random effect (no sampling weight)	Fixed-effect (no sampling weight)	Fixed-effect with sampling weight and cluster correlation
Area of perennial crop land per capita (m²)				0.151***	0.110***	0.112***
				[0.024]	[0.034]	[0.035]
Forestry land per capita (m²)				−0.008	−0.026	−0.033***
				[0.013]	[0.019]	[0.010]
Area of aquaculture water surface per capita (m²)				0.139***	0.011	0.013
				[0.049]	[0.064]	[0.065]
Road to village (yes = 1)				25.578	−3.501	73.475
				[86.985]	[109.139]	[132.414]
Distance to nearest daily market (km)				−11.793**	−2.211	−3.582
				[4.970]	[6.066]	[3.269]
Red River Delta				Base—omitted		
North East				−710.320***		
				[125.288]		
North West				−1176.680***		
				[194.597]		
North Central Coast				−683.058***		
				[132.610]		
South Central Coast				−124.728		
				[142.225]		

Table A9.3
(continued)

Explanatory variables	Random effect (no sampling weight)	Fixed-effect (no sampling weight)	Fixed-effect with sampling weight and cluster correlation	Random effect (no sampling weight)	Fixed-effect (no sampling weight)	Fixed-effect with sampling weight and cluster correlation
Central Highlands				−580.157*** [173.332]		
North East South				1154.754*** [133.819]		
Mekong River Delta				107.106 [116.963]		
Urban				2193.406*** [116.780]		
Time effect (2006 variable)	616.732*** [40.860]	621.270*** [40.475]	615.082*** [53.511]	467.003*** [41.131]	533.584*** [41.117]	519.708*** [57.590]
Constant	4276.946*** [53.202]	4296.294*** [28.803]	4548.855*** [24.810]	5860.681*** [207.203]	7511.981*** [314.251]	8091.677*** [450.432]
Observations	8432	8432	8432	8432	8432	8432
Number of i	4216	4216	4216	4216	4216	4216
R-squared	0.05	0.04	0.04	0.43	0.16	0.15
Hausman test χ^2 (prob)		159.9 (0.000)		443.4 (0.000)		

Source: Estimation from panel data VHLSSes 2004 and 2006.
Note: Standard errors in parentheses.
*significant at 10 percent; **significant at 5 percent; ***significant at 1 percent.

Table A9.4
Regressions of the ratio of working members and the number of working members

Explanatory variables	Working members/total members			Working members		
	Random effect (no sampling weight)	Fixed-effect (no sampling weight)	Fixed-effect with sampling weight and cluster correlation	Fixed-effect Poisson (no sampling weight)	Random effect (no sampling weight)	Fixed-effect with sampling weight and cluster correlation
International remittances (thousand VND)	-0.000006*** [0.000001]	-0.000006*** [0.000001]	-0.0000007*** [0.000002]	-0.000014*** [0.000003]	-0.000013*** [0.000004]	-0.000017*** [0.000005]
Members younger than 16/total household members	0.392005*** [0.014255]	0.540145*** [0.027693]	0.567058*** [0.032548]	-2.353461*** [0.048023]	-1.708024*** [0.093696]	-1.567524*** [0.110482]
Members older than 60/total household members	-0.255982*** [0.012320]	-0.257242*** [0.030087]	-0.262890*** [0.047100]	-0.730356*** [0.041473]	-0.572812*** [0.101798]	-0.560986*** [0.108241]
Household size	-0.078676*** [0.005209]	-0.098372*** [0.009231]	-0.102891*** [0.012423]	0.541307*** [0.017555]	0.531192*** [0.031233]	0.475342*** [0.063409]
Household size squared	0.004704*** [0.000464]	0.006061*** [0.000802]	0.006380*** [0.001073]	-0.001434 [0.001563]	0.001198 [0.002713]	0.006005 [0.006576]
Members with technical degree/total members	0.044635*** [0.015900]	0.096389*** [0.023870]	0.102978*** [0.027643]	0.140401*** [0.053645]	0.332328*** [0.080763]	0.350237*** [0.091373]
Members with postsecondary/total members	0.017463 [0.023317]	0.260835*** [0.044027]	0.260499*** [0.053764]	0.103101 [0.078559]	0.854753*** [0.148962]	0.836195*** [0.170325]
Area of annual crop land per capita (m²)	0.000007*** [0.000002]	0.000004 [0.000003]	0.000006* [0.000003]	0.000010* [0.000005]	0.00000 [0.000009]	0.000003 [0.000010]

Table A9.4
(continued)

Explanatory variables	Working members/total members			Working members		
	Random effect (no sampling weight)	Fixed-effect (no sampling weight)	Fixed-effect with sampling weight and cluster correlation	Fixed-effect Poisson (no sampling weight)	Random effect (no sampling weight)	Fixed-effect with sampling weight and cluster correlation
Area of perennial crop land per capita (m^2)	0.000003 [0.000002]	0.000003 [0.000003]	0.000005* [0.000003]	0.000004 [0.000007]	0.000003 [0.000010]	0.000009 [0.000008]
Forestry land per capita (m^2)	0.000001 [0.000001]	0.000001 [0.000002]	0.000001 [0.000001]	0.000007* [0.000004]	0.000007 [0.000005]	0.000007 [0.000007]
Area of aquaculture water surface per capita (m^2)	0.000004 [0.000004]	0.000008 [0.000006]	0.000005 [0.000008]	0.00001 [0.000014]	0.000022 [0.000019]	0.000013 [0.000026]
Road to village (yes = 1)	0.000026 [0.007144]	0.002227 [0.009349]	0.001892 [0.010078]	0.002863 [0.024130]	-0.001004 [0.031632]	0.013625 [0.034266]
Distance to nearest daily market (km)	0.000098 [0.000409]	-0.001141** [0.000520]	-0.001336*** [0.000423]	-0.001812 [0.001381]	-0.005351*** [0.001758]	-0.006548*** [0.001896]
North East	0.032107*** [0.010025]			0.126874*** [0.033700]		
North West	0.031512** [0.015582]			0.091586* [0.052389]		
North Central Coast	-0.022212** [0.010604]			-0.121797*** [0.035645]		
South Central Coast	-0.003892 [0.011373]			-0.039766 [0.038228]		
Central Highlands	0.01318 [0.013877]			-0.052701 [0.046656]		

Table A9.4
(continued)

Explanatory variables	Working members/total members			Working members		
	Random effect (no sampling weight)	Fixed-effect (no sampling weight)	Fixed-effect with sampling weight and cluster correlation	Fixed-effect Poisson (no sampling weight)	Random effect (no sampling weight)	Fixed-effect with sampling weight and cluster correlation
North East South	-0.033159*** [0.010705]			-0.132133*** [0.035987]		
Mekong River Delta	-0.012134 [0.009366]			-0.006609 [0.031489]		
Urban	-0.081426*** [0.009449]			-0.263615*** [0.031831]		
Time effect (2006 dummy)	-0.016156*** [0.003439]	-0.013672*** [0.003522]	-0.011090*** [0.003882]	-0.044927*** [0.011654]	-0.028738** [0.011917]	-0.022221* [0.012944]
Constant	0.999363*** [0.016803]	0.990560*** [0.026919]	0.988902*** [0.033991]	0.889214*** [0.056623]	0.603264*** [0.091079]	0.677731*** [0.145530]
Observations	8432	8432	8432	7998	8432	8432
Number of i	4216	4216	4216	3999	4216	4216
R-squared	0.22	0.13	0.14	0.62	0.57	0.39
Hausman test χ^2 (prob)	72.7 (0.000)			272.8 (0.000)		

Source: Estimation from panel data VHLSSes 2004 and 2006.
Note: Standard errors in parentheses.
*significant at 10 percent; **significant at 5 percent; ***significant at 1 percent.

Table A9.5
Regressions of annual working hours

Explanatory variables	Annual working hours per working member			Annual working hours per capita		
	Random effect (no sampling weights)	Fixed-effect (no sampling weights)	Fixed-effect (sampling weights and cluster correlation)	Random effect (no sampling weight)	Fixed-effect (no sampling weights)	Fixed-effect (sampling weights and cluster correlation)
International remittances (thousand VND)	-0.0115***	-0.0109***	-0.0110**	-0.0068**	-0.0055	-0.0023
	[0.0019]	[0.0024]	[0.0045]	[0.0027]	[0.0035]	[0.0065]
Members younger than 16/ total household members	-840.5761***	-637.4136***	-612.3833***	126.7249***	17.7247	-16.5051
	[30.9290]	[60.8238]	[62.2531]	[42.7032]	[89.1169]	[92.7447]
Members older than 60/ total household members	-692.9007***	-615.2529***	-643.0128***	-722.2424***	-591.9096***	-668.4195***
	[26.6990]	[66.0831]	[115.9812]	[36.6304]	[96.8226]	[148.3619]
Household size	-64.3343***	-77.4442***	-82.7503***	134.2960***	128.6281***	145.3145***
	[11.3086]	[20.2755]	[27.8351]	[15.6676]	[29.7070]	[33.4032]
Household size squared	2.9546***	3.9353**	4.6391**	-11.2184***	-10.0354***	-10.9687***
	[1.0067]	[1.7610]	[2.3511]	[1.3961]	[2.5802]	[2.7208]
Members with technical degree/total members	106.1335***	186.4422***	195.8052***	68.2896	77.6263	63.1636
	[34.5807]	[52.4285]	[58.8290]	[48.3976]	[76.8164]	[74.3786]
Members with postsecondary/total members	144.966***	621.331***	587.845***	111.616	366.885***	269.328
	[50.5980]	[96.7001]	[118.6326]	[69.9148]	[141.6816]	[166.6653]
Area of annual crop land per capita (m2)	-0.0037	-0.0013	0.0001	-0.0148***	0.0009	0.003
	[0.0035]	[0.0061]	[0.0074]	[0.0048]	[0.0089]	[0.0096]

Table A9.5
(continued)

Explanatory variables	Annual working hours per working member			Annual working hours per capita		
	Random effect (no sampling weights)	Fixed-effect (no sampling weights)	Fixed-effect (sampling weights and cluster correlation)	Random effect (no sampling weight)	Fixed-effect (no sampling weights)	Fixed-effect (sampling weights and cluster correlation)
Area of perennial crop land per capita (m2)	-0.0041 [0.0043]	0.0041 [0.0065]	0.0068 [0.0061]	-0.0062 [0.0060]	0.0067 [0.0095]	0.0088 [0.0094]
Forestry land per capita (m2)	-0.0006 [0.0023]	0.0019 [0.0035]	0.004 [0.0040]	-0.0058* [0.0033]	-0.003 [0.0051]	0.0003 [0.0084]
Area of aquaculture water surface per capita (m2)	0.0037 [0.0087]	0.0256** [0.0121]	0.0207 [0.0187]	0.0008 [0.0123]	0.0468*** [0.0177]	0.0397** [0.0199]
Road to village (yes = 1)	32.2659** [15.5647]	27.4813 [20.5340]	30.0836 [21.2196]	63.0966*** [21.9999]	56.6440* [30.0857]	55.3039* [31.6430]
Distance to nearest daily market (km)	-1.0156 [0.8911]	-1.2624 [1.1414]	-1.0739 [1.4364]	-1.554 [1.2630]	1.1297 [1.6723]	1.7424 [2.0353]
North East	71.1442*** [21.6774]			47.1721 [29.3908]		
North West	0.0205 [33.7013]			-41.2948 [45.7492]		
North Central Coast	-34.4369 [22.9265]			-1.3202 [31.0523]		
South Central Coast	-7.6895 [24.5881]			18.1579 [33.3017]		
Central Highlands	-6.9438 [30.0125]			-20.608 [40.7286]		

Table A9.5
(continued)

Explanatory variables	Annual working hours per working member			Annual working hours per capita		
	Random effect (no sampling weights)	Fixed-effect (no sampling weights)	Fixed-effect (sampling weights and cluster correlation)	Random effect (no sampling weight)	Fixed-effect (no sampling weights)	Fixed-effect (sampling weights and cluster correlation)
North East South	72.9059***			187.3539***		
	[23.1476]			[31.3731]		
Mekong River Delta	−74.4765***			−128.4896***		
	[20.2564]			[27.4979]		
Urban	120.5362***			414.8475***		
	[20.4997]			[28.3175]		
Time effect (2006 variable)	8.8296	10.4994	11.2493	33.5535***	25.9731**	21.4611
	[7.5328]	[7.7359]	[9.3207]	[11.0055]	[11.3344]	[13.7098]
Constant	1485.59***	1469.28***	1472.23***	1343.03***	1425.39***	1407.75***
	[36.4743]	[59.1247]	[81.8643]	[50.5076]	[86.6274]	[98.4460]
Observations	8432	8432	8432	8432	8432	8432
Number of i	4216	4216	4216	4216	4216	4216
R-squared	0.21	0.17	0.17	0.16	0.08	0.08
Hausman test χ^2 (prob)	48.8(0.000)			89.3 (0.000)		

Source: Estimation from panel data VHLSSes 2004 and 2006.
Note: Standard errors in parentheses.
*significant at 10 percent; **significant at 5 percent; ***significant at 1 percent.

Notes

1. There are earlier versions of the survey available. However, due to changes in the households interviewed, it is not possible to match the 2006 survey with surveys conducted earlier than 2004.

2. $US1 is equivalent to 15,777 and 16,054 VND in 2004 and 2006, respectively.

3. It should be noted that we treat international remittances as an exogenous transfer of income by migrants. We do not control for home earnings of migrants had those migrants stayed and worked at home, as has been done by, for example, in Adams, Cucuecha, and Page 2008. We ignore home earnings of migrants had they not migrated because this factor induces severe methodological difficulties. Probably our methodology implies that the results overestimate the possible positive effects of international remittances.

4. In order to examine the robustness of our bootstrap technique, we also tried to bootstrap households.

5. We tested whether international remittances have a different impact in rural and urban areas by including interaction terms for international remittances and a dummy for living in an urban area. These estimates indicate that the effects of remittances do not differ between urban and rural areas. We therefore present only the estimates for the entire sample.

6. Estimates available from the authors on request. Corresponding author: Nguyen Viet Cuong. Email: c_nguyenviet@yahoo.com.

7. The government of Vietnam does not allow the use of laborers under fifteen years old.

8. We used Hausman specification tests to test the differences in coefficients between the random and fixed-effect regressions. The test statistics strongly reject the null hypothesis that the differences in coefficients between two regressions are not systematic. Thus we use the fixed-effect regressions.

References

Acosta, P. 2007. What Is the Impact of International Remittances on Poverty and Inequality in Latin America? World Bank Policy Research Working Paper 4249.

Adams, R. 2006. International Remittances and the Household Analysis and Review of Global Evidence. *Journal of African Economies* 15 (2): 396–426.

Adams, R., A. Cuecuecha, and J. Page. 2008. The Impact of Remittances on Poverty and Inequality in Ghana. World Bank Policy Research Working Paper 4732.

Adams, R., and J. Page. 2005. Do International Migration and Remittances Reduce Poverty in Developing Countries? *World Development* 33:1645–1669.

Anyanwu, J.C., and A.E.O. Erhijakpor. 2010 Do International Remittances Affect Poverty in Africa? *African Development Review* 22 (1): 51–91.

Azam, J. P., and F. Gubert. 2006. Migrants' Remittances and the Household in Africa: A Review of Evidence. *Journal of African Economies* 15 (2): 426–462.

Bugamelli, M., and F. Paternò. 2005. Do Workers' Remittances Reduce the Probability of Current Account Reversals? World Bank Policy Research Working Paper, No. 3766.

Cattaneo, C. 2009. International Migration, the Brain Drain and Poverty: A Cross-Country Analysis. *World Economy* 32 (8): 1180–1202.

Chami, R., C. Fullenkamp, and S. Jahjah. 2003. Are Immigrants Remittance Flows A Source of Capital for Development? International Monetary Fund Working Paper, WP/03/189.

Cordova, E., and A. Olmedo. 2006. International Remittances and Development: Existing Evidence, Policies and Recommendations. INTAL/ITD Occasional Paper No. 41.

Cox, D., Z. Eser, and F. Jimenez. 1998. Motives for Private Transfers over the Life Cycle: An Analytical Framework and Evidence for Peru. *Journal of Development Economics* 55:57–80.

De Vasconcelos, P. 2005. Improving the Development Impact of Remittances. Paper presented at United Nations Expert Group Meeting on International Migration and Development, July 6–8.

Deaton, A. 1997. *The Analysis of Household Surveys*. Baltimore: Johns Hopkins University Press.

Edwards, A. C. and M. Ureta. 2003. International Migration, Remittances and Schooling: Evidence from El Salvador. *Journal of Development Economics* 72:429–461.

Foster, J., J. Greer, and E. Thorbecke. 1984. A Class of Decomposable Poverty Measures. *Econometrica* 52:761–765.

Heckman, J., R. Lalonde, and J. Smith. 1999. *The Economics and Econometrics of Active Labor Market Programs*, ed. A. Ashenfelter and D. Card. Handbook of Labor Economics 3. Amsterdam: Elsevier Science.

Nguyen, V. C. 2008. Do Foreign Remittances Matter to Poverty and Inequality? Evidence from Vietnam. *Economic Bulletin* 15 (1): 1–11.

Niimi, Y., T. H. Pham, and B. Reilly. 2008. Determinants of Remittances: Recent Evidence Using Data on Internal Determinants in Vietnam. World Bank Policy Research Working Paper 4586.

Orozco, M. and R. Fedewa. 2005. Leveraging Efforts on Remittances and Financial Inter-mediation. Report Commissioned by the Inter American Development Bank.

Phuong, N. T., T. N. T. M. Tam, N. T. Nguyet, and R. Oostendorp. 2008. Determinants and Impacts of Migration in Vietnam. DEPOCEN Working Paper Series No. 2008/01.

Rapoport, H., and F. Docquier. 2005. The Economics of Migrants' Remittances. IZA Dis-cussion Paper No. 1531.

Ratha, D., and W. Shaw. 2007. South-South Migration and Remittances. World Bank Working Paper No. 102.

Rodriguez, E. R. 1996. International Migrants' Remittances in the Philippines. *Canadian Journal of Economics. Revue Canadienne d'Economique* 29:427–432.

Solimano, A. 2003. Remittances by Emigrants: Issues and Evidence. Presented at WIDER Conference: Innovative Sources for Development Finance, Helsinki, May 17–18.

Stahl, C. 1982. Labour Migration and Economic Development. *International Migration Review* 16:868–899.

Stahl, C. W., and F. Arnold. 1986. Overseas Workers' Remittances in Asian Development. *International Migration Review* 20:899–925.

Vietnamese Academy of Social Sciences. 2007. *Vietnam Poverty Update Report. Poverty and Poverty Reduction in Vietnam 1993–2004.* Hanoi: National Political Publisher.

World Bank. 2005a. *World Development Indicators 2005.* Washington, DC: World Bank.

World Bank. 2005b. *Global Economic Prospects Report 2006: Economic Implications of Remittances and Migration.* Washington, DC: World Bank.

World Bank. 2008. *Migration and Remittances Factbook, 2008.* Washington, DC: World Bank.

10 Mortgage Finance in Central and Eastern Europe—Opportunity or Burden?

Thorsten Beck, Katie Kibuuka, and Erwin R. Tiongson

Household indebtedness has grown rapidly in recent years in a number of countries in Central and Eastern Europe and the Baltic region, especially in many of the new European Union (EU) member countries. Between 2001 and 2006, for example, household debt grew at an average rate of close to 40 percent across these countries while rising only by 11 percent in the older EU member countries. Though household debt levels in the new EU countries (about 11 percent of GDP, on average) are still not at the level of more advanced economies (close to 50 percent of GDP), there are significant variations across new EU countries. Much of the growth in household indebtedness has been driven by increasing mortgage debt, underpinned by the availability of a broad range of mortgage instruments.[1] On the one hand, this increase in access to credit by households can be seen as relaxing the financing constraints of households and helping smooth their consumption over the business cycle and lifetime; on the other hand, household over-indebtedness is typically seen as a root cause of the current global financial distress. This chapter uses household data from the EU Statistics on Income and Living Conditions (EU-SILC) to address the welfare and stability implications of increasing household indebtedness in the new EU member countries.[2]

The macro- and microeconomic consequences of rising household access to credit and indebtedness can be significant. However, it is not clear a priori whether benefits or costs dominate. On the one hand, the rising indebtedness could reflect the benefits of financial deepening, allowing households to smooth consumption and achieve home ownership without significant previous saving periods. A dwelling can constitute an important—if not the most important—asset for households, and access to and cost of financing the acquisition of a dwelling therefore has important repercussions for household welfare. On the

other hand, although a dwelling can be one's most important asset, the loan on the dwelling can also be the largest liability for the household, with implications for its financial vulnerability. The implications for financial stability of rapidly rising household indebtedness and the exposure of banking industries to vulnerable households and "risky" borrowers are causes for concern. The poverty and social implications of a rising debt burden can be enormous, especially in a significant economic slowdown, credit tightening, or a macroeconomic crisis.[3] The adverse welfare implications of rising debt burdens for households might be further compounded by rising energy and food prices, as we saw in 2007–2008.[4]

The costs and benefits of rapidly increasing mortgage holdings and household indebtedness can be compared to a similar debate on financial sector deepening in general. Financial deepening is associated with faster economic growth and reduction in poverty levels (Beck, Levine, and Loayza 2000; Beck, Demirgüç-Kunt, and Levine 2007),[5] rapidly increasing credit levels have at the same time been found to be good predictors of crises (Demirgüç-Kunt and Detragiache 1998). The rise in household lending is also related to the process of financial deepening. As financial systems deepen and economies develop, a larger share of bank lending typically goes to households as opposed to enterprises (Beck et al. 2011).

To date, little is known about the incidence of household indebtedness and its distribution in the new EU countries. Although some institutions have called for greater use of microdata to assess household indebtedness and overall financial stability, current assessments of the financial risks faced by the banking sector have been largely based on macroeconomic data, including in many advanced economies.[6] Aggregate or macroeconomic indicators based on average household indebtedness, however, mask the likely concentration of borrowing among selected households, including among those that are more vulnerable or less able to service their debt in the event of an economic slowdown. Debt holding could vary significantly across household income groups, age, and other demographic groups. To answer the questions listed previously on the welfare and stability implications of increasing household indebtedness, microlevel data are therefore necessary.[7]

This chapter documents the recent rapid increase in access to consumer and mortgage credit by households in the new EU member countries, compares use of mortgage credit by households of different

characteristics across old and new EU member countries, and assesses whether mortgage holding can result in a financial burden, at least during the period preceding the current global financial crisis. We use aggregate data as well as household-level data in our analysis. Specifically, we use aggregate lending data across European countries to document recent trends and data from the EU-SILC to explore the benefits and costs of mortgage holding at the household level across countries.

The development of mortgage markets in the transition economies has been part of the overall process of financial deepening in the region. Although financing for the purchase of houses was previously available in some Central European countries such as Hungary or Slovenia, it was not allocated on a market basis (Roy 2008). However, even before 1990, there was a wide variation in tenure status. According to Struyk (1996), 84 percent of houses in Bulgaria were privately owned but this figure was only 26 percent in Russia. If not privately owned, housing was provided by cooperatives or directly by the government. In most countries, the transition process included the privatization of the state-owned housing stock and its distribution to the population. This privatization did not, however, necessarily imply that households immediately used their houses as collateral to obtain financing.

These questions are of immediate policy relevance beyond the economies of Central and Eastern Europe and the Baltics. First, recent research for the United States has shown that the product variety introduced in the 1980s (such as variable rate mortgages) and the liberalization of the market has benefitted homeowners, as their borrowing capacity was increasingly based on their expected lifetime income rather than their current income (Gerardi, Rosen, and Willen 2009). Second, the recent mortgage crisis in the United States has also shown the risk of greater access to mortgage credit. Specifically, mortgage debt beyond a certain threshold ratio of disposable income and with variable interest payment makes households very vulnerable to shocks and can convert the opportunities offered by a mortgage into a financial burden (Mian and Sufi 2009).

In the absence of microdata, the cross-country literature on household credit has focused on aggregate data. Beck et al. (2011) show that the positive effect of financial development on growth and its dampening effect on income inequality have been driven by enterprise credit, while a deeper household credit segment is associated with more consumption smoothing over the business cycle. Beck et al. (2009b) show

that the composition of overall bank lending in enterprise and house-hold credit is mostly driven by socioeconomic and demographic country characteristics and less by policy variables. Jappelli, Pagano, and di Maggio (2008) find that information-sharing arrangements (such as credit bureaus) and judicial enforcement are positively related to household indebtedness and negatively related to defaults. Simi-larly, Warnock and Warnock (2008) find that credit information systems, strong legal rights for both borrowers and lenders (e.g., bankruptcy law), and macroeconomic stability all serve to promote housing finance systems. Wolswijk (2006) analyzes mortgage debt holding among households in the older member states of the EU and finds that finan-cial deregulation, among other practices, have been important drivers of mortgage debt growth.

Regression analyses of tenure status—that is, the determinants of being a mortgage holder—show that there are still significant structural differences between old and new EU countries. Specifically, the prob-ability of being a mortgage holder is *less* sensitive to income and age in the new than in the old EU countries. In general, it is more difficult to explain variations in tenure status in the new EU countries than in the old ones. More important, we find no evidence that prospective, rather than current, income determines the use of mortgage finance in any of the new EU countries, though this seems generally true for the older EU members as well. Our empirical analysis also suggests that in spite of the rapid aggregate increase in mortgage finance, mortgage holders are not more likely to report financial burden or incur arrears than renters or outright owners. In fact, the likelihood of financial dis-tress among mortgage holders in the new EU member countries fell between 2005 and 2007, possibly reflecting the generally strong income growth experienced by these countries over this period.

Although this chapter represents significant progress in understand-ing the benefits and costs of increasing access to household and more specifically mortgage credit, some caution is warranted in interpreting the results. First, given the nature of the EU-SILC surveys as instru-ments to measure living standards and poverty incidence, we do not have as much information on households' financial assets, liabilities, and flows as we would like. Second, although we have three years of data, these are repeated cross-sections and we do not have the longi-tudinal dimension available. Finally, our sample ends in 2007, so the results reported here refer to the period before the onset of the global financial crisis.

Data

We utilize both aggregate and household-level survey data in our empirical analysis. Specifically, we use information from the European Credit Research Institute (ECRI) to illustrate aggregate trends in household and mortgage lending across the new EU member states over time and in comparison with the old EU member states. Although data are available for 1995 to 2007 for many Western European countries, they are available for most transition economies starting only in the late 1990s. We complement these aggregate data with data on the share of foreign exchange loans and the share of variable interest rate loans in total mortgage lending, hand-collected from country-specific sources. Although such aggregate data allow us to make cross-country comparisons, they do not allow us to make in-depth assessment of the benefits and costs of mortgage holdings. We therefore use these data largely for illustrative and motivational purposes before proceeding to the use of microdata for a deeper analysis.

To explore the relationship between household characteristics, mortgage holdings, and financial vulnerability, we utilize information from the databases of the EU-SILC, an annual EU-wide household survey anchored in the European Statistical System. This survey is conducted by national statistical offices and has a cross-sectional as well as a longitudinal dimension, that is, subsamples of households are surveyed over several years. The EU-SILC was initiated in 2003, but the new EU member countries undertook their first surveys only in 2005. At the time of our analysis, data was available for 2005, 2006, and 2007 for both old and new EU members. Specifically, we have survey data available for the following Western European and South European countries: Austria, Belgium, Cyprus, Denmark, Finland, France, Great Britain, Greece, Ireland, Italy, Luxembourg, the Netherlands, Portugal, Spain, and Sweden. We have survey data for eight countries that joined the EU in 2005: the Czech Republic, Estonia, Hungary, Latvia, Lithuania, Poland, the Slovak Republic, and Slovenia.[8]

The EU-SILC is a census-based stratified survey with at least 3,500 households per country. It collects timely and comparable data on income, expenditures, and social exclusion in countries of the European Union. Critically, the survey contains information about (1) whether households own with or without mortgage or rent their current residence, (2) whether they are in arrears on different credit obligations, and (3) whether they see their housing costs as a financial burden. In

addition, the EU-SILC database provides information on several types of variables: those measured at the household level (including household size, composition, and others) and basic individual and demographic characteristics of household members (including education, health status, access to health care, detailed labor market activity, and age). In our analysis, we focus on households rather than individuals. Where we use individual-level information, we use the information provided by either the household head (if he or she is the one responding to the survey) or the information provided by the household member with the highest income.

The EU-SILC database offers certain advantages for our purposes as well as limitations. The main strength of the database is that it is consistent across twenty-three countries, thus allowing us valid comparisons between the new EU members in Central and Eastern Europe and the Baltic region and the old EU member countries in Western Europe. Further, most survey questions are asked in all countries, which again enables us to undertake cross-country comparisons. Finally, there are detailed questions both on the tenure status as well as on a large array of sociodemographic variables and indicators of financial burden and vulnerability that are directly relevant to our analysis.

However, there are some weaknesses in the available data. First, data for the new EU member countries are available only since 2005, which constrains a more in-depth analysis and testing of hypotheses over time. The EU-SILC database includes a longitudinal component, but this is yet to be made available in the public domain. Second, the focus of the EU-SILC survey is not access to financial services or financing constraints but rather social exclusion and poverty, so many of the variables do not correspond to exact measures as used in other country-specific studies and as required to test specific theories. For example, we have information on mortgage interest payments but not total mortgage payments (including principal repayment).[9] We also lack information on the access to and use of other financial services by the household. Third, we do not have the necessary information to control for the stratification, so the standard errors in our regressions are most likely underestimated. Finally, because these are survey data, the volume of household loans and mortgages may not necessarily correspond fully to aggregate data from the banking sector. Nonetheless, they do provide a useful statistical portrait of the distribution of household debt (see, e.g., NBS 2006; Beer and Schürz 2007).

Mortgage Credit across Europe: The Aggregate View

Although the new EU countries have, on average, experienced a rapid increase in household credit, there are large variations across countries. This section documents aggregate trends in household credit across the new EU member countries, contrasting and comparing them with Western Europe as appropriate.

Household credit to GDP increased from less than 5 percent in 2000 to over 25 percent of GDP in 2007 across the new EU countries, while at the same time increasing from 42 percent to 50 percent in Western Europe (figure 10.1). Behind this average statistic, however, is a wide variation. Household credit to GDP reached over 40 percent in 2007 in Croatia, Estonia, and Latvia, yet it was less than 20 percent in Romania and Slovakia. The difference is even starker when relating household credit to disposable income. Although it reached 64 percent in Latvia and 79 percent in Estonia, household credit accounted for only 23 percent of disposable income in Romania. But even among the old EU members, there is substantial variation in household credit, ranging from 30 percent in Italy to 124 percent in Denmark.

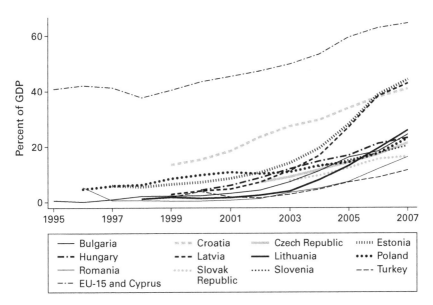

Figure 10.1
Total credit to households, 1995–2007.

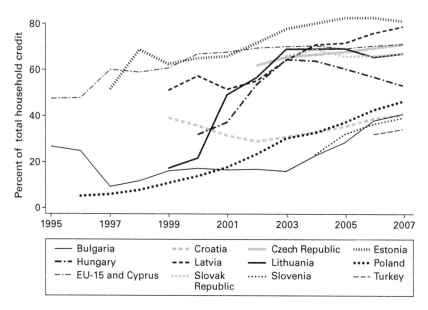

Figure 10.2
Mortgage credit to households, 1995–2007.

The share of mortgage credit in total household credit also varies significantly across the new EU member countries (figure 10.2). Although mortgage credit constituted 80 percent of household credit in Estonia in 2007, it constituted less than 20 percent in Romania. In Western Europe, the share of mortgage credit in total household credit ranged from 54 percent in Austria to almost 90 percent in the Netherlands. On average, mortgage credit constituted 56 percent of total household credit in the new EU countries in 2007, compared to 72 percent in Western Europe. This suggests that mortgage credit is only one component—though an important one—of overall household credit.

The rapid increase in the importance of household credit has gone hand in hand with a decreasing importance of enterprise credit in overall bank lending (figure 10.3). Although the share of household lending in total bank lending in the old EU countries has stayed relatively constant over the period 2000–2007, at around 55 percent, it has increased from 22 percent in 2000 to 54 percent in 2007 among the new EU countries of Central and Eastern Europe. Behind this rapid increase in household lending is an overall strong lending growth in the new EU countries, from 17 percent of GDP in 2000 to 55 percent in 2007.

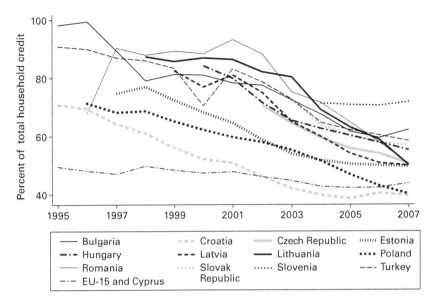

Figure 10.3
Credit to enterprises, 1995–2007.

One important difference between mortgage markets in the old and new EU countries, with implication for both affordability and household vulnerability, is the currency in which mortgages (and household loans in general) are denominated. In the old EU countries, almost all household and mortgage loans are denominated in local currency; in contrast, a large proportion of mortgage loans in the new EU countries are denominated in foreign currency, mostly euros or Swiss francs (table 10.1). The share of foreign exchange mortgage loans, however, varies enormously among the new EU countries, ranging from less than 1 percent in the Czech Republic to more than 50 percent in Hungary and almost 90 percent in Romania. This percentage seems especially risky in the case of Hungary and Poland, where a large share of these foreign currency–denominated loans is in Swiss francs, which are typically more volatile than the euro (ECB 2009). The share of variable interest rate loans also varies greatly, at close to 80 percent in Hungary, Slovakia, and Slovenia; only a third of mortgage loans in France and Denmark are variable interest, but 95 percent are in Portugal.

The rapid credit growth—especially in household credit—and the high share of foreign exchange loans point to the growing role of foreign-owned banks in the new EU countries over the past decade. Foreign

Table 10.1
Share of foreign currency–denominated loans

	Banks loans to households	Mortgage loans	Variable interest rates
New EU countries			
Bulgaria	29.82	36.00	
Czech Republic	0.10	0.10	
Estonia	82.35		
Hungary	70.21	46.30	73.60
Latvia	87.38		
Lithuania	61.64		
Poland	39.83	54.90	
Romania	58.73	88.50	
Slovak Republic	2.79	4.60	78.00
Slovenia			78.00
Other countries			
Armenia	23.58		
Croatia	69.10	88.10	95.60
Kazakhstan	50.80		
FYR Macedonia	44.30		
Russia	10.00	20.90	
Turkey	0.70	6.60	
Ukraine	71.90		
Belgium			32.40
Denmark			30.00
France			32.00
Ireland			64.40
Italy			86.90
Netherlands			36.00
Portugal			95.40
United Kingdom			34.90

Sources: European Central Bank; National Central Banks; UniCredit.
Variable interest rate data sources: Bank of Slovenia 2008; Croatian National Bank 2008; EMF 2006; Schich and Ahn 2007.
Note: The variable rate refers to an interest rate that remains unchanged for up to one year. Data for Croatia and Slovenia refer to 2007.

banks have played a critical role in breaking the vicious cycle of connected lending from formerly state-owned banks to formerly (or still) government-owned enterprises, fostering broader access to credit and thus promoting private sector development in these economies.[10] Under competitive pressure and having access to cheaper funding sources and better lending technologies than domestic banks, foreign banks also introduced household lending, which was previously almost unheard of. Because the deposit base did not experience the same growth as lending, foreign banks have relied mostly on financing from their parent banks. The current global crisis, on the other hand, has shown the risk of this rapid financial deepening, with fragility not only on the macroeconomic level but also on the household level. We explore this in greater depth later in this chapter. Another factor behind the rapid increase in mortgage finance is the rapid improvement in the contractual framework underlying mortgage finance (EBRD 2007), although further reforms are needed to fully establish clearly defined property rights.

The rapid increase in household credit is however partly also demand driven, that is, driven by higher incomes as well as by higher expected future incomes. Reliance on foreign currency loans at significantly lower interest rates can be explained by the rational expectation of appreciating local currencies following the Balassa-Samuelson hypothesis. The aggregate numbers presented in this section show the rapid increase in household indebtedness over the past years. They do not, however, give any insight into the distribution of access to credit and indebtedness within countries and the effect thereof on welfare and fragility. We turn to these questions now.

Who Has Access to Mortgage Finance?

Mortgage debt holdings vary significantly across countries as well as within countries by selected household characteristics. Using EU-SILC survey data, this section utilizes graphs and multinomial probit regressions to explore household characteristics that can explain mortgage debt holding. In particular, we compare the significance and elasticity of these different characteristics across countries. We distinguish between renting, owning with mortgage, and owning without mortgage and relate an array of household and individual characteristics to this tenure status.

Figure 10.4 shows the distribution of renters, outright owners, and owners with mortgages across countries in our sample of EU-SILC

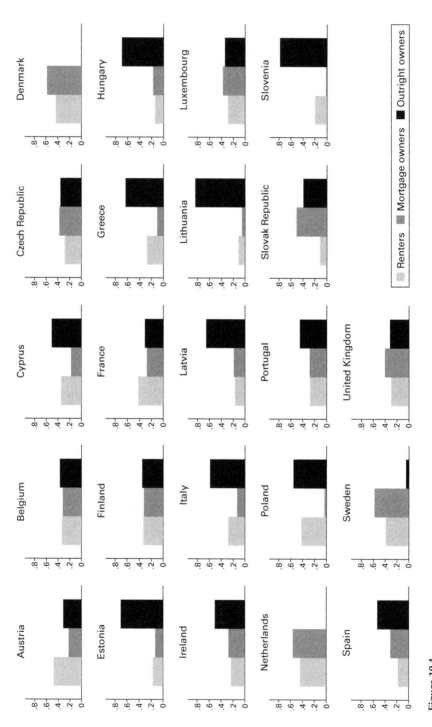

Figure 10.4
Share of renters, mortgage owners, and outright owners, 2007. *Source:* EU Statistics on Income and Living Conditions (EU-SILC), 2007

countries for 2007.[11] We note two countries in Western Europe without any outright owners in our database—Denmark and the Netherlands—and thus only renters and mortgage holders.[12] In 2007, the share of mortgage holders varied from 1.9 percent in Slovenia to 57.6 percent in Denmark; the share of renters ranged from 10.7 percent in Lithuania to 48 percent in Austria. There has been an increasing trend over the three years we have data for; the average share of mortgage holders increased from 31.7 percent (old EU member countries) and 12.9 percent (new EU countries) in 2005 to 32.4 percent (old EU countries) and 18.3 percent (new EU countries) in 2007. We also note the relatively high share of outright owners in many new EU countries, which could be a legacy of housing privatization in the transition process. Plotting the share of mortgage holders against the ratio of mortgage credit to GDP shows a positive correlation suggesting that the EU-SILC surveys capture aggregate trends in the population (figure 10.5). This information also suggests that the depth and breadth of mortgage markets coincide broadly.

Figure 10.6 shows the weighted variation of tenure status across income deciles across the twenty-three surveys for 2007. We can see

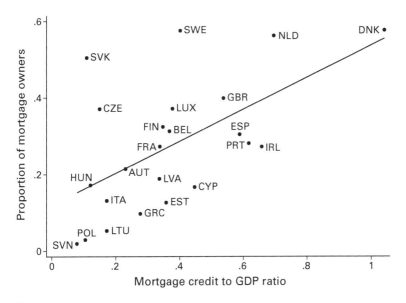

Figure 10.5
Share of mortgage owners and mortgage credit to GDP ratio, 2007. *Source:* EU Statistics on Income and Living Conditions (EU-SILC), 2007, and ECRI—Lending to Households in Europe, Statistical Package 2008

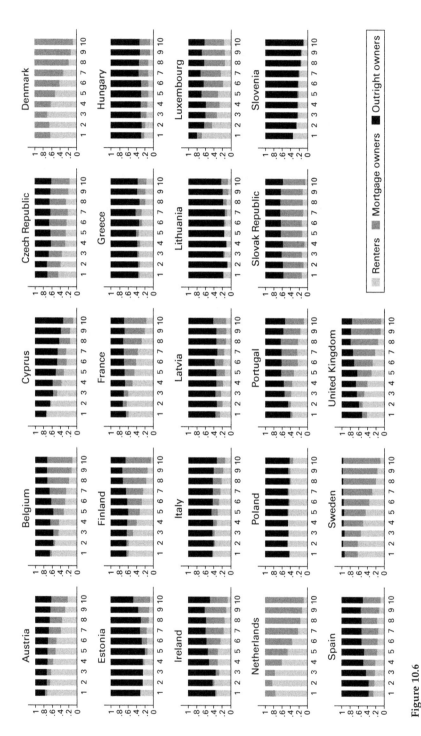

Figure 10.6
Tenure status by income decile, 2007. *Source:* EU Statistics on Income and Living Conditions (EU-SILC), 2007

some general trends but also some pronounced differences across countries. In most countries, richer households are less likely to rent and more likely to hold mortgages, whereas there is no clear relationship between outright ownership and income across countries. Although the sensitivity of tenure status to income varies significantly across countries, these relationships do not seem to vary significantly between Western European countries, on the one hand, and new EU member countries, on the other hand. However, we confirm earlier findings that mortgage holdings are significantly lower at all income quintiles in the new EU member countries, whereas outright ownership is typically higher in transition economies. Figure 10.7 shows the variation of tenure status across age brackets of the household head. Specifically, we split the sample according to the age of the household head, forming brackets of (1) below 35 years, (2) between 35 and 44 years, (3) between 45 and 54 years, (4) between 55 and 64 years, and (5) 65 years and older. There are some general trends, such as outright ownership increasing with age and renting decreasing with the age of the household head. The share of households with mortgages first increases then decreases with the age of the household head. Although this finding most likely reflects patterns of mortgage holding over the life cycle in Western and Southern Europe, it might reflect also exclusion of older households from the mortgage market in the new EU member countries. Tenure status does not vary as much across age brackets in the new EU countries as it does in Western and Southern Europe.

Many household and individual characteristics are correlated with tenure status and are also correlated with each other. To formally explore the relationship between household characteristics and the decision to rent, own outright, or own with a mortgage, we first run multinomial regressions of the form shown in equation 10.1:

$$y = X\beta + \varepsilon, \tag{10.1}$$

where y can take on three values: 0 if the household rents the dwelling, 1 if the household owns the dwelling it lives in and holds a mortgage, and 2 if the household owns the dwelling without holding a mortgage; X is a set of household characteristics. Given the unordered nature of the three choices, we use multinomial regressions. For two countries— Denmark and the Netherlands—we use simple logit regressions, as the survey sample in these countries does not include any owners without mortgages. We run separate regressions for each survey, yielding a total of sixty-nine regressions. Although we focus mostly on the 2007 results,

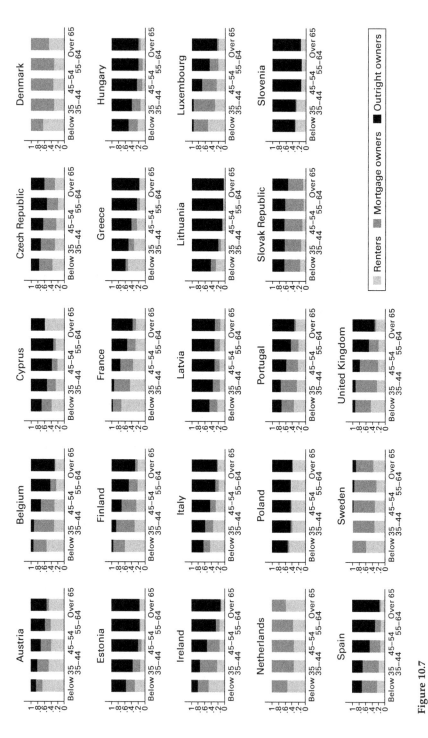

Figure 10.7
Tenure status owners by age group, 2007. *Source:* EU Statistics on Income and Living Conditions (EU-SILC), 2007

we make comparisons across survey years, for which there may be some notable trends. All the results make use of household weights provided in each survey.[13] The probability that a household will choose one of the three options is shown in equation 10.2:

$$\text{prob } (y = i \mid X) = \exp(X\beta_i) / [1 + \Sigma \exp(X\beta_{i})] \quad i = 0,1,2. \qquad (10.2)$$

Given that the probabilities add up to 1, we normalize $\beta_1 = 0$, which allows us to derive two log-odds ratios:

$$\log[p_j(X, \beta) / p_0(X, \beta)] = \exp (X\beta_i) \quad i = 1,2, \qquad (10.3)$$

where p_j denotes the response probability in equation 10.2.[14]

By construction, the log-odds ratios do not depend on the third omitted choice—a rather strong condition—which we test using a Hausman test, comparing the log-odds ratios from the full model with logit estimates from a restricted model in which we leave out households taking the third choice. Because in most cases we reject the independence of irrelevant alternatives and thus the validity of the multinomial regressions, we also report the results of nested multinomial regressions. In the case of nested regressions, we use the decision to rent or own as branches, with mortgage holding being one of two choices in the "own-branch."

We include an array of household and individual characteristics. First, we include information on the type and size of the household; specifically, we include dummy variables for whether the household is (1) a one-person household or (2) a family without dependent children, with (3) family with dependent children being the omitted category. The choice of owning or renting might depend on altruistic inheritance motives but also on geographic mobility, which in turn might depend on the household type. We expect families with dependent children to be less mobile and more likely to commit to a house. We also control for the number of household members, which might influence both the choice as well as the affordability of tenure status. Although larger families might be more likely to prefer owning a house, they might be less likely to afford it. Second, we include dummies for the location of the residence by including a dummy for urban areas. Availability of dwellings and tenure status might vary across urban and rural areas, although theory does not make any prediction a priori and this relationship might vary across countries. Third, we include a dummy variable for house, as opposed to apartment, as the tenure status might vary with the dwelling type. We expect apartment residents to be more

likely to rent, as apartments are often seen as transitory housing arrangements. Fourth, we include several characteristics of the household head, such as age (in logs), gender, education status (captured by dummy variables for secondary and university education), and the current employment status. Current employment status is captured by dummy variables for (1) working full-time, (2) working part-time, (3) unemployed, and (4) retired, with (5) other being the residual category. Employment status might influence the affordability of the tenure status beyond income. Finally, and most important, we include household income, expecting a higher likelihood of owning than renting as household income increases as well as a higher likelihood of owning without a mortgage.[15]

We also use the regression analysis to test several hypotheses on access to mortgage finance and its covariants. Traditional mortgage lending criteria base the mortgage finance approval and amount on current employment and income. From the consumer's perspective, however, the mortgage should be based on lifetime income and thus income expectations over the course of the mortgage. One way to test what determines mortgage finance access would be by examining the coefficients on income, age, and education and their interactions. If households are able to borrow only on their current income, then we should find a positive and significant coefficient on income with insignificant coefficients on education and its interaction with age or income. If households are able to borrow based on their expected lifetime income, we expect a smaller coefficient on current income and a negative coefficient on its interaction with education; the coefficient on age might be positive, and its interaction with education should be negative. This hypothesis implies that higher education is significantly correlated with higher income growth over the lifetime.

Table 10.2 provides descriptive statistics on the different household characteristics for 2007. Tables A10.1 and A10.2 report descriptive statistics for 2005 and 2006, respectively. We note that the average age is around fifty years. The share of female respondents is higher in the new EU countries, where the household size is also greater, but average income is—unsurprisingly—lower. The share of respondents with secondary education is higher in the new EU countries, and the average share of respondents with university education is at a similar levels. More respondents in the old EU countries live in houses than in the new EU countries; household composition is, on average, similar

between old and new EU countries. There is, on average, a higher share of full-time employees, but also retirees in the new than the old EU countries; a greater share lives in urban areas in the old EU countries. Critically, there is even more variation between members of each group in terms of household characteristics than there is between the two groups.

Table 10.3 presents the results of the multinomial regressions: panel A reports the log-odds ratios between renters and mortgage holders and panel B reports the log-odds ratios between outright owners and owners with a mortgage. We report estimates for separate regressions across the twenty-three countries in 2007; results for 2005 and 2006 are reported in tables A10.3 and A10.4, respectively.[16] We report marginal effects rather than coefficients to gauge both the statistical and economic significance of the estimates. As discussed previously, we also report the results of the Hausman tests, comparing the log-odds ratios from the full model with logit estimates from a restricted model without the third option. We note that the Hausman test is rejected for most countries, suggesting the need for a nested model, which we report in table 10.4. In the following sections, we discuss the findings, focusing on cross-country and cross-time differences in coefficient size and significance and comparing and contrasting old and new EU members.

The regression results in table 10.3 show some country traits that are consistently related to tenure status across countries and others that are either insignificant or related to tenure status with different signs across countries. First, there is a strong relationship between income and tenure status; households with higher incomes are more likely to have a mortgage, both in old and new EU countries. However, the elasticity is, on average, higher in the old EU countries (0.083) than in the new EU countries (0.046); that is, the sensitivity of tenure status to income is not as strong in the new EU countries. In addition, the relationship between income and tenure status is insignificant in several new EU countries such as Hungary, Latvia, and the Slovak Republic. Second, in most countries, mortgage holders are older, with the notable exceptions of Denmark, Cyprus, Hungary, and the Slovak Republic, where the relationship between age and tenure status is insignificant, and in the Netherlands, where the relationship is reversed. Third, there is little evidence that households headed by females are less likely to have a mortgage relative to households headed by males, except in Belgium,

Table 10.2
Descriptive summary statistics (weighted averages: explanatory variables)

Country	age	female	hhsize	lnincome	secedu	teredu	house	apartment
Recently added EU countries								
Czech Republic	50	0.33	2.52	9.06	0.84	0.16	0.43	0.56
Estonia	50	0.46	2.32	8.72	0.59	0.36	0.31	0.69
Hungary	51	0.45	2.60	8.75	0.68	0.25	0.64	0.34
Latvia	50	0.48	2.64	8.49	0.64	0.32	0.28	0.72
Lithuania	51	0.45	2.57	8.50	0.39	0.50	0.41	0.59
Poland	51	0.42	2.84	8.72	0.56	0.23	0.44	0.55
Slovak Republic	51	0.40	2.82	8.77	0.78	0.21	0.47	0.53
Slovenia	51	0.42	2.82	9.71	0.72	0.23	0.69	0.31
EU-15 and Cyprus								
Austria	51	0.35	2.32	10.19	0.69	0.30	0.51	0.48
Belgium	51	0.34	2.31	10.10	0.47	0.39	0.71	0.26
Cyprus	50	0.27	2.94	10.19	0.42	0.30	0.73	0.25
Denmark	50	0.41	2.01	10.28	0.75	0.25	0.62	0.37
Finland	50	0.42	2.12	10.12	0.49	0.31	0.57	0.43
France	51	0.38	2.27	10.09	0.52	0.31	0.59	0.40
Greece	52	0.30	2.68	9.71	0.39	0.24	0.45	0.55
Ireland	49	0.35	2.83	10.49	0.38	0.36	0.96	0.04
Italy	54	0.34	2.44	10.02	0.54	0.18	0.41	0.53
Luxembourg	50	0.30	2.47	10.78	0.44	0.28	0.65	0.33
Netherlands	50	0.31	2.26	10.19	0.54	0.34	0.68	0.26
Portugal	52	0.35	2.75	9.49	0.29	0.14	0.62	0.38
Spain	50	0.29	2.75	9.88	0.41	0.30	0.34	0.66
Sweden	51	0.39	2.11	10.09	0.54	0.36	0.48	0.51
United Kingdom	51	0.36	2.35	10.32	0.69	0.31	0.82	0.18

Source: EU Statistics on Income and Living Conditions (EU-SILC) database, 2007.
Note: Data used to create dummy variables—urban and rural—are not available for the Netherlands and Slovenia.

hh1	hhnodep	hhdep	fulltime	parttime	unemp	retired	other	urban	rural
0.24	0.41	0.36	0.62	0.01	0.04	0.28	0.05	0.37	0.39
0.34	0.32	0.34	0.65	0.03	0.02	0.25	0.05	0.50	0.50
0.24	0.38	0.37	0.56	0.02	0.04	0.30	0.09	0.35	0.45
0.25	0.34	0.40	0.64	0.03	0.03	0.25	0.04	0.49	0.51
0.27	0.32	0.41	0.64	0.02	0.03	0.27	0.05	0.42	0.58
0.25	0.33	0.40	0.51	0.03	0.03	0.28	0.16	0.46	0.43
0.24	0.37	0.39	0.64	0.01	0.02	0.32	0.02	0.29	0.23
0.21	0.37	0.43	0.60	0.01	0.03	0.34	0.02		
0.35	0.35	0.30	0.52	0.05	0.04	0.34	0.03	0.41	0.35
0.34	0.35	0.31	0.49	0.08	0.06	0.30	0.06	0.56	0.04
0.16	0.36	0.48	0.69	0.03	0.02	0.23	0.03	0.59	0.29
0.44	0.29	0.27	0.53	0.05	0.03	0.25	0.13	0.36	0.24
0.39	0.35	0.26	0.54	0.05	0.05	0.25	0.10	0.29	0.54
0.34	0.34	0.32	0.51	0.05	0.04	0.35	0.04	0.50	0.17
0.20	0.46	0.34	0.57	0.03	0.02	0.29	0.08	0.43	0.44
0.21	0.33	0.46	0.55	0.10	0.05	0.14	0.16	0.34	0.37
0.29	0.38	0.33	0.54	0.03	0.02	0.29	0.12	0.44	0.17
0.29	0.33	0.38	0.62	0.04	0.02	0.22	0.10	0.49	0.20
0.35	0.35	0.30	0.48	0.14	0.01	0.19	0.18		
0.17	0.41	0.42	0.60	0.04	0.04	0.28	0.04	0.45	0.25
0.17	0.45	0.37	0.62	0.03	0.04	0.23	0.08	0.54	0.27
0.39	0.32	0.29	0.53	0.09	0.02	0.26	0.09	0.22	0.68
0.30	0.37	0.30	0.52	0.07	0.02	0.26	0.13	0.76	0.05

Table 10.3
Panel A: Multinomial regressions (log-odds ratio between renters and mortgage holders [marginal effects])

Country	lage	female	hhsize	lnincome	hhnodep	hhdep	house	secedu	teredu
Recently added EU countries									
Czech Republic	−0.1905***	0.0141	−0.0088	−0.1391***	−0.0475**	−0.0008	−0.2820***		−0.5195***
Estonia	−0.2852***	0.0081	−0.0506***	−0.0358**	−0.0976***	−0.0155	0.0374**		0.2462
Hungary	−0.0695	0.0017	0.0007	−0.0398	−0.0224*	−0.0027	−0.1290***	0.4006	0.2215
Latvia	−0.4303***	−0.0250	0.0117	−0.0982	−0.0480**	−0.0452*	−0.1245***	−0.9904***	−0.9248***
Lithuania	−0.2006***	−0.0183*	−0.0132	−0.0412***	−0.0339**	0.0127	0.0103		0.0793
Poland	−0.2896***	0.0150	−0.0100	−0.0749***	0.0258	0.0394	−0.5823***	−0.5512	−0.5621***
Slovak Republic	−0.1963	−0.0150	0.0004	0.0114	−0.0307*	0.0298	−0.0964***	0.1450	0.7868
Slovenia	−0.1687*	−0.0285***	−0.0196***	−0.1244***	−0.0625***	0.0873***	−0.1136***	−0.0579	−0.0918
EU-15 and Cyprus									
Austria	−0.6764**	0.0043	−0.0252**	−0.2457	−0.0187	−0.0102	−0.4861***	−0.9232***	−0.9671***
Belgium	−0.2716**	0.0405*	0.0013	−0.2824***	−0.0722**	−0.0061	−0.4598***	−0.0055	−0.0205
Cyprus	0.0764	0.0133	−0.0288*	−0.1987***	0.0135	−0.0424	−0.2652***	0.4060	0.7276
Denmark	−0.3377	−0.1023***	0.0637***	−0.5600*	0.0810**	−0.0723	0.5214***	−0.9997***	−0.9998***
Finland	−0.3005**	−0.0034	−0.0030	−0.3458***	0.0148	0.0612	−0.3450***	0.2375	0.6248
France	−0.3813***	0.0364*	−0.0039	−0.1541***	−0.0479	−0.0413	−0.4723***	0.9512***	0.9655***
Greece	−0.5006***	−0.0296*	−0.0798***	−0.0014	−0.0890***	0.0461	−0.2025***	0.2732	−0.4130***
Ireland	−0.5735***	0.1005***	0.0192*	−0.1396***	0.0338	0.0289	−0.6699***	−0.2334	0.8394**
Italy	−0.3677***	−0.0094	−0.0226***	−0.0863***	−0.0584***	0.0322	−0.1085***	0.0700	−0.2201**
Luxembourg	−0.2668**	−0.0301	0.0076	−0.3874***	0.0771	0.0547	−0.4626***	−0.5687	−0.9415***
Netherlands	0.3008**	−0.0085	−0.0049	0.3158***	0.0362	0.0535	0.3215***	0.5840	−0.1458
Portugal	−0.2721***	0.0354	−0.0113	−0.1106***	−0.0459	−0.0437	−0.0626***	0.3513	−0.2865
Spain	−0.2110***	0.0263**	0.0012	−0.0799***	−0.0625***	−0.0692***	−0.0618***	−0.2463	−0.0398
Sweden	−0.3274**	0.0204	0.0018	−0.2552***	−0.0195	0.0422	−0.5192***	−0.9495***	−0.8644***
United Kingdom	−0.6659***	0.0336**	0.0062	−0.1588***	−0.0449**	0.0456	−0.4159***	−0.7518***	

Source: EU Statistics on Income and Living Conditions (EU-SILC) database, 2007.
*significant at 90 percent; **significant at 95 percent; ***significant at 99 percent.

fulltime	parttime	unemp	retired	urban	lage*secedu	lage*teredu	inc*secedu	inc*teredu	Hausman F-Statistic	r²
−0.0365	−0.0277	0.1536***	−0.0170	0.0520***		0.0167		0.1138***	0.95	0.31
−0.0130	0.0511	−0.0451	0.0896*	0.0119		−0.0980*		0.0152	0.82	0.20
−0.0434***	−0.0160	−0.0076	0.0117	0.0617***	−0.1125**	−0.0844	−0.0136	0.0084	1.55*	0.11
−0.0311	−0.0035	−0.0086	−0.0399	−0.0460***	0.3202**	0.3600**	0.0386	0.0716	1.06	0.10
−0.0032		0.0018		−0.0013		−0.0692**		0.0175	0.89	0.23
−0.002	0.0161	0.1087**	0.0008	0.2000***	0.1446***	0.1660***	0.0092	0.0200	3.44***	0.32
0.0347	0.0118	0.0542	0.0267	0.0096	0.0855	0.0136	−0.0718	−0.0736	0.75	0.30
0.1402***	0.2500**	0.2302***	0.1853***		−0.0661	−0.1653	0.0086	0.0263	1.47*	0.11
−0.0343	−0.0271	−0.0509	0.0302	0.1659***	0.4344	0.2960	0.0106	0.1328	2.45***	0.25
−0.1544***	−0.1460***	0.0202	−0.0374	0.0456**	−0.2000*	−0.3604***	0.0588	0.0948	1.88**	0.34
0.0209	0.0428	0.1871*	0.1250*	0.0902***	−0.3229***	−0.2526**	−0.0657	−0.0418	1.61**	0.19
0.2031***	0.0947*	−0.0182	0.0969**	−0.0542**	0.4869	0.3635	0.6578**	0.6601**		0.34
−0.0842***	−0.0755*	0.1002**	−0.0726*	0.0717***	−0.2186	−0.4100**	0.0532	0.0700	2.87***	0.32
0.0438	0.0411	0.2284***	0.0172	−0.0053	−0.3743***	−0.3626***	−0.0956*	−0.1190**	2.05***	0.32
−0.0288	0.0180	−0.0434	−0.0603*	0.0371**	0.1672***	0.2712***	−0.1006***	−0.0456	1.91***	0.17
−0.1362***	−0.0661**	0.0274	−0.0186	0.0850***	0.0452	−0.1613	−0.0087	−0.0469	3.05***	0.31
0.0286	0.0388	0.0811**	−0.0240	0.0679***	0.0294	0.0800	−0.0316**	−0.0535**	3.38***	0.13
−0.0365	−0.1484**	0.1576	0.0106	−0.0470	−0.0632	−0.0214	0.1089	0.2617***	1.09	0.35
0.2447***	0.0724**	0.0651	0.0858***		−0.1427	−0.0483	0.0103	0.0648		0.29
−0.0797	−0.0726	0.0101	−0.0109	0.1293***	0.0123	0.1429	−0.0493	−0.0358	2.33***	0.16
0.0213	0.0779*	0.0187	0.0221	−0.0135	0.0107	0.0540	0.0202	−0.0243	1.88**	0.14
−0.0871***	−0.1277***	0.0284	−0.1287***	−0.0394**	0.1942	0.1972	0.0734	0.0722	1.08	0.31
−0.2984***	−0.1915***	0.1615**	0.0158	−0.0096	0.2652***			−0.0285	4.85***	0.32

Table 10.3
Panel B: Multinomial regressions (log-odds ratio between outright owners and mortgage holders [marginal effects])

Country	lage	female	hhsize	lnincome	hhnodep	hhdep	house	secedu	teredu
Recently added EU countries									
Czech Republic	0.1973***	−0.0101	0.0453***	−0.0152	0.0290	−0.1214***	0.7002***		0.4479
Estonia	0.3668***	−0.0163	0.0565***	−0.0212	0.1266***	−0.0044	−0.0520***		−0.2967
Hungary	0.2588***	0.0099	0.0022	0.0244	0.0460**	−0.0473*	0.1333***	0.0637	0.1215
Latvia	0.0808	0.0232	0.0007	−0.1522*	0.0820***	0.0333	0.2193***	−0.0077	−0.0752
Lithuania	0.2215***	0.0155	0.0202**	0.0294**	0.0346**	−0.0290	−0.0084		−0.1828
Poland	0.3170***	−0.0120	0.0176***	0.0654**	−0.0281	−0.0643**	0.5769***	0.6416***	0.5662***
Slovak Republic	0.3462	−0.0218	0.0417***	−0.2012	0.0191	−0.1053***	0.6178***	−0.2883	−0.2234
Slovenia	0.1664	0.0298***	0.0259***	0.0817**	0.0538***	−0.1183***	0.1167***	−0.9303***	−0.9081***
EU-15 and Cyprus									
Austria	0.7034*	−0.0046	0.0376***	0.0035	0.0199	−0.1222***	0.3340***	0.4981	0.0671
Belgium	0.5650***	−0.0239	0.0119	−0.0469	0.1614***	−0.1001**	0.2518***	−0.9115***	−0.9582***
Cyprus	0.0904	0.0015	0.0531***	0.0878**	0.0367	−0.0188	0.2113***	−0.9920***	−0.9209***
Finland	0.8250***	0.0021	0.0119	0.0473	0.0849***	−0.0856***	0.1558***	0.4033	−0.5851
France	0.6918***	−0.0209	−0.0106	0.0439	0.0530**	−0.0284	0.2247***	0.0292	−0.2549
Greece	0.5214***	0.0037	0.0838***	−0.0314	0.0724**	−0.1198***	0.2156***	−0.0665	0.5234***
Ireland	0.8503***	−0.0586*	0.0166	0.0373	0.0042	−0.2083***	0.5183***	0.6455	−0.8552***
Italy	0.5061***	0.0202*	0.0437***	−0.0024	0.0647***	−0.0986***	0.1283***	−0.3768	−0.6931***
Luxembourg	0.8991***	0.0747*	0.0360*	0.1702*	−0.0127	−0.2062***	0.2774***	0.9738***	0.5804
Portugal	0.4245***	0.0107	0.0538***	−0.0248	0.0449	−0.1718***	0.2752***	−0.0309	−0.3417
Spain	0.6515***	0.0193	0.0808***	−0.0601***	0.0481*	−0.1776***	0.0800***	0.2004	−0.4026
Sweden	0.0714***	−0.0047**	−0.0042*	−0.0086*	0.0066	0.0020	0.0391***	0.5376	0.9512***
United Kingdom	0.8818***	−0.0262*	0.0272**	−0.0373**	0.0724***	−0.1529***	0.1969***	0.8422***	

Source: EU Statistics on Income and Living Conditions (EU-SILC) database, 2007.
*significant at 90 percent; **significant at 95 percent; ***significant at 99 percent.

Ireland, Spain, and the United Kingdom: in some countries (Greece, Lithuania, and Slovenia), they are more likely to have a mortgage. In a few countries (Austria, Cyprus, Estonia, Greece, Italy, and Slovenia), larger families are more likely to have a mortgage; in Denmark, such families are more likely to rent. In some countries, especially among new EU countries, families with no dependents are more likely to have a mortgage than to rent. Fourth, in most countries, households living in houses are more likely to be mortgage owners than renters, with the notable exceptions of Denmark, Estonia, and the Netherlands, where the relationship is reversed. On the other hand, there is no clear rela-

fulltime	parttime	unemp	retired	urban	lage*secedu	lage*teredu	inc*secedu	inc*teredu	Hausman F-Statistic	r²
0.0014	0.0808	-0.0458	-0.0061	-0.0390***		-0.0140		-0.0544	9.12***	0.31
-0.0175	-0.0322	0.0430	-0.0436	-0.0153		0.1138**		-0.0179	1.22	0.20
0.0217	-0.0696	0.0322	0.0291	-0.0815***	0.0663	0.0308	-0.0082	-0.0471	1.59**	0.11
0.0119	0.0108	0.0070	-0.0202	-0.1145***	0.0470	0.1136	0.1485*	0.1550*	0.71	0.10
-0.0205		-0.1535		-0.0038		0.0872**		-0.0197	1.73**	0.23
-0.0145	-0.0565	-0.1095**	-0.0149	-0.2015***	-0.1409**	-0.1619**	-0.0194	-0.0236	2.01***	0.32
0.0379	0.0202	0.1297	0.0478	-0.1780***	-0.2994	-0.3168	0.1911	0.1653	2.49***	0.30
-0.1548***	-0.3018***	-0.2449***	-0.1937***		0.0812	0.1762	0.0300	0.0148	1.67**	0.11
-0.1241***	-0.0988**	-0.0880	-0.0460	-0.0637***	-0.4656	-0.3653	0.0979	0.0518	3.09***	0.25
-0.0033	0.0112	0.1021	0.1878***	-0.0642***	0.2008	0.3102**	0.0948*	0.1322**	2.29***	0.34
-0.0885	-0.0298	-0.1728	-0.1028	-0.1157***	0.3496***	0.2398**	0.1422***	0.0838*	0.92	0.19
-0.0177	0.0833*	-0.0143	0.0795**	-0.0300	-0.0375	0.1658	-0.0294	0.0256	2.58***	0.32
-0.0849**	-0.0109	-0.0918***	-0.0184	-0.0053	0.0571	0.0898	-0.0214	0.0402	3.36***	0.32
-0.0628	-0.1398*	-0.0122	0.0079	-0.0363*	-0.2091***	-0.3359***	0.0882***	0.0489	1.51*	0.17
-0.0607	-0.0436	-0.1165	0.1337***	-0.1609***	-0.2227	0.1792	0.0110	0.0558	1.78**	0.31
-0.1004***	-0.1103***	-0.1067**	-0.0131	-0.0771***	-0.0594	-0.1074*	0.0666***	0.1108***	4.23***	0.13
-0.1755***	-0.0352	0.0483	0.0076	-0.0016	-0.1425	-0.0529	-0.0994	-0.0861	1.08	0.35
-0.1275*	-0.0969	-0.0987	-0.0520	-0.1339***	-0.1042	-0.1532	0.0411	0.0999	2.98***	0.16
-0.1255***	-0.1251**	-0.0097	0.0076	-0.0071	-0.1453**	-0.1051	0.0333	0.0810***	2.10***	0.14
-0.0063	0.0040	-0.0004	-0.0030	-0.0011	-0.0450**	-0.0553**	0.0052	0.0072	2.01***	0.31
0.0365	0.1237***	-0.0789	0.2263***	-0.0161	-0.2704***			0.0703***	15.02***	0.32

tionship between living in urban areas and either having a mortgage or being a renter. Urban dwellers are more likely to rent in most countries, but they are less likely to rent in Denmark, Latvia, and Sweden. Fifth, characteristics of the household head seem to matter for tenure status—more so in the old EU countries than in the new EU countries. Full-time workers are more likely to have a mortgage; unemployed are more likely to rent, with the effect for retirees varying across countries. Although the two education dummies—for secondary and tertiary education—enter significantly in the regressions for some countries, their signs vary across countries. Specifically, in Austria,

Table 10.4
Panel A: Nested logit regressions (log-odds ratio between renting and owning)

Country	lage	female	hhsize	lnincome	hhnodep	hhdep	house	secedu	teredu
Recently added EU countries									
Czech Republic	−0.20*	0.16**	−0.09	0.09	−0.48***	−0.05	−2.89***		0.94
Estonia	−3.03**	0.22	−0.63***	0.97***	−1.71***	0.15	0.53**		8.63***
Hungary	−2.42*	−0.16	−0.05	0.48	−0.38	0.94	−1.66***	14.20***	8.27**
Latvia	−0.57	−0.16	0.11	0.39	−0.33	−0.41*	−0.84	7.73	1.84
Lithuania	−14.15	−0.86	−3.89	1.63	−0.48	5.19	0.24		−3.45
Poland	5.52***	0.66	1.49***	−0.65	−0.22	−3.51***	−0.97*	25.55***	9.50*
Slovak Republic	−0.31	−0.22*	0.14	−0.05	−0.30	−0.01	1.12	7.97***	11.62***
EU-15 and Cyprus									
Austria	−0.79	−0.06	−0.25***	0.33	−0.15	0.99***	−2.85***	16.25***	11.00***
Belgium	0.80	0.22**	0.01	−0.14	−0.29*	−0.29	−1.99***	15.15***	14.43***
Cyprus	−4.97	−0.16	−0.43**	1.47	−0.10	0.77	−0.98***	26.76***	17.00***
Denmark	−1.43	0.43***	−0.27***	0.80	−0.35**	0.30	−2.32***	8.69***	6.28***
Finland	5.12***	0.01	0.04	−1.83***	0.60**	0.03	−1.68***	21.43***	18.16***
France	2.12***	0.13	−0.06	−0.55***	0.00	−0.41**	−1.81***	21.59***	18.34***
Greece	0.15	−0.44	−0.31	0.42	−0.65	−0.63	−0.73	19.26	14.35
Ireland	0.45	0.67***	0.17	0.21	0.06	−0.63	−2.59***	21.97***	25.05***
Italy	3.03***	0.15	0.24**	−0.79***	−0.10	−0.84**	0.02	11.92***	7.43***
Luxembourg	1.32***	−0.06	0.05	−0.44***	0.19	0.05	−2.13***	14.90***	6.10*
Netherlands	0.70**	0.03	0.00	−0.06	−0.20*	−0.22	−1.31***	17.05***	20.41***
Portugal	1.47***	0.36**	0.16*	−0.52***	−0.17	−1.16***	1.12***	13.16***	4.87
Spain	−0.80	0.19**	−0.04	0.14	−0.49***	−0.36	−0.46***	7.12***	8.85***
Sweden	1.44***	0.10	0.00	−0.49**	−0.15	0.19	−2.64***	11.77***	11.63***
United Kingdom	−0.65***	0.43***	−0.04	0.36***	−0.43***	0.31**	−1.70***		19.27***

Source: EU Statistics on Income and Living Conditions (EU-SILC) database, 2007.
*significant at 90 percent; **significant at 95 percent; ***significant at 99 percent.

Denmark, Latvia, Sweden, and the United Kingdom, households whose head completed secondary education are more likely to have mortgages; in France, they are more likely to rent. In Austria, the Czech Republic, Denmark, Greece, Italy, Latvia, Luxembourg, Poland, and Sweden, households whose head has university education are more likely to have mortgages; in France and Ireland, they are more likely to rent.

There is little evidence that expected income explains tenure status. In particular, in only a few countries does the interaction between age and the education dummies enter positively and significantly—Latvia,

fulltime	parttime	unemp	retired	urban	suburban	lage*secedu	lage*teredu	inc*secedu	inc*teredu
-0.21	-0.15	1.02***	-0.27*	0.21***			-0.32		-0.01
0.59	-0.14	-0.21	-1.51	0.16			-1.58***		-0.34
-0.16	0.57	-0.44	-0.96	1.20***	0.17	-2.26**	-1.71*	-0.74	-0.33
-0.23	-0.01	0.05	-0.45	-0.79		-0.19	0.45	-0.96***	-0.63
30.88		30.17		1.02			-2.41		1.31
-3.28**	-4.36**	0.36	-1.53	-0.65	0.29	-0.14	-0.10	-3.23***	-1.63**
0.48	0.19	0.88*	0.36	-0.32	-0.02	-0.72	-1.53	-0.62	-0.73
1.16**	1.12*	0.59	-0.48	0.84***	0.75***	-2.24**	-2.34**	-0.97***	-0.49
-0.83***	-0.76***	0.42	-0.56	0.23	0.08	-1.96***	-2.32***	-0.78***	-0.60***
0.53	-0.23	0.39	-0.95	0.98**	-0.38	0.57	2.79	-2.79*	-2.57
-0.86***	-0.42	0.09	-0.42**	0.27**	0.07	0.80	1.32	-1.22**	-1.23**
-0.70***	-0.18	0.62**	0.08	0.36***	0.05	-4.93***	-5.49***	-0.19	0.26
-0.36	-0.05	0.68	0.02	-0.02	0.05	-3.09***	-3.13***	-0.98***	-0.70***
-1.15	-0.56	-0.33	-0.84	-0.03	-0.41	-1.64	-1.49	-1.43*	-0.98***
-1.74**	-0.90*	0.00	0.10	0.14	0.09	-2.82***	-3.10***	-1.23***	-1.41***
-1.04**	-0.70	-0.03	-0.66**	-0.29	-0.41	-2.22***	-2.10***	-0.44***	-0.09
0.28	-0.12	1.62**	-0.08	-0.16	0.03	-1.71***	-1.49**	-0.82***	-0.04
-1.06***	-0.34***	-0.23	-0.45***			-1.30***	-1.70***	-1.25***	-1.48***
-0.90*	-0.45	0.30	0.07	0.53**	0.44**	-1.88***	-0.82	-0.68***	-0.26
0.55**	0.87***	0.54**	-0.12	-0.08	0.00	-0.53*	-0.21	-0.52***	-0.83***
-0.45***	-0.72***	0.16	-0.78***	-0.19**	-0.05	-1.99***	-1.99***	-0.36*	-0.37*
-1.39***	-1.00***	1.65***	-2.02***	0.10			-2.35***		-1.07***

Poland, Greece, and the United Kingdom—providing little evidence that more educated household heads convert from renters to mortgage holders at an earlier age. In Estonia, Hungary, Lithuania, Belgium, Cyprus, Finland, and France, either or both interaction terms even enter significantly and negatively. Similarly, we find positive interaction terms between income and the education dummies only for the Czech Republic, Denmark, and Luxembourg, and the interaction terms enter positively and significantly in Greece and Italy. Overall, this finding suggests that only in a few countries are more educated households more likely to have a mortgage rather than rent at an earlier age

Table 10.4
Panel B: Nested logit regressions (log-odds ratio between owning with and without a mortgage)

Country	lage	female	hhsize	lnincome	hhnodep	hhdep	house	secedu	teredu
Recently added EU countries									
Czech Republic	0.89***	-0.07	0.21***	-0.73***	0.14	-0.68***	4.36***		4.56
Estonia	2.73***	-0.12	0.21***	-0.90***	0.92***	-0.32	-0.40***		2.62
Hungary	1.03***	0.10	0.03	-0.33*	0.08	-0.48***	0.25***	-2.58***	-1.40
Latvia	1.56*	0.03	0.07	-0.63	0.33*	-0.02	1.04***	4.19**	-1.77
Lithuania	2.77***	0.17	0.80***	-0.37	0.02	-1.00***	-0.01		3.01
Poland	1.59***	0.17	0.45***	-0.24	-0.08	-1.07***	0.58***	5.64***	1.29
Slovak Republic	1.38	-0.13	0.23***	-0.99*	0.04	-0.50***	3.20***	-1.39	0.25
EU-15 and Cyprus									
Austria	1.49**	0.04	0.13**	-0.65**	0.00	-0.92***	0.45***	-3.68***	-1.93
Belgium	2.96***	-0.04	0.09	-1.13***	0.71***	-0.68***	0.04	-10.03***	-14.60***
Cyprus	3.54***	0.20	0.24***	-1.14***	0.04	-0.76***	-0.11	-9.24***	-4.76*
Denmark	-3.61	0.22***	-0.12	-1.21	-0.18	0.12	-1.19***	-22.41***	-24.05***
Finland	2.66***	0.04	0.05	-1.01***	0.73***	-0.19	-0.16*	-2.57	-9.60***
France	1.52***	-0.03	-0.10**	-0.49***	0.35***	-0.26	0.30***	-4.16**	-9.64***
Greece	1.37***	-0.29	0.16**	-0.19	-0.09	-0.97*	0.41***	6.42**	6.93***
Ireland	1.79***	0.13	0.19***	-0.45***	0.24	-1.17***	0.36	-0.30	-8.24***
Italy	2.15***	0.14**	0.26***	-0.57***	0.18*	-0.75***	0.41***	-0.12	-3.60***
Luxembourg	2.84***	0.39*	0.24**	-1.08***	0.03	-1.39***	0.92***	-13.38***	-20.45***
Netherlands	-1.72***	0.00	-0.05	-1.96***	0.11	0.04	-0.70***	-16.76***	-14.74***
Portugal	1.16***	0.16	0.25***	-0.47***	0.15	-1.07***	1.35***	1.47	-3.38
Spain	2.30***	0.18**	0.49***	-0.85***	0.07	-1.17***	0.16**	-4.37***	-6.95***
Sweden	2.09***	-0.36*	-0.38**	-1.16***	0.50*	0.23	2.01***	-5.54*	-4.01
United Kingdom	1.99***	-0.32***	0.15**	-0.72***	0.04	-1.06***	-0.18		-13.00***

Source: EU Statistics on Income and Living Conditions (EU-SILC) database, 2007.
*significant at 90 percent; **significant at 95 percent; ***significant at 99 percent.

or at a lower income, with the perspective of higher income growth in the future. However, we do not find more or less evidence in either old or new EU countries.

The log-odds ratios reported in panel B of table 10.3 show the following: first, that richer households are more likely to own without a mortgage than with a mortgage in most but not all countries. Second, in most of the older EU member countries, older households are more likely to be outright owners rather than mortgage holders. Among the new EU countries, this relationship is insignificant in Latvia, the Slovak Republic, and Slovenia. Third, although there is again little evidence

fulltime	parttime	unemp	retired	urban	suburban	lage*secedu	lage*teredu	inc*secedu	inc*teredu
0.32*	0.36	0.38	0.60***	-0.31***			-0.54		-0.26
-0.83	0.34	0.32	1.22*	-0.11			0.08		-0.36
-0.12	-0.36	0.22	0.36**	-0.24***	0.03	0.35	0.29	0.18	0.07
-0.05	0.11	0.09	-0.33	-1.20***		-1.29	-0.42	0.21	0.49
-6.10		-5.85		-0.26			0.10		-0.39
-0.93**	-1.28***	-0.07	-0.41	-0.45***	0.01	0.10	0.19	-0.79***	-0.38*
0.20	0.11	0.55	0.16	-0.98***	-0.14	-1.28	-1.47	0.84	0.70
-0.81**	-0.62*	-0.30	0.05	-0.03	-0.37***	-0.04	-0.30	0.52*	0.45
-0.53*	-0.39	0.90**	1.08***	-0.07	0.20	0.67	0.68	0.72**	1.12***
-0.32	0.16	0.35	0.60	-0.47**	-0.10	-0.96	-1.96***	1.24***	1.11***
-0.45	-0.23	0.05	-0.23	0.14	0.03	3.29	3.55	0.98	1.02
-0.29*	0.26	0.11	0.46***	0.01	-0.12	0.11	0.77*	0.18	0.60***
-0.73***	-0.33	-0.38	-0.12	-0.17*	-0.20**	1.16***	1.50***	-0.08	0.30
-1.25***	-1.06*	-0.46	-0.47	-0.20	-0.37**	-1.15	-1.63***	-0.28	-0.12
-1.13***	-0.62*	-0.64	0.88**	-1.00***	-0.81***	-0.32	1.29**	0.10	0.24
-0.93***	-0.78***	-0.46	-0.33*	-0.56***	-0.42***	-0.41	-0.43	0.11	0.44***
-1.22***	-0.69	0.70	0.16	-0.25	-0.13	0.88	1.50	0.96**	1.39***
-0.49	0.00	-0.05	0.03			1.29***	1.03**	1.18***	1.06***
-0.83***	-0.57	-0.25	0.01	-0.32**	0.03	-0.48	-0.15	0.02	0.41
-0.65***	-0.45	-0.01	0.18	-0.27***	-0.41***	-0.27	0.20	0.52***	0.60***
-0.55	0.24	-0.06	-0.16	-0.17	-0.09	-0.36	-1.21	0.66	0.85*
-0.83***	-0.09	-1.05**	1.30***	-0.10			1.81***		0.56***

of gender differences in tenure status, larger families are more likely to own outright than be mortgage holders, both in old and in new EU countries. Fourth, compared to families with dependents, single people and families without dependents are more likely to be outright owners than mortgage holders in almost all countries. Fifth, in all countries except Estonia and Lithuania, house dwellers are more likely to be outright owners than mortgage holders, and in most countries urban dwellers are significantly more likely to be mortgage holders. Finally, although the employment status of the household head seems to matter in few countries, the education status variables enter often significantly

but with varying signs across countries, as is the case for the interactions of age with the educational dummies.

In summary, we notice some differences between old and new EU countries in these results. The likelihood of ownership with mortgage as opposed to renting increases more rapidly with age in the old than in the new EU countries. The likelihood of owning with mortgage as opposed to renting is also much more sensitive to income in the old than in the new EU countries. We note that the pseudo R-squared measures are, on average, lower for the new than for the old EU countries, with the notable exceptions of the Czech and Slovak Republics and Poland, suggesting that tenure status is more difficult to explain in new than in old EU countries with household characteristics. Comparing the survey results across different years for the new EU countries does not yield any major differences (tables A10.3 and A10.4). As the results of the Hausman test reject the null hypothesis of independence of irrelevant alternatives in most cases, we turn to nested regressions. In this case, we first test the difference between owning and renting (panel A of table 10.4) before testing the difference between owning without and with mortgage (panel B of table 10.4).[17]

The log-odds ratios between renting and owning in panel A of table 10.4 suggest that in many—though far from all—of the old EU countries, richer households are more likely to own, while among the new EU countries, this relationship is significant only for Estonia, where richer households are more likely to rent. Although there is a positive relationship between age and renting in the old EU countries, among the new EU countries this association holds only for Poland, while in the Czech Republic, Estonia, and Hungary, older households are more likely to own. In addition, this result is very different from the non-nested regressions in table 10.3, in which we found that older households are more likely to have a mortgage than to rent; here we find that they are more likely to rent as opposed to own (with or without mortgage). In only a few countries is there a significant relationship between gender of the household head or household size and the log-odds ratio between renting and owning. Interestingly, in several countries, female-headed households are more likely to rent; the relationship between household size and tenure status varies across countries. For many countries, we find that households with no dependents are significantly more likely to own, with the exception of Finland, where this relationship is reversed. In some new and old EU countries, house dwellers are significantly more likely to own than to rent. The relation-

ship between education and tenure status is highly significant in most countries, with more educated households significantly more likely to rent than to own. Employment status, the location of the dwelling (urban vs. rural), and the household type enter significantly in some countries, but not with consistent signs across countries. Finally, we find negative interaction terms between age and education and age and income in almost all countries, suggesting that the relationship between tenure and income is stronger for more educated households and that more educated households are also more likely to move into ownership status as they grow older. However, neither of these results points to expected income as criterion for tenure status.

Panel B of table 10.4 shows logs-odds ratios between owning with and without mortgage, demonstrating the importance of controlling for the nested nature of the tenure decision. Unlike the results reported in panel B of table 10.3, we now find that richer households that own are more likely to have a mortgage in most countries, especially in the old EU countries, which might be explained with the tax advantage of mortgage payments. As in table 10.3, however, older households that own are actually more likely to be outright owners. As before, we find the relationship between gender and tenure status to be insignificant in most countries; larger households are more likely to own in most countries in both old and new EU economies. In many countries, households with dependents are more likely to own with rather than without mortgage, and in most countries, house owners are more likely to be outright owners. Full-time employees are more likely to own with a mortgage, as are urban dwellers in many countries. In most old EU countries, more educated households are more likely to be outright owners; few new EU countries show any significant relationship between education and tenure status. Finally, as before, few of the interaction terms between age and income, on the one hand, and education dummies, on the other hand, enter significantly.

In summary, the results of the nested logit regressions confirm the conclusions from the multinomial regressions that tenure status is less sensitive to income and to age in the new EU countries. Overall, the explanatory variables have less power in the new EU countries in explaining cross-household variation in tenure status. We do not find much evidence in most of the old or any of the new EU countries that prospective rather than current income determines access to mortgage finance. Comparing the results across surveys in different years, we do not find many significant differences (tables A10.5 and A10.6). The

lower ability of our variables to explain cross-household variation in tenure status in the new EU countries can be explained both by historic and policy legacies (inherited housing, rental subsidy programs, etc.) as well as financial systems that are still in the process of developing.

Can Mortgages Turn into a Financial Burden?

The main benefit of a mortgage loan, as of loans for consumer durables such as cars, is that the consumer is not forced to save the whole amount for the good or house up front but can smooth payments over time. In the case of mortgages, the underlying asset—the house—typically appreciates over time, both in real and nominal terms, at least in the medium to long term. However, although a mortgage can help mitigate liquidity constraints and help realize large investments in housing earlier, mortgage debt holding itself may turn into a financial burden. If the income stream used to make repayment is subject to macroeconomic shocks, in the absence of a savings buffer a household may fall into financial distress. These shocks can be channeled through income shocks (such as an economic slowdown) or through exchange rate (if the mortgage is in foreign currency) or interest rate (in case of variable-interest mortgages) shocks. Further, if the mortgage payments represent a large share of disposable income, rising debt burden might curb the household's ability to respond to shocks to other expenditure categories, such as rapidly rising food and energy prices, as were observed in 2007 and 2008.

In this section, we assess whether mortgage holders are more subject to financial distress than non–mortgage holders, be they renters or owners without mortgage. Specifically, we use different financial burden and vulnerability measures and test for the marginal effect of being a mortgage holder on financial distress controlling for numerous other household characteristics. In the existing literature on household loan delinquency, the relevant threshold used to identify household borrowers in financial distress or at risk of default has been based on three primary approaches. First, some studies have used the concept of a "financial margin" (e.g., Johansson and Persson 2006; Vatne 2006; Żochowski and Zajączkowski 2007, 2008) or the disposable income net of debt service payments and average basic living costs. Second, some studies have employed a more arbitrary approach, using some indicative threshold debt service obligation as a share of disposable income,

typically around 30 percent (e.g., Beer and Schürz 2007). A third approach analyzes actual financial distress, as evidenced by mortgage payment arrears and other types of payment arrears.[18] The analysis in this section falls under this third approach. We control for the same variables that we used as explanatory variables in tables 10.3 and 10.4 and also control for the possible endogeneity of the tenure status with a two-stage least squares regression.

We use several measures of financial vulnerability. Our first measure is FINBURDEN, an ordinal response to the question of how burdensome the total housing cost is. Responses include: 3 = a heavy burden, 2 = somewhat a burden, 1 = not a burden at all, with higher values thus indicating a higher burden. Although this is a subjective measure of financial burden, we also use several objective measures of financial vulnerability. First, we use three binary variables indicating whether a household has (1) arrears on mortgage or rent payments, (2) arrears on utility payments, or (3) arrears on hire purchase installments or other loan payments. Second, we use a binary variable indicating whether a household had any arrears on one of the previously mentioned payments. Finally, we use an indirect indicator of financial vulnerability: a binary variable indicating whether a household has unmet medical needs due to lack of finance. As medical care should be high on the priority list of any household, not being able to meet medical needs due to lack of financial resources certainly indicates financial vulnerability.

There is a large variation across countries in indicators of financial burden and vulnerability, as reported in table 10.5. Here we report data for 2007; tables A10.7 and A10.8 report the same statistics for 2005 and 2006, respectively. The average self-reported burden varies from 1.3 in Denmark to 2.6 in Cyprus. Self-reported burdens are significantly higher in the new EU countries than in the old EU countries, with little variation over time. In 2007, the share of population that has (1) arrears on mortgage or rent payments, (2) arrears on utility payments, or (3) arrears on hire purchase installments or other loan payments varied from 2.7 percent in Luxembourg to 26.6 percent in Greece. Although in 2005, the share of population with arrears was, on average, significantly higher in the new EU countries (16.0 percent) than in the old EU countries (9.7 percent), there was no significant difference in 2007 due to a subsequent drop of this share in the new EU countries, possibly reflecting the strong income growth experienced by most of these countries over this period. In 2007, the new EU countries still had, on average, a higher share of the population with arrears on utility bills, while there

Table 10.5
Descriptive summary statistics (weighted averages: financial vulnerability dependent variables)

Country	finburden	finvul	arrears1	arrears2	arrears3	himedcost
Recently added EU countries						
Czech Republic	2.075	0.051	0.052	0.035	0.065	0.002
Estonia	1.946	0.049	0.047	0.043	0.030	0.011
Hungary	2.221	0.160	0.116	0.149	0.136	0.021
Latvia	2.099	0.103	0.087	0.090	0.049	0.094
Lithuania	2.071	0.087	0.107	0.082	0.045	0.021
Poland	2.284	0.164	0.127	0.151	0.128	0.045
Slovak Republic	2.280	0.066	0.049	0.050	0.039	0.008
Slovenia	2.183	0.129	0.205	0.106	0.142	0.002
EU-15 and Cyprus						
Austria	1.833	0.037	0.031	0.020	0.112	0.005
Belgium	1.901	0.056	0.040	0.040	0.026	0.004
Cyprus	2.600	0.208	0.184	0.093	0.250	0.046
Denmark	1.324	0.052	0.021	0.020	0.035	0.003
Finland	1.902	0.087	0.059	0.042	0.059	0.004
France	1.756	0.088	0.079	0.058	0.049	0.013
Greece	2.224	0.266	0.241	0.168	0.434	0.053
Ireland	1.927	0.075	0.085	0.056	0.029	0.015
Italy	2.534	0.107	0.101	0.088	0.156	0.032
Luxembourg	2.125	0.027	0.026	0.020	0.007	0.002
Netherlands	1.701	0.043	0.028	0.022	0.088	0.002
Portugal	2.030	0.066	0.057	0.050	0.040	0.097
Spain	2.442	0.062	0.062	0.037	0.075	0.000
Sweden	1.503	0.059	0.026	0.033	0.042	0.006
United Kingdom	1.863	0.077	0.058	0.043	0.039	0.000

Source: EU Statistics on Income and Living Conditions (EU-SILC) database, 2007.

was no significant difference in arrears on mortgage/rent payments or hire purchase installment and other loan payments. Across the new EU countries, however, there are stark differences: 16 percent of the population in Hungary and Poland had arrears in 2007, with an increasing trend in Hungary and a decreasing trend in Poland, and the share of population with arrears was 5 percent in Czech Republic and Estonia, with a decreasing trend. There is a large variation across countries on composition of arrears. In Hungary and Poland, arrears on utility bills are typical; arrears on mortgage and rent payments are the most common form of arrears in Estonia, Lithuania, and Slovenia.

The share of households with unmet medical needs due to lack of financial resources is very low—on average, 2.6 percent in the new EU member countries in 2007 and 1.9 percent in the old EU countries. For the new EU economies, however, this share halved between 2005 and 2007. In 2007, the share of households with unmet medical needs due to lack of financial resources was highest in Latvia (9.4 percent) and lowest in the United Kingdom (less than 0.1 percent). These differences might be driven to a large extent by the different health care systems, with countries with government-provided health care likely to have significantly lower shares of population reporting unmet medical needs in the first place.[19]

The different indicators of financial burden and vulnerability are significantly correlated with each other within and across countries. They also provide similar rankings, with Hungary, Latvia, Poland, and Slovenia being the new EU countries with the highest incidence of financial vulnerability across the different indicators and the Czech Republic and Estonia with the lowest incidence. Similarly, among the old EU countries in our sample, Denmark is consistently the country with the lowest incidence of financial burden and vulnerability, and Cyprus and Greece have the highest incidence of financial vulnerability.

Interestingly, there is a negative and often significant correlation between the size of mortgage markets and the share of households that are in default on at least one loan product as well as with the financial burden as reported by households. We find this negative correlation both across the sample of all countries as well as within the subsample of new EU countries. On the aggregate level, a deeper mortgage market therefore does not seem to be associated with higher financial vulnerability of households.

How do financial burden and arrears vary across income and age groups? Figure 10.8 shows a significant negative correlation of income

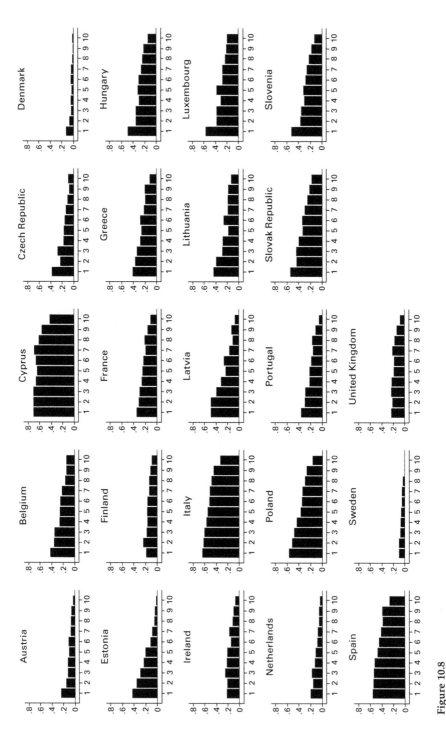

Figure 10.8
Share of households for whom FINBURDEN=3 by income decile, 2007. *Source:* EU Statistics on Income and Living Conditions (EU-SILC), 2007

with financial burden across all countries in 2007. Here we show the average weighted survey response across income deciles for all surveys in 2007; the share of households reporting that housing costs are a heavy financial burden decreases with income in most countries, although the decrease is not always linear. There do not seem to be significant differences across countries. Similarly, figure 10.9 shows that, on average, arrears in payments decrease with the income deciles, though not monotonically, most likely due to the small number of households with arrears. Figure 10.10 shows that the financial burden is, on average, not correlated with the age of the household age, with the exception of Denmark, Ireland, Netherlands, Norway, Sweden, and the United Kingdom, where we see a decline in self-reported financial burden with the age of the household head. In none of the new EU countries can we see a clear relationship between self-reported financial burden and age. On the other hand, figure 10.11 shows that with few exceptions—most prominently Greece—there is a negative relationship between the age of the household head and the likelihood that the household is in arrears. These graphs show us the distribution of financial burden and vulnerability across the general population; we now turn to the question of whether tenure status is significantly associated with financial burden and vulnerability.

We use regression analysis to test whether mortgage holders report a higher financial burden or are more likely to incur arrears, thus controlling for an array of other household and individual characteristics that might also affect a household's financial burden and the likelihood of arrears. We use probit regressions for the binary indicators of financial vulnerability and ordered probit regressions for the subjective indicator of financial burden. The general regression setup is as follows:

$$FINBURDEN = \beta_1 \cdot MORTGAGE + \beta_2 \cdot RENT + \delta' \cdot X + \varepsilon, \qquad (10.4)$$

where $RENT$ and $MORTGAGE$ are binary variables that take the value 1 if household is a renter or has a mortgage, respectively; X is a vector of household and individual characteristics of the household head. We run separate regressions for each survey; that is, we have three coefficient estimates on $MORTGAGE$ for each country and for each dependent variable. β_1 indicates whether mortgage holders are significantly more likely to report a financial burden or be financially vulnerable than outright owners, and we also test for the significance of the difference between β_1 and β_2, thus testing whether mortgage owners report higher financial burden and are more likely to be financially

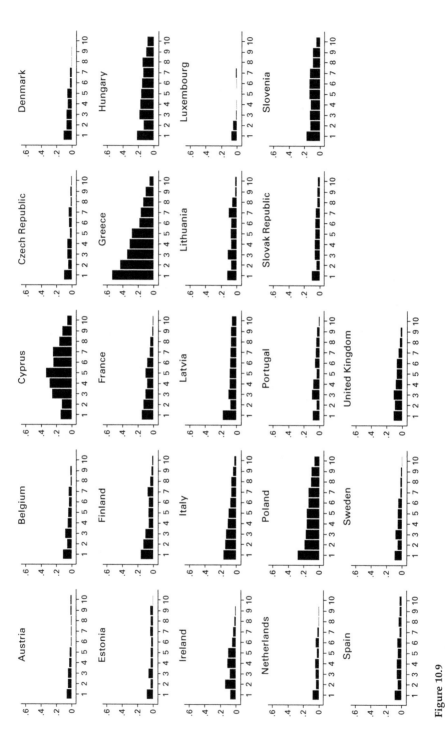

Figure 10.9
Share of households that have any bills in arrears by income decile, 2007. *Source:* EU Statistics on Income and Living Conditions (EU-SILC), 2007

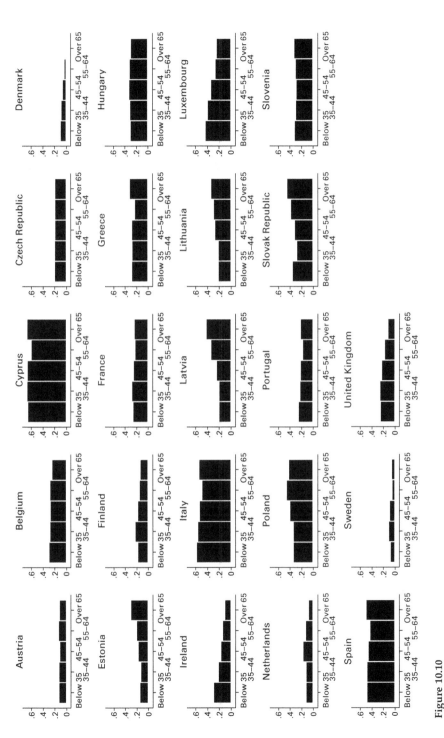

Figure 10.10

Share of households for whom FINBURDEN = 3 by age group, 2007. *Source:* EU Statistics on Income and Living Conditions (EU-SILC), 2007

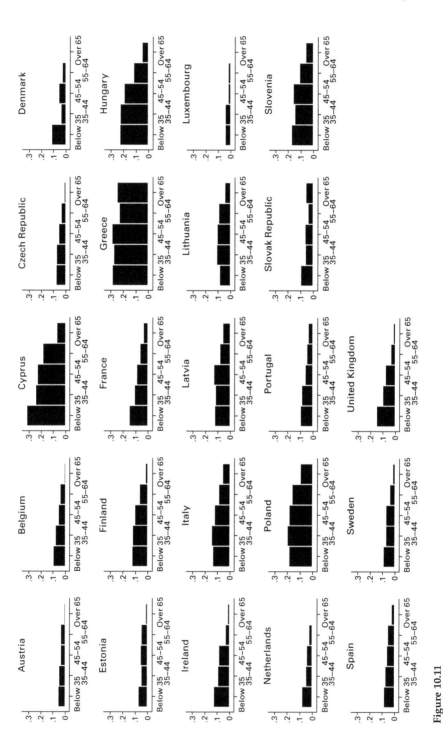

Figure 10.11
Share of households that have any bills in arrears by age group, 2007. *Source:* EU Statistics on Income and Living Conditions (EU-SILC), 2007

vulnerable than renters. As in the previous regressions, we weight observations according to their representativeness.[20] Rather than reporting coefficient estimates, we report marginal effects for the binary indicators, thus indicating the increase or decrease in percentage points on the likelihood of arrears or unmet medical needs for financial reasons if a household holds a mortgage. In the case of the subjective measure of financial burden, we report the difference in percentage points in the likelihood that a household reports a heavy financial burden if it holds a mortgage, as opposed to not holding a mortgage.[21] We focus on the results for 2007 in the main text, but we report estimates for 2005 and 2006 in tables A10.9 and A10.10, respectively.

To avoid confounding the relationship between mortgage holding and financial vulnerability with the impact of other household characteristics on financial vulnerability, we control for the same household characteristics as in the previous section. We expect larger families with more dependents to be more likely to report a financial burden and incur arrears and households with lower income and whose head is not full-time employed or draws on a stable retirement income to have higher financial burden and higher likelihood of arrears. The location and type of the dwelling, as well as other characteristics of the household head (age, gender, and education) do not have an a priori positive or negative impact on financial burden and arrears.[22]

The regressions results in table 10.6 show similarities but also differences between old and new EU countries. First we find substantial variations across countries in the relationship between tenure status and financial burden. In Belgium, Estonia, France, Ireland, Lithuania, the Netherlands, Poland, and Sweden, we find that mortgage holders report a lower financial burden than outright owners, with the reverse relationship in Austria, Cyprus, Finland, Greece, Hungary, Italy, Latvia, Portugal, Slovenia, Spain, and the UK. When comparing mortgage holders with renters, we find that in Hungary, Greece, Ireland, Luxembourg, and Poland, mortgage holders report, on average, a lower financial burden than renters and that in Austria, Cyprus, Italy, Lithuania, Portugal, Slovenia, and Spain, they report, on average, a higher financial burden than renters. Only in Austria, Cyprus, Italy, Portugal, Slovenia, and Spain—and in none of the new EU countries—do mortgage holders report the highest financial burden compared to the other two groups.

Turning to actual arrears, we find that in most countries mortgage holders are significantly more likely to incur arrears than outright

Table 10.6
Ordered probit and probit regressions (financial vulnerability regressions [marginal effects])

Country	finburden				finvul				arrears1	
	mortgage	renter	Pseudo r²	t-test	mortgage	renter	Pseudo r²	t-test	mortgage	Pseudo r²
Recently added EU countries										
Czech Republic	-0.0253	0.0737	0.08	0.69	0.0185**	0.0531***	0.16	-4.63***	-0.0271***	0.17
Estonia	-0.1512*	0.0040	0.12	-0.52	0.0171	0.0241**	0.10	-0.40	-0.0369	0.15
Hungary	0.0437***	0.0825***	0.07	1.66*	0.0444***	0.0687***	0.13	-1.30	0.0878***	0.13
Latvia	0.0217**	0.0518**	0.09	-0.32	0.0566***	0.0769***	0.09	-0.75	0.0344	0.09
Lithuania	-0.0118***	-0.0424*	0.07	3.89***	0.0329	0.0289	0.08	0.09	0.1195**	0.34
Poland	-0.1706**	0.0886***	0.08	-4.09***	0.0672***	0.0325***	0.09	1.23	-0.0615**	0.13
Slovak Republic	-0.0539	0.0484	0.06	-0.88	0.0041	0.0774***	0.10	-5.76***	0.0555***	0.15
Slovenia	0.1375***	0.0435	0.06	4.58***	0.0401	0.0261**	0.09	0.38	0.1278**	0.16
EU-15 and Cyprus										
Austria	0.0523***	0.0001	0.06	6.54***	0.0347***	0.0226***	0.14	0.65	-0.0107	0.10
Belgium	-0.0525***	0.1200***	0.05	1.37	0.0258***	0.0752***	0.19	-5.29***	0.0297***	0.16
Cyprus	0.0920***	-0.0448	0.10	6.47***	0.0892***	0.0136	0.10	2.72***	-0.0760**	0.11
Denmark	-0.0247		0.07		-0.0369***		0.24		-0.0048	0.24
Finland	0.0458***	0.0567***	0.06	1.54	0.0562***	0.1043***	0.17	-4.30***	0.0426***	0.15
France	-0.0131***	0.0668***	0.04	0.85	0.0040	0.0643***	0.14	-5.59***	-0.0450***	0.11
Greece	0.0522***	0.0845***	0.06	1.67*	0.2553***	0.1578***	0.16	2.72***	0.0206	0.18
Ireland	-0.0458***	0.2174***	0.09	-2.46**	0.0164	0.0892***	0.26	-3.89***	0.0494**	0.20
Italy	0.2176***	0.0821***	0.08	13.94***	0.0925***	0.0987***	0.13	-1.41	0.0491***	0.11
Luxembourg	0.0066	0.0661	0.08	3.64***	0.0082	0.0265	0.19	-2.07**	0.0133*	0.19
Netherlands	-0.0897***		0.05		-0.0418***		0.13		-0.0265***	0.12
Portugal	0.1007***	-0.0261	0.10	8.50***	0.0311**	0.0508***	0.10	-1.24	-0.0070	0.14
Spain	0.1106***	-0.0450**	0.06	10.48***	0.0585***	0.0625***	0.09	0.29	-0.0080	0.09
Sweden	-0.0894***	0.0914***	0.07	-7.90***	0.0210	0.0935***	0.14	-7.46***	-0.0224**	0.11
United Kingdom	0.0256***	0.0782***	0.06	0.74	0.0216**	0.1150***	0.21	-9.64***	-0.0602***	0.16

Source: EU Statistics on Income and Living Conditions (EU-SILC) database, 2007.
*significant at 90 percent; **significant at 95 percent; ***significant at 99 percent.

| arrears2 | | | | arrears3 | | | | himedcost | | | |
mortgage	renter	Pseudo r²	t-test	mortgage	renter	Pseudo r²	t-test	mortgage	renter	Pseudo r²	t-test
0.0067	0.0312***	0.17	-4.46***	0.0091	0.0512**	0.10	-2.88***	-0.0009	-0.0001	0.14	-1.50
0.0086	0.0117	0.10	-0.20	0.0154	0.0393**	0.15	-1.03	-0.0005	0.0076**	0.19	-1.19
0.0294**	0.0537***	0.13	-1.39	-0.0271*	0.0136	0.09	-1.67*	0.0070*	0.0046	0.09	0.42
0.0371**	0.0475***	0.10	-0.45	0.0265	0.0321	0.09	-0.19	0.0399***	0.0395***	0.15	0.04
0.0081	0.0190	0.09	-0.31	-0.0037	0.0219	0.07	-0.77	-0.0009	-0.0067	0.13	0.77
0.0437*	0.0216**	0.09	0.87	0.0119	0.0401***	0.07	-0.90	0.0149	0.0053	0.10	0.67
0.0014	0.0424***	0.11	-3.89***	-0.0125	0.0109	0.09	-2.54**	-0.0021	0.0047	0.20	-2.62***
0.0436	-0.0043	0.08	1.61	-0.0422	0.0327	0.06	-1.21				
0.0054	0.0051	0.13	-0.08	0.1047*	0.0440	0.17	0.97	0.0019	0.0007	0.07	0.47
0.0154**	0.0489***	0.16	-4.17***	0.0121	0.0246*	0.16	-1.42	0.1137***	0.1810***	0.29	-0.89
-0.0154	0.0057	0.07	-1.24	-0.0236	0.0153	0.10	-1.05	-0.0003	0.0080	0.10	-0.70
-0.0157***		0.28		-0.0294***		0.20		-0.0006		0.18	
0.0320***	0.0175**	0.10	1.99**	0.0120	0.0526***	0.14	-3.27***	0.0014	0.0030*	0.12	-1.04
-0.0128*	0.0215**	0.12	-5.03***	0.0027	0.0296**	0.09	-2.72***	0.0043	0.0107***	0.14	-1.75*
0.0234	0.0924***	0.28	-3.28***	0.1153**	0.0929**	0.11	0.42	0.0134	0.0208**	0.08	-0.58
0.0011	0.0428***	0.26	-3.40***	0.0000	0.0072	0.19	-1.03	0.0033	0.0023	0.39	0.35
-0.0659***	0.0725***	0.12	-1.31	0.0163	0.0351*	0.09	-0.86	0.0177***	0.0224***	0.09	-1.10
0.1392**	-0.0907*	0.20	-1.48	-0.0060***		0.28			0.0016**	0.34	
-0.0208***		0.13		-0.0442**		0.14		0.0000		0.27	
0.0046	0.0190*	0.10	-1.26	0.0129	0.0285*	0.12	-0.95	0.0350**	0.0616***	0.09	-1.56
-0.0191***	0.0244***	0.07	-0.49	0.0265*	0.0581***	0.06	-1.53				
-0.0047	0.0152	0.13	-3.98***	0.0098	0.0753**	0.16	-7.94***	-0.0016	0.0039	0.15	-3.64***
-0.0074	0.0482***	0.17	-5.80***	-0.0003	0.0519***	0.15	-6.36***				

owners. In most of the old EU countries, on the other hand, mortgage holders are less likely to incur arrears than renters, with the notable exceptions of Cyprus and Greece, where the relationship is reversed. In the Czech and Slovak Republics, mortgage holders are less likely to incur arrears than renters, and there is no significant difference between these two groups in the other new EU countries. Turning to specific arrears, we find that in most countries, mortgage holders are less likely to incur arrears on their mortgage payments than renters on their rent. It is only in Cyprus that mortgage holders are more likely to incur arrears than renters. In the case of arrears on utility bills, we find mixed evidence across countries on whether owners with or without mortgage are more likely to incur arrears; mortgage holders are, on average across countries, either less likely to incur arrears on utility payments than renters or there is no significant difference. Concerning arrears on hire purchase installments or other loans, we find significant differences between the three groups in few countries. Similarly, the probability of unmet medical needs for financial reasons is significantly higher for mortgage holders in few countries; renters are more likely to report unmet medical needs for financial reasons than outright owners in quite a few countries. When considering the relationship between mortgage holdings and financial burden and vulnerability over time, thus comparing results in tables 10.6 and tables A10.9 and A10.10, we find that if there has been any trend within the group of new EU countries, there has been a decrease in financial vulnerability—that is, in the likelihood of incurring arrears—for mortgage holders between 2005 and 2007, in both the statistical as well as the economic sense.

The control variables, which for ease of presentation are not reported, vary greatly in statistical significance across countries, years, and financial vulnerability measures. However, income, household size, and tertiary or postsecondary education are significant in at least 60 percent of all the financial vulnerability regressions over the three years. As anticipated, higher incomes, smaller household sizes, and tertiary education are, on average, associated with lower levels of financial burden and vulnerability. In addition to these variables, having a full-time job was consistently significant in 2007; in particular, those with full-time employment are, on average, less likely to be financially vulnerable. Interestingly, this variable did not register significantly in the majority of these regressions for 2005 and 2006. Of these significant characteristics in 2007, household size is more likely to contribute to financial vulnerability, on average, in the new EU countries. More than 80

percent of the regressions for these countries reported these variables as statistically significant, as opposed to 60 percent in old EU countries. Meanwhile, tertiary education is more significant on average in old EU countries (60 percent in old EU compared to 45 percent in new EU). Full-time employment in both groups is significant in 60 percent of all regressions. Unsurprisingly, income is the biggest determinant of financial burden and vulnerability in this analysis as it entered significantly into at least 90 percent of the regressions over all countries and all years.

Comparing the relative financial burden and arrear probability of mortgage holders to the other two groups, there is no evidence that mortgage holders in countries with larger mortgage markets are more likely to report financial burden or incur arrears. When comparing mortgage holders to outright owners, there is a negative or insignificant correlation between the size of the mortgage markets and the coefficient estimate on the mortgage coefficient in the financial burden and arrears regression. Comparing mortgage holders with renters, there is a positive correlation with the size of the mortgage markets; that is, there is some evidence that mortgage holders suffer from higher financial burden and are more likely to incur arrears in countries with larger mortgage markets. However, this inference does not extend to the new EU countries, where we find a negative correlation in the financial burden regression and most of the coefficient estimates are insignificant in the arrears regression.

The regression results reported in table 10.7 show even more strongly that being a mortgage holder does not imply a higher financial burden or a higher likelihood of incurring arrears. Here, we present two-stage least squares regressions. Specifically, we compute the predicted probability of (1) being a mortgage holder, (2) being an outright owner, and (3) being a renter from the nested multinomial regressions in table 10.4 and use these instead of the actual dummy variables in table 10.6. To satisfy the over-identifying conditions, we drop regressors that did not enter significantly in table 10.6 and that vary across countries. In most countries, we find either a negative or insignificant coefficient on the mortgage dummy in the financial burden regressions, indicating that the predicted likelihood of being a mortgage holder does not imply a higher financial burden than being an outright owner. Only in the Slovak Republic, Belgium, Cyprus, Greece, Spain, and the United Kingdom is the likelihood of being a mortgage holder significantly associated with a higher financial burden. Similarly, with the exception

Table 10.7
Two-stage least squares regressions (financial vulnerability regressions [marginal effects])

Country	finburden p(Mortgage)	p(Rent)	Pseudo r²	t-test	finvul p(Mortgage)	p(Rent)	Pseudo r²	t-test	arrears1 p(Mortgage)	Pseudo r²
Recently added EU countries										
Czech Republic	0.0259	−0.0567	0.08	0.65	0.0026	0.0330	0.14	−0.66	0.0872	0.15
Estonia	−0.2403***	0.3102**	0.11	−2.92***	0.0031	0.0491	0.09	−0.55	−0.0905**	0.10
Hungary	0.1746	−0.1711*	0.06	1.81*	−0.1388	0.0734	0.12	−0.93	0.0952	0.10
Latvia	−0.4368***	−0.0052	0.08	−2.17**	0.0781	0.0037	0.06	0.79	0.0679	0.07
Lithuania	0.2804	0.0394	0.07	−0.72	0.1015	−0.0985	0.08	0.87	−0.0832	0.26
Poland	−0.5140***	0.0870	0.08	−5.03***	−0.1950**	0.0458***	0.09	−2.48**	0.0713	0.10
Slovak Republic	0.2575**	0.0930	0.06	0.58	−0.0659	0.1788**	0.08	−1.59	0.0333**	0.11
EU-15 and Cyprus										
Austria	0.0450	−0.0057	0.06	1.03	0.0285	−0.0555*	0.13	2.49**	0.0047	0.12
Belgium	0.0875***	−0.0077	0.04	1.78*	0.0287	0.0577***	0.16	−1.10	−0.0144	0.13
Cyprus	0.1998**	−0.0912	0.08	2.40**	0.0340	−0.0522	0.09	0.55	0.1916**	0.06
Denmark	−0.0098		0.08		−0.0452***		0.18		−0.0172***	0.18
Finland	0.0201	0.1025**	0.04	−1.25	−0.1244**	0.0754*	0.15	−2.88***	−0.0573*	0.13
France	0.0362	0.0079	0.03	0.39	0.0020	0.1077***	0.12	−3.15***	0.0101	0.09
Greece	0.2276*	−0.0035	0.05	1.58	0.3357**	0.0826*	0.13	1.49	0.0955	0.18
Ireland	−0.0199	0.0353	0.07	−0.66	−0.0083	0.1187***	0.21	−2.78***	0.0410	0.16
Italy	0.0783	0.0584	0.04	0.16	−0.0186	0.1579***	0.10	−3.29***	−0.0382	0.09
Luxembourg	0.0941	−0.0664	0.08	1.17	0.0155	0.0034	0.17	0.64	0.0116	0.16
Netherlands	−0.1724***		0.04		−0.0667***		0.10		−0.0428***	0.09
Portugal	0.0079	−0.0294	0.07	0.45	0.0112	0.1083***	0.08	−1.46	0.0104	0.13
Spain	0.2978***	−0.2811*	0.04	2.76***	0.0095	0.0801*	0.07	−1.30	0.0014	0.08
Sweden	0.0679	0.0353***	0.06	0.58	0.1294*	0.0897**	0.11	0.39	0.0139	0.08
United Kingdom	0.1507***	0.0563	0.05	2.16**	0.0928***	0.0872***	0.18	0.15	0.0136	0.12

Source: EU Statistics on Income and Living Conditions (EU-SILC) database, 2007.
*significant at 90 percent; **significant at 95 percent; ***significant at 99 percent.

arrears2				arrears3				himedcost			
p(Mortgage)	p(Rent)	Pseudo r^2	t-test	p(Mortgage)	p(Rent)	Pseudo r^2	t-test	p(Mortgage)	p(Rent)	Pseudo r^2	t-test
0.0188	0.0154	0.15	0.06	0.0002	0.0508	0.07	−0.45	−0.0025***	0.0077	0.07	−2.54
−0.0091	0.0601	0.10	−0.85	−0.0359	0.0085	0.11	−0.33	0.0131	−0.0137	0.18	1.35
−0.3048	−0.0031	0.12	−1.37	−0.1129	0.0395	0.08	−0.55	−0.0574	−0.0191	0.09	−0.73
0.0511	−0.0171	0.09	0.83	0.1138	0.0452	0.06	0.53	0.0745	0.0061	0.14	0.84
0.0520	−0.1019	0.08	0.68	−0.0532	0.0359	0.04	−0.38	−0.0460	−0.0301	0.13	−0.13
−0.2675***	0.0446	0.09	−3.58	−0.0817	0.1153	0.06	−1.55	−0.0547**	0.0133	0.10	−1.17
−0.0835**	0.1720	0.09	−2.03	−0.0303**	0.1135	0.07	−2.49	0.0049	0.0074	0.18	−0.16
0.0150**	0.0157	0.15	−0.07	−0.1631	0.0694	0.13	−1.12	0.0058	−0.0030	0.06	1.01
0.0330***	0.0321	0.14	0.04	0.0072***	0.0379	0.13	−1.49	−0.0022***	0.0021	0.19	−3.45
−0.0238	0.0324	0.07	−0.61	−0.0511	−0.0175	0.09	−0.15	−0.0307	0.0393	0.09	−1.27
−0.0035		0.18		−0.0278		0.14		−0.0012		0.13	
0.0034	−0.0256	0.09	0.73	−0.0805***	0.1361	0.13	−3.90	−0.0028**	0.0063	0.10	−1.93
−0.0255***	0.0445	0.09	−0.76	0.0218**	0.0451	0.06	−0.68	−0.0048***	0.0152	0.11	−2.76
0.0116	0.0202	0.27	−0.09	−0.4762	0.0461	0.10	−1.53	0.0064	0.0037	0.07	0.06
0.0119***	0.0594	0.23	−2.01	−0.0579	0.0191	0.20	−2.72	0.0039	0.0047	0.38	−0.10
0.0020***	0.1383	0.10	−2.92	−0.0785	0.0369	0.09	−0.58	−0.0127	0.0199	0.08	−1.15
0.0149	−0.0014	0.14	1.09	0.0002	0.0012	0.15	−0.20	0.0008	−0.0008	0.17	0.41
0.0151		0.10		−0.0457		0.11		0.0000		0.34	
0.0242*	0.0582	0.08	−1.47	−0.0092**	0.0942	0.05	−1.92	0.0305*	0.0791	0.07	−0.87
0.0047	0.0171	0.06	−0.57	−0.0601***	0.2618	0.05	−2.84	0.0000	0.0000	0.24	−1.85
0.0446***	0.0296	0.10	0.31	0.1551	0.0637	0.10	0.77	0.0400*	0.0105	0.11	1.06
0.0346***	0.0444	0.15	−0.40	0.0118***	0.0608	0.11	−2.61	−0.0001**	−0.0002	0.22	0.86

of Belgium, Cyprus, Hungary, Spain, and the United Kingdom, pre-dicted mortgage holders do not report a higher financial burden than predicted renters. In Estonia, Latvia, and Poland, predicted mortgage holders report significantly lower financial burden than predicted renters.

Turning to actual arrears, the likelihood of being a mortgage holder is positively and significantly associated with a higher probability of arrears only in Greece, Spain, and the United Kingdom but none of the new EU countries. When comparing the predicted probabilities of being a mortgage holder and being a renter, it is only in Cyprus that the former is associated with a higher arrear probability than the latter. Similarly, it is only in Cyprus that the probability of incurring mortgage arrears is higher than the probability of incurring rent arrears. Similarly, in comparison to outright ownership and renting, the likelihood of holding a mortgage is not associated with a higher probability of incur-ring arrears on utility payments, with the exceptions of Austria and Belgium. The same relationship applies to arrears on hire purchase and other loans, with the exception of Sweden. There are few significant differences in unmet medical needs for financial reasons across the three groups, and the economic effects are typically very small. The two-stage least squares regression results for 2005 and 2006 (tables A10.10 and A10.11, respectively) confirm these findings in broad terms for the two earlier years.

In summary, there is no consistent evidence that mortgage holders are more likely to report financial burden than non–mortgage holders in old or new EU member countries. Mortgage holders experienced higher arrears in the new EU countries in 2005, but the difference com-pared to non–mortgage holders lost significance by 2007. Taken all together, the evidence presented in this section does not offer convinc-ing evidence that the recent deepening of mortgage markets in the new EU countries has contributed to financial vulnerability, at least in the period preceding the global financial crisis. Interestingly, rather than one of the new EU member countries of Central and Eastern Europe, it is Cyprus that shows a significantly higher financial burden and vulnerability for mortgage holders than for other groups.

Conclusions

This chapter assessed the benefits and costs of increasing mortgage holding in the new EU countries of Central and Eastern Europe and the Baltic region. Many of the same characteristics that explain tenure

status in the old EU countries also explain tenure status in the new EU countries, although we generally find that these characteristics have lower explanatory power in the new EU countries. In addition, we find tenure status to be less sensitive to income and age in the new EU countries than in the old ones. Across old and new EU countries, we find little evidence that mortgage holders face higher financial burdens or experience a greater likelihood of incurring arrears compared to non–mortgage holders or renters.

This chapter is a first step in better understanding the determinants and consequences of households' access to mortgage markets across countries. More complete data on households' mortgage payments and the use of other financial services will help us gain more insights. Data for years after 2008 will allow the effect of the crisis on different household groups to be better assessed, especially by comparing mortgage holders to others. Making the longitudinal dimension available will allow for the testing of additional hypotheses on financing constraints and tenure status. Finally, combining supply data on mortgage characteristics and interest rates with demand data as provided by EU-SILC will help us gain a more complete picture of housing finance and its economic consequences for households.

Appendix

Table A10.1
Descriptive summary statistics, 2005 (weighted averages: explanatory variables)

Country	age	female	hhsize	lnincome	secedu	teredu	house	apartment
Recently added EU countries								
Czech Republic	50	0.33	2.52	8.82	0.84	0.15	0.43	0.56
Estonia	51	0.48	2.40	8.35	0.57	0.37	0.31	0.68
H`ungary	51	0.45	2.47	8.58	0.73	0.18	0.64	0.36
Latvia	50	0.48	2.56	8.10	0.49	0.32	0.28	0.72
Lithuania	50	0.47	2.53	8.04	0.42	0.47	0.40	0.59
Poland	51	0.45	2.84	8.36	0.56	0.20	0.43	0.56
Slovak Republic	50	0.42	2.90	8.45	0.82	0.18	0.52	0.48
Slovenia	51	0.42	2.80	9.54	0.56	0.21	0.67	0.33
EU-15 and Cyprus								
Austria	51	0.33	2.34	10.18	0.68	0.31	0.51	0.48
Belgium	51	0.35	2.32	10.04	0.47	0.37	0.73	0.25
Cyprus	50	0.26	2.97	10.00	0.41	0.29	0.75	0.22
Denmark	50	0.41	2.02	10.22	0.75	0.25	0.61	0.37
Finland	50	0.42	2.14	10.05	0.50	0.29	0.57	0.42
France	51	0.38	2.30	10.06	0.54	0.27	0.59	0.40
Greece	52	0.30	2.67	9.63	0.38	0.23	0.45	0.55
Ireland	49	0.35	2.85	10.31	0.37	0.35	0.95	0.04
Italy	53	0.34	2.48	9.98	0.55	0.16	0.47	0.51
Luxembourg	50	0.28	2.51	10.73	0.44	0.27	0.67	0.32
Netherlands	50	0.31	2.29	10.12	0.54	0.34	0.68	0.25
Portugal	51	0.34	2.79	9.41	0.27	0.15	0.63	0.36
Spain	50	0.29	2.83	9.75	0.36	0.29	0.36	0.64
Sweden	51	0.40	2.08	10.02	0.53	0.34	0.49	0.51
United Kingdom	50	0.37	2.31	10.20	0.61	0.39	0.81	0.19

Source: EU Statistics on Income and Living Conditions (EU-SILC) database, 2005.
Note: Data used to create dummy variables—urban, suburban, and rural—are not available for the Netherlands and Slovenia.

hh1	hhnodep	hhdep	fulltime	parttime	unemp	retired	other	urban	rural
0.23	0.42	0.35	0.61	0.02	0.05	0.27	0.04	0.38	0.39
0.31	0.31	0.37	0.61	0.04	0.03	0.27	0.05	0.48	0.52
0.29	0.37	0.34	0.54	0.05	0.04	0.30	0.07	0.35	0.43
0.25	0.37	0.37	0.62	0.03	0.05	0.28	0.03	0.48	0.52
0.28	0.31	0.41	0.59	0.04	0.05	0.27	0.05	0.41	0.59
0.25	0.32	0.42	0.48	0.03	0.05	0.29	0.15	0.46	0.42
0.24	0.33	0.43	0.61	0.01	0.04	0.32	0.02	0.27	0.25
0.21	0.36	0.43	0.59	0.01	0.03	0.35	0.02		
0.34	0.35	0.31	0.56	0.04	0.03	0.33	0.03	0.40	0.36
0.34	0.35	0.31	0.49	0.07	0.08	0.30	0.07	0.57	0.04
0.16	0.36	0.48	0.68	0.03	0.02	0.23	0.04	0.59	0.30
0.44	0.29	0.27	0.54	0.05	0.04	0.25	0.12	0.36	0.35
0.38	0.34	0.27	0.54	0.05	0.06	0.25	0.10	0.30	0.53
0.31	0.35	0.34	0.52	0.05	0.05	0.34	0.04	0.50	0.17
0.20	0.44	0.36	0.58	0.02	0.02	0.29	0.09	0.42	0.58
0.22	0.34	0.44	0.56	0.08	0.04	0.14	0.18	0.35	0.37
0.28	0.39	0.33	0.53	0.03	0.03	0.29	0.12	0.44	0.18
0.29	0.34	0.37	0.62	0.04	0.02	0.22	0.11	0.50	0.19
0.35	0.35	0.31	0.47	0.12	0.02	0.13	0.26		
0.17	0.41	0.42	0.61	0.04	0.04	0.28	0.04	0.44	0.25
0.16	0.45	0.37	0.61	0.03	0.04	0.24	0.09	0.53	0.27
0.42	0.29	0.29	0.54	0.07	0.03	0.25	0.11	0.21	0.66
0.31	0.37	0.29	0.49	0.08	0.02	0.24	0.18	0.77	0.05

Table A10.2
Descriptive summary statistics, 2006 (weighted averages: explanatory variables)

Country	age	female	hhsize	lnincome	secedu	teredu	house	apartment
Recently added EU countries								
Czech Republic	50	0.33	2.52	8.94	0.85	0.15	0.43	0.56
Estonia	50	0.48	2.36	8.53	0.57	0.37	0.30	0.69
Hungary	51	0.44	2.61	8.72	0.68	0.23	0.67	0.33
Latvia	50	0.47	2.63	8.25	0.64	0.33	0.29	0.71
Lithuania	50	0.46	2.55	8.23	0.42	0.48	0.39	0.61
Poland	51	0.43	2.84	8.60	0.56	0.21	0.44	0.56
Slovak Republic	51	0.43	2.88	8.61	0.79	0.19	0.51	0.49
Slovenia	51	0.43	2.82	9.61	0.62	0.22	0.70	0.30
EU-15 and Cyprus								
Austria	51	0.34	2.33	10.15	0.70	0.29	0.51	0.48
Belgium	52	0.33	2.31	10.08	0.46	0.38	0.74	0.25
Cyprus	50	0.26	2.97	10.10	0.41	0.30	0.74	0.24
Denmark	50	0.42	2.02	10.25	0.75	0.25	0.62	0.37
Finland	50	0.42	2.13	10.08	0.49	0.31	0.57	0.43
France	51	0.39	2.29	10.08	0.54	0.28	0.60	0.40
Greece	52	0.30	2.68	9.68	0.40	0.23	0.45	0.55
Ireland	49	0.34	2.85	10.38	0.37	0.35	0.95	0.04
Italy	53	0.34	2.46	9.99	0.54	0.17	0.43	0.52
Luxembourg	50	0.30	2.47	10.75	0.44	0.27	0.66	0.32
Netherlands	50	0.31	2.27	10.14	0.54	0.34	0.69	0.26
Portugal	52	0.35	2.76	9.42	0.27	0.14	0.65	0.34
Spain	50	0.29	2.79	9.81	0.38	0.29	0.37	0.63
Sweden	51	0.40	2.11	10.02	0.55	0.37	0.50	0.49
United Kingdom	50	0.36	2.34	10.23	0.65	0.35	0.81	0.18

Source: EU Statistics on Income and Living Conditions (EU-SILC) database, 2006.
Note: Data used to create dummy variables—urban, suburban, and rural—are not available for the Netherlands and Slovenia.

hh1	hhnodep	hhdep	fulltime	parttime	unemp	retired	other	urban	rural
0.24	0.41	0.35	0.61	0.02	0.04	0.28	0.05	0.37	0.40
0.33	0.31	0.36	0.64	0.03	0.03	0.25	0.05	0.49	0.51
0.25	0.37	0.38	0.55	0.02	0.04	0.31	0.08	0.35	0.44
0.24	0.35	0.40	0.64	0.03	0.04	0.26	0.03	0.48	0.52
0.28	0.30	0.42	0.63	0.02	0.04	0.27	0.05	0.41	0.59
0.25	0.32	0.42	0.50	0.03	0.03	0.28	0.16	0.46	0.43
0.24	0.34	0.42	0.62	0.02	0.03	0.32	0.01	0.26	0.25
0.20	0.38	0.41	0.60	0.01	0.03	0.34	0.01		
0.35	0.35	0.30	0.54	0.05	0.04	0.34	0.04	0.41	0.35
0.33	0.35	0.31	0.49	0.07	0.06	0.31	0.07	0.56	0.04
0.16	0.37	0.47	0.70	0.03	0.02	0.23	0.02	0.59	0.29
0.44	0.29	0.27	0.53	0.05	0.03	0.25	0.14	0.36	0.34
0.39	0.35	0.27	0.54	0.05	0.05	0.26	0.10	0.29	0.54
0.31	0.35	0.34	0.52	0.05	0.05	0.34	0.05	0.49	0.17
0.20	0.45	0.35	0.58	0.03	0.02	0.29	0.09	0.41	0.45
0.22	0.34	0.45	0.58	0.07	0.04	0.14	0.17	0.35	0.37
0.29	0.38	0.33	0.54	0.03	0.03	0.29	0.11	0.44	0.18
0.29	0.34	0.37	0.61	0.05	0.02	0.22	0.10	0.49	0.20
0.35	0.35	0.30	0.47	0.14	0.02	0.19	0.17		
0.17	0.42	0.42	0.60	0.04	0.04	0.28	0.04	0.40	0.29
0.16	0.45	0.38	0.61	0.02	0.04	0.23	0.09	0.53	0.28
0.41	0.29	0.30	0.53	0.08	0.02	0.26	0.11	0.21	0.64
0.30	0.38	0.29	0.50	0.07	0.02	0.25	0.16	0.77	0.05

Table A10.3
Panel A: Multinomial regressions, 2005 (log-odds ratio between renters and mortgage holders [marginal effects])

Country	lage	female	hhsize	lnincome
New EU Countries				
Czech Republic	−0.2534***	0.0095	0.0030	−0.1868***
Estonia	−0.1701***	−0.0028	−0.0246***	−0.0159
Hungary	−0.2323***	−0.0176*	−0.0095	−0.0376
Latvia	−0.2000***	0.0382**	0.0081	−0.0311
Lithuania	−0.2716***	−0.0346***	−0.0165**	−0.0342***
Poland	−0.2704***	0.0138	−0.0200***	−0.0523**
Slovak Republic	−0.3695***	−0.0550***	−0.0244***	
Slovenia	−0.1418***	−0.0112	−0.0377***	−0.0168
EU-15 and Cyprus				
Austria	−0.2042***	0.0067	−0.0387***	−0.1687***
Belgium	−0.5392***	0.0462**	−0.0204	−0.2190***
Cyprus	−0.0998	−0.0159	−0.0079	−0.1792***
Denmark	1.1392	−0.1038***	0.0620***	0.5896**
Finland	−0.5927***	0.0043	−0.0113	−0.2502***
France	−0.4434***	0.0310*	−0.0291**	−0.1053**
Greece	−0.3803***	−0.0141	−0.0722***	0.0030
Ireland	−0.5264***	0.0259	0.0029	−0.0659**
Italy	−0.3474***	−0.0143	−0.0151**	−0.0809**
Luxembourg	−0.2086*	−0.0808**	−0.0074	−0.1946**
Netherlands	0.3940***	−0.0684***	0.0290**	0.2696**
Portugal	−0.2499***	0.0152	0.0051	−0.1297**
Spain	−0.2461***	−0.0024	−0.0186***	−0.0769**
Sweden	−0.4169**	0.0465**	0.0097	−0.1165*
United Kingdom	−0.7063***	0.0202	0.0006	−0.1273**

nhnodep	hhdep	house	secedu	teredu	fulltime
-0.0250	-0.0235	-0.2708***		-0.4032***	0.0243
-0.0720***	-0.0554***	0.0155		0.0795	-0.0900***
-0.0234*	0.0005	-0.1278***	-0.3171	-0.0637	-0.0080
-0.0544**	-0.0540*	-0.1626***	-0.0868	-0.2184	-0.0593
-0.0507***	0.0012	0.0108		-0.1377	-0.0292
0.0453**	0.0478**	-0.6144***	-0.3846	-0.3613*	0.0134
-0.2369***	-0.0962***	-0.0645***	-0.3431		-0.0798*
-0.0500***	0.0890***	-0.1792***	0.7582***	0.9552***	0.0622*
-0.0113	0.0130	-0.4904***		0.2252	0.0314
-0.0159	0.0664	-0.4962***	0.4386	-0.2780	-0.1352***
0.0083	-0.0881**	-0.2166***	0.3999	0.4291	-0.0691
-0.0034	-0.1880***	0.5353***	0.9999***	0.9996***	0.2028***
0.0196	0.0719*	-0.3478***	0.5301	0.2103	-0.2002***
-0.0669**	0.0179	-0.5021***	0.9539***	0.9332***	-0.1116***
-0.0385	0.0665*	-0.1556***	0.8484***	0.4796	0.0014
-0.0025	0.0586*	-0.6633***	0.7508*	0.5408	-0.2043***
0.0658***	0.0164	-0.1335***	-0.1101	-0.2359***	0.0290*
0.0032	0.0085	-0.5284***	0.8019*	-0.2943	-0.0383
0.0064	-0.0431	0.3462***	0.8541***	-0.0612	0.2457***
0.0866***	-0.1205***	-0.0337	-0.1770	-0.0277	-0.0241
0.0318*	0.0004	-0.0476***	-0.1912	-0.1055	-0.0309
0.045	-0.0411	-0.5563***	-0.7319	-0.5136	-0.1386***
0.0351*	0.0831***	-0.4215***	-0.6757***		-0.3818***

Table A10.3
(continued)

Country	lage	female	hhsize	lnincome	hhnodep	hhdep	house	secedu	teredu
Recently added EU countries									
Czech Republic	-0.2534***	0.0095	0.0030	-0.1868***	-0.0250	-0.0235	-0.2708***		-0.4032***
Estonia	-0.1701***	-0.0028	-0.0246***	-0.0159	-0.0720***	-0.0554***	0.0155		0.0795
Hungary	-0.2323***	-0.0176*	-0.0095	-0.0376	-0.0234*	0.0005	-0.1278***	-0.3171	-0.0637
Latvia	-0.2000***	0.0382**	0.0081	-0.0311	-0.0544**	-0.0540*	-0.1626***	-0.0868	-0.2184
Lithuania	-0.2716***	-0.0346***	-0.0165**	-0.0342***	-0.0507***	0.0012	0.0108		-0.1377
Poland	-0.2704***	0.0138	-0.0200***	-0.0523**	0.0453**	0.0478**	-0.6144***	-0.3846	-0.3613*
Slovak Republic	-0.3695***	-0.0550***	-0.0244***		-0.2369***	-0.0962***	-0.0645***	-0.3431	
Slovenia	-0.1418***	-0.0112	-0.0377***	-0.0168	-0.0500***	0.0890***	-0.1792***	0.7582***	0.9552***
EU-15 and Cyprus									
Austria	-0.2042***	0.0067	-0.0387***	-0.1687***	-0.0113	0.0130	-0.4904***		0.2252
Belgium	-0.5392***	0.0462**	-0.0204	-0.2190***	-0.0159	0.0664	-0.4962***	0.4386	-0.2780
Cyprus	-0.0998	-0.0159	-0.0079	-0.1792***	0.0083	-0.0881**	-0.2166***	0.3999	0.4291
Denmark	1.1392	-0.1038***	0.0620***	0.5896**	-0.0034	-0.1880***	0.5353***	0.9999***	0.9996**
Finland	-0.5927***	0.0043	-0.0113	-0.2502***	0.0196	0.0719*	-0.3478***	0.5301	0.2103
France	-0.4434***	0.0310*	-0.0291**	-0.1053**	-0.0669**	0.0179	-0.5021***	0.9539***	0.9332**
Greece	-0.3803***	-0.0141	-0.0722***	0.0030	-0.0385	0.0665*	-0.1556***	0.8484***	0.4796
Ireland	-0.5264***	0.0259	0.0029	-0.0659**	-0.0025	0.0586*	-0.6633***	0.7508*	0.5408
Italy	-0.3474***	-0.0143	-0.0151**	-0.0809***	-0.0658***	0.0164	-0.1335***	-0.1101	-0.2359**
Luxembourg	-0.2086*	-0.0808**	-0.0074	-0.1946**	0.0032	0.0085	-0.5284***	0.8019*	-0.2943
Netherlands	0.3940**	-0.0684***	0.0290**	0.2696***	-0.0064	-0.0431	0.3462***	0.8541***	-0.0612
Portugal	-0.2499***	0.0152	0.0051	-0.1297***	-0.0866***	-0.1205***	-0.0337	-0.1770	-0.0277
Spain	-0.2461***	-0.0024	-0.0186***	-0.0769***	-0.0318*	0.0004	-0.0476***	-0.1912	-0.1055
Sweden	-0.4169**	0.0465**	0.0097	-0.1165*	-0.045	-0.0411	-0.5563***	-0.7319	-0.5136
United Kingdom	-0.7063***	0.0202	0.0006	-0.1273***	-0.0351*	0.0831***	-0.4215***	-0.6757***	

Source: EU Statistics on Income and Living Conditions (EU-SILC) database, 2005.
*significant at 90 percent; **significant at 95 percent; ***significant at 99 percent.

fulltime	parttime	unemp	retired	urban	lage*secedu	lage*teredu	inc*secedu	inc*teredu	Hausman F-Statistic	r²
0.0243	0.0066	−0.0223	0.0685	0.0996***		−0.0583		0.1067**	1.05	0.24
−0.0900***	−0.0230	−0.0304	−0.0214	−0.0324**		−0.0518		0.0112	1.70**	0.21
−0.0080	0.0484	0.0251	0.0508**	0.0428***	0.0698	−0.0298	0.0049	−0.0125	2.29***	0.12
−0.0593	−0.0777*	−0.0673*	−0.0789*	−0.0260	0.0324	0.0810	−0.0307	−0.0497	0.95	0.09
−0.0292		−0.0212		−0.0137		0.0190		0.0070	0.74	0.22
0.0134	−0.0216	0.0647*	0.0048	0.1871***	0.0632	0.0883	0.0149	−0.0056	4.37***	0.34
−0.0798*	−0.0256	−0.0953***	−0.0006	0.0602***	0.2157***		−0.0886**	−0.0328	4.57***	0.17
0.0622*	0.2351**	0.1258*	0.0729		−0.0947**	−0.1347**	−0.0542***	−0.0533**	1.81**	0.15
0.0314	0.0368	0.1555**	0.0830	0.1475***		−0.1346*		−0.0084	2.21***	0.25
−0.1352***	−0.1247***	−0.0623	−0.0243	0.0428**	−0.1451	0.0738	−0.0810	0.0008	1.67**	0.35
−0.0691	−0.1187**	0.1033	0.0181	0.0703***	−0.0995	−0.1612*	−0.0202	−0.0149	1.29	0.16
0.2028***	0.1360***	−0.0244	0.1517***	−0.0313	−1.0301	−0.9949	−0.4199	−0.3710		0.35
0.2002***	−0.1296***	0.0066	−0.0305	0.0562***	−0.1245	−0.2312	−0.0148	−0.0001	2.62***	0.31
0.1116***	−0.0882*	0.0607	−0.0760*	0.0024	−0.3185***	−0.3562***	−0.0953***	−0.0931*	2.03***	0.32
0.0014	0.0865	0.0806	0.0028	0.0718***	−0.0311	0.0097	−0.0892***	−0.0619**	1.09	0.13
−0.2043***	−0.0851***	−0.0133	−0.0344	0.1004***	−0.0099	−0.0435	−0.0964***	−0.0432	3.32***	0.28
0.0290*	0.0761***	0.0748***	−0.0321**	0.0507***	0.0709*	0.0351	−0.0284*	−0.0352	4.02***	0.12
0.0383	−0.0455	0.1971	−0.0586	−0.0315	−0.1852	−0.0306	−0.0547	0.0585	0.68	0.35
0.2457***	0.1462***	−0.0591	0.0755***		−0.2294***	−0.1074	−0.0162	0.0852		0.29
0.0241	−0.0829	−0.0677	−0.0046	0.1860***	0.0369	0.1034	−0.0071	−0.0612	1.47*	0.19
0.0309	0.0164	0.0283	−0.0068	−0.0051	0.0211	0.0616	0.0123	−0.0147	2.73***	0.15
0.1386***	−0.1522***	0.0279	−0.0593	−0.0236	0.1607	0.2078	0.0101	−0.0399	2.16***	0.31
0.3818***	−0.2447***	0.0225	−0.0166	−0.0150	0.2805***			−0.0355	4.76***	0.32

Table A10.3
Panel B: **Multinomial regressions, 2005** (log-odds ratio between outright owners and mortgage holders [marginal effects])

Country	lage	female	hhsize	lnincome	hhnodep	hhdep	house	secedu	teredu
Recently added EU countries									
Czech Republic	0.2574***	0.0041	0.0321**	0.0677**	0.0271	-0.0594	0.5884***		0.8488***
Estonia	0.2328***	-0.0012	0.0304***	-0.0378**	0.0996***	0.0366	-0.0288*		-0.1745
Hungary	0.1254	0.0052	0.0239***	-0.1594	0.0306	-0.0628**	0.1120***	-0.6720	-0.9360***
Latvia	0.1815***	-0.0453***	-0.0036	0.0059	0.0479**	0.0305	0.1674***	-0.4582	-0.7367***
Lithuania	0.2860***	0.0327***	0.0203***	0.0152	0.0426**	-0.0261	-0.0084		-0.0729
Poland	0.2917***	-0.0067	0.0231***	0.0420**	-0.0395**	-0.0555**	0.6128***	0.4187*	0.1289
Slovak Republic	0.2313***	0.0285	0.0529***		0.2265***	0.1037***	0.4044***	0.2565	
Slovenia	0.1678***	0.0146	0.0385***	0.0153	0.0397**	-0.1094***	0.1867***	-0.7034***	-0.9190***
EU-15 and Cyprus									
Austria	0.2094***	0.0090	0.0449***	0.0801***	0.0224	-0.1294***	0.3545***		-0.5646***
Belgium	0.6986***	-0.0062	0.0466***	-0.0349	0.0685**	-0.2316***	0.2864***	-0.9813***	-0.7037**
Cyprus	0.2976***	0.0226	0.0316***	0.0349	0.0044	-0.0375	0.1570***	-0.6674**	-0.7840**
Finland	0.7958***	0.0144	0.0151	0.0421	0.0421	-0.0835**	0.1804***	-0.4694	-0.8413**
France	0.7209***	-0.0021	0.0012	0.0154	0.1026***	-0.0235	0.2065***	-0.0154	-0.2465
Greece	0.3201***	0.0091	0.0688***	-0.0335	0.0169	-0.1400***	0.1666***	-0.7204***	-0.6621**
Ireland	0.8212***	0.0056	0.0258**	-0.0255	0.0386	-0.2204***	0.4648***	0.0243	-0.4000
Italy	0.5062***	0.0186*	0.0368***	-0.0180	0.0609***	-0.1021***	0.1615***	-0.1632	-0.6996**
Luxembourg	0.7133***	0.0307	-0.0031	0.0212	0.0828*	-0.0651	0.3013***	-0.9093***	-0.5908
Portugal	0.4229***	0.0090	0.0478***	-0.0587***	0.0732*	-0.1439***	0.3265***	0.4172	-0.3553
Spain	0.5651***	0.0249	0.0797***	-0.0593***	0.0457*	-0.1801***	0.0868***	0.0183	-0.3163
Sweden	0.1073**	-0.0062	-0.0085	0.0221	0.0082	-0.0131	0.0444***	0.8609**	0.9971**
United Kingdom	0.8130***	0.0005	0.0192**	-0.0679***	0.0764***	-0.1442***	0.1799***	0.9659***	

Source: EU Statistics on Income and Living Conditions (EU-SILC) database, 2005.
*significant at 90 percent; **significant at 95 percent; ***significant at 99 percent.

fulltime	parttime	unemp	retired	urban	lage*secedu	lage*teredu	inc*secedu	inc*teredu	Hausman F-Statistic	r²
-0.0258	0.0535	0.0250	-0.0415	-0.1097***		-0.0881		-0.1202**	3.96***	0.24
0.0713*	-0.0378	0.0436	0.0133	0.0300**		0.0837*		-0.0190	0.65	0.21
-0.0172	-0.0587	-0.0267	0.0006	-0.0400***	0.1118	0.2545**	0.1424	0.1944*	2.48***	0.12
0.0511	0.0929**	0.0721	0.0771*	0.0186	-0.0003	-0.0427	0.0362	0.0570*	0.46	0.09
0.0221		0.0029		0.0126		-0.0061		-0.0037	1.13	0.22
-0.0255	0.0212	-0.0898***	-0.0103	-0.1821***	-0.0697	-0.0755	-0.0164	0.0065	2.49***	0.34
0.0810	0.0556	0.0360	0.0156	-0.1187***	-0.1148		-0.0059	-0.0233	10.30***	0.17
-0.0959***	-0.2574**	-0.2096**	-0.1215**		0.0762*	0.1375**	0.0563***	0.0445	1.88**	0.15
-0.0625	-0.0495	-0.0862	0.0084	-0.0758***		0.1495**		0.0316	2.13***	0.25
0.0569	-0.0412	0.0239	0.1427***	-0.0488**	0.2080	0.0611	0.1580**	0.1253*	2.31***	0.35
-0.0428	-0.0110	-0.1098	-0.0310	-0.1112***	0.1001	0.1239	0.0460	0.0674	2.05***	0.16
-0.0204	0.0268	0.0034	0.0298	-0.0241	0.0871	0.3399***	0.0134	0.0461	3.13***	0.31
-0.0270	0.0484	-0.0696*	-0.0006	0.0068	0.0121	0.1141	0.0164	0.0154	2.80***	0.32
-0.0461	-0.0647	-0.0934	-0.0241	-0.0821***	-0.0121	-0.0249	0.0873***	0.0834**	1.76**	0.13
-0.0544	0.0078	-0.0364	0.2068***	-0.1677***	-0.2133**	-0.0410	0.0501	0.0540	2.52***	0.28
-0.0682***	-0.1057***	-0.0573	0.0249	-0.0518***	-0.1359***	-0.0876	0.0768***	0.1091***	5.04***	0.12
0.1480***	-0.0458	-0.0701	-0.0146	0.0040	0.2475	0.2383	0.0596	0.0274	1.03	0.35
0.2307***	-0.0378	-0.2982***	-0.1984***	-0.1664***	-0.1718**	0.0015	0.0269	0.0624	2.96***	0.19
0.0874***	-0.1229***	-0.0851*	0.0382	-0.0240*	-0.0663	-0.1295**	0.0180	0.0735***	3.01***	0.15
0.0186	-0.0108	0.0383	0.0177	-0.0130*	-0.0443	-0.0732	-0.0290*	-0.0317**	1.59**	0.31
0.1076***	0.2245***	0.0700	0.2677***	-0.0252*	-0.2665***			0.1144***	9.79***	0.32

Table A10.4
Panel A: Multinomial regressions, 2006 (log-odds ratio between renters and mortgage holders [marginal effects])

Country	lage	female	hhsize	lnincome	hhnodep	hhdep	house	secedu	teredu
Recently added EU countries									
Czech Republic	-0.2284***	-0.0160	-0.0111	-0.1279***	-0.0670***	-0.0076	-0.2734***		-0.4526***
Estonia	-0.2921***	0.0025	-0.0402***	-0.0518	-0.0820***	0.0031	0.0381**	-0.4777	-0.1999
Hungary	-0.1530***	-0.0100	-0.0096	-0.0226	-0.0358***	-0.0125	-0.12***	0.0507	-0.0791
Latvia	-0.2663**	0.0084	0.0040	-0.0093	-0.0333*	-0.0339	-0.1296***	-0.3599	-0.1874
Lithuania	-0.1655***	-0.0277***	-0.0157**	-0.0308***	-0.0326***	-0.0030	0.0128		-0.0037
Poland	-0.2196***	0.0210	-0.0181***	-0.0839***	0.0306	0.0523**	-0.5958***	-0.0408	-0.5135***
Slovak Republic	-0.5318**	-0.0251**	-0.0032	0.0750	-0.0199	0.0381*	-0.1114***	-0.8940	-0.1563
Slovenia	-0.1245***	0.0003	-0.0373***	-0.0004	-0.0670***	0.0705***	-0.0872***	0.7900***	0.9712**
EU-15 and Cyprus									
Austria	-1.2767	0.0092	-0.0250*	-1.9602***	-0.0505*	-0.0135	-0.4781***	-1.0000	-1.0000
Belgium	-0.3224**	0.0334	-0.0247	-0.1925**	-0.0442	0.0456	-0.5021***	0.0336	0.0135
Cyprus	0.0159	0.0072	-0.0146	-0.1968***	0.0602*	-0.0471	-0.2319***	0.9305***	0.8724**
Denmark	0.1007*	-0.1098***	0.0819***	0.2343***	0.0018	-0.1940***	0.5194***		-0.0015
Finland	-0.2824*	0.0002	-0.0118	-0.2720***	0.0220	0.0718*	-0.3208***	0.8040***	0.9368**
France	-0.4545***	0.0638***	-0.0158	-0.1641***	-0.0471*	0.0100	-0.4982***	0.9064***	0.9407**
Greece	-0.3211***	-0.0430**	-0.0815***	0.0121	-0.0714**	0.0288	-0.1654***	0.8618***	0.2360
Ireland	-0.4601***	0.0561**	0.0185*	-0.1235***	-0.0341	0.0055	-0.6479***	0.3920	0.7084
Italy	-0.3815***	-0.0126	-0.0235***	-0.0924***	-0.0583***	0.0278	-0.1128***	-0.4355**	-0.2274*
Luxembourg	-0.1814*	-0.0490	0.0282	-0.2724***	0.0264	-0.0171	-0.5028***	0.8920***	-0.6124**
Netherlands	0.3258***	-0.0363*	-0.0217	0.1451**	0.0272	0.0883*	0.3812***	-0.8784***	-0.9380**
Portugal	-0.2731***	0.0216	-0.0094	-0.1075***	-0.0072	-0.0314	-0.0537**	0.0818	0.7502**
Spain	-0.1729***	0.0239*	-0.0057	-0.0771***	-0.0669***	-0.0572**	-0.0449***	-0.2863	0.0998
Sweden	-0.4284**	0.0035	-0.0061	-0.1266	-0.0721**	-0.0389	-0.5426***	-0.7485	-0.7752**
United Kingdom	-0.8167***	0.0295*	0.0088		-0.0820***	0.0237	-0.4289***	-0.9062***	

Source: EU Statistics on Income and Living Conditions (EU-SILC) database, 2006.
*significant at 90 percent; **significant at 95 percent; ***significant at 99 percent.

fulltime	parttime	unemp	retired	urban	lage*secedu	lage*teredu	inc*secedu	inc*teredu	Hausman F-Statistic	r²
-0.0476	-0.0270	0.0634	0.0116	0.1109***		0.0083		0.0966***	0.97	0.26
-0.0637**	-0.0244	-0.0280	0.0318	-0.0146	0.0630	-0.0159	0.0216	0.0323	1888.07***	0.18
-0.0319*	-0.0524**	0.0146	0.0436**	0.0659***	-0.0610	-0.0223	-0.0203	0.0010	1.86**	0.13
-0.0767*	-0.0407	-0.0624*	-0.0862***	-0.0448***	0.1418	0.1140	-0.0357	-0.0488	1.05	0.07
-0.0015		-0.0227		-0.0233**		-0.0223		0.0047	1.03	0.24
0.0207	-0.0253	0.0976**	0.0156	0.2000***	0.0153	0.0737	0.0158	0.0445	2.99***	0.32
-0.0329	-0.0562**	-0.0521**	-0.0346	0.0172	0.4221**	0.3552*	-0.1178	-0.1358	1.25	0.29
0.1010***	0.1746*	0.1794**	0.1637***		-0.1311***	-0.1968***	-0.0524***	-0.0361	1.57*	0.10
-0.0432	-0.0906	0.0913	0.0584	0.1479***	1.1195	0.9986	1.7892**	1.8079**	3.86***	0.24
-0.1744***	-0.1624***	-0.0823**	-0.0661	0.0572***	-0.2079	-0.3132**	0.0167	-0.0010	1.73**	0.35
0.0973*	0.0877	0.0876	0.1964***	0.0866***	-0.3356***	-0.2513***	-0.0565	-0.0310	2.18***	0.16
0.1702***	0.0992	0.0338	0.0927*	-0.0702***		-0.0351		0.0210		0.37
0.1473***	-0.0834**	0.0931*	-0.0655*	0.0919***	-0.3296**	-0.4673***	0.0110	0.0062	2.93***	0.31
0.0610	-0.1209**	0.0393	-0.0779	0.0092	-0.2911***	-0.2854***	-0.0628	-0.1220**	1.62**	0.32
0.0159	0.0330	0.0591	-0.0559*	0.0662***	-0.0267	0.0794	-0.0988***	-0.0872***	1.10	0.14
0.1598***	-0.0464	-0.0403	-0.0406	0.0969***	-0.0922	-0.2177**	-0.0174	-0.0025	2.59***	0.28
0.0399**	0.0570*	0.1120***	-0.0464***	0.0732***	0.1182***	0.0594	-0.0133	-0.0325	3.32***	0.13
0.0037	-0.1749***	0.0173	0.0014	-0.0399	-0.0903	-0.0439	-0.0916	0.1169*	0.96	0.35
0.2257***	0.0950***	-0.0003	0.0657**		-0.1629	0.0180	0.2239***	0.2162***		0.31
0.0836	-0.1100*	-0.0905	-0.0471	0.1604***	0.0456	0.0779	-0.0370	-0.1589***	1.66**	0.19
0.0512**	0.1007**	0.0515	0.0494*	-0.0063	0.0184	-0.0522	0.0254	0.0041	2.31***	0.14
0.1163***	-0.0747**	0.0627	-0.1424***	-0.0663***	0.1991	0.1729	-0.0082	0.0365	1.44*	0.33
0.4009***	-0.2297***	-0.0308	-0.0458*	-0.0272*	0.3641***		-0.0963***	-0.1390***	13.4***	0.33

Table A10.4
Panel B: Multinomial regressions, 2006 (log-odds ratio between outright owners and mortgage holders [marginal effects])

Country	lage	female	hhsize	lnincome	hhnodep	hhdep	house	secedu	teredu
Recently added EU countries									
Czech Republic	0.2519***	0.0208	0.0381***	0.0265	0.0405	−0.0898**	0.6088***		−0.1990
Estonia	0.2298***	−0.0027	0.0458***	−0.0372	0.1030***	−0.0157	−0.0474***	−0.5223	−0.8001***
Hungary	0.1414**	0.0077	0.0211***	−0.1182**	'	−0.0724***	0.1083***	−0.9260***	−0.9197***
Latvia	0.0605	0.0302	−0.0040	−0.0213	0.0745***	0.0251	0.2284***	−0.2548	−0.8046***
Lithuania	0.1691***	0.0279***	0.0172**	0.0212**	0.0345***	−0.0009	−0.0132		−0.6783
Poland	0.2426***	−0.0176	0.0216***	0.0821***	−0.0263	−0.0613**	0.5926***	0.4126	0.5389***
Slovak Republic	0.7571*	−0.0014	0.0362***	0.0077	−0.0115	−0.0826***	0.5959***	0.9146***	0.9877***
Slovenia	0.1460***	0.0037	0.0377***	−0.0075	0.0700***	−0.0750***	0.0965***	−0.7970***	−0.9451***
EU-15 and Cyprus									
Austria	0.6515	0.0217	0.0446***	0.2535	0.0348	−0.1480***	0.3496***	0.0000	0.0000
Belgium	0.5760***	−0.0154	0.0425***	−0.1560	0.1143***	−0.1659***	0.2832***	−0.9742***	−0.9915**
Cyprus	0.2300***	−0.0015	0.0296**	0.0722**	0.0078	−0.0043	0.1668***	−0.9598***	−0.8109**
Finland	0.8166***	0.0088	0.0189**	0.0480	0.0465**	−0.0929***	0.1383***	0.0323	−0.6641**
France	0.8020***	−0.0247*	−0.0129	0.0081	0.1047***	−0.0080	0.2099***	−0.0027	−0.3105
Greece	0.2693***	0.0431**	0.0850***	−0.0497**	0.0230	−0.1193***	0.1726***	−0.7836***	−0.7469**
Ireland	0.8663***	−0.0519*	0.0196	−0.0263	0.0478	−0.2036***	0.4784***	−0.1067	−0.7416**
Italy	0.5573***	0.0207*	0.0428***	0.0060	0.0500***	−0.1061***	0.1387***	0.2681	−0.5568**
Luxembourg	0.7725***	0.0541	−0.0212	0.0854	0.0432	−0.0383	0.2832***	−0.4913	0.1179
Portugal	0.4818***	−0.0137	0.0620***	−0.0549**	−0.0073	−0.2329***	0.3152***	−0.0053	−0.6773**
Spain	0.6083***	−0.0087	0.0717***	−0.0360*	0.0415	−0.1691***	0.1051***	0.4272	0.1789
Sweden	0.0875*	0.0015	−0.0015	−0.0072	0.0043	−0.0156*	0.0483***	0.8637	0.7084
United Kingdom	0.8303***	−0.0135	0.0148		0.0886***	−0.1324***	0.2001***	0.9009***	

Source: EU Statistics on Income and Living Conditions (EU-SILC) database, 2006.
*significant at 90 percent; **significant at 95 percent; ***significant at 99 percent.

fulltime	parttime	unemp	retired	urban	lage*secedu	lage*teredu	inc*secedu	inc*teredu	Hausman F-Statistic	r²
-0.0226	-0.0450	-0.0355	-0.0454	-0.1474***		0.0708		-0.0294	8.11***	0.26
0.0685**	0.0418	0.0408	0.0048	0.0204	0.0421	0.1354*	0.0310	0.0212	1.33	0.18
-0.0004	0.0287	-0.0109	0.0103	-0.0608***	0.1454**	0.1464**	0.1147**	0.1360***	1.98***	0.13
0.0994*	0.0264	0.0802	0.0767	-0.0035	0.0722	0.1812	0.0085	0.0552	0.91	0.07
-0.0082		-0.0622		0.0219**		0.0361		-0.0036	0.95	0.24
-0.0296	0.0020	-0.0907**	-0.0233	-0.1970***	-0.0192	-0.0662	-0.0280	-0.0558*	1.73**	0.32
0.0681	0.0765	0.0308	0.0639	-0.0882***	-0.6625	-0.7351	-0.0228	0.0092	3.28***	0.29
-0.1114***	-0.1908*	-0.2158**	-0.1704***		0.1200***	0.1704***	0.0582***	0.0401	1.60*	0.10
-0.1032*	-0.133***	-0.1598**	-0.0691	-0.0711***	-0.4666	-0.3479	-0.1646	-0.1571	3.42***	0.24
0.0362	-0.0509	0.0610	0.1914***	-0.0670***	0.2081	0.2625	0.1696*	0.2631***	2.25***	0.35
-0.2310***	-0.2080***	-0.1814*	-0.2058***	-0.1085***	0.2418***	0.1117	0.1170***	0.0815*	1.45*	0.16
-0.0268	0.0237	-0.0642	0.0019	-0.0391**	0.0288	0.1886	-0.0232	0.0514	2.43***	0.31
-0.0855**	0.0055	-0.0536	-0.0702**	-0.0157	0.0071	0.0009	0.0102	0.0736**	3.15***	0.32
-0.0143	-0.0147	-0.0436	0.0411	-0.0832***	0.0362	-0.0758	0.0819***	0.1113***	1.51*	0.14
-0.0535	-0.0952	-0.0782	0.0096	-0.1754***	-0.1571	0.0709	0.0752*	0.0719	1.30	0.28
-0.1117***	-0.1374***	-0.1278***	0.0147	-0.0812***	-0.1951***	-0.1205**	0.0569***	0.0896***	4.70***	0.13
-0.1773***	-0.0778	-0.1344	0.0044	-0.0221	0.0739	0.0153	0.0461	-0.0261	1.13	0.35
-0.1776***	-0.1358	-0.1356	-0.1543*	-0.1694***	-0.1151	0.0087	0.0506	0.1773***	2.64***	0.19
-0.1219***	-0.0643	-0.0703	0.0322	-0.0028	-0.1731***	-0.1232*	0.0142	0.0215	2.30***	0.14
-0.0091	-0.0142***	-0.0136***	-0.0012	0.0035	-0.0572	-0.0415	-0.0018	0.0006	1.35	0.33
0.0376	0.0934***	0.0251	0.2498***	-0.0229*	-0.2802***		-0.0562***	0.0340**	12.09***	0.33

Table A10.5
Panel A: Nested logit regressions, 2005 (log-odds ratio between renting and owning)

Country	lage	female	hhsize	lnincome	hhnodep	hhdep	house	secedu	teredu
Recently added EU countries									
Czech Republic	−0.08	0.03	0.32***	−0.36**	−0.48**	−0.76**	−21.9***		−3.61
Estonia	−2.77	0.09	−0.37***	0.97	−1.86**	−0.69	0.53		5.99*
Hungary	−19.53***	0.15	−1.72***	5.23**	2.38*	6.47***	0.30	13.27*	42.05***
Latvia	−3.31	1.25	−0.86	0.26	1.09	3.10	−2.74*	−22.09	−11.12
Lithuania	−0.31	−0.36	−0.11	0.21	−1.22	−0.80	0.33		15.69
Poland	6.26***	1.14**	0.83***	−1.04*	1.55*	−1.37	1.38	19.64***	−0.39
Slovak Republic	−1.37**	−0.46**	0.63***	−0.57*	−0.38	−0.74*	17.07***	14.49***	14.85***
EU-15 and Cyprus									
Austria	−2.60***	−0.55	−0.52***	0.18	−0.01	3.21***	−3.12***		19.03**
Belgium	−0.49	0.26***	−0.05	0.39	−0.23	0.04	−2.18***	22.59***	15.24**
Cyprus	−2.05	−0.12	−0.17	0.58	0.13	0.27	−0.98***	11.14***	13.46**
Denmark	0.39	0.44***	−0.27***	0.13	0.04	0.83***	−2.37***	11.10***	13.40**
Finland	−0.06	0.05	−0.06	0.04	−0.09	0.23	−1.55***	21.60***	21.16**
France	−0.61	0.12	−0.13***	0.34	−0.43***	0.03	−2.19***	20.43***	20.30**
Greece	−0.33	−0.08	−0.36	0.41**	−0.43	−0.35	−0.51	19.50	14.06
Ireland	1.20*	0.33**	0.15	0.12	0.16	−0.83**	−2.93***	27.46***	17.85**
Italy	2.19	−0.01	0.17	−0.69	−0.37***	−0.74	−0.20	9.78***	7.16**
Luxembourg	0.80*	−0.40**	−0.07	−0.17	−0.03	−0.02	−2.39***	14.43***	6.71*
Netherlands	−2.25***	0.41***	−0.45***	0.90***	−1.25***	−0.79***	−0.17		14.02**
Portugal	1.75***	0.25*	0.25***	−0.72***	−0.19	−1.36***	1.41***	11.81***	9.53**
Spain	−0.37	0.03	−0.10	0.03	−0.26**	−0.05	−0.32***	7.81***	8.77**
Sweden	0.86	0.16	0.05	−0.09	0.08	−0.25	−2.74***	14.88***	13.77**
United Kingdom	−0.67***	0.20***	−0.04	0.42***	−0.34***	0.37***	−1.74***		17.63**

Source: EU Statistics on Income and Living Conditions (EU-SILC) database, 2005.
*significant at 90 percent; **significant at 95 percent; ***significant at 99 percent.

fulltime	parttime	unemp	retired	urban	suburban	lage*secedu	lage*teredu	inc*secedu	inc*teredu
-0.28	0.15	-0.20	-0.75**	0.45***			-0.43		0.57*
-0.74	0.41	-0.71	-0.85	-0.28			-1.51***		-0.07
2.74	3.18	-0.11	-5.87*	-0.16	0.79	7.69	3.23	-4.03	-5.25**
-1.48	-6.60	-4.59	-2.90	0.94		-1.41	-0.39	3.09	1.51
0.23		0.88		-0.31			-2.19*		-0.99
-2.49**	0.27	-4.82***	-0.71	0.16	0.50	-2.11	0.44	-1.61**	-0.64
-0.42	-0.89	-0.59	-1.19*	-1.52***	-1.75***	0.89		-0.29	
3.01*	2.92*	2.36	-4.25*	1.02***			-1.84*		-1.19***
-0.53***	-0.40*	0.02	-0.96**	0.10	-0.10	-1.96***	-0.85*	-1.58***	-1.28***
-0.28	-0.24	1.08	-0.46	0.70**	0.10	-0.31	0.29	-1.02**	-1.42*
0.88***	-0.63**	0.06	-0.71***	0.24*	0.21*	-0.84	-0.99	-0.88	-1.08
0.81*	-0.55**	0.17	-0.97**	0.18	-0.13	-2.71***	-2.85***	-1.06**	-1.00**
0.14	-0.04	0.64**	-0.70***	0.05	0.07	-2.42***	-2.41***	-1.10***	-1.15***
0.23	0.92	0.74	-0.19	0.17	-1.32	-2.28	-1.86	-1.13	-0.76***
2.30***	-1.24***	-0.55	1.54*	-0.07	-0.11	-3.05***	-2.48***	-1.67***	-0.96***
0.17	0.16	0.70***	-0.26	0.04	-0.20	-2.07**	-2.11**	-0.23	0.01
0.14	0.39	1.48**	-0.54*	-0.13	0.00	-1.34***	-0.69	-0.91***	-0.38
1.25***	-0.57***	0.84***	-0.64**	-0.01			-1.29***		-0.93***
0.51	0.58	-0.51	-0.14	0.84***	0.54***	-1.97***	-0.64	-0.52**	-0.77***
0.12	0.54*	0.70***	-0.28*	-0.13	-0.15	-0.79***	-0.45	-0.50***	-0.72***
0.91***	-1.01***	0.38	0.06	-0.24*	-0.20	-1.61**	-1.45**	-0.91***	-0.89***
1.84***	-1.39***	0.58**	-1.92***	0.15*			-1.99***		-1.04***

Table A10.5
Panel B: Nested logit regressions, 2005 (log-odds ratio between owning with and without a mortgage)

Country	lage	female	hhsize	lnincome	hhnodep	hhdep	house	secedu	teredu
Recently added EU countries									
Czech Republic	-0.20***	0.01	-0.07**	-0.07***	0.07*	0.13**	2.94***		1.07
Estonia	2.65***	0.02	0.15*	-0.82***	0.86**	-0.34	-0.52***		3.79
Hungary	2.00***	-0.04	0.21***	-0.55**	-0.32***	-0.83***	-0.17*	-1.44*	-4.96***
Latvia	0.81*	-0.29	0.26**	-0.02	-0.42	-1.00**	0.46	7.83*	4.61
Lithuania	3.20***	-0.10	0.38**	-0.92***	-0.48	-1.77***	0.17		5.58**
Poland	1.38***	0.25**	0.21***	-0.26**	0.31*	-0.37*	1.01***	3.12**	-1.70
Slovak Republic	0.12	-0.01	0.10***	-0.03	0.15**	-0.04	2.04***	-1.17***	-1.40**
EU-15 and Cyprus									
Austria	0.42***	0.11	0.08*	-0.09	-0.03	-0.74***	0.18*		-2.92**
Belgium	3.19***	0.16	0.22***	-1.24***	0.35**	-1.21***	0.17	-13.16***	-11.94**
Cyprus	2.74***	0.11	0.19***	-0.85***	-0.23	-1.07***	0.06	-0.19	-2.74
Finland	-3.29	0.21	-0.12	-1.32	0.02	0.39	-1.21***	-21.07***	-20.55**
France	2.18***	0.05	0.02	-0.71***	0.04	-0.52*	0.05	-9.34***	-15.14**
Greece	2.03***	0.08	-0.05	-0.73***	0.52***	-0.08	-0.11	-10.73***	-14.69**
Ireland	0.78**	-0.02	0.05	-0.04	-0.24	-0.93**	0.40***	7.74***	3.96
Italy	1.41***	0.11	0.14***	-0.33***	0.29*	-1.06***	-0.04	1.60	-4.99**
Luxembourg	2.57***	0.09	0.28***	-0.81***	0.04	-0.95***	0.53***	-0.15	-4.40**
Portugal	3.01***	0.06	0.01	-1.11***	0.42	-0.60	1.00***	-18.88***	-22.63**
Spain	2.04***	-0.16	0.27***	-1.14***	0.68***	-0.53**	2.68***		-11.79**
Sweden	1.44***	0.10	0.27***	-0.60***	0.27	-1.06***	1.74***	3.34*	-0.89
United Kingdom	2.04***	0.14*	0.41***	-0.72***	0.14	-1.01***	0.27***	-3.08***	-4.10**

Source: EU Statistics on Income and Living Conditions (EU-SILC) database, 2005.
*significant at 90 percent; **significant at 95 percent; ***significant at 99 perent.

fulltime	parttime	unemp	retired	urban	suburban	lage*secedu	lage*teredu	inc*secedu	inc*teredu
0.10	-0.04	0.06	0.24***	-0.01			-0.03		-0.11
-0.46	-1.14	0.75	-0.27	-0.20			0.22		-0.60**
-0.34*	-0.33	0.07	0.62***	0.10	-0.04	-0.68	-0.12	0.35	0.49*
0.35	1.74	1.21	0.67	-0.32		0.28	0.12	-1.04***	-0.66*
-0.22		-0.21		-0.06			-0.52		-0.48
-0.59**	0.08	-1.21***	-0.15	-0.16	0.05	-0.26	0.39	-0.30*	-0.07
0.01	-0.09	0.01	-0.15*	-0.16*	-0.14**	-0.04		-0.01	
-0.57**	-0.51*	-0.27	0.59**	-0.08			0.32		0.16**
0.66**	-0.59**	-0.03	0.84***	0.08	0.23	0.71	0.51	1.03***	0.97***
-0.65	-0.29	-0.55	0.19	-0.53***	-0.45***	-0.74	-1.12*	0.30	0.65**
0.48	-0.36	0.01	-0.41	0.13	0.11	3.05	2.99	0.93	0.88
-0.66***	-0.25	-0.03	0.10	-0.06	-0.24*	1.11***	2.25***	0.44	0.56***
-0.59**	-0.04	-0.52	-0.18	0.00	0.01	1.35***	2.05***	0.50***	0.60**
0.46	0.44	0.03	-0.22	-0.27*	-3.93***	-1.36***	-1.11**	-0.27	0.00
0.76***	-0.38*	-0.54*	1.27***	-0.87***	-0.76***	-0.07	0.73**	-0.15	0.15
0.56***	-0.49**	0.09	-0.04	-0.45***	-0.48***	-1.01***	-0.80**	0.39	0.71***
0.94**	-0.47	0.34	-0.08	-0.36*	-0.34	2.25***	2.75***	0.95***	1.14***
0.16	-0.27	-0.16	0.35*	-0.33***			0.37		0.95***
0.98***	0.16	-1.37***	-0.50	-0.35***	0.07	-0.79***	0.27	-0.05	0.03
0.76***	-0.68***	-0.51**	0.18	-0.28***	-0.27***	-0.02	-0.26	0.30***	0.48***

Table A10.6
Panel A: Nested logit regressions, 2006 (log-odds ratio between renting and owning)

Country	lage	female	hhsize	lnincome	hhnodep	hhdep	house	secedu	teredu
Recently added EU countries									
Czech Republic	-0.50***	0.02	-0.09	0.20***	-0.62***	-0.11	-3.71***		2.11
Estonia	-5.11**	-0.01	-0.79***	1.71***	-3.03**	0.39	1.09**		7.86*
Hungary	-3.46	-0.12	-0.41	0.68	-0.03	1.67	-1.04***	8.06***	11.61
Latvia	-1.17	-0.11	0.05	0.35	-0.56	-0.31	-1.98	2.32	6.79***
Lithuania	-3.34	-0.52	-0.65	0.94	-1.51	0.22	0.45		12.06
Poland	4.43*	0.53	0.82***	-0.02	0.85	-1.71*	-0.16	19.09**	6.91
Slovak Republic	-1.77	-0.29**	0.19**	0.89	-0.36*	-0.12	3.64*	6.99***	11.16***
EU-15 and Cyprus									
Austria	0.44	-0.18	-0.25***	-0.25	0.26	1.62***	-3.21***	13.47***	10.36**
Belgium	0.44	0.20**	-0.08	0.06	-0.18	-0.09	-2.22***	15.10***	15.83***
Cyprus	-2.55	0.08	-0.20	0.60	0.01	0.23	-0.86***	20.33***	13.10**
Denmark	0.06	0.53***	-0.49***	0.24***	-0.49***	0.54**	-2.42***		10.92**
Finland	3.90***	0.06	0.00	-1.33***	0.36	0.06	-1.60***	20.42***	17.46**
France	0.19	0.27***	-0.09*	0.05	-0.21	0.01	-2.18***	20.00***	21.62***
Greece	-9.52*	-1.41	-1.42	1.64	3.79	6.04**	-5.68	-27.55	-23.90
Ireland	0.12	0.34**	0.17**	0.22	-0.40**	-0.44	-2.67***	21.31***	22.34***
Italy	3.55***	0.13	0.26*	-0.95***	-0.37**	-1.15**	0.19	9.79***	6.48**
Luxembourg	1.09**	-0.26	0.09	-0.35**	0.01	-0.10	-2.37***	18.68***	8.58***
Netherlands	-1.94***	0.36***	-0.36***	0.74***	-0.97***	-0.53**	-0.24		12.00**
Portugal	1.94***	0.10	0.22**	-0.70***	0.02	-1.30***	1.36***	11.35***	10.92**
Spain	0.34	0.19**	0.06	-0.26	-0.46***	-0.60**	-0.21*	4.12***	7.17**
Sweden	1.10	-0.03	-0.01	-0.23	-0.29	-0.33	-2.45***	12.76***	11.76**
United Kingdom	-0.87***	0.31***	-0.04	0.52***	-0.52***	0.20	-1.75***		18.87***

Source: EU Statistics on Income and Living Conditions (EU-SILC) database, 2006.
*significant at 90 percent; **significant at 95 percent; ***significant at 99 percent.

fulltime	parttime	unemp	retired	urban	suburban	lage*secedu	lage*teredu	inc*secedu	inc*teredu
-0.27	-0.12	0.78***	-0.26	0.67***			-0.24		-0.19
-0.36	-0.06	-1.71	-3.79*	-0.45			-1.42*		-0.25
0.20	-0.57	-0.12	-1.26	0.84***	0.64**	-1.00	-0.56	-0.32	-0.89
-0.68	-0.19	-0.57	-0.66	-0.08		0.08	-0.43	-0.32	-0.66
1.44		1.98		-0.39			-2.82*		-0.22
-2.68*	-3.52*	0.64	-1.70	-0.07	-0.29	0.07	1.55	-2.79**	-2.23*
-0.22	-0.81	-0.56	-0.48	-0.84***	-0.88***	1.07	0.01	-1.43	-1.48
1.55*	1.57*	1.61	-0.16	0.81***	0.45**	-2.92	-2.81	-0.40	-0.22
-0.95***	-0.87***	-0.19	-0.74**	0.30	0.09	-1.92***	-2.10***	-0.82***	-0.85***
1.39*	1.01	1.24	0.07	0.92**	0.34	-0.55	0.80	-1.81*	-1.55*
-1.14***	-0.68**	-0.14	-0.60***	0.26**			-0.59*		-0.89***
-1.10***	-0.44	0.28	-0.35	0.35***	-0.21	-4.33***	-4.73***	-0.34	0.02
0.08	-0.23	0.46	-0.54**	0.15	0.16	-2.56***	-2.41***	-1.01***	-1.27***
7.96	-10.72	-9.01	-7.90	-0.90	-2.51	6.84	12.97	0.84	-1.58
1.57***	-0.53	-0.29	-0.70***	0.60**	0.48*	-3.00***	-3.38***	-1.05***	-1.02***
1.12*	-0.87	0.19	-0.62**	-0.31	-0.47	-2.47***	-2.45***	-0.14	0.14
0.53	-0.33	0.94*	-0.32	-0.21	-0.07	-1.36***	-1.25**	-1.30***	-0.35
1.17***	-0.77***	-0.46	-1.06***	-0.03			-1.35***		-0.70***
1.16**	-0.43	-0.44	-0.57	0.60***	0.50**	-1.70***	-0.52	-0.58**	-0.95***
0.47**	0.88***	0.60**	0.18	-0.12	-0.13	-0.69*	-1.12***	-0.16	-0.33
0.65**	-0.68	0.05	-0.66	-0.22	0.00	-1.71**	-1.63**	-0.64**	-0.58*
1.95***	-1.27***	0.49*	-2.11***	0.08			-2.45***		-1.01***

Table A10.6
Panel B: Nested logit regressions, 2006 (log-odds ratio between owning with and without a mortgage)

Country	lage	female	hhsize	lnincome	hhnodep	hhdep	house	secedu	teredu
Recently added EU countries									
Czech Republic	0.68***	0.06	0.06	−0.49***	0.19	−0.14	3.16***		−3.83
Estonia	2.40***	0.10	0.24***	−0.83***	1.13***	−0.23	−0.45***		0.51
Hungary	1.18***	0.02	0.19***	−0.21	−0.17	−1.02***	0.06	0.43	−3.97**
Latvia	0.35	0.25*	−0.03	0.07	0.40**	0.05	1.09***	3.12**	−1.83
Lithuania	2.80***	0.18	0.35	−0.70**	0.60	−0.44	−0.12		4.73
Poland	1.21*	0.13	0.26***	−0.02	0.22	−0.57**	0.81***	3.60	0.58
Slovak Republic	0.46	−0.04	0.19***	−0.60	−0.12	−0.46***	3.58***	−3.83***	−4.49***
EU-15 and Cyprus									
Austria	0.43	0.11	0.13**	−0.17	−0.29*	−1.30***	0.66***	−3.91***	−0.98
Belgium	3.30***	−0.01	0.23***	−1.27***	0.49***	−1.01***	−0.11	−7.29***	
Cyprus	2.80***	0.03	0.15**	−0.85***	0.14	−0.64*	−0.13	−6.60***	−2.28
Denmark	−1.12***	0.11	0.12	−2.28***	0.86***	0.79**	−1.09***		−16.80***
Finland	2.50***	0.08	0.08**	−0.90***	0.53***	−0.24	−0.17**	−4.10*	−11.82***
France	2.70***	0.03	−0.13**	−0.91***	0.65***	0.08	−0.08	−9.10***	−12.25***
Greece	0.73**	0.11	0.10	−0.13	−0.40	−0.57	0.45**	3.36	2.93
Ireland	2.45***	−0.09	0.18***	−0.73***	0.14	−1.17***	0.38	−2.72	−7.55**
Italy	2.26***	0.13**	0.25***	−0.61***	0.00	−0.89***	0.50***	−0.09	−3.84***
Luxembourg	2.94***	0.22	−0.05	−1.07***	0.26	−0.46	0.92***	−18.42***	−17.71***
Netherlands	1.43***	−0.14	0.10	−0.90***	0.52***	−0.72***	2.68***		−11.69***
Portugal	1.53***	−0.04	0.30***	−0.59***	0.07	−1.33***	1.58***	1.12	−4.82*
Spain	2.22***	0.03	0.41***	−0.79***	0.04	−1.13***	0.37***	−4.16***	−3.81***
Sweden	0.99	−0.15	−0.08	−0.59	0.22	−0.78	0.91	−3.16	−6.11***
United Kingdom	1.86***	−0.09	0.10*	−0.71***	0.14	−0.91***	−0.12		−11.57***

Source: EU Statistics on Income and Living Conditions (EU-SILC) database, 2006.
*significant at 90 percent; **significant at 95 percent; ***significant at 99 percent.

fulltime	parttime	unemp	retired	urban	suburban	lage*secedu	lage*teredu	inc*secedu	inc*teredu
0.12	-0.32	-0.26	0.36	-0.84***			0.48		0.20
-0.15	-0.18	0.83	1.53**	0.16			0.16		-0.18
-0.27	0.00	0.18	0.68***	0.00	-0.06	0.15	0.28	-0.22	0.20
0.27	-0.12	0.10	0.02	-0.33***		-0.01	0.58	-0.48	-0.20
-1.25		-1.61		-0.14			0.65		-0.89**
-0.80**	-1.00**	0.02	-0.48	-0.27*	-0.13	0.30	0.76	-0.71**	-0.61*
0.04	-0.11	0.04	-0.15	-0.56***	-0.39***	-0.04	-0.31	0.53	0.70
-0.99**	-0.94**	-0.51	-0.05	-0.08	-0.25***	0.77	0.36	0.19	0.09
-0.79***	-0.74***	0.19	1.01***	0.07	0.28	0.10	-0.09	0.69***	1.23***
-0.89	-0.45	-0.58	0.27	-0.54***	-0.48***	-0.83	-1.46***	0.96***	0.73***
1.03***	0.43	0.76**	1.30***	0.09			0.96***		1.31***
-0.49**	0.01	-0.23	0.07	-0.01	-0.12	0.45	1.07**	0.18	0.67***
-0.94***	-0.46	-0.60*	-0.79***	-0.23**	-0.22*	1.00**	0.97**	0.47**	0.77***
0.78***	1.03*	0.89*	0.72***	0.12	0.25	-0.65	-1.23**	-0.16	0.08
-1.16***	-0.83***	-0.77*	-0.14	-1.03***	-0.79***	-0.60	0.28	0.48**	0.60***
-0.97***	-0.93***	-0.38	-0.21	-0.58***	-0.47***	-0.74***	-0.45	0.24	0.50***
-1.08***	-0.94**	-1.00	0.11	-0.53**	-0.36*	1.85**	1.60*	1.07***	1.10***
-0.01	-0.07	1.26*	0.87***	-0.22**			0.77*		0.78***
1.07***	-0.48	-0.53	-0.47	-0.34***	0.18	-0.42	0.57	0.03	0.30
-0.60***	0.00	-0.35	0.41**	-0.25***	-0.40***	-0.32	-0.25	0.51***	0.45***
0.54	-1.47**	-1.28**	-0.25	0.26	-0.13	0.66	1.71	0.01	-0.11
0.63***									

Table A10.7
Descriptive summary statistics, 2005 (weighted averages: financial vulnerability dependent variables)

Country	finburden	finvul	arrears1	arrears2	arrears3	himedcost
Recently added EU countries						
Czech Republic	2.116	0.096	0.094	0.063	0.112	0.003
Estonia	2.075	0.105	0.097	0.097	0.067	0.027
Hungary	2.097	0.148	0.122	0.132	0.145	0.031
Latvia	2.193	0.227	0.230	0.182	0.156	0.167
Lithuania	2.226	0.203	0.183	0.196	0.115	0.044
Poland	2.326	0.237	0.205	0.215	0.201	0.077
Slovak Republic	2.314	0.123	0.081	0.090	0.039	0.029
Slovenia	2.220	0.137	0.206	0.113	0.138	0.000
EU-15 and Cyprus						
Austria	1.861	0.030	0.021	0.016	0.091	0.003
Belgium	1.978	0.069	0.045	0.053	0.053	0.009
Cyprus	2.527	0.194	0.185	0.089	0.233	0.035
Denmark	1.314	0.074	0.032	0.030	0.042	0.002
Finland	1.919	0.103	0.066	0.064	0.085	0.028
France	1.712	0.095	0.083	0.064	0.051	0.015
Greece	2.169	0.336	0.236	0.276	0.318	0.040
Ireland	1.936	0.084	0.089	0.061	0.039	0.013
Italy	2.491	0.110	0.101	0.090	0.148	0.039
Luxembourg	1.997	0.036	0.032	0.028	0.020	0.002
Netherlands	1.810	0.055	0.037	0.030	0.067	0.002
Portugal	2.032	0.062	0.052	0.045	0.038	0.036
Spain	2.407	0.055	0.062	0.033	0.078	0.004
Sweden	1.609	0.093	0.060	0.052	0.092	0.007
United Kingdom	1.895	0.060	0.065	0.001	0.025	0.001

Source: EU Statistics on Income and Living Conditions (EU-SILC) database, 2005.

Table A10.8
Descriptive summary statistics, 2006 (weighted averages: financial vulnerability dependent variables)

Country	finburden	finvul	arrears1	arrears2	arrears3	himedcost
Recently added EU countries						
Czech Republic	2.115	0.073	0.067	0.050	0.105	0.002
Estonia	2.037	0.064	0.054	0.057	0.047	0.024
Hungary	2.105	0.143	0.094	0.130	0.123	0.017
Latvia	2.155	0.140	0.094	0.129	0.053	0.121
Lithuania	2.211	0.135	0.097	0.129	0.072	0.052
Poland	2.306	0.201	0.189	0.183	0.149	0.063
Slovak Republic	2.355	0.090	0.074	0.059	0.044	0.026
Slovenia	2.229	0.127	0.205	0.105	0.114	0.000
EU-15 and Cyprus						
Austria	1.830	0.029	0.024	0.016	0.094	0.004
Belgium	1.964	0.063	0.043	0.046	0.050	0.006
Cyprus	2.636	0.196	0.198	0.092	0.229	0.035
Denmark	1.308	0.058	0.020	0.028	0.035	0.002
Finland	1.908	0.092	0.072	0.040	0.054	0.016
France	1.756	0.088	0.080	0.060	0.054	0.016
Greece	2.199	0.311	0.181	0.266	0.278	0.052
Ireland	1.968	0.076	0.076	0.062	0.034	0.013
Italy	2.486	0.113	0.104	0.093	0.131	0.033
Luxembourg	2.063	0.023	0.016	0.017	0.013	0.002
Netherlands	1.743	0.050	0.029	0.027	0.089	0.002
Portugal	1.999	0.062	0.048	0.047	0.027	0.036
Spain	2.423	0.055	0.056	0.034	0.068	0.002
Sweden	1.549	0.075	0.039	0.043	0.066	0.013
United Kingdom	1.894	0.055	0.058	0.002	0.024	0.001

Source: EU Statistics on Income and Living Conditions (EU-SILC) database, 2006.

Table A10.9
Ordered probit and probit regressions, 2005 (financial vulnerability regressions [marginal effects])

Country	finburden mortgage	renter	Pseudo r²	t-test	finvul mortgage	renter	Pseudo r²	t-test	arrears1 mortgage	Pseudo r²
New EU Countries										
Czech Republic	-0.0025**	0.0335	0.07	1.43	0.0200	0.0589***	0.13	-2.93***	-0.0535***	0.16
Estonia	-0.0980	-0.0619***	0.12	3.20***	0.0151	0.0312	0.10	-0.55	-0.0580*	0.21
Hungary	0.0191**	0.0014	0.06	1.49	0.1078***	0.0738***	0.12	1.50	-0.0509**	0.11
Latvia	-0.1037	0.0569	0.08	-0.47	0.1204***	0.0967***	0.10	0.40	-0.0427	0.07
Lithuania	-0.0761	0.0036	0.09	0.50	0.1442***	0.0395	0.08	1.69*	0.0039	0.28
Poland	-0.1257	0.0978**	0.08	-3.04***	0.0586	-0.0130	0.08	2.46**	-0.0827***	0.12
Slovak Republic	-0.0074*	-0.0494***	0.04	3.49***	-0.0053	0.0261	0.05	-2.31**	-0.0263**	0.12
Slovenia	0.0520**	0.0487	0.06	2.07**	0.1402***	0.0488***	0.09	2.50**	-0.0004	0.09
EU-15 and Cyprus										
Austria	0.0508***	-0.0095	0.04	6.46***	0.0105	0.0265***	0.14	-2.63***	-0.0069	0.14
Belgium	-0.0037***	0.1049***	0.05	3.83***	0.0243**	0.0659***	0.17	-3.72***	-0.0057	0.18
Cyprus	0.1595***	-0.0481	0.06	7.65***	0.1205***	0.0578***	0.11	2.68***	0.0865***	0.12
Denmark	-0.0688		0.08		-0.0438***		0.19		-0.0122*	0.17
Finland	0.0297***	0.0707***	0.05	1.66*	0.0725***	0.1508***	0.18	-6.99*	-0.0495***	0.13
France	-0.0179***	0.0754***	0.04	0.44	0.0202*	0.0857***	0.16	-6.88***	-0.0513***	0.13
Greece	-0.0685	0.0757**	0.04	-2.74***	-0.0616**	0.0941***	0.08	-4.56***		0.10
Ireland	-0.0130***	0.1981***	0.09	0.58	0.0446***	0.1203***	0.24	-4.24***	-0.0515***	0.17
Italy	0.1612***	0.0305***	0.05	12.90***	0.0702***	0.0845***	0.13	-1.88*	-0.0429***	0.13
Luxembourg	0.0199***	0.1048***	0.07	2.11**	0.0089	0.0256**	0.15	-1.61	-0.0267***	0.18
Netherlands	-0.1145***		0.05		-0.0477***		0.14		-0.0315***	0.14
Portugal	0.0708***	0.0541***	0.09	4.14***	0.0348***	0.0167	0.06	1.51	0.0126	0.11
Spain	0.0782***	-0.0194	0.04	6.94***	0.0250***	0.0601***	0.11	-3.30***	-0.0253**	0.08
Sweden	-0.1126**	0.1220***	0.06	-8.32***	0.0468*	0.1183***	0.13	-5.48***	-0.0329***	0.15
United Kingdom	0.0105***	0.0900***	0.05	0.08	0.0284***	0.1305***	0.20	-11.24***	-0.0823***	0.16

Source: EU Statistics on Income and Living Conditions (EU-SILC) database, 2005.
*significant at 90 percent; **significant at 95 percent; ***significant at 99 percent.

arrears2				arrears3				himedcost			
mortgage	renter	Pseudo r²	t-test	mortgage	renter	Pseudo r²	t-test	mortgage	renter	Pseudo r²	t-test
0.0015	0.0254**	0.11	-2.25**	0.0210	0.0210	0.10	0.00	0.0022	0.0042	0.06	-0.71
0.0001	-0.0020	0.11	0.09	0.0149	0.0276	0.06	-0.28	-0.0104	-0.0071	0.17	-0.61
0.0712***	0.0452***	0.12	1.29	0.0814***	0.1023**	0.06	-0.34	0.0184**	0.0202***	0.07	-0.17
0.0742**	0.0640***	0.11	0.17	-0.0848**	0.0086	0.04	-1.99**	-0.0268	0.0261*	0.12	-1.41
0.1009*	0.0082	0.08	1.58	0.0928*	0.0356	0.05	0.76	0.0753**	0.0056	0.09	1.76*
0.0084	-0.0463	0.09	2.00**	0.0425	0.0678	0.06	-1.00	0.0912**	0.0328*	0.06	1.45
-0.0176	0.0038	0.05	-1.83*	-0.0163*	0.0127	0.06	-3.23***	-0.0062	-0.0064	0.09	0.09
0.0850***	0.0157	0.08	2.38**	-0.0121	0.0015	0.05	-0.35			0.32	
-0.0005	0.0071*	0.15	-1.64	0.0836	0.0967***	0.22	-1.73*	0.0029*	0.0000	0.19	2.51**
0.0112	0.0473***	0.15	-3.68***	0.0071	0.0280*	0.15	-1.51	0.0077**	0.0065**	0.19	0.35
0.0076	0.0289**	0.11	-1.51	-0.0115	0.0251	0.09	-1.18	0.0009	0.0169***	0.13	-1.93*
-0.0062		0.17		-0.0355***		0.17		-0.0015*		0.17	
0.0346***	0.0716***	0.15	-4.42***	0.0400***	0.1243***	0.12	-5.83***	0.0168**	0.0145**	0.11	0.07
0.0004	0.0331***	0.14	-4.51***	0.0139	0.0337**	0.10	-2.16**	0.0047	0.0113***	0.16	-1.99**
-0.0845***	0.0500**	0.09	-4.32***	-0.1216***	0.0326	0.07	-3.59***	-0.0156**	0.0128*	0.11	3.05***
0.0159*	0.0542***	0.21	-2.97***	0.0044	0.0345***	0.28	-3.23***	0.0099**	0.0143**	0.13	0.50
0.0340***	0.0556***	0.12	-2.62***	0.0156	0.0942***	0.10	-3.65***	0.0308***	0.0246***	0.09	0.55
0.0052	0.0141	0.10	-0.91	0.0106	0.0181	0.12	-0.65	0.0270**	0.0612**	0.41	0.41
-0.0255***		0.13		-0.0268		0.08		-0.0010		0.17	
0.0032	0.0053	0.08	-0.23	0.0078	0.0013	0.09	0.59	-0.0033	0.0183***	0.13	3.63***
-0.0027	0.0217***	0.10	-3.87***	-0.0003	0.0791***	0.09	-3.91***	0.0013	0.0037**	0.10	-1.14
0.0208	0.0592***	0.11	-3.88***	0.0671*	0.1527***	0.12	-4.81***	0.1699***	0.2167***	0.13	-1.08
0.0003	-0.0005	0.09	1.60	0.0040	0.0400***	0.10	-6.75***	0.0003	0.0005	0.14	-0.38

Table A10.9
Ordered probit and probit regressions, 2006 (financial vulnerability regressions [marginal effects])

Country	finburden				finvul				arrears1	
	mortgage	renter	Pseudo r^2	t-test	mortgage	renter	Pseudo r^2	t-test	mortgage	Pseudo r^2
Recently added EU countries										
Czech Republic	-0.0060***	0.0611	0.08	1.73*	0.0101	0.0476***	0.17	-4.40***	-0.0293***	0.20
Estonia	-0.1187	-0.0445***	0.11	2.55**	-0.0201*	0.0218*	0.12	-2.81***	-0.0469***	0.23
Hungary	0.0089**	0.0097	0.07	2.23**	0.0629***	0.0547***	0.11	0.43	-0.0323*	0.09
Latvia	-0.0257	0.0393	0.08	1.08	0.0546***	0.0881***	0.11	-1.47	-0.0071	0.13
Lithuania	-0.0131*	-0.0605**	0.09	2.98***	0.0550	0.0223	0.10	0.60	0.3340	0.19
Poland	-0.1033	0.0861***	0.07	-1.43	0.0528*	0.0464***	0.10	0.11	-0.0914***	0.10
Slovak Republic	-0.0033*	0.0221	0.06	0.58	0.0520***	0.0917***	0.08	-1.53	-0.0260**	0.09
Slovenia	0.1041***	0.0282	0.05	3.01***	0.0237	0.0351***	0.08	-0.41	-0.1353***	0.12
EU-15 and Cyprus										
Austria	0.0521***	-0.0137	0.05	5.29***	0.0169**	0.0218***	0.20	-1.76*	0.0003	0.15
Belgium	-0.0133***	0.0971***	0.04	3.57***	0.0357***	0.0647***	0.18	-2.90***	-0.0153**	0.14
Cyprus	0.1031***	-0.0289	0.09	5.73***	0.0979***	0.0349*	0.11	2.52**	0.1168***	0.13
Denmark	-0.0759		0.08		-0.0479***		0.17		-0.0101**	0.16
Finland	0.0326***	0.0691***	0.05	2.02**	0.0673***	0.1313***	0.19	-5.18***	-0.0470***	0.14
France	-0.0216***	0.0622***	0.04	0.54	0.0198***	0.0822***	0.16	-7.33***	-0.0530***	0.12
Greece	-0.1043	0.0900***	0.08	-1.94*	-0.1322***	0.0971***	0.15	-6.61***		0.20
Ireland	-0.0105***	0.2213***	0.10	-0.75	0.0137	0.1002***	0.22	-5.04***	-0.0582***	0.18
Italy	0.1994***	0.0195***	0.06	16.04***	0.0755***	0.0960***	0.12	-2.48**	-0.0600***	0.09
Luxembourg	0.0423***	0.0651	0.07	2.71***	-0.0182***	0.0088	0.18	-3.73***	-0.0123**	0.24
Netherlands	-0.1015***		0.05		-0.0459***		0.13		-0.0324***	0.14
Portugal	0.0564***	0.0416***	0.09	4.76***	0.0276**	0.0094	0.06	1.46	0.0232**	0.09
Spain	0.0746***	-0.0077	0.05	5.27***	0.0525***	0.0641***	0.09	-0.38	-0.0175*	0.08
Sweden	-0.1002***	0.1002	0.05		-0.0822***		0.12		-0.0384***	0.14
United Kingdom	0.0054***	0.1043***	0.05	-0.07	0.0282***	0.1066***	0.20	-9.72***	-0.0650***	0.16

Source: EU Statistics on Income and Living Conditions (EU-SILC) database, 2006.
*significant at 90 percent; **significant at 95 percent; ***significant at 99 percent.

arrears2				arrears3				himedcost			
mortgage	renter	Pseudo r²	t-test	mortgage	renter	Pseudo r²	t-test	mortgage	renter	Pseudo r²	t-test
-0.0009	0.0190**	0.15	-3.09***	0.0120	0.0217	0.13	-0.48	0.0002	-0.0005	0.12	0.92
-0.0268***	0.0134	0.13	-3.73***	-0.0084	0.0289	0.14	-1.64	-0.0060	0.0077	0.22	-2.26**
0.0392***	0.0322**	0.11	0.40	0.0145	0.0663*	0.08	-1.31	0.0067	0.0129***	0.07	-0.86
0.0310**	0.0728***	0.11	-1.95*	0.0029	0.0596***	0.09	-2.26**	0.0006	0.0343***	0.16	-1.96**
0.0577	0.0022	0.11	1.08	0.0473	0.0272	0.08	0.33	-0.0017	-0.0110	0.12	0.46
0.0148	0.0317***	0.10	-0.67	-0.0215	0.0343**	0.06	-1.57	-0.0132	-0.0050	0.09	-0.62
0.0250***	0.0396***	0.08	-0.69	0.0099	0.0294*	0.07	-1.28	-0.0008	0.0040	0.12	-0.95
0.0068	0.0149	0.07	-0.31	0.0278	-0.0344**	0.07	1.56				
0.0009	0.0049**	0.22	-1.56	0.1148	0.1075***	0.23	-1.99**	-0.0008	-0.0001	0.19	-1.22
0.0160**	0.0329***	0.17	-2.15**	0.0086	0.0198	0.14	-0.94	0.0029*	0.0057***	0.24	-1.23
-0.0102	0.0211*	0.08	-2.05**	-0.0377	0.0046	0.11	-1.33	-0.0005	0.0016	0.11	-0.27
-0.0236***		0.18		-0.0333***		0.14		-0.0004***		0.18	
0.0309***	0.0218***	0.11	1.29	0.0171	0.0694***	0.15	-4.71***	-0.0036	0.0053	0.08	-1.87*
0.0034	0.0466***	0.16	6.20***	-0.0033	0.0197*	0.13	-3.12***	0.0077**	0.0157***	0.14	-2.27**
-0.1175***	0.0659***	0.16	-5.69***	-0.2192***	-0.0004	0.18	-6.07***	0.0023	0.0186**	0.07	-1.10
0.0053	0.0628***	0.22	-4.29***	-0.0010	0.0327***	0.17	-3.19***	0.0035	0.0051	0.14	-1.10
0.0415***	0.0627***	0.12	-2.52**	0.0044	0.0415**	0.08	-1.86*	0.0227***	0.0234***	0.08	-0.30
-0.0139**	0.0064	0.15	-3.03***	-0.0047	0.0133*	0.19	2.19**	0.0255**	0.1011**	0.29	-0.47
0.0221***		0.12		-0.0661**		0.08		-0.0002		0.20	-2.24**
-0.0010	-0.0038	0.05	0.30	0.0127	0.0059	0.10	0.75	0.0249***	0.0244***	0.14	
0.0193***	0.0298***	0.07	-0.98	0.0289**	0.0636***	0.08	-1.72*	0.0014	0.0008	0.12	0.25
	0.0514***	0.11		-0.0733***		0.15			0.0178***	0.10	0.75
0.0002	-0.0005	0.10	1.32	0.0130**	0.0328***	0.10	-3.67***	0.0005	0.0011*	0.13	-0.81

Table A10.10
Two-stage least squares regressions, 2005 (financial vulnerability regressions [marginal effects])

	finburden				finvul				arrears1	
Country	p(Mortgage)	p(Rent)	Pseudo r^2	t-test	p(Mortgage)	p(Rent)	Pseudo r^2	t-test	p(Mortgage)	Pseudo r^2
Recently added EU countries										
Czech Republic	−1.0385*	−0.1352	0.06	−1.60	0.0848*	−0.0649	0.12	1.08	0.0638**	0.14
Estonia	−0.1015	−0.0054	0.11	−0.45	−0.1785**	−0.0012	0.09	−1.38	−0.1905*	0.05
Hungary	0.02909	0.0017	0.06	0.17	0.3833**	0.0853	0.10	−2.57**	0.1145	0.08
Latvia	−0.6449**	−0.0988	0.08	−1.64	−0.2680	0.0983	0.09	−1.34	0.0612	0.06
Lithuania	−0.2587	0.1828	0.09	−1.80*	0.1173	0.1942*	0.07	−0.32	−0.1849	0.13
Poland	−0.7706***	0.0828	0.06	−6.17***	−0.4515***	−0.2443**	0.08	−1.53	0.5092**	0.12
Slovak Republic	0.6020	−0.2389***	0.04	1.50	0.0386*	0.0557	0.04	−0.35	0.1167	0.09
EU-15 and Cyprus										
Austria	−0.0062	0.0096	0.03	−0.39	0.0435	0.0034	0.11	1.28	0.0359**	0.11
Belgium	0.0935**	0.0365	0.05	0.91	0.0074	0.0595***	0.15	−1.61	0.0332	0.14
Cyprus	0.3377**	0.0266	0.05	1.27	0.0601	−0.0989	0.10	1.59	0.1264	0.10
Denmark	−0.0174		0.07		−0.0811***		0.15		−0.1000***	0.16
Finland	0.0448	0.0986	0.04	−0.55	−0.0184	0.1578***	0.14	−3.07***	−0.0189	0.11
France	0.0763**	0.0094	0.04	1.51	−0.0835*	0.1083***	0.14	−399***	0.0135	0.10
Greece	−0.0316	−0.0286	0.04	−0.02	−0.0350	0.0993	0.07	−0.70	0.0654	0.10
Ireland	0.0709	0.0998***	0.08	−0.37	0.0162	0.0612***	0.20	−0.90	0.0582	0.13
Italy	−0.2132**	0.1285	0.04	−2.28**	−0.0944**	0.2026***	0.11	−4.75***	−0.0714	0.12
Luxembourg	0.1585***	0.0309	0.06	1.56	0.0047	0.0111	0.12	−0.15	0.0798**	0.12
Netherlands	−0.1789***		0.04		−0.0455***		0.11		−0.0380***	0.11
Portugal	0.1000***	0.0074	0.07	1.33	0.0362	−0.0092	0.05	1.04	0.0359	0.09
Spain	0.0772	−0.0826	0.03	0.92	0.0160	0.0809*	0.08	−1.30	−0.0076	0.05
Sweden	0.2170**	0.0903***	0.05	1.10	0.4231***	0.0745***	0.11	2.49**	0.3083***	0.13
United Kingdom	0.1668***	0.1053***	0.05	1.28	0.0503**	0.0900***	0.14	−1.65*	−0.0012	0.11

Source: EU Statistics on Income and Living Conditions (EU-SILC) database, 2005.
*significant at 90 percent; **significant at 95 percent; ***significant at 99 percent.

arrears2				arrears3				himedcost			
p(Mortgage)	p(Rent)	Pseudo r^2	t-test	p(Mortgage)	p(Rent)	Pseudo r^2	t-test	p(Mortgage)	p(Rent)	Pseudo r^2	t-test
0.0002	0.0069	0.10	−0.06	0.0657	−0.0624	0.09	0.57	−0.0009	0.0114	0.03	−1.17
−0.0897	0.1102	0.09	−1.92	0.0937*	−0.2109	0.04	1.71	−0.0083	−0.0164	0.15	0.15
−0.4262	0.0754	0.11	−2.15	0.1199	0.0173	0.02	0.38	−0.0626	0.0139	0.05	−1.35
−0.1635	0.1345	0.10	−1.20	−0.3989	−0.0621	0.03	−0.94	−0.4378	0.0907	0.11	−1.21
0.1147	0.1422	0.07	−0.12	−0.2144	0.1169	0.04	−1.28	0.1646***	−0.1387	0.09	3.44
−0.4375***	−0.2753	0.09	−1.22	−0.2656	0.2438	0.05	−2.21	−0.0047	0.0058	0.06	−0.15
0.1744	0.0140	0.04	0.58	−0.0206	0.0216	0.03	−1.11	−0.0755	−0.0119	0.07	−0.57
0.0491	−0.0212	0.14	2.93	0.1217	0.0502	0.18	0.55	−0.0023	0.0025	0.14	−1.03
0.0041***	0.0384	0.13	−1.23	`	0.0783	0.14	−1.86	−0.0026**	0.0077	0.16	−1.44
−0.0196	−0.0272	0.10	0.10	−0.1762	−0.1123	0.09	−0.42	−0.0090	0.0016	0.12	−0.37
−0.0386		0.14		−0.0524		0.13		−0.0015		0.08	
−0.0108**	0.0731	0.12	−1.64	−0.1344***	0.1074	0.09	−2.74	−0.0081	0.0185	0.09	−0.88
−0.0539***	0.0434	0.13	−2.65	−0.0012***	0.0517	0.08	−2.07	−0.0128***	0.0223	0.14	−4.95
−0.2487	0.0388	0.08	−1.86	0.2041**	−0.2427	0.06	2.27	−0.0116	−0.0110	0.09	−0.01
−0.0058	0.0218	0.19	−0.72	0.0001***	0.0328	0.24	−1.38	0.0096***	0.0240	0.07	−1.37
−0.0645***	0.1514	0.11	−3.92	−0.2783***	0.3291	0.08	−2.73	0.0234	0.0216	0.08	0.05
−0.0132	0.0099	0.08	−0.98	0.0013	−0.0142	0.05	0.58	−0.0002*	0.0003	0.39	−1.57
−0.0350		0.10		−0.0554		0.04		0.0000		0.06	
−0.0475***	−0.0772	0.08	0.88	0.0405	−0.0239	0.06	1.51	−0.0029**	0.0305	0.11	−1.62
0.0036	0.0295	0.08	−0.67	−0.0395***	0.2728	0.05	−2.45	0.0017	−0.0016	0.06	0.29
0.1669**	0.0888	0.09	0.83	0.1293***	0.0964	0.10	0.17	0.0127***	0.0124	0.10	0.01
0.0004	−0.0011	0.01	0.91	0.0345***	0.0384	0.08	−0.29	0.0003	−0.0009	0.08	0.96

Table A10.11
Two-stage least squares regressions, 2006 (financial vulnerability regressions [marginal effects])

Country	finburden p(Mortgage)	p(Rent)	Pseudo r²	t-test	finvul p(Mortgage)	p(Rent)	Pseudo r²	t-test	arrears1 p(Mortgage)	Pseudo r²
Recently added EU countries										
Czech Republic	-0.0473	-0.0426	0.08	-0.03	0.0860***	-0.1305**	0.16	2.46**	0.0020	0.18
Estonia	-0.2231**	0.2851**	0.10	-2.65***	-0.0889**	0.0815	0.11	-1.86*	-0.1507**	0.15
Hungary	0.0107	-0.0120	0.07	0.12	-0.2481*	0.0677	0.10	-1.90*	-0.0803	0.07
Latvia	-0.2277*	-0.0216	0.07	-1.23	0.0155	0.0749	0.09	-0.54	-0.2912**	0.11
Lithuania	-0.3614**	-0.1271	0.09	-0.87	0.0342	0.0426	0.09	-0.04	-0.0054	0.09
Poland	-0.4520***	0.0260	0.07	-3.40***	-0.2721**	0.0477***	0.10	-2.59***	0.1028	0.07
Slovak Republic	0.0789**	-0.3338**	0.05	2.06**	0.0257	-0.0488	0.06	0.45	0.0890	0.07
EU-15 and Cyprus										
Austria	0.0046	0.0081	0.05	-0.06	0.0100	0.0446**	0.16	-1.27	0.0341***	0.14
Belgium	0.1484***	0.0379	0.04	0.93	-0.0050	0.0391***	0.16	-1.77*	0.0257	0.13
Cyprus	0.1165	-0.1261*	0.08	1.42	0.1402	-0.0747	0.10	2.04**	0.2389***	0.08
Denmark	-0.0369***		0.07		-0.0590***		0.12		-0.0089	0.13
Finland	0.0755**	0.0270	0.04	0.62	0.0276	0.0693***	0.16	-1.08	0.0204	0.12
France	-0.0547	0.1391**	0.03	-1.69*	-0.0413	0.0862***	0.14	-2.89***	0.0381**	0.08
Greece	-0.3330*	0.1004**	0.08	-2.25**	-0.8502**	0.2246**	0.14	-2.65***	-0.0025	0.20
Ireland	-0.0679	0.1150***	0.09	-2.31**	-0.0703	0.0820***	0.18	-2.80***	0.0829**	0.15
Italy	0.2246***	0.0876	0.04	1.23	-0.0753**	0.1245***	0.10	-3.35***	-0.2033***	0.08
Luxembourg	0.1810***	-0.0393	0.06	2.58***	0.0162	0.0169*	0.14	-0.03	0.0136*	0.22
Netherlands	-0.1489**		0.05		-0.0920***		0.10		-0.0446*	0.10
Portugal	0.0400	-0.1067*	0.08	2.23**	-0.0044	0.0934***	0.05	-2.28**	-0.0097	0.07
Spain	0.1129	-0.4729**	0.05	3.02***	-0.0336	0.0572	0.06	-1.36	-0.0377	0.07
Sweden	0.1316	0.0492***	0.05	0.76	0.0502	0.0780***	0.10	-0.24	0.1074**	0.12
United Kingdom	0.1580***	0.0711***	0.05	2.68***	0.0488***	0.0672***	0.15	-1.03	0.0043	0.11

Source: EU Statistics on Income and Living Conditions (EU-SILC) database, 2006.
*significant at 90%; **significant at 95%; ***significant at 99%.

arrears2				arrears3				himedcost			
p(Mortgage)	p(Rent)	Pseudo r²	t-test	p(Mortgage)	p(Rent)	Pseudo r²	t-test	p(Mortgage)	p(Rent)	Pseudo r²	t-test
0.0204	−0.0392	0.14	0.82	0.0558	−0.0816	0.11	0.75	−0.0012	−0.0005	0.03	−0.04
−0.1255*	0.0946	0.12	−2.62	0.0680	−0.0904	0.12	1.34	−0.0039	−0.0311	0.20	0.52
−0.2796	0.0940	0.11	−2.32	0.2199	−0.0269	0.06	1.40	−0.0402	0.0112	0.06	−2.28
−0.0484	−0.0262	0.10	−0.21	0.0329	0.0182	0.03	0.12	−0.1449*	0.1530	0.16	−1.78
0.0269	−0.0398	0.11	0.29	0.1072	0.1445	0.08	−0.13	−0.3750*	−0.0741	0.12	−1.64
−0.1983**	0.0326	0.10	−1.89	−0.1627**	0.0512	0.06	−1.44	0.0774	0.0025	0.08	0.97
0.0004	−0.0777	0.07	0.62	−0.0208	0.0569	0.04	−0.94	0.0357***	−0.0907	0.11	2.07
0.0290	−0.0011	0.17	2.38	−0.0762***	0.1519	0.19	−2.06	0.0013	−0.0044	0.17	1.10
−0.0158	0.0139	0.16	−1.49	−0.1012***	0.1173	0.13	−3.49	−0.0027	0.0018	0.21	−1.41
0.0279	0.0258	0.07	0.03	0.1340	−0.0604	0.10	1.31	−0.0456	−0.0169	0.11	−0.85
−0.0217		0.14		−0.0266		0.11		−0.0017		0.02	
0.0348***	0.0646	0.10	−0.82	−0.0452***	0.0835	0.12	−2.66	−0.0229**	0.0239	0.07	−2.98
−0.0340***	0.0411	0.14	−2.04	0.0252***	0.0492	0.11	−0.65	−0.0021***	0.0126	0.11	−1.84
−0.4497***	0.1645	0.15	−1.85	−0.8408	0.0548	0.14	−1.60	−0.0426*	0.0408	0.06	−0.84
−0.0872***	0.0571	0.19	−4.55	−0.0203***	0.0424	0.14	−2.18	0.0041	−0.0073	0.12	0.73
−0.0461***	0.0907	0.10	−2.65	−0.0738***	0.2331	0.07	−2.01	0.0074**	0.0419	0.07	−1.28
0.0171	0.0103	0.08	0.44	0.0109***	0.0257	0.11	−1.35	0.0004**	0.0008	0.27	−0.77
−0.0232		0.09		−0.1206		0.05		−0.0012		0.13	
−0.0135	0.0436	0.04	−1.67	−0.0327***	0.0872	0.10	−3.34	0.0071	0.0167	0.10	−0.38
−0.0190	0.0052	0.06	−0.46	−0.0951	0.1859	0.07	−1.94	0.0003	0.0064	0.10	−0.93
0.1008***	0.0371	0.08	0.82	0.1900***	0.0685	0.12	0.94	−0.0851**	0.0633	0.08	−2.20
0.0002	−0.0005	0.07	0.53	0.0383***	0.0243	0.09	1.32	−0.0006	−0.0001	0.14	−3.32

Notes

We gratefully acknowledge outstanding research assistance by Naotaka Sugawara, technical advice by Ed Al-Hussainy, and financial support by the DECRG Research Support Budget (RF-P115252-RESE-BBRSB). We received valuable comments and suggestions from Asad Alam, Jean-Jacques Dethier, Anna Gueorguieva, and two anonymous reviewers during initial stages of this research. Some of the preliminary results of this research have been used as background information in a recently completed regional report, "The Crisis Hits Home: Stress Testing Households in Europe and Central Asia" (Report No. 50158-ECA). This chapter's findings, interpretations, and conclusions are entirely those of the authors and do not necessarily represent the views of the World Bank, its executive directors, or the countries they represent.

1. See ECB 2009 and Roy 2008.

2. See ECB 2009 for a discussion on housing finance in the euro zone.

3. A significant share of household debt in the new EU countries for which data are available are foreign currency–denominated and have adjustable interest rates, exposing them to exchange rate and interest rate shocks.

4. In fact, a new World Bank regional study has just been completed precisely to investigate the macroeconomic risks faced by countries in Eastern and Central Europe and the likely welfare consequences should the risks materialize, with special emphasis on an assessment of household indebtedness (World Bank 2009).

5. A strand of the literature has also documented the welfare consequences of constrained access to credit. See for example Kang and Sawada (2008) and Sawada et al. (2007).

6. See Gyntelberg, Johansson, and Persson (2007); IMF (2006, 61); and BIS 2007 on the need for microdata in assessing financial stability.

7. To date, most microlevel studies focus on one country, such as Żochowski and Zajączkowski (2007) on Poland, NBS (2006) on the Slovak Republic, CNB (2009) on the Czech Republic, Beer and Schürz (2007) on Austria, and Holló (2007) on Hungary. These studies do *not* assess the drivers of household debt holding and, because they are country-specific, do not explore cross-country differences in household indebtedness. In addition, a recent study of Bosnia and Herzegovina (Chen and Chivakul 2008) looks at household credit market participation (self-reported desire to borrow) and credit constraint (whether refused a loan). Even in more advanced economies outside Central Europe, analyses of microdata on household debt have been few and very recent. See, for example, BIS (2007) and Dynan and Kohn (2007). Crook (2006) reports that most studies using survey data focus on the United States, though there are some limited recent work on the United Kingdom and Italy.

8. Although Cyprus is also a new EU country, we group it together with the old EU countries because of its level of economic and financial development. At the time of the first wave of EU-SILC (2005), Bulgaria and Romania were not yet members of the EU. Data for Germany were excluded in the database received from Eurostat.

9. We therefore do not include measures of debt payment–income ratios in our analysis.

10. See Beck (2009) for an overview of financial sector transformation in the transition economies, including the role of foreign banks.

11. We weight all household observations according to the weights given in the survey.

12. This result is most likely due to the fact that mortgage interest payments are completely tax-deductible in these countries and both have very high marginal tax rates.

13. As mentioned previously, we do not have sufficient information on the stratification in order to correct the standard errors for cluster effects, which might result in a downward bias in our standard errors.

14. See Woolridge (2001) for a discussion.

15. As for some surveys in which some of the categories are very small or some of the dummy variables are highly correlated with each other, in some cases we had to drop some variables from the specification in order for the model to converge.

16. For Denmark and the Netherlands, we do not report the log-odds for outright owners in panel B as these two countries do not include any such households.

17. As in table 10.3, Denmark and the Netherlands are not included in panel B. In addition, we had to drop Slovenia as the results did not converge.

18. Cash-flow difficulties have been analyzed, for example, by La Cava and Simon (2005) using Australian microdata and Whitley, Windram, and Cox (2004) using household survey data from the United Kingdom.

19. The low share in the United Kingdom is certainly due to the availability of the National Health Services.

20. As noted earlier, we do not have stratification information and the standard errors are therefore most likely to be underestimated.

21. Because it is not possible to compute such an effect in the 2SLS regressions—as there we work with continuous predicted variables rather than dummies—we report marginal effects on the coefficients.

22. See Anderloni and Vandone (2008) for a literature review of studies of household indebtedness and different variables that are typically included.

References

Anderloni, Luisa, and Daniela Vandone. 2008. Household Over-Indebtedness in the Economics Literature. Universit'a degli Studi di Milano Working Paper 2008–46.

Bank of International Settlements (BIS). 2007. Measuring the Financial Position of the Household Sector. Proceedings of the IFC Conference, Basel, August 30–31, 2006, IFC Bulletin No. 26.

Bank of Slovenia. 2008. Financial Stability Review. Ljubljana: Bank of Slovenia.

Beck, Thorsten. 2009, Finance in Transition. A Long Road with More Challenges Ahead. Unpublished mimeo.

Beck, Thorsten, Berrak Buyukkarabacak, Felix Rioja, and Neven Valev. 2011. Who Gets the Credit? And Does It Matter? Household vs. Firm Lending across Countries. *The B.E. Journal of Macroeconomics* 12 (1): 542–545.

Beck, Thorsten, Aslı Demirgüç-Kunt, and Ross Levine. 2007. Finance, Inequality and the Poor: Cross-Country Evidence. *Journal of Economic Growth* 12:27–49.

Beck, Thorsten, Ross Levine, and Norman Loayza. 2000. Finance and the Sources of Growth. *Journal of Financial Economics* 58:261–300.

Beer, Christian and Martin Schürz. 2007. Characteristics of Household Debt in Austria: Does Household Debt Pose a Threat to Financial Stability? *Monetary Policy and the Economy*, 2nd Quarter: 58–79.

Croatian National Bank. 2008. Financial Stability Report. Zagreb: Croatian National Bank.

Czech National Bank (CNB). 2009. Financial Stability Report 2008/2009. Prague: Czech National Bank.

Chen, Kechen, and M. Chivakul. 2008. What Drives Household Borrowing and Credit Constraints? Evidence from Bosnia and Herzegovina. IMF Working Paper No. 08/202. Washington, DC: International Monetary Fund.

Crook, Jonathan. 2006. Household Debt Demand and Supply: A Cross-Country Comparison. In *The Economics of Consumer Credit*, ed. Giuseppe Bertola, Robert Disney, and Charles Grant, 63–92. Cambridge, MA: MIT Press.

Demirgüç-Kunt, Aslı, and Enrica Detragiache. 1998. The Determinants of Banking Crises: Evidence from Developing and Developed Countries. *IMF Staff Papers* 45 (1): 81–109.

Dynan, Karen E., and Donald L. Kohn. 2007. The Rise in U.S. Household Indebtedness: Causes and Consequences. Finance and Economics Discussion Series No. 37. Washington, DC: Federal Reserve Board.

European Central Bank (ECB). 2009. *EU Banking Sector Stability*, November. Frankfurt: European Central Bank.

European Bank for Reconstruction and Development (EBRD). 2007. Mortgages in Transition Economies: The Legal Framework for Mortgages and Mortgage Securities. London: European Bank for Reconstruction and Development.

European Mortgage Federation (EMF). 2006. Study on Interest Rate Variability in Europe. Brussels: EMF.

Gerardi, Kristofer, Harvey Rosen, and Paul Willen. 2010. The Impact of Financial Innovation on Consumers: The Case of the Mortgage Market. *Journal of Finance* 65 (1): 333–360.

Gyntelberg, Jacob, Martin Johansson, Mattias Persson. 2007. Using Housing Finance Micro Data to Assess Financial Stability Risks. *Housing Finance International* (September): 3–8.

Holló, Dániel. 2007. Household Indebtedness and Financial Stability: Reasons to Be Afraid? *MNB Bulletin*, November. Budapest: National Bank of Hungary.

International Monetary Fund (IMF). 2006. Czech Republic, Republic of Estonia, Hungary, Republic of Latvia, Republic of Lithuania, Republic of Poland, Slovak Republic, and Republic of Slovenia—Export Structure and Credit Growth. IMF Country Report No. 06/414. Washington, DC: International Monetary Fund.

Jappelli, Tullio, Marco Pagano, and Marco di Maggio. 2008. Households' Indebtedness and Financial Fragility. Working Paper No. 208. Centre for Studies in Economics and Finance.

Johansson, Martin W., and Mattias Persson. 2006. Swedish Households' Indebtedness and Ability to Pay: A Household Level Study. *Sveriges Riksbank Economic Review* 3:24–40.

Kang, S. J., and Y. Sawada. 2008. Credit Crunch and Household Welfare: The Korean Financial Crisis. *Japanese Economic Review* 59 (4): 438–458.

La Cava, Gianni, and John Simon. 2005. Household Debt and Financial Constraints in Australia. *Australian Economic Review* 38 (1): 40–60.

Mian, Atif, and Amir Sufi. 2009. The Consequences of Mortgage Credit Expansion: Evidence from the 2007 Default Crisis. *Quarterly Journal of Economics* 124 (4): 1449–1496.

National Bank of Slovakia (NBS). 2006. *Report on the Results of the Slovak Financial Sector Analysis.* Bratislava: National Bank of Slovakia.

Roy, Friedeman. 2008. Mortgage Markets in Central and Eastern Europe: A Review of Past Experiences and Future Perspectives. *European Journal of Housing Policy* 8 (2): 133–160.

Sawada, Y., K. Nawata, M. Ii, and J. Lee. 2007. Did the Credit Crunch in Japan Affect Household Welfare? An Augmented Euler Equation Approach Using Type 5 Tobit Model. CIRJE Discussion Papers F-Series No. 498. Tokyo: University of Tokyo.

Schich, Sebastian, and Jung-Hyun Ahn. 2007. Housing Markets and Household Debt: Short-Term and Long-Term Risks. *Financial Market Trends*, no. 1: 191–214.

Struyk, Raymond. 1996. *Economic Restructuring of the Former Soviet Bloc: The Case of Housing.* Washington, DC: Urban Institute Press.

Vatne, Bjørn Helge. 2006. How Large Are the Financial Margins of Norwegian Households? An Analysis of Micro Data for the Period 1987–2004. *Norges Bank Economic Bulletin* 77 (4): 173–180.

Warnock, Francis, and Veronica Warnock. 2008. Markets and Housing Finance. *Journal of Housing Economics* 17:239–251.

Whitley, John, Richard Windram, and Prudence Cox. 2004. An Empirical Model of Household Arrears. Bank of England Working Paper No. 214 London: Bank of England.

Wolswijk, Guido. 2006. Determinants of Mortgage Debt Growth in EU Countries. *European Journal of Housing Policy* 6 (2): 131–149.

Woolridge, Jeffrey. 2001. *Econometric Analysis of Cross Section and Panel Data.* Cambridge, MA: MIT Press.

World Bank. 2009. The Crisis Hits Home: Stress Testing Households in Europe and Central Asia. Report No. 50158-ECA.

Żochowski, D., and S. Zajączkowski. 2007. The Distribution and Dispersion of Debt Burden Ratios among Households in Poland and Its Implications for Financial Stability. IFC Bulletin No. 26. Basel: BIS.

V More than Products

11 Measuring Personality Traits and Predicting Loan Default with Experiments and Surveys

Dean Karlan, Sendhil Mullainathan, and Omar Robles

Intuition suggests that certain personality types are predisposed to loan default. Accurately identifying these personality types could have profound implications for consumer banking policy and important lessons for our understanding of why credit markets may fail. Specifically, we discuss two types of moral hazard: a more deliberate or conscious decision to shirk or not repay (e.g., strategic default) versus a less deliberate series of acts of financial or time mismanagement that lead to the inability to repay. Our experiments are designed to measure each separately and—particularly in the case of individual mismanagement—to assess whether the individual is self-aware of his or her mistakes. This second aspect of self-awareness is important in terms of its theoretical implications, in that it determines whether the information on type is hidden from both the lender and the borrower or just the lender.

We used two experiments and one survey to create personality measures of subjects. In the first experiment, we tried to identify subjects with higher moral standards. During the experiment, subjects were intentionally given too much cash during a transaction at the bank; subjects were encouraged to believe this was a result of a clerical error by the bank's cashier (hereafter referred to as bank error). We focused on subjects who returned and reported the bank error after first exiting the bank with additional cash, as once the individual has left the bank the perceived likelihood of being penalized for taking the extra cash should fall. Thus, for this group of individuals, the high psychosomatic moral cost can be understood as the driving force behind the decision to return. Using the above experiment to measure moral standards, or psychosomatic cost of moral defection, we find that those who voluntarily return to the bank to acknowledge the error are less likely to default, and if they do, they default on a smaller amount.

In our second experiment, we tried to identify subjects that were not able to complete a future task (complete a text-back[1] message survey exactly seven days later) and those who were naïve about the likelihood that they would complete the task. In this experiment, individuals were randomly assigned to one of two groups: those asked to respond in exactly seven days (the control group) and those given the choice to respond in exactly seven days or complete the survey immediately at the bank for significantly less compensation. Those who choose the text-back option but failed to actually text back can be classified as naïvely over-optimistic subjects. Those who choose to complete the survey immediately can be classified as being rationally aware, or pessimistic, about their ability to meet future commitments. We then attempt to link these personality traits to the probability of loan default. We expect that the naïvely over-optimistic subjects will be more likely to believe they can make a higher stream of loan payments than their circumstances permit and thus more likely to default on loans. We expect that rationally aware subjects will be less likely to default on loans. We find that the subjects who chose to text back were not more likely to actually text back than the control group, which suggests the presence of subjects with naïvely optimistic beliefs. In addition, consistent with our theory, we find that rationally aware subjects—those who did not choose the text-back option—were less likely to default relative to the other groups.

Finally, we used a survey to explore the relationship between psychological measures and behavior in both our experiments and loan default. We first attempted to use measures of social capital to predict default in individual loans, as compared to previous work mapping measures of social capital to predict default on group loans (Karlan 2005). We found that social capital is less predictive in individual loans, which makes sense, as the burden of default falls on the bank and not individuals within the participant's social network. We also incorporated recent work in psychology to examine the relationship between personality index measures and behavior in real-world settings. Several studies have been able to predict school- or job-related behavior using these personality measures.[2] Yet few studies have analyzed the link between personality measures and undesirable behavior. Salgado (2002) examined the relationship between personality measures and counterproductive behavior such as absenteeism, accidents, deviant behaviors, and turnover. The results of that meta-analysis showed that

conscientiousness consistently predicted deviant behaviors. Although we find no evidence that personality measures are good predictors of loan default, we discovered other interesting links between the personality measures and the classes of subjects we identified in our experiments.

Setting

The experiments took place from 2005 to 2006 in various locations across the island of Luzon in the Philippines.[3] A regional bank, the Rural Bank of Mabitac, provided us with the financial transaction data through one year after the experiment for all of the subjects involved in our experiment.[4] Experiments and surveys were conducted by the bank immediately after subjects had received approval for a new individual loan. This bank was an ideal setting for our experiment due to its high default rate of 71 percent (in which "default" is defined as not completing full payment on or before the maturity date of loan). Because we do not have financial transaction data for the period after the maturity dates of loans, we are unable to report the overall final default rate (i.e., those who never completed payment).

All participants were recipients of short-term individual loans that were commonly renewed from two to five times a year. Summary information on the characteristics of the participants is available in table 11.1. Over 77 percent of the participants were female, of whom 82.2 percent were married and 74.5 percent had secondary or postsecondary education. The average income for the sample was within the ninth decile of the population according to the 2006 Philippine Census (i.e., on the wealthy side but not the wealthiest). Given that there is a relatively large middle class in the Philippines and that these data come from different sources, they are likely to be biased high (applicants have an incentive to overstate income on loan applications in order to get larger loans). The vast majority of subjects were entrepreneurs, and the most common form of business was "corner stores."

Experiments and Results

Bank Error
The first experiment was focused on the influence of a borrower's moral standards or high psychosomatic costs of immoral behavior on

Table 11.1
Summary statistics (means and standard deviations)

Demographic information		
Observations		725
Age		40.80
		(9.45)
Female		77.4%
Education (last level completed)		
	Elementary	22.0%
	High school	45.3%
	College	29.2%
	Other	3.5%
Marital status		
	Single	9.5%
	Married	82.2%
	Widowed or separated	8.3%
Household members (including head)		5.08
		(1.93)
Children		2.25
		(1.33)
Financial information		
First-time borrower		37.2%
Average previous loan cycles		3.87
		(3.29)
Average loan size (in thousands)[1]		1,868
		(1,665)
First cycle default rate		0.26
		(0.44)
Annual default rate		0.71
		(0.45)
Household weekly income[2]		
	P5,000 or less	40.1%
	P5,000–10,000	25.6%
	P10,000–15,000	11.1%
	P15,000 and up	23.1%
Household income source		
	Buy and sell	8.4%
	Sari-Sari store[3]	44.2%
	Other[4]	47.4%
Unexpected reduction in income[5]		50.3%
Held voluntary savings account at bank		52.4%

[1]The exchange rate between US$ and Pesos is P42 to the dollar during the period of the experiment.
[2]Average annual household income in ninth decile is P292,000 according to the 2006 census. This corresponds to an average weekly income of approximately P5,615. *Source:* National Statistics Office, Republic of the Philippines.
[3]Sari-Sari stores are neighborhood shops for various kinds of household items.
[4]"Other" includes all other categories. Each has a share of less than 3.0 percent.
[5]An unexpected reduction in income over the six months prior to the survey date.

strategic default; these character traits were assessed at a bank branch when the subject was compensated for completing an initial survey. The subject had just met with the loan officer to initiate or renew a loan and was asked to fill out an initial survey on individual and household characteristics. The subject was also told that this survey was voluntary, that participation would not influence the loan decision, and that all answers would be confidential and not shared with the bank. A loan officer informed the subject that he would receive compensation of P30.00 (US$0.60) in exchange for participating in the survey. The officer then conducted the survey and gave the subject a claim stub that stated "Thank You. Claim your P30.00 from the cashier."[5] Both the verbal instruction by the loan officer as well as the written instruction on the claim stub informed the subject that the bank had pledged P30.00. The subject was instructed to hand the stub to the bank cashier in exchange for the promised P30.00. In each case, the cashier handed the subject P50.00 (two P20.00 bills and one P10.00 bill or coin) and instructed the subject to sign the claim stub upon receipt of the money.[6] If a subject alerted the cashier to the error and returned the excess compensation of P20.00, the cashier was instructed to say "Oh, thank you" and make no acknowledgment of the intentional bank error. If a subject did not alert the cashier to the excess cash, then the subject was allowed to leave without interruption.

We classify the subject's behavior into three possible reactions. The subject either: (1) acknowledged and immediately returned the excess cash; (2) exited the bank without acknowledging or returning the excess cash; or (3) exited the bank but returned later in the day to acknowledge and return the excess cash.[7]

We argue that the first two of the three aforementioned actions reveal little information about a subject's moral standards or psycho-somatic moral costs. First, there is no certainty that subjects who left the bank were aware of the excess cash when doing so. Second, the subject's chosen action may also reflect the expected consequences of taking the cash or revealing the bank error. The subject's choice will depend on the perceived likelihood and severity of being penalized, the benefit from obtaining the excess cash, as well as the potential for guilt or some other psychosomatic cost. Because we cannot distinguish between these motivations, the act of immediately revealing the bank error uncovers little information about the subject's psychosomatic costs. We might expect that the majority of subjects who chose to return the excess cash were motivated by the cost-benefit analysis (the

risk of being penalized exceeds the benefit of taking the excess cash) given that the amount of excess cash was insignificant relative to the size of each subject's loan (0.001 percent, on average) and therefore also insignificant relative to the value of a continued relationship with the bank.

The third reaction (returning excess cash after exiting the bank), however, does reveal information about the subject's moral standards or psychosomatic costs. We can organize this group of subjects into two classes: those who exited the bank knowing about the excess cash, and those who exited the bank not knowing about the excess cash. The former case implies that the subject initially intended to take the excess cash but changed his mind after exiting the bank. The latter case implies that the subject realized he had the excess cash after exiting the bank and subsequently decided to return it. We contend that for either class of subjects, the perceived risk of being penalized for taking the excess cash is lower ex post. This issue raises the overall expected value of the choice to take (or keep) the excess cash. Because the subjects in this group have a higher expected value for keeping the cash but return it anyway, we can infer that on average they have higher psychosomatic costs from taking the excess cash relative to subjects who reveal the bank error immediately (and also, of course, relative to subjects who take the cash).

We note that failure to notice the excess cash quickly may also be indicative of simply being unorganized. If it were the case that such individuals were somewhat (only "somewhat" because they do have to notice the error a few minutes later) unorganized, this result would counteract the hypothesis, as such a characteristic is potentially positively correlated with default or missed loan payments.

We put forward the following hypothesis:

Hypothesis #1 (Bank Error): Returning to the bank to give back the excess cash is negatively correlated with loan default.

The mean default rates in table 11.2 suggest that, as predicted, the aforementioned subjects were significantly less likely to default within one year of the experiment than were the other groups. In table 11.3 we display the results of probit regression analysis to determine the subjects' likelihoods of default and tobit regression analysis to analyze the fraction of the principal defaulted (given censoring at zero). Separate analysis was done on default in the first loan cycle (panel A) and over the course of the first year (panel B). There is no indication in panel

Table 11.2
Bank error experiment (mean outcomes)

	First cycle		First year	
Bank error experiment	Default	Fraction defaulted	Default	Fraction defaulted
Never return	0.26	0.08	0.71	0.18
Return immediately	0.26	0.09	0.72	0.18
Return later	0.31	0.04	0.56	0.08
Return (immediately or later)	0.26	0.08	0.71	0.17
Diff: ret immed & ret later	−0.05	0.05	0.16	0.10
\mid t-statistic \mid	0.79	1.41	2.39	2.86
Diff: never ret & ret later	−0.05	0.04	0.15	0.10
\mid t-statistic \mid	0.68	1.27	2.11	3.10

Notes: Means are based on 725 observations. "Default" is defined as having an unpaid balance on a loan at the contracted end date. "Fraction defaulted" is the ratio of the unpaid balance to the principal.

A that any of the three groups of subjects were more or less likely to default on the first loan cycle after the experiment, but panel B shows that the longer-term effect on repayment over one year is strong and significant statistically: subjects who returned the excess cash ex post were 15.1 percent less likely to default within the first year of the loan. The lack of predictive power for *immediate* default potentially indicates that trustworthiness and morality do not lead to more default immediately after disbursal than later or that if anything, morality is more influential on default in later loan cycles. This option could be an indication of strategic behavior from the beginning—to wait until loan sizes are larger before defaulting—or could simply be a function of more time being needed to improve efficiency of estimates of default. Economically, the effect is large: the amount of the default as a percentage of the principal was 15 percent lower for those marked as trustworthy. Thus we contend that on average, subjects who return the cash after exiting the bank have higher psychosomatic costs, which in turn makes them less likely to default. The true effect of high psychosomatic costs may be understated, as customers who returned to the bank may have been less aware, counteracting some of the reduction in default rate caused by higher psychosomatic costs.

Table 11.3
Bank error experiment econometric results

Panel A: First loan cycle	Probit: default				Tobit: fraction defaulted		
	(1)	(2)	(3)	(4)	(5)	(6)	(7)
Return	0.000	0.002			0.011		
	(0.035)	(0.035)			(0.057)		
Return later			0.049	0.054		-0.016	-0.001
			(0.075)	(0.076)		(0.117)	(0.116)
Return immediately			-0.005	-0.004		0.009	0.013
			(0.035)	(0.036)		(0.059)	(0.058)
Controls	No	Yes	No	Yes	Yes	No	Yes
Observations	725	725	725	725	725	725	725

Panel B: First year	Probit: default				Tobit: fraction defaulted		
	(1)	(2)	(3)	(4)	(5)	(6)	(7)
Return	-0.004	-0.002			-0.004		
	(0.036)	(0.036)			(0.050)		
Return later			-0.156**	-0.151**		-0.162***	-0.150***
			(0.080)	(0.081)		(0.052)	(0.052)
Return immediately			0.012	0.013		-0.001	0.002
			(0.037)	(0.037)		(0.025)	(0.024)
Controls	No	Yes	No	Yes	Yes	No	Yes
Observations	725	725	725	725	725	725	725

Notes: Robust standard errors reported in parentheses. "Default" is defined as having an unpaid balance on a loan at the contracted end date. "Fraction defaulted" is the ratio of the unpaid balance to the principal. The controls include ln(age), number of previous loan cycles, and indicators of high school completion and a business income shock within the last six months prior to the experiment.
Hypothesis #1 (bank error): Returning to the bank to give back the excess cash is negatively correlated with default. Results of panel B analysis find support for this hypothesis; clients who returned to the bank were 15.1% less likely to default (column 4) and the amount of the default, as a

Timed Response Survey

The second experiment was focused on unintentional default: we examined the link between both a subject's ability to meet future commitments and a subject's perception of his or her ability to meet future commitments with the likelihood of default. The subjects were asked to participate in a second, shorter survey upon completion of the first survey but prior to receiving the excess cash in the bank error experiment. The survey contained two short questions on client satisfaction with multiple-choice responses: the first question required a one-digit response (1–5) and the second question required a single-letter response (A–E). The subjects were randomly assigned to one of two groups: group A was given the survey and instructed to text back the responses exactly one week in the future using his or her cell phone.[8] Subjects were informed that P50.00 (US$1.00) would be deposited in the person's savings account at the bank if the text was received on the specified date;[9] otherwise, no payment would be made to the subject.[10] Group B was given an identical survey but had a choice regarding timing and payment: the person could either complete the survey immediately at the bank for P30.00, or they could text back the response exactly one week in the future for P50.00.

The experiment yields five pools of people, outlined in the following table: (1) those in group A (who had no choice about when to respond) and were successful; (2) those in group A who were unsuccessful; (3) those in group B (who had a choice on when to respond) who chose to complete the survey immediately; (4) those in group B who chose to text back in a week and were successful; and (5) those in group B who chose to text back in a week and were unsuccessful. The following table presents a discussion of how these five experiment outcomes identify various personality types and ensuing predictions regarding correlation with default:

Treatment group	Choice	Experiment success	#	Personality inference	Predicted loan behavior
A: No choice	n/a	Successful	1	Good at implementing future plans (assumes cost of responding is lower than opportunity cost of time, which may be correlated with ability to repay)	Low default rate
		Unsuccessful	2	Bad at implementing future plans (assumes cost of responding is lower than opportunity cost of time, which may be correlated with ability to repay)	High default rate
B: Choice	Choose immediate	N/A	3	Either (a) very high discount rate or (b) bad at (or pessimistic about) implementing future plans and self-aware	(a) Ambiguous[11] and (b) Low default rate
	Choose text back	Successful	4	Good at implementing future plans and self-aware	Low default rate
		Unsuccessful	5	Bad at implementing future plans and not self-aware	High default rate

The choice made by subjects in group B—to immediately complete the survey or to text back the response to the survey—depends on both the discount rate and the self-perceived likelihood of completing the task.[12] Subjects with a sufficiently high discount rate might find it optimal to forego 40 percent of the payout to avoid waiting a week for payment and complete the survey immediately. Subjects who believe they have a low likelihood of success may also find it optimal to complete the survey immediately, and subjects who believe they have a high likelihood of success will choose to text back the response.

If subjects' perceptions are correctly realized, we should see a higher rate of text-back success in group B relative to group A due to self-selection; this means that we would expect to see a higher success rate in group B for those who opt to text back in a week than in group A who are randomly assigned to have to text back in a week (i.e., all of group A).

The results of our analyses are presented in table 11.4.

Hypothesis #2 (Bad Implementers Default): Within group A (those with no choice as to whether to do the survey now or later), those who failed to text back (group 2) are more likely to default than those who succeed (group 1). Within group B (those with a choice as to whether to do the survey now or later), those who failed to text back (group 5) are more likely to default than those who succeed (group 4).

There is weak evidence that the subjects who successfully texted back were less likely to default than those who did not. The difference is not statistically significant at 90 percent, but the individuals who failed to text back (group 2) did have a greater likelihood of default than those who successfully texted back, particularly in the first cycle. Within group B, the evidence is similar; among those who texted back, the first-cycle default rate is 18 percent, compared to 28 percent among those who were unsuccessful. The differential reverses after one year (although it is neither near the level of statistical significance nor of the magnitude found from the first experiment). The fraction defaulted is consistently higher through the first year for those who failed to text back.

Hypothesis #3 (Self-Aware Test): Group 3 is less likely to default than group A (no choice treatment group). Group 3 contains individuals bad at implementing future plans but self-aware, so they may seek out only loans they expect to repay. Note this hypothesis has an important

Table 11.4
Text-back experiment outcomes (means and standard errors)

		Mean (standard error)		Mean (standard error)	
		First cycle		First year	
		Default	Fraction defaulted	Default	Fraction defaulted
Treatment group A					
	No choice, all	0.28	0.09	0.73	0.17
		(0.02)	(0.01)	(0.02)	(0.01)
(1)′	Group 1: no choice, successful	0.22	0.07	0.70	0.15
		(0.05)	(0.03)	(0.06)	(0.02)
(2)′	Group 2: no choice, unsuccessful	0.30	0.10	0.74	0.18
		(0.03)	(0.02)	(0.02)	(0.01)
Treatment group B					
(3)′	Group 3: choose now	0.20	0.05	0.69	0.17
		(0.04)	(0.01)	(0.04)	(0.02)
	Choose text-back, all	0.26	0.10	0.69	0.18
		(0.03)	(0.02)	(0.03)	(0.02)
(4)	Group 4: choose text-back, successful	0.18	0.07	0.75	0.16
		(0.06)	(0.02)	(0.07)	(0.03)
(5)	Group 5: choose text-back, unsuccessful	0.28	0.09	0.67	0.19
		(0.03)	(0.01)	(0.04)	(0.02)

Notes: Means are based on 725 observations. "Default" is defined as having an unpaid balance on a loan at the contracted end date. "Fraction defaulted" is defined as the ratio of the unpaid balance to the principal.
Hypotheses presented using difference of mean and $|t\text{-}statistic|$.
*significant at 10 percent; **significant at 5 percent; ***significant at 1 percent.

Hypothesis #2 (bad implementers):								
$(1) \neq (2)$	−0.07	−0.04	−0.03	−0.03				
and	1.18	0.83	0.58	1.16				
$(4) \neq (5)$	−0.10	−0.03	0.08	−0.02				
	1.33	0.77	0.99	0.58				
Hypothesis #3 (self-aware test):								
$(3) \neq$ pool of (1) and (2)	−0.09*	−0.04*	−0.04	−0.01				
	1.88	1.88	0.94	0.35				
Hypothesis #4 (sorting of self-aware):								
Success rates of group B \neq group A		Group B: 79.5%	Group A: 82.8%					
Hypothesis #5 (Bad impl effect strongest with sorting):								
$	(4) \neq (5)	>	(1) \neq (2)	$	0.03	0.01	0.04	0.01
	1.19	0.95	1.51	0.37				

confound, in that group 3 also contains those with high discount rates (i.e., those who are unwilling to wait a week for higher future payment) and thus this is not a clean test of this hypothesis.

We find evidence for Hypothesis #3. Group 3, composed of self-aware bad implementers, are nine percentage points less likely to default. The one-year results, however, are nearly half the size and not significant statistically.

Hypothesis #4: (Sorting of the Self-Aware): Group A is more likely to fail to text back than pooled groups 4 and 5 (text-back pool of group B) because the choice to opt out of the future plan likely removes self-aware bad implementers from this group B pool.

There is some evidence to support Hypothesis #4 based on the average success rates. Although 79.5 percent of subjects in group B failed to text back after having made the choice to text back, 82.8 percent of subjects in group A failed to text back.

Hypothesis #5 (Bad Implementers Effect Strongest with Sorting): Because bad but self-aware implementers select out of the text-back pool (and are in group 3), the differential between group 5 and group 4 default will be more than the differential between group 2 and group 1 default.

The results of our analysis show that the default differential for the first cycle is three percentage points higher for group B than group A. When considering the data from the first year, this differential is four percentage points and is slightly stronger statistically.

Surveys

Social Capital
For the third part of the study, we administered a survey with the social capital questions from the General Social Survey (GSS) on trust, fairness, and helpfulness to predict default.[13] One definition of individual-level social capital is the social skills and networks that enable an individual to overcome imperfect information problems and form contracts with others.[14] Trust and trustworthiness are two critical ingredients of individual social capital. Previous literature has examined the link between the GSS questions and the trust game[15] as well as the GSS questions and real-life outcomes or decisions. Glaeser et al. (2000)

found that more positive answers to the GSS questions predicted trustworthy behavior in a trust game but not trusting behavior. Because the difficulty of observing or enforcing credit market contracts can be mitigated by increased social connections, there should exist a positive relationship between loan compliance and measures of social capital. Karlan (2005) used the GSS to predict real financial decisions on a micro level and found evidence that more positive answers to the GSS questions predicted higher repayment on group loans and higher savings levels (for savings then held as collateral for the group loans).

The results of our probit regression analysis in table 11.5 indicate that social capital does not predict default on individual loans, unlike the result for group loans from Karlan (2005). This result may occur

Table 11.5
General Social Survey and default

	Probit			
	First cycle default		First year default	
	(1)	(2)	(3)	(4)
GSS index	−0.021		0.023	
	(0.016)		(0.017)	
GSS #1: People can be trusted		−0.025		−0.011
		(0.024)		(0.030)
GSS #2: People try to be fair		0.016		0.046*
		(0.021)		(0.030)
GSS #3: People are helpful		−0.013		0.002
		(0.024)		(0.031)
Controls	Yes	Yes	Yes	Yes
Observations	712	712	712	712

Notes: Robust standard errors reported in parentheses. The three General Social Survey questions are: (1) "Generally speaking, would you say that most people can be trusted or that you can't be too careful in dealing with people?"; (2) "Do you think most people would try to take advantage of you if they got a chance, or would they try to be fair?"; (3) "Would you say that most of the time people try to be helpful, or that they are mostly just looking out for themselves?" Subjects may either agree, disagree, or give a neutral response. The responses were standardized with mean zero and variance 1. The GSS index was calculated as the sum of the three responses (+1) Agree, (−1) Disagree, and (0) Neither, and standardized with mean zero and variance 1. The controls include ln(age), number of previous loan cycles, and indicators of high school completion and business income shock within the last six months prior to the experiment.
*significant at 10 percent; *significant at 5 percent; **significant at 1 percent.

because social capital makes people less likely to default when the burden falls on people within their network, as is the case with group lending. However, in the case of individual loans, the burden falls on the bank, which is likely to be outside of a subject's social network.

Personality Index
In the final part of the study, we examined the relationship between personality index measures and behavior in financial settings using the Big Five personality index model. The Big Five personality index model is a hierarchical model developed from statistically aggregate clusters of descriptors of personality.[16] The model summarizes personality into the following five factors:

1. *Openness* is a dimension of personality that distinguishes imaginative, creative people from down-to-earth, conventional people. Describes the breadth, depth, and complexity of an individual's mental and experiential life (Caspi et al. 1994).

2. *Conscientiousness* concerns the way in which one controls, regulates, and directs one's impulses. Primarily describes tasks and goal-directed behavior and socially prescribed impulse control.

3. *Extraversion* is marked by pronounced engagement with the external world.

4. *Agreeableness* reflects individual differences in concern with cooperation and social harmony.

5. *Emotional stability* refers to the tendency to experience negative emotions (anxiety, sadness, irritability, and nervous tension).

Recent research has looked at the Big Five's predictive power in personality disorders and job performance. Barrick and Mount (1991, 1998) found that conscientiousness showed consistent relations with all performance criteria for all occupational groups. Extraversion was a valid predictor for occupations involving social interaction (e.g., management and sales). Furthermore, extraversion and openness to experiences were valid predictors of training proficiency criteria. However, little systematic research on personality measures has been directed at whether the Big Five are predictive of counterproductive behaviors. Salgado (2002) found (1) that conscientiousness predicted deviant behaviors (e.g., theft, drug, and alcohol use) and turnover and (2) that extraversion, openness, agreeableness, and emotional stability predicted turnover.

We examined the Big Five's ability to predict default and behavior in our experiments using the Ten-Item Personality Index (TIPI), a brief measure of the Big Five factor model developed by Gosling, Rentfrow, and Swann (2003). The TIPI uses a seven-point scale from 1 (strongly disagree) to 7 (strongly agree) for each of ten descriptive items. Pairs of items compose each of the five factors of personality, similar to the bipolar markers in Goldberg (1992). Gosling, Rentfrow, and Swann (2003) provide evidence that the instruments reach adequate levels in terms of: (1) convergence with widely used Big Five measures in self, observer, and peer reports, (2) test-retest reliability, (3) patterns of predicted external correlates, and (4) convergence between self and observer ratings.[17]

The results examining the predictive power of the five factor personality index model on default and behavior in our experiments are presented in table 11.6. We found no evidence that personality measures were strong predictors of default in the first cycle or first year after the survey using probit regression analysis.

We can speculate that there is little to no deliberate default in our sample according to Salgado's results or that there *is* deliberate default and our results contradict that of Salgado (2002). We used a multinomial probit regression to examine the predictive power of the bank error outcomes normalized on the choice to return the excess cash prior to exiting the bank. We found evidence that *Agreeableness* and *Openness* were weakly negatively correlated with never returning the excess cash (relative to returning it at the moment of the disbursement), perhaps because individuals who rated themselves as being highly agreeable or open were concerned with cooperation and maintaining social harmony.

In the case of the text-back experiment, we found that *Emotional Stability* (i.e., calmness vs. anxiety or irritability) was positively correlated with the choice to text back. Alternatively, this result suggests that individuals who rated themselves as being relatively anxious were more likely to choose to complete the survey at the bank rather than text back a response. This finding is consistent with our premise that some of the group B individuals who chose to complete the survey at the bank may have done so because of a very high discount rate. *Openness* was correlated with actual success in the choice to text back, possibly due to an association between *Openness* and crystallized intelligence, which is the ability to use skills, knowledge, and experience (Geary 2005).[18] Crystallized intelligence relies on the ability to

Table 11.6
Ten-Item Personality Index (TIPI)

	Probit		Mprobit		Probit	
	First cycle	First year	Bank error		Group B	
	default	default	Later	Never	Choice	Success
	(1)	(2)	(3)	(4)	(5)	(6)
Extraversion	-0.002	0.012	0.004	0.008	0.014	-0.002
	(0.017)	(0.018)	(0.097)	(0.075)	(0.027)	(0.018)
Agreeableness	-0.008	-0.016	-0.025	-0.135*	-0.005	0.012
	(0.020)	(0.020)	(0.127)	(0.082)	(0.033)	(0.024)
Conscientiousness	-0.027	0.018	-0.096	0.014	-0.032	-0.01
	(0.020)	(0.020)	(0.117)	(0.084)	(0.033)	(0.024)
Emotional stability	0.011	0.021	-0.052	0.041	0.060**	0.017
	(0.020)	(0.020)	(0.121)	(0.081)	(0.030)	(0.022)
Openness	0.019	0.033*	0.026	-0.152**	0.024	0.037*
	(0.018)	(0.018)	(0.111)	(0.075)	(0.027)	(0.021)
Controls	Yes	Yes	Yes	Yes	Yes	Yes
Observations	657	657	657	657	308	308

*significant at 10 percent; **significant at 5 percent; ***significant at 1 percent.
Notes: Robust standard errors reported in parentheses. Columns 3 and 4 are the results of a multinomial probit on the individual's action in the bank error experiment, with a base outcome of returning the excess cash immediately after the experiment. Column 5 examines the likelihood of choosing the text-back option when prompted with a choice to complete the survey immediately or text back a response. Column 6 only examines the likelihood of successfully texting back given that the individual made the choice to text back. The TIPI measure of personality index contains two polar questions for each personality category. The corresponding questions are averaged together to get a measure of each category of the personality index. Each item was standardized with mean zero and variance 1. The controls include ln(age), number of previous loan cycles, and indicators of high school completion and business income shock within the six months prior to the experiment.

access memory. As a result, it is possible that lack of success in the text-back experiment may be due to an inability to remember how or when to text back the survey results, particularly as it is an uncommon act.

Overall, however, the correlations between personality measures and repayment were weak and did not conform to a precise theory. This result could be due either to a default driven by nonchoice circumstances (shocks in one's life that are not correlated with personality) or to measures that do not successfully identify personality traits in this context or implementation.

Conclusion

We used field experiments and surveys to identify character elements that may predict the likelihood of default in individual loans. In the first experiment, we identified the class of subjects with high psychosomatic costs from taking excess cash when a bank error was made in their favor. We find this measure to be positively correlated with default on loans over one year. In the second experiment, we identified the class of subjects that was less naïve about their own ability to meet future commitments. We then used that information to predict the likelihood of default in the first loan cycle. We also explored the relationship between psychological measures and behavior in both our experiments and in the case of default on individual loans and found little correlation for both measures of social capital and personality measures. From a policy perspective, given the growth of cell phone ownership and introduction of mobile banking, these experiments do suggest that credit scoring approaches could benefit from further exploration and identification of type-revealing surveys and screening devices.

Notes

We thank Carissa Feria, Matthew Grant, Tomoko Harigaya, Nicole Mauriello, Sang Seok Lee, and Hannah Trachtman for excellent research assistance. This article has benefited from the comments of Nava Ashraf, Lucas Coffman, Justin Ho, Asim Khwaja, Kirk Moore, and participants at the Harvard Economic Development workshop. Any and all errors are the authors' own. All views expressed in this paper are those of the authors and do not necessarily reflect the views or policies of the U.S. Bureau of Labor Statistics.

1. "Texting back" refers to the act of communication via Short Message Service (SMS) on mobile telephones.

Figure 11.1
Map of field experiment areas in Luzon Island, Philippines. *Notes:* There were eight branches used in the experiment: Cabuyao, Calamba, Los Baños, Tanay, Santa Maria, Siniloan, Paete, and Infanta. The locations of Cabuyao and Siniloan are approximated on this map. *Source:* Google Maps (http://maps.google.com)

2. Zimmerman (2008) found that neuroticism best predicted (negatively) employees' intentions to quit, whereas the traits of conscientiousness and agreeableness best predicted (negatively) actual turnover decisions. He found that employees who were low on neuroticism were more likely to quit for reasons other than dissatisfaction with their jobs or not being able to perform their jobs well. The direct effects on turnover suggest that individuals who were low on agreeableness or high on openness were more likely to engage in unplanned quitting. See Barrick and Mount (1991) for more.

3. See figure 11.1 for a map of the eight branch locations on the island of Luzon in the Philippines.

4. The bank was established in the early 1970s and regulated by the government. It typically offers ninety-day term loans and voluntary savings. Only individual loans with a start and maturity date within a one-year period were included in the analysis.

5. All communication in verbal or written form was in Tagalog, the official language of the Philippines.

6. The two bills should be easily differentiable by the different images and colors.

7. There were no reports of subjects who attempted to return the money the day after initially leaving the branch.

8. All subjects were required to have access to a cell phone to participate in this experiment.

9. The bank required all loan recipients to have a savings account.

10. The instructions specifying the expected date for the response, the phone number, and the amount to be deposited were all clearly specified on each copy of the survey that was provided to subjects.

11. It is ambiguous whether individuals with high discount rates should be more or less likely to default. On the one hand, they likely place a high value on access to credit; on the other hand, their higher value of short-term consumption may increase their inability to meet future obligations.

12. We are not concerned about the potential for a liquidity constraint because the payout is an insignificant proportion (0.001 percent) of the loan that is received the same day.

13. See Sobel 2002 for more information on the social capital literature. See Krishna and Shrader 2000 and Grootaert and van Bastelaer 2001 for discussions on measuring social capital.

14. See Fukuyama 1995 and Ostrom 1990 for work on social capital frameworks.

15. The trust game extends the dictator game one step by having the reward that the dictator can (unilaterally) split between him- or herself and a partner, partially decided by an initial gift from that partner.

16. The most recent account of the Big Five personality dimensions was developed by Goldberg (1981) but first identified by Norman (1963). This model has become widely used in the psychology field (for reviews, see John and Srivastava 1999 and McCrae and Costa 1999) but not unanimously (see Block 1995).

17. Although long instruments tend to have better metric properties than short instruments, the time and costs associated with short instruments are much lower.

18. Crystalized intelligence is distinct from fluid intelligence, which is the ability to reason independent of knowledge. It is worth noting that *Openness* is only weakly correlated with general intelligence.

References

Barrick, M. R., and M. K. Mount. 1991. The Big Five Personality Dimensions and Job Performance: A Meta-Analysis. *Personnel Psychology* 44:1–26.

Barrick, M. R., and M. K. Mount. 1998. Five Reasons Why the "Big Five" Article Has Been Frequently Cited. *Personnel Psychology* 51:849–858.

Block, J. 1995. A Contrarian View of the Five-Factor Approach to Personality Description. *Psychological Bulletin* 117:187–215.

Caspi, A., O. John, T. Moffitt, R. Robins, and M. Stouthamer-Loeber. 1994. The "Little Five": Exploring the Nomological Network of the Five-Factor Model of Personality in Adolescent Boys. *Child Development* 65:160–178.

Fukuyama, Francis. 1995. *Trust: The Social Virtues and The Creation of Prosperity*. New York: Free Press Paperbacks.

Geary, D. C. 2005. *The Origin of Mind: Evolution of Brain, Cognition, and General Intelligence*. Washington, DC: American Psychological Association.

Glaeser, Edward L., David I. Laibson, Jose A. Scheinkman, and Christine L. Soutter. 2000. Measuring Trust. *Quarterly Journal of Economics* 115:811–846.

Goldberg, Lewis R. 1981. Language and Individual Differences: The Search for Universals in Personality Lexicons. In *Review of Personality and Social Psychology, Vol. 1*, ed. Ladd Wheeler, 141–165. Beverly Hills, CA: Sage.

Goldberg, Lewis R. 1992. The Development of Markers for the Big-Five Factor Structure. *Psychological Assessment* 4: 26–42.

Gosling, S. D., P. J. Rentfrow, and W. B. Swann, Jr. 2003. A Very Brief Measure of the Big-Five Personality Domains. *Journal of Research in Personality* 37:504–528.

Grootaert, Christiaan, and Thierry van Bastelaer. 2001. Understanding and Measuring Social Capital: A Synthesis of Findings and Recommendations from the Social Capital Initiative. Social Capital Initiative Working Paper No. 24.

John, O. P., and S. Srivastava. 1999. The Big Five Trait Taxonomy: History, Measurement, and Theoretical Perspectives. In *Handbook of Personality: Theory and Research*, ed. L. A. Pervin and O. P. John, 102–138. New York: Guilford Press.

Karlan, D. 2005. Using Experimental Economics to Measure Social Capital and Predict Financial Decisions. *American Economic Review* 95 (5): 1688–1699.

Krishna, Anirudh, and Elizabeth Shrader. 2000. Cross-Cultural Measures of Social Capital: A Tool and Results from India and Panama. Social Capital Initiative Working Paper No. 21. Social Development Department, World Bank, Washington, DC.

McCrae, Robert R., and Paul T. Costa, Jr. 1999. A Five-Factor Theory of Personality. In *Handbook of Personality: Theory and Research*, ed. L. A. Pervin and O. P. John, 139–153. New York: Guilford Press.

Norman, Warren T. 1963. Toward an Adequate Taxonomy of Personality Attributes: Replicated Factor Structure in Peer Nomination Personality Ratings. *Journal of Abnormal and Social Psychology* 66:574–583.

Ostrom, Elinor. 1990. Social Capital: A Fad or a Fundamental Concept? In *Social Capital: A Multifaceted Perspective*, ed. Partha Dasgupta and Ismail Serageldin, 172–214. Washington, DC: The World Bank.

Salgado, J. 2002. The Big Five Personality Dimensions and Counterproductive Behavior. *International Journal of Selection and Assessment* 10:117–125.

Sobel, J. 2002. Can We Trust Social Capital? *Journal of Economic Literature* 40: 139–154.

Zimmerman, R. D. 2008. Understanding the Impact of Personality Traits on Individuals' Turnover Decisions: A Meta-Analytic Path. *Personnel Psychology* 61 (2): 309–348.

12 Valuing Financial Literacy

Shawn Cole, Thomas Sampson, and Bilal Zia

In recent years, financial literacy has come to play an increasingly prominent role in financial reform in both developed and developing countries. The U.S. government, for example, created the President's Advisory Council on Financial Literacy in January 2008 to promote programs that improve financial education at all levels of the economy and to help increase access to financial services. In the developing world, the Indonesian government declared 2008 "the year of financial education" with a stated goal of improving access to and use of financial services through increasing financial literacy. In 2007, the Reserve Bank of India launched an initiative to establish Financial Literacy and Credit Counseling Centers throughout the country, which would offer free financial education and counseling to urban and rural populations.

Both international and private organizations are also pushing heavily for financial literacy programs across the globe. For instance, a World Bank trust fund financed by the Russian government recently approved a $15 million Financial Literacy Program to support an international program on financial literacy and financial education. The Citigroup Foundation is halfway through a ten-year, $200 million Global Financial Education Project supporting financial literacy programs in sixty-five countries around the world.

Much of this attention on financial literacy is motivated by a compelling body of household survey evidence. Surveys from developed countries demonstrate a strong association between financial literacy and household well-being: households with low levels of financial literacy tend to not plan for retirement (Lusardi and Mitchell 2007a), borrow at higher interest rates (Lusardi and Tufano 2008; Stango and Zinman 2009), acquire fewer assets (Lusardi and Mitchell 2007b), and participate less in the formal financial system relative to their more

financially literate counterparts (van Rooij, Lusardi, and Alessie 2011; Hogarth and O'Donnell 1999).

In the developing world, we conduct the first survey to measure financial literacy in a developing country through a nationally representative household survey in Indonesia (Cole, Sampson, and Zia 2011). We combine this survey in Indonesia with rural household survey data from India and find that levels of financial literacy are substantially lower in these two developing countries than in developed countries such as the United States. Yet, just as in the United States, we find that education, cognitive ability, and wealth are all positively associated with financial literacy and that financial literacy predicts demand for financial services. Similarly, Klapper and Lusardi (2010) conduct a survey to measure financial literacy in Russia and find the levels to be fairly low: only 47 percent of respondents can answer a simple question about inflation. Consistent with all previous survey evidence, the authors find that financial literacy is significantly related to participation in financial markets and negatively related to the use of informal sources of borrowing.

This overwhelming and consistent survey evidence has prompted many organizations to advance financial literacy programs as a low-cost intervention to enhance household financial outcomes and overall welfare. The recent worldwide attention and the accompanying funds that are being channeled toward financial literacy programs call for a careful study of program impacts and the precise mechanisms through which they affect financial behavior. Specifically, for policy to be better designed and better targeted, the causal channel between financial literacy and use of financial services must be identified.

Survey-based analysis can go only so far in establishing a causal link between better financial literacy and greater use of financial services. Indeed, the positive correlations reported in survey analyses may be driven by omitted variables or endogenous selection. For instance, people who choose to participate in surveys or literacy seminars may be quite different from those who do not participate in terms of interest in financial matters. Further, survey evidence cannot distinguish the direction of causality: greater financial literacy may lead to greater use of financial services or, just as likely, individuals who use more financial services may score better on financial literacy assessments based on their experience in financial markets.

Experimental studies on financial literacy, similar to medical drug trials, allow for the establishment of a causal relationship between

financial literacy and financial market participation. Such experiments overcome the problems of selection and endogeneity that are associated with survey analysis. Using this methodology, we directly test the role and the relative importance of financial literacy and prices in determining demand for banking services in Indonesia. We find that financial literacy education has only modest effects, improving the likelihood of opening a bank account only among households with low initial levels of education and financial literacy. On the other hand, small financial incentives have large effects, significantly increasing the share of households that open a bank account within the subsequent two months. These results hold in the long term as well, as substantiated by our follow-up survey two years later.

These results suggest that financial literacy programs may be more effective if they are targeted at particular subgroups of individuals. Additionally, a more comprehensive financial literacy program that is delivered over several weekly sessions, rather than a single session of a few hours, may be required to improve households' financial attitudes and behavior, which can be quite rigid and difficult to change.[1]

What Do We Know? Review of Experimental Evidence on Financial Literacy

In the developed world, research evidence that financial education can affect decision making comes from a randomized evaluation conducted at a major university in the United States. Duflo and Saez (2003) implemented an "encouragement design" in which they randomly offered some administrative employees a small financial incentive ($20) to attend a session on retirement products. Those who received the incentive were significantly more likely to attend the training session. Further, the session had a small but significant impact on their savings decisions, as more individuals in the treatment group enrolled in tax-deferred retirement accounts. Also in the United States, Bertrand and Morse (2011) consider the effects of providing information on the costs of payday borrowing. Their results indicate that an information treatment reinforcing the adding up of interest over time reduces the likelihood that an individual renews a payday loan.

In developing countries, much less is known about the impact of financial literacy programs, although the findings have likewise been mixed. Our study in Indonesia is the first experimental evaluation of its kind in a developing country setting. Many more studies focus

instead on business literacy programs for small and microenterprises. For example, Karlan and Valdivia (2011) find that a business education program improves record keeping, though not profits, among women microfinance borrowers in rural Peru; Bruhn and Zia (2011) find significant impacts of a business training program on business investment and production processes among young entrepreneurs in Bosnia and Herzegovina; and Drexler, Fischer, and Schoar (2010) find that a rule-of-thumb training for microentrepreneurs in the Dominican Republic increases the likelihood that they keep accounting records and calculate monthly revenues. In a similar vein, Bruhn, Karlan, and Schoar (2010) conduct a randomized evaluation of on-site business mentoring in Mexico and find positive effects on productivity and profitability.

Such entrepreneurial training programs typically incorporate some aspects of what is usually considered financial literacy (e.g., learning how to separate business and financial accounts, understanding financial statements) with other elements of better business practices (e.g., how to market products better, sales techniques). Thus, these studies identify the overall impact of the business training program being evaluated and cannot isolate the impact of financial literacy training by itself.

Few ongoing studies attempt to look at other aspects of financial literacy and financial behavior. We are doing follow-up work in India and South Africa in which we conduct a randomized evaluation of a video-based financial literacy training program that includes modules on loans, savings, budgeting, and insurance. Elsewhere, Hastings and Mitchell (n.d.) are conducting an experiment among Chilean households to determine whether financial literacy has an effect on an individual's ability to make optimal financial decisions, and Karlan, McMillan, and Kutsoati (n.d.) are carrying out a randomized control trial in Ghana, providing rural bank customers with six 15-minute financial literacy lessons to investigate the impact of financial education on bank savings account adoption, selection of savings products, and frequency of deposits. These ongoing studies will make very important contributions to the evidence base on financial literacy.

Survey Evidence from Indonesia

Household-level data was collected in Indonesia as part of the World Bank's Access to Finance survey, a nationally representative survey designed to measure the use of and attitude toward financial services.

Additionally, the survey measures financial literacy and cognitive ability levels; 112 villages were selected through stratified sampling, and from each village 30 households were randomly selected to participate in the survey for a total sample size of 3,360 households. The survey took place between July and December 2007.

On the use of financial services, only 41 percent of the households in the survey sample report having a bank account. However, 29 percent of those that do not currently have a bank account had one at some point in the past. In addition, 51 percent of the households report having a savings account with a nonbank institution, but only 13 percent have advanced savings instruments, such as certificates of deposit or mutual funds. For loans, informal credit is much more common, as 52 percent of the households have loans from microfinance institutions, moneylenders, or other informal sources, whereas only 25 percent have a formal sector loan. The most common source of informal credit is family and friends. Almost half of the households report having some form of insurance policy such as health or asset insurance.

Among survey respondents who have bank savings accounts, the most common reason cited for having one are: for security (53%), for predicted future needs (42%), for money transfers (37%), and for emergency needs (31%). When asked about their reason for not having a bank account, 92 percent of unbanked households responded that they do not have enough money. Furthermore, 71 percent of currently unbanked households who did have an account at some point in the past report that they had stopped using the account because of lack of money. As for insurance, not enough money is again the most frequent reason given, representing 59 percent of the households who do not have any insurance.

This survey is also the first nationally representative household survey on financial literacy in a developing country. Financial literacy is measured using methods consistent with previous surveys in the United States. It is captured through the following set of four questions: (1) "Suppose you borrow Rupiah 100,000 from a moneylender at an interest rate of 2 percent per month, with no repayment for three months. After three months, do you owe less than Rupiah 102,000, or more than Rupiah 102,000?" (2) "If you have Rupiah 100,000 in a savings account earning 1 percent interest per annum, and prices for goods and services rise 2 percent over a one-year period, can you buy more than, less than, or the same amount of goods in one year as you

could today, with the money in the account?" (3) "Is it riskier to plant multiple crops or one crop?" and (4) "Suppose you need to borrow Rupiah 500,000. Two people offer you a loan. One loan requires you to pay back Rupiah 600,000 in one month. The second loan requires you to pay back in one month Rupiah 500,000 plus 15 percent interest. Which loan represents a better deal for you?"

The average score for these financial literacy questions is 2.1 out of 4. It should be noted, however, that all questions were multiple choice and that two questions had two possible answers and two questions had three possible answers. As a result, random guessing on these financial literacy questions would yield an average score of 1.67. Of the survey respondents, 78 percent were able to answer the question involving compound interest correctly, and only 28 percent answered the question on risk diversification correctly.

In addition to financial literacy, the survey also measures cognitive ability through a series of eight mathematics questions. The average score for these mathematics questions is 6.5 out of 8. Almost all survey participants responded correctly to addition questions ("What is 4 + 3?"), whereas many more had difficulty with multiplication ("What is 3 × 6?") and division ("What is one-tenth of 400?"). Because respondents were not allowed to ask their friends or neighbors for help, it is reasonable to think that in situations in which collaboration is possible, they will perform better when answering these mathematics questions.

The survey also collected standard data on household demographic information, wealth, and income. About 58 percent of the sample is rural, and the average household size is three; 39 percent of households have a nonfarm enterprise. Eighty percent of the survey respondents completed primary school, but only 33 percent completed high school education. Monthly per capita household expenditure is about $90, and the average annual household income is $1,315.

Correlates of Financial Literacy

The data on financial literacy levels, cognitive ability, household wealth, and demographic information collected in the survey enable us to examine the factors that predict financial literacy. Splitting the survey sample by household per capita expenditure shows that the richer half performed significantly better than the poorer half on all four financial literacy questions. The results are similar when splitting the sample by

cognitive ability. Specifically, the differences between the subsamples of high and low cognitive ability are about twice as large as those between the subsamples of high and low per capita expenditure. This finding suggests that cognitive ability may play an important role in determining financial literacy.

More formally, estimates from regressing our measure of financial literacy on various individual characteristics confirm that greater household per capita expenditure, cognitive ability, and education are all positively correlated with higher financial literacy levels. Although wealth and cognitive ability are some of the most important predictors of financial literacy, estimates show that cognitive ability has a substantially stronger association with financial literacy relative to wealth. Additionally, we find that rural households and those with a female household head have significantly lower financial literacy levels. In contrast, households that own a nonfarm enterprise exhibit higher levels of financial literacy.

We also estimate whether household characteristics and financial literacy predict the use of various financial services, particularly bank accounts, formal and informal loans, and insurance. We find that higher per capita expenditure is a strong predictor of the use of such financial products and that greater cognitive ability predicts the use of formal loans and insurance. Education, on the other hand, is positively associated with having a bank account, formal credit, and insurance but is negatively correlated with informal credit use. We also find that greater financial literacy is significantly correlated with a greater use of bank savings accounts, although the magnitudes of the estimates suggest that it is a much less important predictor than wealth.

Finally, we explore the relationship between various household characteristics, financial literacy, and the demand for financial services, particularly commitment savings products, deposit collector services, and retirement savings. Regression estimates show that higher household per capita expenditure is associated with greater interest in these financial products, but there is no evidence that education and cognitive ability have a significant effect. We also find a higher financial literacy level to be a strong predictor of the demand for savings products. Additionally, lack of knowledge about how a bank operates was the second most common reason for not having a bank account among survey respondents. These results provide support for the idea that financial literacy training could increase the share of households possessing a bank account.

Experiment Design

To test whether financial literacy acts as a barrier to opening a bank account, we conduct a randomized experiment in Indonesia alongside the household survey. This experiment enables us to investigate whether financial literacy training programs do lead to greater financial access by comparing outcomes for the treatment and control groups. That is, the outcomes of both groups will be identical unless literacy training has an effect. We study the use of savings accounts, which is one of the most basic but perhaps also the most valuable financial service. We choose to study savings accounts as an outcome because it can be an efficient savings technology for households, providing security from theft and often interest payments, as well as a means for sending and receiving payments. It also allows individuals to build a relationship with the bank, with the potential to facilitate access to credit and other financial services in the future, which may in turn improve household welfare. Transactions and savings accounts are the first and most obvious way in which household participation in the formal financial sector begins.

For the experiment, we worked with Microfinance Innovation Center for Resources and Alternatives (MICRA), an international nonprofit organization based in Jakarta that provides consulting and training programs to banks and microfinance organizations in Indonesia. Together with MICRA, we offered free financial literacy education to the unbanked households from our survey. The training curriculum was customized and developed by MICRA and was adapted from training materials developed by a consortium of Microfinance Opportunities, the Citigroup Foundation, and Freedom from Hunger. It was designed for unbanked individuals, with the specific goal of teaching households about the costs and benefits of opening a bank savings account. These literacy seminars are two or three hours in length, are group based, and are held at a convenient village location on a weekend.

The experiment took place in the sixty-four villages from the island of Java that were part of the Access to Finance survey. Thirty households were sampled in each village for a total of 1,920 households. Of these, 1,173 did not have a bank account at the time of the survey. After completing the survey, each of these unbanked households was offered the opportunity to participate in the experiment. The experiment participants were then assigned to either treatment or control groups; the treatment group was offered free financial literacy education. The

financial literacy training session in each of the sixty-four villages was held within one month of the date when the survey was conducted.

As a secondary experiment, study participants were also randomly assigned a financial incentive level for which either Rupiah 25,000 ($3), 75,000 ($8), or 125,000 ($14) was offered with equal probability for opening a bank account within two months of the intervention. These financial incentives were randomly assigned to participants independent of whether they were offered financial literacy training. Thus it allows for directly comparing the effects of financial literacy education relative to financial incentives. To receive this incentive, the household was required to fill out a postage-paid mail-in form with name and bank account number. The survey firm then transferred the appropriate incentive amount to the participant's bank account upon receipt of this form.

At the time of the study, Indonesia's largest bank, the Bank Rakyat Indonesia, offered a "SIMPEDES" account, which required a minimum deposit of Rupiah 10,000. This account did not charge any fees as long as the client made no more than four deposit and withdrawal transactions per month. This account paid no interest for deposit levels below Rupiah 100,000 and had increasing interest rates for balances greater than this amount.

Unfortunately, there is evidence that the surveyors were collaborating with the households to ensure that households received high incentives. As a result, 23 villages had to be dropped from the experiment sample, leaving a survey sample of 1,230 individuals, of which 736 did not have a bank account. Out of these 736 unbanked households, 564 agreed to participate in the experiment; 274 of these experiment participants were assigned to the treatment group and were invited to the financial literacy training program. The rest were assigned to the control group and were not invited to the training program.

The outcome of interest in this experiment is whether a household opened a bank savings account, which we measure based on the financial incentive claims. After verifying the identity of the claimant and the existence of a bank account, we were left with forty-nine claims that came from eligible households that had indeed opened a bank account, which represent 9 percent of the participants.

Experiment Results

Table 12.1 reports results of our randomized experiment, measuring the effect of offering financial literacy training and financial incentives

Table 12.1
Experimental results: The effect of financial literacy education and incentives on the opening of bank accounts

Dependent variable: Opened bank account?	(1)	(2)	(3)	(4)	(5)	(6)
Financial literacy invitation?	-0.020	-0.022			0.022	0.029
	(0.027)	(0.028)			(0.028)	(0.034)
Incentive = 75,000			0.054**	0.048*	0.065*	0.066*
			(0.024)	(0.026)	(0.036)	(0.037)
Incentive = 125,000			0.092***	0.088***	0.136***	0.137***
			(0.026)	(0.029)	(0.036)	(0.033)
(Incentive = 75,000)* Financial literacy invitation					-0.021	-0.036
					(0.047)	(0.052)
(Incentive = 125,000)* Financial literacy invitation					-0.090	-0.101
					(0.057)	(0.062)
Constant	0.097***	-0.444	0.035**	-0.447	0.024	-0.455
	(0.017)	(0.306)	(0.014)	(0.308)	(0.017)	(0.303)
Household controls		YES		YES		YES
Observations	564	564	564	564	564	564
R-squared	0.001	0.068	0.018	0.082	0.023	0.089

Notes: This table reports the results from a randomized experiment measuring the effect of offering financial literacy training and financial incentives on respondents' decision to open a bank account. The dependent variable is an indicator for whether the respondent opened a bank account. A linear probability model is used. Standard errors, clustered at the village level, are given in parentheses beneath each point estimate. *** indicates statistical significance at the 1 percent level, ** at the 5 percent level, and * at the 10 percent level.

on respondents' decision to open a bank account. Take-up of the financial literacy education is high; approximately 69 percent of respondents invited to attend the program in fact attended the training. Yet the experiment results show that for the general population, the training program we offered has a precisely estimated zero effect on the likelihood of opening a bank savings account.

However, it is possible that financial literacy training is more effective for specific subgroups of the population. For example, our survey data, as well as those from the United States and other developed countries, indicate that education is an important factor in determining financial literacy. Additionally, because the training curriculum was developed for individuals with low levels of financial literacy, the training program might have been more effective for this group.

Splitting the sample of experiment participants into those with and without formal schooling, we find, as before, that the training program has no effect on literate households. However, for households that report having received no schooling, we find that the financial literacy program has a substantial effect. Specifically, the likelihood that these households open a bank savings account increases by 12 percent as a result of the financial literacy training program. Similarly, we explore the possibility that financial literacy training has a positive impact on participants who have low initial levels of financial literacy as measured in the baseline survey. Again, we find that the training program has no impact on individuals with above-average financial literacy, whereas the subpopulation of individuals with below-average financial literacy do benefit from the program; they are 5 percent more likely to open a bank savings account. Overall, these results suggest that financial literacy training has a substantial effect among uneducated and financially illiterate households.

Financial incentives, on the other hand, have a very large and significant effect on inducing households in the general population to open a bank account. We find that even the smallest incentive payment of $3 has a positive effect on the likelihood of opening a bank savings account. Additionally, a household receiving the middle incentive of $8 is 5.4 percentage points more likely to open a bank savings account compared to a household receiving the smallest incentive of $3. Furthermore, increasing the incentive from $3 to $14 also increases the share of households that open a bank savings account from 3.5 percent to 12.7 percent, representing a change of almost 260 percent. This effect is quite large, as it implies that moving

from the low incentive ($3) to high incentive ($14) level has an effect equivalent to increasing household expenditure by two-thirds of a standard deviation.

These results suggest that the financial literacy training program delivered to the general population will not produce significant effects but a program targeted at those with low education and financial literacy levels may increase the demand for financial services. These results hold up in the long term, as evidenced by a follow-up survey we conducted two years after the experiment.

However, even if financial literacy programs are carefully targeted, they may still not be cost effective. In our experiment, the training program cost $17 per head to deliver. For those participants with low levels of financial literacy at baseline—that is, those below the median score in the financial literacy assessment of the survey—the training program increased the likelihood of opening a bank account by 5 percent. This finding implies that the cost per head of effectively delivering the program is $17/0.05 = $340.

In contrast, for the subsample of individuals with low financial literacy levels, increasing the financial incentives from $3 to $14 raises the probability of opening a bank account by 7.6 percent, so the cost per bank savings account opened is $11/0.076 = $145. Thus, providing financial incentives instead is more than 2.5 times cheaper in inducing households to open a bank account relative to training programs targeted at the financially illiterate. However, this calculation does not take into account any extra benefits that households may reap in the future from the financial literacy education course, such as better internal savings or higher informal savings. Nevertheless, it does suggest that financial literacy programs are a relatively expensive way to increase financial access.

Conclusion

A compelling body of survey evidence, mainly from developed countries, demonstrates a strong association between financial literacy and financial behavior, thus spurring governments, nonprofits, and international and private organizations to promote financial literacy as a means of expanding the depth and breadth of the financial system. In Indonesia, using a new nationally representative household survey, we find that financial literacy is indeed a powerful predictor of the demand for formal savings, loans, and insurance services.

To measure the causal impact of financial literacy and financial incentives on the likelihood of opening formal savings accounts, we conduct a randomized evaluation alongside the household survey. We find that the financial education program has no effect on the likelihood of opening a bank account for the general population but is effective for specific segments of the population, particularly the uneducated and those with low initial financial knowledge. However, for the average population or for literacy programs administered en masse, there is a clear upper bound on how much should be spent on such programs if the goal is to improve banking access. Results from our experiment indicate that for the average population, financial incentives are a more effective and feasible mechanism for drawing households into the formal financial system.

Although our results show a very weak causal link between greater financial literacy and better financial access, a few caveats are in order. It should be taken into account that our metric of measurement may be somewhat imperfect. For example, financial literacy may make households better financial planners, make them save more informally, and may lead to improvements in welfare that are not captured in our study of formal bank accounts. To measure external benefits of financial literacy programs, we are repeating our research exercise in India and South Africa with detailed follow-up surveys to measure such benefits.

Another important aspect to consider is that perhaps a more comprehensive financial literacy training program is necessary to change financial behavior among households. An in-depth training program that is delivered over several weekly sessions, rather than a single session of two to three hours, might be more effective in increasing the demand for financial services. However, longer courses will also be more expensive to provide. With this in mind, we are currently testing a video-based delivery mechanism in India and South Africa that has the potential to be easily replicated at low cost.

The jury is still out on whether financial literacy is a useful and cost-effective tool for promoting financial access. The studies mentioned here and many more that are in development will enhance our understanding of what works, how it works, and for whom it works.

Note

1. Our complete analysis is available in Cole, Sampson, and Zia 2011. This chapter is a derivative of the aforementioned publication.

References

Bertrand, Marianne, and Adair Morse. 2011. Information Disclosure, Cognitive Biases, and Payday Borrowing. *Journal of Finance* 66 (6): 1865–1893.

Bruhn, Miriam, Dean Karlan, and Antoinette Schoar. 2010. What Capital is Missing in Developing Countries? *American Economic Review Papers and Proceedings* 100 (2): 629–633.

Bruhn, Miriam, and Bilal Zia. 2011. Stimulating Managerial Capital in Emerging Markets: The Impact of Business and Financial Literacy for Young Entrepreneurs. World Bank Policy Research Working Paper Series No. 5642.

Cole, Shawn, Thomas Sampson, and Bilal Zia. 2011. Prices or Knowledge? What Drives Demand for Financial Services in Emerging Markets. *Journal of Finance* 66 (6): 1933–1967.

Drexler, Alejandro, Greg Fischer and Antoinette Schoar. 2010. Keeping It Simple: Financial Literacy and Rules of Thumb. Centre for Economic Policy Research (CEPR) Discussion Paper No. DP 7994.

Duflo, Esther, and Emmanuel Saez. 2003. The Role of Information and Social Interactions in Retirement Plan Decisions: Evidence from a Randomized Experiment. *Quarterly Journal of Economics* 118:815–842.

Hastings, Justine, and Olivia Mitchell. N.d. Financial Literacy, Short-Run Impatience, and the Determinants of Savings and Financial Management. Ongoing project.

Hogarth, J. M., and K. H. O'Donnell. 1999. Banking Relationships of Lower-Income Families and the Governmental Trend toward Electronic Payment. *Federal Reserve Bulletin* (July): 459–473.

Karlan, Dean, Margaret McMillan, and Edward Kutsoati. N.d. Savings Account Labeling and Financial Literacy Training for Susu Customers in Ghana. Ongoing project.

Karlan, Dean, and Martin Valdivia. 2011. Teaching Entrepreneurship: Impact of Business Training on Microfinance Clients and Institutions. *The Review of Economics and Statistics* 93 (2): 510–527.

Klapper, Leora and Annamaria Lusardi. 2010. Financial Literacy and Participation: Evidence from an Emerging Market. Ongoing project.

Lusardi, Annamaria, and Olivia S. Mitchell. 2007a. Financial Literacy and Retirement Preparedness: Evidence and Implications for Financial Education. *Business Economics* 42 (1): 35–44.

Lusardi, Annamaria, and Olivia S. Mitchell. 2007b. Baby Boomer Retirement Security: The Roles of Planning, Financial Literacy, and Housing Wealth. *Journal of Monetary Economics* 54 (1): 205–224.

Lusardi, Annamaria, and Peter Tufano. 2008. Debt Literacy, Financial Experience, and Over-Indebtedness. Working paper.

Stango, Victor, and Jonathan Zinman. 2009. Exponential Growth Bias and Household Finance. *Journal of Finance* 64 (6): 2807–2849.

van Rooij, Maarten, Annamaria Lusardi, and Rob Alessie. 2011. Financial Literacy and Stock Market Participation. *Journal of Financial Economics* 101 (2): 449–472.

13 Use of Biometric Technology in Developing Countries

Xavier Giné, Jessica Goldberg,
Shalini Sankaranarayanan, Peter Sheerin, and
Dean Yang

The success of governments in combating corruption or delivering public services efficiently relies on positive and accurate identification of their citizens and the ability to cross-reference databases and information across government departments and agencies. This functioning is possible only if a national system that allows individuals to be uniquely identified exists, which is unfortunately not the case for many developing countries.

As a result, government programs work in isolation, each with its own database of beneficiaries, often not digitized, that cannot be merged with others. These databases typically contain data entry mistakes as well as duplicate and dead entries, causing substantial mistargeting of beneficiaries and pilferage in the delivery of public services.

In these places, the implementation of a unique identification system could dramatically improve the efficiency of the government as well as the market: credit and insurance markets could expand, as financial institutions would be more willing to provide services and the labor market would work better as employers could verify diplomas and certificates.

One way to establish the identity of individuals is through their biometrics. A biometric is a measure of identity based on a physiological (fingerprint, face, eye iris or retina) or behavioral (speech or signature) characteristic. It is an effective personal identifier because it is unique to and embodied in each person, so it cannot be forgotten, lost, or stolen like other conventional identification methods.

Biometric identification requires a device such as a camera or a scanner to capture the image, recording, or measurements of an individual's characteristics and computer hardware and software to extract, encode, store, and compare these characteristics. Because the process

is automated, biometric decision making is generally very fast, in most cases taking only a few seconds in real time (U.S. General Accounting Office 2002). Recent advancements in recognition technology coupled with increases in digital storage capacity and computer processing speed have made biometric technology feasible in many identification applications.

Criminal identification is far and away the oldest and most widespread large-scale identification use of biometric systems to identify suspects. The technology is also used to gain access to facilities and to authenticate individuals accessing computers and networks. For example, more than half the nuclear power plants in the United States employ biometric hand geometry systems (U.S. General Accounting Office 2002). Many federal agencies in the United States, such as the Office of Legislative Counsel of the U.S. House of Representatives, the Department of Defense, the Department of Energy, and the Department of Justice, are adopting biometrics recognition systems to protect confidential files and documents.

In addition, biometric technology has been used in developed countries to combat fraud. Leading banks and other financial institutions are piloting biometric recognition systems to authenticate ATM users and to combat credit and debit card fraud. Hand geometry and iris and facial recognition have been deployed at ATMs in North America, Europe, and Asia. Even firms that offer Internet shopping are considering biometric technologies to authorize various types of transactions.

Biometrics can also be used in monitoring and surveillance applications. For example, biometrics can be added to time and attendance processes to prevent hourly employees from punching time cards for their absent friends, which costs employers hundreds of millions of dollars annually. It is also being used by major casinos in North America to spot known cheaters.

Finally, biometric technologies are being used in countries as diverse as India, South Africa, the Philippines, and Spain as the basis for the national identification system, eliminating the need for multiple identification mechanisms. Biometrics can help determine whether applicants are already enrolled under a different identity and can thus prevent individuals from cheating public sector benefits programs by collecting benefits under multiple identities. With more accurate data on beneficiaries and allocation of benefits, government officials may have less room for diverting public resources (Atanassova et al., forthcoming; Bertrand et al. 2007; Niehaus and Sukhtankar 2009; Olken

2006; Reinikka and Svensson 2004). In India, the implementation of the biometrics-based Multipurpose National Identity Card will replace all other forms of identification and enable citizens to access public services and subsidies on food, energy, and education that now suffer from major pilferage (Chilukuri and Nandakumar 2009; The Hindu 2009; Planning Commission 2005).

In this chapter, we focus on the potential of biometric technology in improving the credit market in Malawi, a country without a unique identification system. In these places, identity fraud—the use of someone else's identity or a fictitious one—to gain access to services unavailable to the individual is rather common. Lenders tell anecdotes of past borrowers purposefully defaulting and trying to obtain a fresh loan from the same or another institution, and although such practices might be less common in developing countries because markets are less developed, one could imagine sick individuals without coverage using the insurance policy of their healthier friends or relatives. The response of lenders and insurance companies has been to restrict the supply of such services. Indeed, Africa and Malawi in particular have one of the lowest levels of credit penetration in the world.

In the case of credit, biometric technology can make the threat of future credit denial credible because it makes it easier for financial institutions to withhold new loans from past defaulters and to reward responsible past borrowers with increased credit. As a result, individuals might take out smaller loans or avoid borrowing altogether; borrowers might have greater incentives to ensure that production is successful, either by exerting more effort or choosing less risky projects, and—whenever production could cover the loan repayment—might be less likely to default intentionally or opportunistically.

Use of Biometric Technology in the Rural Credit Markets of Malawi

Giné, Goldberg, and Yang (forthcoming) implemented a field experiment with smallholder paprika farmers who applied in 2007 for an agricultural input loan from a government lender, MRFC. Farmers in the study were randomly allocated to either a control group or a treatment group in which each member had a fingerprint collected as part of the loan application. Both treatment and control groups were given a training session on the importance of credit history in ensuring future access to credit.

The authors chose fingerprint recognition over face, iris, or retina recognition because it is one of the cheapest, best known, and most widely used technologies. Fingerprinting technology extracts features from impressions made by the distinct ridges on the fingertips and has been commercially available since the early 1970s. There are more than seventy-five fingerprinting companies, which ensures a very competitive market. An image of the fingerprint was captured by a portable optical scanner attached to a laptop, then enhanced and converted into a template. Optical technology is the oldest and most widely used; it requires that the finger be placed on a coated platen that is typically made of hard plastic. In most devices, a charged coupled device converts the image, with dark ridges and light valleys, into a digital signal. The brightness is adjusted automatically or manually to produce a usable image.

During enhancement, "noise" caused by things such as dirt, cuts, scars, and creases or dry, wet, or worn fingerprints is reduced, and the definition of the ridges is enhanced. To minimize noise, farmers were instructed to wash their thumbs before placing them on the scanner, and the scanner was also cleaned after each impression.

The industry uses three main metrics to determine the accuracy of a given technology: failure to enroll rate (FTER), false match rate (FMR), and false nonmatch rate (FNMR). FTER measures the probability that a person will be unable to enroll primarily due to insufficiently distinctive biometric data. During the collection process in Malawi, only about 2 percent of the sample of the 1,600 fingerprinted farmers had the left thumbprint recorded, rather than the required right thumbprint, because the scanner failed to capture it. As it turns out, many farmers grow tobacco, which requires heavy use of fingers in the transplanting of seedling. Over the years, the fingerprint ridges become too worn to be captured.

A false match occurs when a system incorrectly matches an identity, and FMR is the probability of individuals being wrongly matched. They may occur because there is a high degree of similarity between two individuals' characteristics. False nonmatches occur because there is not a sufficiently strong similarity between an individual's enrollment and the recorded fingerprint.

The fingerprint identification software in Malawi uses an algorithm based on the extraction of minutiae points relating to breaks in the ridges of the fingertips. During demonstration sessions, everyone selected was correctly identified, so both the FMR and the FNMR rate were zero, albeit with a small sample.

The study shows that for the subgroup of farmers with the highest ex ante default risk, fingerprinting led to increases in the repayment rates of about 40 percent. By contrast, fingerprinting had no impact on repayment for farmers with low ex ante default risk. These higher repayment rates are due to fingerprinted borrowers requesting smaller loan sizes and devoting more land and other inputs to paprika.

A rough cost-benefit analysis of the pilot experiment suggests that the benefits from improved repayment greatly outweigh the costs of equipment and fingerprint collection.

The results suggest that biometric technology can improve repayment, but if these data are not shared with other lenders (or even other institutions such as utilities, durable goods stores, etc.), one cannot prevent defaulters from accessing a loan or services from these other institutions. A credit bureau that allows the sharing of credit information across institutions can help enhance the culture of repayment and facilitate access to finance nationwide. The key input into a credit bureau is accurate identification data, so biometrics can serve as the basis for such identification systems as the ones in Uganda and Nigeria (Mylenko 2007).

The following section describes the benefits of credit reporting as well as some of the arguments against it.

Credit Reporting

Credit information systems refer to databases of information on borrowers in a financial system. Information in these systems is available on individual consumers and/or firms and can be drawn from creditors as well as from public information sources (Miller 2003, 27).

As mentioned, financial markets are characterized by the problem of asymmetric information between borrowers and creditors. Creditors have less information on borrowers and their ability and willingness to make good on debt obligations than borrowers do themselves. Credit information sharing systems can reduce the extent of asymmetric information by making a borrower's complete credit history available to existing and potential lenders.

Historically, the concept of credit information sharing was pervasive between trade creditors and merchants, who exchanged negative lists of information on common debtors among their respective communities to reduce the risk of delinquencies and nonpayments. Lenders armed with this data avoided lending to high-risk individuals with

poor repayment histories, defaults, or bankruptcies. In more advanced economies, credit scoring and advanced quantitative models appeared on the banking scene in the mid-1900s and simplified the underwriting process by taking away the subjective judgment aspect that traditionally defined lending processes. The resulting automation of screening new applicants and credit granting processes enabled the lending community to widely expand its portfolios at reduced costs.

Although the objective of a credit information sharing system is to compile information from creditors and accessible public information sources on borrower credit histories, credit information sharing systems have developed in different parts of the world at different times, often for different reasons. In some countries, credit information databases reside within central banks and are primarily used for systemic risk monitoring of large exposures. In others—including the United States, where credit bureaus first emerged in the early 1900s—credit reporting has thrived in the private sector and involves the compilation of information on small-ticket consumer and small business loans.

Benefits of Credit Information Sharing

Over the years, much has been written about the benefits of credit information sharing. These can be broadly summarized in the following categories:

Advantages to Lenders

1. Lenders can make more informed credit granting decisions with information on borrower credit histories. This decision making lowers the risk associated with incorrect credit risk assessments and inappropriate approvals. Consequently, lenders can lower the level of nonperforming loans in their portfolios and maintain higher-quality loan portfolios (Jappelli and Pagano 1993; Padilla and Pagano 1997, 2000; Djankov, McLiesh, and Shleifer 2007; and McIntosh and Wydick 2007).

2. Lenders stand to benefit from operational efficiencies introduced by automated screening and lending processes. Luoto, McIntosh, and Wydick (2007) find that the introduction of a major Guatemalan microfinance lender's branches into a credit reporting system increased the number of applications processed per loan officer per month by 55 percent, implying huge operational efficiency gains to the lender. Of banks surveyed in thirty-four countries in 2001–2002 by the World Bank, approximately 50 percent indicated that they had witnessed a

decline in operating costs by more than 25 percent as a result of the use of credit registries.

3. McIntosh and Wydick (2005) show that credit bureaus can help microlenders identify pockets of overindebtedness among their clients, as they are aware of all other outstanding debt obligations of their clients, and consequently place limits on new credit. McIntosh, de Janvry, and Sadoulet (2006) show that credit information sharing can encourage consumers to meet their obligations when they know that noncompliance with obligations will be entered into a database and accessed by creditors and potentially by service suppliers.

4. The availability of credit information sharing systems may lead creditors to shift from collateral-based lending policies to more information-based lending policies, which can impact the cost of credit and service. Collateral-based lending, which is still very prevalent all over the world, is problematic in the case of borrowers without sufficient collateral, who risk being denied access to formal financial services. Collateral is also problematic for lenders, as the costs of collecting on collateral and the time and effort involved can be significant. Another issue with collateral-based lending is that the most acceptable forms of collateral continue to remain land and buildings, and therefore there is a mismatch in what can be used as collateral and the types of collateral firms typically hold. Safavian, Fleisig, and Steinbuks (2006) look at enterprise survey data on sixty low- and middle-income countries and find that although 22 percent of assets held by private firms are composed of land and building, the majority of firms' assets are of a movable nature, including machinery and receivables, which are not typically accepted as usable forms of collateral for bank loans.

Lending decisions that are facilitated by the use of credit information data can have significant cost savings for lenders. The resultant cost savings enables lenders to diversify their product offerings and develop products that are more targeted and suited to meeting the needs of their borrower clients (Jappelli and Pagano 2002).

Advantages to the Market and Growth in Private Credit

Empirical research shows that credit information sharing is critical for small businesses to lower financing constraints. According to a study by Love and Mylenko (2004) based on information from 5,000 firms in 51 countries, the percent of firms reporting financing constraints declined from 49 percent in countries without credit information

sharing systems to 27 percent in countries that did have such systems. The same study showed that the probability of a small firm obtaining a bank loan increased from 28 percent in countries without credit bureaus to 40 percent in those that did have credit bureaus.

Djankov, McLiesh, and Shleifer (2007, 5) find that better creditor rights and the presence of credit registries are associated with a higher ratio of private credit to GDP. Additionally, private credit to GDP ratios rise following improvements in creditor rights or the introduction of credit bureaus. Love and Mylenko (2004) and Jappelli and Pagano (2006) also find that higher lending is associated with the presence of credit registries (specifically, private credit registries). Turner and Varghese (2007) look at the use of credit information sharing in Latin America and the Caribbean and show that there are statistically significant increases in private sector lending (as a share of GDP) associated with increased rates of coverage by private bureaus. As one moves to full-file coverage, private sector lending can rise by sixty percentage points of GDP, all else being equal (Turner and Varghese 2007).

Advantages to the Borrower
Another benefit of instituting a credit reporting system is that it acts as a borrower disciplining device. Credit information sharing systems enable the creation of "reputational collateral." Borrowers understand that delinquencies or late payments detract from the value of such reputational collateral and have a greater incentive to meet their debtor obligations (Miller 2003; Padilla and Pagano 2000).

It is also in the interest of nondefaulting consumers to have their histories available so that creditors with whom they have relationships know that they are creditworthy. Borrowers whose information is reported on a credit reporting system can thus obtain lower rates and better conditions for various financial products.

Evidence against Information Sharing
The benefits of credit information sharing notwithstanding, researchers have also questioned the legitimacy of information sharing. Gehrig and Stenbacka (2001) find that information sharing in the financial services industry leads to relaxation of competitive practices as relationship lending becomes less important. In other words, information sharing weakens competition for the formation of banking relationships by serving as an institutional mechanism for redistribution of surplus from talented entrepreneurs to banks. The implied anticom-

petitive effects reduce the social returns of information sharing. It also leads to exclusion of creditworthy borrowers from the credit market. The authors argue that information sharing increases prices for borrowers without credit histories and undermines the importance of banking relationships.

Jappelli and Pagano (2002) find that lenders are generally averse to information sharing due to fear of competition and poaching of clients. They lose monopoly power developed with exclusive access to customer information. Unless there are specific provisions to protect lenders—as in the case of the United States, where traditionally rules limited branching across states—lenders would be hesitant to share information. In the United States, credit bureaus existed in the early 1920s. In Europe, on the other hand, banks were traditionally allowed to compete nationally, thus causing credit bureaus to develop later and on a smaller scale. If there is a dominant bank (as in the case of Italy), there can be hesitance to join a bureau. The Italian credit bureau, CRIF, was established in 1990 by small and medium-sized banks in the northeastern part of Italy. These banks had little to fear from others, due to the highly localized nature of markets. However, big nationwide banks joining the bureau over the years shows that the estimated benefits of joining it outweighed the costs (Jappelli and Pagano 2002).

Other factors determining the extent (or limit of) sharing of information between creditors are determined by borrower mobility (which is a big factor in the case of the European Union and the global economy at large) and population heterogeneity (Jappelli and Pagano 1993).

Some of the other drawbacks that have been identified are as follows: information sharing does not address some causes of over-indebtedness (unexpected life events, etc.); borrowers may not be happy with personal data being shared because of privacy concerns; higher risk of identity thefts; consumer associations are not convinced that credit data accurately reflects individual situations; and consumers may be excluded from services due to information sharing between financial institutions and service providers (DG Internal Markets and Services 2009).

Challenges notwithstanding, credit reporting systems are still recognized as effective tools for mitigating adverse selection and moral hazard problems in credit-related decision-making processes. The rapid growth in the number of credit reporting systems worldwide, both privately operated and central bank operated, is a testament to this effectiveness. The use of automated credit information tools and credit scoring applications enables creditors to acquire information

quickly and at a lower cost. In the old days of relationship lending, banks relied on the personal knowledge and relationships built with customers by loan officers to assess and process loans. In fact, this form of loan assessment and approval still exists in several parts of the world where credit bureaus do not exist or do not function as required.

As the world moves on to complex financial markets in which lenders are driven by competition to improve operating margins and increase profitability, tools that enhance automated screening procedures and the ability of lenders to make quicker lending decisions become invaluable. Credit information sharing systems form one set of such tools that can enhance the effectiveness of the lending sector. Over the past few years, the world has definitely seen an upward trend in the development of credit reporting systems worldwide, and their importance cannot be undermined.

Negative and Positive Credit Reporting

Negative information sharing includes simple statements of past defaults or arrears and is also known as black or negative data. Positive information sharing includes detailed reports on an applicant's assets and liabilities, guarantees, debt maturity structure, pattern of repayments, employment, family history, account balances, number of inquiries, debt ratios, on-time payments, credit limits, account type, loan type, lending institution, interest rates, public record data, and other information and is also known as full-file information sharing. Several OECD countries, including the United States, the United Kingdom, and most other European countries, permit positive reporting. The United States represents what may be the most open credit information sharing environment thanks to the Fair Credit Reporting Act, originally enacted in 1970, which set the extension of credit as a primary objective for lenders.

Empirical research (Barron and Staten 2003; Jappelli and Pagano 2000; Love and Mylenko 2004; Turner and Varghese 2007) indicates that positive information sharing can lead to a significant reduction in bad debt rates, a reduction in the likelihood that credit is extended to bad borrowers, and an increase in the number of better-quality customers becoming eligible for credit. Turner and colleagues (2009) explain how negative-only reporting fails to accurately depict any one individual's entire credit history because the reporting of negative data is contingent on the occurrence of a negative event, such as a delinquency or a late payment. For the majority of borrowers, however, such events are

rare. A data furnisher that provides negative-only information fails to include information about accounts that have never entered these conditions. Therefore, a credit file that is derived from negative-only information excludes all positive repayment behavior as well as evidence of the existence of accounts that are current. In a negative-only system, consumers who have no credit history are equivalent to consumers who have established credit accounts and have met their obligations to repay without an occurrence of delinquency, default, collection, or bankruptcy. This partial survey of a person's credit history provides a less robust prediction of credit risk and is a very poor indicator of credit capacity.

The major benefit of an increased level of information sharing is the ability to more accurately assess credit risk and capacity, which results in fewer incorrect credit granting decisions and lesser instances of borrower defaults. Turner and Varghese (2007) have also shown that full-file reporting allows for the extension of credit to traditionally excluded borrower groups, including women, racial minorities, low-income borrowers, and younger segments of the population.

In addition to positive and negative credit reporting, information sharing can be comprehensive across financial sectors such as banking, retail, credit cards, and insurance or can be limited to certain sectors as defined by data sharing regulations or by market outcomes. Comprehensive reporting across financial sectors has been empirically shown to increase access to credit, provide fairer access to credit, and decrease risk through fewer lender mistakes and fewer borrower defaults. The more inclusive and comprehensive the information a lender has on a borrower's complete financial and payment history, the better lending decisions can be made (Barron and Staten 2003; Love and Mylenko 2004; Turner et al. 2009).

Traditionally, private bureaus did not capture information on micro and small business segments of the economy; this job naturally fell beyond the purview of central bank–operated registries. Increasingly, however, as the benefits of comprehensive credit reporting are becoming known, credit information sharing systems have started collecting data from microfinance institutions and small- and medium-sized businesses to bolster their databases. Several developing market credit bureaus such as those in India, Turkey, and Saudi Arabia have been incorporating small business credit reporting in their business plans to avoid these mistakes (IFC 2006).

In addition to developing comprehensive credit information sharing systems, operators are looking at nontraditional or alternative sources of information to bolster information on clients with limited credit histories. An alternative lies in data collected from the services sector, such as utility payments and telecom bills, all of which are much more prevalent than financial accounts. PERC studies have shown that segments of the U.S. population that are least likely to be in the mainstream credit market such as ethnic minorities, lower-income households, the young, and the elderly benefitted most from the addition of nonfinancial information to their credit files (Turner et al. 2006, 2008).

Challenges in the Implementation of Biometric Systems

Despite the encouraging results from the pilot in Malawi and the success of biometric technology in controlled laboratory environments, there are still a few concerns and challenges when collecting and using biometrics in actual environments with plans for a major scaling-up to establish an identification system at a national level:

• *Not everyone can be enrolled in a fingerprint-based identification system.* Fingerprints can be unrecognizable due to cuts or burns or extreme weight gain or loss. In addition, older individuals may have poor fingerprints, and the operation of fingerprint readers may be jeopardized due to arthritis. In some areas recovering from years of conflict, individuals may lack fingers altogether. In other cases, skin pigmentation obfuscates the possibility of getting readable prints. In the most comprehensive study to test the process and customer attitude during the recording of biometric information, the UK Passport Service Trial reports an enrollment success rate of 100 percent for the 9,250 nondisabled participants and 96 percent for the 750 disabled participants. Interestingly, the enrollment rate is much lower among the black population. As already mentioned, in the Malawi pilot only 2 percent of the sample had another fingerprint recorded than the required one.

• *The accuracy of biometric technology remains to a large extent untested.* Biometric companies report very high accuracy rates from highly controlled trials that typically use artificially generated data. However, because the performance of a technology depends greatly on the context, trials using real-life data are far less impressive. For example, the UK Passport Service Trial reports that only 80 percent of the cases

could be correctly verified, younger individuals being more successful than older. According to a recent review of available systems, only a handful of products achieved an equal error rate of under 3 percent, and the performance of most was much worse.[1] Some experts have also warned about the use of fingerprinting as evidence in the judiciary process. Among the numerous cases of mistaken identification through fingerprinting, that of Brandon Mayfield is particularly indicative. Following the Madrid bombings of March 11, 2004, Spanish National Police managed to lift a fingerprint from an unexploded bomb. Three highly skilled FBI fingerprint experts declared that Oregon lawyer Brandon Mayfield's fingerprint was a match to the crime scene sample, describing the match as "absolutely incontrovertible" (Harden 2004). As a former U.S. soldier, Mayfield's fingerprints were in the national fingerprint system. Mayfield was imprisoned for two weeks. The fingerprint, however, was not his. Mayfield was himself a convert to Islam who had once represented a convicted Taliban sympathizer in a child custody dispute. So when Mayfield's personal information was combined with the crime scene evidence, the FBI was convinced of his culpability. The cautionary tale is that as the collection of biometric information increases, and as it moves from law enforcement to civilian applications, the error rate involved in its usage may significantly increase.

• *Individuals may have a negative attitude toward providing their biometrics.* People may be reluctant to place their fingers on the scanners due to hygiene concerns. More important, there is the widespread public perception that fingerprinting is linked to the criminal justice process. In conflict-affected countries stricken by ethnic infighting, individuals may refuse to provide biometrics for fear of persecution by authorities or others who gain illegal access to such biometric records. Finally, during the Parliamentary debates concerning the ID Cards Bill in the United Kingdom, 55 percent of respondents of a poll thought that the collection of biometric information was an infringement of civil liberties. In Malawi, the authors did not encounter any resistance from the farmers, perhaps because it was a very novel technology.

• *The cost of collecting biometrics can be high.* The estimates are sparse and detailed cost-benefit analyses have not been systematically conducted. However, the costs of using different types of biometric technology including basic fingerprinting techniques and voice and iris recognition software can be prohibitively expensive. In India, there are

legitimate concerns that the costs of rolling out biometric technology could mean a huge opportunity cost for the provision of social benefits for more than 700 million Indians living in poverty. In the UK, a critical report by several researchers at the London School of Economics (LSE) found that the government underestimated the implementation cost of the ID Cards Bill. The report suggests that the cost of the ten-year rollout would be between £10.6 billion and £19.2 billion, excluding public or private sector integration costs.

• *Biometric technology is not infallible.* Although biometric technology can be a big step toward combating issues of identity theft, fraud, and money-laundering efforts, it is essentially a technological application. As is the case with any other technology, it can be hacked or, infiltrated and runs the risk of allowing data to fall into the wrong hands. Because biometric technology is at present being piloted on a large scale only in some pockets of the world, legitimate concerns on privacy do arise. For example, it is possible to imagine that workers on the ID database could be corrupted, threatened, or blackmailed. After all, the perpetrators of 80 percent of all computer security lapses are not hackers but employees. Optical scanners that use minutiae-based and pattern-matching technologies such as the ones in the Malawi pilot have been tricked into accepting reactivated latent prints or artificial fingers with forged fingerprints. Latent fingerprints were reactivated by simply breathing on the sensor or by placing a water-filled plastic bag on the sensor's surface. Latent fingerprints were also reconstructed and authenticated by dusting the sensor's platen with commercially available graphite powder and lifting with adhesive tape. Artificial fingers made with candle wax or gelatin and the fingerprints of enrolled individuals have also successfully fooled the system (Thalheim, Krissler, and Ziegler 2002).

• *It is important that a common platform be used if biometrics data is merged with other datasets.* Biometric data is stored in formats that may be incompatible with the information systems of other government agencies, so an effort must be made for compatibility if the data have to serve as the basis for a national identification system.

Conclusions

Biometric technology presents a valuable data capture interface, but it is only a technology. As such, it cannot alone be the panacea for all

government and market inefficiencies. It even doesn't resolve by itself the challenges inherent in building identification systems, as other factors affect data quality. Even countries with national ID forms of some sort struggle constantly with compliance of data providers and with data information sharing laws, regulations, or simple industry codes of conduct.

Despite these concerns, biometric technology presents an exciting and innovative opportunity for increased access to financial markets and better public service delivery. Whether it can be scaled up effectively and be used to resolve identification and authentication issues remains to be seen.

Notes

We appreciate comments from David Rohrbach. This chapter was funded by the World Bank Research Committee, the Korean Trust Fund for ICT4D, USAID's BASIS AMA CRSP research facility, and the USAID Malawi country office.

1. The equal error rate (EER) refers to the point at which FMR equals FNMR.

References

Atanassova, Antonia, Marianne Bertrand, Sendhil Mullainathan, and Paul Niehaus. Forthcoming. Targeting with Agents. *American Economic Journal: Economic Policy*.

Barron, J. M., and Michael Staten. 2003. The Value of Comprehensive Credit Reports: Lessons from U.S. Experience. In *Credit Reporting Systems and the International Economy*, ed. M. Miller, 273–310. Cambridge, MA: MIT Press.

Bertrand, Marianne, Simeon Djankov, Rema Hanna, and Sendhil Mullainathan. 2007. Obtaining a Driver's License in India: An Experimental Approach to Studying Corruption. *Quarterly Journal of Economics* 122 (4): 1639–1676.

Chilukuri, Krishna K., and Vignesh Nandakumar. 2009. Unique ID for Indians—Boon or Bane? *Wall Street Journal*. http://online.wsj.com/article/SB125474159669964289.html.

DG Internal Markets and Services. 2009. Report of the Expert Group on Credit Histories. http://ec.europa.eu/internal_market/consultations/docs/2009/credit_histories/egch_report_en.pdf.

Djankov, S., C. McLiesh, and A. Shleifer. 2007. Private Credit in 129 Countries. *Journal of Financial Economics* 84 (2): 299–329.

Gehrig, Thomas, and Rune Stenbacka. 2001. Information Sharing in Banking: A Collusive Device? CEPR Discussion Paper no. 2911. London: Centre for Economic Policy Research. http://www.cepr.org/pubs/dps/DP2911.asp.

Giné, X., J. Goldberg, and D. Yang. Forthcoming. Credit Market Consequences of Improved Personal Identification: Field Experimental Evidence from Malawi. *American Economic Review*.

Harden, Blaine. 2004. FBI Faulter in Arrest of Ore. Lawyer. *Washington Post*, November 16, A02.

The Hindu. 2009. Unique ID Will Enable More Effective Public Delivery. Karan Thapar of CNN-IBN Interviews UIA Chairman Nandan Nilekani in Devil's Advocate. http://www.hindu.com/thehindu/nic/nandannilekani.htm.

International Finance Corporation (IFC). 2006. *Credit Bureau Knowledge Guide*. Washington, DC: IFC.

Jappelli, Tullio, and Marco Pagano. 1993. Information Sharing in Credit Markets. *Journal of Finance* 48:1693–1718.

Jappelli, Tullio, and Marco Pagano. 2000. Information Sharing in Credit Markets: A Survey. CSEF Working Papers 36, Centre for Studies in Economics and Finance (CSEF), University of Naples, Italy.

Jappelli, Tullio, and Marco Pagano. 2002. Information Sharing, Lending and Defaults: Cross-Country Evidence. *Journal of Banking & Finance* 26:2017–2045.

Jappelli, Tullio, and Marco Pagano. 2006. The Role and Effects of Credit Information Sharing. In *The Economics of Consumer Credit*, ed. Giuseppe Bertola, Richard Disney, and Charles Grant. 347–371. Cambridge, MA: MIT Press.

Love, I., and Nataliya Mylenko. 2004. Credit Reporting and Financing Constraints. World Bank Policy Research Working Paper No. 3142.

Luoto, J., C. McIntosh, and B. Wydick. 2007. Credit Information Systems in Less-Developed Countries: Recent History and a Test. *Economic Development and Cultural Change* 55 (2): 313–334.

McIntosh, C., A. de Janvry, and E. Sadoulet. 2006. How Increasing Competition Among Microfinance Institutions Affects Incumbent Lenders. *Economic Journal* 115:987–1004.

McIntosh, C. and Bruce Wydick. 2005. Competition and Microfinance. *Journal of Development Economics* 78:272–298.

McIntosh, C. and Bruce Wydick. 2007. Adverse Selection, Moral Hazard, and Credit Information Systems. November. http://stage-cpe.ucsd.edu/assets/002/6938.pdf.

Miller, Margaret, ed. 2003. *Credit Reporting Systems and the International Economy*. Cambridge, MA: MIT Press.

Mylenko, Natalia. 2007. Developing Credit Reporting in Africa: Opportunities and Challenges. *Access Finance* 19. World Bank.

Niehaus, Paul, and Sandip Sukhtankar. 2009. Corruption Dynamics: The Golden Goose Effect. BREAD working paper no. 223. Bureau for Research and Economic Analysis of Development, Duke University, Durham, NC.

Olken, Benjamin A. 2006. Corruption and the Costs of Redistribution: Micro Evidence from Indonesia. *Journal of Public Economics* 90 (4–5): 853–870.

Padilla, A. Jorge, and Marco Pagano. 1997. Endogenous Communication among Lenders and Entrepreneurial Incentives. *Review of Financial Studies* 10 (1): 205–236.

Padilla, A. Jorge, and Marco Pagano. 2000. Sharing Default Information as a Borrower Discipline Device. *European Economic Review* 44 (10): 1951–1980.

Planning Commission. 2005. *Performance Evaluation of Targeted Public Distribution System (TPDS)*. New Delhi: Government of India.

Reinikka, Ritva and Jakob Svensson. 2004. Local Capture: Evidence from a Central Government Transfer Program in Uganda. *The Quarterly Journal of Economics* 119 (2): 678–704.

Safavian, Mehnaz, Heywood Fleisig, and Jevgenijs Steinbuks. 2006. Unlocking Dead Capital. How Reforming Collateral Laws Improves Access to Finance. World Bank View Point Note No. 307. http://siteresources.worldbank.org/INTTOPCONF3/Resources/307Safavian_Fleisig_Steinbuks.pdf (accessed August 15, 2012).

Thalheim, Lisa, Jan Krissler, and Peter-Michael Ziegler. 2002. Body Check: Biometric Access Protection Devices and Their Programs Put to the Test, trans. Robert Smith. *c't Magazine* 11:114.

Turner, M., and R. Varghese. 2007. *Economic Impacts of Payment Reporting Participation in Latin America*. Chapel Hill: Political and Economic Research Council.

Turner, Michael, Robin Varghese, Alyssa Stewart Lee, and Patrick Walker. 2006. Give Credit Where Credit is Due: Increasing Access to Affordable Mainstream Credit Using Alternative Data. PERC. http://perc.net/files/downloads/alt_data.pdf (accessed August 15, 2012).

Turner, Michael, Robin Varghese, Alyssa Stewart Lee, and Patrick Walker. 2008. You Score, You Win: The Consequences of Giving Credit Where Credit Is Due. PERC Press. http://perc.net/files/downloads/web_layout-you-score.pdf (accessed August 15, 2012).

Turner, Michael, Robin Varghese, Patrick Walker, and Katrina Dusek. 2009. Optimal Consumer Credit Bureau Market Structure in Singapore: Theory and Evidence. PERC.

U.S. General Accounting Office. 2002. Using Biometrics for Border Security. Washington, DC.

14 Accessing Credit from Banks, Microfinance Institutions, and Informal Groups: What Is the Role of Social Capital?

Anni Heikkilä, Panu Kalmi, and
Olli-Pekka Ruuskanen

Broadening financial sector outreach in the developing world is an important policy objective and topic for academic research.[1] Despite the relevance of the topic, empirical studies on financial sector outreach have been limited, due to difficulties in data collection. This problem has been recognized, and recent years have witnessed several parallel exercises to collect data on financial sector breadth (for a review, see Honohan 2008). Recent cross-country studies on financial sector outreach utilize both data provided by bank regulators and surveys of households or individuals (e.g., Beck, Demirgüç-Kunt, and Martinez Peria 2007; Claessens 2006; Honohan 2008). Most microlevel studies on financial sector outreach in developing countries utilize financial access or usage questions that are embedded within general household surveys or specialized financial access surveys (recent work includes, amongst others, Aktaruzzaman 2009; Al-Hussainy et al. 2008, including both micro and cross-country models; Basu and Srivastava 2005; Cull and Scott 2009; Heikkilä, Kalmi, and Ruuskanen 2009; Johnston and Morduch 2008; Kumar et al. 2005).

Guiso, Sapienza, and Zingales (2004), as well as Calderon, Chong, and Galindo (2002) provide evidence that social capital plays an important role in the determination of financial development.[2] Guiso, Sapienza, and Zingales (2004) study the importance of social capital for households' use of checks, investment in cash and in stock, access to institutional credit, and use of informal credit. They carry out their study in a developed country context, using data from Italy. Calderon, Chong, and Galindo (2002) examine links between trust and various measures of financial development in a cross-country analysis. From the development economics perspective, a limitation of the study of Calderon, Chong, and Galindo (2002) is that they exclude all the least developed countries (LDCs) from their analysis.

So far, the literature on financial access in developing countries has not considered social capital among the determinants of financial access. Lack of research on the role of social capital for financial access is somewhat surprising, given the importance of social capital in the development literature (e.g., Woolcock and Narayan 2000). Social capital has a prominent role in the microfinance literature; however, this literature typically examines the effect of social capital (or social ties) on repayment performance in joint-liability lending (recent work includes, among others, Ahlin and Townsend 2007; Cassar, Crowley, and Wydick 2007; Karlan 2007; Van Bastelaer and Leathers 2006). Perhaps the major reason for the lack of attention to the role of social capital for access to finance is the scarcity of datasets containing information on both social capital and financial access. FinScope Uganda 2006 data are an exception, as they include information on both access to credit from various types of financial institutions and respondents' social capital.

In this chapter, we examine how social capital affects access to credit from different types of financial institutions in Uganda. To the best of our knowledge, this chapter and Heikkilä, Kalmi, and Ruuskanen 2009 are the first empirical studies that consider the impact of social capital on access to credit in a developing country setting. Like Heikkilä, Kalmi, and Ruuskanen (2009), we include both individual and aggregate measures of social capital in our analysis. We define individual social capital as "the quantity and quality of an individual's social connections." These connections are valuable because they allow individuals to reap economic and noneconomic returns from interactions with others (Glaeser, Laibson, and Sacerdote 2002). As does much of economics literature (e.g., Knack and Keefer 1997; La Porta et al. 1997), we use generalized trust as our measure of aggregate social capital. By "generalized trust," we mean general interpersonal trust between people, not merely trust between people who are socially close to each other. Our measure of access to credit compares those who have taken loans from a certain type of financial institution to those who have taken loans only from family members, friends, shops, private moneylenders, or other sources that are not financial institutions.[3]

In the empirical analysis of this chapter, we examine the probability that an individual has accessed loans from formal, semiformal, or informal financial institutions and how the level of social capital influences his or her access to credit from different sources. We find that individual social capital is positively associated with access to credit from

informal financial groups when compared to formal institutions or other sources of credit that are not financial institutions. This finding gives support to our expectation of the importance of the members' individual social capital for the lending activities of informal groups. Individual social capital has a positive association also with access to semiformal institutions when compared to sources of credit that are not financial institutions. General interpersonal trust that prevails in the region has a positive association with access to credit from formal institutions but remains insignificant for semiformal institutions and informal groups. This finding is consistent with our expectation that general interpersonal trust matters most for formal financial institutions, as their lending business relies more on impersonal economic exchange than the lending business of other types of financial intermediaries.

How Does Social Capital Affect Access to Credit?

Social capital is a popular research topic in many social sciences, despite the prevailing ambiguity in the content of the term itself. In the large body of research inspired by the influential work of Putnam (1993, 2000), social capital is understood as a community-level attribute. However, several authors—including Bourdieu (1986); Glaeser, Laibson and Sacerdote (2002); and Portes (1998)—define social capital at the level of individuals. Glaeser, Laibson and Sacerdote (2002) show that the formation of social capital can be analyzed using a microeconomic model of optimal individual investment decisions. Even prior to this contribution, Glaeser et al. (2000) concluded that social capital is an individual-level variable that can be studied with the tools of price theory. In this chapter, we acknowledge that social capital can be defined both at the level of individuals and at the aggregate (community) level. As we explain later in this chapter, both individuals' social connections and the generalized trust that prevails in the region are likely to matter for access to credit from different financial institutions, and therefore we include both types of social capital measures in our analysis.[4]

In developing countries such as Uganda, borrowers typically cannot pledge sufficient physical collateral to secure their loans, so financial institutions need other ways to assess and ensure their clients' creditworthiness and incentives to pay back the borrowed money. Even when sufficient physical collateral is available, weak judicial systems

and hence difficulties and costs related to contract enforcement are likely to increase financial institutions' need to make sure that their borrowers are trustworthy clients.[5] Individual social capital can serve as such a nonmonetary signal for borrowers' creditworthiness.

The importance and value of individual-level social capital is likely to vary across different contexts. As highlighted by Ghatak and Guinnane (1999) and Van Bastelaer (2000), many microfinance institutions rely heavily on social capital and especially on the ability to enforce social sanctions against borrowers who do not repay their loans. On the other hand, there are reasons why social capital is likely to be even more important for informal groups and a lot less important for commercial banks. We argue that both the need and ability of different institutions to screen borrowers based on their social capital differ, and therefore we expect the importance of individual social capital to credit access to vary across institutions.

Informal financial groups, such as rotating savings and credit associations, represent an extreme case in their reliance on borrowers' individual social capital. They typically operate in a very limited geographical area, and the members share a common bond and know each other well. Therefore, the ability to join such groups—and thus access credit—is likely to be related to individual social capital, that is, the extent and quality of social networks that the potential member possesses. Informal groups are typically not registered enterprises; hence their contracts may not be legally enforceable, and they need to depend almost entirely on the ability to impose social sanctions. This view emphasizes the importance of social capital in the member selection stage for these institutions.

Social capital is also important for semiformal financial institutions. Microfinance institutions practicing group lending are often based on close social ties among group members. Even though the lending institutions may not have much information about the borrower characteristics, they can elicit this information through the design of groups. Often the borrowers form the groups themselves, in which case a borrower candidate with a lot of individual social capital is more likely than a candidate with low social capital to be able to join a borrowing group.[6] Microfinance institutions that practice individual lending, as well as credit cooperatives, often require two cosigners for loans. Therefore, a borrower candidate with a large number of trusted social contacts is more likely than a less well connected candidate to get the required guarantors for his or her loan and thus access credit. Semifor-

mal financial institutions can rely on legal sanctions to some extent, and they often also demand some physical collateral from their borrowers. However, enforcing their contracts through legal proceedings is costly when the overall legal enforcement is poor, which also justifies the importance of social capital and the threat of social sanctions for these institutions.

In contrast, formal financial institutions such as commercial banks are more likely to be able to rely on physical collateral requirements as a borrower screening device rather than utilizing less tangible social connections among the borrowers (or social connections between the loan officer and the loan applicant, if no guarantors are required).[7] By offering better terms and larger loans than other lenders, formal financial institutions can select clients who are likely to be able to offer sufficient physical collateral. It would probably be hard for formal institutions to screen their borrowers based on individual social capital because these institutions usually have branches in large towns where social networks are more dispersed and they typically have more customers per branch than less formal financial institutions. Formal financial institutions may also be in the best position to enforce their contracts through courts, even though they are also likely to suffer from the general inefficiency of the judicial processes in a country like Uganda.

Summing up, the viability of informal institutions' lending activities relies to a great extent on social ties and trust among the borrowers, so these institutions are likely to screen their members thoroughly based on individual social capital. Semiformal institutions are also likely to screen their borrowers based on individual social capital. However, semiformal institutions can often require some physical collateral from their borrowers, and they are able to enforce their claims in courts (at least to some extent), so they have also recourses other than social sanctions available. Formal financial institutions are most likely to get full collateral protection for their loans, and due to their urban operating environment, it would also be hard for them to rely on social capital in their borrower selection process. Thus, we expect individual social capital of borrowers to be most important for informal financial groups and least important for formal institutions, with semiformal institutions falling between these two extremes.

Turning to general interpersonal trust, the framework of Guiso, Sapienza, and Zingales (2004) provides a basis for our hypothesis on the effect of generalized trust on access to credit from financial institutions. They argue that due to the trust-intensive nature of the lending

business, higher social capital that can be characterized by higher generalized trust prevailing in the area positively affects the supply of loans to households. They find support for this hypothesis in their empirical estimations. Their measures of social capital are voter turnout and blood donation at the province level and the World Values Survey measure of general interpersonal trust at the regional level. These measures of social capital are related to the willingness to make anonymous contributions to the common good and general trust in people, rather than trusting just friends and family. One way of interpreting the results of Guiso, Sapienza, and Zingales is that the requirement of general interpersonal trust in lending may be more pronounced when the relationship between the lender and the borrower is more anonymous.

The argument of the importance of generalized trust for more anonymous lending business is consistent with the findings of La Porta et al. (1997), which indicate that higher generalized trust facilitates impersonal economic exchange. Considering the typology of financial institutions discussed previously, we may interpret these results as predicting that generalized trust would be especially important for the viability of formal financial institutions that rely least on their borrowers' individual social capital. Semiformal institutions and informal groups are likely to rely on social networks and personal relationships in their borrower screening, so we would assume that generalized trust remains a smaller role for these institutions.

Financial Sector in Uganda

Uganda has enjoyed steady economic growth during its twenty-three years of postconflict recovery. However, the country is still predominately rural, with 70 percent of the labor force engaged in farming and an urbanization rate of merely 15 percent, one of the lowest in Africa. The poverty rate is also relatively high at 31 percent (Uganda Bureau of Statistics 2009). However, the country has a relatively diverse financial sector considering its low overall level of development, with a number of different types of financial institutions operating in the country. Figure 14.1 depicts different financial institution and group types and other sources of credit used in Uganda.

Formal financial institutions are regulated by the Bank of Uganda. There are twenty-two commercial banks (Tier 1), three credit institutions (Tier 2), and three microfinance deposit-taking institutions (Tier

Formal institutions		Semiformal institutions		Informal groups/ organizations	
Commercial banks, credit institutions	Microfinance deposit-taking institutions (MDIs)	Credit-only microfinance institutions (MFIs)	Savings and credit cooperatives (SACCOs)	Groups, e.g., ROSCAs, ASCAs, savings clubs	Loans taken from friends, relatives, employer, shops, moneylenders, etc.

Regulated by Bank of Uganda

Figure 14.1
Financial institutions and other sources of credit used in Uganda. *Source:* FinScope
Uganda 2006

3) in the country. Semiformal financial institutions are licensed or registered under an Act of Parliament (Tier 4) but are not supervised by the Bank of Uganda. This category is made up of savings and credit cooperatives (SACCOs) and credit-only microfinance institutions, which are allowed to make loans but not to collect deposits for intermediation.[8] It has been estimated that there are more than 1,300 such institutions operating in Uganda (Kavuma 2009).

Informal financial groups and organizations consist of all those groups that are not under the supervision of the Bank of Uganda and are not registered under Acts or Statutes enacted by the Parliament of Uganda. They fall into several categories. Most of these are voluntary groups of members from the same location, which usually meet regularly. Rotating savings and credit associations (ROSCAs), accumulating savings and credit associations (ASCAs), and savings clubs are examples of informal financial groups. Because they are informal, it is difficult to estimate how many are operating in the country. However, the FinScope 2006 survey indicates that over a fifth of the adult population belongs to these informal groups (Steadman Group 2007).

An influx of foreign banks increased the competition in the formal banking sector, which resulted in a rapid expansion of banking networks in the country, with the number of bank branches growing to 332 by the end of March 2009. However, most of the branches are still concentrated in capital or district centers, offering the rural population only limited access to the banking network (Bank of Uganda 2009).

Despite recent developments, the Ugandan banking system is still less developed than that of neighboring Tanzania and Kenya in terms of private credit to GDP (which was 5 percent in Uganda in 2004). Uganda also has a very low loan-deposit ratio, suggesting that the intermediation of deposits into private sector loans is limited. Also, the

contractual and informational framework is challenging for the Ugandan banks, which results in high lending costs for both borrowers and lenders (Beck and Hesse 2009).

An indication of the challenges mentioned thus far is the modest outreach of the lending sector in Uganda. According to the FinScope survey of 2006, only 7 percent of Ugandan adults who borrow have loans from formal institutions, 7 percent from semiformal institutions and 11 percent from informal groups. This finding is in contrast to the apparent need for credit, which is indicated by the great majority of Ugandan borrowers having a loan exclusively from a source that is not a financial institution, such as family, friends, private moneylenders, or shops (Steadman Group 2007).

Data

Measure of Access to Credit from Different Sources
Our dependent variable, *loans from different sources*, indicates the distribution of Ugandan borrowers according to the formality of the lender. The source of this variable is the FinScope Uganda 2006 survey, which is a nationally representative, individual-level, cross-sectional survey of access, demand, and use of financial services in Uganda.[9] The survey was conducted in October–November 2006 in all the fifty-six districts of Uganda that were covered during the 2002 census. Every Ugandan aged 18 and over had an equal chance of ending up in the survey sample. The final sample size was 2,959 people (Steadman Group 2007.)

The dependent variable has four categories: borrowers of formal financial institutions; borrowers of semiformal institutions; borrowers of informal groups/organizations; and borrowers who have taken loans only from family members, friends, shops, employer, private moneylenders, or other such sources that are not financial institutions. The last category includes borrowers who have applied for loans from different types of institutions and been turned down as well as borrowers who have never tried to get loans from institutions (maybe because they expect that the application would be turned down or because they don't need loans from institutions). We made the categories of the dependent variable mutually exclusive. Hence, in cases in which the respondent reports that he or she has taken loans from several sources, we have counted only the most formal source of credit used.[10]

We include both current and past loans in our dependent variable for two reasons. First, consumer loans in developing countries are often

small and have a short payback period, so including only current borrowers would reduce the number of borrower observations on questionable grounds (i.e., including those currently paying back their loans but excluding those who happen to have finished paying theirs a short time ago). Second, FinScope questions on the amount of loans taken from different lenders ask about the "most recent loan you have taken," which means that the loan may no longer be effective.

The frequency distribution of the dependent variable is given in table 14.1. The total number of observations is 1,128. The base category of the variable, *loans from family, shops, moneylenders*, is clearly the largest category, including 64.5 percent of the observations. The category *loans from formal institutions* has more observations (15.9 percent) than *loans from semiformal institutions* (8.5 percent) and *loans from informal groups/organizations* (11.2 percent) categories. Because our variable counts only the most formal loan taken for each respondent, the share of borrowers from formal institutions is somewhat exaggerated compared to all other borrower categories.

Measures of Social Capital and Other Independent Variables

Our *individual social capital* variable is based on the following attitudinal statement in the FinScope data: "I have many stable friendships and we support and trust each other." Thus our individual social capital variable measures the quantity and quality of the respondent's social connections and also includes elements of trust within the network of friends.[11] The definition of "individual social capital" we use in this study is similar to the one we use in Heikkilä, Kalmi, and Ruuskanen 2009, and it is also in line with much of the previous literature that views social capital as an individual-level characteristic (e.g., Glaeser, Laibson, and Sacerdote 2002; Karlan 2005).

Our *generalized trust* variable is based on the World Values Survey (WVS) question "Generally speaking, would you say that most people can be trusted or that you need to be very careful in dealing with people?" The trust scores indicate the percentage of respondents who state that "most people can be trusted." The WVS survey was carried out in sixteen districts of Uganda in 2001.[12] These sixteen districts cover 46 percent of the FinScope sample population; for the remaining 54 percent, we calculated a province-level average of the available district-level scores. We also use the WVS trust scores—that is, generalized trust—as our measure of aggregate social capital in Heikkilä, Kalmi, and Ruuskanen 2009.

Table 14.1
Summary statistics of the dependent variable

	Frequency	Percent	Cumulative
Loans from formal institutions	179	15.9	15.9
Loans from semiformal institutions	96	8.5	24.4
Loans from informal groups/organizations	126	11.2	35.6
Loans from family, shops, moneylenders	727	64.5	100.0
Total	**1128**	**100**	

Table 14.2 presents the summary statistics of social capital and other independent variables. All our individual- and household-level control variables are taken from the FinScope survey (for a more detailed description of the variables, see the table A14.1). In table 14.3, we compare the means of individual social capital and generalized trust in different borrower categories (according to the dependent variable). Informal groups' borrowers appear to have clearly higher individual social capital than that of any other borrower category, and the difference is statistically significant in all comparisons. Individual social capital of formal and semiformal institutions' borrowers is almost at the same level, and it is significantly higher in both of them compared to borrowers who have taken loans from sources that are not financial institutions. Generalized trust is higher for formal institutions' borrowers than for any other borrower category; however, the difference is (weakly) significant only when formal institutions' borrowers are compared to borrowers who have taken loans from sources that are not financial institutions.

Empirical Results

In this section, we present estimation results of a multinomial logit model. Our dependent variable in table 14.4, *loans from different sources*, has four categories: (1) includes borrowers of formal institutions, (2) borrowers of semiformal institutions, (3) borrowers of informal groups/ organizations, and (4) borrowers who have taken loans only from sources that are not financial institutions. Category 4 is the base category in the estimation. We regress the dependent variable on the level of individual social capital; generalized trust; and several individual, household-level, and regional control variables. The reported coefficients in different columns of table 14.4 indicate the change in the log

Table 14.2
Summary statistics of independent variables

Variable	Observations	Mean	Standard deviation	Minimum	Maximum
Individual social capital	1128	0.73	0.45	0	1
Generalized trust	1128	7.82	2.28	2.7	16.4
Female	1128	0.53	0.50	0	1
Married	1128	0.63	0.48	0	1
Age	1128	35.04	13.94	18	95
Household head	1128	0.58	0.49	0	1
Self-employed	1128	0.40	0.49	0	1
Paid employment	1128	0.17	0.38	0	1
Agricultural production	1128	0.32	0.47	0	1
Primary education	1128	0.50	0.50	0	1
Secondary education or more	1128	0.36	0.48	0	1
Literate	1128	0.67	0.47	0	1
Wealth	1128	1.35	0.89	0	3
Rural	1128	0.70	0.46	0	1

Table 14.3
Social capital of borrowers, according to the formality of the lender

Borrower category	Variable	Obs.	Mean	Standard deviation	Min	Max
Loans from formal institutions	Individual social capital	179	0.78	0.42	0	1
	Generalized trust	179	8.15	2.63	2.7	16.4
Loans from semiformal institutions	Individual social capital	96	0.79	0.41	0	1
	Generalized trust	96	7.59	2.67	2.7	16.4
Loans from informal groups/ organizations	Individual social capital	126	0.91	0.28	0	1
	Generalized trust	126	7.71	2.40	2.7	15.4
Loans from family, shops, moneylenders	Individual social capital	727	0.67	0.47	0	1
	Generalized trust	727	7.78	2.11	2.7	16.4

Table 14.4
Loans from different sources (multinomial logit estimates)

	Formal institutions	Semiformal institutions	Informal groups/ organizations
Individual social capital	0.3260	0.4533*	1.3579***
	(0.2314)	(0.2674)	(0.3790)
Generalized trust	0.1040*	0.0375	0.0291
	(0.0536)	(0.0658)	(0.0903)
Female	−0.0998	0.1319	−0.1229
	(0.2770)	(0.2492)	(0.3256)
Married	−0.0376	0.1432	0.1445
	(0.2748)	(0.3510)	(0.2348)
Age	0.2013***	0.2359***	0.1082**
	(0.0324)	(0.0730)	(0.0456)
Age squared	−0.0017***	−0.0025***	−0.0009**
	(0.0004)	(0.0009)	(0.0005)
Household head	−0.4571	−0.2686	−0.6700**
	(0.3154)	(0.3469)	(0.3238)
Self-employed	0.3518	0.0536	0.4099
	(0.4421)	(0.4417)	(0.4315)
Paid employment	−0.1625	−0.7396	0.1186
	(0.5262)	(0.6200)	(0.6085)
Agricultural production	−1.3692***	−0.6697	−0.2755
	(0.4704)	(0.5048)	(0.4711)
Primary education	0.8146	0.9289	0.2035
	(0.5621)	(0.6386)	(0.3459)
Secondary education or more	1.7984***	0.5025	0.3010
	(0.5334)	(0.6750)	(0.4869)
Literate	0.9815***	0.8733***	0.3023
	(0.3646)	(0.3271)	(0.3823)
Wealth quintile 3	1.1522***	−0.1985	0.3443
	(0.3724)	(0.4013)	(0.2960)
Wealth quintile 4	1.0891***	0.1951	−0.2001
	(0.4059)	(0.3839)	(0.4162)
Wealth quintile 5	1.7558***	−0.2937	−0.5487
	(0.4610)	(0.5312)	(0.6101)
Rural	−0.1185	0.3441	0.0346
	(0.2164)	(0.3290)	(0.3244)
Baseline probabilities	0.0071	0.0179	0.0262

Notes: Number of observations in the estimation is 1,128. The dependent variable takes value 1 if the respondent has loans from formal financial institutions, 2 if loans from semiformal institutions, 3 if loans from informal groups/organizations, and 4 if loans from noninstitutional sources such as family members, shops, moneylenders. Category 4 is the base category. Baseline probabilities are calculated keeping all dummy variables at value 0 and continuous variables at their sample means. For a description of all the other variables, see the appendix. Controls also include five provincial dummies. The standard errors reported in parentheses are corrected for the potential clustering of the residual at the district level.
*significant at the 10 percent level; **significant at the 5 percent level; ***significant at the 1 percent level.

of the odds ratio, which is the ratio of the probabilities P(loans from XX institution)/P(loans from noninstitutional sources), when the independent variable changes by one unit. However, to facilitate the interpretation of the main results, we calculate odds ratios of getting loans from XX institution compared to loans from noninstitutional sources by exponentiating the reported coefficients. In table 14.4, we also report the baseline probabilities that are calculated for a hypothetical observation for which all dummy variables are set to 0 and continuous variables at their sample mean values. The baseline probability for the omitted category (loans from sources other than financial institutions) is 0.949.

Comparing access to credit from different financial institutions versus noninstitutional sources of credit, we find that individual social capital is most clearly associated with access to credit from informal groups/organizations. The coefficient of individual social capital is positive and significant at the 1 percent level in the "Informal groups/organizations" column of table 14.4. For instance, when the odds ratio for our hypothetical baseline observation for having credit from informal groups rather than credit from noninstitutional sources is only 0.028, the odds ratio increases to 0.107 when individual social capital increases from 0 to 1; that is, the odds ratio increases almost fourfold from its baseline value. The positive coefficient of individual social capital is (weakly) significant at the 10 percent level in the "Semiformal institutions" column. The coefficient indicates an increase in the odds ratio of almost 60 percent when individual social capital increases from 0 to 1. The coefficient of individual social capital in the "Formal institutions" column is not significant. We also tried a specification where the base category was formal institutions and found that individual social capital has a positive and significant coefficient in the informal groups category but not in the comparison between semiformal and formal financial institutions. Thus, the strongest result from these estimations is that individual social capital is important for accessing credit from informal groups or organizations when compared with formal institutions or sources of credit other than financial institutions.

In the second row of table 14.4, we report the results concerning generalized trust. The only statistically significant result here is in the "Formal institutions" column, where the generalized trust coefficient is (weakly) statistically significant at the 10 percent level. This finding is consistent with our expectation that general interpersonal trust would matter mostly for formal financial institutions, as they rely more

on impersonal economic exchange than other types of financial inter-
mediaries. An increase in the trust score from its sample mean 7.82 by
one unit to 8.82 would increase the odds of having formal credit com-
pared to noninstitutional credit by around 11 percent. In their study,
Guiso, Sapienza, and Zingales (2004) found that higher trust measured
by the WVS trust score has a positive—yet not statistically significant—
effect on having access to credit from a financial institution. Guiso,
Sapienza, and Zingales did not distinguish between loans from differ-
ent types of financial institutions, so we cannot directly compare their
result to ours.

We briefly comment on the results concerning our control variables.
Age has a positive and nonlinear relationship with access to credit from
all types of financial institutions (age and its square are significant in
all columns of table 14.4). Being employed in agricultural production
is associated with reduced access to credit from formal financial institu-
tions. Secondary education is associated with improved access to loans
from formal financial institutions. Also, increased household wealth is
associated with better access to loans from formal financial institutions,
which is consistent with the argument that wealthier people can use
part of their wealth as collateral for their loans, and that insufficient
wealth creates a barrier for access to loans from the formal financial
sector.

Conclusions

This chapter examined the impact of individual social capital and
general interpersonal trust on access to credit from different types of
financial institutions in Uganda. We extended the analysis of Heikkilä,
Kalmi, and Ruuskanen (2009) to consider differences between various
financial institution types when examining the impact of social capital
on access to credit in a developing country setting. Our empirical
results provide support for our expectation that individual social
capital of borrowers and generalized trust prevailing in the region play
different roles in the lending business of different types of institutions.
We found a positive and significant association between the individual
social capital of the borrower and his or her access to loans from infor-
mal financial groups. A positive but weaker association was also found
between individual social capital and access to semiformal institutions'
loans. The only significant result we got with the generalized trust

variable is its positive association with access to credit from formal financial institutions.

The significance of individual social capital for access to credit from informal groups highlights the extent to which such informal organizations need to rely on social cohesion and trust between the group members. It is natural that these unregulated groups and organizations must be selective regarding whom they accept as their members, as social sanctions are the only effective way for them to punish nonperformers. The lending business of semiformal institutions does not rely as heavily on borrowers' common bond as does the lending of informal groups, because semiformal institutions typically also require some physical collateral from the borrowers. However, the personal guarantor system that is often used in semiformal institutions makes the individual social capital of the borrowers important also for these institutions. In formal financial institutions, the lending business is likely to be more impersonal in nature. This impersonal nature may be partly due to their reliance on physical collateral and legal sanctions and partly due to their urban operating environment, where it is much harder for loan officers to know their clients based on overlapping social networks. Hence it is not surprising that generalized trust is more important for the lending business of formal institutions compared to less formal institutions, which rely on social ties and trust within personal networks.

Potentially the most interesting policy implications of this study are related to the future of different types of financial institutions and the role of social capital in broadening access to finance. Borrowers' individual social capital is likely to be at least a partial substitute for physical capital in the lending business of semiformal and informal financial institutions; thus, individual social capital may improve access to credit in circumstances in which formal institutions would be unwilling to operate. However, if semiformal and informal financial institutions purposefully select individuals with high social capital as their clients, individuals with weaker social connections may find it difficult to join these institutions. Low levels of individual social capital may even slow down the growth of more informal institutions in certain areas. Even if formal financial institutions apply strict selection criteria that many borrowers cannot currently meet, such as regular incomes or valuable collateral, they may still have a future role in broadening access to credit for people with weaker social connections.

Appendix

Table A14.1
Variable descriptions and data sources

Variable	Description
Loans from different sources	Categorical variable based on the following questions in the FinScope Uganda 2006 survey: Do you currently have loans from XX institution? If not currently, have you previously had loans from XX institution? For the most recent loan from XX type of institution, what was the amount borrowed? Category (1) includes current and previous borrowers of formal institutions, (2) current and previous borrowers of semiformal institutions, (3) current and previous borrowers of informal groups/organizations, and (4) borrowers who have only taken loans from sources that are not financial institutions. The categories are mutually exclusive, hence only the most formal source of loans used is taken into account for each respondent.
Individual social capital	Indicator variable based on responses to the following statement in the FinScope Uganda 2006 survey: "I have many stable friendships and we support and trust each other."
Generalized trust	An index of the level of trust based on the World Values Survey for Uganda, carried out in 2001. The sample size was 1,002 and the survey was conducted in sixteen districts of Uganda. The question asked from the respondents was: "Generally speaking, would you say that most people can be trusted or that you need to be very careful in dealing with people? 1 = Most people can be trusted, 2 = Need to be very careful." The trust score is calculated as the percentage of people who answer "most people can be trusted."
Female	Indicator variable equal to one if the FinScope Uganda 2006 survey respondent is female.
Married	Indicator variable equal to one if the FinScope Uganda 2006 survey respondent is married.
Age	Respondent's age in the FinScope Uganda 2006 survey.
Household head	Indicator variable equal to one if the FinScope Uganda 2006 survey respondent is household head.
Self-employed	Indicator variable equal to one if the FinScope Uganda 2006 survey respondent is self-employed. "Self-employed" equals one for people who have responded that their main source of income is one of the following: running own business, trading in agricultural produce bought from others, trading in livestock products bought from others, trading in fish bought from others.
Paid employment	Indicator variable equal to one if the FinScope Uganda 2006 survey respondent is working for somebody else. "Paid employment" equals one for people who have responded that their main source of income is one of the following: working on other people's farms, working in other people's homes doing domestic work, working for an individual in a private business, employed in the formal sector like in an office.

Table A14.1
(continued)

Variable	Description
Agricultural production	Indicator variable equal to one if the FinScope Uganda 2006 survey respondent is employed in agricultural production. "Agricultural production" equals one for people who have responded that their main source of income is one of the following: sell produce from own farm (cash crops or food crops), sell own livestock, sell products from own livestock, fishing.
Primary education	Indicator variable equal to one if the FinScope Uganda 2006 survey respondent has gone to primary school (has not necessarily completed it) but has no higher level of education.
Secondary education or more	Indicator variable equal to one if the FinScope Uganda 2006 survey respondent has gone to secondary school (has not necessarily completed it) or has higher level of education than secondary school.
Literate	Indicator variable equal to one if the FinScope Uganda 2006 survey respondent can both read and write.
Wealth	Categorical variable indicating household wealth of the FinScope Uganda 2006 survey respondents, based on the wealth index definition of the Uganda Bureau of Statistics. The wealth index includes variables related housing and household characteristics, e.g. materials used for construction of the housing unit and nutrition of the household members. FinScope Uganda 2006 data includes wealth quintiles, based on which we have formulated the wealth indicator variable: 0 = first and second wealth quintiles (grouped due to small number of observations in the first quintile), 1 = third wealth quintile, 2 = fourth wealth quintile, 3 = fifth wealth quintile.
Rural	Indicator variable equal to one if the FinScope Uganda 2006 survey respondent lives in a rural area.
Province	Categorical variable indicating the province where the FinScope Uganda 2006 survey respondent lives: 1 = Central Kampala, 2 = Other Central Regions, 3 = Eastern Uganda, 4 = Northern Uganda, 5 = Western Uganda.

Notes

We thank Karen Ellis, Pertti Haaparanta, Ari Hyytinen, Derek Jones, Antti Kauhanen, Päivi Kankaanranta, and Otto Toivanen for useful comments. We also benefited from the comments of the participants of the World Bank Conference on Measurement, Promotion, and Impact of Access to Financial Services in Washington, DC, and the participants of the HECER-WIDER Autumn Seminar 2008 in Helsinki. This research is supported by the Academy of Finland (Projects No. 122398 and 120234).

1. For a discussion on the importance of broad financial services outreach, see Beck, Demirgüç-Kunt, and Martinez Peria 2007 and Cull and Scott 2009.

2. There are also recent papers examining the role of social connections (Hong, Kubik, and Stein 2004) or trust (Guiso, Sapienza, and Zingales 2008) as a determinant of stock market participation.

3. For different definitions of the term "financial access," see Claessens 2006, Honohan 2008, and World Bank 2008.

4. Glaeser, Laibson, and Sacerdote (2002) highlight the challenges in the aggregation of individual social capital because aggregate social capital should also include the cross-person externalities generated by individual social capital. These challenges are why we use completely different measures for individual and aggregate social capital and are not willing to formulate aggregate social capital by aggregating our individual social capital variable.

5. Kaufmann, Kraay, and Mastruzzi present comparative data on institutional quality covering 212 countries. One of their indices is Rule of Law, which measures "perceptions of the extent to which agents have confidence in and abide by the rules of society, and in particular the quality of contract enforcement, the police, and the courts, as well as the likelihood of crime and violence" (2008, 7). On a standardized scale with zero mean, Uganda receives in 2007 a score of –0.54, well below the average on the world scale. However, it is only slightly less than neighboring Tanzania and higher than its other neighbors (Kenya, Rwanda, Sudan, and the Democratic Republic of the Congo).

6. It should also be noted that the groups are not always formed by members but are sometimes formed by the institution in a fairly random manner (see, e.g., Karlan 2007), in which case the groups cannot be regarded as screening devices.

7. Glaeser et al. (2000) show in experiments that social connections between individuals predict trust and trustworthiness, and hence we would assume that a loan officer is more likely to approve a credit applicant to whom he or she is socially connected.

8. For a discussion on the types of formal financial providers and microfinance institutions in Uganda, see Braun and Hannig 2006. They also discuss in detail the creation of the Microfinance Deposit-Taking Institutions (MDI) Act of 2003. Report of a Census of Financial Institutions in Uganda (Ministry of Finance, Planning and Economic Development 2006) discusses especially the role of Tier 4 financial institutions.

9. FinMark Trust has carried out or is currently carrying out FinScope surveys in fourteen African countries and in Pakistan; see http://www.finscope.co.za.

10. It is not uncommon for respondents to have taken loans from several types of institutions. For example, 25 percent of formal institution borrowers in the FinScope data have also taken loans from semiformal institutions, and 18 percent of semiformal borrowers also have loans from informal groups.

11. Examples of other attitudinal statements available in the FinScope data are: "I participate in communal work," "I attend parties," "I attend cultural functions," and "I participate in sporting activities." The problem with these statements is that they may measure also other things than individual-level social capital, such as wealth of the household or consumption of services (see Glaeser, Laibson, and Sacerdote 2002).

12. These data are available at http://www.worldvaluessurvey.org.

References

Ahlin, Christian, and Robert M. Townsend. 2007. Using Repayment Data to Test Across Models of Joint Liability Lending. *Economic Journal* 117 (517): F11–F51.

Aktaruzzaman, Khondker. 2009. Determinants of Demand and Supply of Microcredit: Does Education Matter? Evidence from Rural Bangladesh. In *Essays on Microcredit in Rural Bangladesh*. Helsinki: University of Helsinki.

Al-Hussainy, Edward, Thorsten Beck, Aslı Demirgüç-Kunt, and Bilal Zia. 2008. Household Use of Financial Services. Mimeo., World Bank.

Bank of Uganda. 2009. State of Ugandan Economy 2008/2009. Bank of Uganda Research Function.

Basu, Priya, and Pradeep Srivastava. 2005. Scaling-Up Microfinance for India's Rural Poor. World Bank Policy Research Working Paper No. 3646.

Beck, Thorsten, Aslı Demirgüç-Kunt, and Maria Soledad Martinez Peria. 2007. Reaching Out: Access To and Use of Banking Services across Countries. *Journal of Financial Economics* 85 (1): 234–266.

Beck, Thorsten, and Heiko Hesse. 2009. Why Are Interest Spreads So High in Uganda? *Journal of Development Economics* 88 (2): 192–204.

Bourdieu, Pierre. 1986. The Forms of Capital. In *Handbook of the Theory and Research for the Sociology of Education*, ed. J. G. Richardson, 241–258. Westport, CT: Greenwood Press.

Braun, Gabriela, and Alfred Hannig. 2006. Creating a Separate Tier: The Micro Finance Deposit-Taking Institutions Act, 2003. In *Transforming Microfinance Institutions: Providing Full Financial Services to the Poor*, ed. Joanna Ledgerwood and Victoria White, 441–458. Washington, DC: The World Bank.

Calderon, Cesar, Alberto Chong, and Arturo Galindo. 2002. Development and Efficiency of the Financial Sector and Links with Trust: Cross-Country Evidence. *Economic Development and Cultural Change* 51 (1): 189–204.

Cassar, Alessandra, Luke Crowley, and Bruce Wydick. 2007. The Effect of Social Capital on Group Loan Repayment: Evidence from Field Experiments. *Economic Journal* 117 (517): F85–F106.

Claessens, Stijn. 2006. Access to Financial Services: A Review of the Issues and Public Policy Objectives. *World Bank Research Observer* 21 (2): 207–240.

Cull, Robert, and Kinnon Scott. 2009. Measuring Household Usage of Financial Services: Does It Matter How or Whom You Ask? World Bank Policy Research Working Paper No. 5048.

Ghatak, Maitreesh, and Timothy W. Guinnane. 1999. The Economics of Lending with Joint Liability. *Journal of Development Economics* 60 (1): 195–228.

Glaeser, Edward L., David Laibson, and Bruce Sacerdote. 2002. An Economic Approach to Social Capital. *Economic Journal* 112 (483): F437–F458.

Glaeser, Edward L., David I. Laibson, José A. Scheinkman, and Christine L. Soutter. 2000. Measuring Trust. *Quarterly Journal of Economics* 65 (3): 811–846.

Guiso, Luigi, Paola Sapienza, and Luigi Zingales. 2004. The Role of Social Capital in Financial Development. *American Economic Review* 94 (3): 526–556.

Guiso, Luigi, Paola Sapienza, and Luigi Zingales. 2008. Trusting the Stock Market. *Journal of Finance* 63 (6): 2557–2600.

Heikkilä, Anni, Panu Kalmi, and Olli-Pekka Ruuskanen. 2009. Social Capital and Access to Credit. Mimeo., Helsinki School of Economics.

Hong, Harrison, Jeffrey D. Kubik, and Jeremy C. Stein. 2004. Social Interaction and Stock-Market Participation. *Journal of Finance* 59 (1): 137–163.

Honohan, Patrick. 2008. Cross-Country Variation in Household Access to Financial Services. *Journal of Banking & Finance* 32 (11): 2493–2500.

Johnston, Don, Jr., and Jonathan Morduch. 2008. The Unbanked: Evidence from Indonesia. *World Bank Economic Review* 22 (3): 517–537.

Karlan, Dean S. 2005. Using Experimental Economics to Measure Social Capital and Predict Financial Decisions. *American Economic Review* 95 (5): 1688–1699.

Karlan, Dean S. 2007. Social Connections and Group Banking. *Economic Journal* 117 (517): F52–F84.

Kaufmann, Daniel, Aart Kraay, and Massimo Mastruzzi. 2008. *Governance Matters VII: Aggregate and Individual Governance Indicators for 1996-2007*. Washington, DC: World Bank.

Kavuma, John. 2009. *Draft National Development Plan*. Kampala: National Planning Authority of Uganda.

Knack, Stephen, and Philip Keefer. 1997. Does Social Capital Have a Pay-off? A Cross-Country Investigation. *Quarterly Journal of Economics* 112 (4): 1251–1288.

Kumar, Anjali, Thorsten Beck, Cristine Campos, and Soumya Chattopadhyay. 2005. Assessing Financial Access in Brazil. World Bank Working Paper No. 50.

La Porta, Rafael, Florencio Lopez-de-Silanes, Andrei Shleifer, and Robert W. Vishny. 1997. Trust in Large Organizations. *American Economic Review* 87 (2): 333–338.

Ministry of Finance, Planning and Economic Development. 2006. *Report of a Census of Financial Institutions in Uganda*. Kampala: Ministry of Finance, Planning and Economic Development.

Portes, Alejandro. 1998. Social Capital: Its Origins and Applications in Modern Sociology. *Annual Review of Sociology* 24:1–24.

Putnam, Robert D. 1993. *Making Democracy Work: Civic Traditions in Modern Italy*. Princeton, NJ: Princeton University Press.

Putnam, Robert D. 2000. *Bowling Alone: The Collapse and Revival of the American Economy*. New York: Simon & Schuster.

Steadman Group. 2007. *FinScope Uganda: Demand, Use and Access to Financial Services in Uganda, Report for Financial Sector Deepening Project Uganda*. Kampala: The Steadman Group.

Uganda Bureau of Statistics (UBOS). 2009. *Statistical Abstract 2009*. Kampala: Uganda Bureau of Statistics.

Van Bastelaer, Thierry. 2000. Does Social Capital Facilitate the Poor's Access to Credit? A Review of the Microeconomic Literature. World Bank Social Capital Initiative Working Paper.

Van Bastelaer, Thierry, and Howard Leathers. 2006. Trust in Lending: Social Capital and Joint Liability Seed Loans in Southern Zambia. *World Development* 34 (10): 1788–1807.

Woolcock, Michael, and Deepa Narayan. 2000. Social Capital: Implications for Development Theory, Research and Policy. *World Bank Research Observer* 15 (2): 225–249.

World Bank. 2008. *Finance for All? Policies and Pitfalls in Expanding Access*. Washington, DC: World Bank.

VI Conclusion

15 Ten Research Questions

Jonathan Morduch

High-quality evidence on the state of financial access around the world is advancing rapidly, as the chapters of this book illustrate.[1] A happy consequence of increasing knowledge is the ability to better recognize what we don't yet know. Here are ten questions—some micro, some macro—that need answers if we are to make informed decisions on how to improve financial access.

1. Does financial access—evaluated in typical settings with a long enough time horizon to see change—substantially improve the well-being of customers?

The most fundamental, unresolved question concerns impact. Does expanding financial access really make a notable difference to families and communities? And, if so, how and when?

Muhammad Yunus (1999) and other early microcredit advocates took us down a narrow path. Yunus's stress on "microcredit for microenterprise" continues to play well with the public, but we're learning that the rhetoric does an injustice to the complicated reality of how low-income families actually use financial services. The notion that microcredit loans are sought exclusively for business investment fails in the data, whether asked directly (Collins et al. 2009) or derived indirectly (Karlan and Zinman 2011).

That takes us to the question of what borrowers are in fact doing with their loans when they're not funding business. One important use is to pay for big, lumpy expenses including healthcare costs, school fees, and home repair. In a survey of customers of Mongolia's XacBank, for example, Attanasio et al. (2011) find that about half of all microcredit business loans were used for household ends, not for business investment. Leading nonbusiness uses include purchases of household assets such as video players, radios, and large domestic appliances. A second

type of use is to pay down more expensive loans. A third type is to help smooth seasonal ups and downs of consumption. The uses make perfect sense from the standpoint of economic theory, but they make microcredit advocates nervous.

Advocates worry that borrowers cannot repay loans if there's no major business investment in the picture, but they miss the larger picture. The evidence in Collins et al. (2009) suggests that borrowers repay microcredit loans with money earned in various wage and self-employment activities. Even if a particular loan is not used to *fund* self-employment, income from self-employment may nevertheless provide an important way to repay the loan. The distinction too often gets lost. From the bank's perspective, the central question should be whether the household can generate the cash flow to service the loan (and whether it will be in a position to apply that cash flow to loan repayments), not whether the loan is used for a particular purpose. The XacBank customers described in Attanasio et al. (2011) still repay their loans, even when the loans are not used to finance business. Grameen Bank, for its part, reports loan repayment rates close to 100 percent, even though at least one survey from Grameen suggests that many loans do not go to business purposes (in a small sample collected by Stuart Rutherford, about half of loans are used for nonbusiness purposes; Collins et al. 2009).

Given the complexity of what access to finance means for households, decent evaluations with clear bottom lines are needed to anchor conversations. But so far, evaluations have done little to settle the question of whether microfinance "works." We have an older set of studies that had hoped to measure the impact of microfinance on consumption or income but were compromised in one way or another, usually by not making comparisons to credible control groups; Armendáriz and Morduch (2010) provide an overview, and Roodman and Morduch 2011 demonstrate the lack of robustness of the well-known estimation of Pitt and Khandker (1998).

As control groups have become more credible, evidence of net impact has become weaker. Coleman's (2006) work in Northeast Thailand shows how this works. He finds that microfinance borrowers are already much wealthier than their neighbors before they gain access to microfinance. These wealthier households tend to see gains from access to microfinance, but their less wealthy neighbors do not on average. The overall finding is of no significant average impacts (Coleman 1999).

The push for randomized trials reflects the sense that they do far better in terms of credibility, but researchers are often forced to grab opportunities where they arise and thus tend to investigate narrow populations and short-term outcomes. One thing we have learned from randomized trials is that internal validity is crucial. We've also learned that internal validity is no substitute for external validity (Cartwright 2007), and it is questions around how—and if—results extend to other contexts that leave the literature unsettled.

Truth be told, however, the most unsettling finding is the lack of strong positive results. Neither the randomized trial completed by Banerjee et al. (2009) in Hyderabad nor that by Crépon et al. in Morocco (2011), for example, find much in the way of strong impacts. The most positive finding so far is that of Attanasio et al. (2011) in their eighteen-month study of XacBank in Mongolia, though even here the story is mixed. Attanasio and colleagues find that access to microcredit group loans increased food consumption (and increased the quality of foods consumed as well). The result comes from both greater home production and from more spending. The effect is large: total food consumption in treatment villages was 17 percentage points higher than in control villages. Yet no such increase is found for households that receive microcredit loans using an individual-loan method (rather than a group method with joint liability). Nor does the early research find evidence of a parallel increase in income, even for households borrowing under the group lending method.[2]

Taking a structural approach, Kaboski and Townsend (2011) find in Thailand that credit constraints are rife and that microcredit access raises consumption. But when costs are compared to benefits, the costs of running the programs are 30 percent higher than the cumulative benefits. Studies like these are forcing most academics to revise downward their expectations for microcredit impacts, but these are still early days in the evaluation literature.[3]

2. How much does consumption smoothing contribute to the welfare of families?

There are clear theoretical linkages between consumption smoothing, financial access, and improved well-being. Modern economics is built around the premise that households seek to maximize utility, not income. A core economic task of a household, rich or poor, is matching the availability of resources with the timing of consumption needs. This task is especially burdensome for poor households who have to piece

together uneven cash flows using a handful of imperfect financial tools. A key role of access to predictable, reliable, and convenient financial services is thus to smooth consumption (Collins et al. 2009).

All the same, the links are not well established empirically. People with more assets appear better able to smooth consumption, but it is unclear how much of that is self-insurance, how much is help from neighbors and relatives, and what the costs of the strategies are. Households can go to great lengths to smooth consumption, often using expensive or risky alternatives (such as moneylenders or asking neighbors to hold cash), but we don't have good measures of how much consumption smoothing affects household welfare. Even if average consumption over the year is unchanged, welfare can rise substantially if its distribution improves within the year. At present, we have little handle on relative magnitudes.

As to the reverse chain of causation, we have much further to go in describing the path from consumption smoothing to asset holding and profitability. We have bits of evidence (e.g., Samphantarak and Townsend 2010 for Thai data) and need more on the ways that having a stable, predictable, reliable financial life carries over to investment choices.

The most interesting recent work is by Cole, Giné, and Vickery (2011), who extend their work on rainfall insurance in south India to determine the impact of access to insurance on production choices. They examine whether farm households with insurance will shift toward riskier (and more profitable) crops once insurance is available. They find a large and positive effect, with the share of households planting a (relatively risky) cash crop rising to 55 percent from 48.6 percent in the control group. The size is relatively large, given the nature of the intervention, though it's unlikely to be transformative in itself. Still, the result stands as the most convincing link so far between financial access, risk reduction, and more profitable production choices for low-income households.

3. Why do so many micro businesses stay micro?

In the large microfinance markets of Asia, a common but seldom-discussed observation is that the microenterprises nominally tied to microcredit borrowing rarely grow substantially, especially after the first few years. There are many possible reasons to explain this finding, including borrowers' simple lack of imagination, lack of management capacity, low profitability at scale, limited ability to hire trusted workers,

risk aversion, lack of access to sufficient capital for productive growth investments, poor policy environments, and insufficient access to larger markets.

What role do financial institutions play? Making microcredit loans more flexible may help, although microfinance institutions worry that being more flexible may increase risk and costs.[4] Field, Pande, and Papp (2009) studied 169 microcredit groups in West Bengal, India. Of these, eighty-four were allowed a two-month grace period before loan repayments started. Those given the grace period were twice as likely to start a new business, but the treatment group was also substantially more likely to default: four months after the final installment was due, 11 percent of the treatment group had failed to repay in full, compared to 3 percent of the control group. (It's unclear how much the result reflects the impact of effectively increasing loan sizes, rather than adding flexibility per se.)

The lack of growth may also be due to competing household needs such as childcare. Even if financial access makes a big impact at first, the long-run impact hinges on the extent of continuing gains.

4. Is small and medium enterprise (SME) finance an alternative strategy to microfinance?

If micro businesses tend to stay micro, perhaps there are better options? Critics of the hoopla around microcredit suggest that job creation is better done by larger enterprises (e.g., Karnani 2007). The rush to support SMEs has been given attention by the G-20 countries and is tied in part to the idea that SMEs can contribute to the goal of poverty reduction by employing low-skill workers. But can they? It's an empirical question that has been met with little evidence so far.

One piece of data comes from McKenzie and Woodruff (2008), who use data on tens of thousands of Mexican microenterprises to find marginal returns to capital of 15 percent per month for investment levels below $200 and weak evidence of scale economies when investments get up to about $1,000–$2,000. The implication is that there are not strong gains to increasing scale. By this evidence, the Mexican microenterprises do not seem to be destined to generate low returns simply because they cannot grow large enough. There are no poverty traps here.

Bauchet and Morduch (2011) approach the question not by looking at returns but by considering the structure of employment. They investigate data on the employees of SMEs supported by BRAC Bank in

Bangladesh. Their conclusion is that these employees are far more educated and skilled than microcredit borrowers; in line with this finding is that SME employees come from households that are considerably less poor on average. The average employee of a small enterprise in the BRAC Bank sample is a semi-skilled twenty-six-year-old male with almost five years of formal education. Bangladeshi microcredit borrowers, in contrast, are mostly women, and about half have no formal education and most have few professional skills. Bauchet and Morduch (2011) find that just 7 percent of SME employees in their sample are women.

In sum, the two groups—SME employees and microcredit borrowers—look very different in the Bangladesh surveys. Will these kinds of results hold up elsewhere, particularly in Latin America and Eastern Europe, where the gender and education profiles of microcredit borrowers are different from that in South Asia?

More important, if SMEs won't generate much poverty reduction through direct employment, can they create enough of a difference by spurring regional demand and broadening the base of economic growth?

5. Which financial services are most valuable to the poorest?

Credit is just one useful financial service, but credit has been the first focus of microfinance institutions because there's a business model that makes lending possible, not because it is necessarily most important for customers. Customers pay handsomely for access to credit. Regulations also often make it much easier to lend than to take deposits (because the risk rests with the lender).

Saving programs have emerged, and some advocates now claim that deposit services deserve claim to being the most fundamental need for poor families—and for the poorest, specifically. But the picture developed by Collins et al. (2009) pushes against that view. We argue that a range of financial devices are sought and used together, with different degrees of substitution and complementarity. None has clear primacy.

Programs in locales around the world have experimented with a variety of "credit plus" offerings (notably credit with education) to target poorer populations with mixed results and only recently have a few methodologically sound studies begun reporting evidence. We are just beginning to shine a light on what combination of services, financial and otherwise, will help the poorest build assets and graduate into more standard microcredit and other financial products.

One concern is that the optimal mix may not be commercially viable. The costs of building groups, disbursing, collecting, and monitoring may overwhelm the return on very small loans at even the highest viable interest rates—and certainly if interest rates are lowered to maximize social impact.

Microfinance has always been a balancing act in which economic reality is balanced against expanding the social good. But making the right choices also necessitates stepping away from economic reality to assess what could be optimal in a less constrained world.

6. Are borrowing and saving complements or substitutes?

In developed economies, households often use both savings and borrowings to produce large amounts of capital to buy fixed assets such as houses and vehicles. House buyers, for example, make a down payment from their savings and borrow the rest. Saving and borrowing are thus complements in this context.

Behavioral economics provides another mechanism through which saving and borrowing act as complements: for households that are loathe to draw down their hard-earned savings, the ability to borrow—and thus to leave their stash of savings untouched—can function as a helpful way to maintain accumulations. Were households more confident in themselves, or if they had better mechanisms to achieve discipline, "borrowing to save" would be less useful, but in an imperfect world it can be the best of an array of imperfect strategies (Morduch 2010).

In other contexts, borrowing and saving are depicted as alternative activities. In making intertemporal choices, consumers eager to consume today will draw down savings or borrow; consumers focused on consuming at later dates will instead save. This rock of neoclassical theory takes as given that consumers are wage earners, not entrepreneurs (more precisely, it takes as given that income is exogenous). For the self-employed (such as small-scale microcredit borrowers), income is instead endogenous, and they routinely seek to borrow in order to generate income for the future. In this case, borrowing is a forward-looking household activity, not one driven by immediate consumption needs. As Bauer, Chytilová, and Morduch (2012) find, it is the more patient villagers in their sample who are most likely to borrow, even more so than their impatient neighbors.

Bauer, Chytilová, and Morduch (2012) draw a second connection between loans and saving, arguing that microcredit borrowing can compensate for the lack of disciplined ways to save. In villages in

Karnataka, India, the evidence is consistent with pent-up demand for better ways to save. But until better mechanisms emerge, the microcredit borrowing process can function as an imperfect alternative. The argument is that microcredit allows households to convert small amounts of money today into the promise of large future cash flows, just as savings does (Rutherford 2001). In this way, saving and borrowing are substitute activities.

To the extent that this conclusion is generalizable, as poor households gain more access to better savings products, will they switch away from credit products? What will this effect mean for the microcredit business model? Answering those questions requires a better understanding of how borrowing and saving interact.

7. When and how does financial literacy really matter?

The evidence on financial education has, to date, not been encouraging. As Cole, Sampson, and Zia write in chapter 12, being financially *literate* clearly helps, but the value of financial *education* is a different question. We know the desired outcome (literacy) but not a reliable way to get there enough of the time; nor is it clear that literacy is enough. Behavioral economics teaches us that consumers also need ways to implement ideas, especially when temptations and distractions are difficult to keep at bay.

Intuition tells us that improved financial decision making through training would have powerful effects, and there's some evidence in that line. Karlan and Valdivia (2011), for example, randomly selected microcredit borrowers in Peru to receive free business training on issues like cash management, business choice, and marketing. Some, but not all, econometric specifications show that those who got the training earned greater profits, especially in bad months.

But the result from Peru stands out in a landscape in which most studies show no real impact. So where exactly are existing financial literacy programs going off track? Is it curriculum? Is it delivery? Is it context?

It's plausible that financial literacy training is most effective when delivered just in time, but rarely are financial literacy training programs paired with quality financial products that make consumer choices meaningful. If a person understands compounding interest but cannot gain access to an interest-bearing savings account, the understanding can have little welfare impact.

Still, there should be situations in which some measure of financial literacy should matter—for instance, training on good financial management for shopkeepers. Drexler, Fischer, and Schoar's (2010) results

are mixed, but they indicate that impact is possible if we solve the curriculum, delivery, and context puzzles. In their case, having simple rules of thumb were particularly valuable. Working with a microfinance institution in the Dominican Republic, they find that providing admonitions to take simple steps like separating business and personal accounts had impacts, even when teaching a list of detailed financial concepts did not.

8. Can the expansion of microfinance add up to macro impacts?

The most basic question is the micro one: whether microfinance typically yields notable impacts on the lives of low-income families. The logical following question is: to the extent that micro impacts emerge, how do those impacts add up? Is there a reasonable case that expanding microfinance can make a dent in regional or national economic growth rates? In national-level poverty rates?

There are two complementary research strategies. One is cross-country research, which tends to show positive correlations between financial expansion and the reduction of inequality (Demirgüç-Kunt and Levine 2009 provide an overview). The work doesn't connect the dots from microfinance explicitly, but it does help frame issues. The second approach connects the dots by imposing structure on the relationships. A good example is the general equilibrium analysis of Buera, Kaboski, and Shin (2011). They find that increasing financial access leads to macro impacts but that the magnitudes are small.

The work will be more meaningful as the penetration of finance expands to include more of today's unbanked population. As that happens, it will become more pressing to begin sorting out what this all adds up to.

9. Can increasing access enhance or jeopardize the stability of financial systems?

Regulators hope that expanding financial access will also provide greater stability to the overall financial system. This result would occur as the market becomes larger and more diverse and thus better able to withstand difficulties in any particular corner. The range of depositors would enlarge, as would the kinds of financial institutions in the market. Greater competition among providers would create pressure for quality competition.

That's the rosy scenario. The financial crisis of 2007–2008 in the United States is a contrasting reminder that expanding access and increasing stability do not necessarily go hand in hand. In the United

States, the expansion of mortgage finance opened the way for new home buyers to engage in speculative and ill-advised real estate investments, eventually fueling the drama behind the financial crisis (McLean and Nocera 2010). The financial crisis was created by a range of forces— including fundamental structural inequalities exacerbated by poor oversight, misaligned incentives, and some measure of outright fraud— so generalization should proceed with caution (Rajan 2010). Still, the crisis underscores the larger point: regulators need a deeper understanding of what can happen to the stability of financial systems when millions of new participants enter.

Debates over the benefits and risks of commercialized microfinance as a gateway for financial access have raged since the early days of microfinance. Neither the 2010–2011 crisis in Andhra Pradesh nor prior crises in Nicaragua, Bosnia, Nigeria, and other locales have resolved those debates. Clearly, there can be a relationship between striving for profitability, fast growth, and poor practices leading to over-indebtedness of clients and portfolio deterioration.

Yet despite the warning signs and many public pledges by various industry actors to work on client protection approaches and social metrics, problems arise regularly. Is there an optimal mix of priorities that protects clients yet meets the goals for rapid expansion in the number of clients who have access to formal financial services? Is microfinance, like other financial services, likely to experience repeated cycles of boom and bust?

10. What should regulators do?

There's not enough academic research on the regulation of financial inclusion. Many of the questions might seem too applied for some research-minded economists, but that leaves regulators with few guideposts. It also seems short-sighted.

Regulation is always a question of trade-offs between competing goals. Within microfinance, for example, there is evidence that the supervision and monitoring that is part of prudential regulation increases costs substantially for microfinance institutions. That regulation-induced increase, in turn, appears to push profit-minded institutions to preserve profits by reducing outreach to their poorer customers and women. By a similar token, institutions that tilt toward being "socially minded" tend to reduce profit rather than outreach (Cull, Demirgüç-Kunt, and Morduch 2011). The alternative—less regulation in order to increase outreach—carries plenty of dangers. Those are difficult trade-offs to

make, and there is as of yet not enough empirical evidence to describe optimal regulatory schemes for microfinance.

Add to this uncertainty the largely uncharted roles of large nonprofit institutions. Regulatory schemes are generally designed around reining in the reckless behavior of profit-seeking banks. But nonprofits react to regulation differently. Should they therefore be regulated by different agencies, those more familiar with the unique behavior of nonprofits? Or should they be regulated by finance ministries and central banks as are others that provide financial services? Moreover, how do profitable nonprofit institutions affect competitive markets?

Microfinance promises to marry the social and the commercial. It has always been an uneasy alliance (Cull, Demirgüç-Kunt, and Morduch 2009), but one that has genuinely succeeded in delivering reliable services globally. The preceding ten questions show that there remain fundamental uncertainties about how it all adds up, but that does not diminish the remarkable institutional and organizational successes of the global microfinance movement.

Moving forward will require understandings that are both fine-grained and "big picture." In many ways it is the middle ground—understandings of organizations and their incentives—that is most deserving of greater attention. This will require applying a corporate finance lens and an industrial organization lens to the new, inclusive financial landscapes. Looking forward, this is likely where we will find the most intellectually interesting inquiries of all.

Notes

1. I appreciate editorial input from Timothy Ogden.

2. As I write this, Attanasio et al. 2011 is just being circulated in draft form, and it will surely generate much interest, discussion, and clarification. If the past is a guide, there will be questions about the relatively short length of exposure to the treatment and the small sample (just forty villages: ten in the control group, fifteen with group lending and fifteen with access to an individual lending methodology). The small sample size is on the low end of what is usually accepted for levels of statistical power in experimental designs.

3. Although the new evaluation literature focuses rightly on study design, a complementary concern rests with data accuracy. The work of Cull and Scott in chapter 4 and Collins in chapter 5 point to important practical steps for collecting sharper data on financial variables—especially with regard to informal mechanisms and the broad range of semiformal options. Together with others, including Samphantarak and Townsend (2010) and de Mel et al. (2009), the studies give us a better grounding for mapping theory and data. Improved data on cash flows, microenterprise finance, and the use of financial services will be one part of answering the impact question.

4. Part of developing financing products that allow small businesses to grow will be finding ways to better assess risk. That's why the results from the work of the Entrepreneurial Finance Lab on producing psychometric tests to judge repayment risk, currently being piloted by Standard Chartered Bank in several African countries, will be interesting to follow.

References

Armendáriz, Beatriz, and Jonathan Morduch. 2010. *The Economics of Microfinance*. 2nd ed. Cambridge, MA: MIT Press.

Attanasio, Orazio, Britta Augsburg, Ralph De Haas, Emla Fitzsimons, and Heike Harmgart. 2011. Group Lending or Individual Lending? Evidence from a Randomised Field Experiment in Mongolia. European Bank for Reconstruction and Development, working paper.

Banerjee, Abhijit V., Esther Duflo, Rachel Glennerster, and Cynthia Kinnan. 2009. The Miracle of Microfinance? Evidence from a Randomized Evaluation. Cambridge, MA: MIT Department of Economics and Abdul Latif Jameel Poverty Action Lab, working paper.

Bauchet, Jonathan, and Jonathan Morduch. 2011. Is Micro Too Small? Microcredit vs. SME Finance. Financial Access Initiative working paper. New York University.

Bauer, Michal, Julie Chytilová, and Jonathan Morduch. 2012. Behavioral Foundations of Microcredit: Experimental and Survey Evidence from Rural India. *American Economic Review* 102 (2): 1118–1139.

Buera, Francisco, Joseph Kaboski, and Yongseok Shin. 2011. The Macroeconomics of Microfinance. University of Notre Dame, Department of Economics, working paper.

Cartwright, Nancy. 2007. Are RCTs the Gold Standard? *Biosocieties* 2:11–20.

Cole, Shawn, Xavier Giné, and James Vickery. 2011. How Does Risk Management Influence Production Decisions? Evidence from a Field Experiment. Harvard Business School, World Bank, and Federal Reserve Bank of New York, working paper.

Coleman, Brett. 1999. The Impact of Group Lending in Northeast Thailand. *Journal of Development Economics* 60:105–141.

Coleman, Brett. 2006. Microfinance in Northeast Thailand: Who Benefits and How Much? *World Development* 34 (9): 1612–1638.

Collins, Daryl, Jonathan Morduch, Stuart Rutherford, and Orlanda Ruthven. 2009. *Portfolios of the Poor: How the World's Poor Live on $2 a Day*. Princeton, NJ: Princeton University Press.

Crépon, Bruno, Florencia Devoto, Esther Duflo, and William Pariente. 2011. *Impact of Microcredit in Rural Areas of Morocco: Evidence from a Randomized Evaluation*. Cambridge, MA: MIT Press.

Cull, Robert, Aslı Demirgüç-Kunt, and Jonathan Morduch. 2009. Microfinance Meets the Market. *Journal of Economic Perspectives* 23 (1): 167–192.

Cull, Robert, Aslı Demirgüç-Kunt, and Jonathan Morduch. 2011. Does Regulatory Supervision Curtail Microfinance Profitability and Outreach? *World Development* 39 (6): 949–965.

de Mel, Suresh, David McKenzie, and Christopher Woodruff. 2009. Measuring Microenterprise Profits: Must We Ask How the Sausage is Made? *Journal of Development Economics* 88 (1): 19–31.

Demirgüç-Kunt, Aslı, and Ross Levine. 2009. Finance and Inequality: Theory and Evidence. *Annual Review of Financial Economics* 1: 287–318.

Drexler, Alejandro, Greg Fischer, and Antoinette Schoar. 2010. Keeping It Simple: Financial Literacy and Rules of Thumb. CEPR Discussion Paper No. DP7994.

Field, Erica, Rohini Pande, and John Papp. 2009. Does Microfinance Repayment Flexibility Affect Entrepreneurial Behavior and Loan Default? IFMR working paper.

Kaboski, Joseph, and Robert Townsend. 2011. A Structural Evaluation of a Large-Scale Quasi-Experimental Microfinance Initiative. *Econometrica* 79 (5): 1357–1406.

Karlan, Dean, and Martin Valdivia. 2011. Teaching Entrepreneurship: Impact of Business Training on Microfinance Clients and Institutions. *Review of Economics and Statistics* 93 (2): 510–527.

Karlan, Dean, and Jonathan Zinman. 2011. List Randomization for Sensitive Behavior: An Application for Measuring Use of Loan Proceeds. *Journal of Development Economics* 98 (1): 71–75.

Karnani, Aneel. 2007. Microfinance Misses Its Mark. *Stanford Social Innovation Review* 5 (3): 34–40.

McKenzie, David, and Christopher Woodruff. 2008. Experimental Evidence on Returns to Capital and Access to Finance in Mexico. *World Bank Economic Review* 22 (3): 457–482.

McLean, Bethany, and Joseph Nocera. 2010. *All the Devils are Here: The Hidden History of the Financial Crisis*. New York: Portfolio.

Morduch, Jonathan. 2010. Borrowing to Save. *Journal of Globalization and Development* 1 (2). DOI: 10.2202/1948-1837,1153.

Pitt, Mark M., and Shahidur R. Khandker. 1998. The Impact of Group-Based Credit on Poor Households in Bangladesh: Does the Gender of Participants Matter? *Journal of Political Economy* 106 (5): 958–996.

Rajan, Raghuram. 2010. *Fault Lines: How Hidden Fractures Still Threaten the World Economy*. Princeton, NJ: Princeton University Press.

Roodman, David, and Jonathan Morduch. 2011. The Impact of Microcredit on the Poor in Bangladesh: Revisiting the Evidence. Center for Global Development and Financial Access Initiative, working paper.

Rutherford, Stuart. 2001. *The Poor and their Money*. Delhi: Oxford University Press.

Samphantharak, Krislert, and Robert Townsend. 2010. *Households as Corporate Firms: An Analysis of Household Finance Using Integrated Household Surveys and Corporate Financial Accounting*. Cambridge: Cambridge University Press.

Yunus, Muhammad. 1999. *Banker to the Poor: Microlending and the Battle against World Poverty*. New York: PublicAffairs.

Contributors

Thorsten Beck, CentER and European Banking Center, Tilburg University, and CEPR

Miriam Bruhn, World Bank

Alberto Chaia, McKinsey & Company

Stijn Claessens, International Monetary Fund, University of Amsterdam, and CEPR

Shawn Cole, Harvard Business School

Daryl Collins, Bankable Frontier Associates

Robert Cull, World Bank

Aparna Dalal, Financial Access Initiative

Aslı Demirgüç-Kunt, World Bank

Erik Feijen, World Bank

Xavier Giné, World Bank

Tony Goland, McKinsey & Company

Jessica Goldberg, University of Michigan

Maria Jose Gonzalez, McKinsey & Company

Anni Heikkilä, Aalto University School of Economics and HECER

Patrick Honohan, Central Bank of Ireland

Panu Kalmi, University of Vaasa

Dean Karlan, Yale University

Katie Kibuuka, World Bank

Michael King, Trinity College Dublin

Leora F. Klapper, World Bank

Robert Lensink, Wageningen University and University of Groningen

Inessa Love, World Bank

Jonathan Morduch, New York University

Sendhil Mullainathan, Harvard University

Georgios A. Panos, University of Aberdeen Business School and CELMR

Omar Robles, United States Bureau of Labor Statistics

Olli-Pekka Ruuskanen, University of Tampere

Thomas Sampson, Harvard University

Shalini Sankaranarayanan, International Finance Corporation

Robert Schiff, McKinsey & Company

Kinnon Scott, World Bank

Peter Sheerin, International Finance Corporation

Erwin R. Tiongson, World Bank

Nguyen Viet Cuong, Wageningen University

Marrit van den Berg, Wageningen University

Dean Yang, University of Michigan

Bilal Zia, World Bank

Index

Printed in the United States
by Baker & Taylor Publisher Services